Computational Intelligence in Archaeology

Juan A. Barceló
Universitat Autònoma de Barcelona, Spain

INFORMATION SCIENCE REFERENCE

Hershey · New York

Acquisitions Editor: Kristin Klinger
Development Editor: Kristin Roth
Senior Managing Editor: Jennifer Neidig
Managing Editor: Jamie Snavely
Assistant Managing Editor: Carole Coulson
Copy Editor: Katie Smalley
Typesetter: Elizabeth C Duke
Cover Design: Lisa Tosheff
Printed at: Yurchak Printing Inc.

Published in the United States of America by
    Information Science Reference (an imprint of IGI Global)
    701 E. Chocolate Avenue, Suite 200
    Hershey PA 17033
    Tel: 717-533-8845
    Fax: 717-533-8661
    E-mail: cust@igi-global.com
    Web site: http://www.igi-global.com

and in the United Kingdom by
    Information Science Reference (an imprint of IGI Global)
    3 Henrietta Street
    Covent Garden
    London WC2E 8LU
    Tel: 44 20 7240 0856
    Fax: 44 20 7379 0609
    Web site: http://www.eurospanbookstore.com

Library of Congress Cataloging-in-Publication Data

Computational intelligence in archaeology / Juan A. Barcelo, editor.

    p. cm.

  Summary: "This book provides analytical theories offered by new and innovative artificial intelligence computing methods in the archaeological domain. This stimulating, must-have title is full of archaeological examples that allow academicians, researchers, and students to understand a complex but very useful data analysis technique to the field of archaeology"--Provided by publisher.

  ISBN 978-1-59904-489-7 (hardcover) -- ISBN 978-1-59904-491-0 (e-book)

  1. Archaeology--Data processing 2. Computational intelligence. 3. Archaeology--Philosophy. I. Barceló, Juan A.

 CC80.4.C645 2008

 930.1028'5--dc22

                        2007048405

British Cataloguing in Publication Data
A Cataloguing in Publication record for this book is available from the British Library.

All work contributed to this book set is original material. The views expressed in this book are those of the authors, but not necessarily of the publisher.

Table of Contents

Section II
Learning and Experimentation in Historical Sciences

Section III
Practical Examples of Automated Archaeology

Foreword

I wish to thank Juan A. Barceló for asking me to write the foreword to his fine book on *Computational Intelligence in Archaeology*. As he writes in the prologue, we might sometimes disagree, but he still regards himself as a kind of "gardinist" in his more modern world. One example is the place we both gave to the conference on computer applications and quantitative methods in archaeology (http://caa. leidenuniv.nl). Barceló indicates that he attended nearly all the annual meetings of that series since 1991. I personally was invited to present the initial paper of the 2002 meeting of that conference, as an interim report on the logicist program. There are differences between that program and those that formed the basis of all the computer applications discussed at this conference. Before going into them, I shall first summarize Barceló's views here presented on the subject.

* * * *

Section I, *From Natural Archaeology to "Artificial" Intelligence*, establishes first the automated form of archaeology in an Input →STATE → Output format. The analysis of such forms calls for some inferences that are social interpretations of the input data, that is, 'inverse engineering' distinct from 'real' data. The major question is problem solving in the brain and by the machine. The answer here is the machine, but with a difference between expert systems, in which the mechanisms of human conceptualization are lacking (as in our view of expert rules), and a neurocomputational one where the "rational" automated archaeologist makes more sense.

Section II, *Learning and Experimentation in Historical Sciences*, takes on this neurocomputational framework of study through the concept of "inverse reasoning," an inverse engineering based on 'the generalization of input-output mappings connecting cause and effect in certain fields of regularity. Inverse reasoning starts not with observations but with conjectures, hence a predictive task depending on social processes more than on the accumulation of data. The 'Introduction to neurocomputing' is a way to answer this schematic representation between neurons from input detectors to integrated outputs (there are many ways to account for the relation between neural including the recurrent networks, which I shall not summarize here).

Section III, is titled *Practical Examples of Automated Archaeology*. The starting point is a recall of the principle of visual and non-visual analysis in automated archaeology, from observable effects to unobservable causes. The automated archaeologist should first find the social cause of what it 'sees' and extract from that analysis a number of unobservable questions which should be included in the initial computer classification of the data. Examples are given for shape analysis, texture and compositional analyses, spatiotemporal analysis. In this last case, the most provocative of all questions asked along this book is raised: "Can an automated archaeologist not only 'forecast' the future, but even explain how our social action will be?" The provisional answer to that problem tends to call more on studies of social causation than on particular objects. In other words, we should concentrate on the function of the objects mentioned as inputs in order to convert into output actions that seem reasonable, that is, neither too general nor too specific. Some of the material elements in given social activity will be used to guide inferences and to fill gaps in the knowledge of the element's function.

Section IV consists of the Conclusions. Summarizing the argument, the automated archaeology actually sees humans acting socially and perceives their variation in time backwards, explaining it through some causes. This may be understood as seeing the past or the present. In this second case, the inverse reasoning or inverse engineering approach is used to simulate unobservable mechanisms that link the input (observation) with the output (explanation), or to predict properties of parts of the social process from properties of other parts. The case of organized "libraries" of internal representations of various prototypical perceptual situations has not been discussed here.

The last section of the book *Towards a Computational Philosophy of Science* is particularly interesting to understand its purpose. First, an artificial archaeologist is defined as "a physically instantiated system that can perceive, understand and interact with its environment, and evolve in order to achieve human—like performance in activities requiring context—(situation and task) specific knowledge." Second, we therefore need "a theory of why a specific computation or a group of related computations performed by a system that has (those) abilities." Among them, "computer programs (that) do work in real science, not only in archaeology " that is, "not simulating or reproducing the way archaeologists think today because we are doing archaeology in the wrong way." Thirdly, in this purpose, "the robot scientist can infer hypotheses with integrated reasoning, perception, and action with a uniform theoretical and implementation framework (derived) from cognitive robotics. Computational cognitive models of archaeological abilities should be based on the study of particular human capabilities and how humans solve certain tasks, but still models will never be like human archaeologists, nor do I pretend to substitute human scientific endeavor by slave androids." Finally, in other words, the preference is "to discuss how to design the theory of the computation (knowledge level) rather than the possible implementation (physical level) "hence a " top-down strategy" with three kinds of assumptions: social activity, rather strong and daring; a more predictive hypotheses; or closely related to them but in terms that run the risk of certain distortions.

* * * *

I wish now to go back to the logicist program and its interim report presented at the CAA 2002 meeting which I attended (Doerr & Sarris, 2003). The main point was to recall the two 'natural kinds' developed by Jerome Bruner in his theory in *Actual Minds, Possible Worlds* (1986): one is the logic-scientific way used in the "hard" sciences, the other is the way of thought presented in the liberal kinds such as the 'soft' studies including literature. The example given by Bruner belonged all to the narrative kinds, which made it difficult to know whether a 'third' way of knowledge was possible existing beyond his two natural kinds, covering 'between' the two other points. Bruner was wise enough to avoid that question so that I myself had to propose an answer; it consisted in focusing that the logico-scientific part was applicable to our studies as well, while seeing in their case a large number of 'complements' differently named, from the more advanced to the more journalistic or literary ones. Our research on 'Conceptual modeling and digitalization' was logic-scientific in this case, but it did not hesitate to raise questions about the many computer works presented at the same meeting (Gardin, op. cit, p. 5-11).

Yet my view is "wrong" according to Barceló because "it lacks the mechanism of human conceptualization," as done in his understanding of computational intelligence. I accept this criticism given the fact that " problem solving never ends."

My understanding then went back to my initial book presented in 1980, Archaeological Constructs: an aspect of theoretical archaeology. The analysis was a set of basic data used in the picture (declaration propositions) without explicit antecedents in the discourse, followed by inferences practiced by the author (rewriting, derivation, detachment) to reach his conclusion or hypothesis according to his way of presenting the argument (mode empiric-inductive or hypothetic-deductive). The argument itself thus took the form of a sequence of rewriting operations "p→q," read as "IF p, THEN q." Each of the operations mark in the discourse the passage of a set {Pi} to another set {Pj} following a logic of "natural reasoning" as understood in historical disciplines as later named by J.-C. Passeron (1991). Two interesting properties of this sort of writing were named: (a) the function of the parts of discourse that are not present in the logicist modelization, provisionally regarded as 'literary' in a vague sense of the word ; (b) the metatheoretical aspect of the most diverse schools of thought mentioned, for example, 'traditional' or 'new archaeology,' post-processual, marxist, structural, contextual, symbolic, cognitive, and many others.

The next book mentioned was *Expert Systems and Human Sciences: The Case of Archaeology, Produced by Several of us in 1987* (English version in Gardin et al., 1988). In the same year, I was invited by the Société Française de Philosophie to present my views on the 'Questions d'épistémologie pratique dans les perspectives de l'intelligence artificielle.' The name of 'practical epistemology' was essential in all such matters, implying the same relative view of the artificial intelligence to which it was applied. The decisive position then was to show that the use of computers should be regarded as an interesting part of the process but by no means as an essential one since a large number of articles on the problem were raised even before computers were used (ex., Binford, Renfrew), and so forth.

It was only in the 90s that our situation changed in that respect with the appearance of computers in archaeological publications, but not at first in Barceló's views. My first example was an addition of a 'Problème de formes' in a book on the long-term interpretation of certain facts observed in archeological sites of North-eastern Afghanistan, from the Bronze Age to Islamic times (Gardin, 1998). A computer system was envisaged to simulate the 'data' and successive 'inferences' necessary to justify the proposed 'hypothesis,' using ways of presentation that entirely differed from the initial lines. An example of the kind was given by Valentine Roux in a collective publication of the Cornaline de l'Inde using two forms of writing: (a) the presentation of numerous techniques of fabrication (space, artisans, economics, workshops, etc.), followed by socio-historical hypotheses for each one of them; (b) the expression of such constructions by a set of logicist analyses submitted to practical epistemology and to different modes of computer writing. The book published in 2000 followed the same distinction: (a) first came a large set of individual collections (ca. 500 pages, rich in scientific studies of all sorts: psychometric, mathematics, economics, etc.), each ending with the kind of conclusions called 'natural reasoning;' (b) the second part was a CD-ROM in which Roux tried to represent the logico-empirical data mobilized in each of the hypotheses, using the more efficient multimedia required for this work developed by Philippe Blasco under the name of SCD (scientific constructs and data).

Seen like this, the CD-ROM could be understood as a way to replace the book rather than to complete it. The opinion of Roux was that this way of thinking was erroneous, as much as trying to distinguish the respective merits of models and literature in the human sciences. The position taken after the publication of the Cornaline de l'Inde was to considerably reduce the purpose of the objects and ideas presented in such books, while trying to observe the principle of 'conceptual modeling and digitalization' adopted for the logico-scientific part of the work. A new collection came out called Referentiel at the Maison des Sciences de l'Homme, in which the CD-ROM became the major part of the argument delivered on the left-hand side of the book in a logic-empirical form. An added part was available on the right-hand side, limited to a few dozens papers written in linear format to expose the author's complements (e.g., history of the methods used, their conception and structure, suggestions for future research, etc.). The first study of Referentiel was published after a thesis on the technical tradition of modern ceramics observed in the Senegal valley (Gelbert, 2003). Others followed on the archaeology of Bronze Age in the Middle East (Boileau, 2005), the relation between India and South-East Asia in and after the passage to the first millennium (Bellina, 2007), the sequence of medieval traditions in Central France till the present (Zadora, in press), and so forth. The SCD format is still a relatively fixed way of presenting the logic-empirical reasoning, but with differences in some applications, where inverse reasoning may lead to the varied predictive analysis in Barceló recommendations.

Another development is oriented in the same program in the name of Archaeotek, the European Association for the Archaeology of Techniques. Its purpose is to encourage studies in a special journal of new works on the logicist analysis of archaeology of techniques (in English only). An article recently published (Gardin, Roux 2004) presents this project, its origin and attended programs, together with the reasons expected against its formal applications (op. cit., p. 35 – 39). Some of them may have to do with the historical and social exploitations in the internal analysis of the observed features, in which case the Archaeotek Journal approaches the phenomenon of computational intelligence. The existing examples already published raise different technical problems leading to interesting discussions of their rewriting procedures. In such features, it may happen that 'new ways of thinking old concepts' are formed, as required in Barceló's computable archaeology. A true intelligent machine thus appears in his own sense of the word, "based on the study of particular human capabilities and how humans solve certain tasks, but such models will never be like human archaeologists" as understood in his notion of artificial intelligence.

This book has a subtitle on Investigations at the Interface between Theory, Technique and Technology in Anthropology, History and the Geosciences. I regret not being able to extend this foreword to this large subject, except perhaps regarding my own views on ethnoarchaeology. We all know that many studies come out on surface features, characterizations, production systems and social groups in ethnoarchaeology, but with few correlates on regularities between material cultures and dynamic phenomena. This problem has been described recently by Valentine Roux in an interesting article on 'Ethnoarchaeology: a Non-Historical Science of Reference Necessary for Interpreting the Past' (Roux, 2007). In reading it, I could not avoid some thought on the inverse reasoning recommended by Barceló for the computer systems, namely 'the observation of the presence of actions that were probably performed in the past' using the computational intelligence. However, the fact that it is regarded as a non-historical science of references is another question, which I prefer to leave opened.

Similar questions have been raised at the Commission IV of the International Congress on Prehistorical and Protohistorical Sciences that took place last year in Portugal (Lisbon, 2006). The following title was asked: "Reconstruction, simulation, reconstitution: how 'real' is our thought? How 'imaginary' is our view of the past?" The first seven papers tried to answer that point with reference to the 'new paradigm of technology.' My own position was that the problem could be raised in the wider perspective of cognitive archaeology presented by James Bell and Colin Renfrew. It was not evident that the inferences or imaginary visions of such 'paradigms' had more or less reality than the modes of writing or reasoning of another order in which technology did not have the same place. Moreover, 10 papers presented under the title of "Emergence of cognitive abilities" seemed to prefer a more general answer with reference to wider ways of thought—neurophysiology, ethology, and so forth—than to the new paradigms of technology. Computer technique is then a particular detail of the 'reality' artificially observed using different 'paradigms' in each case. This view is again in favor of Barceló's view on computational intelligence in archaeology based on models that are never like human archaeologists although they are able to solve certain human tasks.

Jean-Claude Gardin
Former Research Director at
Centre National pour la Recherche Scientifique
Ecole de Hautes Etudes en Sciences Sociales

REFERENCES

BELLINA, B. (2006). Echanges culturels de l'Inde et de l'Asie du Sud-Est (VIè siècle avant notre ère – VIè siècle de notre ère), Paris: Editions de la Maison des Sciences de l'Homme.

BOILEAU, M.-C. (2005). Production et distribution des céramiques au IIIè millénaire en Syrie du Nord-Est, Paris: Editions de la Maison des Sciences de l'Homme.

BRUNER, J. (1986). Actual minds, possible worlds. Cambridge, MI: Harvard University Press.

DOERR, M., & SARRIS, A. (eds.) (2003). CAA 2002, The Digital Heritage of Archaeology, Athens (Greece): Hellenic Ministry of Culture.

GARDIN, J.-C. (1980) Archaeological constructs: An aspect of archaeological theory. Cambridge,UK: Cambridge Univ. Press.

GARDIN, J.-C. (1998). Prospections archéologiques en Bactriane orientale (1974-1978), vol. 3: Description des sites et notes de synthèse. Editions Recherche sur les Civilisations, Paris.

GARDIN, J.-C. et al. (1987). Systèmes experts et sciences de l'homme. Paris: Editions Eyrolles.

GARDIN, J.-C., & ROUX, V. (2004). The Arkeotek project: A european network of knowledge bases in the archaeology of Techniques. Archeologia e Calcolatori, 15, 25-40.

GELBERT, A. (2003). Traditions céramiques et emprunts techniques ; étude ethnoarchéologique dans les hautes et moyennes vallées du fleuve Sénégal. Paris: Editions de la Maison des Sciences de l'Homme.

PASSERON, J.-C. (1991). Le raisonnement sociologique. L'espace non-poppérien du raisonnement naturel. Paris: Nathan.

ROUX, V. et al. (2000). Cornaline de l'Inde. Des pratiques techniques de Cambay aux techno-systèmes de l'Indus. Paris: Editions de la Maison des Sciences de l'Homme.

ROUX, V. (2007). Ethnoarchaeology: a Non-Historical Science of Reference necessary for Interpreting the Past. Journal of Archaeological Method and Theory, 14(2).

Preface

Is it possible to build a machine to do archaeology?
Will this machine be capable of acting like a scientist?
Will this machine be able to understand the way humans acted, or how humans think they acted in the past?

This book tries to offer some possible answers to these questions and to investigate what it means to solve "automatically" archaeological problems.

Don't panic! Even if those questions would have a positive answer, I am not arguing that an artificial archaeologist will replace human archaeologists, because it will work better and cheaper than we will. We all know that artificial intelligence will eventually produce robots whose behavior may seem dazzling, but it will not produce robotic persons. Automatic archaeologists will DO a lot, but they will not BE a lot. Computational mechanisms cannot carry by themselves the weight of a scientific explanation.

I have tried to create an analogy with an "intelligent" machine, in order to understand the way we think. We should imagine an automated or artificial archaeologist as a machine able to act as any of us, human archaeologists, learning through experience to associate archaeological observations to explanations, and using those associations to solve archaeological problems. It should have its own "cognitive core" and should interact with the world to make changes or to sense what is happening. In so saying, I am not arguing that machines run as human brains or that computer representations should be isomorphic to "mental" states. Rather, I want to understand reasoning processes by understanding the underlying abstract causal nature behind what archaeologists do. If a computer can be programmed to perform human-like tasks, it will offer a "model" of the human activity that is less open to argument than the verbalized explanations that are normal in philosophy. The purpose is then to understand how intelligent behavior is possible in archaeology.

I am just arguing that the activity of machine and human automata can be described and analyzed in the same terms. The idea of an intelligent robot should be seen as a model of archaeologist's behavior rather than an explanation of his or her mind. Computer hardware and programming techniques enable the model builder to construct virtual creatures that behave in intelligent and flexible ways under natural conditions. They provide powerful (and perhaps indispensable) tools for building such creatures, but they can play no role as explanatory kinds by themselves.

In some way, computational intelligence provides social scientists with a set of tools with the same degree of finesse as those used in current qualitative studies and with the same mobility, the same capacities of aggregation and synthesis, as those used in quantitative studies by other social sciences. The limitations of these tools and methods are the same as those of any instrument from any scientific discipline. Instead of being restricted to the usual representational schemes based on formal logic and ordinary language, computational approaches to the structure of archaeological reasoning can include many useful representations such as prototypical concepts, concept hierarchies, conceptual spaces, production rules, associative memories, causal networks, mental images, and so on. Researchers concerned with the growth of scientific knowledge from a computational perspective can go beyond the narrow resources of inductive logic to consider algorithms for generating quantitative laws, discovering causal relationships, forming concepts and hypotheses, and evaluating competing explanatory theories. This book presents tools and methods that liberate us from the narrow constraints of words by enforcing rigor in a non-classical way, namely via the constraint of computational realizability.

Maybe some of you will say that we do "not yet" have automatic archaeologists, but we should hurry up to the engineering department and build them for having someone able to substitute us in the tedious task of studying ourselves and our past. Other readers will claim: "fortunately, such a machine will never exist!" "Why we need such an awful junk? Computers cannot emulate humans." These critics seem to think that computer programs are guilty of excessive simplification, of forcing knowledge, or distorting it, and of failing to exploit fully the knowledge of the expert, but it seems to me that it is archaeology, and not computer programs, what is "narrow minded." The saddest thing is that archaeologists do not know how they know archaeological matters.

The so called "intelligent" machines incite instinctive fear and anger by resembling ancestral threats, a rival for our social position as more or less respected specialists. But robots are here, around us. I have never heard of a claim against washing machines selecting "intelligently" the best way to wash a specific tissue, or a photo camera with an "intelligent" device measuring luminance and deciding by itself the parameters to take the picture. So, why have fear of a machine classifying a prehistoric tool and deciding "intelligently" its origin, function and/or chronology? Rather than arguing whether a particular behavior should be called intelligent or not, a point that is always debatable, I try to provide answers to the following question: Given some behavior that we find interesting in some ways, how does the behavior come about? Rather than use intuition as the sole guide for formulating explanations of past human behavior, we need a theory of why a specific computation or a group of related computations should be performed by a system that has certain abilities.

The discussion is between what is considered an artificial way of reasoning (computer programs), and a natural way of reasoning (verbal narrative). Critics of computationalism insist that we should not confound scientific statements with predicate logic operations, since discursive practices or argumentations observed in a scientific text are not "formal." By that reason, they are tributary, to a certain extent, from the Natural Language and the narrative structure (literary) of which scientific texts derive. I take the opposite approach: scientific problem solving stems from the acquisition of knowledge from a specific environment, the manipulation of such knowledge, and the intervention in the real world with the manipulated knowledge. The more exhaustive and better structured the knowledge base, the more it emulates a scientific theory and the easier will be the solution to the scientific problem, and more adequate the interpretations we get.

My personal approach is based on a fact that archaeologists could not evaluate 15 years ago: computer programs do work in real science, not only in archaeology. Maybe they are more successful in other "harder" sciences, but we cannot deduce from this fact that archaeology is a different kind of science. We should instead rebuild archaeology. Simulating or reproducing the way archaeologists think today is not the guide to understand archaeology, because we are doing archaeology in the wrong way! Computable archaeology, if you do not like the expression "automatic archaeology," is the proper way of exploring new ways of thinking old concepts.

In other scientific domains the performance of humans at a particular task has been used to design a robot that can do the same task in the same manner (and as well). In many different domains it has been shown how 'robot scientists' can interpret experiments without any human help. Such robots generate a set of hypotheses from what it is known about a scientific domain, and then design experiments to test them. That is, a robot scientist can formulate theories, carry out experiments and interpret results. For instance, the robot biochemist developed by Ross King of the University of Wales at Aberystwyth, and his colleagues, does everything a flesh-and-blood scientist does—or, rather, it does what philosophers of science say that scientists ought to do. That is, it formulates hypotheses from observations, conducts experiments to test them, and then formulates new hypotheses from the results. And, it does so as effectively as a person. The intellectual input comes from deciding, on the basis of the results obtained, which experiments to do next until you have filled in all the blanks. The robot scientist was able to do this. It was fitted with artificial intelligence software that could perform the logical processes involved in making such decisions, and this software was given a representation of the pathway chosen (one of those by which amino acids, the building blocks of proteins, are made) from which to work. The robot scientist can infer hypotheses to explain observations, infer experiments that will discriminate between these hypotheses, actually do the experiments and understand the results.

Consequently, the design of an automated archaeologist should not be considered a mere science fiction tale. It is a technological reality. Research in cognitive robotics is concerned with endowing robots and software agents with higher level cognitive functions that enable them to reason, act and perceive in changing, incompletely known, and unpredictable environments. Such robots must, for example, be able to reason about goals, actions, when to perceive and what to look for, the cognitive states of other agents, time, collaborative task execution, and so forth. In short, cognitive robotics is concerned with integrating reasoning, perception and action within a uniform theoretical and implementation framework. The question of whether it is possible to such machines to automate the scientific process should be of both great theoretical interest and increasing practical importance because, in many scientific areas, data are being generated much faster than they can be effectively analyzed.

The book is divided into four parts. The first one introduces the subject of "artificial intelligence" within the apparently restricted domain of archaeology and historical sciences. This introductory part contains two chapters. The first one, "'Automatic' Archaeology: A Useless Endeavor, an Impossible Dream, or Reality?" provides an overview of the approach. After discussing the basic concepts of automata theory, the first elements of a formalization of archaeological reasoning are presented. The very idea of archaeological problems is introduced from the point of view of cause-effect analysis and social activity theory. The relationship between archaeological, anthropological, and historical problems is studied in detail, to serve as a basis for a presentation of how a mechanical problem solving procedure would look like in those domains. The chapter ends with a very short presentation of the diversity in current Artificial Intelligence theory and techniques.

The second chapter, "Problem Solving in the Brain and by the Machine," presents the classical artificial intelligence approach to problem solving as search and planning. Rule-based systems are discussed, focusing in its philosophical foundations. Jean Claude Gardin's logicist analysis is used as a relevant archaeological example, together with some of the current expert systems used in practical archaeology. A final debate leads the reader to a discussion about "rationality" and the shortcomings of traditional artificial intelligence and expert systems.

The second section of the book is the most technical one and presents a detailed but understandable account of learning algorithms and neural networks. It has been divided into two chapters. The third chapter, "Computer Systems that Learn," develops the criticism of the classical approach to "intelligent robotics," presenting the way computer systems and "intelligent" robots may learn. Learning is here presented as a predictive task that can be simulated by computers. Many archaeological cases are used through this chapter to understand the algorithmic nature of experimentation and discovery tasks.

The fourth chapter, "An introduction to Neurocomputing," offers a presentation of neural networks. After discussing in plain language what neural networks are, some algorithms are introduced with a minimum of mathematical jargon, here reduced to the basic arithmetic operations. Backpropagation networks are exhaustively analyzed, together with radial basis functions, self-organized maps, Hopfield networks, and other advanced architectures.

Section III constitutes the core of the book, and discusses different examples of computational intelligence in archaeology, with cases concerning rock-art, lithic tools, archeozoology, pottery analysis, remote sensing, ancient settlement investigation, funerary ritual, social organization in prehistoric societies, etc. It has been divided into six chapters.

In Chapter V, "Visual and Non-Visual Analysis in Archaeology," some of the elements introduced in chapter I are developed. A general approach towards an "intelligent" pattern recognition system is presented, discussing the differences between a true visually based system and another one, which uses identified previously—instead of visual—data. This chapter serves as an introduction to the following ones, where practical and relevant examples of archaeological neurocomputing are shown in the domains of shape, texture, composition, spatiotemporal and functional analysis.

Chapter VI, "Shape Analysis in Archaeology," defines the concept of "shape" and presents different approaches to shape representation, analysis, and interpretation. Emphasis has been placed on the analysis of three-dimensional objects and the study of complex shapes.

Chapter VII, "Texture and Compositional Analysis in Archaeology," defines the concepts of "texture" and "composition." It also presents many archaeological applications of neurocomputing in these domains.

Chapter VII, "Spatiotemporal Analysis," has been written in order to explain the way spatial and temporal data (frequencies and densities of archaeological findings, for instance) can be analyzed using neural networks and other similar technologies. The spatial interpolation problem is posed, and different methods for finding a solution are evaluated, showing many real examples. Remote sensing also finds its place in this chapter. Time series and chronological problems are also a form of interpolation problem. Neural networks can be used to solve it, but we also need specifically organized networks to deal with recursiveness and related questions. The focus is on spatiotemporal explanatory models, not only from a strictly archaeological point of view but with a more general social science and historical perspective.

In Chapter IX, "An Automated Approach to Historical and Social Explanation," visually based explanatory approaches are substituted by a more general account of simulation and modeling, which illustrates how social processes can be simulated as computational mechanisms to be understood. The idea of social classification is discussed, and many examples of simulating social interaction using "populations" of computer programs are finally presented.

To conclude our journey into the automatization of scientific reasoning, the book ends with a Section IV that presents a theoretical discussion on the philosophy of social sciences and the benefits of computers and nonlinear algorithmic approaches. This part is composed of a single chapter that explores the theoretical consequences that may arise when using computational intelligence technologies to study the human past. Here the "robot" analogy gives its place to a proper account of a Computational Philosophy of Archaeology and related sciences.

It is important to take into account that this is a book on "computational intelligence" in archaeology, and not on "computer applications in archaeology." I have focused the text on the very concept of "explanation," and what it really means to explain archaeological (and historical) data. Therefore, important and usual concepts that are not properly related to "explanation" have less relevance. The reader may ask why I have not included more references to fashionable and apparently modern issues like geographic information systems, visualization and virtual reality. The answer is that these subjects appear in the book, but in a different envelope, insisting in their contributions to archaeological explanation. Therefore, GIS techniques have been included in Chapter VIII on spatiotemporal explanation, and all the discussion on virtual reconstructions has a more logical place in Chapter VI on shape analysis, but it is also analyzed in Chapter X. The reader is referred to other books for the practical side of data bases, GIS, CAD and visualization software. This is a book on the interface between technique and theory. Although some "how-to" is presented, and many practical applications are referred, the book merely opens a door, encouraging the reader to begin a research along this line.

Do not look for a classic presentation of the archaeological practice. This is an unconventional book with very little respect for tradition. In a first reading, the text may seem highly skewed towards computational intelligence, with very little traditional archaeological stuff. Even the number of traditional archaeological references is surprisingly small. This is because my goal has been to open new grounds in archaeology and the social sciences. Technology is not the solution, but it is the way we have to follow if we want to rethink the way archaeology has been done. This emphasis on new ways to understand ancient times explains the apparently minor relevance of traditional aspects. However, they are not absent. They have acquired a new appearance, as a careful reading will prove.

This is not an encyclopedia of archaeological methods and explanations. I could not present all aspects of the archaeological research process nor all available computer science methods. Because any book needs to be focused, I have had to obviate many important aspects that in other circumstances would be interesting. If a majority of readers find the book relevant, and I have the chance to do more research work in this "computable" archaeology, new chapters on archaeological site formation processes or intelligent virtual archaeology environments will follow. The technology is evolving, and each day sees some new advancement. For all information that couldn't be included in the book, and for periodic updates of theories, techniques and technologies, the reader is referred to its related Web page: http://antalya.uab.cat/perhistoria/Barcelo/IGIBook.html.

Acknowledgment

No book is the work of its author alone. Moreover, a book like this, which is based on the investigations of so many researchers from so many different disciplines, is no exception to the rule. I cannot mention every person that sent me their work material and gave me permission to quote some aspects of their research. Although their names are not written on these pages, all of you are acknowledged for your help. I apologize if my presentation of their research does not give justice to those investigations.

This book is the result of a continuing effort since 1989, when I began to explore the possibilities of artificial intelligence in archaeology. I had the chance to work at that time in Paris, with Jean Claude Gardin, Henri-Paul Francfort, and Marie-Salomé Lagrange, who introduced me to the world of expert systems. Jean Claude has also agreed to write a foreword to this book, and I thank him for all he has done. Even if we may not always agree, I believe I am still a sort of "gardinist" in this modern academic world of labels and classifications.

After such introductory work, many friends in the archaeological discipline helped me to understand what it really means to be an archaeologist. I have collaborated or debated with people like María Eugenia Aubet, Luis-Felipe Bate, Hans-Peter Blankholm, Igor Bogdanovic, Ignacio Clemente, Xavier Clop, Ana Delgado, Jose Antonio Esquivel, Jordi Estevez, Maurizio Forte, Sorin Hermon, Luis Lumbreras, Gian Carlo Macchi, Laura Mameli, Glauco Mantegari, Jorge Marcos, Miquel Molist, Eduardo Moreno, Franco Nicolucci, Giuliano Pelfer, Pier-Giovanni Pelfer, Raquel Piqué, Billy Reynoso, Nick Ryan, Maria Saña, Stephanie Spars, Xavier Terrades, Iraida Vargas, Gonçalo Velho, and Assumpció Vila, among others at different places and diverse archaeological sites from Syria to Patagonia. Some of them allowed me to experiment with my technologically-inspired ideas in their projects. The contribution of Jordi Estévez and Raquel Piqué stands out, however. We have been working together for many years in several ways, both teaching at the Universitat Autònoma de Barcelona in Spain, and doing research on the same projects. In some ways, my views on archaeology and computing come from such collaboration.

Since 1991, I have been teaching "artificial intelligence techniques in archaeology" to graduate students at the Universitat Autònoma de Barcelona. Although many students were only moderately interested on that subject, Ferran Borrell, Iván Briz, Florencia Del Castillo, Alfredo Maximiano, Jordi Pijoan-López, Andrea Toselli, David Travet, Oriol Vicente, and Esther Verdún decided that the subject was interesting enough to learn a bit more, and they all began to investigate in their own way. They helped me to focus my attention in directions that I had never explored before. Two of them merit special mention. I have been working with Jordi Pijoan-López for many years on our project on neural networks for use wear analysis. Now, he has finished his PhD, and I was also finishing this book. We have made many things together, and many more wait to be done. Alfredo Maximiano was the last to join our laboratory on quantitative archaeology. Perhaps I have worked with him more than with any other. He is no longer my student, but a colleague looking for a way in his own, and a friend in many subjects, especially on spatial analysis. He has been able to understand my cryptic thinking, when I couldn't understand what

I was thinking about. If my discussion on spatial analysis has some coherence, it is due to him. Jordi and Alfredo: thanks for everything, but of course, you do not have responsibility for the way I describe what we had been working on together.

Parts of this book comes from a former publication in Spanish. At that time, Professor María Eugenia Aubet from the Universitat Pompeu Fabra in Barcelona contributed to the funding and publication of that research. Afterwards, the Spanish Ministry for Education and Research, and the Spanish Ministry for Culture funded all my investigations through successive research grants awarded to me or to my colleagues Jordi Estévez and Assumpció Vila. The Catalan Government and the European Union also funded the acquisition of some software I have been using throughout the book, and provided grants and fellowships so some graduate students could work with me.

As lecturer at the Department of Prehistory, at the Universitat Autònoma de Barcelona, and head of its Quantitative Archaeology Lab, my institution also merits acknowledgement. The working conditions could not be any better and the University itself has funded some parts of the research presented in this book. Our research group is associated with the corresponding unit at the Institució Milà i Fontanals (Spanish National Research Council). Many aspects of the book come from our collaborative work, and the Institució has funded some aspects of this research.

This book would have been very different without the Computer Applications and Quantitative Methods in Archaeology Society. I participated in a conference in 1991 for the first time, in Oxford. Since that time, I have attended nearly all the annual meetings. It was there that I presented my first papers, and where the subject of artificial intelligence in archaeology evolved through time.

Some friends and colleagues read some earlier drafts of the book and made very interesting comments. I acknowledge the efforts by Geoff Carver, James Doran, John Fulcher, and Glauco Mantegari. Special thanks to Flavia Mameli for her help in grammar checking.

I am also grateful to the IGI Global, for accepting this book for publication, especially when I was losing any hope of seeing it in print. The publisher sent the book to three anonymous referees, who made important suggestions that I have tried to follow to ameliorate the book. Special thanks to all staff at IGI Global, especially to Jessica Thompson, my managing development editor.

This is a long list of acknowledgements, but no person or institution is responsible for any inexactitudes, errors, or mistakes that may remain in the text.

Far from the scientific background, I would never have finished this book without the love and patience of my family, although most of them didn't read a single line of it. My parents, my mother in law, my sisters, and sisters-in-law were always near me, giving full support when I needed it.

In the end, nobody deserves more acknowledgement and deep gratitude than Laura and Martí. With her immense love, Laura encouraged me to begin, to continue, and to finish what seemed at the very beginning to be a never ending story. She also discussed with me many aspects of the book. Being very critical with the "automatization" prospect, she helped me to clarify ideas, and to analyze previously unsuspected consequences of my former attitudes. Martí arrived in this world when the book was already on the desk, and when the writing seemed harder. It is not easy to write a book and take care of a child at the same time. I apologize for not playing with him as much as he needed. Even on weekends, neural networks seemed more important than telling him stories or playing with his building blocks. For those reasons, it is you, Martí, more than any other, that I dedicate this book.

The book is finally finished. I can forget about robots and archaeology for a while. I can come back to you again, my beloved Laura and Martí.

Section I
From Natural Archaeology to "Artificial" Intelligence

Chapter I
"Automatic" Archaeology:
A Useless Endeavour, an Impossible Dream, or Reality?

AUTOMATA: THE AWFUL TRUTH ABOUT HUMANS AND MACHINES

Let us begin with a trivial example. Imagine a machine with artificial sensors, a brain, and some communication device. Suppose that such a machine is able to "see" prehistoric artifacts made of flint. The purpose of this automated archaeologist should be to "explain" the function of archaeological material. It decides consequently to measure, for instance, three properties: shape, texture, and size. The shape sensor will output a 1 if the prehistoric tool is approximately round and a −1 if it is more elliptical. The texture sensor will output a 1 if the surface of the artifact is smooth and a −1 if it is rough. The size sensor will output a 1 if the artifact is greater than 20 cm, and a −1 if it is less than 20 cm. The three sensor outputs will then be fed as input to the thinking core of the robot, whose purpose is to execute a function deciding which kind of tool has been discovered buried at this precise location. An input pattern is determined to belong to class *Knife* if there is a function, which relates incoming inputs with an already defined concept "knife," or otherwise a "scraper." As each observed element passes through the sensors, it can be represented by a three dimensional vector. The first element of the vector will represent shape, the second element will represent texture, and the third element will represent size.

$$P = \begin{pmatrix} Shape \\ Texture \\ Size \end{pmatrix}$$

Therefore, a prototype knife would be represented by

$$P_1 = \begin{pmatrix} -1 \\ 1 \\ 1 \end{pmatrix}$$

and a prototype scraper would be represented by

$$P_2 = \begin{pmatrix} 1 \\ -1 \\ 1 \end{pmatrix}$$

The task of this automated archaeologist will be to assign to any artifact, represented by some features, visual or not, some meaning or explanatory concept. In other words, the performance of such an automated archaeologist is a three-stage process: Feature extraction, recognition, and explanation by which an input (description of the archaeological record) is transformed into an explanatory concept, in this case, the *function* of an archaeologically perceived entity (Figure 1). In order for the system to make a decision as to whether the object is a knife or a scraper, input information should be recognized, that is "categorized," in such a way that once "activated" the selected categories will guide the selection of a response.

Let us move to a more interesting example. Imagine a specialized mobile robot equipped with video cameras, 3D scanners, remote sensors, excavator arms, suction heads and tubes, manipulation hands for taking samples exploring in the search of evidence for archaeological sites, excavating the site by itself, describing the discovered evidence, and analyzing samples and materials (Barceló, 2007). Or even better, imagine a team of robots doing different kinds of archaeological tasks, those tasks that, up to now, have been a matter of human performance. The idea is to develop an exploration system that allows a robot to explore and extract relevant features from the world around it, expressing them in some specific way. This unit should use visual and non-visual information to make decisions about how to find archaeological evidence. This specialized robot will use stereoscopic CCD cameras, laser rangers, sonar, infrared sensors, georadar, magnetometers,

and construct a multidimensional representation of geometric space. From this representation, it will recognize locations, plan trajectories, and distinguish objects by shape, color, and location. The robot should acquire a sense of general spatial awareness, and to be able to do it, it probably needs an especially fine representation of the volume around it to precisely locate archaeological objects and structures and visually monitor performance. In other words, the first member of our team has to learn how to find an archaeological site, based on the perceived properties of the observed archaeological elements.

The second member of the team emulates what most archaeologists think is the definition of their job: *the* excavation *of an* archaeological site. Archaeological robots should do much more than just explore and visualize what is observable. They should take samples from the ground, and they should dig and unearth material evidence. When evaluating the differences between visual and non-visual information, the robot takes the decision of removing what prevents the visualization of the archaeological evidence: earth. The explorer becomes an excavator.

It is easy to see that this team of robots also needs some specialized understanding component. This component is concerned with a specific mechanism able to identify archaeological evidence, and to solve specific goals linked to this distinction. The automated archaeologist should correlate evidence and explanation adequately in order to generate a solution to an archaeological

Figure 1.1. The performance of an automated archaeologist as a three-stage process

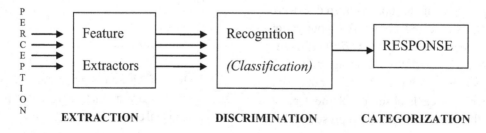

problem. In the same way, our intelligent machine should have the ability to reflect on what it has done, to explain what it is doing and why, to answer questions about why it did not do something and explain what would have happened if it had done something different, or describe what someone else had done wrong. A computer program will implement this understanding component. It is important to keep these two ideas distinct. A cognitive function is an abstract mathematical description of what to do and how to accomplish the task; the computer program is a concrete implementation, running on the agent hardware architecture. What is difficult is to discover (or to *learn*) such a function, but once we have it, it is very easy to implement it in software or hardware circuitry.

This example of the team of explorer-excavator-explanator robots may seem science fiction by the way, it is! However, actual technology allows the construction of such a machine, allowing us going even further. We can imagine an "intelligent machine" able to translate any visual and non-visual information about the material outcomes of social action into a causal explanation of the actions having generated those observables. Given a detailed description of burials, bodies and grave goods, such a machine should be able to explain the kind of society, which most reliably performed such a ritual activity in the past.

Archaeological research involves an intricate set of interrelated goals, and therefore, an intricate set of interrelated *problems*. We want to produce knowledge, to preserve data, and to prevent the loss of information about past human behavior. Why can't intelligent machines contribute in such an effort? We can create a specialized automated archaeologist to solve each kind of problem types in archaeology (see Table 1).

Table 1. Problem types in archaeology (adapted from Root-Bernstein, 1989; Wagman, 2002)

TYPE	GOAL TO BE ACHIEVED	MACHINE TASK
Definition	What is society? What is a social class? What is an archaeological site? What is a tool?	Invention of concept or taxonomy
Theory	How do we explain the distribution of this pottery type? Why do these objects have this shape?	Invention of theory
Data	What information is needed to test or build a theory?	Observation, experiment
Technique	How can we obtain data? How do we analyze it? How may the phenomenon best be displayed?	Invention of instruments and methods of analysis and display
Evaluation	How adequate is a definition, theory, observation or technique? Is something a true anomaly or an artifact?	Invention of criteria for evaluation
Integration	Can two disparate theories or sets of data be integrated? Does Binford contradict Hodder?	Reinterpretation and rethinking of existing concepts and ideas.
Extension	How many cases does a theory explain? What are the boundary conditions for applying a theory or a technique?	Prediction and testing
Comparison	Which theory or data set is more useful?	Invention of criteria for comparison
Application	How can this observation, theory or technique be used?	Knowledge of related unsolved problems
Instrument	Do these data disprove the theory? Is the technique for data collection appropriate?	Recognition that problem is insoluble as stated

Simply stated, an *automaton* is a discrete processing mechanism, characterized by internal states. Bright (1958) divided machines up into 17 types. For the purpose of this book, I follow Collins and Kusch (1998) classification of machines in five types:

- **Behavers:** Machines that just do something.
- **Disjunctive behavers:** Machines that do something according to a predetermined list of choices.
- **Feedback behavers:** Machines that respond to anything within a preconceived range of sensed stimuli. Note that the behavior of a feedback behaver is not predictable in advance.
- **Learning behavers:** Machines that take information from their environment and their users, or both, and incorporate this in their design.

It is necessary to insist in the fact that an automated archaeologist is a computer program that *acts* (Stein, 1995). In our case, what the machine does is a kind of *epistemic action* (Kirsch & Maglio, 1995). Expressed in its most basic terms, the epistemic action to be performed may be understood in terms of *predicting* which explanations should be generated in face of determined evidence. In that sense, explanations are for our automatic archaeology machine a form of acting. Explanation is not an explanatory structure, nor something that explains, but a process of providing understanding. Explanation is something that people *do*, not an eternal property of sets of sentences (Thagard, 1988).

We can define an automated *explanation* as some *function* that maps any given stimulus to a response (Aleksander & Morton, 1993). Explanation involves activating an input-output function (*explanans*) that enables any automaton, be it human or robotic, to deal with a situation (*explanandum*) for which understanding is needed.

What gives its truly "intelligent" character to the automated archaeologist is the non-trivial connection between perception (data) and action (explanation) (Brady, 1985). If we assume that archaeological knowledge is just something that goes through a mechanism from an input sensor to an output actuator or "explanator," during which it is processed, then the robot task would be the "interpretation of the change experimented by this knowledge under a given goal" (Kitamura & Mizougouchi, 2004). The automated archaeologist should also be capable of changing its internal state structure over time according to a set of algorithms that take information from the automaton's own previous state and various inputs from outside the automaton to determine a new state in a subsequent time step. In this way, automated archaeologists will have the capacity to process information from their surroundings and to alter their characteristics accordingly. They will be flexible and efficient abstractions that enable the construction of detailed, complex, and dynamic models.

The possible tasks of such intelligent machines can be divided into three very general categories. If a task involves obtaining information about the empirical characteristics of an archaeological site or some archaeological material and producing a representation useful for other tasks (description, representation, analysis, explanation), then it falls in the SENSE category. If the task is based on processing information and evaluating the possibilities for generating explanations (either from primary data or some previous theoretical knowledge about the material evidence of social action, already implemented in the robot's cognitive core), we say that the cognitive robot is PLANNING its future behavior. Finally, and most importantly, robotic tasks, which produce explanations, fall into the ACT category.

A simple but quite general conception of what it means to act is to produce a specific output pattern for a given input pattern (Figure 2). The input specifies the context, contingencies, or demands of

Figure 1.2. A definition for automaton: Producing a specific output pattern for a given input pattern

the task, and the output is the appropriate response (O'Reilly & Munakata, 2000, p. 147).

An automaton changes its current state over time according to a set of rules that take information from an automaton's own state and various inputs from outside to determine a new state in a subsequent time step. In this way, automata have the capacity to process information from their surroundings and to alter their characteristics accordingly. The essence of the automata approach is in temporal discreteness and its ability to change according to predetermined rules based on internal and external information.

Here lies the cognitive core of our robot. It should store and retrieve abstract, mathematical, or logical descriptions implemented in a computer program, which takes the current observation as input from the sensors and returns an explanation. By applying some input to the system, it will produce new actions in response. The point is that outputs are the resulting actions that a machine performs in some environment as a response to what has been perceived. Thus, an automated archaeologist involves two sets of actions: (1) *Inputs*—the information introduced in the machine (data, "percepts"); (2) *Outputs*—the explanatory action that the machine applies to incoming data. Two factors are responsible for the production of output actions. The first are the input actions, which we have just discussed. The second factor consists of certain properties that the machine has at the time of the input. In other words, there is a set of properties of the machine, called the automaton's *states* that determine which output actions the machine will produce in response

to its input actions. We have consequently two simultaneous mechanisms:

Input x State → Output
Input x State → New State

The activity of an automaton should be divided into two subsets: (1) the set of actions that the machine contributes to any resulting causal interaction with the environment, and (2) the set of changes in the machine itself.

Essentially, the idea is to set up appropriate, well-conditioned, tight feedback loops between input and output, with the actual and past observations as the medium for the loop. In other words, our automatic archaeologist relies on the definition of a set of input events $I_1, I_2, \ldots$ and a set of output events $Z_1, Z_2, \ldots$ and relates the two through the intervention of a set of internal states $Q_1, Q_2, \ldots$ This intervention takes the following form: every pair of elements, one taken from the set of inputs and the other from the set of internal states, represents a possible combination of a present input and a present state. Such a pair is related to a unique "next" state. Outputs can be related directly to the internal states. In this way, the system arrives at an internal state through a chain of inputs, different chains leading to different states (Aleksander & Morton, 1993; Dawson, 2004).

The only way we have to make a machine explain what it perceives is by implementing some algorithms that map any given input sequence to an output action. We can say that an automated archaeologist's activity is described by the function that maps any given percept sequence to explanation. Each time an explanation is asked for some input, the machine does two things. First, it tells its "brain," or cognitive core, what it is being perceived. Second, it executes some "deliberative" procedure to decide what action it should perform. In the process of answering this query, extensive reasoning may be done about the current state of the world, about the outcomes of possible cognitive action sequences, and so on. Once the action is chosen, the automated archaeologist records its choice and executes the explanation. Essentially, the idea seems to set up appropriate, well-conditioned, tight feedback loops between the perceived input and its explanation (Donahoe & Palmer, 1994). For any mapping $m: A \rightarrow B$ in the system, we will call A the stimulus set (or input), and B the response set (or output), and we will consider the mapping m as a behavior. We are replacing the concepts of data and explanation by the concepts of information input and output. In addition, theories about mediating stimulus-response chains would be replaced by theories about internal computations and computational states.

What characterizes an automaton is the fact that, if the machine has some data, the response is completely determined by the data and the machine's state at that time. This deterministic character, however, has been mistaken with simple, direct association of a stimulus with a response, and it is the reason of the poor reputation of automata. Nevertheless, this algorithmic way of perceiving-deciding-and-acting characterizes both human scientists and cognitive robots. Maybe humans do not think that way, but scientific knowledge should be produced in that way. After all, scientific reasoning is an *artificial* way of thinking, and it has nothing to do with common sense, or reasoning in everyday practice.

How must we go about artificially reproducing archaeological reasoning in a robot? The current state of the field is such that no straightforward answer is possible. If we are going to say that an artificial machine thinks like a human, we must have some way of determining how humans think. We need to get inside the actual workings of human minds. It has been said that machines cannot act as humans do. They cannot be involved in "intentional actions" (cf. Collins & Kusch, 1998), because they do not have an understanding of the purpose or motivation of the action. Although machines do not have intentions, they can be made to mimic the mechanism used by humans to produce their own explanations. The boundary between humans and machines is then permeable, at least insofar as machines can be programmed with a surrogate of "intention." The computer's program, which determines the order and/or circumstances in which the operations are performed, can be thought of as a virtual machine. It "models" or imitates a set of relationships that may be quite unlike those expressed in the operation of the physical machine in which it is implemented, as evidenced by the possibility of running the same program on a range of computers with different physical structures (Rutkowska, 1993).

Thirty years ago Dreyfuss (1972) criticized the very idea of "artificial" intelligence, saying that scientists know too little about how the mind works to be able to create the kind of reasoning that humans take for granted. He was not so wrong. No one knows what "thinking" really means anyway, so we cannot answer the question of whether a machine can truly think. This is mostly true in archaeology, history, and the social sciences. The trouble is that we do not know what "archaeological," "historical," "anthropological," or "sociological" reasoning really means. Therefore, before thinking about endowing robots with "real cognition" (whatever that means) a number of fundamental and programmatic issues need to be addressed. *Without an understanding of what archaeology really is, we cannot see how we can successfully fabricate an automated archaeologist.* If archaeology is just excavating old remains, then a robot will do it better than us. What should we do for *studying* old remains? What does it mean to study the past?

ARCHAEOLOGY AS A PROBLEM SOLVING TASK

Let us suppose that our "intelligent machine" is at an archaeological site. It excavates and unearths many things. It sees what a human archaeologist supposes are tools, rubbish generated by some past society, the remains of their houses… Is the automated archaeologist sure that the human archaeologist is right? Why does this object look like a container? Why does this other seem an arrow point? Are those stones being correctly interpreted as the remains of a house? Can "activity areas" be recognized within an ancient hunter-gatherer settlement? Were those remains produced for some social elite in a class society? How can social inequality be discovered?

Most of these questions seem out of order for mainstream archaeological studies. Current archaeological explanations, like most social science explanations, seem addressed to tell us what happens *now* at the archaeological site. They do not tell us what happened in the past, nor *why* or *how*. A substantial proportion of research effort in archaeology and the social sciences isn't expended directly in explanation tasks; it is expended in the business of unearthing the traces of social action, without arguing *why* those actions took place there and then. The fact is that it is very difficult to publish a paper that simply suggests an explanation of social action. Most archaeology journals want reports of excavations and data. *Explanation* is relegated to the "discussion" section, which is generally lose and, frankly, speculative compared to the rest of the paper.

Our automated archaeologist, although it is perfectly capable of doing archaeology in the traditional way, is a bit more ambitious. It considers archaeology as a problem solving discipline, centered on *historical* problems, whose focus is on explaining existing perceivable phenomena in terms of long past causes. The aim of this parable of automated archaeology is to remark the fact that the goal of archaeology is to study social

causation and not just objects. I am programming the automated archaeologist to perform the kind of cognitive tasks I presume define archaeology as a social science: the perceived present is the consequence of human action in the past, interacting with natural processes through time. Human action exists by its capacity to produce and reproduce people, labor, goods, capital, information, and social relationships. In this situation, the obvious purpose of archaeological data is to be used as evidence of past actions. An archeological site is something to be explained.

Any consequence of social action should be considered an *archaeological evidence* or *artifact*: the bones of a hunted animal, the bones of a buried human body, a territory, even an empty place is the consequence of some action; cleaning, for instance. The outcomes of social activity can be anything participating in a transformation process, including both material tools and tools for thinking (e.g., instruments, signs, procedures, machines, methods, laws, and forms of labor organization). Social relationships are then *effects* because they are events produced by social actions. People are the material consequence of human work, too, in the same sense as authority, coercion, information, a village, territory or landscape are *products* of human work.

By assuming that what it perceives in the present are simply the material effects of human work, the automated archaeologist should understand "archaeological percepts" as material things that were products at the very beginning of their causal history. It has to analyze archaeological observables within the context of social activity by identifying the ways people produced (and/or used) the artifact, the needs it served, and the history of its development.

In that sense, *production, use and distribution are the social processes which in some way have produced (*cause*) archaeologically observed properties* (effect) (Figure 1. 3).

Archaeological artifacts have specific physical properties because they were produced so

Figure 1.3. An automated archaeologist analyzes archaeological materials within the context of social activity by identifying the ways people produced (and/or used) the artifact, the needs it served, and the history of its development

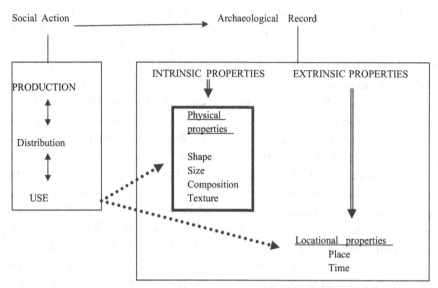

that they had those characteristics and not some other. They were produced in that way, at least partially, because those things were intended for some given uses and not some other: they were tools, or consumed waste material, or buildings, or containers, or fuel, and so forth. If objects appear in some locations and not in any other, it is because social actions were performed in those places and at those moments. Therefore, archaeological items have different shapes, sizes, and compositions. They also have different textures, and appear at different places and in different moments. That is to say, the changes and modifications in the form, size, texture, composition, and location that nature experiences as the result of human action (work) are determined somehow by these actions (production, use, distribution) having provoked its existence.

It is not hard to see that the automated archaeologist has a much more developed definition of archaeology than is usual, that of a discipline dealing with *events* instead of mere objects.

An event instance describes a state or a change in the state of specific object attributes and occurs at a specific time (Doyle, 2006; Findler & Bickmore, 1996). The automated archaeologist defines archaeological events as an expression of the fact that some percept has some feature f in some space and temporal location e, that the perceived entity is in a state s and that the features defining state s of that entity are changing or not according to another space and temporal location e. The fact that a vessel has shape x, and the fact that a lithic tool has texture t are events, because a social action has been performed at this spatial and temporal location (event), resulting in some artifact with, among other things, some specific shape and texture properties. The fact that "a pit has a specific shape," and the fact that "there are some animal bones inside that pit" are also events, because a social action was performed at this spatial and temporal location (event), resulting in a modification of the physical space: first the excavation of a pit, and then an accumulation of garbage items.

In that sense, the automated archaeologist considers archaeology as a problem solving task:

WHY IS THE PRESENT OBSERVATION THE WAY IT IS?
WHAT ACTION OR PROCESS CAUSED WHAT IT IS SEEING NOW?

In other words,

WHY THE OBSERVED MATERIAL ENTITIES HAVE SPECIFIC VALUES OF SIZE, SHAPE, TEXTURE, COMPOSITION, AND WHY DO THEY APPEAR AT SOME SPECIFIC SPATIAL AND TEMPORAL LOCATION?

Archaeology for our intelligent machine equals to solve such *why* questions. Their answer will always imply some kind of *causal affirmation*.

To produce causal affirmations, the cognitive robot should know what a cause is. "Cause" has been defined as "the way an entity becomes what it is" (Bunge, 1959). In our case, *causal affirmation* should refer to the formation process of society. Social action appears as a transformational process to which the automated archaeologist attributes the cause of what it perceives at the archaeological site. Here, what humans did in the past is analyzed morphologically, in terms of the spatiotemporal characteristics of physical mechanisms involved.

In other words, the automated archaeologist will solve the question "*why* archaeological observables are the way they are" in terms of *how* humans acted around them. It is easy to see that the concept of productivity becomes the heart of this kind of causal explanation. *Productivity* has been called a type of cause, which makes things up from other things. It is the idea of productive capability, which is so important in the explanation of social events because the outcomes of any social action come from entities and actions being made up from old entities and old actions.

Thus, the causal affirmation generated by the automated archaeologist will be expressed in terms of *action*. *Social action* can be defined in terms of purposeful changing of natural and social reality (Davydov, 1999; Engeström, 1987; Leont'ev, 1974; Wobcke, 1998,). In fact, it is a pattern of interactions with the world (Hendriks-Jansen, 1996). Social actions are goal-directed processes that must be undertaken to fulfill some need or motivation. They are conscious (because one holds a goal in mind), and different actions may be undertaken to meet the same goal. However, an action can be an intentional action without the actor having to be aware of the intention from moment to moment. Motivations or intentions are not just conditions for developing cognitive activity, but real factors influencing productivity and perceivable structure.

It is therefore important to distinguish between:

- **The causal social actions:** Which are processes and mechanisms capable of transforming reality;
- **Causal interactions:** Which are events whereby the effect of a social action has induced a transformation by virtue of its own invariant change-relating capability (Glennan, 1996, 2002). In some sense, those interactions are the factors explaining *why* a social action was performed at a specific time and place, which is, its *motivation* or *reason*.

The automated archaeologist explains social events by showing how their results and consequences fit into a causal structure, that is to say, a vast network of interacting *actions* and *entities*, where a change in a property of an entity dialectically produces a change in a property of another entity. What the automated archaeologist needs to compute is the definition of a complex system that produces the recognized evidence by the *interaction* of a number of actions and entities, where the interactions between them can be characterized by direct, invariant and change-relating generalizations. For example, consider what the main recognizable features of a cup are. Each has a crucial function assigned to it: the flat bottom is for standing the cup on a surface; the handle is for grasping the cup when lifting; the inside is for containing the liquid; the rim is for supporting the cup against the lips when drinking. The assignment of causal interactions to features *defines* the object as a cup (Leyton, 1992, 2005). We may argue, then, that the *use* of a cup is specified in terms of the actions applied to it, for example, standing up, lifting, and so forth, and in terms of the resulting actions that the cup applies back to the environment, for example, conveying the liquid upward. All that means that we are describing the cup in terms of five components:

1. INPUTS: e.g., standing up, lifting, etc.
2. OUTPUTS: e.g., conveying liquid
3. STATES: physical characteristics of the cup, e.g., its shape
4. FIRST CAUSAL RELATIONSHIP:
   e.g., lifting (input) acts on shape (state) →
   conveying liquid (output)
5. SECOND CAUSAL RELATIONSHIP:
   e.g., lifting (input) acts on shape (state) →
   shape does not change (dynamics: next state).

Clearly, nothing is gained if the automated archaeologist introduces as an explanation of how some *x* occurs, an indicator that some *y* occurred (where *x* and *y* refer to different acts, events or processes). Such descriptive mechanisms, even if true, are not explanations but are themselves something to be explained. Statistical regularities do not explain, but require explanation by appeal to the activities of individual entities and collections of entities. Studies offering models for the detection of event-related properties typically fail to distinguish between description and explanation. Usually the only explanation given for how the event in question was perceived was

to describe some hypothetical mechanism that undergoes a given state transition whenever the event undergoes a correlated transition. For instance, the *cause* of a table is not the fact that a board is fixed to four wood legs, and this appearance is regularly associated with what some people refer as "table." The cause of the table lies in the fact that a carpenter, in a specific place and time, did a work action whose goal was to establish a physical and durable relationship between a specific board and some specific wood legs. The wheel of the potter is not the cause of the shape of a vessel; the condition for the existence of a vessel with that shape are a series of working actions made by one or several social agents with a determined goal, and in specific circumstances in which certain techniques and instruments were used.

The simplest way to understand social activity is to realize that in the case of many types of actions, the *same action* can be carried out by an indefinite number of *different behaviors*. At the same time, the same behavior may be the instantiation of many different actions. The presence of variability is characteristic of intentional activity. The variability with which an action of some kind can be realized is thus part of what this kind of action means for the agent. Social activity is characterized by essential variability in the behaviors with which they are executed. The goal-directed nature of actions involves varying behavior to carry out the same action in relation to a situation. Some tools have different use wear texture, *because* they have been used to cut different materials; some vases have different shapes *because* they have been produced in different ways; graves have different compositions *because* social objects circulated unequally between members of a society and were accumulated differentially by elites.

The automated archaeologist looks for changes in the temporal and spatial trajectory of some properties of an entity, which appear to be *causally* linked to changes in properties of another entity. This is what the automated archaeologist considers *a causal transformation.* Careful examination shows that not every observed change is a causal transformation. Transformation means changing an object internally, making evident its essence, and altering it (Davydov, 1999). Many changes of natural and social reality carried out by people or by natural factors affect the object externally without changing it internally. Such changes can hardly be called transformations. Therefore, in order to discern causal effects from accidental changes, the automated archaeologist needs a more strict definition of causal transformation.

This is the reason of emphasizing the use of invariant change-relating capabilities to characterize social events. The automated archaeologist adds the additional stipulation that a relationship between two (or perhaps more) actions and entities should involve an *intervention* if it pretends to explain how one effect brings about a related effect. An *intervention* is an idealized manipulation that determines whether changes in some variable are causally related to changes in another variable. The emphasis on the nature of *interventions* is related to a focus on *practice*: to the automated archaeologist humans are what they do, the way they do it, and also the way they have actually changed the way they did before. What humans did and the way they did it is firmly and inextricably embedded in the social matrix of which every person is a member. This social matrix has to be discovered and analyzed by the cognitive robot. Consequently, it is not possible to understand how people act and work if the unit of study is the unaided individual with no access to other people, or to artifacts for accomplishing the task. The unit of analysis is object-oriented action mediated by human produced tools and signs. Thus, the automated archaeologist is motivated to study context to understand relations among individuals, artifacts, and social groups.

Because of this focus on social actions as *practiced* by human actors in reference to other human actors, the automated archaeologist should take into account that social action has purpose

in mind of the people involved in the action or causal process. Activity theory (Davydov, 1999; Engeström, 1987, 1999; Leont'ev, 1974; Nardi, 1996; Zinchenko, 1996) emphasizes human motivation and purposefulness. Those researchers suggest that social activity is shaped primarily by an intention held by the subject; in fact, humans are able to distinguish one activity from another only by virtue of their differing motivations or intentions.

That is to say, social actions cannot be understood without a frame of reference created by the corresponding social motivation or *intention*. Leont'ev, one of the chief architects of activity theory, describes *social activity* as being composed of subjects, needs, motivations, goals, actions and operations (or behavior), together with mediating artifacts (signs, tools, rules, community, and division of labor) (Leont'ev, 1974). A subject is a person or group engaged in an activity. An intention or motivation is held by the subject and it explains activity. Activities are realized as individual or cooperative *actions*. Chains and networks of such actions are related to each other by the same overall object and motivation. For their part, actions consist of chains of operations, which are well defined behaviors used as answers to conditions faced during the performing of an action. Activities are oriented to motivations, that is, the reasons that are impelling by themselves. Each motivation is an object, material or ideal, that satisfies a need. Actions are the processes functionally subordinated to activities; they are directed at specific conscious goals. Actions are realized through operations that are the result of knowledge or skill, and depend on the conditions under which the action is being carried out.

One social need or motivation may be realized using different actions, depending on the situation. On the other hand, the same action can be associated to different motivations, in which case the action will have a diverse meaning in the context of each motivation. For instance, if the motivation (activity) is "building a house," one of its goals (actions) will be "fixing the roof," the skill (operation) can be hammering, or making bricks, or cutting wood. In the same way:

A person may have the object of obtaining food, but to do so he must carry out actions not immediately directed at obtaining food... His goal may be to make a hunting weapon. Does he subsequently use the weapon he made, or does he pass it on to someone else and receive a portion of the total catch? In both cases, that which energizes his activity and that to which his action is directed do not coincide. (Leont'ev, 1974, quoted by Nardi, 1996, p. 73-74)

The frontier between intentional activity and operational behavior is blurred, and movements are possible in all directions. Intentions can be transformed in the course of an activity. An activity can lose its motivation and become an action, and an action can become an operation when the goal changes. The motivation of some activity may become the goal of an activity, as a consequence of which the later is transformed into some integral activity. Therefore, it is impossible to make a general classification of what an activity is, what an action is and so forth, because the definition depends on what the subject or object in a particular real situation is.

Since social activity is not relative to one individual, but to a distributed collection of interacting people and the consequences of their actions, the automated archaeologist will not study how social activities took place by understanding the intentions or motivations of individual agents alone, no matter how detailed the knowledge of those individuals might be. To capture the *teleological,* or purposive aspect of behavior, it should investigate collective action, that is, why different people made the same action, or different actions at the same place and at the same time. Its research goal should be to explain the sources or causes of that variability, and not exactly the inner *intentions* of individual action. Some relevant questions to

be solved are: Why this group of people always hunted rabbits when living in those mountains? Why funerary practices are so different among different social classes? Why this people used the same instruments to prepare their food, whereas this other group of people used a very different toolbox for the same task? How was social hierarchy? Why some people accumulated more capital than others? Why the social elite had more chances of survival than the rest of society? Why social action changes through time and space, and how other actions were performed in such a way that they caused the performance of a new action?

The automated archaeologist moves the unit of analysis to the system and finds its center of gravity in the functioning of the relationships between social activities, social action, operations, and social actors. The unit of analysis is thus not the individual, nor the context, but a relation between the two. The term *contradiction* is used to indicate a misfit within the components of social action; that is, among subjects, needs, motivations, goals, actions and operations, and even mediating artifacts (division of labor, rules, institutions, etc.), and produces internal tensions in apparently irregular qualitative changes, due to the changing predominance of one over other. Social activities are virtually always in the process of working through contradictions, which manifest themselves as problems, ruptures, breakdowns, clashes, and so forth. They are accentuated by continuous transitions and transformations between subjects, needs, motivations, goals, behavior, signs, tools, rules, community, division of labor, and between the embedded hierarchical levels of collective motivation-driven activity, individual goal-driven action, and mechanical behavior driven by the tools and conditions of action. Here lies the true nature of social causality and the motivation force of change and development: there is a global tendency to resolve underlying tension and contradictions by means of change and transformation. To discover the *cause* of observed changes and transformations, the cognitive robot should look for tensions and contradictions between the components of social activity.

An important aspect of this way of understanding social causality is that it forces the analysis to pay attention to the flux of ongoing activities, to focus on the unfolding of real activity in a real setting. In other words, social activities are not isolated entities; they are influenced by other activities and other changes in the environment. The automated archaeologist uses a very specific notion of context: the activity itself is the context. What takes place in an activity system composed of objects, actions and operations, *is* the context. People interact, influence others, reinforce some actions, interfere with others, and even sometimes prevent the action of other people. People consciously and deliberately generate contexts (activities) in part through their own objects; hence, context is not just "out there" (Nardi, 1996). Context is not an outer container or shell inside of which people behave in certain ways. It is constituted through the performance of an activity involving people and artifacts.

Therefore, the relationship between *social actions as cause* and *social actions as effect* appears to be extraordinarily complex, because the aspects of social action we are interested in are divisible in components with their own dynamics, often contradictory. On the other hand, external influences change some elements of activities, causing imbalances between them.

To sum up, we have to build a cognitive robot which should not only be able to explain existing perceivable phenomena in terms of their causes, but in terms of the human purposeful activity and operational behavior performed in the past and responsible of what has been performed until the present. The automated archaeologist will base its reasoning about social causality by accepting that each social behavior is by definition uniquely constituted by the confluence or interaction of particular factors that come together to form one "situation" or *event*. Such factors, mostly contradictory among themselves, are the same

components of social activity we have enumerated so far. That means that to know the cause of social actions, the automated archaeologist should specify an indivisible conjunction of particularities giving rise to a unique situation where social activity takes place.

That means that the automated archaeologist should study a *double causality chain*:

- What is the causal process or processes responsible of the actual appearance of what it "perceives" in the present?
- What is the causal process or processes responsible of human activity performed in the past?

In the same way as human archaeologists, an automated archaeologist needs to document *what, where and when* before explaining *why* some social group made something, and *how*. Only after solving preliminary perceptual recognition (*what?*), the automated archaeologist can ask more general problems about the cause for social actions (*why?*). It is obvious that solving the first kind of problem is a condition to solve the second.

The following pages will try to offer an account of the first kind of problem (*archaeological recognition*). The study of the cause of social activity will be put off until the last chapters of the book.

WHY ARCHAEOLOGICAL OBSERVABLES ARE THE WAY THEY ARE? THE MECHANICAL NATURE OF ARCHAEOLOGICAL RECOGNITION

As we have seen throughout this book, human and machine archaeologists seem to be interested in knowing *why* what they (we) archaeologically "see" or "perceive" (shape, size, composition, texture, location of archaeological elements), predict the way things having those properties had been produced or used in the past (Figure 1.4). I am using here the term *percept* to refer to the archaeologist's data inputs at any given instant. Following Leyton (1992), I understand the task of perception to be the recovery of *causal interactions*. That is, the role of perception is to unpack time from this memory.

The main assumption is that some percept (*archaeological description*) is related to a causal affirmation about the causal event (social action) having produced the perceived evidence (*archaeological explanation*). In our case, it implies to *predict* the cause or formation process of some archaeological entity given some *perceived* evidence of the effect of this causal process. In its most basic sense, then, the task may be reduced to the problem of detecting localized key perceptual stimuli or features, which are unambiguous cues to appropriate causal events. For instance, a distinctive use wear texture on the surface of a lithic tool, and not on others predict that these tools have been used to process fresh wood, and we infer that at some moment a group of people was cutting trees or gathering firewood. Alternatively, we can consider that the shape of some pottery vases predicts their past use as containers for wine, and then we have traces of wine production and trade; the composition of some graves predicts the social personality of the individual buried there and hence the existence of social classes. Here the output is not the object (trees or firewood, wine, social elite), but a cause: cutting trees or gathering firewood, wine production and trade, social power and coercion.

Interpretations of this kind typically constitute what we may call *inverse engineering*. Inverse problems refer to problems in which one has observations on the response, or part of the response, of a system and wishes to use this information to ascertain properties that are more detailed. It entails determining unknown *causes* based on observation of their *effects*. This is in contrast to the corresponding direct problem, whose solution involves finding effects based on a complete description of their causes. That is to say, the automated archaeologist has to be able to infer the motivations and goals of social action based on perceived material transformations, which are the consequence of such motivations and goals. When the relevant properties of the social action and their motivations are assumed known, as well as the initial and boundary conditions, a model then predicts the resultant effect: how reality has been transformed.

There is usually an enormous number of material effects of a past event that are individually enough (given the right theoretical assumptions) to infer the social action's occurrence *there* and *then*: the presence of a house means that someone built it when other people lived there for some time, and abandoned it after that. The trick is finding such material clues of past action, in terms of the perceived modifications caused by the same action, and preserved until today. In

Figure 1.4. Archaeological explanation as an Input-Output function

PERCEPTION: Input

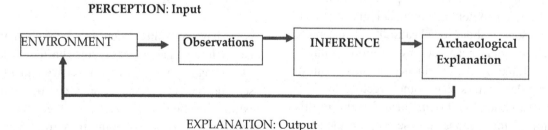

EXPLANATION: Output

other words, the automated archaeologist looks for "a smoking gun:" "a trace(s) that unmistakably discriminates one hypothesis from among a set of currently available hypotheses as providing "the best explanation" of the traces thus far observed" (Cleland, 2002, p. 481). Instead of inferring test implications from a target hypothesis and performing a series of experiments, the automated archaeologist focus its attention on formulating mutually exclusive hypotheses about social action in the past and searching for evidentiary traces in the present to discriminate among them. This places the automated archaeologist in the position of criminal investigators. Just as there are many different possibilities for catching a criminal, so there are many different possibilities for establishing what caused the perceptual properties of material effects of past actions. Like criminal investigators, the automated archaeologist collects observables, considers different suspects, and follows up leads. Unlike stereotypical criminal investigations, however, a smoking gun for a historical hypothesis merely picks one hypothesis as providing the best explanation currently available; it does not supply direct confirming evidence for a hypothesis independently of its rivals.

Any one of a large of contemporaneous, disjoint combinations of traces is enough to conclude that the event occurred. The automated archaeologist does not need to perceive every sherd of pottery, bone, or stone in order to infer that people lived there and did something. A surprisingly small number of appropriately dispersed fragments will do. The over determination of causes by their effects makes it difficult to fake past events by engineering the appropriate traces since there will typically be many other traces indicating fakery. This is not to deny that traces may be so small, far flung, or complicated that no human being nor intelligent machine could ever decode them.

Let us consider with more detail archaeological perception, and how it can be implemented in the robot's hardware and software. The first we have to take into account when dealing with

archaeological "perception" is that archaeology is a quintessentially "visual" discipline, because it makes us aware of such fundamental properties of objects as their size, orientation, shape, color, texture, spatial position, distance, all at once. Visual cues often tell us about more than just optical qualities. In particular, the mechanical properties of a thing of any kind are often expressed in its image.

If human archaeologists have eyes, automated archaeologists have diverse onboard sensors. The sensor is a device that measures some visual attribute of the world. Regardless of sensor hardware or application, they can be thought of the way a robot interacts with the world. If human archaeologists have a brain to think on what they see, in a cognitive robot the sensor observation should be intercepted by a perceptual mechanism, which extracts the relevant percept of environment for the problem solving behavior (Figure 1.5). This percept is then used by the inference mechanism, which leads to explanation.

Explanation occurs when a perceptual input matches a perceptual memory containing a description of each causal event the system is expected to *recognize* or *identify*. Visual recognition means here the reasoning process during which the social action's *observable* effects are used to specify the conceptual identity of the causal action. At this level, we should distinguish:

- Event recognition can be defined as the process of finding and "labeling events [in the real world] based on known causal models," that is event recognition is the process of deciding what category of causal processes an observed effect belongs to.
- Event identification can be defined as the process of deciding which individual event it is, rather than deciding what category of causal processes it belongs to.

Historically, the traditional approach to explaining what has been perceived was cat-

Figure 1.5. Mechanizing the process of perception-explanation

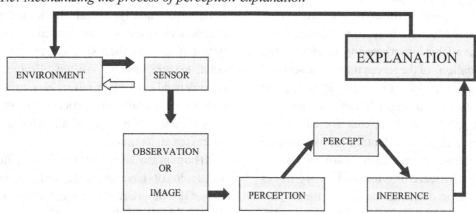

egorization in the guise of *associationism* and unconscious inference. That is, the meaning of an object was thought to be accessed by its visual appearance's activating a category representation that was linked to known interpretations via associations in memory. This is the basics of what has been called *pattern matching*. Pattern matching is actually a very broad concept, and it is useful to distinguish among types of matching. *Pattern completion* has been defined as the mapping of an incomplete pattern onto a completed version of the same pattern. *Pattern transformation* is the mapping of one pattern onto a different, related pattern. *Pattern association* is the arbitrary mapping of one pattern onto another, unrelated pattern. Finally, *pattern recognition* has been defined as the mapping of a specific pattern onto a more general pattern (that is, the identification of an individual as an exemplar of a class). In statistical terms, one first extracts a sufficient set of characteristic features from the primary input patterns, and then applies statistical decision theory for the identification and the classification of the latter.

Comparing an internal model with an external input is assumed the basis for perception understanding. The recognition of one input constitutes an internal cue, which facilitates explanation together with the external cues available from

outside the brain. The outcomes of preliminary classifications should be combined to obtain patterns that are more global. They will in turn serve as input patterns to higher-level recognition devices. Thus, a problem will be solved by explaining something, and with the help of that result, explaining further.

There is nothing wrong in this approach, except of the limitations of current memory: just objects from our current life. The idea is that any general rules for organizing perceptions and spatiotemporal variability are of little help, if such rules are not integrated with previous knowledge of the complex series of causal processes involved in the formation of the archaeological record. Consequently, the automated archaeologist should determine whether visual data "it currently sees" corresponds to a causal event, "it already knows." Recognition requires knowledge about how social action happens, and about the specific changes generated by all related social and natural processes.

The automated archaeologist is then defined as a machine consisting of a number of representations and processes, or on a more abstract level, as a set of maps which can be classified into three categories: (a) the visual competences that map different visual features to each other, (b) the problem solving routines which map visual features to explanatory concepts or representations of various kinds residing in memory, and (c) the learning programs that are responsible for the development of any map. To design or analyze such a vision system amounts to understanding the mappings involved.

Palmer and Kimchi (1986) have analyzed some of the implicit assumptions that underlie this information processing approach to cognitive behavior:

- **Informational description:** Explanations can be functionally described as informational events, each of which consists of three parts: the input information, the operation performed on the input, and the output information. That means that what our robot explains can be specified as an operation that transforms an initial ensemble of input information into output information. If the input/output mapping is well defined, there will be a way of specifying the operation such that knowing the input and the operation determines the output.

- **Recursive decomposition:** It is used to generate more complex descriptions of what goes inside an input/output mapping. The important concept introduced by this assumption is that one can define an input/output mapping in terms of a number of smaller input/output mappings inside it, plus a specification of how they are interconnected. These smaller mappings can be considered as stages, each of which is assumed independent of other stages to some degree. What this assumption asserts is that any complex informational event at one level can be specified more fully at a lower level by decomposing it into a number of component informational events. Because decomposition is recursive, any stage can be further decomposed into a hierarchy of lower level stages and the ordering relations among them. Successive decompositions re-

move some of the complexity that is *implicit* within a single input/output mapping and makes it *explicit* through the connections among the operations at the next lower level of analysis.

- **Physical embodiment:** In the physical system whose behavior is being described as informational events, information is carried by states of the system (called *representations*), while operations that use this information are carried out by changes in state (called *processes*). Information and operations are, technically speaking, entities in the abstract domain of information processing descriptions, whereas representations and processes are entities in the physical world when viewed as embodiments of information and operations.

Here are some basic examples. Archaeologists use shape as a visual feature to identify animal and human bones according to a reference database: all bones in a human or animal skeleton. In this case, archaeologists are lucky: anatomy provides the necessary theory to find equivalences between shape and explanation: a bone has the shape it has *because* of the particular evolution of the animal species. The shape of the bone (and other visual features as size, porosity, composition, etc.) is the key for understanding some characteristics of animal behavior, which are based on the particular way this animal species has evolved. Furthermore, the particular variations of the visual features describing this particular bone can be used to infer some specificities of its individual behavior. This is the case, for instance of human paleopathology or labor-induced alterations on bone morphology.

The problem is quite different in other archaeological domains. We see that a particular pottery vase is a *bowl*, because its shape is quite similar to bowls I have at home. However, I do not have any explanatory theory relating shape to function. I do not know why this particular ancient vase is a bowl because it is not related to the way a vase with a similar shape is being used in the present. Even, not all bowls can be used in the same way. This trouble is also typical of most kinds of archaeological material, be it the remains of a house, a garbage pit, or a whole site. We need some reference model if we want to recognize what we are seeing archaeologically, but this reference model is usually built subjectively. This is the classical approach of typological reasoning. The archaeologist takes all known shapes and organizes them according to some criteria known to him or her. The typology only accounts for shape differences.

More interesting would be the organization of a systematic description of the morphometry of pottery vases, and an exhaustive investigation of the way vases with a similar morphometry have been used in specific and well-documented contexts. Then, by using ethnoarchaeological analogies, a reference knowledge base on shape and function can be built.

Even better is the approach followed in lithic use wear studies. Here, the use of the tool is not matched to ethnoarchaeologically recorded cases, but to an experimental reference knowledge base, where some traces are repeatedly associated with some ways of using a tool (cutting wood, scraping leather, etc.) in a specifically designed experiment.

If we consider those cases as examples for a forthcoming archaeological recognition system, the automated archaeologist must have the following components to be able to *perceive* and explain what it has perceived (Figure 1.6):

* A knowledge base or causal model
* A feature detector
* A hypothesizer
* A hypothesis verifier

The model database should contain all the models known to the system. The information in the model database depends on the approach used for the recognition. It can vary from a qualitative or functional description to precise parametric equations. The feature detector applies operators to the input and identifies locations of features that help in forming causal event hypotheses. Using the detected features in the input, the hypothesizer assigns likelihoods to those events that may have produced the observed evidence. The knowledge base is organized using some type of indexing scheme to facilitate elimination of unlikely causal events candidates from possible consideration. The verifier then uses causal theories to verify the hypotheses and refines the likelihood of explanations. The system then selects the causal event with the highest likelihood, as the correct event.

The mechanism works in the following way (Alexandrov & Gorsky, 1991). To recognize a social action, the robot should compare the perceived hierarchy of the visual features of a social action effect with many hierarchies stored in memory. On the one hand, the automated archaeologist creates a group of possible percepts with each salient feature in the perceptual sequence. The most important details possessing the most valuable information are identified in the first step. Hypotheses on the percept arising after one has recognized each individual percept are important, even when the robot still has not discovered what the perceived element really is. If the type of the perceived element is known approximately, then it is often possible to say in advance, where additional key distinctive properties are to be found. It means that in remembering how a causal process produces its effects, the automated archaeologist can weight the significance of perceived features differently for correct identification. By the way, maybe these "significant" features will later create the same natural classifications—the causal events will group themselves according to their most similar details.

This is a prototype-based approach, where archaeological events are grouped into classes, such as a class of work actions (hunting, butchery, coercion, social reproduction, etc.). Each group

Figure 1.6. A model for an archaeological recognition system

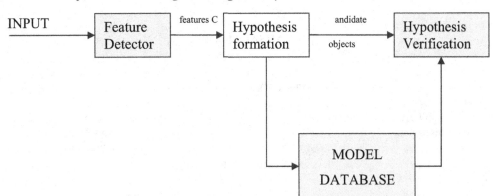

of equivalent events is represented by a single class prototype. As we have already discussed, the first stage in recognizing new archaeological evidence consists of comparing it against the class prototypes, rather than against already known individual events. The best matching prototype is identified, and further processing is then limited to the class represented by this prototype (Figure 1.7). On some occasions the classification may happen to be ambiguous, that is, a number of prototypes may compete for the best match. In this case, subsequent processing will be directed to a number of classes rather than a single one.

However, establishing the desired correspondence between the archaeological evidence and their causal explanation is not an easy task. A direct matching between a perceived input and explanatory stored patterns is insufficient for various reasons (Adelson, 2001; Fernmüller, & Aloimonos, 1995; Jain et al., 1995; Marr, 1982; Palmer 1999; Ullman, 1996):

- The space of all possible visualizations of all causal events is likely to be prohibitively large. It therefore becomes impossible to test a shape for property P by simply comparing it against all the members of S stored in memory. To be more accurate, the problem lies in fact not simply in the size of the set

S, but in what may be called the size of the *support* of S. When the set of supports is small, the recognition of even a large set of objects can still be accomplished by simple means such as direct template matching. This means that a small number of patterns is stored and matched against the figure in question. When the set of supports is prohibitively large, a template matching decision scheme will become impossible. The classification task may nevertheless be feasible if the set of shapes sharing the property in question contains regularities. This roughly means that the recognition of property P can be broken down into a set of operations in such a manner that the overall computation required for establishing P is substantially less demanding than the storing of all the shapes in S.

- Finding solutions by inverse engineering may also seem an impossible task because of the non-uniqueness difficulties that arise. Non-uniqueness means that the true solution cannot be selected from among a large set of possible solutions without further constraints imposed (Thornton, 2000). This undesirable behavior is due to noise in the measurements, and insufficient number of measurements.

Figure 1.7. Archaeological explanation as pattern matching

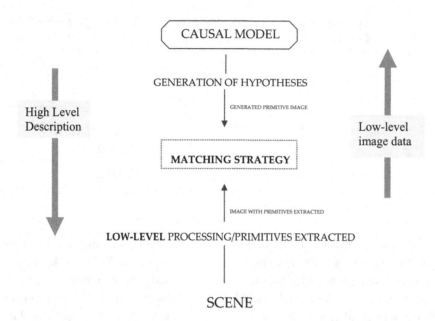

- The material traces to be recognized will often not be sufficiently equivalent to any already known causal model. For instance, DVD players, computers, and shoeboxes have visual features (shapes) that are about as unrevealing of their function as they could possibly be. Although we might be able to figure out their functions after extended viewing and interaction, if we did not know them already, its explanation will be impossible. Therefore, the relationship shape-explanation seems to be too ambiguous to base archaeological explanations.

- How do relate between them the many visual appearances that the same causal event can generate (Kersten, et al., 2004)? That is to say, the objective ambiguity of visual data arises when several different causal events could have produced the same archaeological visual features.

- The automated archaeologist generally does not know the most relevant factors affecting the shape, size, texture, composition, and spatiotemporal location of material consequences of social action. Instead, it extracts from the environment sparse and noisy measurements of perceptual properties, and an incomplete knowledge of relational contexts. The trouble here includes which features are selected for correspondence, and how to determine the match between image and model features. What simple properties would distinguish, for example the territory of a hunter-gatherer society from the territory of a chiefdom-kind of society? How do the effects of economic intensification distinguish in terms of simple visual properties from the effects of self-subsistence? How do exchanged goods differentiate from stolen goods? To make such recognitions, it appears that a more precise description of visual features, rather than a restricted geometric invariance (shape) would be necessary. In some cases, simple invariant properties may be common to all the archaeologically observable material consequences of a single action. In other, less restricted cases, such invariance may not exist. In archaeological event recognition, there is no particular reason to assume the existence of relatively simple properties.

- There is a necessity to establish correspondence with not just one, but multiple internal models. To select the correct model, correspondence must be established between the viewed archaeological evidence and all the different candidate models that need to be considered. As we will see in Chapter IV, the alternative is to evaluate in parallel multiple competing alternatives.

- Specific to the archaeological case, we should take into account that the visible properties of the archaeological record are not always the result of purposeful human activity. The problem is that although many types of social activities, actions, and operative behaviors leave memory, many other types of processes do not. In fact, there are many types of processes whose effect is to actually wipe out memory. An aggregation of bones or artifacts may not reflect past human social action, but rather post depositional processes: fluvial, transport, solifluction, rodent activity, contemporary farming, etc. Most post depositional processes have the effect of disordering artifact patterning in the archaeological record, and increasing entropy. Loss, discard, reuse, decay, and archaeological recovery are numbered among the diverse formation processes that in a sense, mediate between the past behaviors of interest and their surviving traces in the present.

Instead of relying exclusively on bottom-up processing of the perceptual input, the recognition process can be aided by using the results of accumulated past experience with the same or similar objects. That is to say, an automated archaeologist can use previous "correct" solutions to increase its problem solving abilities and to recognize new percepts. When faced again with a similar input, the computation will follow the sequence that proved successful in the past rather than search anew for a possible link between the input and a stored representation. Relationships between the given stimuli and those occurring because of problem solving are registered, and invariants are sought for classes of stimuli. If such invariants are found, they are abstracted, and these, in turn, determine the contents of perception in terms of visual features that can be used to recognize classes of traces for which a comparable consequence of a certain action can be anticipated. In this view, perceptions that underlie recognition serve to anticipate explanations (Hoffman, 1996).

By treating perceptual recognition as a form of probabilistic inference, various conclusions may be assigned subjective probabilities of correctness based on given observations. Archaeologically-perceived evidence is not determined univocally by human labor; there is only certain probability that this specific material entity had been produced when a concrete action or series of actions have been performed, among many others. If and only if the perceived trace could not have produced in absence of that action (probability=0), then the automated archaeologist will be reasonably sure that the percept can be recognized as having been determined by that action. Consequently, probabilities can be used to infer the most appropriate solution to the problem at hand, which may not even be based on the highest probability (Kersten et al., 2004; Lowe 1990). If we accept that automated recognition can never be made absolutely reliable, it is necessary to describe the goal of recognition as maximizing the probabilities of a correct identification and providing a confidence measure for each identification.

The admittedly strange idea that what the robot "sees" is a probabilistic manifestation of its past "experiences" with similar inputs, rather than a logical analysis of what now perceives in this actual case may be difficult to accept. Percepts are neither correct nor incorrect representations of reality but simply a consequence of having incorporated into visual processing the statistics of visual success or failure (Hoffman 1996; Purves & Lotto, 2003). Of course, this utilitarian-cum-probabilistic approach to perception does not imply that the mechanisms of perceptual problem solving are completely chaotic and unlawful in character (Ramachandran, 1990). That is to say, "visual features" should be viewed as emergent properties of sensory fields, not static things in the environment that are merely detected, selected, or picked up. In this conception of perceptual problem solving, the automated archaeologist should see its empirical significance, or more formally, the probability distribution of the possible sources of the stimulus, in response to any given stimulus. Understanding what a robot can see and why will depend on understanding the probabilistic relationship between stimuli and their sources during the automated archaeologist past experience. As a result, the percepts that are entertained would accord with the accumulated experience of what

the visual and non-visual inputs in question had typically signified in the history of this individual automated archaeologist.

These ideas suggest that the perceptual structure underlying object recognition may be described as expectations of certain stimulations at certain locations in a still unstructured global stimulus distribution (Hoffman, 1996)(Figure 1.8).

Anticipatory explanations can be modeled as a kind of "mechanical intention." What the robot knows from its experience determines which set of explanations should be active based on the robot's internal goals and objectives. In those circumstances, "intelligence" arises from the interactions of the robotic agent with its environment, that is, with what it has perceived. It is not a property of either the agent or the environment in isolation but is rather a result of the interplay between them. As a result, when using a robot for perceiving archaeological data, we get the ability to see the *possibilities* for action, and not merely seeing what *already exists*.

At the end, one may question whether perception is driving problem solving (explanations) or vice versa. Two different ways of solving

Figure 1.8. Perceptual structure underlying object recognition

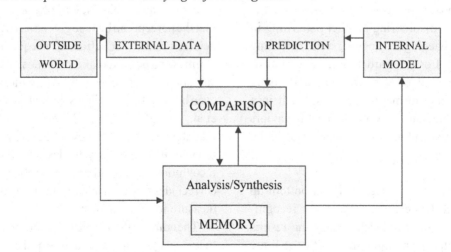

perception problems have resulted (Arkin, 1998, p. 265-266):

- **Action-oriented perception:** In which problem solving needs to determine the perceptual strategies used. Action-oriented perception requires that perception be conducted in a top down manner, with perceptual control and resources determined by an already defined causal theory. The underlying principle is that perception is predicated in the structure of explanation: Only the information germane for a particular explanation need be extracted from the input data. Instead of attempting to interpret almost everything a percept contains, an advantage is gained by recognizing that perceptual needs depend on what an agent is required to do within the world. This is in contrast to more traditional computer vision research, which to a large extent takes the view that perception is an end in itself or that its sole purpose is to construct a model of the world without any understanding of the need for such a model.

- **Active perception:** In which perceptual requirements dictate the automated archaeologist's problem solving strategy. It focuses primarily on the needs of perception, rather the needs of action. The question changes from the action-oriented perspective of "how can perception provide information necessary for problem solving?" to "how can problem solving support perceptual activity?" An active perceptual system is a system that is able to manipulate its incoming sensory information in a controlled manner in order to extract useful data, based on traces gathered from other input data and with the aim of efficiently accomplishing an explanation with respect to the available resources (Fernmüller & Aloimonos, 1995; Tsontos, 1990, 2001). Therefore, an active approach is a *selective one*, and the issues of planning causal sequences become of primary importance, as well as focusing the attention on useful pieces of information. Active perception is thus defined as an intelligent data acquisition process, intelligent in its use of sensors guided by feedback and a priori knowledge.

These two viewpoints are not mutually exclusive; indeed active perception and action-oriented perception are intimately related. What the automated archaeologist needs to know to accomplish its tasks still dictates perceptual requirements, but active perception provides the perceptual processes with the ability to control the problem solving system to make its task easier as well.

According to this way of thinking, a social action is archaeologically recognized according to a stepwise and expectation-bound differentiation of visual information in which each given state defines the starting conditions for the generation of further information.

Archaeological perception (automated or not) is not a clear window onto past realities. The reason is that perception is *under specified* (or *under constrained* or *under determined*) by the visual data captured from the empirical world. That means that archaeological explanation cannot be reduced to a mere "see" and "understand" because what we, or the robots, *perceive* is not necessarily identical to what the robots (or we) *see*. In order to perceive, one must understand the world. To recognize objects, the automated archaeologist must know what it is looking at. To know what it is looking at, it must already be able to see it, but it cannot if it does not know what to see. In other words, to recognize some pottery sherds as a vase, the automated archaeologist must know what a vase is, and which kind of vase *was*. To explain archaeological evidence from a grave, the robot has to know *why* such an individual was buried with those grave goods, who was she, and who were the people that performed such a funerary ritual.

The world is not data, but a set of perceptual information waiting for an observer that imposes order by recognizing an object and by describing it. Global percepts are *constructed* from local information, and such a construction process depends on the interaction of the automated archaeologist with the external context. Perception is constructed according to individual history of practical experiences (Florian, 2002). Hence, the perception problem is reduced to recognizing what situation(s) the robot is in and then choosing one action (or perhaps many) to undertake. As soon as the robot finds itself in a new situation, it selects a new and more appropriate action. That means that, what is recognized, is always known in terms directly related to an agent's current possibilities for future action (Anderson, 2003).

The idea that perception depends on the interaction of the observer with the world is now a popular one (Clancey, 1997; Gibson, 1979; O'Reagan & Noë, 2001; Pfeiffer & Scheier, 1999; Purves & Lotto, 2003, among many others). Perceiving is an act, not a response; an act of attention, not a triggered impression; an achievement, not a reflex (Gibson, 1979). As a mechanical system, robots seem to lack perceptual capabilities at all; that is, they do not *know* anything about the scenes they record. Photographic images merely contain information, whereas sighted people and animals acquire knowledge about their environments. It is this knowledge that should enable cognitive robots to act appropriately in a given perceived situation.

Perceptions are internal constructions of a hypothesized external reality. Unless the perceiver makes assumptions about the physical world that gave rise to a particular image, perception just is not possible (Vision, 1997, p. 22). It should be axiomatic then that perception is not passive but active. Automated perception should be conducted on a need-to-know basis. That means that automated perception has to be considered as a holistic, synergistic process deeply intertwined with the complete agent's cognitive system, be-

cause perceptual needs are predicated upon the agent's motivational and behavioral requirements (Arkin, 1998, p. 238).

Visual experience is a mode of activity involving practical knowledge about currently possible behaviors and associated sensory consequences. Visual experience rests on know-how, the possession of skills. The experience of seeing occurs when the outside world is being probed according to the visual mode. In this sense, seeing is a way of acting. As the automated archaeologists look at archaeological visual data, it should question different aspects of the scene. As soon as it does so, each thing it asks about springs into awareness, and it is perceived because knowledge is now available about how the external world will change when it manipulates the thing it sees. Perceiving the world is not a reflection of the content of some knowledge base, but rather, it is due to the structure of the world itself and the robot's ability to act intelligently with respect to it.

Perception and cognitive problem solving are then closely linked. If perception has to be tied to action, then an artificial archaeologist should be an entity situated and surrounded by the real world. It should not operate upon abstract representations of reality, but rather upon reality itself. That means that the robot should have a physical presence (a body), which influences its dynamic interactions with the world (Anderson, 2003; Brooks, 1999; Noë, 2004; Pfeiffer & Scheier, 1999). Situated activity means that robot's actions are predicated upon the situations in which it finds itself.

THE SCIENCES OF THE ARTIFICIAL

Two different views on perception and explanation were presented in the previously mentioned section:

1.   Information is viewed as something that can be stored, coded, matched, and displayed.

That means that information is derived from external objects and flows into the system via the senses. It is denotational because it is an *encoding*. The robot's memory is just a storehouse of denotational encodings.

2. Information is not given but created as transformations of stimuli. Information does not exist in the world waiting to be extracted by a rational agent, but, rather, the agent is situated in meaningful contexts, in which information should be defined *as a function of* the local needs and concerns of the agent. Perceiving a world implies distinguishing "possibilities for action" and not naming or identifying *per se*. That is to say, it can be understood as recognizing the circumstances to act with or upon. This means that the contents of perception (and, hence, the structure of the phenomenal world) is largely determined by the self-organized dynamics of the cognitive system and pre-rational dispositions that are embodied in the cognitive agent. Being a perceiver, the automated archaeologist should literally create a phenomenal world, because the process of perception first defines relevant distinctions in the sensory environment.

Consequently, two different, opposite approaches to build "intelligent" machines appear:

1. We can build an automated archaeologist simply by telling it what it needs to know,
2. Or we can build it as a *learning* machine.

As we will see in this book, both approaches have their advantages. They are often presented as competing paradigms, but since they attack cognitive problems on different ways, we should see them rather as complementary methodologies. Chapter II shows how to define an automated archaeologist by adding one by one the sentences that represent the designer's knowledge of the en-

vironment or domain. This is called the declarative approach to system building. Successive chapters will criticize this approach and an alternative will be presented.

The declarative or model-based approach is based on the idea that knowledge exists before experience (Plato's philosophy). It consists of descriptions of how the world appears, such as the shape of the tool is associated with its past function, and descriptions of how to behave in certain situations, such as how an archaeologist infers the kind of society having produced the remains of an ancient settlement. In this approach, it is assumed that knowledge is stored as fixed packages in specific memories or knowledge-bases. Descriptions of regularities in the world and regularities in the robot's behavior are called knowledge, and located in the robot's memory. In the first years of Artificial Intelligence (1960-1980) it was hoped that if we could represent the knowledge necessary to describe the world and the possible actions in a suitable formalism, then by coupling this world description with a powerful inference machine one could construct an artificial agent capable of planning and problem solving. In our specific case, the automated archaeologist should be feed with: (a) an a priori causal model of how, when and where social action modifies matter in some specific way, to be able to suggest those actions as the cause of the observed modification without performing the action by itself, and (b) a notion of distance between the goal to be attained (the cause) and the current state (the observation).

It is assumed that the robot can not explain nothing without an operationalization of low level concepts ("pottery," "tool," "activity area," "landscape," and high-level ("hunting," "killing," "fighting," "reproducing," "power," "chiefdom," "authority," "poverty") or any other similar. That means that our robot should store a priori knowledge of patterns that it expects to encounter. Such declarative knowledge takes the form of propositions converted only slowly into action by means of general interpretative procedures (algorithms). Designing the representation language to make easy to express this knowledge in the form of sentences simplifies the construction problem enormously. Although there are many criticisms to this approach, its advantage is that it is a practical and efficient way to reproduce "intelligent" or rational decision making (see next chapter for appropriate examples). It is then the most appropriate simulation of human "rationality," defined in terms of *searching* for the best solution. According to that view, scientific theories may be considered as complex data structures consisting of highly organized packages of declarative facts, procedures and well defined goals.

However, it has been argued that such a *declarative* framework cannot sufficiently account for cognitive process, because it neglects their creative, or *constructive*, aspects. Paraphrasing Wittgestein, we may ask: what does it mean to know what a lithic tool is, what an activity area is, what a territory is? What does it mean to know something and not be able to say nothing? Is this knowledge equivalent to an unformulated definition? If it were formulated, should a machine be able to recognize it as the expression of some background knowledge?

Within the last two decades, the view of problem solving based on pre-fixed plans and searching in restricted knowledge-bases using well-defined operators for activating already existing sequence of explanations has come under scrutiny from both philosophers and computer scientists. The reliance on declarative expressions (logical formulae) seems to be misplaced. The fundamentally unrepeatable nature of everyday life and human existence gives reality a significance that cannot be understood in terms of pre-defined, well-structured declarative expressions. This position argues that a person's understanding of things is rooted in the practical activity of coping with the everyday world. Explanation cannot be properly understood, if considered independently of the context in which it occurs. The historical, cultural, and social context of the interactions of a cognitive system is crucial to the understanding of the ongoing process.

All that means that although the automated archaeologist should use some form of knowledge base, this should not be identified with explicit, passively stored descriptions and well-defined rules. Our automated archaeologist should focus on the outside world, how this world constrains and guides its explanatory behavior. We have to take into account inarticulable "knowledge" closely related to regulating behaviors and coordinating perceptual-explanation interactions.

One of the benefits of this approach is that the mode of processing it proposes is continuous with processes occurring in the external world. The automated system we would like to build is the agent-in-the-right-context, an agent constructing descriptions by adapting old ways of perceiving, by putting models out into the world as artifacts to manipulate and rearrange, and by perceiving generated descriptions over time, relating them to past experiences or future consequences.

A theory of *situated* cognition has been proposed, claiming that every human thought and action is adapted to the environment, that is, situated, because what people *perceive*, how they *conceive of their activity,* and what they *physically do* develop together. Our names for things and what they mean, our theories, and our conceptions *develop in our behavior* as we interact with and perceive what others and we have previously explained and done. Explanation in this view emerges *dialectically* (reciprocally) from the interaction of the machine with its context: the elements that are perceived constrain what the agent can do, and what it does (thinks and/or explains) constrains what it perceives. Action enters as a variable into perception no less that perception enters as a variable into action.

Thus we have the possibility of *situating* automated archaeologists in the world in which we humans do (and did) things, where we have skills and social practices that facilitate our interaction with the objects we want to study. Knowledge goes well beyond a mere process of mapping of observations from the environment to the cognitive domain. It is rather the result of an interaction of processes *within* the cognitive reality. Hence, the structure of the cognitive system itself plays a dominating role in this process of construction, whereas the influence of the environment is rather marginal: it provides a kind of *boundary condition* that perturbs the organism's internal dynamics; it influences, but does not control the structure of the cognitive reality. Because of constructing knowledge, the cognitive system is able to act within these conditions.

Rodney Brooks suggests that if we want to reproduce human intelligence in a machine, we should make emphasis on three central aspects: development, interaction, and integration. Development forms the framework by which machines should imitate the way humans successfully acquire increasingly more complex skills and competencies. Interaction should allow robots to use the world itself as a tool for organizing and manipulating knowledge, it allows them to exploit humans for assistance, teaching, and knowledge. Integration should permit the automated archaeologist to maximize the efficacy and accuracy of complementary mechanisms for perceiving and acting (Brooks, 1999; Brooks et al., 1998).

If we build an "intelligent" robot based on those aspects, we will obtain a machine, which is not born with a complete reasoning, motor or sensory systems. Instead, it should undergo a process of development where it will perform incrementally more difficult tasks in more complex environments en route to an advanced state. In other words, our robot should be capable of improving its capabilities in a continuous process of acquiring new knowledge and skills, and reacting to unusual events such as incomplete input, lack of prior knowledge (DeCallataÿ, 1992). To fulfill this requirement, it is suggested that an automated archaeologist should not be fully programmed since the beginning, but it still be built developmentally. The gradual acquisition of interpretive skills and the consequent gradual expansion of the automated archaeologist capacities to explain archaeological observables (creating more and more self-training data as it does so) will define then the cognitive behavior of our machine. This strategy facilitates learning both by providing a structured decomposition of skills and by gradually increasing the complexity of the task to match the competency of the system. Behaviors and learned skills that have already been mastered prepare and enable the acquisition of more advanced explanations by providing subskills and knowledge that can be re-used, by placing simplifying constraints on the acquisition, and by minimizing new information that must be acquired.

Chapters III and IV have been written with idea to show that an automated archaeologist is a computer system that *learns* to solve archaeological problems. Learning is there defined as the process of improving the execution of a task, without the need of reprogramming. The robot should be capable of modifying what it knows in terms of what it learns, and it will learn when it uses actual knowledge in a situation where that knowledge may be modified, according to some general goal. Consequently, the automated archaeologist should be able to criticize what it has predicted. In other words, declarative knowledge should not substitute perception. In a sense, what is being argued is the possibility of a hypothetical-inductive reasoning, able to generate conjectures and refutations. Explanations are algorithmically produced, and refuted with situated data, that is information perceived in an experimental or controlled context.

DIRECTIONS FOR FURTHER RESEARCH

The theoretical position taken here and throughout the book has its most obvious origins in the works of three very different scholars: the late David

Clarke, Jean Claude Gardin, and Jim Doran. In some ways, the book can be considered as an homage and update of the original suggestion by David Clarke, who considered the faculty of mathematics to be the proper place for studying archaeology, and that cybernetics was the most convenient approach to investigate ancient remains (Clarke, 1968, 1972, 1973). Jean Claude Gardin took an explicitly non-quantitative approach to archaeological reasoning, but he was the very first scholar addressing the need of "automatization." His investigations are covered in Chapter II. Finally, Jim Doran has all the credits for beginning the integration of Artificial Intelligence in Archaeology. From his first papers (Doran, 1970a, 1970b, 1972, 1977) he explored the possibilities of computer modeling and simulation. His most recent investigations are presented in Chapter IX. Although the three approaches are very different, they constitute the prehistory of automated archaeology, what at that time (and even today!) may seem impossible.

This chapter has only an introductory character. I have tried to present some of the main subjects that will be analyzed in depth throughout the book. Chapters V through IX present additional material, but it should be taken into account that research in this area is still in its beginnings, and that aspects like active vision, multi-dimensional representations, scene understanding, haptic interfaces, and so forth. need further investigation. In any case, what it lacks is technology. Theoretical basis on observations are already well established.

At the end of the chapter, the diversity of artificial intelligence is presented as an open gate to a new world. I have tried to present it in very schematic terms, both the classical approaches to symbol processing, and the new artificial intelligence based on context situation. Materials here presented are only introductory. Other comments and suggestions for further research will be presented at the end of the respective chapters.

REFERENCES

ADELSON, E.H. (2001). On seeing stuff: The perception of materials by humans and machines. In B. E. Rogowitz & T. N. Pappas (Eds.), *Human vision and electronic imaging VI*. Proceedings of the SPIE, Vol. 4299, (pp. 1-12).

ALEKSANDER, I., & MORTON, H. (1993). *Neurons and symbols. The stuff that mind is made of*. London: Chapman and Hall.

ALEXANDROV, V.V., & GORSKY, N.D. (1991). *From humans to computers. Cognition through visual perception*. Singapore: World Scientific.

ANDERSON, M.L. (2003). Embodied cognition: A field guide. *Artificial Intelligence, 149*, 91-130.

ARKIN, R.C. (1998). *Behavior-based robotics*. Cambridge, MA: The MIT Press.

BARCELÓ, J.A. (2007). A science fiction tale? A robot called archaeologist. In A. Figueiredo & G. Velho. Tomar (Eds.), *The wolds is in your eyes. Proceedings of the XXXIII Computer Applications and Quantitative Applications in Archeology Conference* (pp. 221-230). Portugal: CAA Portugal.

BRADY, M. (1985). Artificial intelligence and robotics. *Artificial Intelligence and Robotics, 26*, 79-121.

BRIGHT, J.R. (1958). *Automation and management*. Graduate School of Business Administration, Boston: Harvard University.

BROOKS, R. (1999). *Cambrian intelligence: The early history of the new AI*. Cambridge: The MIT Press.

BROOKS, R.A., C. BREAZEAL (FERRELL), R., IRIE, C., KEMP, M., MARJANOVIC, B., SCASSELLATI et al. (1998). Alternate essences of nitelligence. *Proceedings of the 15th National Conference on Artificial Intelligence (AAAI-98)* (pp. 961-976). Madison, Wisconsin.

BUNGE, M. (1959). *Causality. The place of causal principle in modern science*. Cambridge, MA: Harvard University Press.

CLANCEY, W.J. (1997). *Situated cognition: On human knowledge and computer representations*. Cambridge, UK: Cambridge University Press.

CLARKE, D.L. (1968). *Analytic archaeology*. London: Methuen & Co.

CLARKE, D.L. (1972). Models and paradigms in contemporary archaeology. In D.L. Clarke (Ed.), *Models in archaeology* (pp. 1-61). London: Methuen and Co.

CLARKE, D.L. (1973). Archaeology: The loss of innocence. *Antiquity, 47*, 6-18.

CLELAND, C.E. (2002). Methodological and epistemic differences between historical science and experimental science. *Philosophy of Science, 69*, 474-496.

COLLINS, H., & KUSCH, M. (1998). *The shape of actions. What human and machines can do*. Cambridge, MA: The MIT Press,

DAVYDOV, V. (1999). The content and unsolved problems of activity theory. In Y. Engeström, R. Miettinen, & R.L. Punamäki (Eds.), *Perspectives on activity theory*. Cambridge, UK: Cambridge University Press,

DAWSON, M.R.W. (2004). *Minds and machines. Connectionism and psychological modeling*. London: Blackwell Pub.

DeCALLATAŸ, A. M. (1992). *Natural and artificial intelligence. Misconceptions about brains and neural networks*. Amsterdam: North Holland,

DONAHUE, J.W., & PALMER, D.C. (1994). *Learning and complex behaviour*. Boston: Allyn and Bacon,

DORAN J. E. (1970a). Systems theory, computer simulations and archaeology. *World Archaeology, 1*(3), 289-298.

DORAN J. E. (1970b). Archaeological reasoning and machine reasoning. In J.C. Gardin (Eds.), *Archaeologie et Calculateurs* (pp 57-67). Paris: CNRS.

DORAN, J. E. (1972). Computer models as tools for archaeological hypothesis formation. In D.L. Clarke (Ed.), *Models in archaeology* (pp 425-451). London: Methuen and Co.

DORAN, J. E. (1977) Automatic generation and evaluation of explanatory hypotheses. In M. Borillo, W. Fernandezde la Vega, & A Guenoche (Eds.), *Raisonnement et methodes mathematiques en archaeologie* (pp. 172-181). Paris: CNRS.

DOYLE, J. (2006). *Extending mechanics to minds. The mechanical foundations of psychology and economics*. Cambridge, UK: Cambridge University Press.

DREYFUSS, H.L. (1972). *What computers can't do*. New York: Harper and Row.

ENGESTRÖM, Y. (1987). *Learning by expanding. An activity-theory approach to developmental research*. Helsinki: Orienta-Konsultit.

ENGESTRÖM, Y. (1999). Activity theory and individual social transformation. In Y. Engeström, R. Miettinen, & R.L. Punamäki (Eds.), *Perspectives on activity theory*. Cambridge, UK: Cambridge University Press.

FERMÜLLER, C., & ALOIMONOS, Y. (1995). Vision and action. *Image and Vision Computing, 13*, 725-744.

FINDLER, N.V., & BICKMORE, T. (1996). On the concept of causality and a causal modeling system for scientific and engineering domains, CAMUS. *Applied Artificial Intelligence, 10*, 455-487.

FLORIAN, R.V. (2002). Why it is Important to Build Robots Capable of Doing Science. In C. G. Prince, Y. Demiris, Y. Marom, H. Kozima, & C. Balkenius (Eds.), *Proceedings of the Second International Workshop on Epigenetic Robotics:*

Modeling Cognitive Development in Robotic Systems (pp. 27-34). Lund University Cognitive Studies 94.

GIBSON, J.J. (1979). *The ecological approach to visual perception.* Boston, MA: Mifflin.

GLENNAN, S. (1996). Mechanisms and the nature of causation. *Erkenntnis, 44,* 49-71.

GLENNAN, S. (2002). Rethinking mechanistic explanation. *Philosophy of Science, 69,* 342-353.

HENDRIKS-JANSEN, H. (1996). *Catching ourselves in the act. Situated activity, interactive emergence, evolution, and human thought.* Cambridge, MA: The MIT Press.

HOFFMAN, J. (1996). Visual object recognition. In W. Priz & B. Bridgeman (Eds.), *Handbook of perception and action. Volume 1* (pp. 297-344). New York: Academic Press.

JAIN, R., KASTURI, R., & SCHUNK, B.G. (1995). *Machine vision.* New York: Prentice Hall, Inc.

KERSTEN, D., MAMASSIAN, P., & YUILLE, A. (2004). Object perception as Bayesian inference. *Annual Review of Psychology, 55,* 271-304.

KIRSCH, D., & MAGLIO, P. (1995). On distinguishing epistemic from pragmatic action. *Cognitive Science, 18,* 513-549.

KITAMURA, Y., & MIZOGOUCHI, R. (2004). Ontology-based systematization of functional knowledge. *Journal of Engineering Design, 15*(4), 327-351.

LEONT'EV, A. (1974). The problem of activity in psychology. *Soviet Psychology, 13*(2), 4-33.

LEYTON, M. (1992). *Symmetry. Causality, mind.* Cambridge, MA: The MIT Press.

LEYTON, M. (2005). Shape as memory Storage. In C. Young (Ed.), *Ambient intelligence for scientific discovery* Berlin: Springer.

LOWE, D.G. (1990). Visual recognition as probabilistic inference from spatial relations. In A. Blake & T. Troscianko (Eds.), *AI and the eye.* New York: John Wiley.

MARR, D.H. (1982). *Vision. A computational investigation into the human representation and processing of visual information.* San Francisco, CA: W.H. Freeman.

NARDI, B.A. (1996). Studying context: A comparison of activity theory, situated action models and distributed cognition. In B.A. Nardi (Ed.), *Context and consciousness. Activity theory and human-computer interaction.* Cambridge, MA: The MIT Press.

NOË, A. (2004). *Action in perception.* Cambridge, MA: The MIT Press.

O'REGAN, J.K., NOË, A. (2001). A sensorimotor account of vision and visual consciousness. *Behavioral and Brain Sciences, 24,* 939–1031.

O'REILLY, R.C., & MUNAKATA, Y. (2000). *Computational explorations in cognitive neuroscience.* Cambridge, MA: The MIT Press.

PALMER, S. (1999). *Vision science. Photons to phenomelogy.* Cambridge, MA: The MIT Press.

PALMER, S.E., & KIMCHI, R. (1986). The information processing approach to cognition. In T.J. Knap & L.C. Robertson (Eds.), *Approaches to cognition: Contrasts and controversies.* Hillsdale, NJ: Erlbaum Publ.

PFEIFFER, R., & SCHEIER, C. (1999). *Understanding intelligence.* Cambridge, MA: The MIT Press.

PURVES, D., & LOTTO, R.B. (2003). *Why we see what we do. An empirical theory of vision.* Sunderland, MA: Sinauer Associates, Inc.

RAMACHANDRAN, V.S. (1990). Visual perception in people and machines. In A. Blake &T.

Troscianko (Eds.), *AI and the eye* (pp. 21-77). John Wiley: New York.

ROOT-BERNSTEIN, R.S. (1989). *Discovery: Inventing and solving problems at the frontiers of scientific knowledge.* Cambridge, MA: Harvard University Press.

RUTKOWSKA, J.C. (1993). *The computational infant.* London: Harvester Wheatsheaf.

STEIN, L.A. (1995). Imagination and situated cognition. In K.M. Ford, C. Glymour & P.J. Hayes (Eds.), *Android epistemology.* Menlo Park/Cambridge/London: AAAI Press/the MIT Press.

THAGARD, P. (1988). *Computational philosophy of science.* Cambridge, MA: The MIT Press.

THORNTON, C. (2000). *Truth from trash. How learning makes sense.* Cambridge, MA: The MIT Press.

TSOTSOS, J.K. (1990). Analyzing vision at the complexity level, *behavioral and brain sciences, 13*(3), 423 - 445.

TSOTSOS, J.K. (2001). Motion understanding: Task-directed attention and representations that link perception with action, *International Journal of Computer Vision, 45*(3), 265-280.

ULLMAN, S. (1996). *High-level vision. Object recognition and visual cognition.* Cambridge, MA: The MIT Press.

VISION, G. (1997). *Problems of vision. Rethinking the causal theory of perception.* Oxford, UK: Oxford University Press.

WAGMAN, M. (2002). *Problem-solving processes in humans and computers. Theory and research in psychology and artificial intelligence.* Westport, CN: Praeger Publ.

WOBCKE, W. (1998). Agency and the logic of ability. In W. Wobcke, M. Pagnucco, & C. Zhang (Eds.), *Agents and multi-agent systems: Formalisms, methodologies, and applications.* Berlin: Springer.

ZINCHENKO, V.P. (1996). Developing activity theory: The zone of proximal development and beyond. In B.A. Nardi (Eds.), *Context and consciousness. Activity theory and human-computer interaction.* Cambridge, MA: The MIT Press.

Chapter II
Problem Solving in the Brain and by the Machine

LOOKING FOR SOLUTIONS

What does an "intelligent" human being when she tries to solve a problem? In general, she uses the word "problem" to mean different things:

- As a question to be answered,
- As a series of circumstances that hinder the attainment of an objective,
- As a proposition directed to verify the way some results are known.

Research in cognitive sciences suggests "Problem solving is any goal-directed sequence of cognitive operations" (Anderson, 1980, p. 257). According to Sloman (1987) "to *have* a goal" is to use a symbolic structure represented in some formalism to describe a state of affairs to be produced, preserved or prevented. Then, any rational agent, be artificial or natural, has a "problem" when an intention or goal cannot be achieved directly. Jackson (1983) summarizes this type of approach as:

PROBLEM= GOAL+OBSTACLE

When a specific goal is blocked, we have a problem. When we know ways round the block or how to remove it, we have less a problem. In our case, the automated archaeologist *wants* to know the cause of the observed material outcomes of social action. What blocks this goal is a lack of knowledge: it does not know the particular mechanism that caused in the past what it sees in the present. To remove this obstacle it must learn some specific knowledge: *how* a causal process or processes generated the specific measurable properties determining the observed evidence. To the automated archaeologist, problem solving has the task of devising some causal mechanism that may mediate between the observation and its cause or causes. Consequently, explanatory mechanisms taken in pursuit of that goal can be regarded as problem solving. In other words, explanation is a kind of problem solving where the facts to be explained are treated as goals to be reached, and hypotheses can be generated to provide the desired explanations (Thagard, 1988).

Problem solving has been defined as the successive addition of knowledge until the obstacle, which prevented goal achievement, is surmounted (Newell & Simon, 1972). A cognitive machine will solve a problem just by adding knowledge to a situation where it identifies some lack of knowledge. Therefore, a foundation prescriptive rule, one that is so obvious that we always forget it in real life: if you want to solve problems effectively in a given complex domain, you should have as much knowledge or information as you can about that domain.

We cannot use any bit of knowledge we wish, because there is only a finite set of right answers to a problem. Looking for the needed knowledge constitutes part of the procedure. The less knowledge available, the more "problematic," and troublesome is the solution and the more difficult will be to produce a result. In this sense "problematic" means "poor in knowledge." This is true for archaeology as for any other scientific discipline. It is true for both humans and for robots!

When there is insufficient knowledge, a problem cannot be solved. The robot needs specific knowledge for specifying what it knows and what it wants to do (goal). Acquiring this knowledge implies solving a previous problem (sub-goal). Each of the new sub-goals defines a problem that can be attacked independently. Problem decomposition constitutes, at the same time, a problem. Finding a solution to each sub-goal will require fewer steps than solving the overall compound goal. The idea is:

TO DECOMPOSE THE PROBLEM
    If you want to reach the objective *G,*
    And, it is not fulfilled using the
            previous condition *C,*
    Then,
            Look for sub-goal *C*
            Once *C* has been attained,
            Then,
                    Proceed until *G.*

When the solution of each sub-goal depends in a major way of the solution of other sub-goals, and the best solution requires trade-offs between competing constraints, it is most efficient to solve all the goals incrementally in parallel. This allows information about the results to accrue in each sub-problem and to affect the emerging decisions about the remaining sub-problems. This procedure illustrates several important points about problem solving. First, it should be explicitly guided by knowledge of what to do. Second, an initial goal can lead to subsequent sub-goals that effectively decompose the problem into smaller parts. Third, methods can be applied *recursively.*

Problem solving always begins with the identification of the difficulty or obstacle that prevent goal achievement. Once identified, we appeal to available information—previous knowledge—and we decide the starting point of the procedure. As we have already seen, in archaeology, this obstacle is a lack of knowledge on the social cause of some perceived features. Therefore, we need external information (expertise, already solved problems, known cases, scientific knowledge, etc.) so that we can make inferences and possibly choose what to do next. Any information missing from the problem statement has to be inferred from somewhere. All these sources of information together constitute the "space" in which problem solving takes place (Robertson, 2001; Wagman, 2002).

We need a full and exhaustive problem space. We can think of such a problem space as the equivalent of a problem solver's memory: a large encyclopedia or library, the information stored by topics (nodes), liberally cross-referenced (associational links), and with an elaborate index (recognition capability) that gives direct access through multiple entries to the topics (Simon, 1996, p. 88). The idea seems to be that solutions to a problem exist before the problem at some location in this problem space.

In archaeology, the problem space is constituted by those valid scientific facts, possible interpretations, and work hypothesis related to a specific subject. When considering historical problem solving through the looking glass of problem spaces, it appears that the temporality of social action is a sizable structure. It consists of:

1. A space of alternative social actions that could have been occurred,
2. A space of alternative circumstances (external factors) that could have resulted,
3. A space of alternative consequences of the events that actually happened,
4. A description of how all the possible causal interactions, between all the possible actions and circumstances, determine the consequences,
5. A description of how all the possible causal interactions, between all the possible actions and circumstances, determine a new event, that is, a change of state in the social system of agents, actions, consequences and external factors.

For instance, the problem space for a given automated archaeologist will include all activities that can generate specific use-wear traces on the surface of lithic tools, or all the places in a region from which a specific pottery type may come from. The machine needs a set alternative possible solutions (possible, probable and improbable *causes* for the artifact) and deciding which of them is the most appropriate in the case in question, according to certain well specified criteria. This mechanism can be described using a single verb: *searching for the best solution*. Many problems can be represented as involving a search for a suitable series of operations that will transform the starting state of the problem (the GIVENS) into a state that meets the goal requirements (SOLUTION). Given a well-defined problem space, the cognitive robot engages in a *search* to find a path through alternative knowledge bits that will lead to a solution. In other words, within a given a universe (U), it is necessary to find in a set of possible solutions (X), the elementary x that fulfill conditions $K(x)$, which tell us whether this particular x is the solution we are looking for. Of course, we are speaking of a *metaphorical* search in a *metaphorical* space, where goals are seen as spatial locations and event sequences as *metaphorical* paths leading from one state of the problem to another (Holyoak, 1990).

It is precisely that metaphor of "searching" for solution what gives support to the idea of problem space: search is an enumeration of a set of potential partial solutions to a problem so that they can be checked to see if they truly are solutions, or could lead to solutions (Figure 2.1)

The search process consists of small, incremental changes in the subject's belief that can be modeled as small changes in a set of assertions. Because of those changes, the state of the problem changes too. These successive states of the problem, or changes in the problem givens

Figure 2.1. A general procedure for problem solving

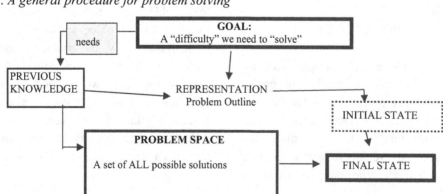

as a result of adding new knowledge into them, can be evaluated by domain-specific additional knowledge and tested to see whether they are goal states.

Consequently, automated problem solving can be described as starting from an initial given situation or statement of a problem (known as the INITIAL STATE of the problem). It coincides with what the logicians designate as *explanans*, this is, what we want to explain. The initial state of an archaeological problem is obvious: the archaeological record, the artifact or the artifact associations we want to explain; for instance, a spatial distribution of artifacts, description of some artifacts shape or texture, and so forth. Such an initial state should be sufficiently precise. It is not a general sentence about some descriptive features, but a precise statement of all physical properties of objects defined according to well-defined locational properties.

The automated archaeologist will advance towards the goal based on the problem situation and some prior knowledge. When it reaches it, it is in the GOAL STATE of the problem. It is expressed in terms of a set of requirements, and it can be defined as "what it wants to get." Therefore, it refers to the *explanandum* (what explains), and designates the final state of the problem. In our case, it is the specific mechanism explaining why the evidence is that way. Such a goal state is defined in terms of those elements that differentiate the most probable cause from alternatives, but less probable ones. The more general be the terms that describe a goal, the wider will be the area of application, and will answer to more problems.

Goals can be formulated explicitly as declarative facts: the function of an ancient sword, for example, is to be used as a social identity symbol; the function of a medieval jar is to contain a liquid. Here, "social identity symbols," and "liquid containers" appear as facts, and questions like "is x a social identity symbol?" or "is y a liquid container?" are the correct representations of some specific research goals. The solution procedure can be expressed in terms of necessary actions needed to *activate* the most appropriated explanatory concept to the case at hand. For instance, to the question "which is the function of this burin?" it corresponds the following action: "by studying use-wear traces, check whether observed texture coincide with the characteristic texture patterns experimentally generated in a laboratory when cutting wood." Here, the goal is not a single conceptual label ("cutting wood"), but a procedure designed to discover if that tool served to this purpose or not.

Once the robot has defined its goals, it should estimate the existing difference between some starting point (input information: perception) and the point to which it wants to arrive (the goal: causal explanation), choosing for this procedure an operator which reduces that difference and makes it move from the starting state until the arrival point or solution. The term operator is used to denote the description of "an action or process that bears some rational relation to attaining a problem solution" (Newell & Simon, 1972, p. 88; Rusell & Norvig, 1995, p. 60). Associated with such cognitive operations is information about prerequisites and the effects of applying them.

The operators are functions that transform a state description representing one state of the problem into one that represents the state resulting after an action. These are models of the effects of actions (Nilsson, 1998, p. 130). However, often the term "solution" is used as referring to two aspects of problem solving: either the final solution -the "answer"- or the means of finding the answer -the "solution procedure"- (Brown & Chandrasekaran, 1989; Holyoak, 1990; Robertson, 2001).

We also need a well-defined criterion to verify any solution proposed, and a recognizable procedure to apply that criterion.

As an additional example of how search is used to solve an archaeological problem, consider the task of determining the chronology of a bronze sword (GOAL: *How old is this bronze sword?*). A morphometric description of that

Figure 2.2. Problem solving in archaeology

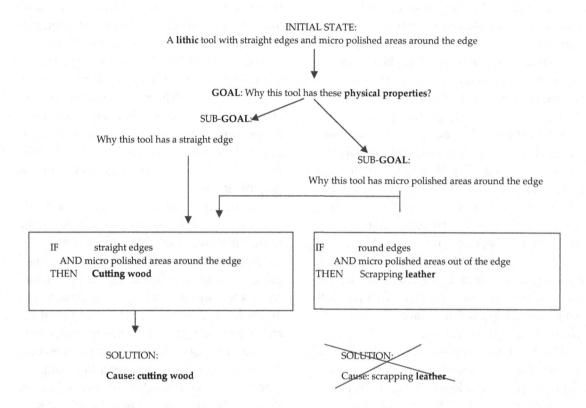

swords constitutes the initial state of the problem. The set of possible solutions contains all possible chronologies: 9th century B.C., 8th century B.C., 7th century B.C., etc. The automated archaeologist needs some knowledge to go from the descriptive features of the sword until the chronological knowledge. If the sword had its fabrication date inscribed, the problem would be easily solved. Imagine, however, that this is not the case. We have not the necessary knowledge.

How do we acquire knowledge to explain the chronology of an ancient sword?

We can achieve this goal by determining the chronology of the context where the sword was found. Possible solutions may be:

- Pottery with painted decoration (9th century B.C.)
- Pottery with incised decoration (8th century B.C.)
- Pottery without decoration (7th century B.C.)

Therefore the sub-goal we have to achieve is:

What kind of decorated pottery is associated with the bronze sword found in that context?

Let us suppose that the sword has been found out of context. It belongs to the private collection of a local fan and nobody agrees on when and where was unearthed. The possible intermediate states are three, one by each type of ceramics that could be have found near the sword. We will appeal now to an analogy:

What sword morphometrically similar to the initial one (A) has been found in a context associated with one of the three previous kinds of pottery?

Suppose we have two examples, a sword associated with painted pottery in context (*B*) and another one associated with undecorated pottery in context (*C*). Here we have the typical case of too many possible solutions. Now, we use a mathematical operator (similarity)

Which description (B) or (C) is more similar to the initial state of the problem (the original sword)(A)?

An automated archaeologist can use a mathematical similarity criterion to establish which of the two swords in known contexts are like the "problematic" one. If the answer is sword (*B*), then using an analogical operator we will apply the chronological knowledge of (*B*) to the original case (*A*). Given that (*B*) is associated to painted pottery, and the presence of this pottery is a truth condition for "CHRONOLOGY=9th century B.C.," it concludes that our sword is nearly 3,000 years old.

Let us consider now how to select among a potentially infinite set of social actions. Imagine our automated archaeologist should explain the formation processes having acted on what today is an archaeological site. How it should explain the presence of a wall, the detection of some pits holes, or the discovery of an accumulation of animal bones near a wall and over a pit hole? Not many professional archaeologists are able to understand and explain those traces. Only experienced researchers can do that, and they can because they have organized all their knowledge, and the knowledge provided by their colleagues,

into a coherent body of alternative solutions. The archaeologist is not a mere database of walls, pit holes or archaeological structures seen somewhere. We organize knowledge into hierarchical networks of observations, middle range descriptions, explanatory and abstract concepts, and the like. We will see in Chapter III how to create generalizations from experimental and controlled observations and how to relate the empirical and the abstract. The results of such learning methods are stored to allow the archaeologist (human or a machine) finding something similar, in which case they it will be applied to specific cases, provided some ideal criteria be fulfilled. This task can be easily implemented in a computer. Similarity and analogy are then among the most useful operators to relate observations with explanations, in the same sense as statistical induction and causal modeling are used as operators for building the space of all solutions.

To explain the cause of social activity is, however, much more difficult. After all, a wall or a pit hole seen here are more or less similar to the wall or pit hole seen there. Traces of building houses, butchering animals, or making tools at some place can be proved similar to the evidence of building or butchering, or making tools at another place. Nevertheless, a social organization having emerged here probably has nothing to do with a social organization having emerged there. It is usual, however, to solve historical problems using some kind of social typologies as problem spaces. For instance, if this group of people hunted rabbits, gathered apples, and killed their human neighbors without arrows, then they are a society *of the X kind*. Concepts like *chiefdom* or *state* have been used in this way. There is nothing intrinsically wrong with this approach. The difficulty is that actual typologies are rather limited and unstructured, and they cannot be used as full problem spaces.

Archaeological problem solving does not have a unique problem space. Different kinds of problem spaces can be visualized, each appropriate for some kinds of domain knowledge and not others. For a search in a problem space to be operationally definable, we need problem states, operators transforming one problem state into a set of successors, and some ordering knowledge that helps to choose between alternatives. For a search to be practical, such mechanisms should not be too complex.

EXPERT SYSTEMS

The procedure required to conclude a successful search (i.e., to solve the problem) can be represented as a series of conditional actions (Lesgold, 1988). The idea is that of a contingent association between a perception or sensory stimulus and an epistemic action as a response.

Some psychologists (among others Anderson, 1983; 1990, Johnson-Laird, 1988; Newell, 1990; Newell & Simon 1972; Simon, 1996) have proposed to represent the association between successive states of the problem under the form of condition-actions pairs. When the current state of the world (the set of true statements describing the world), matches a specified CONDITION, this match should cause a specified ACTION to create another (true) descriptor for the world. A condition-action pair defines a single chunk of problem solving knowledge. Here, conditions are only a specific set of key features, and actions are explanatory concepts associated to those features, and used to reach the goal.

Using the terminology proposed by Post (1943) we may call those conditionals *productions* or *production rules*. Each production is a process that consists of two parts: a set of tests or *conditions* and a set of *actions*. The actions contained in a production are executed whenever the conditions of that production are satisfied. In that sense, the productions operate in complete independence of each other (Simon, 1996, p. 102). They contain an antecedent and a consequent. The antecedent enumerates those situations in which the rule is applicable. When those conditions are "true," we say that the knowledge represented in the rule consequent has been activated. Their fundamental advantage is that of "indexing" available knowledge in terms of associations.

In general, the condition part of a production rule can be any binary-valued (0,1) function of the features resulting from perception of the problem givens. The action part is a primitive action, a call to another production system, or a set of epistemic actions to be executed simultaneously (Nilsson, 1998, p. 27). As actions are executed, inputs and the values of features based on them change.

The underlying logical mechanism is:

IF   FEATURE1 = true
           (object O has Feature1)
    AND   (If Feature1 then Concept X) = true
    AND   GOAL = G
THEN   CONCEPT X =   true
           (the presence of object O allows the use of Concept X in the circumstances defined by Object O, if and only if your goal to achieve was G)

This rule represents the knowledge required for appropriate application of a problem solving operator. The "then" portion of the rule specifies the action to be taken and the expected state change will bring about. The "if" portion consists of a set of clauses describing when the action could and should be invoked. The clauses in the condition of this rule are of two types. The first two describe conditions that must be met before the operator can be applied. The third clause specifies a goal for which the operator is useful. The goal restriction helps to limit search, because it means this rule will only be considered when the relevant goal has arisen (Holyoak, 1990, p. 124).

The associations between the different units of knowledge can be extremely complex: the consequences of determined rules serve as condition of activation of others. For example:

If *A* and *B*, then *C*.
If *x* is *X*, then *D*.

If C and D, then H.
If B, then D.

In this case, A and B are attributes of the real world, and are defined as empirical facts in the problem statement. In this case, A and B "exist," and the first rule is "true." Therefore, the system instantiates this rule and it *activates* unit C. If the automated archaeologist has additional knowledge about the proper nature of entity x (it is an instance of class X), then, the system will instantiate another rule, which activates knowledge D. The effect of this new knowledge unit and unit C, is not to explain A and B, but to *activate* a new concept (H), whose function will be, either to activate a new unit, or to determine if the goal has been reached.

From this discussion, we infer that to activate some specific knowledge to solve a problem, two things are needed: a unit of knowledge and an association between this one and another. In other words, all inference is reduced to establish associations between predefined units of knowledge. If the automated archaeologist does not have explanatory concepts (this is, if we have not provided them previously), it will never get to process the empirical data. In order to know whether a pottery vase dates in 9th century B.C., the automated archaeologist designer should previously define the concept "9th century B.C.," because from this definition the connections will arise that will allow to associate ("to activate") the initial state with the final state of the problem. If the intelligent machine should explain some society as an example of "Chiefdom," the robot builder should know, in a very strict sense, what a "Chiefdom" is and what it looks like. Nevertheless, it is important to take into account that rules merely specify what is characteristic of typical entities, not what is universally true of them. Consequently, production rules provide a rough description of what is typical of some archaeological events, not a definition of them.

In fact, the "activation" of a knowledge unit is much more than the mere execution of computer code. Knowledge activation cannot be defined by direct functional links:

If   OBJECT
Then   CONCEPT

We need an "intelligent" evaluation of possible contexts where this association may be true:

If (x,y,z) are proper empirical features of Object $F1$,
AND (v,w) are proper definition terms of Concept F,
OR   there is some contextual similarity between F and $F1$,
   THEN, $F1$ activates F
      Object ($F1$) is an instance of Concept (F)

Problem solving knowledge is, however, usually very difficult to describe and to use. It comprises all we usually include under the label "experience" or "skill." Therefore, we can distinguish three kinds of production rules:

* About the task,
* About the system,
* About how the system will perform the task,

In any case, it is important to remember that human memory is not a mere storehouse of knowledge. An automated archaeologist should not be seen as a list of rules waiting to be mechanically applied to the archaeological facts. Production rules collect and combine information in appropriate ways to construct new representations in which the next rule will have easy access to the information it requires, but all information must be available. If the production rules are formulated as logical implications and the ACTION adds assertions to working memory, then the act of rule firing corresponds to an application of *modus ponens*. There is however an alternative to prevent the formal character of classical predicate logics: the use of *abductive reasoning*. Josephson et al. (1987) suggest adopting the following pseudo-syllogism to represent the abductive inferences:

D is a collection of data (observations expressed in terms of verbal descriptions, numerical measures or digitized images).

H explains *D* (If *H* were true, then would imply *D*).

None of the Hypotheses explains *D* better than *H*.

Then, *H* is right.

Therefore, two abductively associated knowledge units are two elements between which some relation has been settled down. Such relationship should not necessarily be based on the deep nature of the associated units, but it can be built on an external criterion established by the scientist (Clancey, 1984). Following Thagard (1988), we must admit that what has led us to establish an abductive "connection" is merely a practical motif: *A* explains *B* because *A* fulfils certain requirements. Those requirements can be very diverse, formal or quasi-formal or well derived from the goals formulated upon stating the interpretive problem. In that case, we will designate it as a heuristic requirement. What is certain is that there is not any formal definition of the explanation term. In absence of an operative definition, we should work under the assumption—probably wrong—that an explanation equals to a possible association, in which the adjective "possible" has no relation with "universal truth." What converts this association into possible is that the link does not guarantee that it is a "true" bit of knowledge, but it is the best of all alternatives. In this case, the computer produces what it is sufficiently good, but calculable, instead of what is perfect (truth), but unreachable.

Therefore, by means of associations, the activation or production of an explanation will automatically expand, instantiating those concepts with which it is associated first, and these, as well, will cause the activation of new concepts. In a certain sense, then, we can consider that the activation function acts as "necessary energy" so that the automated archaeologist "thinks" and solves the problem, that is to say, so that it can look for the heuristically better solution.

The mechanism of expansion of the activation function is usually very complex, computationally speaking. In order the automated archaeologist "thinks," its computational brain (inference engine) has to be able to cause a cascade movement between different knowledge units. The result is very similar to a chain reaction, because the activation function extends gradually by all the system through the association between the concepts that have been implemented declaratively (under the form of production rules). If that reaction chain or rule search is too narrow, possibly the system will have very little utility, because we will hardly obtain solutions that, at first sight, seem innovating or, at least, different from the awaited thing. If the search is too ample, too many interpretations could be valid at the same time, and the system will fall in the incoherence. The resolution of this paradox, nevertheless, is beyond the reach of actual computer technology.

This cascade of rule firings and successive expanded explanations can be used to characterize the entire process of problem solving. In this case, we are speaking about a production system, and not a mere set of production rules. In computer terms, we usually refer to such mechanisms as *expert systems*. Every expert system consists of two principal parts: the knowledge base; and the reasoning, or inference engine.

The most important ingredient in any expert system is knowledge. The power of expert systems resides in the specific, high-quality knowledge they contain about task domains. The knowledge base of expert systems contains both factual and heuristic knowledge represented in terms of production rules. *Factual knowledge* is that knowledge of the task domain that is widely shared, typically found in textbooks or journals, and commonly agreed upon by those knowledgeable in the particular field. *Heuristic knowledge* is the less rigorous, more experiential, more judgmental knowledge of performance. In contrast to factual knowledge, heuristic knowledge is largely individualistic. It is the knowledge of good practice, good judgment, and plausible reasoning in the field.

The structure of rules in an expert system, including the distinction between the condition and the action and the order in which conditions are tried, determines the way in which the problem space is searched. This task is carried out by the so-called "reasoning engine," which organizes and controls the steps taken to solve the problem. One common but powerful paradigm involves chaining of IF-THEN rules to form a line of reasoning. If the chaining starts from a set of conditions and moves toward some conclusion, the method is called *forward chaining*. If the conclusion is known (for example, a goal to be achieved) but the path to that conclusion is not known, then reasoning backwards is called for, and the method is *backward chaining*.

For instance, consider the following example of forward chaining (Barceló, 1997):

IF   (*x*) is a settlement,
AND   (*x*) has (*y*) in quantity (*h*),
AND   (*y*) is an object of pottery,
OR   (*y*) is glassware,
AND   (*y*) is dated in the 10th century B.C.,
THEN VERIFY THE ORIGIN OF (*y*).

IF   (*Goal*) is TO VERIFY THE ORIGIN OF (*y*),
AND   (*y*) is made of foreign material,
THEN (*y*) is an Imported Object.

IF   (*y*) is an Imported Object,
AND   (*y*) is similar to the Muslim pottery from the Castle of Silves (Portugal),
THEN (*x*) has Foreign Trade evidence.

In the case of backward chaining, goal-driven search begins with a goal and works backwards to establish its truth. The goal is placed on working memory and matched against the ACTIONS of the production rules. These ACTIONS are matched just as the CONDITIONS of the productions were matched in the data-driven reasoning. When the ACTION of a rule is matched, the CONDITIONS are added to working memory and they become new sub-goals of the search. The new states are then matched to the ACTIONS of other production rules. The process continues until a fact is found, usually in the problem's initial description.

The control structure used for such a reasoning engine is straightforward. The current state of the problem solving is maintained as a set of patterns in *working memory*. Working memory is initialized with the beginning problem description. Production rules correspond to the problem solving planning skills in long-term memory and they are transferred to the working memory when necessary. The patterns in working memory are matched against the conditions of the production rules; this produces a subset of the productions, called the conflict set, whose conditions match the patterns in working memory. The productions in the conflict set are said to be *enabled*. One of the productions in the conflict set is then selected (*conflict resolution*) and the production is fired. That is, the action of the rule is performed, what changes the contents of working memory. After the selected production rule is fired, the control cycle repeats with the modified working memory. The process terminates when no rule conditions are matched by the contents of working memory. In this way, production rules are not changed by the execution of the system; they are invoked by the "pattern" of a particular problem instance, and new skills may be added without requiring "recoding" of the previous existing knowledge.

In addition to the knowledge base and the reasoning engine, an expert system usually integrates:

* **A knowledge acquisition subsystem:** A subsystem helps experts to build knowledge bases. Collecting knowledge needed to solve problems and building the knowledge base continues to be the biggest bottleneck in building expert systems,

- **An explanation subsystem:** It is a subsystem that explains the system's actions. The explanation can range from how the final or intermediate solutions were arrived at to justifying the need for additional data.

The general problem of explanation in an intelligent machine can be viewed as a problem of mapping between the information needed to satisfy the goals and what the machine can provide to meet that information needs. This mapping is complex because neither machine's goals nor its explanatory abilities are static or simple. Both are complex hierarchical structures and both change dynamically. The need for understanding at any particular time (goal) might relate to general world knowledge relevant to the robot's explanatory functionality, or it might relate to understanding the dynamic reasoning processes of the machine itself. Explanations of the reasoning of the system might refer to the details of individual explanations, or they might refer to various higher level strategic procedures carried out by the system, which might be only implicit in the system design. In many ways, the world knowledge and reasoning questions can intertwine, as in the well-known issue of providing the justifications for rule-based actions (Clancey, 1984). In general, the states of rule-based systems change in ways that eliminate potential actions at later points that were possible earlier. During the system's reasoning processes, resources are consumed, knowledge is combined in ways that preclude other combinations, time passes, actions are taken that prevent alternatives, either physically or by meeting the same goals, and so on. As a result, explanations for actions, and especially explanations for actions not taken, need to account for earlier states as well as the current situation (Metzler & Martincic, 1998).

Given the importance, complexity, and especially the heterogeneity of the explanation problem, it is not surprising to find that it has been addressed in a variety of ways as well (Giarratano & Riley, 2004; Tyler, 2007). Some intelligent system architectures have provided useful explanation facilities based directly on their internal data and control structures, such as the rule traces of a rule-based system. Since intelligent systems, especially expert systems are most often based on data and control structures that correspond closely to human articulated knowledge, these structures are relatively understandable and informative to users, at least to expert users. In general however, while such "transparent system" approaches have proven useful, it is well understood today that they are relatively brittle, not providing the flexibility of focus required for general user understanding of an intelligent system. They do not directly deal with the complex issues mentioned previously. For instance, rule trace approaches are essentially chronological rather than dependency based, so that they do not distinguish which are the important events in a long history of past explanations. They deal only with what actually occurred and not with other hypothetical lines of reasoning, and they do not represent the notions of goals or purposes in any manner that directly supports explanation. Some have uncoupled the problem of providing explanation from the system's reasoning by providing alternative reasoning mechanisms that are separate from the expert system's functioning.

"DECONSTRUCTING" ARCHAEOLOGY

Scientific reasoning has been described in terms of problem solving search (Klahr & Dunbar, 1988; Klahr, 2000; Kulkarni & Simon, 1988; Langley et al., 1987; Simon & Lea, 1974; Thagard, 1988; Valdés-Pérez, 1995, 1996; Valdés-Pérez et al., 1993; Wagman, 2000). According to that view, scientific theories may be considered as complex data structures in a computational system; they consist of highly organized packages of rules, concepts, and problem solutions.

The idea is that scientific knowledge directs problem solving search through a space of theoretical concepts. This specific knowledge matches against different possible regularities in the data and take different actions depending on the kind of regularity the system has perceived among external data. Some of this knowledge proposes laws or hypotheses, others define a new theoretical term, and yet others alter the proposed scope of a law. Different data led to the application of alternative sequences of knowledge operators, and thus to different conclusions.

Generating a causal explanation is then a type of problem solving search, in which the initial state consists of some knowledge about a domain, and the goal state is a hypothesis that can account for some or all of that knowledge in a more concise form. A space of instances and a space of hypotheses should then be used, with the search in one space guided by information available in the other. That is to say, the use of instances constrains the search for hypothetical statements of the causal relationship. Hypotheses are evaluated through known instances of the causal relationship. In looking for appropriate instances of examples, scientists are faced with a problem solving task paralleling their search for hypotheses. They must be able to plan by making predictions about which observational (or experimental) results could support or reject various hypotheses. This involves search in a space of data that is only partially defined at the outset. Constraints on the search must be added during the problem solving process. This, in turn, requires domain-general knowledge about the pragmatic constraints of the particular discovery context.

Archaeological explanation can be represented in the same terms, that is to say, as a series of successive actions that lead from the empirical description of an archaeological phenomenon to its interpretation. Those "actions" imply the application of different rules whose function is to put in touch the initial state (description of the phenomenon) with the final state (explanation).

The problem space containing such rules is, in fact, a scientific theory.

This is exactly the proposal by Jean Claude Gardin: the way archaeologists take decisions can be mechanized. Although he never tried to build an automated archaeologist, some of his suggestions are very interesting for our concern (Gardin, 1980, 1991, 1993, 1994, 1998, 2003).

His point of departure was to explore the discursive practices of archaeology. According to Gardin, the concrete expression of reasoning in any dominion of science is the text where the author has expressed the mental operations that have lead him or her from the observation of certain empirical facts, to the affirmation of certain explanatory proposals. This methodology looks for the necessary bridges between facts and theses and the links between explanations. It has been called *logicist analysis* (Gardin et al., 1981). Its goal is to reduce the content of the text in its main components, studying their fundamental connections. The schematization of an archaeological paper is not an abstract or a summary of the paper, but a reformulation of its content in a condensed form. Gardin uses the word "condensation" as in physics: a rearrangement of something into a more compact volume, without loss of substance. He and his colleagues "have deconstructed" numerous scientific works (mainly archaeological) in this way. This approach is precisely a framework for analyzing and modeling the questions and answers that bracket a scientific text, and there is an obvious intuitive link between meaning, questions, and answers. Similar approaches have been those by Stutt (1989), Winder (1996), Orlandi (1997, 2002), Tsaganou et al. (2003), Zhang et al. (2002).

The deconstruction process involves: (1) capturing the source text; (2) capturing, making explicit, and formalizing the textual expertise of human interpreters; (3) defining and evaluating degrees of meaning and the plausibility of interpretations; and (4) implementing a query system for interpretative questions on the computer.

Gardin assumes that our theoretical constructs can be expressed in terms of a "calculus." Archaeological theories can be formulated as computational structures with two components. The first one is a *facts base*, here understood as a set of declarative propositions that include not only descriptions of archaeological materials and their context, with associated archaeometric data, but also a large number of referential statements. Those statements are not usually regarded as "data;" they include primarily vast sets of analogies, "common sense," shared belief, ideologies, and so forth. The second component is an inferential tree made up of rewrite operations, which reproduce the chain of inferences from the archaeological record ("facts," represented as P_o) to different explanatory statements (P_n). Between the extremes of the argumentation, there are intermediate theses (Pi). Scientific reasoning builds chains of oriented propositions $P_o, P_1, P_2..., P_n$ in terms of successive operations $P_i \dashrightarrow P_{i+1.}$

Analogies between logicist analysis and some aspects of artificial intelligence are patent, although both representation schemas evolved in parallel without further implications (Gardin, 1980,123-125, 1991; Gardin et al., 1987). Formal characteristics of expert systems technology appear to be very similar to the general structure of rewrite rules. The "deconstruction" of a scientific text in terms of rewriting operations agrees with the "extraction" of the expert knowledge in terms of production rules. In the same way that the knowledge engineer tries to find out how a human expert thinks before introducing "prior knowledge" inside the computer program, a logicist analyst tries to study what is hidden inside a scientific text written in natural language.

The most interesting analogy between both procedures of representation concerns the common way to deal with the general architecture of reasoning: if the logicist analysis tries to reconstruct that architecture, starting from more or less literary texts, the expert system is able to reproduce it in absence of the investigator. Other parallelisms are registered at different levels of abstraction (see Table 2.1).

What we should compare are the results of "scientific" reasoning: a *text* or a *computer program*. Both are encapsulated knowledge devices. The difference is that in human sciences, *texts* are usually "black boxes," because authors hide their reasoning mechanisms in verbal rhetoric or they make very general references to "common sense," forgetting that a text is not a photograph of a mental state, but a representation of a reasoning process. Expert systems are able to represent scientific reasoning, because it is always mechanical and artificial, and it can be reduced to logical mechanisms.

"Rules" are the key, not laws, which are inviolate, but rules that can be changed and indeed are always changing in a reflexive relationship allowing the expert (human or machine) to accommodate new information. Given some

Table 2.1.

Semiologic	Logicist analysis Database (P_o)	Expert systems Fact base
Representation	expressed in terms of a scientific language (descriptive "code")	expressed in terms of a computer language (programming)
Information	Re-write operations	Production Rules
Processing	$P_i \dashrightarrow P_{i+1}$. Ordered in inductive or deductive chains	IF p THEN q organized in a cascade linking

empirical data (observations) about a particular archaeological case, and some bit of associative knowledge (if…then) (hypotheses and interpretations considered valid in a social, anthropological, or historical theory), the archaeological problem can be explained in terms of the knowledge stored in the rule base. In other words, given some visual input and a candidate explanatory causal model, a correspondence can be established between them. This means that a small number of features are identified as matching features in the input and the model. Based on the corresponding features, a decision rule linking visual features with their causal process (social activity) is uniquely determined. The recovered decision rule is then applied to the model. Based on the degree of match, the candidate causal event is selected or rejected. To be accepted, the match must be sufficiently close, and better than that of competing solutions.

The rules discovered by logicist analysis or implemented in an expert system are subjective, but they are explicit. Anyone can produce the same results, so that although the system is subjective, it will be consistent when different subjectivities (i.e., different individuals) use it. The acceptance of the assumptions on which the problem solution is based leads to consistency, and direct comparability between results produced by different people. This fulfills the basic requirements of objective data within the consensus reality of mutual users of the program. Therefore, expert systems and logicist analysis can extract objective-like data, but the complexity of the dynamic process is retained and the data is produced in the form of probabilities that can be compared as if they are objective data within a defined consensus reality.

Expert systems in archaeology have been accused of excessive simplification, of forcing knowledge, or distorting it, and of failing to exploit fully the knowledge of the expert (Doran, 1988; Francfort, 1993; Gallay, 1989; Hugget & Baker, 1986, Lagrange, 1989c; Shennan & Stutt, 1989; Puyol-Gruart, 1999; Wilcock, 1986, 1990;).

However, there is nothing suspicious in such a technology. The basic idea behind them is simply that expertise, which is the vast body of task-specific knowledge, is transferred from a human to a computer. This knowledge is then stored in the computer and users call upon the computer for specific advice as needed. The computer can make inferences and arrive at a specific conclusion. Then like a human consultant, it gives advices and explains, if necessary, the logic behind the advice. Such a strategy has been successfully applied in many diverse domains as finance, medicine, engineering, legal studies, ecology and biological taxonomy (Liao, 2003, 2005). Why not in archaeology?

Let us see some examples.

AN AUTOMATED ARCHAEOLOGIST, WHICH DISCOVERS THE FUNCTION OF LITHIC TOOLS

The most obvious archaeological application of expert systems technology has been the implementation of typologies. All of us know the troublesome thing that is to classify archaeological artifacts when we are not an expert in that cultural period. In these circumstances, an expert system can replace with advantage a series of books or, even, an expert. Its content is the same one that appears in the reference book, but clearer and better ordered. In the expert system, the classification criteria are, by definition, explicit (in form of rules), whereas in the reference book or table, it is usually very difficult to find out why the archaeologist has classified an object in a group and not in another one. Finally, and, mainly, an expert system is very easy to update, given the modularity of the architecture of the knowledge base.

As an example of automatic typology, we can mention the work by Roger Grace (1989), who has developed an expert system for the classification of the technology and typology of tools. This program is called LITHAN (LITHic Analysis of stone tools).

Observations of the archaeological items are entered on a data card (Figure 2.3).

Metrical and non-metrical attributes of the tools such as length, width, thickness, position and type of retouch, and so forth are entered, by 'pressing' the appropriate button (Figure 2.4). Shape related attributes are recorded as being nearest to the following alternatives.

Rules are then applied to interpret the type, and knapping technology. In the case of tool 33, the expert system explains it as a non-cortical morphological flake that was made using a blade technology with soft hammer and is an end scraper.

Often there is insufficient data to identify such categories as knapping technology or hammer mode, particularly when the tools are broken and the proximal end is missing. In such cases they will be classified as 'indeterminate.'

LITHAN uses production rules like the following:

BLANK TYPE:
    IF   length/width ratio >2,
        AND   width <12 mm,
        THEN put "BLADE LET."
TECH TYPE:
    IF   platform Thickness <5,
        AND   ButtType = "prepared,"

Figure 2.3. Data acquisition initial screen in LITHAN. (© 1989, 1993, by Roger Grace. Figure reprinted with permission of the author). http://www.hf.uio.no/iakk/roger/lithic/expsys.html.

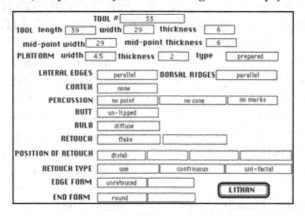

Figure 2.4. Selection of qualitative attributes in LITHAN. (© 1989, 1993, by Roger Grace. Figure reprinted with permission of the author). http://www.hf.uio.no/iakk/roger/lithic/expsys.html.

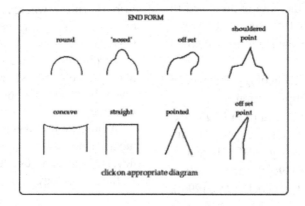

AND   Sides = "parallel" ,
AND   Ridges = "parallel,"
THEN put "TECHBLADE."
HAMMERMODE:
    IF   percussionCone = "no cone,"
    AND   butt = "un-lipped,"
    AND   bulb = "diffuse,"
    THEN put "SOFT HAMMER."
TYPE:
    IF   diff (length - width) > 0,
    AND   distalRetouch = "DISTAL,"
    THEN put "END SCRAPER."

General categories like end-scraper are further subdivided by applying secondary rules:

IF   endForm = "ROUND,"
THEN put "END SCRAPER."
IF   endForm = "CARINATED,"
THEN put "CARINATED END SCRAPER."

There are sub-routines for special categories, cores, burins, arrowheads, and microliths.

Lithic analysis, however, does not end up with shape considerations. Some interpretation about the most probable function of the tool is also necessary. Grace has created therefore the FAST (Functional Analysis of Stone Tools) expert system computer program.

In this case, metrical and non-metrical attributes of use-wear such as grain size, micro-topography, invasiveness, gloss, etc. are also entered, by 'pressing' the appropriate button (Figure 2.5).

The syntax for functional rules is very simply and takes the form of:

IF   (edge angle <30 degrees),
THEN PUT (cutting soft material).
IF   (fractures are absent),
AND   (edge angle >30 and <60),
THEN PUT (medium material).

The parameters contained in these rules are derived from observations of experimental tools. The indications are then counted, again according to a set of rules. If an indication contains two alternatives such as SOFT/MEDIUM for micro rounding, then SOFT would receive 0.5 points but doubled to 1 point because the other surface

Figure 2.5. Selection of qualitative and quantitative attributes in FAST. (© 1989, 1993, by Roger Grace. Figure reprinted with permission of the author). http://www.hf.uio.no/iakk/roger/lithic/FAST.html.

TOOL # 33	TYPE endscraper	EDGE ANGLE	42
GRAINSIZE	fine	LENGTH	28
TOPOGRAPHY	flat	THICKNESS	6
TOPOGRAPHIC FEATURES	absent	PROFILE	0.56
		SHAPE	0.53

EDGE WEAR	VENTRAL macro	micro	DORSAL macro	micro
GLOSS	absent		retouch	
FRACTURES	absent	<5	retouch	retouch
FRACTURE TYPE	absent	flakes	retouch	retouch
ROUNDING	absent	absent	retouch	retouch

MICROTOPOGRAPHY	flat	retouch
DISTRIBUTION	continuous	retouch
DISTRIBUTION TYPE	edge only even	retouch
INVASIVENESS	<0.5	retouch
LINEAR FEATURES	perpendicular	retouch
STRIATIONS	perpendicular	retouch
POLISH DEV.	c	c

is retouched. Each variable counts as two points [except thickness, which has a maximum of 1]. This is because thickness only has two values <4 mm or > 4 mm and is not very discriminatory and consequently less important. Therefore, it carries less 'weight.' The results of the counting rules are entered as SCORES. For instance, if the program has calculated for a single tool 12 indications of scraping, 1 of cutting, 5 of a soft material, 8 of a medium material and 1 of a hard material, then the function rules are applied.

```
IF       "cutting" <4
    AND   "scraping" >8
    AND "grooving" <2
    AND   "whittling" <2
THEN  PUT "SCRAPING"
IF       "soft" >4 and <8
    AND   "medium" >0 and <2
    AND   "hard" = 0
THEN    PUT "SOFT"

IF       "soft" <6
    AND   "medium" >5
    AND   "hard" <4
THEN    PUT "WOOD"
```

Rules that are more complex involve combining motions with materials, and in certain cases also including morphological information concerning the tools:

```
IF     "soft" >2 and <6
    AND   "medium" <8
    AND   "hard" <2
    AND   MOTION "whittling" OR "boring/
    drilling" OR "grooving" OR "chopping/adz-
    ing"
THEN PUT "HIDE"
```

This rule is constructed in this way because whittling, boring, drilling, grooving, chopping and adzing are motions unlikely to be used on hide.

```
IF       "soft" =0,
    AND   "medium" >3,
    AND   "hard" >8,
    AND   MOTION "whittling" OR "cutting"
    OR "piercing" OR "chopping/adzing" OR
    "grooving,"
    AND SUBTYPE "facet" (when referring to
    a burin),
THEN    PUT "STONE."
```

This rule is constructed in this way because whittling, cutting, chopping and adzing are unlikely motions to be used on stone and grooving stone is more likely to be carried out with the burin 'bit' rather than the "facet."

If the scores for motions and materials fall within the parameters in the program then an interpretation will be made of motion, hardness of material and precise worked material. If the scores do not fall within the parameters for motion, hardness or worked material then the program gives 'INSUFFICIENT DATA.' This will apply if there is insufficient use-wear on the tool to be diagnostic or if the use-wear is not consistent with a particular use. That is, it does not match the use-wear of tools in the reference collection of experimental tools from which the parameters were derived. This means the program can suggest a material that has not been studied by experimentation and so is not included in the program.

Since the development of FAST, another expert system for the analysis of use-wear on stone tools has been developed. This program is called Waves (wear analyzing and visualizing expert system, see Dries, 1996). The program is similar in structure to FAST as data are entered by clicking on the appropriate observation from a multiple-choice menu for each variable, and IF-THEN rules are applied in order to match combinations of observations against experimental data. However, it has some other characteristics, which made it more suitable as an example of neural networks. It will be analyzed in detail in Chapter VII.

AN AUTOMATED ARCHAEOLOGIST, WHICH RECONSTRUCTS INCOMPLETE DATA

The archaeological record is fast always incomplete: not *all* past material things have remained until today. Even more, most of those few items from the past that we can observe today are broken. The only possibility to "see what cannot be seen" is as a generalization of fragmented observable data, representing partially the view of a lost physical world reality. This can only be done by generating *simulated* data (Barceló, 2000, 2001). That is to say, the automated archaeologist needs a complete "model" in order to complete damaged input data. The idea is to use a hypothetical model of the thing, and to fit it to the incomplete input data to simulate what is not preserved. We can use the following kinds of knowledge:

a. If all we know to simulate missing data are analogies and some other "similar" cases, then we can build a *qualitative* model. This is the case of ancient buildings. In most cases, preserved remains do not shed light on the structure of vertical walls, which therefore remain unknown. In general, the reconstruction of archaeological badly preserved ancient buildings is largely based on these types of sources:

b. Pictorial evidence from plans and photographs of the building's ruins.

c. Descriptive accounts by modern authors on the ruins in both their existing condition and in their imagined original state.

d. Evidence shown by contemporary buildings in other neighboring places or culturally related areas, which gives clues as to likely construction methods and spatial forms.

e. When old drawings and photographs are not available, external data can be estimated from ethnographic records.

This knowledge can be arranged to constitute an expert system, and then using it to reconstruct archaeological ruins. The problem in all those cases is that theoretical knowledge is not being added to the model in a systematic way. That is to say, knowledge of the model to reconstruct is not organized in rules and facts, but selecting additional information in a subjective way, using what the illustrator wants, and not what the archaeologist really needs.

The problem of visually reconstructing bad preserved archaeological remains is exactly the same problem that any animal brain should solve when dealing with incomplete visual inputs. Because images are not the raw data of perception, it is theoretically possible to rebuild an altered image, using prior-knowledge in the process of image formation from the pattern of luminance contrasts observed in the empirical world. This process is analogous to scientific explanation, and therefore, it involves *induction, deduction* and *analogy*, and therefore we can use *expert systems* to integrate external knowledge to partial input, and then simulate the missing parts of the input. An automated archaeologist should follow the rule: "The most similar is taken for the complete simulation." The procedure is as follows: we transform perceived data as a geometric data set (shape, size, texture), and we try to interpret the visual type, assuming some dependent preference function. Once the type is decided, the closest fit is determined using different numerical techniques (Barceló 2002).

IF b (x,y,z) FITS THEORY,
AND MODEL A IS A PROJECTION OF
    THEORY,
THEN b (SHAPE) DERIVES FROM MODEL
    A.

The expert system inference engine organizes and controls factual knowledge, chaining different IF-THEN rules to form a line of reasoning, as we have seen. For instance:

IF the geometric model of (x) has geometric
    properties A,B,C,
THEN (x) is an example of MODEL AB.C..
IF (x) is an example of MODEL AB.C.,
AND (x) has not property D,
THEN JOIN property D to the geometric model
    of (x).

Where JOIN is an operator implemented as a command able to add some geometric unit to those already present in a preliminary model of the partial input. As a result, some new visual features (property D) are added to the geometrical model of the original data.

To deal with uncertain knowledge, a rule may have associated with it a confidence factor or a weight. For instance:

IF the geometric model of (x) has geometric
    properties A,B,C but not properties D,E,
THEN(x) is an example of MODEL ABC (with
    probability 0.7).
IF the geometric model of (x) has geometric
    properties A,B,C, D,E,
THEN (x) is an example of MODEL ABC (with
    probability 1.0).
IF (x) APPROXIMATELY fits MODEL
    ABC,
THEN VISUALIZE the incomplete parts of (x)
    using A,B,C properties.

The automated archaeologist needs to build the model first, and then use it for simulating the unseen object. It creates a geometric model of the interpreted reality, and then it uses information deduced from the model when available visual data fit the model. In most cases, it creates "theoretical" or "simulated" geometric models. Here "theory" means general knowledge about the most probable "visualization" of the object to be simulated or prior knowledge of the reality to be simulated.

One of the main examples of using expert systems for the simulation of archaeological missing data is the estimation of the general shape of a building by Ozawa (1992, 1996). The geometric model was based on a contour map of keyhole tomb mounds of ancient Japan. When archaeological information is not enough to produce the contour map, an expert system creates an estimated contour map of the original tomb mound in co-operation with archaeologists. The expert system holds the statistical knowledge for classifying any tomb into its likeliest type and the geometrical knowledge for drawing contour lines of the tomb mound. The user for each contour map introduces shape parameters, and the system classifies the mound as one of the seven types, according to specific parameters (diameter, length, weight, height, etc.). The estimated shape layout is then used as input for the 3D solid modeling and rendering (Ozawa, 1992).

Florenzano et al. (1999) give a further advance in this artificial intelligence approach. They use an object-oriented knowledge-base containing a theoretical model of existing architecture. The proportion ratios linking the diverse parts of architectural entities to the module allow a simple description of each entity's morphology. The main hypothesis of this research is about comparing the theoretical model of the building to the incomplete input data (preserved remains) acquired by photogrammetry. Abstract models are organized with the aim of isolating elementary entities that share common morphological characteristics and function, on which rules of composition can be used to re-order the building. The concept of architectural entity gathers in a single class the architectural data describing the entity, the interface with survey mechanisms and the representation methods. Each architectural entity, each element of the predefined architectural corpus, is therefore described through geometrical primitives corresponding to its morphological characteristics: a redundant number of measurable geometrical primitives are added to each entity's definition, as previously mentioned. Related applications are Lewis and Séguin (1998), Drap et al. (2003).

In the case of objects like pottery vases, reconstructions can be easier, because manufactured objects fit better with single geometric models. Therefore, the reconstruction of a given object is most of the times a direct generalization of fragmented observable data by mathematical object description. The fragmented spatial information available can be extrapolated to complete a closed surface. The procedure may be illustrated by the mathematical ovoid and the eggshell compared. The eggshell is a solid formed by a fine closed surface. Continuity and dynamics are bound to the shape of the eggshell, in such a way that it is possible to locate the fragments of a broken eggshell as well as to define the whole by only very few spatial measurements. Evidently, to model the geometry of an eggshell, it is sufficient to pick from the fragments of a broken eggshell some spatial world data to simulate the entire eggshell. The spatial continuity and dynamics of the ovoid is included in the mathematical description, to simulate the missing information. The algorithm for the mathematical ovoid serves as a generalized constructive solid geometry, and just some additional information will tell the specification and the modification of the individual eggshell, its capacity, and the location of the centre of gravity. In other words, an automated archaeologist should create a geometric model (the mathematical ovoid) of the interpreted reality, and then use information deduced from the model to fit the partially observed reality. The idea is very similar to the previous one, but instead of a qualitative model, the automated archaeologist uses geometric models. Several measurements—like volume, width, maximal perimeter, and so forth—are computed from observable data. Comparing the actual measurements or interpolated surface with the parameters and surfaces defining the theoretical model makes simulation possible. Relevant examples are Kampel and Sablatnig, 2002, 2003, 2004, Cooper et al., 2002, Leitão et al., 2002, Leymarie, 2003, Hawarah, et al. 2003,

Melero et al., 2004, Kampel and Melero, 2003, and Moon et al., 2005.

An interesting future development is the possibility of using visualizations in a *case-based reasoning* framework (Foley & Ribarsky, 1994). The fundamental strategy is to organize a large collection of existing images or geometric models as *cases* and to design new visual reconstructions by adapting and combining the past cases. New problems in the case-based approach are solved by adapting the solutions to similar problems encountered in the past. The important issues in building a case-based visualization advisor are developing a large library of models, developing an indexing scheme to access relevant cases, and determining closeness metric to find the best matches from the case library.

AN AUTOMATED ARCHAEOLOGIST, WHICH UNDERSTANDS WHAT AN ARCHAEOLOGICAL SITE WAS

KIVA is an expert system designed to interpret hypothetical archaeological sites based on the current understanding of American Indian Pueblo cultures (Patel and Stutt 1988, Stutt 1989). KIVA takes a description of an American Pueblo Indian site, which includes features, artifacts and ecofacts, and gives an interpretation of the activities that went on at that site when it was occupied in the past.

The system applies the heuristic or transformation rules, which embody the archaeological knowledge about Pueblo sites, to the facts, which constitute the description of a site, in order to produce an interpretation of the site in terms of the activities that may be associated with significant areas. This process forms an essential stage in the derivation of a cultural profile for the site.

The knowledge base of KIVA consists of *facts* about the domain and *heuristic rules* for interpreting those facts. The major part of the *fact frames* consists of two classifications: *features* and *finds*. *Finds* are objects, worked-on or man-made (*artifacts*) and of natural origin. *Artifacts* carry rich information about the technology, economy, and social organization. *Features* refer to the physical characteristics of the site. These include *hole, accumulation* (e.g., debris), *enclosing feature* (e.g., *ring* of stones, *palisades*, area demarcations), and *mound. Features* provide important clues regarding the spatial layout of an archaeological site. For example, the number of rooms in the site, burial places, fire places, etc. At the *cultural profile* level, they provide information on the social organization of the occupants of the site.

Another important classification is that of *activity areas*. These are derived by the system from data about finds and features. There are four basic types of activity areas: *living area*, a large room with a fire pit in it; *storage area*, a small room with no fire pit; *plaza*, the area between rooms; *kiva*, a subterranean room used for religious purposes.

The activity areas are derived from the features using the interpretive rules held in KIVA's knowledge base. These *rule frames* consist of seven sets (or clusters) of rules.

1. **Features rules:** This cluster of rules produces significant areas from the size and placement attributes of features.
2. **Finds rules:** This cluster derives uses of artifacts from their attributes.
3. **Content rules:** This cluster takes individual areas and searches for *finds* and *features* within the area. It also checks that the contents are from the same period in time.
4. **Area rules:** Based on contents, the main activity areas are identified.
5. **Activity rules:** From artifact uses, a different world is created for each possible activity.
6. **Constraint rules:** Expectations derived from the model help prune the worlds.
7. **Site rules:** Worlds are merged to give final interpretation of the site.

Once the raw facts are input, the interpretation can begin. KIVA activates rules in forward chaining to discover areas, based on where activities could take place. This is done using information like the size and location of the feature. Next, *content rules* determine which *finds* and *features* are contained within the significant areas. *Area rules* use this information to detect activity areas. For example, a significant area with a fire pit would be classed as a living room. Then, a world is created in the *world browser* corresponding to each defined *activity area*.

By creating "worlds," it is possible to hypothetically reason about a situation. Thus, when *activity rules* are fired, a child world of an area world is created for each possible activity within the area. An *area world* is comprised of a set of propositions about the area. It contains propositions such as, "the contents of the area are fire pit No. 5" and "the area is a living room" and so on. It does not include propositions about the activity carried out in this area. Activities possible in any given area are derived from the artifacts and features found within the area. A fire pit would suggest cooking activity, for example.

Next, top-down reasoning is employed in a two-stage process to determine which activities are feasible. Firstly, impossible activities are marked as false. Butchering, for instance, cannot be an activity of a living area. This process is achieved by means of constraint rules, which reduce the set of possible activities for an area. Secondly, other rules identify sets of activities that go naturally together and thus provide stronger evidence for a particular activity. Hence, the system suggests that cooking is a possible activity of *area51*, because two of the activities possible at the area, cooking and cutting reinforce each other.

In a penultimate step, site rules eliminate all improbable activities and confirm the most probable ones. For example, the possible activity of *area No. 51* (i.e., cooking) is confirmed by the presence of food preparation as an activity. As a result, the other likely activity (i.e., sleeping) is eliminated as a contending activity. This differs from the previous stage in the reasoning in that all contenders which are not reinforced are eliminated, leaving, if possible, only one contender for each area. Finally, site profiles are derived by combining possible site world/s.

As it has been shown, KIVA is build around an expectation-based model. According to the authors, the approach seems to capture the actual practice of archaeologists. When an archaeologist interprets a site, she has a model of the kind of site determining what she expects to find. Thus, in the example given above, the archaeologist, thinking that she is excavating a Pueblo Indian site, will expect a particular range of artifacts and features. If a find or feature is wrongly identified at some early stage, the application of the fine details of the model will generally serve to correct initial misconceptions.

In archaeological reasoning, therefore, the correct interpretation is the one that subsumes as many of the finds as possible without infringing any constraints on the combination of possible activities on a site (Stutt, 1988, 1989, 1990). KIVA builds up all possible solutions and, from its knowledge of a typical site, picks out the best solution (or solutions). In the above example, the system could apply a set of constraint rules, which includes the knowledge that all Pueblo sites have a cooking area. Thus, it could determine that it is better to believe that the activity carried out in this particular area was cooking since the area has a fire pit and no other area of the site has evidence for this necessary component of a site of this kind. Furthermore, from its knowledge that leather working was never carried out in an area reserved for cooking, it can determine that cooking was the only activity carried out. Since the knowledge which is used to select the possible interpretations is represented explicitly (in what is, in effect, a distributed model of a typical archaeological site) the knowledge of how the

system reached its decision about its reasoning is available for possible use in explanation.

AN AUTOMATED ARCHAEOLOGIST, WHICH EXPLAINS ANCIENT SOCIETIES

PALAMEDE is an expert system capable of measuring some aspects of social dynamics (Francfort, 1987, 1990, 1991, 1997, Francfort, Lagrange & Renaud, 1989). The program calculates the relative value of three main socio-economic functions (residential, productive, prestige) for each archaeological unit and cumulates the results for each of the historical phases.

IF   (x) is a settlement area,
    AND in (x) there is kitchen pottery,
THEN increase 20 points residential indicator
    at (x).

IF   (x) is a settlement area,
    AND in (x) there are tools for manufacturing ornaments,
THEN
    increase10 points productive indicator at (x).

IF   (x) is a settlement area,
    AND dominant pottery at (x) are storing vases,
    AND   prestige indicator >= 40,
THEN
    increase 20 points prestige indicator at (x).

IF   (x) is a settlement area,
    AND productive indicator at (x) >= residential indicator at (x),
THEN
    (x) predominant function is productive.

There are other rules allowing evaluation of the *relative variation* of the values of the three between the different phases. Thirteen kinds of variations are possible, with each function increasing, decreasing, stable, or indefinite.

IF   (A) and (B) are chronological phases,
    AND   (A) is older than (B),
THEN
            CALCULATE:
                Difference of Residential indicators Ri(B)- Ri (A)
                Difference of Productive indicators Pi(B)- Pi (A)
                Difference of Prestige indicators PGi(B)- PGi (A)

IF   (A) and (B) are chronological phases,
    AND   (A) is older than (B),
        AND   Difference of Prestige indicators PGi(B)- PGi (A) > 5%,
THEN
        Prestige increases at (B).

Another set of rules interprets the variations in function and allows conclusions about the value of the variation of specialization of the areas, the amplitude of the variation on a conventional scale and the direction of the variation.

IF   (A) and (B) are chronological phases,
    AND   (A) is older than (B),
        AND "prestige" in (B) increases,
    AND "domestic" in (B) decreases,

THEN
    "specialization" in (B) increases.

The next rules deal with long distance "exchange" at the site, quantified with respect to imports. They give a value to the exchange, a measure of the amplitude and direction of the variation.

Results are printed in the following format:

From phase A to phase B, the domestic indicator increases, the crafts indicator is stable, the prestige indicator decreases; conclusions, at this site, from phase A to phase B, the specialization of the areas diminishes somewhat (-2), the long distance trade diminishes enormously (-4).(Francfort et al., 1989, p. 116).

A second module of PALAMEDE models techno-informational aspects, proceeding from data to notions like "number of technological operations needed to elaborate some item," or "of technological operations needed to elaborate divided by the number of items found at a distinct activity area." In general, the idea is to weight an estimation of the quantity of labor with an estimation of the mass of artifacts generated by such a work. The results follow the previous format:

From phase A to phase B, the volume *of production diminishes greatly (4) when the sophistication of production is stable.* (Francfort et al., 1989, p. 142).

The next module of PALAMEDE evaluates all the architectural and urban features excavated, using indicators, and constructing meta-notions like: architectural technique, urbanism, quantity of work, urban planning, architectural sophistication, degree of monumentality, urban comfort, common ideology, collective control, defense of territory, and the like. As in previous models, the archaeological indicators of meta-notions are compared by phase.

Finally, PALAMEDE produces a synthesis of the historical dynamics at each level: the stability of crafts and the stability of the sophistication of production, for instance, can be related to the absence of urbanism growth, and the lack of common ideologies.

AN AUTOMATED ARCHAEOLOGIST, WHICH UNDERSTANDS EVERYTHING

In the late 1970s, Doug Lenat built a computer program (Eurisko) that discovered things on its own in many fields. To get it to work, he had to give it the power to tinker with its own learning heuristics and its own goals. Often he found it in a mode best described as "dead." Sometime during the night, the program decided by itself that the best thing to do was to commit suicide and shut itself off. More precisely, it modified its own judgmental rules in a way that valued "making no errors at all" as highly as "making productive new discoveries." As soon as Eurisko did this, it found it could successfully meet its new goal by doing nothing at all for the rest of the night (Lenat, 1995a).

People have found many ways to grapple with and resolve conflicting goals short of killing everybody in sight. Surviving and thriving in the real world means constantly making tough decisions, and making mistakes. The only ways not to make mistakes are:

1. Do nothing
2. Make sure there are no living souls left anywhere around you
3. Be omniscient.

Surely, any automated archaeologist will understand that occasional mistakes and inconsistencies are inevitable and can even serve as valuable learning experiences. Anything else leads to the absurdity that holds that one small inconsistency will make the computer self-destruct.

Our human dependence on common sense is very far-reaching. It comes into play with spoken and written language (as when we try to decipher someone's scratchy handwriting) and in our actions (e.g., when driving a car and deciding whether to brake or accelerate or swerve to avoid something). Our simple common-sense models of the world do not just clarify possible ambiguities; they are good enough to provide a context, a way of restricting reasoning to potentially relevant information and excluding irrelevant data.

Before we let automatic archaeologists explain by themselves past human actions, it is necessary that the machine has general common sense about the value of a pottery sherd compared with a simple stone, about adobe walls being more difficult to distinguish than stone walls, and so on. That "and so on" obscures a massive amount of general knowledge of the everyday world without which not any human or machine scientists should be on the road. These examples illustrate how important it is to have a fair amount of common knowledge to understand what the world really is. In other words, before any future "intelligent" machine can be entrusted with absolute power of decision, it would somehow have to acquire this massive prerequisite store of knowledge. You can think of this knowledge as the foundation of consensus reality, things that are so fundamental that anyone who does not know and believe them lives in a different world.

Lenat thinks he is now in a position to specify the steps required to bring a possible intelligent machine into existence:

1. Prime the pump with the millions of everyday terms, concepts, facts, and rules of thumb that comprise human consensus reality—that is, common sense.
2. On top of this base, construct the ability to communicate in a natural language, such as English or Catalan (my own language). Let the intelligent robot use that ability to vastly enlarge its knowledge base.
3. Eventually, as it reaches the frontier of human knowledge in some area, there will be no one left to talk to about it, so it will need to perform experiments to make further headway in that area.

Of course, the first step is both immensely difficult and immensely time-consuming. What are the millions of things that we should use to prime an automated archaeologist's knowledge pump? How should they be represented inside the machine so that it can use them efficiently to deduce further conclusions when needed, just as we would? Who will do the actual entering of all that data? Assuming a large group of individuals (humans) can do this task, how will they keep from diverging and contradicting each other?

It may surprise you to hear that this is not just a fanciful blueprint for some massive future endeavor to be launched when humanity reaches a higher plateau of utopian cooperation. It is, in fact, the specific plan Doug Lenat and his team have been following for the past dozen years: The *CyC* project, a program with common sense (Lenat & Guha, 1990; Lenat, 1995b; Reed & Lenat, 2002; Schneider et al., 2005. See: http://www.cyc.com). The purpose was not to understand more about how the human mind works, nor to test some particular theory of intelligence. Instead, the idea was to build a machine understanding natural language.

The *Cyc* knowledge base is a formalized representation of a vast quantity of fundamental human knowledge: facts, rules of thumb, and heuristics for reasoning about the objects and events of everyday life. It is not a simple set of rules; the system's designers think of it as a sea of assertions. The *Cyc* knowledge base is divided into many (currently thousands of) "microtheories," each of which is essentially a bundle of assertions that share a common set of assumptions; some microtheories are focused on a particular domain of knowledge, a particular level of detail, a particular interval in time, etc. The microtheory mechanism allows *CyC* to independently maintain assertions, which are *prima facie* contradictory, and enhances the performance of the system by focusing the inference process.

At the time of writing, the full version contains over 2.5 million assertions (facts and rules) inter-

relating more than 155,000 concepts. Most of the assertions in the knowledge base are intended to capture "commonsense" knowledge pertaining to the objects and events of everyday human life, such as buying and selling, kinship relations, household appliances, eating, office buildings, vehicles, time, and space. The system also contains highly specialized, "expert" knowledge in domains such as chemistry, biology, military organizations, diseases, and weapon systems, as well as the grammatical and lexical knowledge that enables the natural language processing (parsing and generation) capabilities incorporated into *CyC*'s user interfaces. *CyC*'s ability to reason is provided by an inference engine that employs hundreds of pattern specific heuristic modules to derive new conclusions (deduction) or introduce new hypotheses (abduction) from the assertions in the knowledge base. *CyC*'s inference engine is multi-threaded, which means that it is able to work on multiple tasks (such as question answering or problem solving) at the same time. It is also able to provide complete explanations for its answers, including the names of the sources (e.g., people, published works, Web sites) from which information was obtained. It can even alert the user in cases where both pro and con arguments can be constructed for particular conclusions, perhaps due to differing circumstances or changes in context. Users can modify dozens of parameters to achieve very fine-grained control of inference, if desired.

At its most basic level, you can do only two things with *CyC*: you can tell it things (assert facts and rules) and you can ask it things (query). You cannot directly tell the system what it should do. Its explanatory power comes from its ability:

- To "know" things *you* never told it (because others have, over many years),
- To "know" things it was *never* told (through inference and heuristics modules), and
- To independently draw upon the right combination of knowledge to bring to bear on a problem.

One of the flashiest early uses of *CyC* has been for information retrieval. Imagine a library of captioned images and a user who comes along and types in a word, phrase, or sentence asking for images. Today's software would have to do Boolean searches based on keywords in the query and the captions, perhaps broadening the search a bit by looking up synonyms in a thesaurus or definitions in a dictionary. Alternatively, consider the World Wide Web, whose keyword-based indexing is the only way to search through that immense information space. That's fine if you want to match "a 23rd century B.C. pottery example" against "a scraper used to scrap fresh hide before the invention of agriculture" but it takes something like *CyC* to match assertions like "a privileged social class" against "a man giving orders to kill another person." *CyC* uses common sense to do matches of that sort. To do that, it used a few rules of the sort: "If people kill other people to dominate in a social context, then they are members of a privileged social class."

IS A "RATIONAL" AUTOMATED ARCHAEOLOGIST AN IMPOSSIBLE DREAM?

All those examples should serve us to conclude that expert systems are useful, very useful indeed, because many archaeological problems can be structured in terms of a single template matching mechanism. Incoming patterns are matched against a set of previously memorized templates by means of some explicit rules linking external input and internal explanations. The automated archaeologist asks itself "Is what I'm seeing already contained in my Memory?" That is to say, "Did I know this item before?" If the answer is affirmative, it decides to remember what was memorized at that moment, and find out additional associate affirmations. By making use of some previously stored knowledge, the robot infers from sensory data, what it is that

gave rise to those data. The input pattern is then categorized as belonging to the class captured by that pre-existing explanation.

One major insight gained using expert systems is the importance of domain-specific knowledge in problem solving tasks. Expert knowledge is a combination of a theoretical understanding of the problem and a collection of problem solving rules that experience has shown to be effective in the domain. A doctor, for example, is not effective at diagnosing illness solely because she possesses some innate and universal problem solving skill; she is effective because she is a specialist in some medical domain. Similarly, archaeologists are effective at discovering archaeological items and at explaining them in social-causal terms because they have previous experience with archaeological materials and explanations. The degree of success is based on the quantity and quality of such expert knowledge.

Consequently, expert systems assume that to recognize an archaeological item, and explain its functional or social meaning there is a predefined representation of that item or that interpretation already stored in the memory. The reader may be surprised with this characterization of archaeological problem solving. We have defined a problem as "something we wish to get and we do not know how." Now, it results that "we do not know how" is constituted, in reality, by a set of possible solutions, one of which will become a suitable answer after a specific search procedure and selection mechanism. The world is knowable, only if it is already known. It seems a tricky way to solve problems! Nevertheless, this procedure is at the very core of any scientific reasoning effort in whatsoever discipline. Plato's answer to the possibility of problem solving was that the concepts of mind must have been put into a human being a priori, that is, before the existence of the individual human being. This philosophical concept was named "the realism of ideas." Plato's principle of a priority was used by Minsky as a basis for creating computer artificial intelligence.

For a computer to operate and make decisions in a complicated environment, concluded Minsky, knowledge ought to be placed onto the computer a priori (Minsky, 1968). A system of logical rules is put into the computer, containing all possible situations, for example, all possible readings of sensors of a particular device or system.

That makes expert systems nothing more than a discrete plan for expressing cognitive action, because they contain descriptions of intended courses of behavior. In that case, a specific explanation is created by searching through a space of possible explanations until the knowledge necessary to generate that explanation is discovered. The procedure may be as follows: during sensing, information from various sensors is collected and integrated into a central representation of the environment, the world model that forms the basis for producing explanations. A number of possible explanations are generated and one of them is chosen and finally applied. This requires a great deal of central processing, which is equivalent to a human *rational* mind.

Figure 2.6 shows a general cognitive architecture allowing the automated archaeologist to first plan (deliberate) how to best decompose a given archaeological problem into sub problems for which knowledge already exists and then to enumerate what are the specific linking of sub-explanations that will bring the solution to the preliminary problem. This type of organization can be described as a sequence of THINK, PERCEIVE-EXPLAIN where the comma indicates that rational thinking, that is, conscious problem decomposition, is done at one step, then acquiring data ("perceiving") in terms of a priori background knowledge. In this way, what the automated archaeologist is permitted to sense and understand is denoted. We can describe the idea in more general terms: given knowledge of the material consequences of social action *the automated archaeologist is likely to encounter*, it uses this information to understand what it is seeing.

However, there is a trouble. A big one, indeed! It is obvious that we do not understand past social actions by enumerating *every* possible outcome of *every* possible social action. A template matching scheme like the one we have here presented could work provided we had precompiled rules for all events to be explained. To explain social action produced in the past, the automated archaeologist would need a universal knowledge base covering the entire domain of interaction. Unfortunately, this is almost impossible to achieve, because it implies the existence of an infinite number of rules to have the ability of recognizing each

Figure 2.6. A general cognitive architecture allowing the automated archaeologist to explain archaeological observables

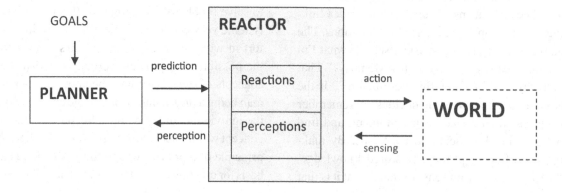

unique archaeological observation for what it is and then selecting an appropriate explanation for each possible historical state. Although the last example—the *CyC* system, with its 2.5 million of rules—seems to be "near" of such a universal knowledge base, the need to formally insert *the entire* world within the automated archaeologist's brain and then maintain every change about it is impossible. This is the reason of many computer failures to understand the real world: it is very easy to forget to put all the necessary details into the world model. Furthermore, the incompleteness of their explicit world models makes expert systems often lack robustness, which means that they lack tolerance of noise and fault tolerance and cannot behave appropriately in new situations. If a situation arises that has not been predefined in its programming, a traditional system breaks down or stops operating. They are incapable of performing appropriately in novel situations, that is, they lack generalization capacity.

Expert systems' relative success is due to their working within a world in which the range of meaning for terms is circumscribed within a carefully selected micro-world. Human archaeologists work in a dynamic world, where perceptions change constantly, and explanations have to be updated concurrently. An expert system is completely different: it should be seen as a series of discrete mappings between aspects of the world and individuated cognitive actions that are based on a closed world assumption which says that the cognitive model (the rule base) contains everything the robot needs to know: there can be no surprises. When the closed world is violated, the robot will not be able to function correctly. The automated archaeologist should not be limited to produce discrete responses to discrete facts, and there should be no assumption that the social history consists of a finite body of facts. Rather, the social world we have to study consists of a rich body of information, some of which crosses the perceptual abilities of our cognitive robot, far greater than ours. The information that is captured by different kinds of specialized sensors provides a broad spectrum about the environment in which the automated archaeologist solves its problems, some of which may be regarded as contextual, depending upon what explanation the machine is looking for. It is up to the machine to learn to identify evidence in an archaeological environment by learning responses to already observed patterns. One advantage of this way of viewing the system's responsiveness to the environment is that the particular response of the system may be influenced by a variety of different factors, some of which we may take to be only indirectly related to the task at hand, but which are able to influence the patterns of activation arising inside the system.

Robots cannot simply be programmed with knowledge, since that would imply a designer-based high-level ontology that would in turn lead to a system incapable of interacting efficiently with the world on its own. A key implication is that the automated archaeologist has to interact with its environment on its own, because solutions to an archaeological problem do not come from nowhere. To predigest the world for a person or a program by supplying readily labeled things and events is to bypass the essential problem that memory must address. Creating a knowledge base is often a scientific effort of empirically constructing and testing models. Very often creating a knowledge base requires inventing new terminology and developing an understanding of causal, temporal, and spatial relations that exceeds what anyone has known before. Indeed, even though many people can readily spout a wealth of rules and relations about their area of expertise, extracting facts and rules from an expert's head is a poor characterization of the archaeologist's task. Therefore, a declarative model of knowledge bears no necessary relation to human knowledge. It has been argued, even, that the contents of an expert system are not knowledge. It is a representation of knowledge (Clancey, 1997). Sometimes, although the knowledge is relevant, its representation is incomplete or not efficient enough.

Explanatory knowledge cannot be defined by necessary and sufficient conditions. Archaeologists do not have exact or complete definitions readily available. They are rather creating the boundaries of their concepts when there is a demand for it. These "blurred" concepts cannot easily be operationalized. Many concepts seem to have a rather "generic" definition, which shapes up by instantiating the concepts with concrete objects. That is our concepts do not have sharp boundaries initially, and that the boundaries are drawn incrementally during use of the concept and probably also during use of other more or less related concepts. In fact, concepts are not fixed entities; rather, they are constructed on each usage by combining attribute values that are appropriate to the context. That raises the question of what mechanism constructs theses unstable concepts. This is obviously not an expert system with its pre-fixed rules and facts!

Scientists do not simply begin with data and then move to theories, but are involved in a continuous loop of data collection and theory formation. There should be no favored starting point, no priority given to any of the activities of problem solving, hypothesis formation or experimentation. Automated problem solving should lead to various kinds of learning, including the formation of hypotheses; the need to test hypotheses leads to the design and execution of experiments and controlled observations; experiments generate problems to be solved, which in turn lead to new hypotheses. In addition, the formation of hypotheses can generate new problems waiting also for their solution, if a new generalization or theory can in turn require explanation (Thagard, 1988).

Consequently, although expert systems are very interesting tools for some determinate tasks, they are not the best model for understanding *how* we are doing archaeology. In that sense, Gardin was wrong: expert systems can (and should) be used for classifying archaeological material, inferring chronology, function and the like, but they are not the best analogy for simulating the way human archaeologists think. Why? Because an expert system is not reasoning about its archaeological or historical rules; it is applying them blindly. Certainly, that is what many professional human archaeologists do, but in so doing, they are as stupid as their mechanic counterpart. A person using such descriptions without knowing what they mean would be quickly uncovered as a charlatan.

What would give a more "intelligent" character to our automatic archaeologist will be not a passive storing of individual rules, but an enhanced ability to learn and to react in a certain way to a certain stimulus. If we want to go beyond the usual archaeological template matching, we should make emphasis not on database consultation, analogy, and decision-making, but on learning and categorizing, and on how meaning can be generalized from known examples of a given concept. That is, the automated archaeologist should develop its own cognitive machinery (what it knows) as opposed to construct a data structure on which a preexisting machinery operates.

This gives rise to an essential question: *where new explanatory predicates come from?*

In the next chapter, we will try to solve such a question using the idea of inverse engineering, which was already presented at the end of Chapter I.

DIRECTIONS FOR FURTHER RESEARCH

Interest on expert systems vanished in recent years, both in computer science and in archaeology (Liebowitz, 1997; Luger, 2005). What seemed at the early 80s an interesting tool, never found in archaeology the place it really merited. I have tried to explain here some aspects of this failure, but the real cause seems to be in the poorly developed formal aspects of our discipline, even today. The post-modern criticism of the early 90s and its reification of subjectivism was an insurmountable obstacle to any effort that tried to analyze "objectively" the way we think. Nevertheless, the work by Jean Claude Gardin and colleagues shows that although most archaeologist still do not know how they think, they are using predicate logics in some way or another.

The actual fashion of bayesian logics and distributed systems (agent-based modeling) is giving a new life to classical artificial intelligence, and the traditional way of understanding explanation as a combination of propositional sentences. The frontiers of classical logics have been overcome however. Alternative ways of explaining, like the logic of possibilism, default logics, non-monotonic reasoning, etc. imply that we have plenty of tools to explore alternative ways of solving archaeological problems.

On the theoretic and technological side, more work is necessary on the proper use of logics in knowledge based systems. In this chapter, I have only presented some basic aspects of inference flow. More research is necessary in the domain of abductive reasoning, and especially on the use of quantifiers and fuzzy logic. Some aspects will be presented in the next chapter, but we still need a deeper understanding of the way to link different propositional statements in a coherent explanation (Levesque & Lakemeyer 2000; Torsun, 1995,).

On the practical side, we can mention different real archaeological applications, whowing that the technology really works, but it also has its limits.

Missikoff (1996, 2003) has investigated some theoretical aspects of automated typologies. As practical applications, we can mention the pioneering work of Bishop and Thomas (1984) on the British Bell Beaker pottery, Joel Mourre (1985) on lithics, Ganascia et al. (1986) on axes of bronze, Markel (1987) on American Indians pipes, Herman (1987) on Cypriot ritual little statues, Steckner (1993) on roman pottery, Barceló (1996) on phoenician pottery sherds, and Kroepelien (1998) on medieval silver vases. Interesting projects were those by Ross (1989), on

the classification and chronology of Anglo-Saxon fibulae, and Gegerun et al. (1990), on orientation of graves in a cemetery. Piqué and Piqué (1993) suggested the use of expert systems to mechanize the process of microscope samples classification for ancient wood taxonomy determination.

VANDAL (Lagrange, 1989a, 1989b; Vitali & Lagrange, 1988,) is a computer program intending to help archaeologists to interpret the results of archaeometric analyses, within the framework of provenance studies. The system produces one (or several) "diagnoses" according to the geographic origin of raw material, from a database of analyzed samples of known origin provided by the user.

Other classificatory programs, this time in zooarchaeology and osteology are those of Brough and Parfitt (1984), Fischer (1985), Maícas (1989), González and Maícas (1991), Mameli et al. (2002). An expert system from the field of paleontology for the determination of a dinosaur species has also been published. It helps the paleontologist to determine creatures from field data (Wichert, 2000). The most recent "intelligent" classifiers go beyond the rule-paradigm, and organize pre-existing knowledge in form of decision trees (Bolla, 2007; Mom, 2007). As we will see in the next chapter, decision trees and rule bases are exchangeable technologies.

Some other systems help scientist to decode decorative patterns in pottery or rock-art. T.I.R.E.S.I.A.S. (Bron et al., 1989, 1991a, 1991b ; Oberlin et al., 1991) interprets the iconography of Greek ceramics. Given an input formed by the iconographic features of the personages who appear represented in one vase in individual, the system answers with a reference to the mythological role present in that scene. Of related interest, Hooker (2002) has built an expert system to classify some celtic coins based on iconographic characteristics. Monteiro (1993) has produced a system to interpret Upper Paleolithic female figurines, and Barceló (1997) a system to classify Bronze Age decorated Stelae. Also related to iconographic interpretation, SUPERIKON

(Lagrange & Renaud, 1983, 1984, 1985, 1987) compares alternative hypothesis of an iconographic explanation.

About the use of expert systems in epigraphy, relevant examples are Siromoney et al. (1985), Terras and Robertson (2005).

In the domain of conservation analysis of archaeological materials, some prototype expert systems have also been proposed (Liberopolou, 1999; Mello & Arias, 1996; Van Balen, 2001).

Of direct interest to archaeologists, are the important applications of expert systems technology to solve geographical and geosciences problems. The idea seems to be building a full geo-expert system to answer questions in a seemingly intelligent way based on facts contained in a GIS and on the procedures and data available in a Digital Remote Sensing System (Filis et al., 2003; Haj-Yehia & Peled; 2004, Pullar, 1997). In earth resources application, GEOMYCIN (Davis & Nanninga, 1985) demonstrated the possibility of incorporating spatial knowledge for land use prediction (forest management). Knowledge based systems for aerial photo interpretation have been developed (McKeown, 1987; McKeown et al., 1985). For remote sensing, expert systems which help to detect relevant features in a landscape have been published (Crowther & Hartnett, 1997; Estes, 1986; Kirby, 1996; Mulder et al., 1988; Peuquet & Guo, 2000; Schiøtz & Peti, 2003; Skidmore, 1989; Soh et al., 2004; Warner et al., 1994; Yialouris et al., 1997; Zhang & Wang, 2003). In the case of archaeological soils interpretation, we can mention the work of Louanna Furbee (Benfer & Furbee, 1989; Benfer et al., 1996; Furbee, 1989). There are some interesting applications in geomorphology, which can be useful to archaeologists (Arentze et al., 1996; Findikaki, 1990; Luckman et al., 1997; Rodriguez-Bachiller & Glasson, 2004, see a review in Witlox, 2005).

Social applications, that is to say, the use of expert systems to explain social action has not yet fully explored. Some preliminary examples are: Banerjee (1986), Carley (1988), Balachandran, et al. (1989), Brent (1989), Guillet (1989a,b).

REFERENCES

ANDERSON, J.R. (1980). *Cognitive psychology and its implications.* New York: W.H. Freeman.

ANDERSON, J.R. (1983). *The architecture of cognition.* Cambridge, MA: Harvard University Press.

ANDERSON, J.R. (1990). *The adaptive character of thought.* L. Hillsdale, NJ: Erlbaum Associates.

ARENTZE, T. A., BORGERS, A. W. J., & TIMMERMANS, H. J. P. (1996a). An efficient search strategy for site-selection decisions in an expert system. *Geographical Analysis, 28*(2), 126–146.

BALACHANDRAN, C.S, FISHER, P. F., & STANLEY, M.A. (1989). An expert system approach to rural development: A prototype (TIHSO). *Journal of Developing Areas, 23,* 259-270.

BANERJEE, S. (1986). Reproduction of social structures: An artificial intelligence model. *The Journal of Conflict Resolution, 30,* 221-252.

BARCELÓ, J.A. (1996). Heuristic classification and fuzzy sets. New tools for archaeological typologies. *Acta Praehistorica Laidensia, 28,* 155-164.

BARCELÓ, J.A. (1997). *Arqueología Automática. El uso de la Inteligencia Artificial en Arqueología.* Sabadell (Spain): Editorial Ausa, (Cuadernos de Arqueología Mediterránea, 2).

BARCELÓ, J.A. (2000) Visualizing what might be. An introduction to virtual reality in archaeology. In J.A.Barcelo, M. Forte & D. Sanders (Eds.), *Virtual reality in archaeology* (pp. 9-36). Oxford: ArcheoPress. British Archaeological Reports (S843).

BARCELÓ, J.A. (2001). Virtual reality for archaeological explanation. Beyond picturesque reconstruction *Archeologia e Calcolatori, 12,* 221-244.

BARCELÓ, J.A. (2002). Virtual archaeology and artificial intelligence. In F. Nicolucci (Ed.), *Virtual archaeology* (pp. 21-28). Oxford: ArchaeoPress. BAR International Series S1075..

BENFER, R.A., & FURBEE, L. (1989). Knowledge acquisition in the Peruvian Andes: Expert systems and anthropology. *AI Expert, 4*(11), 22-30.

BENFER, R.A., FURBEE, L., & BRENT, L.E. (1996). Expert systems and the representation of knowledge. *American Ethnologist, 23*(2), 416-420

BISHOP, M.C., & THOMAS, J. (1984). BEAKER—An expert system for the BB.C. micro. *Computer Applications in Archaeology, 12,* 49-55.

BOLLA, D. (2007). Associative multilingual classification architecture for historical artefact. In A. Figueiredo & G. Velho (Eds.), *The world is in your eyes. Computer Aplicatioins in Archaeology* (pp. 85-94). Tomar, Portugal: CAA Portugal.

BRENT, E. (1989). Designing social science research with expert systems. *Anthropological Quarterly, 62*(3), 121.

BRON, C., CORFU-BRATSCHI, P., & MAOUENE, M. (1989). Hephaistos bacchant ou le cavalier comaste: simulation de raisonnement qualitatif par le langage informatique LISP. *Annali Istituto Universitario Orientale (Archeologia e Storia Antica).* vol. XII: 155-172.

BRON, C., ROGGER, A., & VIRET BERNAL, F. (1991a). Iconographie et Intelligence Artificielle: du signe au sens; compréhension et interprétation d'image. *Aplicaciones Informáticas en Arqueología,* (vol. 1). Bilbao, Spain: Denboraren Argia.

BRON, C., VIRET BERNAL, F., BERARD, A., OBERLIN, A., ROGGER, A., & DE WERRA, D. (1991b). Heraclès chez T.I.R.E.S.I.A.S: Traitement Informatique de Réconnaissance des Elements Semiologiques pour l' Idéntification Analytique des Scènes. *Hephaistos. Kritische Zeitschrift zu Theorie und Praxis der Archäologie, Kunstwissenschaft und angrenzender Gebiete, 10,* 21-33.

BROUGH, D.R., & PARFITT, N. (1984). An expert system for the ageing of a domestic animal. *Computer Applications in Archaeology,* 49-55.

BROWN, D.C., & CHANDRASEKARAN, B. (1989). *Design problem solving. Knowledge structures and control strategies.* London: Pitman.

CARLEY, K. (1988). Formalizing the social expert's knowledge. *Sociological Methods and Research, 17,* 165-232.

CLANCEY, W. J. (1983). The epistemology of a rule-based expert system—a framework for explanation. *Artificial Intelligence, 20,* 215–251.

CLANCEY, W. (1984). Heuristic classification. *Artificial Intelligence, 27,* 289-350.

CLANCEY, W. J. (1997). *Situated cognition: On human knowledge and computer representations.* Cambridge, UK: Cambridge University Press.

COOPER, D. B., WILLIS, A., ANDREWS, S., BAKER, J., CAO, Y., HAN, D. et al. (2002). Bayesian pot-assembly from fragments as problems in perceptual-grouping and geometric-learning. *Proceedings of the 16th International Conference on Pattern Recognition, 3,* 30927–30931.

CROWTHER, P., & HARTNETT, J. (1997). Eliciting knowledge with visualization—instant gratification for the expert image classifier who wants to show rather than tell. *Paper presented at the second annual conference of GeoComputation '97 & SIRC '97,* University of Otago, New Zealand. Retrieved April, 2006, from http://www.geocomputation.org/1997/papers/crowther.pdf

DA MONTEIRO, M. C. (1993). Female Figures of the Upper Paleolithic: One Interpretation through an Expert System. *Aplicaciones Informáticas en*

Arqueología, vol. 2. Denboraren Argia, Bilbao (Spain), pp. 335-355.

DAVIS, J.R. & NANNINGA, P.M. (1985). GEO-MYCIN: Towards a geographic expert system, for resource management, *Journal of Environmental Management*, *21*, 377-390.

DORAN, J.R. (1988). Expert systems and archaeology: What lies ahead? *Computer Applications in Archaeology* (BAR International Series, 393) 237-241.

DRAP, P., SEINTURIER, J., & LONG, L. (2003). A photogrammetric process driven by an expert system: A new approach for underwater archaeological surveying applied to the 'grand ribaud *F*' etruscan wreck. *Conference on Computer Vision and Pattern Recognition Workshop,1*, 16.

ESTES, J. E. (1986). Applications of artificial intelligence techniques to remote sensing. *The Professional Geographer*, *38*, 133-141.

FILIS,I.V., SABRAKOS,M., YIALOURIS, C.P., SIDERIDIS, A.B., & MAHAMAN, B. (2003). GEDAS: An integrated geographical expert database system. *Expert Systems with Applications*, *24*, 25–34.

FINDIKAKI, I. (1990). SISES: An expert system for site selection. In T. J. Kim, J. R. Wiggins, & Wright (Eds.), *Expert systems: Applications to urban planning*. New York:Springer.

FISCHER, M. D. (1985). Expert systems and anthropological analysis. *BICA: Bullettino. Istituto di Corrispondenza Archaeologica*, *4*, 6-14.

FLORENZANO, M.J., BLAISE, J.Y., & DRAP, P. (1999) PAROS. Close range photogrametry and architectural models. In L. Dingwall, S. Exon, V. Gaffney, S. Laflin, M., & Van Leusen (Eds.), *Archaeology in the age of the internet. CAA 1997*. Oxford: British Archaeological Reports (Int. Series, S750).

FOLEY, J., & RIBARSKY, B. (1994). Next-generation data visualization tools. In L.Rosenblum et al. (Eds.), *Scientific visualisation. advances and challenges* (pp.103-127). New York: Academic Press.

FRANCFORT, H.P. (1987). Un système expert pour l'analyse archéologique de sociétés proto-urbaines. Premier étape: le cas de Shortugai. *Informatique et Sciences Humaines*, *74*, 73-91.

FRANCFORT, H.P. (1990). Modélisation de raisonnements interprétatifs en archéologie à l'aide de systèmes experts: conséquences d' une critique des fondements des inférences. In J.C. Gardin & R. Ennals (Eds.), *Interpretation in the humanities: perspectives from artificial intelligence*. The British Library Publications. Library and Information Research Report, 71.

FRANCFORT, H.P. (1991). Palamede—application of expert systems to the archaeology of prehistoric urban civilisations. In K. Lockyear & S. Rahtz (Eds.), *Computer applications and quantitative methods in archaeology-1990*. Oxford: British Archaeological Reports (International Series 565),

FRANCFORT, H.P. (1997). Archaeological interpretation and nonlinear dynamic modelling: Between metaphor and simulation. In S.E Van der Leeuw & J. McGlade (Eds.), *Time, process and structured transformation in archaeology*. Routledge: London.

FRANCFORT, H.P., LAGRANGE,M.S., & RENAUD, M. (1989). *PALAMEDE. Application des systèmes experts à l'archéologie de civilisations urbaines protohistoriques*. Paris: C.N.R.S.-U.P.R. 315. Technical report.

FURBEE, L. (1989). A folk expert system: Soils classification in the colca valley, Peru. *Anthropological Quarterly*, *62*(2), 83-102.

GALLAY, A. (1989). Logicism: A french view of archaeological theory founded in computational perspective. *Antiquity*, 63, 27-39

GANASCIA, J.C., MENU, M., & MOHEN, J.P. (1986). RHAPSODE: un système expert en archéologie *Bulletin de la Societé Préhistorique Française, 83*(10), 363-371.

GARDIN, J.C. (1980). *Archaeological constructs.* Cambridge, UK: Cambridge University Press.

GARDIN, J.C. (1991). *Le Calcul et la Raison. Essais sur la formalisation du discours savant.* Paris, France : Editions de l'Ecole des Hautes Etudes en Sciences Sociales..

GARDIN, J.C. (1993). Les embarrass du naturel. *Archives Européennes de Sociologie XXXIV, 152-165.*

GARDIN, J.C. (1994). Informatique et progrès dans les sciences de l'homme *Revue Informatique et Statistique dans les Sciences Humaines, 30*(1-4),11-35.

GARDIN, J.C. (1998). Cognitive issues and Problems of Publication in Archaeology ." In W.Hensel, S. Tabczynski, & P. Urbanczyk (Eds.), *Theory and practice of archaeological research.* Warszawa: Institute of Archaeology and Ethnology. Polish Academy of Sciences.

GARDIN, J.C. (2003). Archaeological discourse, conceptual modelling and digitalisation: an interim report of the logicist program. In M. Doerr & A. Sarris (Eds.), *The digital heritage of archaeology.* Archive of Monuments and Publications. Hellenic Ministry of Culture.

GARDIN, J.C., GUILLAUME, O., HERMAN, P.O., HESNARD, A., LAGRANGE, M.S., RENAUD, M.et al. (1987). *Systèmes experts et sciences humaines. Le cas de l' archéologie.* Paris, France: Eyrolles.

GEGERUN, A.P., PISLARY, I.A., & POPOVA, T.G. (1990). Archaeological classification and expert systems. In A. Voorrips (Ed.), *New tools from mathematical archaeology.* Krakow, Poland: Polish Academy of Sciences.

GIARRATANO, J., & RILEY, G. (2004). *Expert systems. Principles and programming.* Boston: PWS-KENT Publishing Company,

GONZALEZ, A.M., & MAICAS, R. (1991). DENTALIA, un système expert pour la classification de restes osseux. *Aplicaciones Informáticas en Arqueología,* (vol. 1). Bilbao, Spain: Denboraren Argia.

GRACE, R. (1989). *Interpreting the function of stone tools: The quantification and computerisation of microwear analysis.* Oxford, UK: Archeopress, B.A.R. international series 474.

GRACE, R. (1993). The use of expert systems in lithic Analysis. In *Traces et fonction: les geste retrouvés* (pp. 389-400) Eraul 50, (vol. 2). Liege, Belgium.

GUILLET, D. (1989a). Expert systems applications in anthropology, part one. *Anthropological Quarterly, 62*(2), 57-105.

GUILLET, D. (1989b). Expert systems applications in anthropology, part two. *Anthropological Quarterly, 62*(3), 107-147.

HAJ-YEHIA,B., & PELED, A. (2004). Rule-based system for updating spatial data-base, *XXth ISPRS Congress,* (Vol. XXXV), part B2. Istanbul ,Turkey.

HAWARAH, L., SIMONET, A., & SIMONET, M. (2003). A probabilistic approach to classify incomplete objects using decision trees. In *Database and expert systems applications* (pp. 77 – 87). Berlin: Springer Verlag.

HERMAN, P.Q. (1987). Cas n° 3: Que les ancêtres des figurines chypriotes lèvent le bras. In Gardin, J et al. (ed.), *Systèmes Experts et Sciences Humaines: le cas de l' Archéologie.*

HOLYOAK, K.J.. (1990). Problem solving. In D.N. Osherson & E.E. Smith (Eds.), *Thinking. An invitation to cognitive science* (Vol. 3) (pp. 117-146), Cambridge, MA: The MIT Press.

HOOKER, J. (2002). *Coriosolite Expert System* Retrieved March, 2006, from. http://www. writer2001.com/exp0002.htm

HUGGET, J., & BAKER, K. (1986). The computerized archaeologist: The development of expert systems *Science and Archaeology, 27,* 3-12.

JACKSON, K.F. (1983). *The art of solving problems: Bulmershe-comino problem-solving project.* Reading, UK: Bulmershe College.

JOHNSON-LAIRD, P.N. (1988). *The computer and the mind* Cambridge, MA: Harvard University Press.

JOSEPHSON, J.R., CHANDRASEKARAN, B., SMITH, J.W., & TANNER, M.C. (1987). A mechanism for forming composite explanatory hypotheses. *IEEE Transactions on Systems, Man and Cybernetics, 17,* 445-454.

KAMPEL, M., & MELERO, F.J. (2003). Virtual vessel reconstruction from a fragment's profile. In D. Arnold, A. Chalmers, & F. Nicolucci (Eds.), *VAST2003 proceedings of the 4th International Symposium on Virtual reality, Archaeology, and Intelligent Cultural heritage* (pp. 79-88). Edited by. The Eurographics Association, Aire-la-Ville (Switzerland),

KAMPEL, M., & SABLATNIG, R. (2002). Computer aided classification of ceramics. In F. Niccolucci (Ed.), *Virtual archaeology.* Oxford: ArcheoPress. (BAR Int. Series 1075).

KAMPEL, M., & SABLATNIG, R. (2003). An automated pottery archival and reconstruction system. *Journal of Visualization and Computer Animation,*14(3), 111-120.

KAMPEL, M., & SABLATNIG,R. (2004). New achievments on pottery reconstruction. In Magistrat der Stadt Wien-Referat Kulturelles Erbe-Stadtarchäeologie Wien (Eds.), *Enter the past. The e-way into the four dimensions of cultural heritage.* Oxford: ArcheoPress, (BAR Int. Series, 1227).

KIRKBY, S. D. (1996). Integrating a GIS with an expert system to identify and manage dryland salinization. *Applied Geography, 16,* 289–302.

KLAHR,D. (2000). *Exploring science: The cognition and development of discovery processes.* Cambridge, MA: The MIT Press.

KLAHR, D., & DUNBAR,K. (1988). Dual space search during scientific reasoning. *Cognitive Science, 12*(1), 1-55.

KLAHR, D., FAY, A.L., & DUNBAR, K. (1993). Heuristics for scientific experimentation: A developmental study. *Cognitive Psychology, 13,* 113-148.

KROEPELIEN, B. (1998). Image databases in art history: An expert system for norwegian silver. *Computers and the History of Art Journal, 8*(1), 17-38.

KULKARNI, D., & SIMON, H.A. (1988). The processes of scientific discovery. The strategy of experimentation. *Cognitive Science, 12,* 139-176.

LAGRANGE, M.S. (1989a) Les systèmes experts et la récherche en archéologie et sciences humaines. Un point de vue pragmatique. *Documentaliste,26*(1), 11-15.

LAGRANGE, M.S. (1989b). *VANDAL. Un Système expert d' aide a l' étude de la provenance de ceramiques fondé sur des données archéometriques. Manuel d' Utilisation.* Paris: C.N.R.S.-U.P.R. 315, Technical Report.

LAGRANGE, M.S., & RENAUD, M. (1983). *Simulation du raisonnement archéologique: SNARK, sept archéologues et une pierre gravée.* Document de travail n° 2. CNRS (UPR 315). Paris.

LAGRANGE, M.S., & RENAUD, M. (1984). *SUPERIKON. Un essai de six expertises en iconographie: érudition ou trivialité?* Document de Travail n. 6. C.N.R.S-UPR 315, Paris.

LAGRANGE, M.S., & RENAUD, M. (1985). Intelligent knowledge-based systems in archaeology: A computerized simulation of reasoning by means of an expert system. *Computers and the Humanities, 19*(1), 37-52.

LAGRANGE, M.S., & RENAUD, M. (1987). Cas n° 6, Superikon, essai de cumul de six expertises en iconographie. In *Systèmes Experts et Sciences Humaines. Le cas de l' Archéologie.* Edited by Gardin et al. (1987). Paris: Eyrolles.

LANGLEY, P., SIMON, H.A., BRADSHAW, G.L., & ZYTKOV, J.M. (1987). *Scientific discovery. Computational explorations of the creative process.* Cambridge, MA: The MIT Press.

LEITAO, H. D. DA GAMA, & STOLFI, J. (2002). A multiscale method for the reassembly of two-dimensional fragmented objects. *IEEE Transactions on Pattern Analysis and machine Intelligence, 24*(9), 1239-1251

LENAT, D. B. (1995a). Steps to sharing knowledge. In N.J.I. Mars (Ed.), *Toward very large knowledge bases.* Amsterdam: IOS Press,

LENAT, D. B. (1995b) Cyc: A large-scale investment in knowledge infrastructure. *Communications of the ACM, 38(*11).

LENAT, D.B., & GUHA, R.V. (1990). *Building large knowledge-based systems.* Reading, MA: Addison-Wesley.

LEWIS, R., & SÉGUIN,C. (1998). Generation of 3D building models from 2D architectural plans. *Computer aided Design, 30*(10), 765-769.

LEYMARIE, F. (2003). *Three-dimensional shape representation via shock flows,* PhD thesis. Brown University. Retrieved August, 2007 from http://www.lems.brown.edu/~leymarie/phd/

LIAO, S.H. (2003). Knowledge management technologies and applications—literature review from 1995 to 2002. *Expert Systems with Applications, 25,* 155–164

LIAO, S.H. (2005). Expert system methodologies and applications—a decade review from 1995 to 2004. *Expert Systems with Applications, 28,* 93–103

LIBEROPOULOU, L. (1999). An expert system for the conservation of archeological iron. *Workshop Intelligenza Artificiale per i Beni Culturali.* Bologna (Italy), 14 Settembre 1999

LIEBOWITZ, J. (1997). *Handbook of applied expert systems.* Boca Raton, FL: CRC Press.

LUCKMAN,P.G., GIBSON, R.D., & CHAMARTI,R.R. (1997). A hybrid rule-object spatial modeling tool for catchment analysis. *Paper presented at the second annual conference of GeoComputation '97 & SIRC '97,*University of Otago, new Zealand.

LUGER, G.F. (2005). *Artificial intelligence: Structures and strategies for complex problem solving,* (5th Ed). Reading, MA: Addison-Wesley.

MAÍCAS, R. (1989). Ejemplos de aplicación de inteligencia artificial en arqueología. *Cuadernos de Prehistoria y Arqueología de la Universidad Autónoma de Madrid,16,* 73-80.

MAMELI, L., ESTÉVEZ, J., & GOODALL, N. (2002). An expert system to help taxonomic classification in avian archaeozoology: A first attempt with bird species from tierra del fuego. *Acta Zoologica Cracoviensa, 45,* 383-391

MARKEL, J.L. (1987). *Archaeology and the computer technology revolution.* Ph.D. Dissertation. State University of New York, Buffalo (NY). Ann Arbor, MI: University Microfilms International.

MCKEOWN, D.M. (1987). The role of artificial intelligence in the integration of remotely sensed data with geographic information systems, *IEEE Trans. On Geoscience and Remote Sensing, 25,* 330-348

MCKEOWN, D.M, HARVEY, W.A & MCDER-MOTT, J. (1985). Rule based interpretation of aerial imagery *IEEE Tran. On Pattern Analysis and Machine Intelligence* , *1*(5), 510-585.

MELERO, F.J., LEON, A.J., CONTRERAS, F., & TORRES, J.C. (2004). A new system for interactive vessel reconstruction and drawing. In Magistrat der Stadt Wien-Referat Kulturelles Erbe-Stadtarchäeologie Wien (Eds.), *Enter the past. The e-way into the four dimensions of cultural heritage.* Oxford: ArcheoPress, (BAR Int. Series, 1227).

MELLO, E., & ARIAS, C. (1996). Un sistema esperto a supporto della scelta di intervento conservativo su beni culturali. *Archeologia e calcolatori, 7,* 963-972.

METZLER, P.J., & MARTINCIC, C.J. (1998). QUE: Explanation through exploration. *expert systems with applications, 15,* 253–263

MINSKY, M. (1968). *Semantic information processing.* Cambridge, MA: The MIT Press.

MISSIKOFF, O. (1996). Application of an object oriented approach to the formalization of qualitative (and quantitative) data. *Analecta Praehistorica Leidensia, 28*(I), 263-271.

MISSIKOFF, O. (2003). Ontologies as a reference framework for the management of knowledge in the archaeological domain. In Magistrat der Stadt Wien-referat kulturelles Erbe-Städtarchäologie Wien (Ed)., *Enter the past. The e-way into the four dimensions of cultural heritage* (pp. 35-40). Oxford: ArcheoPress (BAR Int. Series, S1227).

MOM, V. (2007). SECANTO-The section analysis tool. In A. Figueiredo & G. Velho (Eds.), *The world is in your eyes. Computer applications in archaeology* (pp. 95-102). Tomar, Portugal: CAAPortugal.

MOON, H.S., YOU, T., YOO, H.W., SOHN, M.H., & JANG, D.S. (2005). A recovery system of broken relics using least squares fitting and vector similarity techniques. *Expert Systems with Applications,* 28, 469–481

MOURRE, J. (1985). *Le Système Expert SILEX.* Rapport DESS, INRIA, Sophia-Antipolis (France). ISI. Laboratoire pour l'Analyse de Scènes.

MULDER, N.J., MIDDELKOOP, H., & MILTENBURG, J.W. (1988). Progress in Knowledge Engineering for image interpretation and classification. Kyoto: *ISPRS Congress*

NEWELL, A., & SIMON, H.A. (1972). *Human problem solving.* Englewood Cliffs, NJ: Prentice Hall.

Nilsson, N.J. (1998). *Artificial intelligence: A new synthesis.* San Francisco, CA: Morgan Kaufmann Publishers, Inc.

OBERLIN, A., ROGGER, A., DE WERRA, D., BRON-PURY, C., VIRET-BERNAL, F., & BÉRARD, C. (1991). Identifying mythological scenes with artificial intelligence. *Science & Archaeology, 33,* 18-27.

ORLANDI, T. (1997). Informatica, formalizzazione e discipline umanistiche. In T. Orlandi (Ed.), *Discipline umanistiche e informatica. Il problema della formalizzazione*, (pp. 7-17). Roma,

ORLANDI, T. (2002). Is humanities computing a discipline? *Jahrbuch für Computerphilologie, 4,* 51-58

PATEL, J., & STUTT, A. (1988). *KIVA: An archaeological interpreter.* Human Cognition Research Laboratory Technical Report, No. 35. Milton Keynes, UK: The Open University.

PATEL, J., & STUTT, A. (1989). Beyond classification: The use of artificial intelligence techniques for the interpretation of archaeological data. In S.P.Q. Rahtz and J. Richards (Eds.), *Computer Applications and Quantitative Methods in Archaeology.* Oxford: BAR International Series (S548).

PEUQUET, D.J. & GUO, D. (2000). Mining spatial data using an interactive rule-based approach. *GIScience*, 152-153.

PIQUÉ, R., & PIQUÉ, J.M. (1993). Automatic recognition and classification of archaeological charcoals. In J. Andresen, T. Madsen & I. Scollar (Eds.), *Computing the past. Computer applicatons and quantitative methods in archaeology.* Aarhus, Denmark: Aarhus University Press.

POST, E.L. (1943). Formal reductions of the general combinatorial decision problem, *American Journal of Mathematics*, 65, 197-215.

PULLAR, D. (1997) Rule-based modelling. In GIS, *GeoComputation, 97.* Retrieved August, 2007, from *http://www.geocomputation.org/1997/papers/pullar.pdf*

PUYOL-GRUART, J. (1999). Computer science, artificial intelligence and archaeology. In J.A. Barceló, I. Briz & A. Vila (Eds.), *New techniques for old times* (pp. 19-27). Oxford: ArchaeoPress, (BAR International series, 757.

REED, S., & LENAT, D. (2002). Mapping ontologies into cyc. In *AAAI 2002 Conference Workshop on Ontologies For The Semantic Web*, Edmonton, Canada,

ROBERTSON, S.I. (2001). *Problem solving.* Hove: Psychology Press,

RODRIGUEZ-BACHILLER, A., & GLASSON, J. (2004). *Expert systems and geographic information systems for impact assessment.* London: Taylor & Francis.

ROSS, S. (1989). Expert systems for databases in the historical sciences: a case study from archaeology. In *Sciences Historiques, Sciences du Passé et Nouvelles technologies de l'Information. Bilan et Evaluation.* Actes du Congrès International de Lille(France): Centre de Recherches sur la Documentation et l' Information.

RUSSELL, S., & NORVIG, P. (2003). *Artificial intelligence. A modern approach* (2nd. Ed.) Englewood Cliffs, NJ: Prentice Hall.

SCHIØTZ, I.G., & PÈTI, M. (2003). Rule based geoecological mapping on a local scale geography. *Roskilde University Research Report* No. 125. Publications from Geography, Department of Geography and International Development Studies, Roskilde University, Denmark.

SCHNEIDER, D., MATUSZEK, C., SHAH, P., KAHLERT, R., BAXTER, D., CABRAL, J. et al. (2005). Gathering and managing facts for intelligence analysis. In *Proceedings of the 2005 International Conference on Intelligence Analysis,* McLean, Virginia.

SHENNAN, S.J., & STUTT, A. (1989). The nature of archaeological arguments. *Antiquity, 64*(245), 766-777.

SIMON, H.A. (1996). *The sciences of the artificial* (3rd Ed.). Cambridge, MA: The MIT Press.

SIMON, H.A., & LEA, G. (1974). Problem solving and rule induction. A unified view. In L.W. Gregg (Ed.), *Knowledge and cognition.* Hillsdale, NJ: Lawrence Erlbaum Ass.

SIROMONEY, G. CHANDRASEKARAN, R. & SURESH, D. (1985). Developing an expert system for Indian epigraphy. Retrieved July 2006 from http://www.cmi.ac.in/gift/Epigraphy/epig_expertsystem.htm

SKIDMORE, A.K. (1989). Expert system classifies eucalypts forest types using thematic mapper data and a digital terrain model, *Photogrammetric Engineering and Remote Sensing, 55,* 1449-1464.

SLOMAN, A. (1987). Motives, mechanisms, and emotions. *Cognition and Emotion,* 1(3), 217-33.

Soh, L.K., Tsatsoulis, C., Gineris, D., & Bertoia, C. (2004) ARKTOS: An intelligent system for SAR sea ice image classification. *IEEE Transactions on Geoscience and Remote Sensing, 42,* 229–248.

STECKNER, C. (1993). Quantitative methods with qualitative results in expert system. Physical qualities in historical shape design. In *Aplicaciones Informáticas en Arqueología. Teorías y Sistemas* (pp. 486-499). Bilbao, Spain: Denboraren Argia.

STUTT, A. (1988). Second generation expert systems. Explanations, arguments and archaeology. In S.P.Q. Rahtz (Ed.), *Computer applications and quantitative methods in Archaeology.* Oxford: BAR International Series (S446).

STUTT, A.(1989). *Argument in the humanities: A knowledge-based approach.* HCRL Technical Report No. 49. Milton Keynes (UK): The Open University (Human Cognition Research Laboratory).

STUTT, A. (1990). Argument support programs: Machines for generating interpretation. In D.S. Miall (Ed.), *Humanities and the computer. New directions.* Oxford: Clarendon Press.

TERRAS, M., & ROBERTSON, P. (2005). Image and interpretation: Using artificial intelligence to read ancient roman texts. *HumanIT,* 7(3). Retrieved July 2007 from http://www.hb.se/bhs/ith/3-7/mtpr.pdf

THAGARD, P. (1988). *Computational philosophy of science.* Cambridge, MA: The MIT Press.

TSAGANOU,G., GRIGORIADOU,M. CAVOURA,T., & KOUTRA, D. (2003). Evaluating an intelligent diagnosis system of historical text comprehension. *Expert Systems with Applications, 25,* 493–502.

TYLER, A.R. (2007). *Expert systems research trends.* Hauppauge, NY: Nova Science Pub Inc.

VALDÉS-PEREZ, R.E. (1995). Machine discovery in chemistry: New results. *Artificial Intelligence, 65*(2), 247-280.

VALDÉS-PEREZ, R.E. (1996). Computer science research on scientific discovery. *Knowledge Engineering Review, 11,* 57-66.

VALDÉS-PEREZ, R.E. , ZYTKOW,J., SIMON, H.A. (1993). Scientific-model building as search in matrix spaces *Proceedings AAAI-93.* Washington,D.C. [quoted in Wagman 2002].

VAN BALEN, K.E.P. (2001) Learning from damage of masonry Structures. Expert systems can help. In P.B. Lourenço & P. Roca (Eds.), *Historical constructions 2001: Possibilities of numerical and experimental techniques.* Guimarães, Portugal: Publicaçoes de Universidade do Minho.

VAN DEN DRIES, M.H. (1998). *Archeology and the application of artificial intelligence. Case studies on use-wear analysis of prehistoric flint tools.* Archaeological Studies Leiden University No. 1. Holland: Faculty of Archaeology, University of Leiden

VITALI, V., & LAGRANGE, M.S. (1988). VANDAL: An expert system for the provenance determination of archaeological ceramics based on INAA Data. In S.P.Q.Rahtz (Ed.), *Computer applications and quantitative methods in archaeology 1988. .* Oxford: BAR International Series (S446).

WAGMAN, M. (2000). *Scientific discovery process in humans and computers.* Westport, CN: Praeger Publishers.

WAGMAN, M. (2002). *Problem-solving processes in humans and computers. Theory and research in psychology and artificial intelligence.* Westport, CN: Praeger.

WARNER, T. A., LEVANDOWSKI, D. W. BELL, R. & CETIN, A. (1994). Rule-based geobotanical classification of topographic, aeromagnetic and remotely sensed vegetation community data. *Remote Sensing of Environment, 50,* 41 – 51.

WICHERT, A. (2000). A categorical expert system 'Jurassic.' *Expert Systems with Applications, 19,* 149–158

WILCOCK, J. (1986). A review of expert systems: Their shortcomings and possible applications in archaeology *Computer Applications in Archaeology, 13*, 139-144.

WILCOCK, J. (1990). A critique of expert systems, and their past and present use in archaeology. In J.C. Gardin & R. Ennals (Eds.), *Interpretation in the humanities: Perspectives from artificial intelligence*. Library and Information Research Report, 71. The British Library Publications, Wetherby (UK).

WINDER, W. (1996). Texperts. *TEXT Technology*, 6.3. Wright State University.

WITLOX, A. (2005). Expert systems in land-use planning: An overview. *Expert Systems with Applications, 29*, 437–445.

YIALOURIS, C., KOLLIAS, V., LORENTZOS, N., KALIVAS, D., & SIDERIDIS, A. (1997). An integrated expert geographical information system for soil suitability and soil evaluation. *Journal of Geographic Information and Decision Analysis, 1*(2), 90–100.

ZHANG, Q., & WANG, J. (2003). A rule-based urban land use inferring method for fine resolution multispectral imagery. *Canadian Journal of Remote Sensing, 29*(1), 1-13.

ZHANG, C., CAO, C., GU, F., & SI, J. (2002). A domain-specific formal ontology for archaeological knowledge sharing and reusing. In D. Karagiannis & U. Reimer (Eds.), *Practical aspects of knowledge management*: 4th International Conference, PAKM 2002 vol. 2569 (pp. 213-225). Vienna, Austria. Proceedings. Berlin: Springer. Lecture Notes in Computer Science.

Section II
Learning and Experimentation in Historical Sciences

Chapter III
Computer Systems that Learn

INVERSE REASONING

Inverse problems are among the most challenging in computational and applied science and have been studied extensively (Bunge, 2006; Hensel, 1991; Kaipio & Somersalo, 2004; Kirsch, 1996; Pizlo, 2001; Sabatier, 2000; Tarantola, 2005; Woodbury, 2002). Although there is no precise definition, the term refers to a wide range of problems that are generally described by saying that their answer is known, but not the question. An obvious example would be "Guessing the intentions of a person from her/his behavior." In our case: "Guessing a past event from its vestiges." In archaeology, the main source for inverse problems lies in the fact that archaeologists generally do not know why archaeological observables have the shape, size, texture, composition, and spatiotemporal location they have. Instead, we have sparse and noisy observations or measurements of perceptual properties, and an incomplete knowledge of relational contexts and possible causal processes. From this information, an inverse engineering approach should be used to interpret adequately archaeological observables as the material consequence of some social actions.

A naïve solution would be to list all possible consequences of the same cause. This universal knowledge base would contain all the knowledge needed to "guess" in a rational way the most probable cause of newly observed effects. This way of solving inverse problems implies a kind of instance-based learning, which represents knowledge in terms of specific cases or experiences and relies on flexible matching methods to retrieve these cases and apply them to new situations. This way of learning, usually called *case-based learning*, is claimed to be a paradigm of the human way of solving complex diagnostic problems in domains like archaeology. To act as a human expert, a computer system needs to make decisions based on its accumulated experience contained in successfully solved cases. Descriptions of past experiences, represented as cases, are stored in a knowledge base for later retrieval. When the computer sensor perceives a new case with similar parameters, the system searches for stored cases with problem characteristics similar to the new one, finds the closest fit, and applies the solutions of the old case to the new case. Successful solutions are tagged to the new case and both are stored together with the other cases in the knowledge base. Unsuccessful solutions also are appended to the case base along with explanations as to why the solutions did not work.

The suggestion that the intelligent machine should define causal events in terms of the observation of a repeated series of similar events typically relies on a kind of regularity assumption demanding that 'similar problems have similar solutions' (Hüllermeier, 2007; Kolodner, 1993). In other words, a learning machine can be broadly defined as any device whose actions are influenced by past experiences, so that learning procedures changes within an agent that over time enable it to perform more effectively within its environment (Arkin, 1998). The idea is that once a system has a rule that fits past data, if the future is similar to the past, the system will make correct predictions for novel instances (Alpaydin, 2004). This mechanism implies the search for maximal explanatory similarity between the situation being explained and some previously explained scenario (Falkenheimer, 1990).

The trouble is that in most real cases, there are infinite observations that can be linked to a single social action, making them impossible to list by extension. Even the most systematic and long-term record keeping is unlikely to recover all the possible combinations of values that can arise in nature. Thus, the learning task becomes one of finding some solution that identifies essential patterns in the samples that are not overly specific to the sample data. Added complications arise because any inferential task is often fraught with uncertainty. From an analytical perspective, this means that it is quite possible that two similar or even identical samples of prior cases will fall into different classes because there may be ambiguity within the learning sample. If many of our samples are ambiguous for a given set of features, we must conclude that these features have poor explanatory power, and no good solution to the problem may be possible with them alone.

Although we cannot follow the case-based approach in a real research situation, it suggests that an inverse problem can only be solved if there is some prior information about the necessary cause-effect mapping. In other words, the automated archaeologist needs a record of past experiences linking the observed material effects with their cause. It should learn a rule for grouping observable archaeological features in virtue of which they belong to sets of material effects of the same social action. Obviously, the intelligent machine has not enough with rules linking properties observed to co-occur in the instances. We should not forget that, in archaeology we deal with events and not with objects. Consequently, what our automated archaeologist should learn is not a category of similar objects, but the description of a *causal event*. The task is to find perceptual properties that are coherent across different realizations of the causal process.

Robots can potentially learn how to behave either by modifying existing behaviors (adaptation) or by learning new ones. This type of learning can be related to Piaget's theory of cognitive development, in which *assimilation* refers to the modification or reorganization of the existing set of available behaviors, and *accommodation* is the process involved with the acquisition of new behaviors. Robots can also learn how to sense correctly by either learning where to look or determining what to look for.

For instance, the machine will understand what a house, a castle, a burial, a tool are when it learns how a prototypical house, a prototypical castle, a prototypical burial, a prototypical tool have been made, under which social and economic conditions they have existed. Through learning, the automated archaeologist will build a model predicting features that can be perceived in the archaeological record. The automated archaeologist may not be able to identify the causal process completely, but it can construct a good and useful approximation. That approximation may not explain everything, but may still be able to account for some part of the data. Although identifying the complete process may not be possible, an intelligent machine can still detect certain patterns or regularities.

This is exactly what philosophers of science have called *induction* (Bunge, 2006; Genesareth & Nilsson, 1987; Gibbins, 1990; Gillies, 1996; Holland et al., 1986, Langley & Zytkow, 1989; Williamson, 2004; Tawfik, 2004). It can be defined as the way of connecting two predicates to each other, based on a number of examples exhibiting the relevant predicates. Additionally, we can say that induction allows us to conclude that facts similar to observed facts, are true in cases not examined (Pierce, 1878). Inductive learning tools are trained to recognize patterns or to predict outcomes by generalizing from a group of measurements for which the desired outcome is known (training data) to a larger set of circumstances.

Virtually all inductive inferences may be regarded in one sense as either generalizations or specializations. Since Aristotle, generalization has been the paradigmatic form of inductive inference. He and many subsequent logicians discussed the structure and legitimacy of inferences from the knowledge that some observed instances of a kind *A* have a property *B* to the conclusion that all *A* have the property *B*. In the past several decades in philosophy of science, the problem has been conceived in terms of the conditions under which observed instances can be said to confirm the generalization that all *A* are *B*. The underlying assumptions were once suggested by Bertrand Russell (1967):

a. When a thing of certain sort *A* has been found to be associated with a thing of a certain other sort *B*, and has never been found dissociated from a thing of the sort *B*, the greater the number of cases in which *A* and *B* have been associated, the greater is the probability that they will be associated in a fresh case in which one of them is known to be present;

b. Under the same circumstances, a sufficient number of cases of association will make the probability of a fresh association nearly a certainty, and will make it approach certainty without limit.

Consequently, one of the most fundamental notions in inverse reasoning methods is that of similarity: the solutions to an inverse problem

group things together that are similar. Two entities are *similar* because they have many *properties* in common. According to this view:

1. Similarity between two entities increases as a function of the number of properties they share.
2. Properties can be treated as independent and additive.
3. The properties determining similarity are all roughly the same level of abstractness.
4. These similarities are sufficient to describe a conceptual structure: a concept would be then equivalent to a list of the properties shared by most of its instances.

It means that the automated archaeologist has to be able to identify the common property shared by two or more material effects of the same social action to acquire the ability of explaining similar observables as generated by the same cause. In any case, the very idea of similarity is insidious. First, we must recognize that similarity is relative and variable. That means that the degree of similarity between two entities must always be determined relative to a particular domain. Things are similar in color or shape, or in any other domain. There is nothing like overall similarity that can be universally measured, but we always have to say in what respects two things are similar. This kind of judgments will thus crucially depend on the context in which they occur.

In our case, the task will be to find the common structure in a given perceptual sequence under the assumption that structure that is common across many individual instances of the same cause-effect relationship must be definitive of that group (Keselman & Dickinson, 2005). This imply that an automated archaeologist will learn explanatory concepts such as "15th century," "cutting," "killing," "social elite," or any other provided it has enough known instances for the underlying event, and a general background knowledge about how in this situation a human action has generated the observed modification of visual appearances that it is using as perceptual information. That is, the automated archaeologist will learn a mapping from the cause to the effect provided some instances of such a mapping are already known or can be provided by direct experience in the world. When subsequently asked to determine whether novel instances belong to the same causal event, those instances that are similar to instances characteristic of a single event of a single class of events will tend to be accepted. Here, the *givens* -the archaeological description of material consequences of social action- are the condition, and inverse engineering means to find a *generalization* of input-output mappings connecting cause and effect.

Our goal is to program an automated archaeologist in such a way that it be capable of solving specific problems by finding for each domain a general way of relating any particular pattern of observations to one of the specified solutions. The basic representation of the task is therefore quite simple. Each sample of a solved problem consists of: (1) a set of related observations and (2) the corresponding social activity that caused them. For instance, the cause of an animal bone assemblage is the inverse problem we want to solve. The fact that these bones are the consequence of a hunting event is the solution to the problem. This solution will be possible only when our automated archaeologist learn what "hunting" is, or more precisely how to relate the action with its material consequences. This learning has been possible because in the same way as a human archaeologist, the intelligent machine has been trained on a variety of cases in which descriptions of correlated sets of hunting strategies features (supposed to correspond to known instances of human hunting) were fed to the system. These descriptions were obtained by selecting one set of features and stipulating that these describe each prototypical hunting strategy. In case of opportunistic hunting, for instance, carcasses will be presumably butchered unsystematically, and this

fact will be preserved in the number and kind of animal bones, in their fractures, cut marks, and butchery traces. An intelligent machine is then trained on these archaeozoological data -data coming from cases whose formation process is known, a learning set made of ethno-archaeological or experimental data. It never sees a single prototypical "opportunistic hunting strategy," but many instances of approximate examples of opportunistic hunting. It will learn when it will be able to extract the general pattern exemplified in the overall set of instances.

When the automated archaeologist attempts to use a body of observed evidence to discover a way to reconstruct their generative social processes, it exploits certain properties in the data, which can be referred as trends, regularities, similarities and so on. This is the very basics of inverse engineering. The presence of communalities implies a high level of *regularity* in the data, what means that certain characteristics or properties are more probable that others (Zytkow & Baker, 1991, p. 34). In agreement with the most habitual definition of probability, we could affirm, then, that a causal event would exhibit some degree of regularity when the more characteristics are "frequent," and the fewer characteristics are "infrequent" in the known series of observed events. In the same way, we could define the "regularity" of the social action when the material elements used to produce and to reproduce the social group show the same shape, when they have the same size, when their composition and its texture are similar, when we found them in the same place. Associations are likely to be learned if they involve properties that are important by virtue of their relevance to the goals of the system. The propensity, inclination, or tendency of certain states or events to appear together is, then, what we need to learn how the world is.

Regularity has the advantage of increasing useful redundancy into the learning mechanism. When we introduce useful redundancy into an encoding scheme, we want to provide the means whereby a receiver agent can *predict* properties of parts of the message from properties of other parts, and hence generalize how most similar inputs are related to a single output. We must decide whether the number of positive instances and the degree of assessed variability and assessed randomness warrant the potentially useful generalization. These decisions require accurate representations of the variability in the environment and the role of chance, as well as the application of complex inferential rules related to the statistician's law of large numbers.

Nevertheless, nothing is as easy as it seems. If we want to build a computer program that learns from experience, we always should take into account Popperian views about inductivism. Popper said very emphatically, "Induction, that is, inference based on many observations, is a myth. It is neither a psychological fact, nor a fact of ordinary life, nor one of scientific procedure (Popper, 1963, p. 53). In his view, science starts not with observations, as the strict inductivist claims, but with conjectures. The scientist then tries to refute (or falsify) these conjectures by criticism and testing (experiment and observations). The conjecture that has withstood a number of severe tests may be tentatively accepted, but only tentatively. It may break down on the next test or observation. Any refuted (or falsified) conjecture has to be given up, and scientists must try to rectify the situation, either by modifying the old conjecture by producing an entirely new one. The new or modified conjecture is then tested and criticized in its turn, so that science grows and progresses through a never-ending sequence of conjectures and refutations.

Popper is right in the sense that whether learning takes place or not has to do with confirmed or disconfirmed expectations of prior conjectures about what should be learnt, not simple with observations; and it has to do with co-variation detection that leads to improved statistical prediction, rather than with association in the sense of mere occurrence. We should base our approach on the fact that co-variation detection, and hence generalization, are heavily dependent on the initial mental model constructed from prior knowledge (Holland et al., 1986). In other words, the process of solving inverse problems should be based on one's beliefs about the causal structure of some domain of events, and the statistical properties of the observed events. Not only is the degree of generalization from an event governed by one's beliefs about the variability of that kind of event, but also the categorization of events is a highly variable and fluid process. A given event may be categorized in many different ways in a given problem context.

The machine learning approach presented here goes beyond trivial inductivism because I am assuming that learning depends most directly on confirmations and disconfirmations of predictions, rather than on observations or similarities per se. Machine learning is programming computers to optimize a performance criterion using example data or past experience. An automated archaeologist would need then a model defined up to some parameters, and learning would be the execution of a computer program to optimize the parameters of the model using past experience. In any case, machine induction differs from human everyday reasoning in three major aspects. One set of differences has to do with motives and goals of the system. A second has to do with the system's prior experience with the type of concept to be learned (reflected in knowledge available via higher levels in the default hierarchy). The third has to do with the codability of events and event relations that must be incorporated into the concept to be learned (Holland et al., 1986).

INVERSE REASONING AS A PREDICTIVE TASK

Chris Thornton, in a thought-provoking essay suggests that inverse reasoning tasks must be presented in the form of *prediction tasks* (Thornton,

2000). Inverse engineering is a predictive task because its aim is to extract a decision rule from known data that will be applicable to new data (Hitchcock & Sober 2004, Weiss & Kulikowski, 1991; White, 2003). Since knowledge acquisition can always be viewed as the learning of new explanatory or interpretive behavior, we can justifiably treat all learning as some form of behavior adaptation to a specific and well-defined goal. That is, whenever we can specify some learning task sufficiently precisely to get a machine to do it, it is equivalent to having the machine learn to do predictions of a certain kind. We always want the machine to learn a rule of the form "If X, then Y," which is the same, from its perspective, as learning to predict the cause when it sees the material evidence.

Prediction and learning are associated according to the following general principle:

*Given a collection of examples of f, learn a function **h** that predicts the values of f.*

The automated archaeologist has to generalize the set of known examples of f in such a way that **h** can be considered as an agreement of what is common to all f, leaving out the apparently irrelevant distinguishing features (Stary & Peschl, 1995). The function **h** is called a hypothesis, and it will be used to *predict* the most appropriate explanation for new archaeological data not previously seen. In other words, the automated archaeologist will be able to *predict* the social action given an observed material consequence of this action, when it is able to distinguish between events that are consequence of the action, and events that have not been generated by this action or process (White, 2003).

A learning algorithm is presented with a set of input-output pairs that specify the correct output to be generated for that particular input. As we suggested in previous section, this approach to inverse reasoning lead us to the fact that communalities among known instances of the cause-effect relationship are in the basis of the solution process for this kind of problem. In essence, learning in this view amounts to learning a mapping from perceived states to desired actions.

However, not only communality is necessary here, but also some kind of contingent relationship between the observed examples, which will determine the type of association learned. To avoid generating innumerable fruitless hypothesis in its search for useful predictions, an intelligent machine should emphasize constraints that can be derived from the general nature of an information-processing system that pursues goals in a complex environment. Furthermore, it will need some kind of received feedback about its success in attaining its goals (Holland et al., 1986). The central problem of inverse engineering is then to specify constraints that will ensure that the predictions drawn by an automated archaeologist will tend to be plausible and relevant to the system's goals. Which inductions should be characterized as plausible can be determined only with reference to the current knowledge of the system. Inverse engineering is thus highly context dependent, being guided by prior knowledge activated in particular situations that confront the system as it seeks to achieve its goals.

The task can be based on feedback regarding the success or failure of predictions previously generated by the system and tested using some new observed data. The currently active goals of the system, coupled with an activated subset of the system's current store of knowledge provide input to inferential mechanisms that generate plans and predictions about the actual and future observations. The predictions are fed back to other inferential mechanisms along with receptor input. A comparison of predictions and receptor input will yield information about predictive success and failures, which will in turn trigger specific types of inductive changes in the knowledge base.

This approach is also similar to experiment design. Experimental analysis is the process whereby the antecedents of a phenomenon are manipulated or controlled and their effects are measured. Hypotheses investigated in classical experimental science postulate regularities among different repetitions of the same event. A test condition C is inferred from the hypothesis to predict what should happen if C is performed (and the hypothesis is true). In many of these experiments, C is held constant (repeated) while other experimental conditions are varied. Experimentation does not stop with a successful experiment. Scientists continue to fiddle with introducing variations in the conditions while repeating C. They also try removing C while holding conditions constant. When one considers that vast number of additional conditions (known and unknown) that might affect the outcome of an experiment independently of the truth of the hypothesis, all three of these activities make good sense. The experimental evaluation of a hypothesis involves a series of experiments, each one designed in light of the results of previous experiments. In the face of an ostensibly disconfirming result, auxiliary assumptions are modified. Similarly, auxiliary assumptions are also modified in the face of an ostensibly confirming result, and the test condition itself is eventually removed.

The same should be true in the case of archaeology. However, here the meaning of the word "experiment" should change a little. If the automated archaeologist needs observed situations in which a causal relationship is present, its only chances are by rigorous experimentation or through "controlled" observation. In the first case, the cause is replicated in laboratory conditions in order to generate the material effect as the result of a single action, all other actions being controlled. An obvious example is modern use-wear analysis. By replicating lithic tools and using them a determined period of time performing some activity, such as cutting fresh wood, we will be able to test the relationship between kinematics, worked material and observed use-wear on the surface of the tool. It is the archaeologist who makes the tool and who performs the activity. In this way, the

material consequences of cutting fresh wood can be make explicit, and used to discriminate other activity also performed by the archaeologist, for instance, cutting dry bone.

Regrettably, not all social activities performed in the past can be replicated in the present. We cannot replicate human groups, social reproduction processes, or coercive actions, among many others. What cannot be replicated, in many occasions can be observed. Ethnoarchaeology has been defined as the observation in the presence of actions that *were probably performed* in the past. That is to say, it is not a source of analogies, because the observed action is not like the action to be inferred, but a source for hypothesis. "Modern" hunter-gatherers are not necessarily like prehistoric societies whose economic basis was also based on hunting and gathering (Binford, 1968, 1981, 2001a; David, 1992; David & Kramer, 2001; Gándara, 1990, 2006; Gould, 1980; Estevez & Vila, 1995; Vila, 2006; Wylie, 1985; Yellen, 1977). If we use modern ethnographic data to explain by analogy transfer ancient archaeological traces, we are forgetting change, and social dynamics. This is a serious mistake. However, ethnographic and historically preserved ancient written sources can be used as observational situations, in which some causal events took place and they were described. Ethnographical data and historical descriptions are individual instances of the general event the machine should learn. Remember that the task of the automated archaeologist is to find perceptual properties that are coherent across *different realizations* of the causal process. Therefore, the basic problem is distinguishing the social invariants from historical and contextual variability. Here the invariance is a predicate about social action that assigns probabilities (including 1 or 0) to observable outcomes in a series (the more exhaustive possible) of historical situations.

The obstacle that constitutes the basis of the inverse problem is that the needed errors to generalize the input-output mapping are not always provided explicitly in the data (Jordan & Jacobs, 1992), because:

- That specific cause-effect relationship has an unobservable nature. For instance, I cannot see "social power," but its effects.
- The causal process is finished in the present. For instance, Aristotle *wrote* his Metaphysics more than 2,000 years ago. I do not know if he wrote the book, because it is a past action. However, I can infer he is the author because some copies of the book and some contemporary witnesses wrote about Aristotle and his works.
- The causal process is very slow, and I am a finite observer with a short observation span. For instance, mountains and valleys are actual phenomena originated many years ago by the joint effect of geological process, which may be acting here and now, but at a so slow scale, that I cannot perceive its effects during my life span.
- Causal-effect relationships may be holistic (global). I cannot see how human society changes and evolves, because there are more than six thousand million people, and I cannot perceive how social changes affect all of them.

Whether causal prediction is possible has to do with historically or ethnographically confirmed or disconfirmed expectations about what took place. It is not necessarily related to the amount of ethnographic observations or historical descriptions. We have already insisted that inverse reasoning has to do with co-variation detection that leads to improved statistical prediction, rather than with association in the sense of mere occurrence. The use of ethnographic data as a source of positive examples of the event to be learnt is heavily dependent on the initial hypothetical model constructed from prior knowledge. In other words, the process of solving archaeological problems should be based on a previous theory about social processes, and the statistical properties of observed events in experimental replication or ethno-historical sources.

I am assuming that the predictability of causes given an observation of some effects depends most directly on confirmations and disconfirmations of predictions, rather than on the mere accumulation of data. Social action has an intrinsic regularity because collective action is by definition redundant.

Historical predictability critically depends on the ability to accommodate variability in the social domain. If the observed cases for a social event are highly variable with respect to some well-defined features, then predictions whose strength is extreme, and which provide evidence for the causing social action, will acquire more strength than they would if the experimental replications or the observed cases in well-described historical situations were less variable. As a result, archaeologically observed evidence with an extreme strength will provide more evidence for its hypothesized cause (reflected in higher support level) in the former case. The greater the overlap in the features of the material evidence generated by other causal processes, the more difficult it is to generalize positive instances of the relationship. The number of alternative causes also affects the quality of the generalization. Both category overlap and the number of categories will contribute directly to the degree of competition between alternative possible categorizations of instances.

AN INTRODUCTION TO MACHINE LEARNING ALGORITHMS

That concludes the prerequisites for programming an automated archaeologist able to learn to solve archaeological problems. If our aim is to program an intelligent robot, then the question is to implement learning capabilities in the machine. Programming computers to make inferences from data is a cross between statistics and computer science, where statisticians provide the mathematical framework of making inference and computer scientists work on the efficient hardware and software implementation of the inference methods on computers.

We can formalize its inferential task in the following terms:

GIVEN:

An initial description of a theoretical entity

An instance of this entity

An explanation of the association between the concept and its instance

Some operating criteria

DETERMINE:

A generalization of the instance that substitutes initial description and it is related to the explanation and operating constraints.

In other words, the idea is that the automated archaeologist will look for common features between positive examples of the causal relationship to be predicted, and common differences between its negative examples. This task is exactly like an example of a truth-function learning problem

$$
\begin{array}{ccccccc}
1 & 1 & 0 & 1 & 1 & \rightarrow & 1 \\
1 & 0 & 0 & 0 & 0 & \rightarrow & 0 \\
0 & 1 & 1 & 1 & 0 & \rightarrow & 1 \\
1 & 1 & 0 & 0 & 1 & \rightarrow & 0 \\
0 & 0 & 0 & 0 & 0 & \rightarrow & ?
\end{array}
$$

Concept learning problems have the same form, except that target outputs are either "yes" or "no"(or "true"=1 and "false"=0). Inputs that map onto "yes" are treated as positive examples of a particular concept. Inputs that map onto "no" are treated as negative examples (i.e., counterexamples). The process of finding a solution to such a problem is naturally viewed as the process of calculating the *communalities* among positive examples. As such, it is a variation of the philosophical theories seeing *induction* as a process involving the exploitation of similarity.

Let us consider an imaginary case. An automated archaeologist has a sample of instances of historical hunting events, known as the *training set*. Each member of the training set is fully described in terms of some attributes, and the robot is told which members of the set can be interpreted as the consequence of an opportunistic hunting event or a systematic one. Those which are examples of opportunistic hunting are called *positive instances* of the concept "opportunistic hunting," and those which are not are called *negative instances*. The learning problem implies to generate a correct predictive formula, which uses the given attributes for bone assemblages generated by a human group practicing some form of opportunistic hunting. If the attributes were inappropriate for describing the domain, then it would not be possible to generate satisfactory hypotheses. It is important to take into account that the robot is looking for the existence of such an association. It is not imposing an association. Either there is an association or there is not. If there is, it must be possible, at least in principle, to say *what* association is, that is, to give it a formal specification.

The same approach has been followed for solving spatial problems (Gahegan, 2000, 2003). If we have some data providing evidence (positive examples) of a relationship between a location and some value, then, provided this relationship is useful in predicting the desired outcome, a computer program will attempt to learn this pattern. Even if the relationship changes over space, that too can be learned, provided such spatial variability be encoded in the spatial examples presented. In order to be of use, the spatial values must help to characterize the phenomena of interest. This can be achieved if the training sample is randomly distributed within the spatial domain, and hence represents some measure of likelihood of occurrence for the targets. After learning, this will predispose the automated archaeologist to assume that an example belongs to category *C* if its spatial location was helpful in characterizing *C* during the training phase.

These approaches are usually called *supervised* learning, on the grounds that known instances of a cause-effect relationship are like information given to the robot by a teacher or supervisor. In this paradigm, an agent learns to classify stimuli as members of contrastive categories through trial and error with corrective feedback (the teacher) (Gureckis & Love 2003; Perlovsky, 2001). We may think of the teacher as having knowledge of some domain, represented by a set of examples of an *input-output mapping*—experimental replications and/or ethno-historical data. We can build our learning system with the fixed goal of coming to behave in the same way as the teacher, generating the same mapping from perceptual situations to epistemic actions, even when the teacher is no longer present to be observed (Figure 3.1).

Suppose now that the teacher and the intelligent machine are both exposed to a single case or example drawn from what is already known of the domain. By virtue of her or his previous knowledge, the teacher is able to provide with a desired response for that training instance. An error is defined as the difference between the desired response and the actual response of the learner agent in absence of the knowledge provided by the teacher. This adjustment should be carried out iteratively in a step-by-step fashion with the aim of eventually making the learner agent *emulate*

the teacher. The emulation is presumed to be optimum in some statistical sense. In this way, knowledge of the environment available to the teacher is transferred to a problem solver through training as fully as possible. When this condition is reached, we may then dispense with the teacher and let the automated archaeologist deal with new observations completely by itself.

Obviously, the aim of machine learning is rarely to replicate what the teacher teaches but the prediction for new cases. It is usually quite easy to find rules to discriminate or separate data when we know their origin; it is much harder to develop decision criteria that hold up on new cases. That is, the automated archaeologist has to be able to generate the right output for an input instance outside the original set of examples, one set of perceptual properties for which the correct output is not given explicitly.

For best generalization, the automated archaeologist should match the complexity of the hypothesis with the complexity of the function underlying the data. If the hypothesis is less complex that the function, it is *underfitting* the model. If the hypothesis is too complex, or the data is not enough to constrain it, the machine may end up with a bad hypothesis. If there is noise, a too complex hypothesis will be based not only on the underlying function but also on the noise in the data. This is called *overfitting*. In such a case, having more examples, or known instances helps

Figure 3.1. A flow diagram showing the mechanism of supervised learning

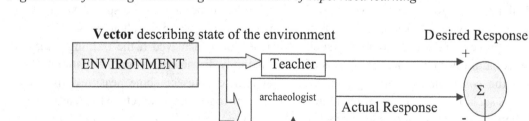

but only to a certain point (Alpaydin, 2004). Consequently, in all inverse engineering or inductive algorithms that are trained from example data, there is a trade-off between three factors:

• The complexity of the hypothesis we fit to data,
• The amount of training data, and
• The generalization error on new examples.

As the amount of training data increases, the generalization error decreases. As the complexity of the model increases, the generalization error decreases first, and then starts to increase.

An intelligent machine can measure the generalization ability of a hypothesis, namely the quality of its inductive bias, if it has access to data outside the training set. We simulate this by dividing the training set we have into two parts. We use one for training (i.e., to find a hypothesis), and the remaining part is called a validation set and is used to test the generalization ability. Assuming large enough training and validation sets, the hypothesis that is the most accurate on the validation set is the best one (the one that has the best inductive bias). This process is called cross-validation.

Consequently, what a machine is capable of learning is influenced by what it is and is not capable of predict. This general principle partially coincides with Binford's suggestion that to develop trustworthy means of knowledge of the past, we need *midrange* investigations, that consist of realistic studies designed to control the relations between the dynamic properties of the past and the static properties of the materials, common to the past and to the present (Binford, 2001b). This affirmation seems to agree with the idea that we propose here: we must construct a causal model that allows predicting when a concrete social action is the cause of a given archaeological artifact. Nevertheless, differences between middle range research and predictive learning as practiced by

our automated archaeologist are very clear and relevant, as we will see in the next pages.

SIMPLE RULE INDUCTION METHODS

The development of inductive learning tools is driven by the need to address a range of complex, nondeterministic problems, where a brute-force search for a truly optimal solution becomes computationally intractable. This need for an approximation solution is the consequence of incomplete or sparse input data, complexity of the explanation to be learnt or both.

The most basic inductive algorithms are designed to find a conjunctive description for a single concept C that covers positive instances of C and that fails to cover negative instances. In this way, we can represent the solution to an inverse problem as a logical conjunction of Boolean features, values of nominal attributes, limits on the values of numeric attributes, or some combination of them. It is usual to refer to each component of such conjunction as a *condition* or a *test*. Briefly, if the new instance matches all conditions in the concept description, it is labeled as a positive instance of the concept C, otherwise it is labeled as negative.

For instance:

• **Given:** A set of positive training instances for the activity "producing pottery containers destined to the transport of liquids."
• **Given:** A set of negative training instances for the activity "producing pottery containers destined to the transport of liquids;" for instance, some instances of pottery containers destined to storing dry goods.
• **Find:** A logical conjunction that, to the extant possible, correctly explains the functionality of novel test cases as pottery vases that were produced in order to transport liquids or as containers for other products.

Algorithms that address this task receive as input a set of positive and negative instances for some class. In response, they must generate an *intentional* description—stated as a logical conjunction—for use in predicting future instances. Note that the goal is not necessarily to find a conjunction that perfectly partition the training cases into positive and negative instances, but to induce a description that accurately classifies novel instances.

One can use a simple trick to extend this scheme to multi-class induction, which requires one to learn descriptions for a set of N concepts rather than for a single concept. For each class C, one treats all instances of the other $N-1$ classes as negative instances of C. Thus, one repeats the basic induction task N times, once for each class. However, this approach can produce descriptions that do not match (and thus fail to classify) some instances and that all match (and thus conflict) on other instances (Langley, 1996).

One can easily identify some major drawbacks of these simple approaches, the most obvious involving their inability to handle situations in which no logical conjunction is consistent with the training data. In noisy domains, even one mislabeled class or feature can seriously derail either technique in its search for consistent descriptions. In some cases, the effect of noise can be even worse, causing the method to eliminate all hypotheses from consideration. Similar problems arise in domains where the target concept is nearly but not perfectly described by a logical conjunction. These problems suggest the need for more robust algorithms that make weaker assumptions about the nature of training data.

A simple way to avoid some of these drawbacks, especially the sensitivity to noise, is by not performing an exhaustive search, but a heuristic one. Heuristic approaches to logical concept induction carry out a partial search through the description space, using an evaluation function that measures the fit to the training data, and selects the best hypotheses at each level. The resulting algorithm is more robust in the presence of noise and target concepts that violate the conjunctive assumption.

This method accepts as input sets of positive and negative instances, along with two sets of concept descriptions, one initialized to the empty set and the other to a set containing a single "null" description with no conditions. The aim of this preliminary hypothesis is to help in the process of specifying candidate descriptions that might still be improved. At each level of its search, the heuristic algorithm considers all specializations of the initial state of the hypothesis that involve the addition of one condition. For each such specialized description S, it is used an evaluation function to measure S's degree of fit to the training data. If the score for S is greater than the score for its parent H, the algorithm adds the hypothesis S to a set of new descriptions that it should consider for further specialization later. If none of the specializations of H score better than their parent, then the new version of the initial hypothesis is accepted, since it cannot be improved further.

After considering all specializations of the current conceptual descriptions, the algorithm checks to see whether any of them have scored better than their parents have. If not, the algorithm simply returns the parent description with the highest score; otherwise, it continues its search. The descriptions generated by this method are not guaranteed to cover all positive instances and no negative instances, nor would this be desirable in domains where the data contain noise or they can only be approximated by a logical conjunction. Nor are the descriptions it generates guaranteed to be minimal, in that some strictly more general descriptions may exist. These are the prices to be paid for carrying out an efficient heuristic search rather than an intractable exhaustive one (Alpaydin, 2004; Han & Kamber, 2001; Hand et al., 2001; Langley, 1996; Mitchell, 1997; Weiss & Kulikowski, 1991; Wittek & Frank, 2005).

One of the most important applications of this approach is the AQ approach by Michalski and colleagues (Kaufman & Michalski, 2000; Michalski & Kaufman, 2001; Michalski, 2004). AQ or A^q stands for algorithm quasi-optimal, as originally developed in 1969, the algorithm creates approximately or strictly optimal solutions of the general covering problem, which subsumes learning rules from examples.

Of related interest is the rule induction method by Clark and Niblett (1989). This algorithm inductively learns a set of propositional "if...then..." rules from a set of training examples. To do this, it performs a general-to-specific beam search through rule-space for the "best" rule, removes training examples covered by that rule, then repeats until no more "good" rules can be found. The original algorithm defined "best" using a combination of entropy (see next section) and a significance test. The algorithm was later improved to replace this evaluation function with the Laplace estimate, and also to induce unordered rule sets as well as ordered rule lists ("decision lists"). See also Agrawal et al. (1993) for a related algorithm to extract association rules.

These rule inductive methods have been used in archaeology from time to time. Mephu Nguifo et al. (1998) show the use of this kind of techniques in the empirical design of a typology of archaeological ceramics from the city of Kerma (Sudan). The archaeological ceramics under study were found in the cemetery of the city of Kerma (Sudan). They are dated from the Ancient and Middle Kerma periods, from 2500–1800 B.C. The overall Kerma ceramic typology being already known, the archaeological problem was how to obtain, through these finds, a more detailed view of the variation of ceramic types according to time, although the definition of these types was not precisely known. Assuming that the north area of the cemetery was the first to be used, and that, as time went, burials progressed towards the south, the ceramics have been dated relatively by successive excavation "sectors" (horizontal stratigraphy). The task of the machine learning program was to discriminate between sectors. The authors define conjecture as a set of examples and counterexamples of a concept (here, of a class or "archaeological sector") to be learned. For instance, a conjecture about class 1 is all the positive instances of class 1, that is, the ceramics described by the archaeological expert ("the teacher" in a supervised learning approach) as belonging to class 1, together with the negative instances of this class, that is, all the ceramics of the other classes. Similarities must be based on attributes which are present at the same time in at least 16 examples and in less than 17 counterexamples of a class. Extracted similarities are called "regularities." A regularity is *valid* if it holds for 'enough' positive instances. It is *pseudocoherent* if it holds for 'few' counterexamples. An example of a regularity extracted for the discrimination of sector 1 is:

The set of attributes: profile simple AND height of top part of body height of lower part of body AND exterior of base non stable (i.e., eggshaped, pointed or rounded) AND rim slope inferior to 20_ is verified in 20 objects, with at least 10 belonging to sector 1, and at most 4 belonging to the other 8 sectors.

When the regularities extracted for a given archaeological sector share a common set of attributes, this set can be said to define a prototype. The prototype of a given sector thus is a fictitious object, which shares a number of attributes with the objects belonging to this sector.

The system classifies new objects by testing their behavior with regard to regularities. If these objects satisfy a number of conditions, they are recognized as examples of a class. If not, they are refused. The conditions consist in numerical thresholds to be satisfied. They concern the percentage of regularities verified by an object.

In a fairly similar way, Gey has used rule association methods to the classification of western

European Bronze Age axes (1800-700 B.C.). The idea was again to test existing typologies for accepting or rejecting them in terms of their coherence and predictive ability (Gey, 1991). Around 100 axes were processed assigned to all identifiable periods within Bronze Age. Artifacts were described in terms of shape, composition, decoration, and so forth. The data were introduced as a semantic network in which an arc between two successive nodes represents a link between an attribute and its value for an individual axe. This representation format can be easily translated to triplets *<entity><relation><entity>*. For instance:

AXE No. 1 HAS   BODY
BODY   HAS   PLANE SUR-
FACE
EXTREME SAME_HEIGTH   RIM
.../...

Shape descriptions are not the only elements in the system. Taxonomies and axioms are also included as meta-knowledge allowing the system to use terms like "extreme," "rim," "surface," etc. as constitutive elements of an axe. Axioms represent known relationships between concepts; they are represented as rules:

IF
    (rim height ?x) AND (extreme height ?x)
THEN
    (Rim) SAME_HEIGTH (Extreme)

IF
    (edge) STATE (used)
THEN
    (object) IS_A (tool)
IF
    (edge) STATE (new)] AND [(hole) INTEN-
TIONAL (no)]
THEN
    object) IS_A (premonetary_item)

Using semantic networks, taxonomies and rules, the system looks for similar objects and generalizes from such equivalence classes. Classes are represented using expressions like:

(axe$_x$ RELATION axe$_y$)

Where the term "relation" refers to three different classification criteria:

-    A spatiotemporal relationship
-    A technological relationship
-    A functional relationship

In this way, the system calculates three different classifications: a first one in which object aggregates contain contemporaneous axes, another, in which axes have been produced in the same way, and the third one in which axes were used in the same way. In each of the three cases, the aim is to calculate the intersection and/or co-occurrence of descriptions between related axes.

In art history, Marie-Salomé Lagrange and Monique Rénaud (Lagrange, 1992; Lagrange & Rénaud, 1987; Sallantin et al., 1991) followed a similar procedure, generalizing a training set containing the architectonic descriptions of medieval churches to find a conceptual description of Cistercian buildings.

A different approach was followed by Nicholas Findler to form kinship concepts by processing examples and counter-examples of patterns of social interaction. In this case, the rule to be induced is essentially the simplest relation applicable between each pair of individuals who are instances of allowed social interactions and relations. For example, *A* could marry *B, C, D,...* but could not marry *U, V, W,...* A possible derived rule may for example be that a male can marry an unrelated unmarried female of the same tribe, a patrilateral cousin or aunt but not a matrilateral cousin or aunt. The program looks at the labels in the exemplary and counter-exemplary cases. It then discards from consideration those labels, that is, rule components that have "uninformative" values (for example, if all marriage statuses—married, not-yet-married, no-longer-married—appear in the central male members' labels in the exemplary cases, marriage status is irrelevant for the rule). On the other hand, if only two out of three values appear, these become a rule component as long as the counter-example cases have only complementary values. It also means that whenever both the exemplar and counter-example cases show an identical value, that value becomes irrelevant. It can happen that *combinations of label values* matter, which the user must flag as a special property, and the program will treat it accordingly. For example, only tribal chiefs can have more than one wife). In this way, the hypothesis of the above marriage rule can be established (Findler, 1992; Findler & Dhulipalla, 1999).

Mennis and Liu (2003) have used the same general approach to induce spatiotemporal rules. A spatiotemporal association rule occurs when there is a spatiotemporal relationship in the antecedent or consequent of the rule. Whereas non-spatial association rule mining seeks to find associations among elements that are encoded explicitly in a database, spatial association rule mining seeks to find patterns in spatial relationships that are typically not encoded in a database, but are rather embedded within the spatial framework of the georeferenced data. These spatial relationships must be extracted from the data prior to the actual association rule mining. There is therefore a trade-off between preprocessing spatial relationships among geographic objects and computing those relationships on the fly. Pre-processing improves performance, but massive data volumes associated with encoding spatial relationships for all combinations of geographic objects prohibits the storage of all spatial relationships. As a case study, the authors used association rule mining (Agrawal et al., 1993) to explore the spatial and temporal relationships among a set of geographic variables that characterize socioeconomic and land cover change.

INDUCING DECISION TREES

Concept hierarchies provide a framework for memory organization, and a considerable amount of machine learning research has taken this approach. Such hierarchies can be represented as a decision tree consisting of nodes and branches. Each node represents a separate concept, typically with its own associated intentional definitions. The links connecting a node to its children specify an "is-a" or subset relation, indicating that the parent's extension is a superset of each child's extension. Typically, a node covers all of the instances covered by the union of its descendents (Langley, 1996; Mitchell, 1997; Weiss & Kulikowski, 1991; Wittek & Frank, 2005). In fact, such a decision tree can be seen as a collection of rules, with each terminal node corresponding to a specific decision rule.

A concept hierarchy uses predictive features or descriptions to sort new instances downward through the tree. One can view these as "tests" that discriminate among the concepts stored at each level, although such tests need not be logical in nature. For instance, consider the simplest and most widely used form of concept hierarchy—the univariate decision tree. This organization divides instances into mutually exclusive sets at each level, splitting on the values of a single predictive feature (thus the term *univariate*). Depending on whether the result of a test is true or false, the tree will branch right or left to another node. At each level, the algorithm uses the predictive features on the alternative nodes to select one to expand, then proceeds to the next level. This continues until reaching a terminal node or otherwise deciding the sorting process has gone deep enough. At this point, the process uses the predictable features associated with the current node to infer attributes missing from the instance, such as the class name. The details of sorting and predicting depend on the nature of the intentional descriptions stored with the nodes. When a terminal node (sometimes referred as a leaf) is reached, a decision is made on the class assignment. As a result, each internal node contains a very simple description for use in sorting. Only terminal nodes include a predictive feature, which specifies the class to predict upon reaching that node. Most presentations of decision trees place the values of the discriminating attribute on the branches leading into nodes, and the attribute itself on the node from which they emanate.

In Figure 3.2, each node represents a single test or decision. In this case, we have a binary tree, because the decision can be either true or false. Circle 1 is the root node and circle 2 is the only non-terminal node. Squares are all terminal nodes. For example, suppose that this tree represents a conceptual hierarchy for determining the social personality of people buried in some graves: *C1* predicts that the burial is the grave of a rich person, and *C2* predicts that the burial is the grave of a poor person. Node 1 is the test of the quantity of labor necessary for building such a burial, and node 2 is the test of a big amount of valuable grave goods. The tree partitions the samples into three mutually exclusive groups, one for each terminal node. There is a first group (*A*) of rich burials in complex graves associated with great amounts of labor in their building. Another group (*B*) of poor people buried in simple graves (low quantity of labor invested in their building), and without a big

amount of grave goods; and finally, a group (*C*) of burials of rich people in simple graves with a big amount of valuable grave goods.

Non-binary decision trees are also widely used. In these trees, more than two branches may leave a node, but again only one branch may enter a node. Figure 3.3 illustrates a non-binary decision tree: node 2 has three branches. In this type of tree, a test performed at a node results in a partition of two or more disjoint sets that cover every possibility, that is, any new case must fall into one of the disjoint subsets. For binary-valued tests, this is equivalent to a true or a false conclusion being reached. In the figure, the values of node 2 are broken into three disjoint sets, for example, test values that are normal (v3), low (v4), and high (v5).

The process of learning the structure of a decision tree or the equivalent rules from data is known as tree or rule induction (Breiman et al., 1984; 1993, Biggs et al., 1991; Buntime & Niblett, 1992; Gilles, 1996; Quinlan, 1986; Wittek & Frank, 2005).

A tree may be induced by selecting some starting feature, splitting that feature into disjoint sets, and then repeating the process for all subsequent nodes. Nodes become terminal and are not split further when all members of the sample belong to one class. Alternatively, nodes become

Figure 3.2. A binary decision tree

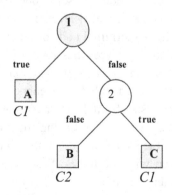

Figure 3.3. A non-binary decision tree

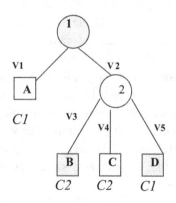

terminal when the number of cases in the remaining group falls below some minimum threshold, and the node is assigned to the class having the greatest frequency at that node. The procedure is top-down. The first level decision tree corresponds to the hypothesis that the single attribute chosen for the root is sufficient for classifying all objects into positive and negative instances. This is simple and general, and will usually be false. The discovery of counter examples leads to the construction of more complicated and specific decision trees.

The simplest technique for splitting the nodes into disjoint groups is to partition the data by the distinct values of the feature. The following explanation may be difficult for some readers. It can be skipped and the rest of the chapter is easily understandable. There is plenty of commercial software that makes the calculations, and the user only needs to concentrate on results. Of course, it would be interesting if the user understands some of the logical steps followed by the algorithm.

In the case of non-binary trees, if all the values of cases $v1$ are members of $C1$, that node becomes a terminal path. The cases having $v2$ include cases of both $C1$ and $C2$, so further splitting of the $v2$ cases must occur. Some test is selected for node 2. This test can assume three distinct values, $v3$, $v4$ and $v5$. A branch from node 2 is created for each of these values. If the cases of each group ($v2$ & $v3$, $v2$ & $v4$, $v2$ & $v5$) belong to a single class, they all become terminal nodes.

After any branch, a decision must be made about the next node to split. The basic approach to selecting a variable is to examine each variable and evaluate its likelihood for improving the overall decision performance of the tree. The underlying concept of any split evaluation is to select a variable and cutoff that will produce the best tree. However, the evaluation function predicts solely based on splitting a single node, without testing possible splits of successor nodes. Thus, the evaluation function is a heuristic that tends to make good judgments with incomplete information.

The most widely used node-splitting evaluation functions work by reducing the degree of randomness or impurity in the current node. The most popular evaluation functions are the *entropy* function and the *Gini* function. The overall goal is to reduce the impurity and randomness of the classes within the current node and future nodes. Because these numbers represent impurity, the smaller the number, the better:

$$\text{ENTROPY:} \qquad -\sum p_j \log p_j \qquad (1)$$

$$\text{GINI FUNCTION:} \qquad 1 - \sum p_j^2 \qquad (2)$$

Given a means of computing the impurity of a node, the learning system selects the next variable or test for splitting as the one that reduces the impurity the greatest. In a binary tree, the reduction in impurity for a given split can be written in the following way:

$$\Delta i(n) = i(n) - p_l\, i(n_l) - p_r\, i(n_r) \qquad (3)$$

Where n is the node being split; p_l and p_r are the probabilities of branching left and right; $i(n)$ is the impurity of the current node n; and $i(n_l)$ and $i(n_r)$ are the impurities of the left and right branch nodes. The probabilities of branching left or right are simply the percentages of cases in node n that branch left or right.

For a non-binary tree, one must consider the impurity of each branch and the likelihood of taking that branch. The likelihood of a branch is merely the percentage of cases from the parent node that take that branch. The impurities of each branch node are summed over all branches, and the reduction in impurity is found by subtracting this sum from $i(n)$ as indicated in the following equation:

$$\Delta i(n) = i(n) - \sum p_k\, i(n_k) \qquad (4)$$

For either type of tree, many different splits are examined, and the variable selected for splitting is the one with the greatest reduction in impurity. For a non-binary tree, the possible split of a variable is immediately determined by the distribution of values of that variable in the node being split. The task of selecting a node is reduced to a simple evaluation of impurity reduction for that variable. For binary trees, a small amount of search is used to examine many different splits. For each split considered, the reduction in impurity is evaluated. The splits that are considered depend on whether the variable is ordered or categorical. For ordered variables, splits for every value found in the sample will be considered. For categorical variables, every possible way of splitting the variable into two sets is considered.

Let us see an archaeological example. Remember that we are following a supervised learning approach to inverse reasoning, therefore we need a set of positive and negative examples of the concept we want to learn. It should be taken into account that Inductive Decision Trees do not generate explanatory hypothesis from data alone. When generating possible explanations, such programs select at each stage an attribute or feature from a set of attributes which is given in advance. The background assumption, which is a substantial one, is that this set of attributes is appropriate for describing the domain in question. If the attributes were inappropriate for describing the domain, then it would not be possible to generate satisfactory hypotheses (Gilles, 1996). In this example, we want to learn a decision rule for determining the chronology of some pottery data set. Stratigraphic and radiocarbon data have allowed the definition of the following training data:

size	*Painted decoration*	*Engraved decoration*	*chronology*
BIG	presence	presence	late
BIG	presence	absence	late
BIG	absence	presence	late
BIG	absence	absence	middle
MEDIUM	presence	presence	late
MEDIUM	absence	presence	middle
MEDIUM	absence	absence	middle
SMALL	presence	presence	early
SMALL	absence	presence	early
SMALL	absence	absence	early

Here we want to generalize the features of potteries with early, middle and late chronologies based on information about the size of the vases, and their decoration. The calculation of entropy allows defining "size" as the attribute with the greater amount of information (0,971), therefore we will split the root node in the following way:

Figure 3.3. A non-binary decision tree for discovering the relationship between pottery and time (1ˢᵗ part)

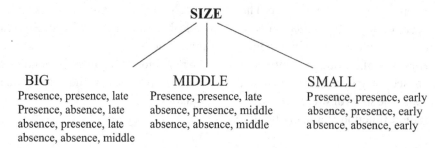

SIZE

BIG
Presence, presence, late
Presence, absence, late
absence, presence, late
absence, absence, middle

MIDDLE
Presence, presence, late
absence, presence, middle
absence, absence, middle

SMALL
Presence, presence, early
absence, presence, early
absence, absence, early

The right node is clearly a terminal node. That is to say, we have already obtained a decision rule:

If size = small, Then Chronology = Early.

We have to split the other nodes to obtain additional rules for generalizing the visual characteristics of late and middle potteries.

The big sized vases node should be split according to the kind of decoration of the potteries. Using the entropy measure, both attributes give a similar value in the increase of information. In the case of the middle sized potteries node, the increase of information using the entropy of painted decoration is greater than using the engraved decorations. Consequently, we can use this attribute in the first place.

Here we have three new decision rules:

If size = big AND painted decoration= Presence, Then Chronology = Late

If size = middle AND painted decoration= Presence, Then Chronology = Late

If size = middle AND painted decoration= Absence, Then Chronology = Middle

One node needs, however, additional splitting. Given that the only remaining attribute is "engraved decoration," we obtain the following complete tree (see Figure 3.5).

This apparently simple algorithm was initially proposed by Hunt (1962; Hunt et al., 1966). Its modern popularity is due to the Ross Quinlan, who ameliorated it in the *C4.5* program (Quinlan, 1986, 1993). There are some inherent weaknesses in the splitting technique that can lead to poor predictions. The obvious difficulty arises with continuous variables. For the continuum of possible values that such features can assume, it is unreasonable to base predictions solely on the values that happen to appear in a small sample. In some cases, the most direct approach is to break the continuous variable into discrete intervals. Another more subtle problem with splitting by attribute value is that it tends to fragment the tree into many smaller groups. The smallest tree among several that have equal error rates will usually do better in prediction. The smaller tree has fewer tests to perform and has larger samples supporting the terminal nodes. Thus with a limited sample, fragmentation is of concern, and one would like to avoid committing the tree to consider

Figure 3.4. A non-binary decision tree for discovering the relationship between pottery and time (2nd part)

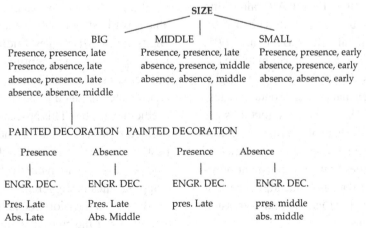

Figure 3.5. A non-binary decision tree for discovering the relationship between pottery and time (3rd part)

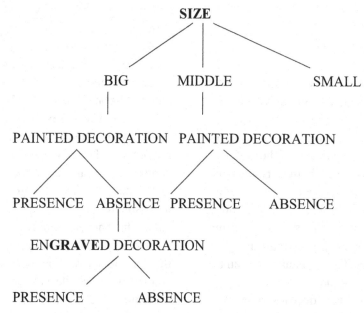

a complete range of values for a test, when a far narrower range, such as an interval of values greater than some threshold, is really of interest. On the other hand, trees that are split by value for non-continuous variables are often more natural and more intuitively understandable.

Much of the recent research has explored variations and extensions of the basic divisive induction of decision trees. Breiman et al. (1984) describe approaches for creating binary trees from numeric attributes. Their CART algorithm creates trees with *n* branches, each with an arbitrary subset of nominal values. Bel et al. (2005) adapted the standard CART algorithm to the use of spatial variables. The authors suggest weighting the samples such that clustered data have less weight than sparse data. Weighted methods are aimed at reducing the bias of the regression tree by taking into account the spatial redundancy of the data. This implies that the equivalent number of independent data is reduced, hence that the variance of the classification and regression parameters is increased.

Another of the most popular and easily available decision tree methods has been called CHAID. To determine the best split at any node, it is possible to merge any allowable pair of categories of the predictor variable (the set of allowable pairs is determined by the type of predictor variable being studied) if there is no statistically significant difference within the pair with respect to the target variable. The process is repeated until not any other non-significant pair is found. The resulting set of categories of the predictor variable is the best split with respect to that variable. Biggs et al. (1991) suggest finding the best split by merging similar pairs continuously until a single pair remains. The set of categories with the largest significance is taken to be the best split for that predictor variable. This process is followed for all predictor variables. The predictor that gives the best prediction is selected, and the node is split. The process repeats recursively until one of the stopping rules is triggered.

Because a decision tree is induced by gradually growing the tree, it is quite natural to try to stop when it is determined that further splits are not likely to be significant. Significance can be measured by a standard statistical test, such as a chi-square test. Once a node split has been selected, the distribution of classes at that node can be compared with those at the resultant split nodes. When the statistical test indicates that further splitting is not significant, no further splitting on that node need be carried out. However, it is quite possible that while the immediate split is not significant, some additional descendant splitting will turn out to be significant. We need consequently more efficient ways for pruning the decision tree.

Among the modern procedures of decision trees induction it should be mentioned the random forest algorithm (Breiman, 2001; Shi & Horvath, 2006). A *random forest* is a classifier that consists of many decision trees and outputs the class that is the mode of the classes output by individual trees. Each tree is constructed using the following algorithm:

1. Let the number of training cases be N, and the number of variables in the classifier be M.
2. We introduce the number m of input variables to be used to determine the decision at a node of the tree; m should be much less than M.
3. Choose a training set for this tree by choosing N times with replacement from all N available training cases (i.e., take a bootstrap sample). Use the rest of the cases to estimate the error of the tree, by predicting their classes.
4. For each node of the tree, randomly choose m variables on which to base the decision at that node. Calculate the best split based on these m variables in the training set.
5. Each tree is fully grown and not pruned (as may be done in constructing a normal tree classifier).

The advantages of random forest are:

- For many data sets, it produces a highly accurate classifier.
- It handles a very large number of input variables.
- It estimates the importance of variables in determining classification.
- It generates an internal unbiased estimate of the generalization error as the forest building progresses.
- It includes a good method for estimating missing data and maintains accuracy when a large proportion of the data are missing.
- It provides an experimental way to detect variable interactions.
- It can balance error in class population unbalanced data sets.
- It computes proximities between cases, useful for clustering, detecting outliers, and (by scaling) visualizing the data.
- Using the previous algorithm, it can be extended to unlabeled data, leading to unsupervised clustering, outlier detection and data views.
- Learning is fast.

Inductive decision trees are increasing their applicability in archaeology. Modern applications range from sex determination of buried human bodies (McBride et al., 2001) to the discrimination of geo-archaeological soil data (Farrigton & Taylor, 2004). In any case, it is in archaeometry where these methods have found its greatest popularity in the recent years (Baxter, 2006; Baxter & Jackson, 2001; Nance, 2000).

Grudzinski and collaborators (Grudzinski et al., 2003; Grudzinski & Karwowski, 2005) also have applied these methods for chronology estimation of archaeological artifacts, using spectroscopic analysis of glass composition. The glass composition has been measured usually in several places: on the original surface of the artifact and on the broken parts. Therefore, several instances in the original database correspond to the same glass object. The measurements of chemical compound concentrations were made using the Energy Dispersive X-ray Fluorescence Spectroscopy. Concentration of the following 26 compounds was measured: Na_2O, MgO, Al_2O_3, SiO_2, SO_3, K_2O, CaO, TiO_2, Cr_2O_3, MnO, Fe_2O_3, CoO, NiO, CuO, ZnO, SeO_3, Br_2O_7, Rb_2O, SrO, ZrO_2 MoO_3, CdO, SnO_2, Sb_2O_3, BaO, and PbO. The original database consists of the description of 555 glass samples. There are approximately 4 samples per glass object. Samples of uncertain chronology have been excluded from the database.

Three main chronological periods are of interest to archeologists:

1. LT C1 - La Tène C1 period, 260 - 170 B.C.
2. LT C2 - La Tène C2 period, 170 - 110 B.C.
3. LT D1 - La Tène D1 period, 110 - 50 B.C.

A preliminary study was performed on the data containing measurements made on both original surface and the broken parts. The authors used the 1R algorithm for decision trees (Witten & Frank, 2005). This algorithm has the characteristics of being based in one single attribute, the one with most discriminative power, building all rules that may be based on that algorithm, and defining the intervals where samples from a single class are prevalent:

IF MnO < 2185.205 THEN La Tène C1 period, 260-170 B.C.

IF 2185.205< MnO< 9317.315 THEN La Tène C2 period, 170-110 B.C.

IF MnO ≥ 9317.315 THEN La Tène D1 period, 110-50 B.C.

These rules predict correctly 100 out of the 143 training samples, and 93 out of 140 test samples.

For a second experiment, only samples with measurements on the glass surface were selected.

C4.5 decision tree was used. Resulting rules are listed below:

If ZrO_2 > 296.1 Then La Tène C1 period, 260-170 B.C. (16/0)

If Na_2O ≤ 36472.22 Then La Tène C1 period, 260-170 B.C. (2/0)

If Sb_2O_3> 2078.76 Then La Tène C2 period, 170-110 B.C. (12/1)

If CdO =0 & Na_2O ≤ 27414.98 Then La Tène C2 period, 170-110 B.C. (12/1)

If Na_2O > 27414.98 & NiO ≤ 58.42 Then La Tène D1 period, 110-50 B.C. (10/0)

If NiO > 48.45 & CdO =0 & BaO =0 & Br_2O_7 ≤ 53.6 & Fe_2O_3 ≤ 12003.35 & ZnO ≤ 149.31 Then La Tène D1 period, 110-50 B.C. (7/0)

These rules predict correctly 54 out of 68 test cases, using 10 features (numbers appearing in brackets: covered cases/Number of mistakes).

For the third experiment, only samples with measurements on the broken parts were selected. The C4.5 decision tree produced 6 rules listed below:

If ZrO_2 > 199.38 & CdO = 0 Then La Tène C1 period, 260-170 B.C. (19/0)

If NiO ≤ 62.23 & CaO ≤ 114121.35 Then La Tène C1 period, 260-170 B.C. (6/0)

If CuO ≤ 5105.37 & MnO > 2546.77 & ZnO ≤ 126.29 Then La Tène C2 period, 170-110 B.C. (15/0)

If SnO_2 > 61.98 & Br_2O_7 ≤ 64.08 Then La Tène D1 period, 110-50 B.C. (10/1)

If Sb_2O_3 ≤ 8246.11 & CuO ≤ 2042.19 & Al_2O_3 > 11525.69 Then La Tène D1 period, 110-50 B.C. (20/0)

Robert Reynolds (1999) has used ID3 decision trees in a more interpretative way. In his study of chiefdoms and state formation in the Valley of Oaxaca (Mexico), each site, for each region and time period, was described in terms of over 100 variables relating to the environment, agriculture, economy (e.g., craft production and trade), and architecture variables. Using these data, the goal was to induce general trends in settlement decision making using decision trees. The author was interested in predicting correctly whether or not a site is likely to have evidence for conflict and raiding in a given time period for a given region of the valley. He used decision trees for such a prediction. The most important variables for understanding prehistoric site location decisions will be found higher up on the tree, while secondary or tertiary variables tend to be found lower down. The expectation, therefore is that need for defense from raiding will gradually "climb the tree" over time. Additionally, the location of sites that are targets for raiding should shift over time in ways that are consistent with the predictions made by the model.

Variables used by Reynolds in this study were: environmental zone (low, alluvium, high alluvium, lower piedmont, high piedmont, mountains), slope (flat, shallow, moderate, steep), hilltop or ridge top (yes, no), soil character (alluvium, bedrock), site located on the boundary between the Loam and the Swampy Region (yes, no), water source (main river, tributary stream, arroyo, spring, well), depth to water table (real number indicating distance), type of irrigation (none, well, valley floor canal irrigation, piedmont canal irrigation, flood water farming, terracing) and land use type (percentage of arable land). Instead of other approaches, Reynolds does not include time as a dependent variable for developing the tree, and consequently, there are neither branches nor nodes for different phases. He prefers to develop a separate analysis for each historical phase, and hence a separate tree for each historical moment. The assumption is that the more frequent and complex the pattern of raiding, the more complicated the tree becomes. The results show that in the oldest period the tree is very simple and that factors most influencing site location are environmental zone and water source: four sites located in the low of high alluvium were

not attacked; three sites whose water source is a main river or a tributary river were not attacked, too. That is to say, at this period almost all of the village sites were located in similar environmental settings for agricultural reasons. The complexity of decision tree increases in the second period, but again environmental zone and water source were the more important factors for site location. There is no interest in increasing the defensibility of sites, what indicates lower levels of raiding. The sites with evidence of raiding are those which seem marginal, and with lower productivity levels than other. Conflict only affects to weakest settlements. The third period shows an intensification of raiding, and now slope is the second most important factor for site location. The increase in the tree complexity shows the complexity of site location decisions, because people should make front to many problems, water source, productivity, defensibility, etc. for locating their homes in the most appropriate location. At the fourth period, when the political organization adopts the form of a complex chiefdom, defensibility of the site becomes of the top most importance, and the main factor to understand site location, but not the only one. Now, 9 variables should be taken into account for appropriate spatial decisions. The assumption is that as social structure and settlement choice become more sophisticated, the patterns of warfare and response may become more predictable in terms of such environmental factors.

Decision trees seem also relevant to paleoecological research (Lenihan & Neilson, 1993). Nevertheless, Jeraj, Szerasko and colleagues (Jeraj et al., 2004) reveal how the binary nature of most decision trees seems not well adapted to stratigraphic correlations. The authors used pollen data for studying spatial and temporal correlations among different trees, shrubs and herbs growing around the study area during Early, Mid and Late Holocene. They try to find regularities and/or dependencies among coexisting plant species through time, with a focus on the period between 8400-3500 BP, to detect changes in the environment caused by human action. The decision tree looked for the relationship between time, stratigraphic depths (between 80 and 500 cm.) from where pollen samples were taken, and vegetation variation, relative pollen frequencies of *pinus, picea, abies, betula, fagus, alnus, corylus, quercus, tilia, carpinus*, other arboreal and non arboreal pollen species at specific stratigraphic depths. The project was based on the application of a variation of Quinlan's C4.5 algorithm called J4.8 (Wittek & Frank, 2005). The unexpected relevance of frequencies of *betula* differentiate the temporal evolution of vegetation changes in two different branches, what is not correct from the point of view of quantitative differences between different species. The procedure does not take into consideration quantitative variation, over emphasizing lower contribution species. As an alternative, instead of binary decision trees, regression trees could give an answer to this problem. These regression trees are a variation of the standard inductive tree where the dependent attribute is a continuous variable. This method has been used in paleoecology, in order to predict the association between the frequencies of fossil findings and environmental variables (Mannila et al., 1998).

This paleoecological case is an interesting example of using the wrong method for solving the wrong kind of problem. It should make us rethink the very idea of machine learning. We are not looking for just a new statistical tool for exploring the data, but we are looking for inducing explanatory predictions for new observations. Decision trees should be used as practical generalization procedures, and not as an exploratory technique. Induction and prediction are only as good as the training data. If there is no interpretive regularity in the data set, the machine learning approach will generalize nothing. We should also take into account that the methods we have been reviewing up to here need some prior knowledge, a teacher or a supervisor, in order to be capable of generalize some particular instances into a prototypical

description of the input-output causal process. Machine learning methods will have a chance for success, only if the database is a real training data set, with observations well correlated to the phenomenon or process to be induced.

An example of what happens when these assumptions are not considered can illustrate this discussion. Fernández Martínez and García de la Fuente (1991) looked for possible associations and dependencies between 25 features describing 389 burials from a Meroitic cemetery in Egypt (3rd-1st centuries B.C.). These features refer to chronology, preservation, qualitative descriptive characteristics of the burial itself, presence/absence of architectonic elements, size, position of the body, skull, hand, and legs, presence/absence of different kinds of grave goods, quantity of grave goods, etc. The idea was to use each of these variables successively as the dependent attribute or knowledge to be predicted in terms of the rest. The failure of the ID3 algorithm application in this context consisted in the poor predictive value of the different rules. For instance, the rules predicting the chronology of a burial in Period 1 were only true in nine out of 52 cases. It is not that the method does not extract enough knowledge, but it extracted too much knowledge, revealing an excessive degree of variability. The failure is in fact a failure of generalization. Cemetery data contained only the descriptions of burials, and it was impossible to extract predictive knowledge that was enough general to be applied to other burials even from the same cemetery and time period.

The success or failure of the simple methods of machine learning we have reviewed up to here are not a consequence of their algorithm, but a consequence of the learning approach considered. Applying ID3, C4.5 or related algorithms to your excavation data is a futile task, because your data are not knowledge to be transformed into predictions, it is perceptual knowledge waiting to be explained in causal terms. You should use laboratory replicated true causal relationships, or observed causal events in an exhaustive set of different situations to obtain predictions before explaining. Only once you have obtained the knowledge, you or your automated machine will explain observed data. After all, a problem solver should know the solution beforehand if it pretends to solve the problem at hand.

Furthermore, it is important to consider that machine learning is not the only solution to a complete automated explanatory machine. After all, it is based on the correlations of observables, and any hypothesis always contains non-observational entities. Specifically if this hypotheses pretends explains something beyond a mere description of present regularities.

CLASSIFICATION AND CLUSTERING

What can we do when the intelligent robot has only input data? When there is no external teacher to oversee the learning process, machine learning textbooks refer to a different way of acquiring knowledge so called *unsupervised* or *self-organized learning methods*. In such an unsupervised or self-organized task, the goal is to identify clusters of patterns that are similar, and using them to generate potential generalizations. The learner agent will suppose there is a structure to the input space such that certain patterns occur more often than others do, and it would look for what generally happens and what does not.

That is to say, a set of explanations will be modeled by first describing a set of prototypes, then describing the objects using these proto-typical descriptions. Each description gives the probabilities of the observable features, assuming that what has been perceived belongs to a group composed of similar looking percepts. The prototype descriptions are chosen so that the information required to describe objects in the class is greatly reduced because they are "close" to the prototype. This information reduc-

tion arises because only the differences between the observed and expected (prototypical) values need to be described. It takes a certain amount of information (in bits) to describe the information required to state the probabilities of the features, given that a new observation belongs to the group of similar objects. However, these probabilities reduce the information needed to describe the objects by first describing each object's prototype membership, then describing how each particular instance differs from the general category (Chee-seman, 1990).

With unsupervised learning, we are not discovering how to instantiate a specific input-output function. Whereas supervised learning involves learning some mapping between input and output patterns, unsupervised learning can be viewed as describing a mapping between input patterns and themselves –i.e., input and output are identical (Chater, 1995; Van Overwalle & Van Rooy, 1998). Once the system has become tuned to the statistical regularities of the input data, it develops the ability to form internal representations for encoding features of the input and thereby to create new categories automatically. Prediction ability is dictated solely by the statistical properties of the set of inputs, and the kind of the statistical rule that governs clustering.

However, before considering another way of learning, the automated archaeologist can always adapt a supervised method to an unsupervised task through a simple transformation. Given k attributes, one runs the algorithm k times, in each case with a different feature playing the role of the class attribute one aims to predict. The result is k different classifiers, each designed to predict accurately one attribute as a function of the others (Langley, 1996).

This distinction between supervised and unsupervised or self-organized learning lead us directly to the concepts of *classification* and *clustering*, because we always can understand the learning task as the partition of an observations set according to the similarity criterion and generating class descriptions from these partitions. Classification is a form of categorization where the task is to take the descriptive attributes of an observation (or set of observations) and from this to label or identify the observation within a different phenomenological domain. The descriptive attributes may be themselves drawn from different data domains, each domain effectively contributing an axis to a combined feature space of all possible object descriptions. Hence, the task of the classifier is somehow to partition this feature space into disjoint regions that each represents a particular class, cluster, or pattern.

The classification problem is just like the supervised learning problem: known cases illustrate what sort of object belongs in which class. The goal in a classification problem is to develop an algorithm which will assign any artifact, represented by a vector x, to one of c classes (chronology, function, origin, etc.). The problem is to find the best mapping from the input patterns (descriptive features) to the desired response (classes). Some finite or infinite set of patterns (binary or real valued vectors) is to be partitioned into classes; a particular problem is then specified by a set of selected training patterns, which are given together with their corresponding class names, and the goal is to classify *all* patterns as correctly as possible. Machine learning, however, differs from statistical classification and clustering in different ways. It is (in comparison at least) robust in the presence of noise; it is flexible as to the statistical types that can be combined; it is able to work with feature spaces of very high dimensionality; it requires less training data, and it makes fewer prior assumptions about data distributions and model parameters (Gahegan, 2000, 2003). Using a machine learning approach to generalization and induction, we are attempting to *learn* a classifier, as distinct from *imposing* or conditioning the classifier. By doing it, we are avoiding some problems whilst making others. Specifically, parametrically based classifiers, such as discriminant analysis, suffer from a number of drawbacks. Firstly, they assume that

values for each data dimension fit a predetermined distribution. This usually implies that categories are both unimodal and symmetric. Unimodality is a particularly demanding constraint in practice, since each class must be constructed from a single region in feature space. Classes should be recognized as such and each distinct region must be defined separately, via its own training examples. Secondly, a large number of training examples are needed to construct the probability density function with defensible confidence.

The purpose of the classification problem is to estimate the probability of membership of the instance in each class. The objective is to build a model with significant predictive power. It is not enough just to find which relationships are statistically significant. That explains why classification and prediction are frequently interrelated. A prediction of an historical event is equivalent to a classification within a given set of events. A prediction of flint knives implies a distinction between longitudinal and transversal use-wear traces, for instance. Conversely, a classification of flint tools also means a prediction of their past function. There are exceptions, of course, where such a relation does not exist.

For classification problems, the supervised task assumes that each training instance includes an attribute that specifies the class of that instance, and the goal is to induce a concept description that accurately predicts this attribute. Clustering is just the statistical way of speaking about self-organized or unsupervised learning: clustering algorithms partition the input space so that diversity may be explicitly recognized and encoded. Clustering is the process of grouping input samples in similarity classes. This approach is popular within statistics: principal component analysis, cluster analysis, and so forth, are good examples. Such methods are based on some distance measure. Each object is represented as an ordered set (vector) of features. "Similar" objects are those that have nearly the same values for different features. Thus, one would like to group samples to minimize intra-cluster distances while maximizing inter-cluster distances, subject to the constraints on the number of clusters that can be formed. Another approach to unsupervised learning, beyond classical statistical procedures are *vector quantization* methods, a general term used to describe the process of dividing up space into several connected regions, using spatial neighborhood as an analogue of similarity (Kohonen, 2001). Every point in the input space belongs to one of these regions, and it is mapped to the corresponding nearest vector. For example, the attributes for "object *A*" are mapped to a particular output unit or region, such that it yields the highest result value and is associated with that object, while the attributes for "object *B*" and so forth. are mapped to different regions (Engel & Van der Broeck, 2001).

One way of understanding the relationship between clustering and unsupervised or self-organized learning is considering Thornton's "fence-and-fill" approach (Thornton, 2000): carving up the input space into simple blocks (with "fences"), and treating every point in the block the same way ("fill"). A particularly simple case of fence-and-fill learning is dividing the input space by straight lines; if this is successful, the problem is said to be linearly separable. It works like this:

1. Use the chosen fence-and-fill method to process the current input data, that is, to find regions of uniformly labeled stimuli.
2. Recode the current input data to draw identically labeled data points closer together. ...
3. Assign the derived data to be the current data and apply the procedure recursively until data are generated that can be satisfactorily processed solely by the fence-and-fill method.

Geometrically, our automated archaeologist should be able to fit shapes of the decision boundaries between the classes formed by lines that are parallel to the axes, yielding rectangular-shaped regions. By fitting enough appropriately sized rectangles, one can approximate any shape and cover any class. The effectiveness and efficiency with which learning systems can cover the data with rectangular-shaped regions will determine the performance of such systems (Weiss & Kulikowski, 1991).

As Thornton notes, unsupervised learning does not have to assume that the clusters it develops at each stage are meaningful in themselves, just that they are going to be useful in deriving a yet-more-accurate cluster at the next step. Thornton does not prove that this kind of "proto-representational learning" will do any better than supercharged fence-and-fill, much less than appropriately chosen pick-and-mix, but I agree that it does have a better *feel* to it that the former, and avoids the latter's need for expert priming.

Consequently, in a purely clustering or unsupervised approach the system would require some estimate of the dispersion of the dimensions defining each category before classification could be justified. A new object would then be classified as an *A* or *B* as a function of the average distance from the central tendency of each of the dimensions underlying category *A* and category *B*, and the dispersion of each of the dimensions around their central tendencies. In addition, knowledge of the dispersion of *A* and *B* can be used to decide whether a novel instance is so unlikely to belong to either known category that a new category concept should be formed to accommodate it.

Archaeologists have been doing clustering to achieve some kind of classification for years, instead of a real conceptual learning (Adams & Adams, 1991; Clarke, 1968; Dunnell, 1971; Doran & Hodson, 1975; Forsyth, 2000; Spaulding, 1953; Vierra, 1982). It is important to understand the difference between clustering and classification. A good classification should both impose structure and reveal the structure already present within the data. With the exception of data reduction tasks, classification techniques are generally favored in analysis since the user retains control over the classes imposed. The outcome from a clustering of a set of data may have little meaning since the resulting clusters are not associated (by design) with any concept arising from the domain of study (although they may be because of inherent structure in the data).

Nevertheless, the acquisition of explanatory knowledge cannot be reduced to clustering, because such methods are limited by the natural grouping of the input data, and they are based on restricting knowledge production to finding regularities in the input. Such regularities are not generalizable out of the specific limits of the input data used. In both cases, a description of the current observation is taken as input and represented by a model of perceptual feature dimensions. Categories and concepts are represented as one or more associated clusters. Initially, the system has only one cluster that is centered upon the first input pattern. As new observations are presented, the system attempts to assign these new items to an existing cluster. When a new item is assigned to a cluster, the cluster updates its internal representation to become the average of all items assigned to the cluster so far. Using supervised classification the system creates a new cluster in response to a surprising misclassification; whereas in an unsupervised clustering approach, a new cluster is created when the model encounters a surprisingly novel observation. Another important difference lies on the fact that supervised learning can be characterized as intentional, in that the automated archaeologist should actively search for rules (using, for instance, some variation of hypotheses testing), on the other hand, unsupervised learning is usually seen as incidental, undirected, observations driven, and incremental accrual of information. Humans seem more likely to aggregate observations in memory in an unsupervised way, whereas we are more likely to segregate observations and deal with exceptions using supervised learning mechanisms. Unsupervised learning is best matched with linear category structures because the optimal clustering solution for a linear category structure involves one cluster per category. On the other hand, nonlinear categories and concepts are not well matched to an unsupervised induction task because nonlinear category structures can only be captured with multiple clusters per category (Gureckis & Love, 2003; Love, 2002).

If, for example, all possible descriptive patterns are provided as well as a number of cases, where the concept C is not present, then learning will be relatively simple. This however, will only be possible if there is some kind of teacher, which prepares the training data on purpose. On the other hand, if some descriptive patterns are not provided in the training data, we cannot expect the learner to know about it. The solution seems to assume that the training examples are chosen randomly, according to the same but still unknown probability distribution according to which the objects are chosen for classification. That is, if there are some frequently occurring descriptive patterns that the learner needs to know about to avoid a large classification error, then the probability to have those patterns included in the training examples is also high. Furthermore, if a particular feature vector were very rare, so that it does not occur among the training examples, then the error, which may be caused by not knowing about it, would be very small. Overall, these probabilistic assumptions allow successful learning, at least if the concept space of the learning task is not too large.

If the automated archaeologist does not have such previous knowledge, that is to say, if it cannot distinguish positive and negative instances of the explanation to be learnt, the explanation cannot be possible. Consequently, we should assume that the starting point must always be the fact that knowledge needed to solve archaeological problems should not only be based on mere correlation or regularity. Archaeological training sets must be built using laboratory replicated tools to experiment the causal association between perceptual features and causal actions. Additionally, when the causal action is not replicable, we can rely on observing how the causal relationship varies in different social situations, known from ethnological and/or historical sources.

PREDICTING COMPLEX RELATIONSHIPS

Although a machine learning approach seems quite appropriate in the case of archaeological research, we should take into account that inductive techniques that rely "only on the input" are of limited utility and that an automated archaeologist must incorporate devices that compare the explanations generated using different mechanisms. The obvious difficulty is that an archaeological explanation cannot be analyzed in terms of simple associations. Explanation is an inference process whose very nature is beyond a mere mapping out of the statistical correlation present in the descriptive features of material traces. Rather they involve identifying and disentangling the *relationships* that exists in the data, utilizing available knowledge about the process that generated those effects.

Just aggregating over many observations is not enough to learn an appropriate explanation, because of the large input space and the ambiguities implicit in it. Consequently, inverse reasoning can be dangerous as a general explanatory mechanism because it leaps from a few experiences to general rules of explanation. If the experiences happen to be untypical, or the conditioning system misidentifies the relevant conditions, predicted behavior may be permanently warped. Even animals and humans are vulnerable to inappropriate learning. Human archaeologists can be victims of self-reinforcing phobias or obsessions, instilled by a few experiences.

To avoid these difficulties, the solution to inverse problems has to work in one of two quite different ways. As we have seen in preceding sections, it may exploit explicit commonalities between observed inputs or we have to look for implicit relationships between them. An alternative way to drawing the explicit/implicit distinction is thus to say that learning can be approached in a *relational* or in a *non relational* form, since in one case we have the exploitation of relational regularities in the data, while in the other we have the exploitation of non relational regularities (associations and similarity effects). Following this argument to its logical conclusion, we can identify two distinct styles of inverse reasoning:

- **Non-relational learning**: Learning oriented toward the exploitation of non-relational regularity (standard statistical classification). The subject learns about the properties of a single stimulus.
- **Relational learning:** Learning oriented toward exploitation of relational regularity (non standard classification). It is the most common type of learning in natural and artificial agents: A subject learns about the relationship between two stimuli, or between a stimulus and a response.

"Relation" is a difficult to define word. Within statistics, we say that two variables are related when they co-vary. That means that they do not share the same values, but when values in one variable are high, so are in the second variable (positive relationship), or alternatively, when values in one variable are high, they are low in the second variable (negative relation). This connection may be constant among all values (monotonic relation), or it may be different for different objects (non-monotonic relation). In general, we say that two objects are related when they are not similar, but there is something connecting them: the paper and the pencil are very dissimilar, but they are related when we use them to write a letter.

For instance, consider an arrow point and a human skeleton. These are objects with different shape, size, texture, and composition. Nevertheless, there is something *relating* them: they have appeared at the same location: in a burial, the arrow point was found inside one of the bones. Both elements are related because they constitute part of the same event, the death of this individual.

We can perceive many sorts of relations between effects of social actions. For example, let us imagine the automated archaeologist studies an "historical crisis:" the human abandonment of certain geographic area during some centuries. The intelligent robot needs to find out what process is responsible for that abandonment: why people left their villages and houses. The cognitive robot will study the cause from what it knows about its effects: the sites that have been abandoned during the period of reference, but were occupied in the immediately previous period. Let us suppose that the automated archaeologist has archaeological data about 25 sites. Five of them were not abandoned nor show any evidence of whatever "crisis." The other 20 archaeological sites neither behaved in the way it was expected and were left, that means, there are no artifacts nor built structures with a date in this period. In both kinds of sites, an archaeological record can be assigned to the period prior to the "crisis," that is to say, the period in which the social dynamics that will conclude in the abandonment of certain sites were already acting. The automated archaeologist will analyze then two events: the way in which the sites of period A (before abandonment) were occupied and the way in which sites of period B (during and/or after abandonment) were occupied or left. The purpose is not to create a classification or typology of archaeological settlements, but to use the differences between both events, with the intention of finding out how an event happened. The hypothesized cause is not a climatic change, but the internal dynamics of that society, characterized by cycles of concentration and dispersal of settlement as a reaction to the increase in social division of labor. The sequence of sites from period A to period B constitutes a process (p) that, in absence of interactions with other processes (for example, climatic change from

A to B), should remained uniform with respect to the characteristic Q (settlement). In presence of other processes (increasing division of labor between producers and non-producers) manifest a modification of Q (settlement) in Q' (non-settlement= abandonment) at the end of the A period (first event), and this modification is transmitted to the B period (second event). The historical trajectory experiments a change of state from the first to the second event in the temporal chain. The social action is causal in the sense in that it is able to transmit its own structure through time.

If the learning task is relational, we know that particular outputs are contingent on relationships described among the inputs, and that the resulting classification is probably not correlated to particular values of each input feature, and therefore should not cluster together in traditional similarity terms. If, on the other hand, the task is non-relational, some of the individual features describing the input are associated with particular outputs; thus, instances of the same concepts tend to share features and to cluster together. From this fact, we may conclude that non-relational learning tends to produce clustering and relational learning *tends* to eliminate it. The basic rule is that the more clustering the instances of an explanation exhibits, the more probable a non-relational learning task implies.

The number of potential relationships in a given scenario is generally unbounded, implying that the number of possible relational regularities is *infinite*. Given the fact that *everything may be related to everything*, this is, in principle, an infinitely hard operation (Thornton, 2000). Does it mean that relational learning is out of the automated archaeologist range? To identify and disentangling the non-explicit *relationships*, we should use available knowledge about the process that generated those effects, because they are not always apparent. If learning proceeds constructively on the identification of certain relationships, then those relationships presumably need to be explicitly identified. This conjures up an image of a machine that is going to using what it knows to learn what it does not yet know. It might use certain known relationships to attempt to exploit certain *unknown* relationships.

The machine learning community has made vast strides, progressing from the simple rule-based and plain inductive approaches to sophisticated concept formation approaches. Most modern research in machine learning is concerned developing theories that provide relational explanations of events and empirical laws. For example, the BACON program (Langley et al., 1987) takes as input a set of independent terms and request the corresponding values of related dependent terms. BACON contains elementary processes for the discovery of simple physical laws. These laws typically involve the establishment of a *predefined* relationship between two variables:

INCREASING: If the values of X increase as the values of Y increase, then define the ratio X/Y and examine its values

DECREASING: If the values of X increase as the values of Y decrease, then define the product XY and examine its values

CONSTANT: If the values of X are nearly constant for a number of values, then hypothesize that X always has this value.

The program constructs a simple factorial design experiment involving all combinations of independent values, and proceeds to collect the co-occurring independent and dependent values, once it knows how to differentiate between the independent and the dependent factors. As it finds laws at each level, the program places conditions on these laws corresponding to the values of the terms that it has not yet varied. As it incorporates these terms to higher-level laws, the conditions are generalized. Thus, BACON gradually expands the scope of its relational learning as it moves to higher levels of description.

Using these mechanisms, a program like BACON has rediscovered a wide range of laws from the history of physics and chemistry (Langley & Zytkow, 1989). The same approach would be applicable in archaeology for discovering similar regularities (Barceló, 1997).

BACON states all relational regularities as either simple constancies or linear functions between two variables. Some other programs go beyond this limitation, either by taking into account more complex functional definitions, or by including hidden or non-observational terms. The FAHRENHEIT system (Langley & Zytkow, 1989) follows the same basic strategy in BACON, but it defines two additional theoretical terms for each law discovered at the lower level. The system treats these terms as dependent variables at the next higher level and attempts to relate their values to those of the varied independent term. That is to say, FAHRENHEIT is able to consider relationships between linear relations.

Valdés-Pérez (1995, 1996a, 1996b, 1999) has programmed systems, which formulate mechanistic hypotheses conjecturing unseen entities. It uses constrained-generation algorithms for generating non-redundant hypotheses under a bias for simplicity (fewer steps and conjectured entities). He describes his system as carrying out a heuristic breath-first tree search with complicated node generators and node evaluators (Valdés-Pérez, 1995).

After such a pioneering work, some new developments were published successively by authors like Falkenheimer (1990), Karp (1990), Rajamoney (1990), Darden et al. 1992, Giza (2002), and Alai (2004). The idea was in all cases moving beyond trivial inductivism and advancing towards a true relational learning.

This modern work on rule discovery in scientific databases illustrates the power of computational methods to circumvent human limitations. Humans are not good at searching massive databases and manipulating sets of rules with many features to make predictions. Cognitive science research has shown that humans have a tendency to focus too rapidly on one hypothesis before doing a systematic search of a hypothesis space. Discovery programs that are more systematic and more thorough than humans are an aid to scientists.

SOME LIMITATIONS OF SUPERVISED LEARNING

Working with fuzzy and rough sets, instead of formally true logical propositions allows the reduction of the supervised learning exigencies.

The fact that explanations can be formulated as vague concepts is only part of the alternative to formal induction. Because any robot explanation is the cumulative product of an extensive event history, it cannot be understood solely by appeals to what is observable at a given moment. Actual observations directly guide explanations but the automated explanation is the result of the present state of the knowledge domain acting on the computer agent that should have been changed by an even-richer history of previous observations. That means that the robot perceived world should be known in terms directly related to the automatic archaeologist's current possibilities for future explanations.

In such circumstances, the pattern of feature values for each case cannot be easily associated with the correct prediction or decision. Furthermore, when archaeological problem solving operates in a *stationary* problem domain (i.e., knowledge whose characteristics do not change with time), the essential nature of the domain can, in theory, be *learned* through a training session with a set of data that is representative of the domain. Frequently, however, the domain of interest is *non-stationary*, which means that the parameters of the information-bearing signals vary with time. In situations of this kind, the traditional methods of supervised learning may prove to be inadequate because the system is not equipped with the necessary means to track the variations of knowledge it needs to build its

predictions. To overcome this shortcoming, it is desirable to relate learned knowledge to variations in training data. In other words, the learning process should never stop, with learning going on while explanation and predictions are being performed by the system.

While maintaining the rational basis of trial-and-error mechanisms characterizing supervised learning algorithms, we need a lightened version of the teacher. Scientific explanation has often be characterized as a process of error correction in which an internal hypothesis or control strategy is formulated and tested, errors are made, and the errors are used to improve the hypothesis. The notion of an error implies the notion of a goal, and it can be described as a *heuristic* process that is driven by errors. When the automated archaeologist learns, it changes the way information is processed by the problem solver. Thus, it is much easier to learn if the problem solver responds to these changes in a graded, proportional manner, instead of radically altering the way it behaves. These graded changes allows the system to try out various new ideas (ways of processing things), and to get some kind of graded, proportional indication of how these changes affect processing. By exploring many little changes, the problem solver can evaluate and strengthen those that improve performance, while abandoning those that do not. Learning is a kind of *heuristic reasoning,* because it depends on using a number of weak, graded signals as "traces" for exploring possibly useful directions to proceed further, and then building on those that look promising.

This alternative version of learning is often referred to as *reinforcement* learning because of its similarity to models used in psychological studies of behavior-learning in humans and animals (Alpaydin, 2004; Donahoe & Palmer, 1994; Kaelbling, 1993; Sutton & Barto, 1998). It is also referred to as "learning with a critic" (Figure 3.6). Instead of a well-organized database of positive and negative instances, the intelligent machine will need some external knowledge, also obtained in laboratory replication or controlled observation conditions converting a *primary reinforcement signal* received from the training data into a higher quality reinforcing knowledge element called the *reinforcement heuristic signal*. Such a system should be designed to learn under *delayed reinforcement*, which means that the automated archaeologist observes a sequence of observations acquired in describable circumstances, which eventually result in the generation of the heuristic reinforcement signal. The goal of learning is to minimize a *cost-to-go* function, defined as the expectation of the cumulative costs of actions taken over a sequence of steps instead of simply the immediate cost. It is motivated by an old psychological concept, the Law of Effect, which states: "applying a reward immediately after the occurrence of a response increases its probability of reoccurring, while providing punishment after the response will decrease the probability" (Sutton & Barto, 1998).

The procedure identifies within input data, properties enabling the prediction and interpretation of those data. When those properties are perceived and responses occur in their presence followed by some kind of reinforcing, cause-effect relations are selected. Some inputs become able to function as what Donahoe and Palmer (1994) call *reinforcers,* as they acquire the ability to evoke cause because of previous success in a prediction task. Reinforcers bring the behavior that precedes them under the control of the environments in which those behaviors took place. Consequently, the appropriate response occurs when the input contains features that have acquired the ability to guide the response. At an explanatory level, if such inputs are present, problem solving occurs. The cumulative effects of selection by reinforcement are effect-cause relationships whose effect components have been enriched by concurrently selected contexts of application. The legacy of

Figure 3.7. A flow diagram showing the mechanism of reinforcement learning

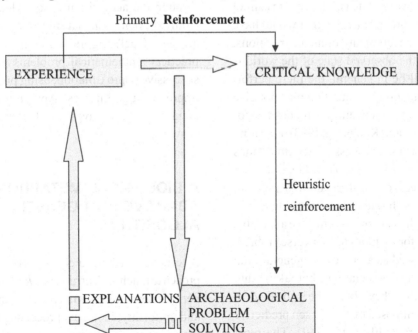

experience is the accumulation of an ever-larger repertoire of effect-cause relations. These relations are selected by reinforcers, which are themselves increasingly the product of previous selections.

Feedback provides information regarding the quality of the explanatory response. It may be as simple as a binary pass/fail or a more complex numeric evaluation. There is no specification as to what correct response is, only how well the particular response worked. The general idea is also related to so called *Hebbian* learning (Hebb, 1949). Co-active representations become more strongly linked, if a given bit of knowledge consistently participates in the firing of another bit of knowledge. Consequently, the connection between both should be in some way strengthened. In the same sense, positive exemplars receive some kind of reinforcement, whereas negative ones are inhibited.

This setting allows for effective function learning, but differs from a system trying to learn from direct supervision alone. The system, finding itself in a particular input situation, must learn a general prediction. It then receives a reinforcement value from what it already knows, indicating how valuable the current world state is. The system cannot deduce the reinforcement value that would have resulted from executing any of its other actions. In addition, if the observed state of the world is noisy, as it will be in general, the mere performance of explanation in a situation may not give an accurate picture of the reinforcement value for that epistemic action (Kaelbling, 1993). Learning does not appear as a process of accumulations of representations of the problem domain; it is a continuous process of transformations of problem solving behavior through continuous change in the capacity of the system to synthesize all. In this way, the search for solutions to an inverse problem can still be viewed as a process of generalizing observed empirical associations, but taking into consideration that they should be subjected to the constraints imposed by the chosen predictive model (Weiss & Kulikowski, 1991). The most

important feature of this definition is its claim that learning cannot be described in isolation. The learner always attempts to improve the behavior of some performance element, which is affected only indirectly through the knowledge base it uses to control its interactions with what it sees. That is to say, the problem solving procedure equals to the cumulative products of selection after a learner has been exposed to a series of mere differential contextual discriminations. Here the idea of "contextual discrimination" is a somewhat diminished version of the set of positive and negative instances. That is, the predicted cause-effect relation depends more on the context in which the guiding input appears than on the input itself (Donahoe & Palmer, 1994).

What the automated archaeologist is doing is making minor adjustments in the present state of its knowledge in order to be more attuned to its accumulated past experiences. Each of these adjustments is neither "true" nor important in itself, but after a series of such changes, a new knowledge emerges. In other words, scientific knowledge is created by improving explanatory performance in a well defined environment through the acquisition of knowledge resulting from experiences in that environment (Holland et al., 1986; Kaelbling, 1993; Langley, 1996). Many practical mathematical problems are solved by successive approximation, using procedures that improve rouge guesses. Applying such refinements repeatedly gives ever better *approximate* answers.

A BIOLOGICAL METAPHOR: ADAPTIVE AND GENETIC ALGORITHMS

A term very useful to characterize this new approach to machine learning is *adaptation*. It means here that learning does not proceed unidirectional and uniformly; instead it proceeds preferentially though steps that specific information indicates might be on the best path to what we want to learn. Learning provides the specific knowledge bits that serve to narrow prediction options and thus provide useful constraints on archaeological problem solving. In so doing, the process of formulating predictions from past experience adopts the form of explanation learning. Learning is then characterized in terms of the modification of responses to subsequent inputs as a function of prior activation history. This can be thought as a form of *self-regulation* (O'Reilly & Munakata, 2000).

Adaptive learning methods are iterative solution techniques that handle a population of individuals, which are evolving according to a given strategy. At each iteration, periods of self-adaptation (random changes) alternate with periods of translation (crossover), and periods of competition (selection). The adaptability of an individual solution to a specific problem represents its ability to survive in an uncertain environment.

Research on adaptive learning mechanisms has been inspired by an analogy with the theory of evolution, and the basic representation and operators reflect this history. They have contributed to so called "genetic algorithms," which imitate how hypothesis are generated, evolve, and compete until the best fitted wins and is selected as the best one to solve the problem at hand (Beer, 1990; Goldberg, 1989; Michalewicz, 1996; Mitchell, 1996; Nolfi & Floreano, 2001; Reynoso & Jezierski, 2002).

The fitness of each member of the population is computed using an evaluation function, called the fitness function measuring how well each individual performs with respect to the task. Its best members are rewarded according to their fitness, and poorly performing individuals are punished or deleted. Over generations, the population improves the quality of its set of solutions. Although such learning algorithms are not guaranteed to yield an optimal global solution, they generally produce high-quality solutions within reasonable amounts of time.

Genetic algorithms usually require specialized knowledge representations (encodings) to facilitate their operation. Knowledge is represented as strings of symbols that correspond loosely to chromosomes. For example, the instance: the archaeological remains of a prehistoric hut, characterized by the presence of two hearths, a great quantity of bovid bones, the presence of arrow points, and the absence of axes might be represented by the vector: 1, 1, 1, 0, with ones and zeros indicating the presence or absence of Boolean features. The encodings typically take the form of position-dependent bit strings in which each bit represents a gene in the string chromosome.

Let us imagine the automated archaeologist has access to a number of archaeological sites described by the presence of following features:

FLORE: 1. Pine, 2. Oak, 3. Birch, 4. Wheat
FAUNA: 1. Rabbit, 2. Sheep, 3. Cow, 4. Deer, 5. Gull 6. Duck
HEARTH: Amount of hearths identified at each site (in units)
TYPE: Presence/Absence of the following tool categories: 1. axe, 2. scraper, 3. arrow point, 4. crucible, 5. hammer
SITE: 1. In the plain, 2. on the top of a hill.
ECONOMIC ACTIVITY: Predominant economic activity: 1. hunting, 2. herding, 3. vegetable gathering, 2. tool manufacturing

The task is to learn the explanatory concept "economic activity," defined in terms of the observable features associated with a characteristic archaeological record of "hunting," "herding," and so forth. An automated archaeologist can solve this generalization problem in the direct crisp way of rule association. Using a genetic algorithm the goal is the same, but the procedure is a bit different.

The idea is to randomly generate and successively modify using mutations and crossovers different predictive rules, until a fitness criterion suggests that the hypothesis is effective enough and not any other genetic modification will make it more adapted to the problem at hand. Crossover involves exchanging information through the transfer of some part of their representation to another individual. This process creates new individuals that may or may not perform better than the parental individuals may. Crossing over individuals and exchanging bit string parts are usually chosen randomly. The net effect is an increase in the overall population. Mutation, a simple probabilistic flipping of bit values in the encoding, affects an individual only and does not increase the overall population size. This random effect provides the ability to escape local minima, a common problem associated with the gradient descent methods. Because the probability of mutation is generally very low and copies of the most fitted individuals result from reproduction, this randomness permits high quality solutions to emerge that would otherwise be unattainable. However, typical adaptive algorithms do not rely heavily on mutation, using it mainly as a backup to preserve some diversity in the population (Langley, 1996).

On each cycle, a genetic algorithm uses an evaluation function to measure the quality of the current description with respect to the training data, giving each competitor an associated score. The method then uses the crossover operator to generate successors for the initial hypothesis. In each case, it selects two descriptions as parents, drawing them at random from the hypothesis set with probability in direct proportion to their relative scores. For each pair of parents, the crossover operator selects a crossover point (or a set of attributes), generates two new descriptions, and adds them to its set of revised hypotheses. The algorithm then mutates each feature in each description with some (low) probability. The algorithm evaluates each of the resulting set of descriptions on the training data in turn, creates yet another set of children hypotheses, and so on, continuing the specified number of iterations.

The use of genetic operators results in varying population of hypotheses over time. Some generalizations have lower fitness than their parents do, but on average the entire population's overall fitness as well as that of the best hypotheses improves with successive generations. If properly designed, the learning system eventually settles on a set of highly fit, near optimal rules with similar bit strings.

The algorithm works in the following way:

FIRST STEP: random definition of predictive rules by randomly linking the decision attribute ("economic activity at the site") and the conditional attributes (flora, fauna, presence of hearths, and presence of tool type).

SECOND STEP. Evaluate random rules by calculating its efficiency (or predictive power).

THIRD STEP. If predictive power is not high enough (user configured threshold), the program should rank the rules according to its probability for firing

$$p = e / E \qquad (5)$$

where e is its rank, and E the sum of ranks for all other rules.

FOURTH STEP. Rules retained in memory cross between them generating new composite rules. A new "generation" of rules is then generated, taking into account the rank of each rule: highest ranked rules have more probabilities for taking part in a new combination. Crossover operator is extensively used, and low degrees of random mutation are also allowed.

Repeat third and fourth step until some rules can pass the user-configured threshold. Each repetition corresponds to a new generation formed by a weighted combination of all rules existing in memory at the former step.

By using this adaptive and heuristic approach, archaeological problem solving is most strongly guided by the particular inputs that were present when predictions succeed. These inputs include not only the nominal discriminative features, but also the contexts in whose presence the discriminative features occur. As prediction proceeds, those inputs that are less reliably present lose their ability to guide the response. The more reliable inputs increasingly block the ability of the less reliable inputs to guide explanation. To insure that the guidance of explanation is restricted to a given set of inputs, the response must be reinforced when a particular subset of stimuli is present, and not reinforced (or differently reinforced) when other stimuli are present.

Papaioannou et al. (2001) describes a semi-automatic system for the reconstruction of archaeological finds from their fragments using a genetic algorithm to estimate the correct relative position between fragments, clustering those fragments that belong to the same entity. After having generated all possible pairs of valid fragments combinations, each pair of combinable fragments is examined in order to determine the relative orientation that corresponds to a best fit, estimating the minimal matching error per facet pair. When all optimal pairwise (fragment facet by fragment facet) matching error values have been calculated and stored in a look-up table, the third stage (full reconstruction) selects those fragment combinations that minimize *a global reconstruction error*, which acts as a fitness function. This reconstruction error equals the sum of matching errors of a given set of fragment pairs. External constraints may contribute to this stage as well, in order to reduce the time needed to produce a correct fragment clustering by eliminating a large number of combinations.

Related applications, also using a genetic algorithm for calculating the best match in object shape reconstruction has been published by Kampel and Melero (2003), and Chaouki and Gaildrat (2005). Yao et al. (2001) have used genetic algorithms in geophysical surveying for improving the location of underground tombs using ground penetrating radar method to survey Chinese Yin Mountain ancient sites. Assuming that the original shape of an ancient building in this region was mostly similar to a hyperbolic curve, a genetic algorithm implements optimal curve fit, and the fitness criterion was established as least squared error method.

Michael L. Gargano has used genetic algorithms to build taxonomies and for solving seriation problems (Gargano & Edelson, 1996; Gargano & Lurie, 2006). The problem of trying to chronologically order graves in a cemetery where each grave contains (or does not contain) a number of different stylistic artifacts (e.g., pottery, jewelry, etc.) of a period has traditionally been called the Petrie Seriation problem. The authors propose an order based hybrid evolutionary modified life cycle model to solve this problem. The problem can be modeled mathematically by an incidence matrix whose rows are the graves and whose columns are a particular artifact type. A chronological ordering of the graves is established by finding a permutation of the rows of the incidence matrix, which minimizes the total temporal range of an artifact type summed over all types of artifacts (i.e., columns). The temporal range of an artifact type is the span from the first appearance to the last appearance of a 1 in the column of the incidence matrix corresponding to that artifact type. This search problem is characterized by a solution space which is generally unstructured (e.g., multimodal) and is intractable for a large number of graves. The solution offered by Gargano and colleagues suggest creating and evolving a population of potential solutions (i.e., sequences of row permutations of the incidence matrix) so as to facilitate the creation of new members by swarming, mating and mutating, or local search. Fitness (or worth) is naturally scored by the Petrie range index of the permuted incidence matrix. In each column j the first row r_f and last row r_l containing a 1 are noted. The Petrie index for that column is $r_l - r_f + 1$. The Petrie range index for the matrix is the sum of these over all columns. This will be the fitness of a permutation (i.e., a possible solution). The smaller the Petrie range index, the better the fitness is (i.e., the better the solution). This method is a hybrid combining swarm methods, genetic algorithms, and local search. An individual population member passes through three phases that are iterated until a satisfactory solution is obtained. As in many processes in nature, each individual member goes through different life cycle paradigms as it evolves. In this adaptive search heuristic, a member goes from a swarm search to a genetic search to a local search and back again reiteratively.

Genetic algorithms have also been used to discovery the underlying spatial trend among a series of locations. The method allows detecting relevant clusters in spatial coordinates (Conley et al., 2005).

Since 1979, Robert G. Reynolds has been applying genetic algorithms to a more social based research (Reynolds, 1979, 1986). The idea was to investigate motivations of economic and social change in the evolution from a hunter-gatherer to agriculture society. In these early applications, Reynolds used a theoretical background from Kent Flannery's theory about the origins of agriculture. It simulates a hunter-gatherer group from the Oaxaca Valley (Mexico). In this area, certain resources were more abundant and easier to manage in specific seasons. The human group should adapt his economic strategy to the annual cycle of natural resources. The adoption of agricultural methods for producing subsistence produces conflicts in the management and planning of other activities, which depend also on the annual cycle. Agriculture needs some labor resources, which traditional were invested in other activities that should be performed at the same period of the annual cycle. In this way, agriculture prevents working in other activities, which are also basic for human survival. Reynolds programmed a computer system that calculated the way in which members of this group would organize their economic activities looking for a balance between agricultural labor investment and investment of labor in other activities. If the model were right, then material predictions made by the program would be like archaeological field observations: the quantities of food remains identified at the archaeological site should be similar to predictions of food consumed made by the program.

The program simulated a group with five or six human agents (according to archaeological estimations at the Guilá Naquitz site), which have access to 10 alternative different economic strategies, or subsistence activities, during a period of four months. It is assumed a dedication of 10 days for each one. Therefore, the group should repeat some of them during the simulated period. The more it applies a determined strategy, the more the activity will influence the predicted contents of the generated archaeological record. Each time a group member performs one of these activities, she/he acquires some quantity of food. An estimation of the quantities of proteins and calories generated by all activities can be used to estimate the degree and quality of subsistence. Another important parameter was the amount of work necessary for obtaining this food. The program uses an estimation of proteins and calories per area unit where the human group is looking for resources. The program also requires information about the degree of "concurrence" between different activities. That is to say, it should know what strategies are available simultaneously, given the environment circumstances in this very moment. Given all those parameters, the aim of the simulation is to estimate and to measure the importance order and contributions of the different activities.

A genetic algorithm randomly assigns a rank order and an intensity value to each of the 10 activities. Using as constraints some knowledge about the group and the environment, this rank order and intensity value will be gradually modified, until arriving to equilibrium;

1. A population of ordered sequence of activities is generated.
2. The efficiency of the sequence is calculated, reconstructing the decision process that would have allowed its adoption in the circumstance at hand.
3. The extracted decision rule is used to generate new economic decisions.
4. Such decisions imply a new modification of the initial sequence of activities.

This way of using genetic algorithms for social simulation evolved in its turn into fully "cultural algorithms," which is the name used by Reynolds in his last publications (Lazar and Reynolds, 2005; Reynolds, 1999; Reynolds & Chung, 1997; Reynolds & Peng, 2005; Reynolds & Saleem, 2005).

LEARNING IN UNCERTAIN CONTEXTS

Although it has been argued that inverse engineering methods provides knowledge allowing the solution of archaeological problems, we have to take into account that such a solution can never be certain because we cannot know the past with certainty. Absolute truth is not to be found in any empirical science, most especially in historical science. What distinguishes the historical sciences from purely laboratory sciences is their inability to know with near certainty the sequence of events that led to the complexity we see today in the present. Although uncertainty has long been recognized as being important in archaeology, it is still a problematic issue. It is not always clear what the term means, how it should be discussed, used, and measured, what its implications are. In general, the assumption seems to be that our knowledge or dataset on the phenomena under discussion is in some way imperfect.

Learning in an archaeological context is fast always uncertain because some indeterminacy may appear between actions of human activity and the visual and structural properties of the material consequences of such an activity. In particular, uncertainty about the initial conditions on which the basic process act limits the completeness of our understanding. With only a partial knowledge of the past, historical science provides a plausible account of the present, but the observed present may not be the only outcome of hypothesized events and processes. Good historical science is *sufficient* to account for the present, but the present is not a necessary consequence of what we know about the past.

Sometimes a social action happens, but the expected material consequence does not take place as expected. Other times, the entity we study does not seem to have experienced any perceptible change allowing the automated archaeologist to know if some social action or sequence of social actions had any causal influence. Even more:

- Diverse actions can determine the existence similar material effects.
- The same action not always will determine the same material effects.

There is always room for individual variation within collective action, and we should be aware that human work depends on the concrete circumstances in which it takes place, that is to say, of the social actions that simultaneously are being performed. For instance, social agents who elaborate pottery to contain liquids, not always will produce vessels with the same shape, size, composition, and texture, neither they should not use these containers in the same place nor waste them in the same way. Furthermore, the consequences of single action may have been altered by the consequences of successive actions, in such a way that effects may *seem* unrelated to causes.

The challenge is to derive a consistent mapping from a potentially infinite set of social actions trough time to a relatively small number of observable outcomes in the present. As a result, causal explanations generated by the automated archaeologist are necessarily as ambiguous as the stimulus (description/measurement of archaeologically observable features) they presumably encode. It is therefore difficult to understand how the information acquired by an intelligent machine could generate a problem solving procedure. This trouble is because the spatiotemporal pattern of empirical features the robot sensors capture does not sufficiently constrain a possible causal interpretation of them. It is difficult to decide among the large number of possible explanations that could fit the variation of input data equally well. Put another way, it is difficult to know what the real underlying causes of the automatic archaeologist perceptions are, and what are mere coincidences or appearances (i.e., noise). The problem is that an infinite number of possible visual features can correspond to a particular material effect of a social action, and even this material outcome can be related in many different ways with many causing social actions. There are millions of reasons why a knife is so long, why this wall is made of adobe and not of stones, why this decorative element was painted in red, etc.

As a result, any mechanism of perceptual recognition is unlikely to be successful, simply because the output in response to a given stimulus can signify any of an infinite combination of features in the real world. It is thus impossible to derive by a process of logic the combination of these factors that actually generated the stimulus.

Archaeological problem solving is even more difficult because what the robot has archaeologically perceived is not a "photograph" of the material effects of social action. There is not any direct, mechanic or necessary connection between cause and effect, that is, between the observation of physical properties and human work responsible of those characteristics. Even worst, the automated archaeologist does not have direct evidence for social actions performed in the past, so it is really a problem how to predict a social action given the presence of its effect. Consequently, regardless of how much evidence is present, the archaeologist, be a human or a machine, cannot read social causes directly from what has been preserved of the material consequences of causes that took place in the past. Determining whether the various frequencies of items in an assemblage or deposit have resulted from differential distribution, differential preservation, or both is the problem. The actual combination of processes that could have given rise to specific physical properties of the archaeological record is nearly infinite, and so one cannot expect to find many simple correspondences between lists of observables and the characteristics of their formation processes. One can hardly argue that uniformitarian principles may be formulated concerning the social scope of human communities, given the profoundly varied nature of social action. In fact, even recent methodological advances provide little or no basis for connecting such inferences to other than non-human process or differential representation and damage morphology. Current middle-range research has only produced simple inferences about the supposed universality human behavior. There are many actions and processes; both social and natural having acted during and after a primary cause, and also primary causes act with different intensities and in different contexts, in such a way that the effects may *seem* unrelated to their causes.

An additional difficulty in inverse engineering concerns the amount of noise in the training data. Increased amounts of noise tend to make learning more difficult overall. In some cases, the presence of noise is the result of the number of irrelevant features or attributes. If the concept to be acquired contains many such features, the learning system can have difficulty distinguishing them from the relevant features that it should use in making predictions. In other cases, noise arises because the learner has access to incorrect feedback. In any case, the perceptual abilities of any human or machine will always be insufficient to characterize completely the state of the external environment (Kaelbling, 1993).

A related issue involves the consistency of the knowledge domain over time. In some cases, a learned concept may suddenly cease to be valid, though it may retain partial overlap with the new situation. Such cases of concept drift can be difficult to distinguish from noise.

Both vagueness and ambiguity present major problems for machine learning. Up to the point that supervised learning approach to solving inverse problems may be too heavy in many circumstances. An algorithmic answer to the inverse problem seems to imply the necessity of formal logics, and this can be misleading in most social science situations, because of the complexity of the input-output relationship to be learnt. For example, vastly different social actions may have produced the same material consequences, at least within the accuracy limit of our observations. Furthermore, the circumstances and contexts (social and natural) where actions were performed and the processes (both social and natural) having acted on that place after the original cause, may have altered the original effects of primary actions. Therefore, a hallmark of most inverse problems is that, if nontrivial and soluble at all, they have multiple solutions. That means that they are affected by the non-uniqueness that may arise. Non-uniqueness means that the true input-output mapping cannot be selected from among a large set of possible mappings without further constraints imposed. While a forward problem has a unique solution, the inverse problem may have many solutions or no solution at all. In fact, the solution of an inverse problem is not a model but a collection of models that are consistent with both the data and the a priori information.

The fact that we cannot *predict* the precise material outcome of a single causal action, does not mean that an archaeological feature cannot be analyzed as caused by a series of social actions and altered by other series (or the same). Although we do not know what single actions

have produced precise material consequences, we can relate the variability of observable features (shape, size, content, composition, and texture) with the variability of social actions through time and space. Consequently, we should infer the variability of social action from the variability of the archaeological record, and we must infer social organization from the variability of inferred social actions.

What we need are inverse reasoning methods that allow an automated archaeologist to predict a cause even when it is not tied universally and directly with its effect. Rather than assuming that data are generated by a single underlying event, it should be assumed that the environment could be modeled as a collection of idiosyncratic "processes," where a process is characterized by a particular probabilistic rule that maps input vectors to output vectors (Jordan & Jacobs, 1992). In other words, the automated archaeologist should be able to generate abstractions that may not exist explicitly in the sensor input, but which capture the salient, invariant visual properties of a generic causal model used as a solution to the perceptual problem. Therefore, what we need is a heuristic classification machine (Clancey, 1984), a classifier which has the smallest probability of making a mistake.

Up to now, we have used standard logics for answering the inductive problem. The prediction that a material effect has been generated by a social action has been presented as a formal proof for the expression:

"percept *a* is member of category *A*"

That means that standard machine learning methods use the mechanism called logical implication. Suppose we have five attributes to determine explanation *A*. The logical implication needed is:

IF   object i has attribute 1
AND   attribute 2

AND   attribute 3
AND   attribute 4
AND   attribute 5
THEN
> object i is an instance of category A.

Let us call this rule "prediction *P*." Archaeological descriptions (attributes) are elements of *P* because they are used in the prediction. A predictive element, such as *attribute 5* may have any number of instances. However, an element must have only one instance in each prediction. Suppose now that given an incomplete observation of the true causal-effect relationship only two attributes have been measured, instead of 5. Following formal *modus ponens* the previously induced rule cannot be fired and object *i* cannot be assigned to category *A*. If we consider items one through five to be of equal importance, and we have to delete attribute 3 to 5 (because only attributes 1 and 2 are present in the observation), the explanation will be impossible because we the automated archaeologist has not enough descriptive information.

This problem can be defined as the *brittleness problem*, that is, the inability of machine learning programs to give a "partial answer" in a graceful way (Sypniewski, 1994). The cause of brittleness in automated explanation is the use of an inadequate assumption about data. If we assume all necessary truths to express the idea of logical necessity are equally important to a proof, we are saying, in effect, that unless we can demonstrate all necessary truths we cannot prove what we are trying to prove. This is the problem of brittleness.

To solve the problem we can consider that *any* element of *P* can be used in the prediction. We do not need that all attributes be present, but the *necessary* elements for predicting the explanation given the observation. No reason exists why we cannot use the accidental elements of *P*, but they cannot substitute for one or more missing necessary attributes. This scenario provides a first glimpse into the definition of *relevance*.

Some elements of *P*, while legitimate members of the prediction do not contribute to it (they are missing in the observed data set). If we remove all members of *P* that are accidents or are unnecessary for predicting, we are left with P^l, which is composed of the necessary elements of *P*; all of them contribute to the prediction. The theory of relevance says that not all members of P^l necessarily contribute to the predictive mechanism in the same way or to the same extent. The extent of that contribution is proved by the importance weight of every attribute or element (E_i). Any E_i that has a larger importance weight than an E_j is more important to a particular *P* than E_j. A predictive element that is irrelevant has an importance weight of 0.0; the same value has an attribute with missing value.

It is important to realize that no item of data has an intrinsic importance weight. All weights are relative to some *P*. Also, note that a particular situation may provide elements whose combined importance weights exceed 1.0. In those cases more data are available than is strictly necessary for a prediction.

The degree to which an attribute contributes to predict an explanation should be determined empirically. When we replicate in the laboratory (experimentation) or we control a series of observations (ethno-historical sources) the training data we need for learning the causal explanations, we will gather information about the elements of a prediction. If we introduce this material into a matrix, we see that some bits of information fill one cell of the matrix and some bits fill more than one cell. The number of cells filled with a particular piece of data or knowledge is a rough gauge of the importance of that particular piece of data or knowledge. As a rule, the more often a particular piece of data or knowledge appears in our hypothetical grid or matrix, the less important it is. We can say that if two predictions differ only by one item of data or knowledge, then this piece of knowledge is the most important item for that prediction. Consequently, a strong importance weight is equivalent to a branch point in a decision tree.

Accordingly, the solution of archaeological inverse problems should be approached within a probabilistic framework (Kaipio & Somersalo, 2004; Tarantola, 2005). At one level, the major task of the system may be described as reducing uncertainty about the knowledge domain. In order to accomplish this, the system must learn about the variability characteristic of various properties and relationships, gaining knowledge of what falls inside the range of permissible variation for a category and what falls outside, in the region of the unclassifiable or intrinsically uncertain. In this way, our computational system will be able to learn partially predictive rules even if some irreducible amount of error variance cannot be accounted for.

Statistical inversion theory reformulates inverse problems as problems of statistical inference by means of Bayesian statistics. In Bayesian statistics, all quantities are modeled as random variables. The randomness, which reflects the observer's uncertainty concerning their values, is coded in the probability distributions of the quantities. From the perspective of statistical inversion theory, the solution to an inverse problem is not a single estimate but a probability distribution of the quantity of interest, which can be used to produce estimates when all information available has been incorporated in the model. In other words, learning the mapping

$$m : A \rightarrow B$$

amounts to learning the probability distribution $P(a,b)$ of the observation/explanation pairs. There are at least two different ways of doing this. One is to let the system model the average mapping from observations to explanations and then apply some distribution with this function as its mean value. The parameters of the distribution may vary with the stimuli so that the system can be more or less certain of whether the mean value is appropriate.

Another approach is to let the system estimate the distribution of the observation/explanation pairs in an analytic form. In this way, since $P(a \mid b) = P(a,b) / P(b)$, the conditional distribution (a posteriori density) can be calculated once some entity has been observed.

The basic and most general idea is quite simple (Tarantola, 2005): we should start with a probability distribution representing the a priori information, and the use of observations will narrow this distribution. The automated archaeologist begins by defining some probabilistic rules that randomly generate models of the system under study. These probabilistic rules should encapsulate all available a priori information on the system: the more a model is (a priori) likely, the more frequently it should appear in the random sample. Any possible model should eventually appear, but very unlikely models should appear very infrequently. Here, a priori information means information that is independent of the data used to modify this a priori information. The intelligent machine should use these probabilistic rules to generate many models. An explanatory theory should be introduced that, given a particular model of the system, is able to predict the result of some observations. Once all this knowledge is available, the problem solver runs a prediction for all the models of the (a priori) sample. For each of the models, this prediction of the observations is compared with the actual observations, and a sensible criterion is applied to decide which models of the a priori sample can be kept (because they fit the data) or must be discarded (because they are unfit). The few models that have been kept represent the most general solution of the inverse problem.

This solution is too abstract to be of interest to solve practical problems. Therefore, we will study alternative ways to deal with uncertainty in training data and explanatory concepts through fuzzy numbers and rough sets.

Fuzzy logic deals with uncertainty. It holds that all things are matters of degree. It measures the degree to which an event occurs, not whether it occurs. Mathematically fuzziness means multi-valuedness or multi-valence and stems from the Heisenberg position-momentum uncertainty principle in quantum mechanics. Multi-valued fuzziness corresponds to degrees of indeterminacy or ambiguity, partial occurrence of events or relations. In 1965, Lofti Zadeh introduced the concept of *fuzzy set*, as a way to represent the logical nature of categories (Zadeh, 1965; Zadeh et al., 1996). Fuzzy sets are constituted by elements; however, those elements are not crisp instances of the categories, but elements that belong only *to a certain degree*. The essence of fuzzy logic is then the notion of fuzzy membership as a continuous value measuring the degree to which element *x* belongs to set *A* (Bezdek & Pal, 1992; Cox, 1993; Dubois et al., 1994; Kosko, 1992, 1993; Ragin, 2000; Smithson, 1988; Tanaka, 2004).

Degrees of truth are often confused with the conditional probabilities of the causal statement of the form $P(Y|X)$, where Y is the cause we would like to condition on X, which is the set of effects we have observed in experimental or ethno-historical circumstances. However, they are conceptually distinct. Fuzzy truth represents membership in vaguely defined sets, not likelihood of some event or condition. To illustrate the difference, consider this scenario: an archaeological artifact has been found in the remains of a house with two adjacent activity areas: room *A* and an open court. The artifact should be either "in room A" or "not in room A." What does happen if the artifact has been found in an imprecise area between room A and the open court? It may be considered "partially in room A," and also "partially in the courtyard." Quantifying this partial state yields a fuzzy set membership. With only a part of it in the court, we might say the artifact is 99 percent "in room A" and 1 percent "in the court," for instance. No prediction will resolve the artifact to being completely "in room A" or "not in room A," as long as it has been found somewhere in between. Fuzzy sets are based on vague definitions of sets, not randomness.

Fuzzy logic permits ambiguous instances to be included in a fuzzy set through a membership value. The degree of membership is given by the membership function, which has a value between 0 and 1. The interpretation is that 0 means no membership (or that the instance is certainly not in the set) and 1 notes complete membership (or that the instance is certainly in the set). A value in between denotes a partial or uncertain membership. Fuzzy logic thus overcome a major weakness of crisp sets: they do not have an arbitrarily established boundary separating members from non-members. I do not think that archaeological predictive explanations have to be intrinsically *fuzzy*, but predictions will only be computed if explanations are described in a fuzzy way. If we do not know how an instance relates with its concept, the relationship is not fuzzy or any other kind. We should know something about the nature of the relationship, before saying that it is crisp or fuzzy. Fuzziness is just one kind of relationship, with a so complex function, full of local values, that it cannot be expressed in any other way.

Let us imagine that *P*, a proof for a predictive assignment, is a set. Then $P = \{attribute\ 1, attribute\ 2, attribute\ 3, attribute\ 4, attribute\ 5\}$, where each attribute or descriptive feature are the elements of proof needed to prove *P* (for example, to prove this artifact is a knife and was used during late Paleolithic times). We can assume that "Paleolithic knives" (*P*) is a fuzzy set, and consequently, each element has a membership value. Given the fact that *P* is fuzzy, the membership value for each element is a continuous number between 0 and 1, meaning the importance weight of that attribute in the logical implication described by *P*. In this case, fuzziness is only a general methodology to compute the sum of partial implications.

We can translate logical implications (proof of predictive assignments) using fuzzy rules, where the output of the rules is a fuzzy set, whose members are the elements of the prediction. Each element, as a member of a fuzzy set, has a fuzzy membership value or importance weight. For instance,

IF   object i's VASE PROFILE is concave (0.875)
       object i's VASE RIM has shape B (0.358)
       object i's VASE MAXIMUM DIAMETER is on top of the pot   (0.47)
THEN
       object i was produced by ACTION A

The values in the rule's antecedent are *fuzzy*, because they belong to a fuzzy set. These values are not the confidence we have in that information, but the importance this prediction has in explanation *A*'s logical implication. To evaluate these rules, a fuzzy logic algorithm computes the degree to which each rule's situation applies. The rule is active to the degree that the IF part is true; this in turn determines the degree to which each THEN part applies. Since multiple rules can be active simultaneously, all of the active rules are combined to create the result. At each cycle, the full set of logical implications is scanned to see which fires. A rule or logical implication will fire when its condition made up of a (fuzzy) logical combination of its antecedents, results in a non-zero value. Each rule therefore samples its inputs and calculates the truth value of its condition from the individual importance weight of each input. In these way, the fuzzy membership function of each element acts as a kind of restriction or constraint on the classification process.

Translating crisp-set membership values (only zero or one) to fuzzy-set membership values (anything from zero to one), we can transform necessary conditions for firing a rule into mere sufficient conditions. Fuzzy systems directly encode structured knowledge in a numerical framework, where each rule stands for an input-output transformation, where inputs are the antecedent of fuzzy rules, and outputs are their consequent. In our case, inputs are the descriptive features we can measure on fragments of broken artifacts, and outputs are an assignation of the fragment to an artifact or class of artifacts. Most fuzzy systems represent inputs and outputs as membership functions whose interactions are the bases for rules. The fuzzy input and desired output ranges are based on fuzzy set values and they are used to create a matrix called *fuzzy associative memory*. When actual input values enter the system, the entire memory fires at once, producing multiple outputs. Each input's membership in the fuzzy input sets must be calculated -this is called the truth value or importance weight-. The information from all inputs is then applied to the rule base, which results, for each system output, in several fuzzy outputs. Since system inputs have multiple fuzzy values and each can be involved in the triggering of multiple rules, since each rule can have several fuzzy input values for its antecedents and each rule also can produce several outputs, and since each output itself has multiple fuzzy values, this process become quite complex.

Fuzzy logic is an organized and mathematical method of handling inherently imprecise concepts. Fuzzy logic and probability refer to different kinds of uncertainty. Fuzzy logic is specifically designed to deal with imprecision of facts (fuzzy logic statements), while probability deals with chances of that happening (but still considering the result to be precise). However, this is a point of controversy. Many statisticians are persuaded that only one kind of mathematical uncertainty is needed and thus fuzzy logic is unnecessary. On the other hand, Bart Kosko (1993) argues that probability is a subtheory of fuzzy logic, as probability only handles one kind of uncertainty. He also claims to have proven a derivation of Bayes' theorem from the concept of fuzzy subsethood.

An alternative to fuzzy logic is rough sets theory, based on a mathematical concept given by Pawlak (1991) (see also Ziarko, 1994). The primary notion of the theory of rough sets is the idea of approximation space: a partition of the domain of interest into disjoint categories. The partition formally represents our knowledge about the domain, for example, in terms of features of objects belonging to the domain. Assume the intention is to discover rules predicting the ancient use of a tool, depending on attributes describing its shape, size, and texture. The attribute *"use"* is selected as a decision attribute (or dependent attribute). The rest of the attributes, *"circularity," "irregularity," "volume," "coarseness," "decoration," etc.* are then the condition attributes (independent attributes). The building of an approximation space implies forming equivalence classes among those traces. They are groups of objects in which the condition attribute values are the same.

An *indiscernibility relation* exists between two objects when all their attribute values are identical with respect to the attributes under consideration, and thus cannot be discerned (distinguished) between by regards of the considered attributes. The discernibility function $f(B)$ computes the minimal sets of attributes required to discern any equivalence class from all the others. Similarly, the relative discernibility function $f(E,B)$ computes the minimal sets of attributes required to discern a given class E from the others. We can then build a *discernibility matrix*. This is a chart where equivalence classes appear on each axis and the values in the chart represent the attributes that distinguish each class from each other.

Classes are considered *vague classes* if there is more than one value for the decision attribute. The lower approximation of X is the collection of objects classified with full certainty as members of the set X. The upper approximation of X is the collection of objects that may possibly be classified as members of the set X. The boundary region comprises the objects that cannot be classified with certainty to be neither inside X, nor outside X. Any subset defined through its lower and upper approximations is called a *rough set*. The rough membership function (RMS) expresses how strongly an element x belongs to the rough set X in view of information about the element expressed by the set of attributes B.

However, not all of the attributes may be necessary to form the equivalence classes. One problem is whether some of the attributes in a decision system are redundant with respect to the object classifications. If an attribute set preserves the indiscernibility relation, then the attributes that form the set are said to be dispensable. All minimal subsets, in terms of size, of attributes that preserve the relation are called *reducts*, and we can define the full set of *reducts* in terms of the discernibility matrix.

Besides the full *reducts* defined above, we can define *reducts* that are relative to a particular object. We call these *object-related reducts*. If indiscernibility is relative to an object x, two other objects y and z are considered to be indiscernible in comparison with x. Reducts that are related to a particular object x are called *x-relative reducts*, since they contain the minimum information needed to select that particular object from other objects in the original training data set. What this implies is that a *relative reduct* contains enough information to discern objects in one class from all the other classes in the information system.

Learning with rough set methodology implies the computation of the full set of reducts, chosing the set of minimal ones, and pruning the data table vertically. Then the *object related reducts* are computed and the exhaustive decision rule system is generated. The goal of the rough sets learning method is to be able to find important dependencies in the data set, even when there is a degree of inconsistency and vagueness in it. Rules represent dependencies in the dataset, which can be used to classify new objects not in the original information system. To transform a *reduct* (relative or not) into a rule, one only has to bind the condition attribute values of the object class from which the *reduct* originated to the corresponding attributes. Then, to complete the rule, a decision part comprising the resulting part of the rule is added. This is done in the same way as for the condition attributes.

It must be emphasized that the concept of rough set should not be confused with the idea of fuzzy set, as they are fundamentally different, although in some sense complementary, notions. The idea behind rough sets is to approximate a set of interest in terms of other sets. Fuzzy sets are good approaches for problems with multiple membership grade requirements, where judgment on set membership grades is possible, and where the ability to deal with vague predicates is required. They are very good for real-valued data. On the other hand, rough sets with the three-valued simplicity, lower, upper, and boundary approximation sets, work well on discrete and categorical data. Rough sets can be useful even with missing data, changes of scale, and problems where membership grades are hard to define, and problems requiring changes in the partition.

Both fuzzy and rough sets approaches have been used in archaeological research. Lazar and Reynolds (2002) have applied rough sets to the study of ancient societies of Highland Meso-america, Valley of Oaxaca. The authors employed rough set concepts in order to represent the domain knowledge. The hypotheses are represented as sets of decision rules and the extracted rules are represented in terms of rough sets.

The goal was to predict the occupation of a terrace in the Monte Albán archaeological site for each archaeological period in order to answer the questions. The analyzed database contains over 2,000 residential sites at the Monte Albán urban center. Each site is comprised of one or more components occupied in one or more archaeological phases, spanning a period from approximately 9000 B.C. to 1500 A.D. Thus, the total spatial and temporal scope is so vast as to make manual interpretation a difficult if not impossible task. In addition, each temporal and spatial instance of a site component can be described in terms of several hundred variables of different types.

The problem to solve here is to discern the differences between the sites occupied in early I and late I periods in terms of the location and cultural attributes. The experts provided a list with the diagnostic pottery types for these two periods. Predominant type from Early I period, from 500 B.C. to 300 B.C., is named Ia, and ceramic types from Late I period, from 300 B.C. to 200 B.C., combines Ib and Ic since a clear distinction between Ib and Ic cannot be made with the available data. Two binary variables were constructed for Early I and Late I for each site. A zero means that the site was not present in the respective period, and 1 means present. Since there are not any sites present in Early I period and absent in Late I period, the authors recoded the two variables in the following way:

0   means the site is present in both early I and late I,

1   means the site is present in late I, but not in early I,

2   means the site is present neither in early I nor in late I, and

3   was designated for site present in early I and not in late I.

This configures the decision attribute. Only the sites with values 0 and 1 for the decision attribute were selected for further processing. Out of the 92 attributes, only 74 were selected because some of them were not significant for the concrete problem. For this experiment, 875 sites were processed, 306 sites with a 0 value, and 569 with a 1 value for the decision attribute.

The *reducts* gives an idea about the most important variables, related to the decision the researchers want to make. They are related primarily with location; that is, east square number and area designation, with elevation, vegetation, structures presents in the site and tools. The authors picked the 20 attributes in the smallest *reduct*, and using the *object-related reducts*, they generated an exhaustive set of decision rules. It contained 16,574 rules. The rules were divided in two subsets, one for decision attribute value 0, and one for the decision attribute 1. After that, they performed a quality-looping filter and kept approximately 20 rules for each class. Some of the rules are shown below:

IF   east square No.10, AND damage due to erosion and plowing (none), AND plaster floor or floors visible on the surface (present), AND pottery density (sparse to light),
THEN the site is present in both early I and late I.

IF   "barranca" or wash adjacent (absent), AND special resources (none), AND presence of well-defined structure or structures less than 1 meter (present), AND plaster floor or floors visible on the surface (present),
THEN the site is present in both early I and late I.

IF   east square No.10, AND area designation (2), AND damage due to erosion and plowing (none), AND plaster floor or floors visible on the surface (present),
THEN the site is present in both early I and late I.

IF   elevation of the terrace in meters above the valley floor, is up to 375, AND "barranca" or wash adjacent (absent), AND vegetation (grass and brush), AND prevailing wall orientations (none), AND number of whole or fragmentary "manos" (1),
THEN the site is present in both early I and late I.

There are not many other applications of this uncertainty tool in archaeology. Of related interest can be the prediction of soil characteristics based on chemical, biological and mineralogical composition (Ding et al., 2006).

Fuzzy sets have more applications in archaeology, probably because it is a more general approach than rough sets. The idea is that of learning instead of general rules, fuzzy definitions for archaeological classes of artifacts (Borodkin & Garskova, 1995; Canal & Cavazzoni, 1990; Pop et al., 1995).

Barceló (1996) has used fuzzy functions to predict the shape of phoenician pottery vases from the observation of broken sherds. Determining shape from part of a vessel is limited by the fact that potters made vessels for different purposes starting with a few basic shapes. Since potters worked by combining standard elements—base, bodies, rims, handles and so on—it has not always been possible to infer the complete shape from the fragments present in a deposit, because rims and bases of similar size and shape might actually have come from vessels of differing size and shape. If one is trying to study pottery shapes using only fragmented material, then the definite absence of certain features may become as important a point to record as their presence. The usual assumption that all attributes have equal relevance is wrong in that case. The solution was to consider that the explanation (the shape of the whole pot) is a fuzzy set, and building predictive rules in terms of fuzzy sets.

Another application of fuzzy methods to build typologies has been published by Hermon and Nicolucci (2002, 2003). The idea is to study archaeological artifacts as object classes with no exactly defined boundaries between them. For example, the descriptive variable "angle of retouch," extensively used in definitions of flint tool types, may have several potential values, like "abrupt," "semi-abrupt" or "low," which not always correspond to exact angles, or, even if so, when translated into real work, few are the typologists who actually measure them. The problem becomes more serious if these variables are used as defining criteria of types, sometimes with a blur boundary between them: a scraper versus a retouched flake, or truncation. The authors introduce the idea that "several truths" are possible, and they build a typology so that an item can be fuzzy assigned into more than one category. If there are some doubts for the explanation of an item, there is no need to firmly decide, but instead this doubt can be expressed by assigning the element to more than one single and crisp category. Hermon and Nicolucci calculate a fuzzy "reliability" index for each artifact taking into account the spread of possibilities assigned to each item (the number of different assignments, considered possible for that item). In this way, an archaeological inventory list would emphasize alternative classifications and it would be based on the reliability index for each element. There are several immediate implications to the use of fuzzy membership rules: problematic ascriptions are easily identified (low reliability index) and can be further excluded prior drawing conclusions from the analyzed assemblage. Moreover, modal categories can be easily identified and decided upon their integration into a single type.

Hermon and Niccolucci approach has been also applied to other categories of archaeological research, notably to the analysis of survey data and the definition of chronological maps that express the level of confidence on survey data (Farinetti et al., 2004).

Nicolucci and colleagues (Crescioli et al., 2000; Nicolucci et al., 2001) suggest the necessity of fuzzy logic to estimate how much a funerary sample is representative of the community. The authors show how some attributes of burials can be transformed into fuzzy entities: gender and age of the deceased, burial in a tomb, and the chronology of the burial. Such entities are in fact fuzzy labels and fuzzy values. A fuzzy label in this context is a nominal element and a number in [0,1]. The nominal elements are chosen from the common domain, so different instances of the fuzzy label consist of the same nominal elements, possibly with different coefficients. Regarding fuzzy values, the required function is approximated by a piecewise linear function. This fuzzy description is only used for data query, and not for predicting relationships. That is to say, the authors estimate demographic trends (numbers of individuals) as a weighted addition of fuzzy categories.

Beaver (2004) has also used fuzzy sets for interpreting bone density measures, meat utility indexes and percentage of survivorship of animal bones in archaeological contexts. The key contention is here that the relationship between the frequency of different skeletal parts, their utility and their survivorship in the archaeological record are not the result of deterministic linear or curvilinear relationships distorted by noise, but they are the result of a limiting relationship between the causal and outcome variables.

Spatial analysis has also been an area of application for fuzzy logic. Archaeologists have been very interested in considering imprecise locations of archaeological sites and/or imprecise chronologies in terms of fuzzy membership rules (Borodkin, 1999; Ergin et al., 2004; Foody, 2003; Hatzinikolaou et al., 2003; Loots et al., 1999; Reeler, 1999). Using these tools and methods, site location prediction is made possible, even in the case of imprecise training data. For instance, Hatzinikolaou et al. (2003) used a general database with archaeological sites in the island of Melos (Aegean Sea), where the sites were grouped in two major categories, according to the classification of a site survey:

- Settlements
- Special purpose sites, including agricultural units, mining units and observatories

The decision attribute is the nature of the site, whereas the conditional attributes are expressed as different GIS thematic layers with spatial information about the geographical location of streams, springs, agricultural land, obsidian sources, slope, hills, bays, capes. The geographical location (x, y) of the main center in the island (Philakopi) was also entered as another conditional attribute. All those attributes were *fuzzified* using the imprecise category of "distance," with just two fuzzy values: "short" and "long." Using the percentage of certainty assigned by a group of human experts about the relevance of such attributes, fuzzy predictive rules were extracted:

- If the distance from a stream is *short* and distance from agricultural land is *short* and slope is *smooth* then it is a settlement with 60 percent certainty
- If the distance from a stream is *short* and distance from a bay is *short* and slope is *smooth* then it is a settlement with 80 percent certainty
- If it is a hill and distance from a bay is short then it is a settlement with a 70 percent certainty
- If distance from a spring is short and distance from agricultural land is short and slope is smooth then it is a settlement with a 60 percent of certainty
- If distance from a cape is short and it is visible from Phylakopi then it is a special purpose site with 85 percent certainty
- If distance from agricultural land is short and slope is smooth and distance from a spring is short, then it is a special purpose site with 85 percent certainty

Leonid Borodkin (1999) has published a very interesting work that goes well beyond passive classification of observed data. The goal of his project was to determine the "fuzzy boundaries" within which two distinctive types of economic development: the manorial and the peasant types. The conditional attributes used considered the range and intensity of hired labor, the nobility's role in landownership, the availability of land, and certain characteristics differentiating peasant households:

- The proportion of peasant households with one horse or with none;
- The proportion of peasant households with four or more horses;
- The ratio of nobles' land to all cultivated land;
- The ratio of hired agricultural laborers to all local workers in agriculture;
- The number of agricultural workers per cultivated area;

- The ratio of sold land (privately owned) to all privately owned land;
- The ratio of lands rented by peasants to peasant parcels of land;
- Average wages of day laborer.

Working from these variables, the author divided Russian provinces into two groups, depending on the predominant kind of economic system. Baltic provinces were assigned to the manorial variant and the Steppe provinces served to characterize peasant variant, given historical descriptions. These two groups provided the decision attribute the system generalized in a fuzzy way, given a fuzzy membership value for each one.

Arkadiusz Salski and colleagues (Salski, 1992, 1996, 2002; Salski & Kandzia, 1996; Salzki et al., 1996) have applied these ideas of uncertain reasoning in environmental studies. Environmental data or classes of ecological objects can be defined as fuzzy sets with not sharply defined boundaries, which reflect better the continuous character of nature. Ecological data are often presented with a semblance of accuracy when exact values cannot be ascertained. They can be estimated subjectively (e.g., the plants cover about 20 percent of the surface area) or inter- or extrapolated. Using the usual sharp cluster analysis, these difficulties often cannot sufficiently be taken into account. Conventional clustering methods, which definitely place an object within only one cluster, are not particularly useful for a classification of ecological data. With fuzzy clustering, it is no more essential to definitely place an object within one cluster, since the membership value of this object can be split up between different clusters. In comparison to conventional clustering methods the distribution of the membership values thus provides additional information; the membership values of a particular object can be interpreted as the degree of similarity between the object and the respective clusters (Salski & Kandzia, 1996).

For a general overview of fuzzy methods in paleoecology, see Jackson and Williams (2004).

DIRECTED GRAPHS AND PROBABILISTIC NETWORKS

Let us transform into a graphical model the previous example on the chronological statement of a series of potteries based on size and decoration (Figure 3.7). The idea is to transform the original decision tree (Figure 3.3), where arcs had no meaning at all, into a directed graph, where an arrow will denote an influence. "Big size influences late chronology" means that knowing the right size of the vase ("big") would directly affect the automated archaeologist's expectation about the value of chronology ("late"). Here we are assuming that "influence" expresses knowledge about "relevance."

When an influence diagram like this receives probabilistic information about the degrees of influence between variables, it becomes a Bayesian Network. Bayesian networks are directed acyclic graphs whose nodes represent variables, and whose arcs encode the conditional dependencies between the variables (Castillo et al., 1997; Jordan, 1999, 2001; Neapolitan, 1990, 2003; Pearl, 1988). The arcs in a Bayesian network specify the independence assumptions that must hold between the random variables. These independence assumptions determine what probability information is required to specify the probability distribution among the random variables in the network: two variables are independent if all the paths between them are blocked (given the edges are directional). If node X_i has no parents, its local probability distribution is said to be *unconditional*, otherwise it is *conditional*. In this way, conditional independence is represented by the graphical property of *d*-connection:

1. X and Y are *d*-connected by S if and only if there is an active path between X and Y given S. Intuitively, X and Y are d-connected if and only if information can "flow" from X to Y
2. X and Y are *d*-separated given S if and only if X and Y are not *d*-connected given S.
3. X and Y are independent given S if and only if X and Y are d-separated given S and X and Y are not d-connected given S

The main use of probabilistic or Bayesian networks is when the user knows some evidence that has actually been observed, and wishes to infer the probabilities of other events, which have not yet been observed. For instance, what is the probability that in later assemblages only big sized vases were present? That means to compute every hypothesis's *belief* (the node's conditional probability) given the evidence that has been observed so far. This process of computing the *posterior* distribution of variables given evidence is called probabilistic inference.

We need archaeological observations to define such conditional probabilities. Using the data, we know that the probability of finding big sized potteries in late contexts is 0.75, whereas the probability of finding medium sized potteries in the same assemblages is only of 0.25. What are then the chances that big sized vases be the dominant pottery type at that chronological moment, con-

Figure 3.7. An influence diagram showing the pottery-chronology relationship from Figure 3.3

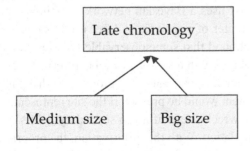

ditioned on the chance that other sizes were also present at the same time?

For decades, Bayes' theorem has been used to perform probabilistic inference in this type of situation (Buck et al., 1996). It allows to update the values of all the other probabilities in the graphical model, and to answer probabilistic queries about them.

The probability of a joint event is determined by:

$$P(E_1, E_2) = P(E_1) P(E_1 | E_2) \qquad (6)$$

It can also be expressed as:

$$P(E_1, E_2) = \frac{P(E_1, E_2)}{P(E_1)} \qquad (7)$$

Suppose our automated archaeologist is studying a prehistoric cemetery and is trying to infer the social status of buried people. Several archaeological observables are related through inference chains. For instance, whether or not an individual can be conceptualized as a "rich man" or member of some social elite has a direct influence both on whether his body was cremated, and on the amount of labor that was invested in the burial rite. In turn, the probabilities for those events have a direct influence on whether there are decorated urns to contain the cremated remains of the individual. In addition, the amount of labor that invested in the burial rite has a direct influence on the visibility of the burial. In this situation, the automated archaeologist would need to do probabilistic inference involving features that are not related via a direct influence. It would determine, for instance, the conditional probability both of cremation and a great quantity of grave goods (what supposes a huge amount of labor) when it is known that the individual was a "rich man," there is a decorated urn in the grave, and the grave was very visible. Alternatively, having observed the poor visibility of the grave, the absence of cremation, and the absence of decorated urn it would be necessary to infer the conditional

probability of the social status of the inhumated individual, and the amount of labor invested in the rite. Yet, the cremation or inhumation of the body has no influence on the visibility of the grave. Therefore, the conditional probabilities cannot be computed using a simple application of Bayes' theorem (Figure 3.8).

Obviously, in order to fully specify the Bayesian network and thus fully represent the joint probability distribution, it is necessary to further specify for each node X the probability distribution for X conditional upon X's parents (Figure 3.9). That is to say, one must give the prior probabilities of all root nodes (nodes with no predecessors) and the conditional probabilities of all non-root nodes given all possible combinations of their direct predecessors. If the variables are discrete, as in this case, it can be represented as a table, which lists the probability that the child node takes on each of its different values for each combination of values of its parents. The skeptic might still wonder how the numbers that are still required are obtained. In this case, it has been done just by measuring the frequency of different kinds of burials. The problem is with the non-observable or conceptual nodes, like the "rich man." In such cases, we should base our analysis in prior knowledge (ethno-archaeological analogy, for instance), or accept that such probabilistic values can be elicited from an expert in terms of *beliefs* or accepted uncertainty. We have already commented some aspects of this problem in the section on fuzzy logic.

John O'Shea (2004) has followed this approach in his analysis of ship archeology. This author uses a Bayesian network to estimate the character of wreck sites. After establishing the likelihood that some observable features would be found with a sail or steam boat, respectively, the network estimates the probability that each element would be present, if the site represents a true wreck site or if it is a secondary debris accumulation. With this information, the program estimates the probability that each feature will or

Figure 3.8. An influence diagram showing the dependences between variables in a burial archaeological analysis

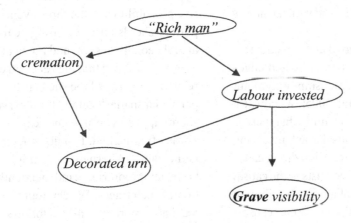

Figure 3.9. Estimating the probability distribution for X conditional upon X's parents in a Bayesian network

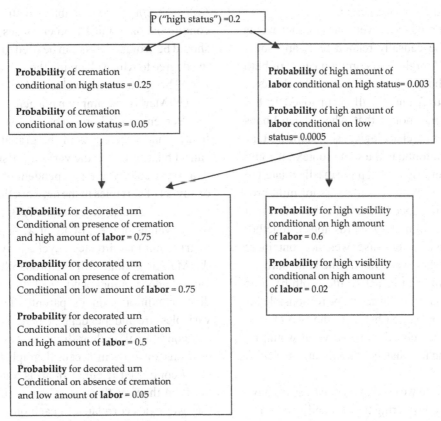

will not appear in the archaeological assemblage. It is then simply a matter of filling in the blanks to indicate what kind of site it is, and which features are, or are not, observed.

We can make a step beyond and consider that such a network of variables and directed edges represents cause-effects relationships (Glymour, 2001; Pearl, 2000; Sloman, 2005; Woodward, 2003). In this case, we are assuming that there is an arrow from X to Y in a causal graph involving a set of variables V just in case X is a direct cause of Y relative to V. The model consists in the causal graph together with the probability distribution of each variable conditional on its direct causes. Probabilistically speaking, if X causes Y, the occurrence of X will change the probability that Y will occur. When we see that X is correlated to Y, that is to say, the probability if X is consistently related to the probability of Y, we can conclude that X caused Y (or vice-versa).

There is a problem, nevertheless. Other events might also be causally related to Y, and some other event Z might be a common cause of both X and Y. Although X does not cause Y, whenever Z occurs both X and Y will occur together. For example, I may notice that when sheep bones are found at an archaeological site, some pottery vases are also found in the same context. It could be that the herding of sheep is causally related to the presence of pottery containers for milk processing, for instance. It could be, however, that sheep bones and pottery sherds appear together at garbage pits. Pottery vases were not containers for milk, but they were transformed into garbage when they finished its active life. Both become refuse material, and this might be responsible for the spatial correlation between the two events. X would be correlated to Y and yet it would be wrong to conclude that there was a causal relation between them.

Clearly, what we need in these cases is to have some way of considering the probability of X and Y relative to the probability of Z. Consider the case of the location of the sheep bones and the pottery sherds. How could I find out which causal hypothesis is correct? I could observe the relative probabilities of the three events. If I observe pottery sherds only appearing near sheep bones at archaeological sites, and not near bovid or pig bones, I conclude that the function of the pottery related to the use of the sheep is the cause of this particular spatial location. If I observe that pottery sherds appear with any other kind of material, but always fragmented, I could conclude that refuse is the cause. Alternatively, I might observe that both factors contribute independently to the location of such traces. We can represent this sort of reasoning more formally as follows. If X, Y, and Z are the only variables and X is only correlated to Y conditional on Z, Z "screens off" X as a cause of Y, and Z rather than X is the cause. If X is correlated to Y independent of Z, then Z does not screen off X and X causes Y. For each causal link *Cause* → *Effect*, the probability distribution of Y conditional on X and Y's other causes $Z_1, \ldots, Z_k$ should be provided; this can be used to determine the degree to which changing the value of X from x to x' brings about the value y of Y.

The Markov assumption is a generalization of the "screening off" property we just described. It says that if the edges of the graphs represent causal relations, then the various possible values of any variable, X, are independent of the values of any set of variables in the network that does not contain an effect (a descendant of X), conditional on the values of the parents of X. A probability distribution in a directed acyclic graph satisfies the Markov condition if the probability of each variable/node is independent of its non-descendents conditional on its parents. That means, variables are independent of their non-effects, and conditional on their direct causes.

Consequently, in a causal graph two nodes are *d*-connected if either there is a causal path between them or there is evidence that renders the two nodes correlated to each other. To put it another way, if two things can cause the same state of affairs and have no other connection, then the two things are independent. This fact leads to a Causal Faithfulness assumption: the only independencies are those predicted by the Markov assumption. Both assumptions encode the intuition of screening off. Given the values of the direct causes, learning only the value of a non-effect does not help in the prediction.

For instance, suppose the automated archaeologist has observed an archaeological object with shape *s*. There are two possible causes for this: it was manufactured either to cut or to scrap. Which is more likely?

In this example, the two causes "compete" to "explain" the observed data. Hence, *cutting* and *scrapping* become conditionally dependent given that their common child, *shape s*, is observed, even though they are marginally independent. Here we have evidence of an effect (shape *s*), and want to infer the most likely cause. This is called diagnostic, or "bottom up," reasoning, since it goes from effects to causes; it is the basis of the inverse reasoning approach presented in this chapter. Bayes nets can also be used for causal, or "top down," reasoning. For example, we can predict the probability that an artifact will have shape *s* given the amount of evidence for scrapping or cutting activities at place. Hence, Bayes nets are often called "generative" models, because they specify how causes generate effects. The graph allows an automated archaeologist predict the causal consequences of an historical event without actually having to perform it. The coherence of probabilistic inference throughout the causal

Figure 3.10. An influence diagram showing the relationship between cause and effect

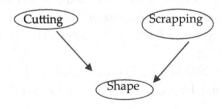

graph allows a wide range of predictions: transitive causal inferences become possible. If *A* causes *B* and *B* causes *C* then *A* will cause *C*.

There are many distinct causal maps representing exactly the same set of independence relations, and thus the same set of distributions. Just as one might want a procedure that computes probabilistic inferences across *d*-separated directed edges, one might want an algorithm that computes all the graphs that represent a given set of independence relations. The causal inductive procedure consists in finding the class of directed graphs—or under some approaches the 'best' directed graph—whose probabilistic independencies implied via the causal Markov assumption are consistent with independencies inferred from the data. That means that a causal graph will be constructed by considering the patterns of associations among events and by assuming that these patterns of association indicate causal structure in a reliable way. The input is a set of independence relations over a set of variables and its output is a set of graphs or networks over *d*-separated variables, or Markov equivalent (Neapolitan, 2003; Pearl, 2000; Spirtes et al. 2000).

Suppose we have a population involving three variables *X1, X2, X3*, and suppose the independence relations in this population are as given in Box 3.1.

There are nine influence graphs supporting the Markov assumption that might have produced data with these independencies. Their only shared feature is that each has some direct connection between X1 and X3 and between X2 and X3. Adding some formal constraints, like the faithfulness condition—all independencies in the data are implied via the causal Markov condition—the set of nine can be reduced to a singleton: $X_a X_b \rightarrow X_c$. In this example, we have managed to infer that both *X1* and *X2* are direct causes of *X3* from a single marginal independence between *X1* and *X2*. Other constraints can also be applied, such as:

Box 3.1.

All Possible Independences among X1, X2, X3	Not In Population	In Population
X1 _||_ X2	+	
X1 _||_ X3	+	
X2 _||_ X3	+	
X1 _||_ X2 | X3		+
X1 _||_ X3 | X2		+
X2 _||_ X3 | X1		+

- Ninimality (no subgraph of the causal graph also satisfies the causal Markov assumption),
- Linearity (all variables are linear functions of their direct causes and uncorrelated error variables),
- Causal sufficiency (all common causes of measured variables are measured),
- Context generality (every individual possesses the causal relations of the population),
- No side effects (one can intervene to fix the value of a variable without changing the value of any non-effects of the variable), and
- Determinism.

However, these extra assumptions are less central than the causal Markov assumption. Approaches differ as to which of these extra assumptions adopt and the assumptions tend to be used just to facilitate the inductive procedure based on the causal Markov assumption, either by helping to provide some justification for the inductive procedure or by increasing the efficiency or efficacy of algorithms for causal induction.

Due to the existence of the causal Markov counterexamples, we cannot be sure that the induced graph will represent the real causal relations amongst the variables. Hence, the induced causal graph should be viewed as a tentative hypothesis, in need of evaluation, as occurs in the hypothetic-deductive method. Evaluation takes place in the prediction and testing stages. If the hypothesis is disconfirmed, rather than returning to the induce stage, local changes are made to the causal graph in the amend stage, leading to the hypothesis of a new causal theory (Williamson, 2005).

Learning the structure of a Bayesian network (i.e., the graph) is another example of machine learning under uncertain conditions. Beginning with statistical data and background knowledge, an automated archaeologist must discover all the possible causal structures that might have generated these data. Assuming that the data is generated from a Bayesian network, an optimization based search method will find the structure of the network. However, the fewer assumptions it makes constraining the class of possible causal structures, the weaker inferential results.

We can see how this approach is different to most inductive procedures so far reviewed (Bowes et al., 2000). Instead of logical rules, a causal induction approach can distinguish different kinds of relationships between variables:

- Either *A* causes *B* or *B* causes *A,* but the direction is indeterminate; that is to say, the variables are associated but the causal nature of the association is undetermined;
- *A* (genuinely) causes *B* (common cause ruled out);
- A hidden common cause has been detected and the procedure cannot go further;

- *A* potentially causes *B* (common cause not ruled out).

Causal inference algorithms produce fewer and more concise relationships between variables than association rules. They reveal underlying causal structure among variables, not just apparent surface associations. The ability to reveal the existence of hidden common causes outside of known data is a promising tool. With causally sufficient data, the intelligent machine will compute conditional probabilities allowing the representation of causal effects generated by the modification of one variable on other variables in the set. This provides much more useful functionality than association rules. Furthermore, the causal structure revealed by the Bayesian network combined with the minimal set of conditional probabilities is clearer than a potentially big number of association rules. The more rigid statistical basis for causal inference leaves less to the user to determine which discovered relationships are valid and which are not.

In spite of their remarkable power and potential to address inferential processes, there are some inherent limitations and liabilities to Bayesian networks. The main problem refers to the quality and extent of the prior beliefs used in Bayesian inference processing. A Bayesian network is only as useful as its prior knowledge be reliable. Either an excessively optimistic or pessimistic expectation of the quality of these prior beliefs will distort the entire network and invalidate the results. Related to this concern, there is the selection of the statistical distribution necessary to model the data. Selecting the proper distribution model to describe the data has a notable effect on the quality of the resulting network. It is important to remark that local probability distributions contain information relevant to the individual causal links, but no information bearing on the truth or falsity of the causal Markov condition. If, for example, the hypothesized model predicts that *C* causes *E*, and an experiment is performed

which shows that changing the value of *C* does not change the distribution of *E*, controlling *E*'s other direct causes, then this evidence alone may be enough to warrant removing the arrow from *C* to *E* in the causal model. Finding out that the dependence between *C* and *E* is explained by non-causal relationships between the variables might also lead to the retraction of the arrow from *C* to *E*. The causal Markov assumption may motivate adding a new common cause variable or a new arrow if two variables are not found to be screened off by their current common causes. Finding physical mechanisms may suggest adding new arrows, while agency considerations may warrant changing directions of arrows. The point is that the same procedures that were used to draw predictions from a causal model may be used to suggest alterations if the predictions are not borne out.

There are not many applications of this technology in archaeology or in any related social sciences (Buck et al., 1996; Dellaportas, 1998; Fan & Brooks, 2000). There are, however, some relevant examples in ecological modeling to depict the influence of habitat or environmental predictor variables on ecological response variables (Marcot et al., 2006). In such uses, Bayesian networks predict the probability of ecological responses to varying input assumptions such as habitat and population-demographic conditions. A standard prototypical example would be the following one. Imagine a Bayesian network built around five random variables "hunting-gathering," "agriculture," "wild Animal bones," "store pits" (Figure 3.11).

In such a model, "hunter-gatherer," and "agriculture" are independent. This is to say that there is no event, which affects both the inference that a settlement has hunter and gathering traces and agriculture ones. As well, "agriculture" and "wild animal bones" are independent given "hunting-gathering," because the presence of wild animal bones is hardly the consequence of agricultural activities.

DIRECTIONS FOR FURTHER RESEARCH

This chapter has presented the very basics of the mechanization of inductive explanation. The classical concept of induction has been reviewed from the point of view of "inverse reasoning." As such, the chapter forms an ensemble with the previous one, where more "deductive" or "abductive" aspects of reasoning were presented.

In the same way as in the previous chapter, here I have only sketched the subject. Both from the theoretical and the technological point of view there is much more to be said. I have followed the approach by Holland et al. (1986) among others, which understand "induction" in terms of iterative knowledge revision and modification and not as a single-step operation of generalization, as it was traditionally analyzed in classical predicate logics. The prospect for a true mechanized explanation has been explored, but there is much more to be explored. Only the simplest algorithms have been reviewed. Computer scientists are intensively exploring this subject and there are many new mechanisms and technologies for knowledge expansion through iterative and recursive revision. The huge number of publications make impossible that we can review the entire field in a single chapter. The purpose was only to introduce the newcomer reader to this fascinating domain. Free computer programs like *Weka* or *Tanagra* can be explored to discover how to extract meaning and knowledge from archaeological data.

Bayesian networks and probabilistic causal models are among the most interesting new methods for inducing explanations from observations. This chapter contains only a very sketchy introduction. There are many computer programs to advance in the archaeological applications. The reader is addressed to the free program *GeNie* to learn more about that. The theoretical aspects of causal modeling, and the way that modern inductive reasoning is related to discovering causal explanations has only begun to be explored by authors like Glymour, Pearl, Sloman, Spirtes, Williamson, and Woodward. In most cases, however, these authors do not have a true historical approach. In this aspect, there is much to be studied from the point of view of historians and archaeologists.

In any case, if the inverse problem idea is correct, we can rephrase the general explanatory problem in the social sciences more specifically. How does an automated archaeologist recover causal explanations from observed data? How can it learn a new cause-effect relationship? Hume posed the most famous of these problems, that we only directly perceive correlations between events, not their causal relationship. How can a robot make reliably correct inferences about whether one event caused the other, and how can it dynamically correct errors when we make them?

Figure 3.11. A directed graph representing factor explaining the presence of store pits at an archaeological site, conditional on the economic activities that took place there.

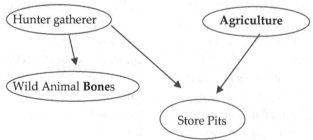

Causation is not just association, or contiguity in space, or priority in time, or all three. The problem is that our evidence is usually reduced to such correlations. It can get worse. In many cases, we make inferences about causes that are themselves unobservable. We not only assume that one event causes another, but we assume that this happens because of unobserved, and sometimes unobservable, intervening causes. Moreover, causal structures rarely just involve one event causing another. Instead, events involve many different causes interacting in complex ways. A system for recovering causal structure has to untangle the relations among those causes, and discount some possible causes in favor of others. Finally, many causal relations may be stochastic rather than deterministic. Given the "noise" in the data, the evidence for even deterministic causal relations will usually be probabilistic. Even if one event does deterministically cause another it is unlikely that we will always observe the two events co-occur. The system must be able to deal with probabilistic information.

I am proposing that to build an automated archaeologist, we make certain assumptions about how patterns of events indicate causal structure. Broadly speaking, there are some assumptions necessary to solve the general problem of discovering causal relations. First, we might propose what we will call substantive assumptions. Some perceptual features of events might be taken to indicate causal structure. Alternatively, we might propose what we will call formal causal assumptions, which posit constraining relations between causal dependencies and patterns of associations. These assumptions would say that certain patterns of association or contingency among events reliably indicate causal relations. It is important to realize that this sort of account would NOT reduce causal structure to patterns of association or define causal structure in terms of association or probability. The idea is that an automated archaeologist should make certain fundamental assumptions about how patterns of contingency are related to causal processes, in much the same way that our human visual system makes assumptions about how two-dimensional sensory information is related to three-dimensional space. Those assumptions may turn out to be wrong in individual cases, just as they may turn out to be wrong in the visual case. Overall, these assumptions may lead to accurate representations of the causal structure of the world.

Some of the troubles prefigured at the end of the previous chapter have not been solved. Inverse reasoning methods are still based on a linguistic assumption. The minimum units of meaning are still propositional sentences. This is a limitation. We have to explore an alternative to inverse reasoning that is not based on words or sentences, but on numbers and vectors. Next chapter offers an introduction to it.

REFERENCES

ADAMS, W.Y., & ADAMS, E.W. (1991). *Archaeological typology and practical reality.* Cambridge, UK: Cambridge University Press.

AGRAWAL, R., IMIELINSKI, T., & SWAMI, A. (1993). Mining association rules between sets of items in large databases. In *ACM SIGMOD Int. Conference on Management of Data* (pp. 207-216). Washington DC, USA.

ALAI, M. (2004). A.I., scientific discovery and realism. *Minds and Machines,* 14, 21–42.

ALPAYDIN, E. (2004). *Introduction to machine learning.* Cambridge, MA: The MIT Press.

ARKIN, R.C. (1998). *Behavior-based robotics.* Cambridge, MA: The MIT Press.

BARCELÓ, J.A. (1996). Heuristic classification and fuzzy sets. New tools for archaeological typologies. *Acta Praehistorica Leidensia, 28,* 155-164.

BARCELÓ, J.A. (1997). *Arqueología automática. El uso de la inteligencia artificial en arqueología* Sabadell (Spain): Editorial Ausa, (Cuadernos de Arqueología Mediterránea, 2).

BAXTER, M.J. (2006). A review of supervised and unsupervised pattern recognition in archaeometry. *Archaeometry, 48*(4), 671–694.

BAXTER, M.J., & JACKSON, C.M. (2001). Variable selection in artefact compositional studies. *Archeometry, 43*(2), 253-268.

BEAVER, J.E. (2004). Identifying necessity and sufficiency relationships in skeletal-part representation using fuzzy-set theory. *American Antiquity, 69*(1), 131-140.

BEER, R.D. (1990). *Intelligence as adaptive behavior: An experiment in computational neuroethology.* New York: Academic Press.

BEL, L., LAURENT, J.-M., BAR-HEN, A., ALLARD, D., & CHEDDADI, R. (2005). A spatial extension of CART: application to classification of ecological data. In P. Renard, H. Demougeot-Renard, & R. Fridevaux (Eds.), *Proc. Vth Eur. Conf. Geostatistics for Environmental Applications* (pp. 99-109). Berlin: Springer.

BEZDEK, J.C., & PAL, S.K. (1992). *Fuzzy systems for pattern pecognition.* Piscataway, NJ: IEEE Press.

BIGGS, D., DE VILLE, B., & SUEN, E. (1991). A method of choosing multiway partitions for classification and decision trees. *Journal of Applied Statistics, 18*, 49-62.

BINFORD, L. R. (1968). Methodological considerations of the archaeological use of ethnographic data. In L.R. Binford (Ed) *An archaeological perspective.* New York, Academic Press.

BINFORD, L.R. (1981). Behavioural archaeology and the Pompeii premise. *Journal of Archaeological Research,* 37, 195-208.

BINFORD, L.R. (2001a). Where do research problems come from? *American Antiquity, 66*(4), 669-678.

BINFORD, L.R. (2001b). *Constructing frames of reference: An analytical method for archaeological theory building using hunter-gatherer and environmental data sets.* University of California Press.

BORODKIN, L. (1999). Defining agricultural regions in Russia: Fuzziness in multivariate classification of historical data. *History and Computing, 11*(1-2), 31-42.

BORODKIN, L.I., & GARSKOVA, (1995). Analytical procedure for multidimensional hierarchical data. In *Statistical Analysis of Burial Customs of the Sarmatian Period in Asian Sarmata (6th -4th Centuries B.C.* pp. 63-114.). Napoli: Istituto Universitario orientale.

BOWES, J., NEUFELD, E., GREER, J.E., & COOKE, J. (2000). A Comparison of Association Rule Discovery and Bayesian Network Causal Inference Algorithms to Discover Relationships in Discrete Data. In *Advances in Artificial Intelligence: 13th Biennial Conference of the Canadian Society for Computational Studies of Intelligence, AI 2000, Montréal, Quebec, Canada, May 2000. Proceedings* Berlin: Springer Lecture Notes in Computer Science, Vol 1822.

BREIMAN, L. (2001). Random forests. *Machine Learning, 45*(1), 5-32.

BREIMAN, L., FRIEDMAN, J.H., OLSHEN, R.A., & STONE, C.J. (1984). *Classification and regression trees.* Belmont, CA: Wadsworth.

BUCK, C.E., CAVANAGH, W.G., & LITTON, C. (1996). *Bayesian approach to intrepreting archaeological data.* London: John Wiley.

BUNGE, M. (2006). *Chasing reality: Strife over realism.* University of Toronto Press.

BUNTINE, W., & NIBLETT, T. (1992). A further comparison of splitting rules for decision-tree induction. *Machine Learning, 8*, 75-86.

CANAL, E., & CAVAZZONI, S. (1990). Antichi insediamenti antropici nella laguna di Venezia: analisi multivariata di tipo fuzzy C-means clustering. *Archaeologia e Calcolatori, 1,*. 165-177.

CASTILLO, E., GUTIÉRREZ, J.M., & HADI, A.S. (1997). *Expert systems and probabilistic network models.* New York: Springer-Verlag.

CHAOUKI M., & GAILDRAT, V.,(2005). Automatic classification of archaeological potsherds. In *The 8th International Conference on Computer Graphics and Artificial Intelligence*, 3IA'2005 (pp. 135-147) Limoges, France, 11 mai 12 mai 2005. Edited by Dimitri Plémenos, MSI Laboratory.

CHATER, N. (1995). Neural networks: The new statistical models of mind. In J.P. Levy, D. Bairaktaris, J.A. Bullinaria & P. Cairns (Eds.), *Connectionist models of ,emory and language.* London: UCL Press.

CHEESEMAN, P. (1990). On finding the most probable model. In J. Shrager & P. Langley (Eds.), *Computational models of scientific discovery and theory formation.* San Francisco, CA: Morgan Kaufmann.

CLANCEY, W. (1984). Heuristic classification. *Artificial Intelligence, 27*, 289-350.

CLARK, P., & NIBLETT, T. (1989). The CN2 induction algorithm, *Machine Learning, 3*(4), 261-283.

CLARKE, D.L. (1968). *Analytic archaeology.* London: Methuen and Co.

CONLEY, J., GAHEGAN M., & MACGILL, J. (2005). A genetic approach to detecting clusters in point datasets. *Geographical Analysis, 37*(3), 286-314.

COX, E. (1993). *The fuzzy systems handbook. A practitioner's guide to building, using and maintaining fuzzy systems.* New York: Academic Press.

CRESCIOLI, M., D'ANDREA, A., & NICOLUCCI, F. (2000). A GIS-based analysis of the Etruscan cemetery of Pontecagnano using fuzzy logic. In G. Lock (Ed.), *Beyond the map: Archaeology and spatial technologies.* Amsterdam (Holland); IOS Press.

DARDEN, L., MOBERG, D., THADANI, S., & JOSEPHSON, J. (1992). *A computational approach to scientific theory revision: The TRANSGENE experiments* (Tech. Rep. 92-LD-TRANSGENE). Laboratory for Artificial Intelligence Research. Columbus, OH: Ohio State University.

David, N. (1992). Integrating ethnoarchaeology: A subtle realist perspective. *Journal of Anthropological Archaeology, 11*, 330-359.

DAVID, N., & KRAMER, C. (2001). *Ethnoarchaeology in action.* Cambridge, UK: Cambridge University Press.

DELLAPORTAS, P. (1998). Bayesian classification of Neolithic tools, *Applied Statistics, 47*, 279-297.

DING, J.M., WANG, Y.H., & DING L.X. (2006). Significance of expansive soil classification indexes analysed by rough sets. *Rock And Soil Mechanics, 27*(9), 1514-1518.

DONAHUE, J.W., & PALMER, D.C. (1994). *Learning and complex behaviour.* Boston, MA: Allyn and Bacon.

DORAN, J., & HODSON, F.R. (1975). *Mathematics and computers in archaeology.* Edinburgh, UK: Edinburgh University Press,

DUBOIS, D., PRADE, H., & SMETS, D. (1994). Partial truth is not uncertainty. fuzzy logic versus posibilistic logic. *IEEE Expert. Intelligent Systems and their applications,9*(4), 15-19.

DUNNELL, R. (1971). *Systematics in prehistory.* New York: The Free Press.

ERGIN, A., KARAESMEN,E., ICALLEF, A., & WILLIAMS, A.T. (2004). A new methodology for evaluating coastal scenery: Fuzzy Logic Systems. *Area, 36,* (4).

ESTEVEZ, J., & VILA, A. (1995). Etnoarqueología: el nombre de la cosa. In J. Estevez & A. Vila. Treballs d'Etnoarqueologia (Eds.), *Encuentros en los conchales fueguinos* (pp. 17-23). 1. CSIC-UAB, Bellaterra (Spain).

FALKENHEIMER, B.C. (1990). Explanation and theory formation. In J. Shrager & P. Langley (Eds.), *Computational models of scientific discovery and theory formation.* San Francisco, CA: Morgan Kaufmann.

FAN, Y., & BROOKS, S. (2000). Bayesian modeling of prehistoric corbelled domes. *The Statistician, 49,* 339-354.

FARINETTI, E., HERMON, S., & NICOLUCCI, F. (2004). Fuzzy logic application to survey data in a GIS environment. In *Beyond the artefact. Computer applications in archaeology.* Budapest (Hungary): ArcheoLingua.

FARRINGTON, O.S., & TAYLOR, N.K. (2004). Machine learning applied to geo-archaeological soil data. In Magistrat der Stadt Wien-Referat Kulturelles Erbe-Stadtarchäologie Wien (Ed.), *Enter the past. The e-way into the four dimensions of cultural heritage* (pp. 456-459). Oxford: Archaeo-Press (BAR International Series, 1227),

FERNÁNDEZ MARTÍNEZ, V., & GARCÍA DE LA FUENTE, M. (1991). El tratamiento informático de datos funerarios cualitativos: análisis de correspondencias y algoritmo ID3 de Quinlan. *Complutum, 1,* 123-131.

FINDLER, N.V. (1992). Automatic rule discovery for field work in anthropology. *Computers and the Humanities, 25,* 285-392.

FINDLER, N.V., & DHULIPALLA, S., (1999). A decision support system for automatic rule discovery in anthropology. *Social Networks, 21,* 167-185.

FOODY, G.M. (2003). Uncertainty, knowledge discovery and data mining in GIS. *Progress in Physical Geography, 27*(1), 113-121.

FORSYTH, H. (2000). Mathematics and computers: The classifier's ruse. In G. Lock & K. Brown (Eds.), *On the theory and practice of archaeological computing* (pp. 31-39). Oxford, UK: Oxford University Committee for Archaeology.

GAHEGAN, M. (2000). On the application of inductive machine learning tools to geographical analysis. *Geographical Analysis, 32*(1), 113-139.

GAHEGAN, M. (2003). Is inductive machine learning just another wild goose (or might it lay the golden egg)? *International Journal of Geographical information Science, 17*(1), 69-92.

GANDARA, M. (1990). La analogía etnográfica como heurística: lógica muestrela, dominios ontológicos e historicidad. In Y. Sugiera & M.C. Sierra (Eds.), *Etnoarqueología: Primer Coloquio Bosch-Gimpera.* México: UNAM.

GANDARA, M. (2006). La inferencia por analogía: más allá de la analogía etnográfica. In *Etnoarqueología de la Prehistoria. Más allá de la analogía* (pp. 14-23). Treballs d'Etnoarqueologia, No. 6, CSIC-UAB, Barcelona (Spain).

GARGANO, M.L., & EDELSON, W. (1996). A genetic algorithm approach to solving the archaeology Seriation problem, *Congressus Numerantium, 119,* 193-203.

GARGANO, M.L., & LURIE, L. (2006). A hybrid evolutionary approach to solving the archaeological Seriation problem. *Congressus Numerantium, 180,* 43-53.

GEY, O. (1991). COCLUSH: Un générateur de classification d'objets structure's suivant différents points de vue. *Actes des 6 Journeés Françaises de l'Apprentissage.*

GIBBINS, P. (1990). BACON bytes back. In J. E. Tiles, G.T. McKee, & G.C. Dean *Evolving knowledge in natural science and artificial intelligence.* London, UK: Pitman.

GILLIES, D. (1996). *Artificial intelligence and the scientific method.* Oxford, UK: Oxford University Press.

GIZA, P. (2002). Automated discovery systems and scientific realism. *Minds and Machines, 12,* 105–117,

GLYMOUR, C. (2001). *The mind's arrows. Bayes nets and graphical causal models in psychology.* Cambridge, MA: The MIT Press.

GOLDBERG, D.E. (1989). *Genetic algorithms in search. Optimization and machine learning.* Redwood City, CA: Addison-Wesley.

GOULD, R.A. (1980). *Living archaeology.* Cambridge, UK: Cambridge University Press.

GRUDZINSKI, K., KARWOWSKI, M., & DUCH, W. (2003). Computational Intelligence Study of the Iron Age Glass Data. *International Conference on Artificial Neural Networks (ICANN) and International Conference on Neural Information Processing (ICONIP).* Istanbul, June 2003, 17-20. Retrieved Agust 2007 from http://www.fizyka.ukw. edu.pl/publikacje/a_s_p.pdf

GRUDZINSKI, K., & KARWOWSKI, (2005). The Analysis of the Unlabeled Samples of the Iron Age Glass Data. In *Intelligent Information Processing and Web Mining, Proceedings of the International IIS: IIPWM'05* Conference held in Gdansk, Poland, June 13-16, 2005., Edited by Mieczyslaw A. Klopotek, Slawomir T. Wierzchon, and Krzysztof Trojanowski. Berlin: Springer (Advances in Soft Computing Series).

GURECKIS, T.M., & LOVE, B.C. (2003). Human unsupervised and supervised learning as a quantitative distinction *International Journal of Pattern Recognition and Artificial Intelligence,* 17(5), 885-901.

HAN, J., & KAMBER, M. (2001). *Data mining. Concepts and techniques.* San Francisco, CA: Morgan Kaufmann.

HAND, D., MANNILA, H., & SMYTH, P. (2001). *Principles of data mining.* Cambridge, MA: The MIT Press.

HATZINIKOLAOU, E., HATZICHRISTOS, T., SIOLAS, A., & MANTZOURANI, E. (2003). Predicting archaeological site locations using GIS and fuzzy logic. In M. Doerr & A. Sarris (Eds.), *The digital heritage of archeology. Computer applications and quantitatiuve methods in archaeology 2002* (pp. 169-178). Archive of Monuments and Publications. Hellenic Ministry of Culture, Heraklion (Greece).

HEBB, D.O. (1949). *The organization of behavior.* New York: John Wiley.

HENSEL, E. (1991). *Inverse theory and applications for engineers.* Englewood Cliffs, NJ: Prentice-Hall.

HERMON, S., & NICCOLUCCI, F. (2003). A fuzzy logic approach to typology in archaeological research. In M. Doerr & A. Sarris (Eds.), *The digital heritage of archeology. Computer applications and quantitatiuve methods in archaeology 2002.* Edited by. Archive of Monuments and Publications. Hellenic Ministry of Culture, Heraklion (Greece), (pp. 307-312).

HERMON, S., & NICCOLUCCI, F. (2002). Estimating subjectivity of typologists and typological classification with fuzzy logic. *Archeologia e Calcolatori,* 13, 217-232.

HITCHCOCK, C., & SOBER, E. (2004). Prediction versus accomodation and the risk of overfitting. *British Journal for the Philosophy of Science,* 55, 1-34.

HOLLAND, J.H., HOLYOAK, K.J., NISBETT, R.E., & THAGARD, P.R. (1986). *Induction. Processes of inference, learning, and discovery.* Cambridge, MA: The MIT Press.

HÜLLERMEIER, E. (2007). *Case-based approximate reasoning.* New York/Berlin: Springer-Verlag.

HUNT, E. B. (1962). *Concept learning: An information processing problem.* New York: John Wiley.

JACKSON, S.T., & WILLIAMS, J.W. (2004). Modern analogs in quaternary paleoecology: Here today, gone yesterday, gone tomorrow? *Annual Review of Earth and Planetary Sciences, 32,* 495-537.

JENSEN, F. V. (2001). *Bayesian networks and decision graphs.* Berlin: Springer.

JERAJ, M., SZERASKO, D., TODOROVSKI, L., & DEBALJAK, M. (2004). Machine learning methods to Paleocological data. In *4th European Conference on Ecological Modelling* September 27 - 29, 2004, Bled, Slovenia. Retrieved February 2007 from http://www-ai.ijs.si/SasoDzeroski/ECE-MEAML04/presentations/039-Jeraj.pdf

JORDAN, M. I. (Ed.) (1999). *Learning in graphical models.* Cambridge, MA: The MIT Press.

JORDAN, M.I., & JACOBS, R.A. (1992). Modularity, unsupervised learning, and supervised learning. In S. Davis (Ed.), *Connectionism: theory and practice.* Oxford:University Press.

KAELBLING, L.P. (1993). *Learning in embedded systems.* Cambridge, MA: The MIT Press.

KAIPIO, J., & SOMERSALO, E., (2004). *Statistical and computational inverse problems.* Berlin: Springer.

KAMPEL, M., & MELERO, F.J. (2003). Virtual vessel reconstruction from a fragment's profile. In D. Arnold, A. Chalmers, & F. Nicolucci (Eds.), *VAST2003 4th International Symposium on Virtual reality, Archaeology and Intelligent Cultural heritage* (pp. 79-88). The Eurographics Association, Aire-la-Ville (Switzerland).

KARP, P.D. (1990). Hypothesis formation as design. In J. Shrager & P. Langley (Eds.), *Computational models of scientific discovery and theory formation* (pp. 275-317). San Francisco, CA: Morgan Kaufmann.

KAUFMAN, K., & MICHALSKI, R. S. (2000). An adjustable rule learner for pattern discovery using the AQ methodology. *Journal of Intelligent Information Systems, 14,* 199-216.

KESELMAN, Y., & DICKINSON, S. (2005). Generic model abstraction from examples. *IEEE Transactions on Pattern Analysis and Machine Intelligence, 27*(7).

KIRSCH, A. (1996). *An introduction to the mathematical theory of inverse problems.* Berlin: Springer.

KOHONEN, T. (2001). *Self-organizing maps* (3rd ed.).Berlin: Springer.

KOLODNER, J. (1993). *Case-based reasoning.* San Francisco, CA: Morgan Kaufmann.

KOSKO, B. (1992). *Neural networks and fuzzy systems. A dynamical systems approach to machine intelligence.* Englewood Cliffs, NJ: Prentice Hall.

KOSKO, B. (1993). *Fuzzy thinking: The new science of fuzzy logic.* New York: Hyperion.

LAGRANGE, M.S. (1992). Symbolic data and numerical processing: A case study in art history by means of automated learning techniques. In J.C. Gardin & C. Peebles (Eds.), *Representations in archaeology* (pp. 330–356). Bloomington, IN: Indiana University Press,

LAGRANGE, M.S., & RENAUD, M. (1987). *TRINITA: un étude de cas en histoire de l' art à l'aide d'un programme d'apprentissage.* Document de Travail n° 7. C.N.R.S.-U.P.R., 315, Paris (France).

LANGLEY, P. (1996). *Elements of machine learning.* San Francisco, CA: Morgan Kaufmann.

LANGLEY, P., SIMON, H.A., BRADSHAW, G.L., & ZYTKOV, J.M. (1987) *Scientific discovery. Com-*

putational explorations of the creative process. Cambridge, MA: The MIT Press.

LANGLEY, P., & ZYTKOW, J. (1989). Data-driven approaches to empirical discovery. *Artificial Intelligence, 40,* 283-312.

LAZAR, A., & REYNOLDS, R.G. (2002). Heuristic knowledge discovery for archaeological data using cultural algorithms and rough sets. In A. Ruhul, S. Sarker, Hussein A. Abbass, & Charles S. Newton (Eds.), *Heuristics and optimization for knowledge discovery (Vol. 2.)* Hershey, PA: Idea Group Publishing.

LAZAR, A., & REYNOLDS, R.G. (2005). Evolution-based learning of ontological knowledge for a large-scale multi-agent simulation. In M. Grana, R.J. Duro, A.D. Aryou, & P.P Wang, (Eds,), *Information processing and evolutionary algorithms-from industrial applications to academic speculation.* Berlin: Springer-Verlag.

LENIHAN, J.M., & NEILSON, R.P. (1993). A rule-based vegetation formation model for canada. *Journal of Biogeography, 20(6),* 615-628.

LOOTS, L., NACKAERTS, K., & WAELKENS, M. (1999). Fuzzy viewshed analysis of the hellenistic city. Defence system at sagalassos. In L. Dingwall, S.Exon, V. Gaffney, S. Laflin & M. Van Leusen (Eds.), *Archaeology in the age of internet. Computer applications and quantitative methods in archaeology 1997* (pp. 63-65). Oxford: ArcheoPress.

LOVE, B. C. (2002). Comparing supervised and unsupervised category learning. *Psychonomic Bulletin & Review, 9,* 829-835.

MANNILA, H., TOIVONEN, H., KORHOLA, A., & OLANDER, K. (1998) Learning, mining, or modeling? A case study from paleoecology. In A. Setsuo & M. Hiroshi (Eds.), *Discovery science* (Vol. 1532, pp. 12-24). Berlin: Springer

MARCOT, B.G., STEVENTON, J.G.D., SUTHERLAND, G.D., & MCKANN, R.K. (2006). Guidelines for developing and updating Bayesian belief networks applied to ecological modelling and conservation. *Canadian Journal of Forestal Research, 36,* 3063-3074.

MCBRIDE, D.G., DIETZ, M.J., VENNEMEYER, M.T., MEADORS, S.A., BENFER, R.A., & FURBEE, N.L. (2001). Bootstrap methods for sex determination from the *Os Coxae* using the ID3 Algorithm. *Journal of Forensic Sciences, 46,* 427-431.

MENNIS, J., & LIU, J. (2003). Mining association rules in Spatiotemporal data, *Proceedings of the 7th International Conference on GeoComputation,* Southampton UK: University of Southampton.

MEPHU NGUIFO, E., LAGRANGE, M.-S., RENAUD, M., & SALLANTIN, J. (1998). PLATA: An application of LEGAL, a machine learning based system, to a typology of archaeological ceramics. *Computers and the humanities,* 31(3), 169-187.

MICHALEWICZ, Z. (1996). *Genetic algorithms + data structures=evolution programs.* Berlin: Springer.

MICHALSKI, R. S., Generating Alternative Hypotheses in AQ Learning, *Reports of the Machine Learning and Inference Laboratory,* MLI 04-6, Fairfax (VA): George Mason University.

MICHALSKI, R. S., & KAUFMAN, K. (2001). Learning patterns in noisy data: The AQ approach. In G. Paliouras, V. Karkaletsis & C. Spyropoulos (Eds.), *Machine learning and its applications* (pp. 22-38). Berlin: Springer.

MITCHELL, M. (1996). *An introduction to genetic algorithms.* Cambridge, UK: Cambridge University Press.

MITCHELL, T.M. (1982). Generalization as search. *Artificial Intelligence, 18,* 203-226.

MITCHELL, T.M. (1987). *Machin Learning.* WCB/MCGraw Hill.

NANCE, J.D. (2000). Elemental composition studies of lithic materials from western Kentucky and Tennessee. *Midcontinental Journal of Archaeology, 25*, 83-100.

NEAPOLITAN R.E. (1990). *Probabilistic reasoning in expert systems.* New York: Wiley.

NEAPOLITAN, R.E. (2003). *Learning Bayesian networks.* Upper Saddle River, NJ: Prentice Hall.

NICOLUCCI, N., D'ANDREA, A., & CRESCIOLI, M. (2001) Archaeological applications of fuzzy databases. In Z. Stancic & T. Veljanovski (Eds.), *Computing archaeology for understanding the past* (pp. 107-116). Oxford: ArcheoPress.

NOLFI, S., & FLOREANO, D. (2000). *Evolutionary robotics. The biology, intelligence, and technology of self-organizing machines.* Cambridge, MA: The MIT Press.

O'SHEA, J. (2004). The identification of shipwreck sites: A Bayesian approach. *Journal of Archaeological Science, 31,* 1533-1552.

PAPAIOANNOU, G., & KARABASSI, E.A. (2003). On the automatic assemblage of arbitrary broken solid artefacts. *Image & Vision Computing, 21*(5), 401–412.

PAWLAK, Z. (1991). *Rough sets: Theoretical aspects of reasoning about data.* Dordrecht (Holland): Kluwer Academic Publishers.

PEARL, J. (1988). *Probabilistic reasoning in intelligent systems.* San Mateo, CA: Morgan Kaufmann.

PEARL, J. (2000). *Causality. Models, reasoning and inference.* New York: Cambridge University Press.

PERLOVSKY, L.I. (2001). *Neural networks and intellect. Using model-based concepts.* New York: Oxford University Press.

PIERCE, C. (1878). Deduction, induction and hypothesis. *Popular Science Monthly, 13,* 470-82.

PIZLO, Z. (2001). Perception as viewed as an inverse problem. *Vision Research, 41*(25), 3145-3161.

POP, H.F., DUMITRESCU, D., & SARBU, C. (1995). A study of roman pottery (terra sigillata) using hierarchical fuzzy clustering. *Analitica Chimica Acta, 310,* 269-279.

POPPER, K. (1963). *Conjectures and refutations: The growth of scientific knowledge.* London: Routledge & Kegan Paul.

QUINLAN, J. R. (1986). Induction of decision trees. *Machine Learning, 1,* 81-106.

QUINLAN, J.R. (1993). *C4.5: Programs for machine learning* San Francisco, CA: Morgan Kaufmann.

RAGIN, C. (2000). *Fuzzy-set social science.* Chicago, IL: University of Chicago Press.

RAJAMONEY, S. (1990). A computational approach to theory revision. In J. Schrager & P. Langley (Eds.), *Computational models of scientific discovery and theory formation* (pp. 225-253). San Francisco, CA: Morgan Kaufmann.

REELER, C. (1999). Neural networks and fuzzy logic analysis in archaeology. In L. Dingwall, S. Exon, V. Gaffney, S. Laflin & M. van Leusen (Eds.), *Archaeology in the age of the internet.* Edited by. Oxford: ArcheoPress.

REYNOLDS, R.G. (1979). *An adaptive computer model of the evolution of agriculture in the valley of Oaxaca, Mexico,* Ph.D. Thesis, University of Michigan, Ann Arbor, MI: University Microfilms.

REYNOLDS, R. G. (1986) An adaptive computer model for the evolution of plant collecting and early agriculture in the eastern valley of Oaxaca. In K. V. Flannery (Ed.), *Guila naquitz: Archaic foraging and early agriculture in Oaxaca, Mexico* (pp. 439-500).. New York: Academic Press.

REYNOLDS, R.G. (1999) The impact of raiding on settlement patterns in the northern valley of Oaxaca: An approach using decision trees. In T.A. Kohler & G.J. Gumerman (Eds.), *Dynamics in human and primate societies. Agent based modeling of social and spatial processes.* Oxford University Press (Santa Fe Institute Studies in the Sciences of Complexity).

REYNOLDS, R.G., & CHUNG, C. (1997). A cultural algorithm to evolve multi-agent cooperation using cultural algorithms. In P. J. Angeline, R. G. Reynolds, J. R. McDonnell, & R. Eberhart (Eds.), *Evolutionary Programming VI* (pp. 323-334). New York: Springer.

REYNOLDS, R. G., & PENG, B. (2005). Knowledge learning and social swarms in cultural algorithms, *Journal of Mathematical Sociology, 29,* pp. 1-18.

REYNOLDS, R.G., & SALEEM, S. (2005). The impact of environmental dynamics on cultural emergence. In L. Booker, S. Forrest, M. Mitchell, & R. Riolo (Eds.), *Perspectives on adaptation in natural and artificial systems: Essays in honor of John Holland* (pp. 253-280). New York: Oxford University Press..

REYNOSO, C., & JEZIERSKI,E. (2002). A genetic algorithm problem solver for archaeology. In G. Burenhult (Ed.), *Archaeological informatics: Pushing the envelope CAA 2001* (pp. 507-510). Oxford: ArchaeoPress.

RUSSELL, B. (1967) (1912). *The problems of philosophy.* Oxford, UK: Oxford University Press.

SABATIER, P.C. (2000). Past and future of inverse problems *Journal of Mathematical Physics, 41,* 4082-4124

SALLANTIN, J., SZCZECINIARZ, J.J., BARBOUX, C., LAGRANGE, M.S., & RENAUD, M. (1991). Théories semiempiriques: conceptualisation et illustrations. *Revue d'Intelligence Artificielle, 5*(1), 9–67.

SALSKI, A. (1992). Fuzzy knowledge-based models in ecological research. *Ecological Modelling, 63,* 103-112.

SALSKI, A. (1996). Fuzzy approach to ecological modelling and data analysis. In *Proceedings of FUZZY'96, Fuzzy Logic in Engineering and Natural Sciences* (pp. 316-325). Zittau (Poland).

SALSKI, A. (2002). Ecological applications of fuzzy logic. In F. Recknagel (Ed.), *Ecological informatics* (pp. 3-14). Berlin: Springer.

SALSKI, A., & KANDZIA, P. (1996). Fuzzy sets and fuzzy logic in ecological modelling. *EcoSys, 4,* 85-97.

SALSKI, A., FRÄNZLE, O., & KANDZIA, P. (Eds.). (1996) Fuzzy logic in ecological modelling. *Ecological Modelling, special issue,* 85(1).

SHI, T., & HORVATH, S. (2006) Unsupervised learning with random forest predictors. *Journal of Computational and Graphical Statistics,* 15(1), 118-138.

SLOMAN, S. (2005). *Causal models. How people think about the world and its alternatives.* New York: Oxford University Press.

SMITHSON, M. (1988). Fuzzy set theory and the social sciences: The scope for applications. *Fuzzy sets and systemsk, 16,* 4.

SPAULDING, A.C.M. (1953). Statistical techniques for the discovery of artifact Types. *American Antiquity, 18,* 305-313.

SPIRTES, P., GLYMOUR,C., & SCHEINES, R. (2000). *Causation, prediction and search.* New York: Springer.

STARY, C., & PESCHL, M.F. (1995). Towards constructivist unification of machine learning and parallel distributed processing. In K.M. Ford, C. Glymour & P.J. Hayes (Eds.), *Android epistemology.* Menlo Park/Cambridge/London: AAAI Press /The MIT Press.

SUTTON, R. S., & BARTON, A.G. (1998). *Reinforcement learning: An introduction* Cambridge MA: The MIT Press.

TANAKA, K. (2004). *An introduction to fuzzy logic for practical application*. Berlin: Springer.

TARANTOLA A, (2005). Inverse problem theory. *Society for Industrial and Applied Mathematics*. Retrieved February 2007 from http://www.ipgp.jussieu.fr/%7Etarantola/Files/Professional/SIAM/index.html

TAWFIK, A. Y., (2004). Inductive reasoning and chance discovery. *Minds and Machines*, 14, 441–451,

THORNTON, C. (2000). *Truth from trash. How learning makes sense*. Cambridge, MA: The MIT Press.

VALDES-PĔRZ, R.E. (1995). Machine discovery in chemistry: New results. *Artificial Intelligence*, 65(2), 247-280.

VALDES-PĔRZ, R.E. (1996a). Computer science research on scientific siscovery *Knowledge Engineering Review*, 11, 57-66.

VALDES-PĔRZ, R.E. (1996b). A new theorem in particle physics enabled by machine discovery. *Artificial Intelligence, 82*(1-2), 331-339,

VALDES-PĔRZ, R.E. (1999). Discovery tools for science applications. *Communications of the ACM, 42*(11), 37-41.

VAN OVERWALLE, F., & VAN ROOY, D. (1998). A connectionist approach to causal attribution. In S. J. Read & L. C. Miller (Eds.), *Connectionist Models of Social Reasoning and Social Behavior* (pp. 143-171). London: Lawrence Erlbaum Associates.

VIERRA, R. K. (1982). Typology, classification, and theory building. In R. Whallon and J. A. Brown (Eds.), *Essays on archaeological typology* (pp. 162-175). Evanston, IL: Center for American Archaeology Press.

VILA, A. (2006). Propuesta de elaboración de la metodología arqueológica. In *Etnoarqueología de la Prehistoria: más allá de la analogía* (pp. 61-76). Treballs d'Etnoarqueologia, 6. CSIC-UAB (Barcelona, Spain).

WEISS, S.M., & KULIKOWSKI, C.A. (1991). *Computer systems that learn*. San Francisco, CA: Morgan Kaufmann.

WHITE, R. (2003). The epistemic advantage of prediction over accomodation. *Mind,* 112, 653-683.

WILLIAMSON, J. (2004). A dynamic interaction between machine learning and the philosophy of science. *Minds and Machines, 14,* 539–549.

WILLIAMSON, J. (2005). *Bayesian nets and causality: Philosophical and computational foundations*. New York: Oxford University Press.

WITTEK, I.H., & FRANK, E. (2005). *Data mining: Practical machine learning tools and techniques* (Second Edition). San Francisco, CA: Morgan Kaufmann.

WOODBURY, K.A. (2002) *Inverse engineering handbook*. Boca Raton, FL: CRC Press.

WOODWARD, J. (2003). *Making things happen. A theory of causal explanation*. New York: Oxford University Press.

WYLIE, A. (1985). The reaction against analogy. *Advances in Archaeological Method and Theory*, 8, 63-111.

YAO, M., MENG, H.Y., ZHANG, L., HUANG, Y., PEI, M., HUANG, Z.J. et al. (2001). Towards improvement in locating of underground tomb relics using EM radar signals and genetic algorithms, *Genetic And Evolutionary Computation Conference Late-Breaking Papers* (pp. 493-498). San Francisco, CA.

YELLEN, J.E. (1977). *Archaeological approaches to the present: Models for reconstructing the past*. New York: Academic Press.

ZADEH, L.A. (1965). Fuzzy sets. *Information and Control. 8*, 338-353.

ZADEH, L.A., KLIR, G.J., Yuan, B (eds.). (1996). *Fuzzy sets, fuzzy logic, and fuzzy systems: Selected Papers by Lotfi A. Zadeh (Advances in Fuzzy Systems - Applications and Theory, Vol 6.* Singapore: World Scientific.

ZIARKO, W. (1994). *Rough sets, fuzzy sets and knowledge discovery.* Berlin: Springer.

ZYTKOW, J.M., BAKER, J. (1991) Interactive mining of regularities in databases. In. G. Piatetsky-Shapiro & W.J. Frawley (Eds.), *Knowledge discovery in databases* Menlo Park, CA: AAAI Press/The MIT Press.

Chapter IV
An Introduction to Neurocomputing

SIMULATING THE BRAIN

Let's build an automated archaeologist!

It is not an easy task. We need a highly complex, nonlinear, and parallel information-processing "cognitive core" able to explain what the robot sees, in terms of causal factors, which not always have an observable nature.

Of course, such a "cognitive core" should not run like a human brain. After all, automated archaeologists do the same tasks as "human archaeologists," but not necessary in the same way. Nevertheless, there is some similitude in the basic mechanism. My suggestion is that an archaeologist, human or "artificial," will perceive archaeological data and, using some basic principles of learning, as those presented in previous chapter, will develop ways of encoding these data to make sense of perceived world. Consequently, we may try to build our artificial archaeologist based on the idea of *learning* and the ability to adapt flexibly epistemic actions to different archaeological problems waiting for a solution.

How much should be programmed in its final form into such a cognitive core and how much will have to be learnt by interacting with some environment, including teachers and other agents? Projects aiming to develop intelligent systems on the basis of powerful and general learning mechanisms start from something close to a "Tabula rasa," however, they risk being defeated by explosive search spaces requiring evolutionary time-scales for success. Biological evolution enables animals to avoid this problem by providing large amounts of "innate" information in the genomes of all species. In the case of humans, this seems to include meta-level information about what kinds of things are good to learn, helping to drive the learning processes as well as specific mechanisms, forms of representation, and architectures to enable them to work. Is it possible to use these ideas for building an "intelligent" machine?

Like its human counterpart, the cognitive core of our automated archaeologist should be made of specialized cells called *neurons* (Figure 4.1). Artificial and biological neurons are relatively similar, and both have the same parts, also called the cell body, axon, synapse, and dendrite (Bechtel & Abrahamson, 1991; Dawson, 2004; Ellis & Humphreys, 1999; O'Reilly & Munakata, 2000; Quinlan, 1991).

Each neuron connects as well as accepts connections from many other neurons, configuring a network of neurons. Those connections are implemented by means of dendrites, while syn-

Figure 4.1. Schematic representation of a neuron

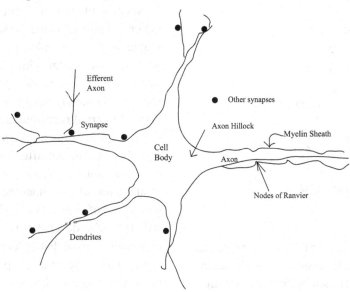

apses are a gateway linked to dendrites coming from other neurons.

We can think about the essential function of each neuron in the network from a computational perspective in terms of a *detector*. First, a detector needs *inputs* that provide the information on which it bases its detection. In human brain, information is expressed in the timing and the frequency neurons communicate among them through electrical pulses. By combining or integrating activation signals or pulses over all the incoming connections (dendrites), each neuron creates some sort of aggregate measure. As a result, the neuron produces a new composite signal, the *output*, transmitted to other neurons, continuing the information-processing cascade through a network of interconnected neurons (Figure 4.2). The chaining of multiple levels of detectors can lead to more powerful and efficient detection capabilities than if everything had to work directly from the raw sensory inputs. However, this chaining implies that the transformation operation is complex because different signals arrive from different sources through different connections, and each

connection modifies the information in a particular way. This style of computing—transforming one pattern into another by passing it through a large configuration of synaptic connections—is called *parallel distributed processing.* As the original input pattern distributed across many neurons pass inward from one specialized neural population to the next, and to the next and the next, the original pattern is progressively transformed at each stage by the intervening configuration of synaptic configurations.

On a neural network, the overall pattern of simultaneous activation levels across the assembled neurons of a given population is the primary unit of representation, and the primary vehicle of semantic content. Such patterns are often referred to as "activation vectors" because they can be usefully and uniquely characterized by a sequence of n numbers, where n = the number of neurons in the representing population. Consequently, concepts may be represented as ephemeral patterns of activation across an entire set of units rather than as individuated elements or symbols. These stable patterns then determine further process-

Figure 4.2. Schematic representation of neuron activity

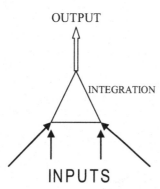

ing, because when activated, they constitute the system's recognition and concurrent understanding of its objective situation, an understanding that produces the system's subsequent behavior. Different patterns capture different aspects of the content of the concepts in a partially overlapping fashion. Alternative concepts are simply alternative patterns of activation. Information processing is the process of evolution in time of conceptual spaces. The primary advantage of a distributed representation is its ability to capture naturally the similarity structure of the represented domain (similar entities can share a greater number of units in the representation than dissimilar entities).

To say that a connectionist explanation is sub-symbolic is to say that the activation values of its individual neurons do not represent interpretable features that could be represented as individual symbols. Instead, each neuron is viewed as indicating the presence of a micro-feature. Individually, a micro-feature is unintelligible, because its "interpretation" depends crucially on the context (i.e., the set of other micro-features simultaneously present, Clark, 1993). However, a collection of micro-features represented by a number of different neurons can represent a concept that could be represented by a symbol in a classical model (Dawson, 2004).

Neurocomputing is the equivalent of *learning*. It consists in the modification of the synaptic gaps

according to some adjustment process sensitive to successful and erroneous performance. In general, upon repeated presentation of various real examples and under the steady pressure of a learning rule or algorithm that makes small adjustments in the network's synaptic connections, the network slowly but spontaneously generates a set of internal representations, one for each of the several features it is required to detect. The overall result is that after learning the network contains a number of processors chained together in such a way as to produce the appropriate outputs given a set of inputs. During learning, a network will typically develop a way of organizing its representations so that different inputs come to be represented as belonging to partitioned classes or groups, which may themselves be hierarchically ordered into various subgroups.

Information is stored in the memory by strengthening the connections between those units that co-occur and weakening the connections between pairs of units in which one is on and the other is off. Consequently, memory refers to the relatively enduring neural alterations induced by the interaction of the system outputs with its inputs coming from an external environment. When a particular activity pattern is learned, it is stored in the brain (artificial or natural) where it can be recalled later when required. Retrieval is assumed to occur when a previously active pattern is reinstated over the set of neurons. As a result, when a new input signal enters the network of interconnected, the signal is transmitted along defined connections, to activate a specific subset of neurons, which represent the explanatory concept.

In this way, a neural network is a distributed memory system that learns by association. Each memory trace is distributed over many different connections, and each connection participates in many different memory traces. The traces of different mental states are therefore superimposed in the same set of neural connections. The neurons themselves can be seen as knowledge micro-features. A particular situation is represented by turning on those micro-features that constitute a description of the represented situation or unit of knowledge. Certain collections of micro-features might represent the physical characteristics of the situation, such as the color or size of an object being viewed, whether some particular object is present, and so on. Other micro-features represent more abstract relational aspects of a situation, such as whether similarity or spatial neighborhood.

The term "connectionism" has been used to refer to reasoning and cognitive activity within this kind of interconnected neural networks. Connectionist systems are automatic problem solvers, which do not contain "words," "images," or surrogates for the external word. They are made of many little parts ("artificial" neurons), each mindless by itself, passing activation or inhibition signals to each other and all of them competing for the right to act and cooperate to send an output signal that can be understood as the solution to the problem. Each neuron by itself can only do some simple thing that needs no mind or thought at all: receive an input from all other units in a connected network and calculate an output. These artificial neurons accept a bunch of numbers (input), and learn to respond to this by producing a number of its own (output). Yet, when we join these units inside a network, this leads to an appearance of intelligent behavior. Vast representational power thus results from very modest resources.

Connectionist systems show how a system might convert a meaningful input into a meaningful output without any rules, principles, inferences, or other sorts of meaningful phenomena in between. A neural network does not contain explicitly represented data structures. Nor does it contain explicitly formulated production rules or procedures, which apply uniformly to all instances of a given class. Any apparent rule activation is an emergent phenomenon, to which only the ideal case of the system will normally conform. The system's knowledge is embodied as a superposi-

tion of individual instances of learning, each of which will cause a slight adjustment to the connection weights between the internal units. Recall is not a matter of looking up the required item in accordance with hierarchical membership criteria; it is more a case of the symbol being recreated if a sufficient number of the units involved in its representation are brought into play.

In these circumstances, "cognition" appears as the emergence of global states in a network of simple components. Neurons mediate between the reception of external stimuli ("observables") and the execution of behavioral responses ("perceptions"). They have no thoughts and no feelings, yet out of them emerge intelligent actions. They are cognitive procedures that act as complex associations between input signals (empirical data) and conceptual or behavioral output. Almost all knowledge is *implicit* in the structure of the device that carries out the task, rather than *explicit* in the states of units themselves. Knowledge is not directly accessible to interpretation, but it is built into the processor itself, in such a way that it determines the course of processing. The automated system learns through tuning of connections, rather than formulated and stored as declarative facts (Rumelhart, 1989).

The claim underlying this principle is that a number of loosely coupled processes running in parallel can control explanation. It postulates that an explicit process that controls all others is unnecessary. Those parallel, loosely coupled processes correspond to non-hierarchical observation-explanation couplings with comparatively little internal processing. This principle contrasts with the traditional view of categorization as a process of mapping a sensory stimulus onto an internal representation. The principle of explaining-as-learning coordination states that problem solving is to be conceived as sensing-action coordination. Note that sensing-acting coordination does not mean simply "explanation." Explanation must be directly guided by the sensory input. Perception and problem solving must now be interpreted from a perspective that includes data acquisition and problem solving processes, especially, learning and prediction. Whatever explanation we are analyzing, we should focus on how the input and knowledge-producing systems are coordinated. Embodiment plays an important role in this coordination.

An archaeological example will help to understand this mechanism for knowledge representation. Imagine the automated archaeologist should learn to identify different kinds of lithic tools, and specify, among other things, which work activity was performed by some prehistoric people using those tools (Figure 4.3). Here, we design an automated archaeologist whose "brain" contains a preliminary subpopulation of neurons to store descriptive features:

shape, size, use-wear, and so forth. Only relatively few neurons are directly connected to the real world as "sensory devices," channels through which empirical data are presented to the system, with the rest gaining their inputs in later stages of processing from other neurons in the network. Those are the *input* neurons and together encode

what the machine visually knows of each tool in a *vector*, that is, a series of numbers indicating the intensity of some physical properties. There is one input vector for each observed exemplar. A second subpopulation of neurons provides a vector encoding of the possible solutions to the problem: arrow point, scraper, and so forth. (Figure 4.4). There are different ways to produce such an encoding: each *output neuron* is a representation for each concept or possible solution, or a single concept is represented in a distributed way through different neurons. That is, we may have four distinct units, one for "knife," another for "arrow point," and a third one for "scraper." This way of encoding the solution is called *localized representation*.

Alternatively, we can have some neurons specialized in detecting different aspects of the solution. For instance: "longitudinal movement," "transversal movement," "work on hard material," "work on soft material." The solution will be a knife, if some input units activate the output units: "longitudinal movement," "work on a soft material," because these are the distinctive

Figure 4.3. The basics of neurocomputing for archaeological reasoning

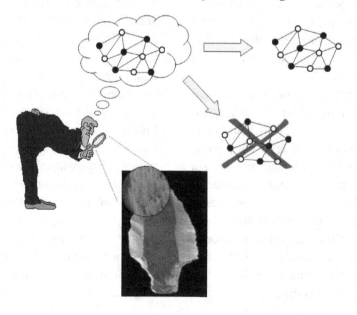

Figure 4.4. An idealized representation of an artificial neural network in archaeology

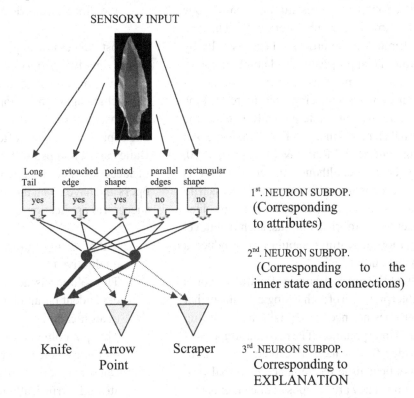

features of using a knife. This is a *distributed representation*. In *distributed* representations, any particular content is encoded by means of a set of simultaneously activated neurons, each of which can participate in the encoding of more than one distinct content. The main characteristic of connectionist systems is their use of distributed representations, where each neuron responds to a variety of different input stimuli, and the fact that many neurons should be active for each input stimulus.

Neural networks process numeric data in a fairly limited range. This presents a problem if data is in an unusual range, if there are missing data, or if data are non-numeric. Fortunately, there are methods to deal with each of these problems. Numeric data are scaled into an appropriate range for the network, and missing values can be substituted for using the mean value (or other statistic) of that variable across the other available training cases (see Bishop, 1995; Hagan et al., 1996). Handling non-numeric data is more difficult. The most common form of non-numeric data consists of nominal-value variables such as *Gender={Male, Female}*. Nominal-valued variables can be represented numerically (presence/absence, 1 or 0), however, neural networks do not tend to perform well with nominal variables that have a large number of possible values. Unconstrained text fields (such as names) cannot be handled and should be discarded. Other kinds of non-numeric data must either be converted to numeric form, or discarded. Dates and times, if important, can be converted to an offset value from a starting date/time. Frequency values can easily be converted.

The central idea is that if a network forms distributed internal representations that encode input features in a combinatorial fashion, then novel stimuli can be processed successfully by activating the appropriate novel combination of representational neurons. Nevertheless, generalization depends on being able to recombine representations that systematically encode the individual elements independent of their specific training contexts (O'Reilly & Munakata, 2000, p. 180). Therefore, although the combination is novel, the constituent features are necessarily familiar and have been trained before to produce or influence appropriate outputs, such that novel combination of features should also produce a reasonable output.

It should be stressed the role of neural networks in the interpretation of archaeological data, in that the user does not need to explain the reasoning behind an interpretation. The network simply acts as a bridge from data to interpretation. Neural networks bear little resemblance to verbal representation. They are composed of elements that are interconnected, rather than ordered in strings and often these units are not even symbols in the ordinary sense. Consequently, it is relatively difficult to work with them. However, these technical difficulties provide many practical advantages. When using neural networks as inverse engineering and problem solving tools for archaeological research, we obtain:

- The capacity for recognizing features or patterns through a veil of noise and distortion, or given only partial information.
- The capacity for seeing complex analogies.
- The capacity for recalling relevant information instantly, as it bears on novel circumstances.
- The capacity for focusing attention on different features of empirical data.
- The capacity for trying out a series of different cognitive "takes" on a problematic situation.

- The capacity for recognizing subtle and indefinable empirical properties.

Most successful applications of neural networks involve pattern recognition, statistical mapping, or modeling. Successful applications can include signal validation, process monitoring, diagnostics, signal and information processing, and control of complex (often nonlinear) systems. Bailey and Thompson (1990) have cited a survey of successful neural-network applications developers and have given the following heuristics for successful applications:

- The problem requires qualitative or complex qualitative reasoning.
- The solution is derived from highly interdependent parameters that have no precise quantification.
- The phenomena involved depend upon multiple-interacting parameters.
- Data are readily available but are multivariate and intrinsically noisy or error-prone.
- There is a great deal of data from specific examples available for modeling.
- Some of the data may be erroneous or missing.
- The phenomena involved are so complex that other approaches are not useful, too difficult, or too expensive.
- Project development time is short, but sufficient network training time is available.

HOW A NEURAL NETWORK WORKS

We can build artificial neurons as pieces of hardware with physical electrical interconnections, or just as software elements able to do input-output computations, and with computable connections implemented as arithmetic or algebraic operations. Let us consider the second case.

For a computing system to be called "artificial neural network" or "connectionist system," it is necessary to have a labeled directed graph structure, consisting of a set of nodes (vertices) and a set of links connecting pairs of nodes. It is the pattern of interconnections what it is represented mathematically as a weighted, directed graph in which the vertices or nodes represent basic computing elements (neurons), the links or edges represent the connections between neurons, the weights represent the strengths of these connections, and the directions establish the flow of information.

The nodes of the graph are either input variables, computational elements, or output variables. Activation values indicate instances. The meaning of nodes (their labels) plays no direct role in the computation: a network's computation depends only on the activation values of nodes and not on the labels of those nodes. However, node labels play an important indirect role, because the nature of the input to the model depends on the labels and the output of a model depends on its input.

To complete specification of the network, we need to declare how the nodes process information arriving at the incoming links and disseminate the information on the outgoing links. The influence diagram of Figure 4.5 provides a functional description of the information flow between the various elements that constitute the model of an artificial neuron.

In the diagram, each node's activation is based on the activations of the nodes that have connections directed at it, and the weights on those connections. The total input to the unit is simply the weighted sum of the separate inputs from each of the individual units. A typical node V_k has an associated node signal I_m, which can be interpreted as the activation value for that particular neuron. A typical directed link originates at node m and terminates on node k; it has an associated weight w_k, which specifies the *strength of the connection*. Its role is to modify the intensity of input signals coming through this particular link. It may be regarded as a factor by which the effects of a signal from one unit to another are amplified or attenuated. In that way, the scalar input I_m is multiplied by the scalar weight w to form V_k. We can modify the activity of the neural network in such a way that some information "weights" more heavily into the firing of some neurons than do others. Thus, by shaping the weights, we may shape the functioning of the neurons.

The incoming weighted input signal goes into a transfer or activation function F, which maps the current state of activation to an output signal U. According to the *integrate-and-fire* model of neural function (O'Reilly & Munakata, 2000, p. 24), each neuron fires, that is to say, it sends an output value in response to the incoming input, if the integrated series of signals arriving from

Figure 4.5. Functional description of the information flow between artificial neurons

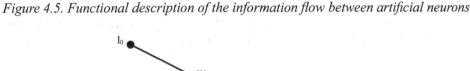
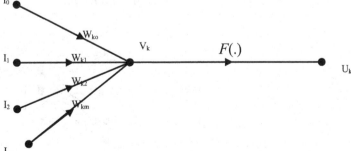

other neurons in the network exceeds a certain threshold. Instead of directly communicating the value of the integrated inputs, neurons have a *firing criterion* that is applied first. The threshold is there so that subsequent neurons are not constantly bombarded with the information that has not enough *intensity* to be concerned. The activation or transfer function executes this firing criterion and produces the neuron's output signal. It may be a linear, a threshold, or a nonlinear sigmoid function. A simple step activation function may be used (i.e., the neuron's output is 0 if the sum of all incoming input is less than or equal to zero, and 1 if the input is greater than 0), although this function is rarely used in artificial neural networks. A much more convenient mathematical form for the activation function is the *sigmoid* logistic nonlinearity:

$$o_i = 1 / (1 + e^{-(vk + \theta_j)/\theta_0}) \qquad (1)$$

This transfer function takes the weighted sum of all incoming inputs v_k squashes the output into the range 0 to 1. The parameter θ_j serves as a threshold or bias (*learning rate*), and it is usually fixed by the user.

To complete this model of an artificial neuron, we need to include some biases or "offset." The bias gives the network an extra variable, and so you might expect that networks with biases would be more powerful (Hagan et al., 1996).

Artificial neurons are connected among them to form a connective system, defined by the parallel distributed flow of activation signals through weighted interconnections. When arranged in an ordered set of neurons called layer, the mechanism is a bit more complex, because we might consider the transformations of the input into an output in terms of successive steps. In such multilayered neural networks, the weights of a layer are associated with the neurons that follow them. Therefore, a layer consists of a set of weights and the subsequent neurons that sum the signals they carry. Successive layers augment the original input pattern, producing a recoding (that is, an internal representation) of the input patterns in some middle (also called hidden) layer in which the similarity of the patterns between units can support any required mapping from the input to the output units. Consequently, activation value in each unit of the hidden layer is a non-decreasing nonlinear function of the product of the input (in the feeding layer) and the connection weight.

Consider the next diagram (Figure 4.7). It shows a graph, whose nodes (artificial neurons) have been organized in three layers, and activation links connect only neurons between layers and not within a layer. It is the most typical organization of a neural network, but not the only one, as we will see later.

Figure 4.6. Neuron activation: Sigmoid logistic nonlinear transfer function

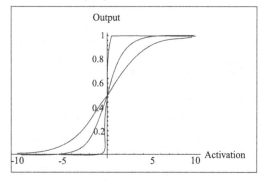

Figure 4.7. A three-layer neural network topology, with a hidden layer

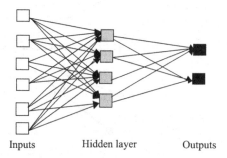

Inputs   Hidden layer   Outputs

In this case there is an input layer of nodes which receives input directly from the environment through dedicated synaptic connections (not depicted in the figure), and typically represents something like pre-processed sensory or empirical data. There is an output layer of units, containing the potential responses; and finally, one layer of intermediate nodes (also called *hidden* units). By the use of such a "hidden layer," simple connectionist networks do not merely store input-output pairs. They allow the emergence of a specific internal structure that generalizes the input-output mappings.

This arrangement of artificial neurons in three consecutive layers can be understood in the following way. An input stimulus from the environment produces some activation level in a given input unit, which then conveys a signal of proportional strength along its connection onto the hidden units. These connections stimulate or inhibit the hidden units, as a function of the strength of the signal, and the efficiency or "weight" of each synaptic connection. A given hidden unit simply sums the *pattern of activations* arriving from the input layer. Which pattern emerges, for a given input, is strictly determined by the configuration of synaptic weights connecting the hidden units. The units in this second or "hidden" layer project in turn to a third population of units, the output layer, which simulate the response containers. In this last layer of the network, the global effect is that an activation pattern across the hidden neurons produces a distinctive activation pattern across the output neurons. As before, exactly what pattern-to-pattern transformation takes place is fixed by the configuration of synaptic weights meeting the output neurons.

The neurons in the input layer may be thought of as "sensory" units, since the level of activation in each is directly determined by aspects of empirical data. The theoretical definition of a neural input is a variable that cannot be influenced by any inner activity of the system (Aleksander & Morton, 1993, p. 222). You may see the input layer as the retina in your eyes, where the raw sensory information is turned into patterns of signals. It is there where the raw external information is turned into quantitative or qualitative vectors. However, rather than representing information as precisely as possible, each neuron in the input layer is sensitive to (activated by) a different set of input signals (its *receptive field*). The receptive field of a neuron generally refers to the spatial and temporal distribution of inputs that affect the firing of that neuron. More generally, this term refers to the set of inputs that activate a given neuron. Input signal is given in terms of a fixed set of representational primitives, i.e., a fixed set of features to which its artificial neurons are seen as sensitive. Such features may include visual ones, like color or size, and non-visual ones, like names or compositional data, or any other information about the archaeological record you can imagine. There should be as many neurons in the first layer as categories to recognize (DeCallataÿ, 1992). We may refer to that configuration of stimulation levels as the *input vector*, since it is just an ordered set of numbers or magnitudes. In this architecture, the fact that a particular unit is active is not very informative; but if a high percentage of the units that are sensitive to a particular input are active, the presence of that input can be inferred with high confidence.

The third layer (output) is devoted to the final recognition of the "solutions." Mathematical theory tells us that we should see output as a separate set of state variables that are influenced both by input and inner state variables. According to this idea, and given that our automatic archaeologist should respond with the *social causes* when it is asked about an *archaeologically observable effect,* these output units contains explanatory concepts: chronologies, functions, social categories, descriptions of social processes or social relationships, and so on.

Intermediate layers in a neural network are needed for technical reasons. They represent the network inner state. An inner state is said to be the instantaneous snapshot of all the system's state variables, a state variable being any variable that has not been designated an input or output variable. We also need a further partition of the inner state into conscious and unconscious state variables. Conscious state variables, through the process of learning, are those that take part in an available representation of the world. Other (hidden units) are the auxiliary state variables that may be needed to label events internally. In this case, it is useful to imagine that the network consists of two classes of neurons, with one class, the *visible* units, corresponding to the possible solutions to the problem (competing hypotheses), and the remaining *hidden* units are used to help storing the input-output patterns.

Hidden neurons are complex features detectors, which may be seen as representational or coding devices. That is, a single hidden unit can be conceived of as standing for something. In this sense, hidden units are thought of as *recoding* the inputs or *internal representations* of the input. Since the output nodes are typically fed only by the hidden units, these internal representations assume a great importance. Because the behavior of hidden units depends on how they are connected to the input nodes, we can sometimes tell something about how a given network parcels up a particular problem by understanding what its hidden units are doing. It is generally accepted that to solve certain problems that are not linearly separable, it is necessary to use a net with one layer (or more) of hidden units. Nets with no hidden layers are used only for solving linear problems, where output concepts are well defined and separated.

The following cases follow this model. Let us begin with an already familiar example. Imagine we are analyzing a prehistoric tool, an arrow point (Figure 4.4). We use several variables to describe it: presence/absence of a long tail, presence/absence of a retouched edge, presence/absence of a pointed shape, presence/absence of parallel edges, presence/absence of rectangular shape, and so forth. Each attribute constitutes a specific

activation level (1,0) for its corresponding neuron in the input layer.

The output layer contains three possible answers: knife, arrow point, and scraper. We can use a similar distributive approach having a different neuron for each feature defining a prototypical knife, arrow point, or scraper, or more easily, just three output neurons, one for each hypothesis.

In this example, activations only flow forward. All "neurons" in the input layer are connected with all units in the intermediate "hidden" layer, and all units in this hidden layer are connected with the neurons in the output layer. No connection is allowed within a layer. In this way, an automatic archaeologist will be able to integrate information from many different sources into a single signal, expressed as the *intensity* of an activation level of some neuron in the system. Consequently, neurons exhibit measurable *tuning curves*, which mean that they respond in a graded fashion to inputs within a range of different parameter values. In this case, the activity pattern of input neurons corresponds to the measures we have taken from the real object. The activity pattern of output neurons corresponds to a double transformation of the input signal: first from the input to the hidden layer, and secondly from the hidden layer to the output. Hidden units here represent the particular nonlinear function between morphological features and inferred functional classes, for instance. It would be even possible to understand the output neurons activation level as the probability value for each explanatory concept. In other words, this neural network is able to answer a functional archaeological problem: given a description of lithic tools in vector format (1s and 0s), the system will produce as an answer the probability that the tool be a knife, an arrow point, and/or a scraper. Provided the correct connection weights among the units, a "solution" will emerge among the output units in response of different input signals.

Suppose now that our automatic archaeologist is able to study the archaeological record without digging (this example is based on a real application by Gorman and Sejnowski, 1988). That means that the system has some remote sensing device producing an input signal to be translated into meaningful output: there is a buried wall or not, there is a buried pavement floor or not. The difficulty is twofold: signals from different archaeological structures may be indistinguishable from magnetic or electrical signals transmitted by the georadar or other remote sensing device. Inputs from each type show wide variation in the character of the remote signal, since walls and floors come in various sizes, shapes, and orientations relative to the incoming input signal. A neural network can be built to solve this problem. A given input signal (from geo-radar, for instance, or magnetic surveying) is run through a frequency analyzer and is sampled for its relative energy levels at a finite number of frequencies (for instance, 30 levels). These values, expressed as fractions of 1, are then entered as activation levels of the respective 30 neurons of the input layer. From here, they are propagated through the network, being transformed by successive weights. The result is a pair of activation levels in two units at the output layer. We need only two units, for we want the network eventually to produce an output activation vector at or near <1,0> when a wall signal is entered as input, and an output activation vector at or near <1,0> when a pavement floor signal is entered as input.

The next example comes from rock-art studies (Barceló, 1995). In this case, the network should be able to explain geographical diversity, chronological variability and social variation from a series of engraved decorations. Input neurons contain the values of some descriptive indexes: the number of symbols engraved; the number of anthropomorphic figures, and so forth. Output units are a binary representation of truth values (1,0) for explanatory concepts: geographical region (four regions), chronology (four temporal phases), presence of imported items among symbols engraved. More about this example and others appear in the next chapters.

Neural networks can be used not only for object classification. Complex social interpretations can also be implemented using this family of nonlinear algorithms. You only need a finite group of competing hypotheses as the output, and a finite set of input units to represent distinctive empirical features of known instances for each hypothesis. For instance, how we can infer the social nature of a cemetery? The answer implies building a set of theoretical social types as output units, and some features describing the shape, the content, and location of graves.

To sum up, all these networks have to be seen as a way to implement input-output functions, where the input is given by the presence/absence or intensity of some observable properties in a real environment and their relationships. The output is seen as an estimation of those properties explaining the existence of entities. Therefore, one of the main advantages of neural networks is that the problem space should not be "stored" physically in the neurons, but specified by states of neural activity that are the result of the neural system's internal organization and dynamics.

Rumelhart and Todd (1993) proposed a general semantics to work with this kind of networks. The model has one bank of input nodes to represent the range of possible subjects, another input bank to represent relations (such as *is a, has-a, can*), and four banks of output nodes, which represent entities, properties, qualities, and actions (Figure 4.8).

Each input or output node represents a single entity, property, relation, quality, or action. In archaeology, the nodes for entities may represent artifacts or any material item to be recognized in the archaeological record. They can be used also to represent people and social categories. Relational nodes answer positively or negatively to relational terms as: *can, is-a, are* and *have*, or even more complex relationships like: *is-made-of, is the consequence-of, generates,* and so forth. The nodes for properties represent components of entities (i.e., wood, pottery, bone, etc.). The

Figure 4.8. An ideal model for a universal neural network

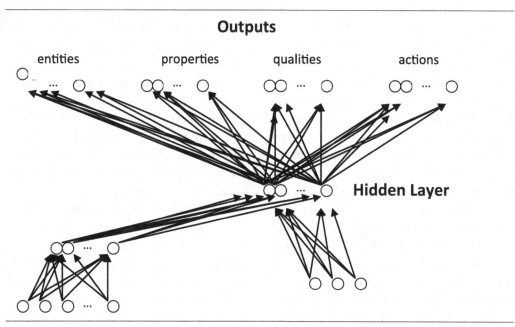

node for qualities may represent adjectives such as red, green, big, far, near. The nodes for actions may be used to represent human activity, that is, "work:" cutting, building, killing, butchering, and so forth. For instance, the expression "a scraper has a transversal retouched edge and it was used to process leather" will be represented with positive values (1s) at those entity neurons in the input layer representing "scrapers." Relation neurons containing "has," and output neurons containing the entity value "leather," the properties neurons "transversal edge" and "retouched edge," and the action neurons "scrapping." The expression "an Empire is a social organization based on territorial expansion and taxation" will be represented with positive values (1s) at those entity neurons in the input layer representing "Empires," and relation neurons containing "is-a," and output neurons containing the entity value "social organization," the properties neurons "territorial expansion" and "taxation," and the action neurons "aggressive," "coactive."

HOW A NEURAL NETWORK LEARNS

Once we have specified the input and output contents, it is time to run the network. Typically, the aim of a neural network is to take a set of input patterns and associate each input pattern with a given output pattern, by spreading excitations and inhibitions (positive and negative numbers) among interconnected nodes. However, a neural network is nothing and does nothing if it has not been previously trained to solve problems. *Learning* in such a neural network means to correlate input with output patterns by slightly changing the values of the connections' weights, so that the application of a set of inputs produces the desired (or at least consistent) set of outputs. The network is able to identify the class of that particular pattern because of the information it has extracted from some training data.

The easiest way to train a neural network is by feeding it with multiple sets of experimental data (laboratory replications) or controlled observations (ethno-archaeological or historical sources) in which the outcomes are known (*supervised learning task)*. That means that before using the network, it must first undergoing a training or learning session, during which a set of input patterns is repeatedly presented to the network, along with the category to which each particular pattern belongs. The more known data presented to the network, the better its performance will be. In the human brain, the initial strengths of the connections reflect the cumulative effects of natural selection. In an artificial neural network simulation, the initial weights are typically assigned small, randomly assigned values at the beginning of learning. Thereafter, the connections weights change based on the degree of correspondence between the activation of the relevant output units by the environment and the activation required for the supervised learning task. A large discrepancy between the output of the network activated by the training stimuli and the output required for the reinforcing stimulus produces large changes in the connection weights within the network. Conversely, when the discrepancy between the output produced by the environment and the required output is small, the weights change very little. This is consistent with selection by reinforcement in that the change in connection weights reduces the discrepancy between the output produced by the environment and the target output required for the reinforcing stimulus.

When a network runs in training mode, both activations and weights will change on each learning trial. After training, the network can be tested by presenting inputs and observing their effects on activations alone. It is important to understand that although both weights and activations can change in response to inputs, their roles are distinct. Activation values are the vehicle for temporary state changes in a network that should tell us which one of a set of possible input patterns has just been processed. Weights are the vehicle for more enduring changes in a network that

make it capable of processing all of the various input patterns on which it has been trained. One similarity between activations and weights is that their changes are determined *locally*; that is, they are based solely on information that is directly available to a particular unit or connection. In the case of a weight change, the outputs of each of the two units between which the connection is being adjusted count as local.

In doing so, the network weights gradually converge to values such that each input vector produces the desired output vector. It is the network, which self-adjusts to produce consistent responses. By adapting its weights, the neural network works towards an optimal solution based on a measurement of its performance.

To get a better idea of how this looks like, we will come back to the arrow point example (Figure 4.4). We want that our automatic archaeologist be capable of distinguishing arrow points from scrapers, because both shapes are related to different uses. First, we should circumscribe the domain by fixing on a prototypical stone arrow point, and a prototypical scraper. These ideal prototypes will be used as the "solution" to the problem. Both kinds of lithic tools will be described in terms of a fixed set of representational primitives (input neurons). Next, we select some arrow points from our excavation data, which we know are approximate to an ideal arrow, and some scrapers, which we know are approximate to an ideal scraper. None of which quite matches its respective prototype. Now assign each individual artifact a category (arrow or scraper). Give the network a series of experiences of individual stone tools by activating simultaneously the units that correspond to the tool description and the unit containing the category. After each such exposure, allow the system to deploy a learning rule to lay down a memory trace in the form of a pattern of altered connectivity and to facilitate recall of the last description. After 50 or so such runs, the system will learn to relate the description with the category, although it has never been exposed to a prototypical arrow point or a prototypical scraper, but only to the excavation data, which are incomplete or distorted instances of the ideal type. The neural network extracts the pattern common to all the slightly distorted or incomplete inputs, producing a general idea of the prototypical member of the set of which the inputs were instances. The process is called "training the network," and it is executed by an auxiliary computer programmed to feed samples from the training set into the network, monitor its responses, and adjust the weights according to the special rule after each trial. Under the pressure of such repeated corrections, the behavior of the network slowly converges on the behavior we desire. That is to say, after several thousands of presentations of recorded inputs and subsequent adjustments, the network starts to give the right answer close to ninety percent of the time.

Remember the remote sensing example. We wanted to build an automated archaeologist able to distinguish buried walls from buried floors and from random noise captured by a geophysical surveying. It would be a miracle if the network made the desired discrimination immediately, since the connection weights that determine its transformational activity are initially set at random values. At the beginning of this experiment, then, the output vectors are sure to disappoint us. Nevertheless, if we proceed to *teach* the network by presenting successively a large set of recorded samples of various (genuine) buried walls remotely sensed signals, from walls of various sizes and orientations, and a comparable set of genuine buried floors signals, the system will be able at the end to recognize appropriately the incoming input.

Unsupervised learning occurs when the network learns in the absence of any form of externally provided feedback (Hinton & Becker, 1992, p. 5). Unsupervised training requires no target vector for the outputs, and hence, no comparisons to predetermined ideal responses. As an example, consider a paleontologist wishing

to determine whether a set of bone fragments belong to the same dinosaur species or need to be differentiated into different species. For this task, no previous data may be available to identify the species for each bone fragment. The scientist has to determine whether the skeletons (that can be reconstructed from the bone fragments) are sufficiently similar to belong to the same species, or if the differences between these skeletons are large enough to warrant grouping them into different species. This is an unsupervised learning process, which involves estimating the magnitudes of differences between the skeletons. One scientist may believe the skeletons belong to different species, while another may disagree, and there is no absolute criterion to determine it correct. The training set consists solely of input vectors. A training algorithm modifies network weights to produce consistent output vectors; that is, both application of one of the training vectors and application of a vector that is sufficiently similar to it will produce the same pattern of outputs. The training process, therefore, extracts the statistical properties of the training set and clusters similar vectors into classes. The resulting model is a network that just looks at the world, and without any further instructions, constructs an internal representation.

The diverse approaches to neurocomputational learning of patterns can be categorized into two general paradigms:

- Associative mapping in which the network learns to produce a particular pattern on the set of input units whenever another particular pattern is applied on the set of input units. The associative mapping can generally be broken down into two mechanisms:
  - **Auto-association:** An input pattern is associated with itself and the states of input and output units coincide. This is used to provide pattern completion, that is, to produce a pattern whenever a portion of it or a distorted pattern is

presented. In the second case, the network actually stores pairs of patterns building an association between two sets of patterns.

- o **Hetero-association:** Is related to two recall mechanisms:
  - *Nearest-neighbor* recall, where the output pattern produced corresponds to the input pattern stored, which is closest to the pattern presented, and
  - *Interpolative* recall, where the output pattern is a similarity dependent interpolation of the patterns stored corresponding to the pattern presented. Yet another paradigm, which is a variant associative mapping is classification, that is when there is a fixed set of categories into which the input patterns are to be classified.

- Regularity detection in which units learn to respond to particular properties of the input patterns. Whereas in associative mapping the network stores the relationships among patterns, in regularity detection the response of each unit has a particular 'meaning.' This type of learning mechanism is essential for feature discovery and knowledge representation.

As it occurs in other machine learning domains, neurocomputational algorithms may be categorized as supervised or unsupervised. For supervised learning, the performance is explicitly measured in terms of a desired signal and an error criterion. For the unsupervised case, the performance is implicitly measured in terms of a learning law and topology constraints. Supervised learning requires pairs of data consisting of input patterns and the correct outputs, which are sometimes difficult to obtain. Unsupervised training classifies input patterns internally and does not exceed expected results. The data requirements for unsupervised training are thus much easier and less costly to meet, but the capability of the network is significantly less than for supervised learning.

THE BACKPROPAGATION LEARNING ALGORITHM

Backpropagation is a special case of *supervised* learning algorithm. To use this approach, we need a feed forward network formed by a minimum of three layers:

- An input layer of descriptive features (measures, observations),
- An output layer for representing "solutions," that is to say, concepts or theoretical entities, and
- A *hidden* layer of units to store the connection weights among input and output units.

Once you have decided that you have a problem, and it can be solved using neural networks because it implies some input-output relationship, you will need to gather data for training purposes. The training data set includes a number of cases, each containing values for a range of input and output variables. For instance, consider a network with three units in the first layer, representing some measures of length, height, and width of archaeological artifacts.

	LENGTH	HEIGHT	WIDTH
ARTIFACT 1	12.5	9.8	25.6
ARTIFACT 2	13.5	8.7	22.6
ARTIFACT 3	10.1	10.2	13.2
ARTIFACT 4	12.1	9.5	25.4
ARTIFACT 5	14.5	7.5	20.0

Here, we are working with a three input unit model (one for each variable), and we know five successive states of activation, one for each observation or artifact. The output of the network will give us the solution to the problem: the *chronology* for those artifacts. They already known values will be stored in another (output) unit.

CHRONOLOGY

ARTIFACT 1	*11*[th] *Century*
ARTIFACT 2	*10*[th]
ARTIFACT 3	*7*[th]
ARTIFACT 4	*11*[th]
ARTIFACT 5	*9*[th]

Let us see how a backpropagation model operates. Present description of the algorithm is based on the original paper by Rumelhart, Hinton and Williams (1986), and the vector notation used by Stone (1986). More mathematical details appear in Caudill and Butler (1992), Haykin (1999), Bishop (1995), Hagan et al. (1996), Mehrotra et al. (1997), Fine (1999), Reed and Marks (1999), and Principe et al. (2000) among others.

The basic learning procedure is a two-stage process. First, an input is applied to the network; then after the system has processed for some time, some neurons are informed of the values they ought to have at this time. If they have attained the desired values, then the weights are changed according to the difference between the actual value the units have attained and the target for those units. This difference becomes an error signal. This error signal is sent back to those units that impinged on the output units. Each such unit receives an error measure that is equal to the error in all of the units to which it connects times the weight connecting it to the output unit. Then, based on the error, the weights into these "second layer" units are modified, and the error is passed back another layer. This process continues until the error signal reaches the input units or until it has been passed back for a fixed number of times. Then a new input pattern is presented and the process repeats. Such a procedure will always change its weights in such a way as to reduce the difference between the actual output values and the desired

output values. The following presentation may be too difficult for some readers. It can be skipped and the rest of the chapter is easily understandable. There is plenty of commercial software that makes the calculations, and the user only needs to concentrate on results. Of course, it would be interesting if the user understands some of the logical steps followed by the algorithm. The same remarks should be made for the presentation of the other algorithms. The reader is advised to read applications Chapters V, VI, and VII to understand some of the procedures presented here:

Step 1. Select the unit with the highest output.

Step 2. If this unit has output greater than or equal to the accepted treshold, and all other units have output less than the reject threshold, assign the class represented by that unit.

Step 3. Calculate actual outputs layer-by-layer, starting on the first hidden layer. The net value of each neuron in it is calculated as the weighted sum of inputs. The net input is then passed through the activation function F to produce output values for each neuron in the first hidden layer. In backpropagation, we usually assume a sigmoid logistic nonlinearity. We assume that each unit provides an additive contribution to the input of units to which it is connected. In such cases, the total input to the unit is simply the weighted sum of the separate inputs from each of the individual units. That is, the inputs from all of the incoming units are simply multiplied by a weight and summed to get the overall input to that unit:

$$net_j = \Sigma w_{ij} o_i \qquad (2)$$

The outputs from neurons in this layer serve as inputs to the next layer (usually the output layer, or a second hidden layer). The process is repeated to obtain the output vector at this layer).

Step 4. Adapt weights. Use a recursive algorithm starting at the output nodes and working back to the hidden layer. Adjust weights by:

$$w_{ij}(t+1) = w_{ij}(t) + \eta \delta_j x_i \qquad (3)$$

In this equation $w_{ij}(t)$ is the weight from hidden unit i from an input to unit j at time t. x_i is either the output of unit i or is an input, η is a scalar constant, which determines the rate of learning, and δ_j is an error term for unit j (it can be seen as the difference between the desired and actual output on input i). If unit j is in the output layer, then:

$$\delta_j = y_j(1 - y_j)(d_j - y_j) \qquad (4)$$

where d_j is the desired output of unit j and y_j is the actual output produced in Step 3. If unit j is an internal hidden layer, then:

$$\delta_j = x_j(1 - x_j)\Sigma_k \delta_k w_{jk} \qquad (5)$$

where k is over all units in the layers above unit j. Internal unit thresholds are adapted in a similar manner by assuming they are connection weights on links from auxiliary constant-valued inputs. Convergence is sometimes faster if a momentum term is added and weight changes are smoothed by:

$$w_{ij}(t+1) = w_{ij}(t) + \eta \delta_j x_i + \alpha(w_{ij}(t) - w_{ij}(t-1)) \qquad (6)$$

where $0 < \alpha < 1$.

Step 5. Repeat by going to step 2. Take another vector input representing the next empirical observation, and start the iterative processing again.

This algorithm can be considered as an iterative process of correction and progressive refinement of an initial matrix of random neural weights. The general idea of this form of weight updating is *gradient descent*. Weight changes at each step are of course minuscule. However, having nudged one weight in a profitable or error reducing direction, we repeat the entire process just described. Proceeding stepwise in this fashion, through every one of the network's connections, produces an ever-so-slightly better performance at the output vector. Next, we repeat this lengthy procedure with a second input-output pair, then a third, a fourth, and so on. That means proceeding in the direction of the steepest descent of error as a function of the weights, to find a global minimum of that function, and minimizing the mean square error between the calculated output and the observed one in an experimental situation.

Fortunately, we can assign the entire business of vector presentation, error calculation, and repeated weight adjustment to a conventional serial computer, and then just stand back and watch the process unfold automatically. All of the input vectors in the training set are paired with their own output vectors and stored in the computer's memory, and the computer is programmed to present each one to the student neural network, compute the error involved in each output, and adjust the weights according to the principles just outlined. After each presentation of each input-output pair, the computer nudges all of the network's weights to slightly happier configuration.

We instruct the computer to keep repeating this procedure, for all the input-output pairs in the training set, until the mean squared error of the network's output performance is made as small as possible. Depending on the complexity of the network, this can take hours, days, or even weeks of furious computing on the best available machines. Nevertheless, it regularly leaves us with a network that has genuinely *learned* the skill or transformational capacity in question. Do not be afraid. With a typical desktop computer, learning a three-layered network with 20 input variables and 7 output units using a databset with 300 training pairs takes less than 3 minutes! However, if you train the network with images (bitmap pictures), training is far more longer (see Chapter VI, p. 212)

HOW GOOD ARE NEURAL NETWORK ANSWERS?

A key question in neurocomputing applications is how to interpret output values. The standard practice is to adopt some activation thresholds or confidence levels that must be exceeded before the unit is deemed to have made a decision. The output neurons have continuous activation values between 0.0 and 1.0, which should be understood in terms of *intensities*: a strong signal if the case is the proper answer and a weak signal if it does not. These graded signals can convey something like the *extent* or *degree* to which something is true.

For a *binomial* (two-class) problem, we can use a network with a single output, and binary target values: 1 for one class, and 0 for the other. We interpret in this way the network's output as an estimate of the likelihood that a given pattern belongs to the '1' class. In order to assign a class from the outputs, the network must decide if the outputs are reasonably close to 0.0 and 1.0. If they are not, the class is regarded as undecided. For a *One-of-N* (multiple class) problem, a class is selected if the corresponding output unit is above the accepted threshold and all the other output units are below the reject threshold. If this condition is not met, the class is undecided. For example, if accept/reject thresholds of 0.95/0.05 are used, an output neuron with an output level in excess of 0.95 is deemed to be on, below 0.05 it is deemed to be off, and in between it is deemed to be undecided. On first reading, we might expect that those networks, whose outputs arrive at threshold minimums (0.5) can be used as a "winner takes all" network. Actually, this is not the case for *one-of-N* encoded networks (it is the case for two-state). You can actually set the accept threshold lower than the reject threshold,

and only a network with accept 0.0 and reject 1.0 is equivalent to a winner-takes-all network. This is true since the algorithm for assigning a class is actually:

Select the unit with the highest output.

If this unit has output greater than or equal to the accept threshold, and all other units have output less than the reject threshold, assign the class represented by that unit.

With an accept threshold of 0.0, the winning unit is bound to be accepted, and with a reject threshold of 1.0, none of the other units can possibly be rejected, so the algorithm reduces to a simple selection of the winning unit. In contrast, if both accept and reject thresholds are set to 0.5, the network may return undecided (if the winner is below 0.5, or any of the losers are above 0.5). This procedure allows us to set some subtle conditions. For example, accept/reject 0.3/0.7 can be read as selecting the class using the winning unit, provided it has an output level at least 0.3, and none of the other units have activation above 0.7. In other words, the winner must show some significant level of activation, for a decision to be reached.

Let us see an example. We are recognizing prehistoric tools in terms of their past function. The hypothesis to test is that the angle between linear use-wear traces and the edge of the tool should be the main feature allowing differentiation between "cutting" and "scraping," because it is the only feature related to the direction of the movement performed with that tool when it was used. Theoretically, we should imagine that an angle between 45 and 90 degrees should correspond to transversal movement, whereas an angle between 0 and 45 correspond to longitudinal movement. Ideally, scrapping is a transversal movement and angle values should be around 90 degrees. Cutting is a longitudinal movement, and its angle values should be around 0. In the middle (45), we should imagine an indeterminacy area.

Barceló and Pijoan-López (2004) have built a very simple neural network connecting a single neuron in the input layer (ANGLE) with two neurons in the input layer: Knives used for cutting (1= Yes, 0 = No) and scrapers used for scrapping (1= Yes, 0 = No). Experimental data were used to teach the network using the backpropagation algorithm. The diagram below shows, schematically, both outputs (longitudinal, transversal), as a function of its input (this is a 1-D representation of the *n*-D input) (Figure 4.9).

Here a cut point appears at angles around 46.5 degrees. In the interval below 46 degrees, tools whose use-wear traces seem to be parallel to the tool's edge, expectations for longitudinal movement are very high, and the output signal sent by the output neuron is higher than 0.5. In the same interval, transversal movement hardly arrives at the 0.5 threshold. The situation is only a bit different for higher angle values, when the use-wear traces main angle is transversal to the tool's edge. In this case, output intensities for longitudinal movement are only slightly below the 0.5 threshold, while, output values for transversal movement, only arrives at the 0.5 level, never beyond. Consequently, the network predicts transversal movement better than longitudinal one (62.132 percent of correct transversal classifications and 48.5 percent of correct longitudinal classifications). Longitudinal expectations decrease smoothly as long angle increases: from 0.6 output signal corresponding to mostly parallel angles (around 25°) to 0.4 at orthogonal angles (higher than 64°). Transversal movement expectations are exactly the opposite; their output intensity values increase as long as the angle becomes more orthogonal.

This highlights the intrinsically probabilistic nature of the visual recognition problem, like all other classification problems. However, the interpretation of output values as intensities does not mean that we can use them as probability estimations. If we need probabilities to tell us how sure (in a formal sense) it is archaeological recognition, then the network's output unit activations should be restricted to fulfill the necessary conditions (Bishop, 1995; Principe et al., 2000). We have to assume that the network has a sufficient number of processing units (neurons) to produce the required map from input space to targets. We also have to assume that training data is sufficient and that the training does indeed take the learning system to the global minimum. The final requirement is that the outputs are between 0 and 1 and that they all sum to 1 for every input pattern (so that each output can represent the probability that the input is in the specified class). To guarantee that

Figure 4.9. Representation of the intensity of the output depending on the input

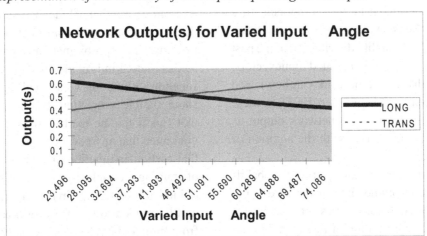

the outputs sum to 1, we may follow Principe et al. (2000) suggestion, and substitute the standard activation function for the so called *softmax activation function*:

$$output = \frac{\exp(\text{net input at output unit }_k)}{\sum_j \exp(\text{net input at output unit }_j)}$$

(7)

where the denominator sums over all network outputs. For the two-class case there is not any relevant difference, since the probability requirements are still met. The probability of class 1 corresponds to its output value, and the probability of class 2 is one minus the value of its output.

This softmax function is similar to the previously presented sigmoid logistic nonlinear, except that the outputs are scaled by the total activation at the output layer (so that the sum of the outputs is 1). It is important to realize that this normalization of activity can be interpreted as competition, because if one neuron produces a larger output, the others are forced to be lower, since the sum is constrained. In fact, any normalization, such as the one imposed in statistics by the probability density function (the area under the curve has to be 1) enforces competition.

The responses of the neural network to input do not "encode" any particular attribute of the data. Rather, the output layer will make sense only when considered as one component in a causal chain that generates responses entirely according to the probability distribution of the past significance of the same or related input vectors. That means that neural network can be viewed as a probabilistic model (Chater, 1995). In these circumstances, we may see network output as an approximate prediction with the addition of random noise.

To sum up, neural networks use of probability theory and prior knowledge expressed in the form of conditional probabilities between causes and effects. The elicitation of these conditional probabilities is however, the weakest point of these networks. Stassopoulou and Petrou (1998) suggest that an appropriate link between Bayesian networks (Chapter III) and multi-layered neural networks will solve the problem. They affirm that there is a direct correspondence between a linearized Bayesian network and the backpropagation architecture, because one can easily work out the relationship between the weights of the neural network and the elements of the conditional probability matrix of the Bayesian network.

WHEN THE NEURAL NETWORK DOES NOT LEARN

Some times, even after many iterations, the neural network does not learn. Minimum square error blocks around 0.40 or something like that, and the difference between desired and calculated outputs does not reduce any more. The fact that a network does not learn may seem at odds with the well-established claim that a multi-layered network, given sufficient units, can learn an input-output whatsoever. For virtually any given function one might represent as an input-output relationship, the theory says, it exists some backpropagation trained network with some configuration of nodes and weights that can approximate it (Hadley, 2000). However, the proofs of Hornik et al. (1989) apply only to theoretical and unreal models that have an arbitrary number of hidden nodes. Such proofs do not show that a *particular* network with fixed resources can approximate any given function. Rather, these kinds of proofs show that for every function within some very broad class there exists some possible connectionist model that can model that function. The mathematical proofs do not guarantee that any particular network can *learn* that particular function given realistic numbers of training examples or with realistic numbers of hidden layers. They in no way guarantee that multilayer feed-forward networks can generalize from limited data. Not any actually instantiated network can literally be a universal function approximator, since the ability to approximate any function depends (unrealistically) on having infinite resources available (Marcus, 2001, pp. 28-29). In this section, we will consider then what neural networks are doing wrong when they do not work properly.

How many weights and training examples does a feed-forward neural network need for recognizing a single isolated class? Delineating a bounded region in a D-dimensional space requires approximately two hyperplanes per dimension. Therefore, a feed-forward neural network needs an order of $2D^2$ weights to define $2D$ hyperplanes for each bounded classification space region. To establish a minimal training requirement for learning an isolated bounded region, the required number of training samples is larger than the number of weights, otherwise the network tend to memorize exactly all the training and fail to "generalize" or to classify correctly any new sample. At least an order of magnitude more training samples than the number of weights in a neural network is required for a robust generalization. This requirement can be prohibitive in archaeological problems were training data are described by hundreds of variables (Reed & Marks, 1999; Perlovsky, 2001).

If the quantity of training instances, and the topology of the network are coherent but the network does not learn, we have to look elsewhere. The first reason for bad running is in the topology of the network. The overriding issue is that, at present, there are almost no guidelines for when a network's architecture is appropriate and when it is not (see, for instance Ripley, 1993, pp. 54-58). Model selection is an important issue, because, if we use an over simplified network, it will not be able to adequately represent the input–output mapping underlying the data. On the other hand, if we use a too complex one, it will extract features from the training set which are peculiar only to that set, and will not generalize well when faced with new data (Penny & Roberts, 1999).

One of the central issues in neurocomputing

is how to set appropriately learning parameters, specially the number of hidden processing elements or neurons. There are two extreme cases. Either the network has too many hidden units to do the job, or it has too few. Understanding each case is important, because correctly setting the number of neurons is still a difficult task at our present state of knowledge. The biggest problem is that the redundant units may have detrimental effects on testing performance (with data that the system has not seen before).

The number of hidden layers and the number of hidden neurons in each layer of a feed-forward neural network are usually determined by a manual trial-and error process. Beginners tend to stick with small networks and reduce the size of the application accordingly. Those with considerable experience with neural networks are usually willing to let the nature of the problem decide the size of the network. With the neural network simulation software available for personal computers and workstations today, a neural network with a thousand neurons and perhaps a hundred thousand connections may no longer be a practical upper limit for non-statistical paradigms such as backpropagation or counter-propagation.

However, as we make bigger and bigger networks with more and more layers and more and more units per layer, the learning will get slower and slower. Even for networks of fixed depth, the learning time (in a serial simulation) is approximately proportional to the cube of the number of connections (Hinton, 1986; Hinton & Becker, 1992). The poor scaling is caused by the fact that the backpropagation process couples all the weights, even in a loosely connected network. Therefore, the number of hidden neurons should be the most reduced possible, given the characteristics of the mapping to be learned. There are several reasons (Zeidenberg, 1990, p. 113). The first is parsimony: both the amount of computer space and the amount of complexity are reduced with a reduction in the number of neurons. In addition, with fewer units, each unit is forced to compute efficiently; no units are wasted, and it is often easier to interpret what each unit is competing. Another reason for keeping the number of hidden units to a minimum is that generalization performance tends to be better when fewer hidden units are present. The disadvantage of using fewer units is that local minima are harder to avoid, and the amount of training time is increased.

Genetic algorithms may provide an effective way to evolve the topology of the neural network. We can first represent a feed-forward neural network as a genotype with chromosomes representing the number of layers, number of nodes, connectivity, and other information about the network. A genetic algorithm can be employed to evolve the initial topology into other topologies until the best topology (in terms of, for example, network complexity, and learning speed) is obtained. The system should consist of two major components: a genetic algorithm engine and a neural network engine. The genetic algorithm engine encodes neural network topologies as genotypes and evolves them through genetic operators. The evolved genotype is then decoded into a neural network by the network decoder (generator) and is then fed to the neural network engine for training. Based on the given training patterns, the engine will train the given neural networks and the resulting networks will then be tested with the given testing patterns. Various statistics such as the size of the network, learning speed, and classification error will be recorded and passed back to the genetic algorithm engine for fitness evaluation. Networks with high fitness will be selected and further processed by various genetic operators. The whole process will be repeated until a network with fitness value higher than the specified requirement is found (Leung, 1997; Zhou & Civco, 1996,).

Beyond the problems derived from complexity and the number of neurons and layers, it is never obvious why the neural network may fail to generalize a given input-output mapping. This point ties in with the allied point that, with complex networks, it may be quite unfeasible to attempt to interpret how the neural network is solving a given problem. In other words, the hidden neurons may become sensitive to extremely subtle and complex regularities in the input-output pairings that are difficult or impracticable to describe (Quinlan, 1991, p. 70).

If the network does not learn, we have to suspect not only on the network parameters, but especially on data. We have to keep in mind that neurocomputational learning is a stochastic process that depends not only on the learning parameters, but also on the initial conditions. The key to success of a neural network based system is the reliability of the data that is presented to it during the training stage of the system's development. Since neural networks learn from the data, the data must be valid for the results to be meaningful. A successful neural network requires that the training data set and training procedure be appropriate to the problem. This includes making the training data set representative of the kinds of patterns the operational network will have to recognize. In order to have extrapolation and interpolation capabilities, neural networks must be trained on a wide enough set of input data to generalize from their training sets. All data that in any way are related to the application should be reviewed and purged of any data that are considered unreliable or impractical for technical or economic reasons. Furthermore, the training set must span the total range of input patterns sufficiently well so that the trained network can generalize about the data.

A very important step prior to neural training is preprocessing of the data. For each feature, the empirical probability distribution should be analyzed. If the distribution is skewed, it is recommended using nonlinear transformations (e.g., taken logarithms) to make it more symmetric. Outliers can be detected e.g. using box plots or statistical tests. These extreme values can be interesting in some applications, but they should be removed prior to training the neural network because they will severely distort the input-output function and can hide the global relational structure. The correlation among features is another important aspect. If several features are highly correlated, this may introduce unwanted emphasis of this aspect of the data. The Pearson correlation coefficient and scatter plots can be used to detect correlation. Some features can then be discarded. Finally, for meaningful distance calculations, the means and variances of the features should be made comparable. This is commonly done using the z-transformation to have zero mean and unit variance for all inputs and thus provide an equal weighting in distances.

One of the most usual problems is that of unbalanced data sets (Barceló et al., 2000). Since a network minimizes an overall error, the proportion of types of data in the set is critical. A network trained on a data set with 900 good cases and 100 bad ones will bias its decision towards good cases, as this allows the algorithm to lower the overall error (which is much more heavily influenced by the good cases). If the representation of good and bad cases is different in the real population, the network's decisions may be wrong. Often, the best approach is to ensure even representation of different cases, then to interpret the network's decisions accordingly.

When there is not enough input for learning input-output pairs, spurious areas are created that produce in-class responses in regions of the input space that do not contain any training data (and therefore are "do not care" regions given the training data). Putting it another way, the machine may not perform very well on data with which it was not trained. If inadequate data are used, correlations become difficult to find. Training time may become excessive when not enough kinds of data exist to make proper associations. This is often the case with backpropagation networks with a very large number of hidden neurons. The negative consequence is memorization of the individual values, and the network may train apparently well but it tests poorly on new data.

If there is uncertainty whether specific data are important, it is usually best to include it because a neural network can learn to ignore inputs that have little or nothing to do with the problem, if enough examples are provided. Using too much or too many kinds of data is seldom a problem if there is adequate data.

If an inadequate number of training examples are available, creating a data set from simulator runs or using expert evaluations of situations may be necessary and acceptable. Several experts can rate examples, and a single network might be trained on the aggregated result of the expert's views. Alternately, a network might be suited for each expert's opinion to see which network gives the best results after training.

Another possible reason for bad learning lies on the fact that neural network's acquired discriminatory capacities are maximally tuned to solving the recognition problems that it typically or most frequently encounters. If, during training, the network encounters data of type A much less frequently than data of type B, then if there are any systematic differences between both types, the network will suffer a performance deficit where data of type A are concerned (Churchland, 1995, p. 52). This phenomenon has been called catastrophic interference (McCloskey & Cohen, 1989). For instance, if the network is learning to recognize different artifact function, it does no good to learn the visual evidence for instruments used to "cut" if in so doing, it forgets instruments used to "scrap." A process is needed for teaching the network to learn an entire training set without disrupting what it has already learned.

An additional problem with training data, the curse of dimensionality, occurs when too many input variables are provided to the network. The risk of ending up with an input-output rule that generalizes poorly on novel data increases with the number of dimensions of the input space. The problem is caused by the inability of existing learning algorithms to cope adequately with a large number of (possibly irrelevant) parameters describing training data (Egmont-Petersen et al., 2002). We can state the hypothesis that artificial neural networks trained through backpropagation depend on correlations between input and output variables. They show that the backpropagation algorithm has very poor generalization ability for statistically neutral problems. Statistically neutral in this context means that no knowledge of the expected output value can be drawn from the knowledge of a single input variable. That means that earning in associative networks is strongly affected by the relationships between members of the input population. In order for the neural network to be effective, the input patterns must be linearly independent of each other. This entire means essentially that for a set of vectors to be linearly independent, no one vector can be a weighted average of the others (Quinlan, 1991, p 55). Highly correlated inputs would tend to limit the efficiency of learning. Those cases that are frequent during the learning phase will leave a greater "impression" in the set of weights than those that are infrequent (Ellis & Humphreys, 1999; Olden et al., 2004).

Neural networks tend to learn the easiest features they can. A mostly quoted illustration (possibly apocryphal) of this is a vision project designed to recognize automatically military weapons. A network was trained on a hundred aerial photographs including weapons, and a hundred not. It achieved a perfect score. When tested on new data, it proved hopeless. The reason? The pictures of weapons were taken on dark, rainy days; the pictures without on sunny days. The network learnt to distinguish the (trivial matter of) differences in overall light intensity. To work, the network would need training cases including all weather and lighting conditions under which it is expected to operate, not to mention all types of terrain, angles of shot, distances.

Networks often fail to learn partitions that reflect the deep facts about the training cases. These are cases in which the target input-output mapping to be learned is based on the recognition

of a feature that is more than first-order, that is, which cannot be defined directly in terms of the primitive attributes appearing in the training examples. In domains organized around interacting rules and features, it can be fatal to allow the net to deal with the complex cases early in its training. In such circumstances, the neural network tries to account for the regularities governed by the complex (second order) features, without yet knowing the basic (first order) ones. Under these circumstances, the second order features are effectively unlearnable and the first-order ones are obscured by the wild hypothesis thrown up in the attempt to cover the second order cases (Clark, 1993).

The topology of the network and the nature of training and testing data are not the only reasons for the wrong functioning of a neural network. The backpropagation method is still not without its drawbacks. It has been observed that an excessive number of running cycles on the training data to insure the lowest minimum square error, sometimes decreases performance on the test data, because minimizing the error measure on a training set does not imply finding a well-generalizable input-output rule. We call this problem the danger of *overfitting* the map f to the particular examples at hand (Ripley, 1993). To be successful, the automated archaeologist should learn the kind of knowledge enabling it to extend its success to other cases. That is, it should not learn only regularities and features in the training data set, but regularities and features that will work in other cases (Clark, 1993, p. 136). When overfitting begins to occur, the validation performance starts to decrease; at this point the neural network is trying to minimize training error on patterns that cannot be generalized to the validation set. It will be able to fit any type of limited data points (e.g., training data) with arbitrary accuracy but will fail to extrapolate well to unseen new observations. This can make the forecaster unstable and therefore of questionable value in real-world applications. If a neuron model drastically overfits the data in *D1*, we would not expect the theory to predict *D2* accurately. After all, overfitting is undesirable precisely because it leads to unreliable predictions.

Neural networks may have a tendency to overfit the training data and to match their discriminant surfaces too closely to the training data. This tends to happen with large networks in particular, and it is not exclusive of supervised learning approaches, but also unsupervised and clustering methods can also overfit the training data. In this latter case, however we have the advantage that a defined region or cluster can contain more than one generator, thereby absorbing any surplus learning capacity so that it does not interfere with convergence.

One way to avoid overtraining is to test periodically predictive performance using some validation test data while training is still in progress. It is supposed that when a neural network's classification performance is tested on "unseen" data (i.e., data not used in training) at regular intervals during the training process and the accuracy for predicting the output given some similar input should improve. However, this may be forcing the neural network to fit the noise in the training data. To avoid this problem, a neural network should periodically stop the training, substitute the test data for one cycle of activations, and record the sum square error. When the sum square error of the test data begins to increase, the training should be stopped. Indeed, if the weights at the previous monitoring are available, they should be used (Caudill, 1991).

After each small step of learning (in which performance of the network on training data improves), one must examine whether performance on test data also improves. If there is a succession of training steps in which performance improves only for the training data and not for the test data, overtraining is considered to have occurred, and the training process should be terminated. The limitation of this approach, however, lies in the fact that in evaluating model fitting and forecasting

performance, only *overall* performance measures such as the sum of squared error (SSE) or the mean squared error (MSE) are used.

Although these measures are useful in reflecting the general modeling and forecasting performance, they do not provide full insights on how and why the overfitting problem arises within the specific forecasting model. In other words, the overall accuracy measures do not delineate a complete picture on the learning and generalizing ability of a model. Therefore, conclusions from a particular application may not be able to generalize to other forecasting situations or even to other data sets from within the same problem domain. Furthermore, overall error measures do not provide insights concerning how to improve forecasting performance.

An additional problem faced by neural networks is the tendency to land in local minima, that is, states that are stable but do not represent the best solution to the constraints. It is a "cul-de-sac," in which for any new learning iteration, the network will be permanently stuck at the point. This is the same problem faced by those human archaeologists, who may persist in some erroneous conclusions. Networks often persist in ignoring or outright misinterpreting salient data until they have escaped the initial configuration into which the learning algorithm initially pushed it. Both human and machines persist in such behavior until they have assumed a more penetrating conceptual configuration, one that responds properly to the ambiguous data (Churchland, 1991). These frustrations finish only when the other weights in the network have evolved to a configuration that finally allows the learning algorithm to appreciate the various examples it has been "mishandling" and to pull the miscreant weights towards more useful values. This fact illustrates that the learning curve is often obliged to take a highly circuitous path in following the local error gradient downwards in hopes of finding a global error minimum.

Perhaps the "easiest" way to deal with a neural network that is stuck in local minima is to start over by reinitializing the weights to some new set of small random values. Geometrically, this changes the starting position of the network so that it has a new set of obstacles and traps to negotiate to proceed until the bottom of the error surface. It is expected (but certainly not guaranteed) that as a result of starting from a new position there will be fewer obstacles in reaching the global minimum of the error surface. The difficulty is that the user must be willing to forego any progress in training and start over on a path that may be no better, or even worse, than the first path. A less drastic approach is to "shock" the neural network by modifying the weights in some small random or systematic way. Again, it is expected (but not guaranteed) that a small move in the error surface will provide a path to the global minimum. A good rule of thumb is to vary each weight by adding a random number of as much as 10 percent of the original weight range (e.g., if the weights range from -1 to +1, add random values to each weight in the range -0.1 to +0.1). Generally, this technique is used when the network has learned most of the patterns before stalling, whereas starting over is used when the network has been unable to learn very few of the patterns. Such changes should be made only after a certain number of learning iterations (Caudill, 1991).

In general, the following rules of thumb are useful to ameliorate the results of a neural network that seems to learn poorly:

- If the results of the training set are adequate but testing results are bad:
  - o The network may be too large and prone to over-fitting the training data. Things to try:
    - Obtain more data
    - Reduce the number of input columns determining which ones are the most important
    - Reduce the number of hidden neurons
    - Try a simpler network architecture
  - o The training data may not be representative of the testing data. Things to try:
    - Randomize the data set.
    - If randomization is not possible, try partitioning the data sets differently.
- If the results of the training set are also inadequate:
  - o The network may not be large or powerful enough. Things to try:
    - Increase the number of hidden neurons
    - Try a more complex network architecture
    - Try adding a second hidden layer
    - Try a more advanced learning algorithm
  - o The data may not contain relevant information. Things to try:
    - Include additional input columns that are relevant
    - Remove inputs columns that are not likely to be relevant
    - Preprocess your data to make the neural network's job easier
- For example, the percentage change of a particular input from one time sample to the next might be more relevant to the desired output than the raw value of that input.

Many years applying neural networks to archaeological problems has allowed me to suggest some addition al advices about how to organize and pre-process data in order to obtain the best results when using backpropagation networks:

- For continuous inputs, look at the data's range and distribution. Consider eliminating inputs with all data concentrated in a single narrow range. For discrete inputs (yes/no or categorical), look at the distribution across various outcomes and consider eliminating variables where almost all outcomes are the same. In many cases, these variables will make the solution more erratic.

- Combine highly correlated inputs together into a single composite. Evaluate cross-correlations between inputs. For categorical data, this may involve creating a derived variable representing input combinations. For continuous variables, this may involve a simple average. This also provides a method for addressing missing data. Experience has shown that the existence of a high degree of redundancy in the data from the monitored variables of a complex process or system can and usually does have an adverse influence of the results of neural network modeling.

- Remove conflicting and duplicated data.

- Neural networks are very sensitive to absolute magnitudes. If one input ranges from 1,000 to 1,000,000 and a second one ranges from 0 to 1, fluctuations in the first input will tend to swamp any importance given to the second, even if the second input is much more important in predicting the desired output. To minimize the influence of absolute scale, all inputs to a neural network should be scaled and normalized, so that they correspond to roughly the same range of values. Common chosen ranges are 0 to 1 or -1 to +1.

- Look inside to determine which variables are the most influential or predictive and try to eliminate them. Although it seems paradoxical, it turns out that sometimes the most predictive variable often relates to some indirect route to the output. The most predictive variable masks more subtle and predictive variable combinations. We often see this when dealing with very noisy data,

as found in image analysis (Gevrey et al., 2003; Olden et al., 2004)

We should look inside our data to obtain a feel for why the network makes mistakes. It is easy to select a dozen or so examples where the network prediction was unacceptable and review the data. We can then search for all other examples with similar inputs and look at the network hidden and output layers; graphing them in Excel as bar or line charts. Coupled with a ranking of each variables influence, we will look for clues as to how correctly and incorrectly classified inputs may differ. Often, this leads to a better problem understanding, and suggests areas where additional data (inputs) may be useful, or raises concerns regarding the neural network's operational use. It also suggests methods in which we might combine or re-code variables at the input stage (Klimasauskas, 2002).

If problems continue, and the network cannot learn, the last way of solving the trouble is to give up on it. An important requirement for the use of a neural network is that the user knows (or at least strongly suspect) that there is a relationship between the proposed known inputs and unknown outputs. This relationship may be noisy but it must exist (Barceló et al., 2000). We certainly would not expect that the factors given for skeletal classification or use-wear determination, for instance, could give an exact prediction, as archaeological interpretations are clearly influenced by other factors not represented in the input set, and there may be an element of pure randomness. It could be argued that certain features simply cannot be learned by connectionist means on the basis of certain bodies of training data, and hence that the only solution is to give up. There is no guarantee the network will succeed in learning to discriminate any kind of input, because there is no guarantee that inputs will differ in any systematic or detectable way.

ALTERNATIVE SUPERVISED LEARNING ALGORITHMS: RADIAL BASIS FUNCTIONS

We can ameliorate the results of a backpropagation neural network if we add a preliminary unsupervised classification of input data to reduce the original variability of the input-output relationship. While the backpropagation algorithm performs a global mapping (i.e., all inputs cause an output), we should experiment with an alternative topology where the network divides the input vectors into similarity classes before calculating outputs. These classes represent the receptive fields for successive layer neurons, and they act as a filter between input data and the hidden layer (Figure 4.10).

A network is presented with a series of input patterns and before calculating the outputs, it must divide them into clusters of similar patterns. The hidden layer contains as many hidden neurons as similarity classes should be used to divide input vectors. There are many well-known algorithms to accomplish this task (Haykin, 1999). In this section we follow the suggestion by Principe et al. (2000, p. 247) to use *K-means* clustering, which is a kind of competitive learning algorithm.

Consequently, hidden units cannot use the usual sigmoid logistic but linear activation function. An appropriated activation rule should assure that on a given trial just one hidden neuron will "win" the others in the hidden layer: the activation of the unit with the greatest net input will go to 1, and the other unit's activation will go to 0. That is the winning unit takes all the activation and inhibits the others. The response surface of a single hidden neuron will be therefore a Gaussian (bell-shaped) function peaked at the centre, and descending outwards (Haykin, 1999; Principe et al., 2000; Schwenker et al., 2001). The name of this activation function, *radial basis function* (RBF), comes from the fact that the output sent by such a neuron is a function of the distance (radius) from the input to the center of the similarity class (cluster) it belongs.

A typical mistake when evaluating this kind of network is to consider that the purpose of such a model is the classification of training data. This classification or clustering is only a requisite to find the best structure for the hidden layer, and has nothing to do with the networks output. The RBF network *clusters* the data (based on a user configured number of optimal centroids), and then *classify* the input vectors based on those clusters. Once the transition from input to the hidden layer has been calculated through the clustering of similar inputs into homogenous receptive fields-, the weights from the hidden to the output layer

Figure 4.10. An alternative kind of network where the input is divided into similarity classes before calculating outputs

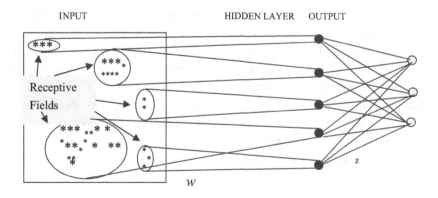

can be optimized using a supervised learning algorithm. This latter transition is usually defined as a standard backpropagation algorithm, or it can be represented as a layer of linear neurons performing a linear transformation of the hidden node outputs (see Bishop, 1995; Haykin, 1999; Hinton & Becker, 1992).

We can understand how this network behaves by following an input vector x through the network to the output y. If we present an input vector to such a network, each neuron in the radial basis layer will output a value according to how close the input vector is to each neuron's weight vector. If an input vector (x) lies near the center of a receptive field, then that hidden node will be activated (Figure 4.11).

Radial basis functions at the hidden layer allow the network to extract properties that are nonlinear functions of the raw input. In this way, hidden layer neurons attempt to tune their activation profiles so that particular units respond maximally to particular patterns in the input set. On the negative side, the kind of neural network we are reviewing here is not inclined to extrapolate beyond known data: the response drops off rapidly towards zero if data points far from the training data are used. In contrast, a backpropagation network becomes more certain in its response when far-flung data is

used. Whether this is an advantage or disadvantage depends largely on the application, but overall the backpropagation's uncritical extrapolation is regarded as a bad point: extrapolation far from training data is usually dangerous and unjustified. In other words, the RBF networks may give an "I don't know" answer, thus hinting the user to disregard the output.

UNSUPERVISED LEARNING ALGORITHMS: SELF-ORGANIZED MAPS

Up to now, we have considered neurocomputational approaches to supervised learning. It is time to consider its alternative. In unsupervised or self-organized learning, networks of neurons are trained without a teacher or a feedback between trial and error. They learn by evaluating the similarity between the input patterns presented to the network. As we argued in Chapter III, transferring the principles of unsupervised learning into data analysis can be done by letting input vectors organize themselves into homogenous groups (self-organized). It means to adjust iteratively similarity relationships as distances in a high dimensional space and producing a low dimen-

Figure 4.11. Typical structure of a radial basis function neural network

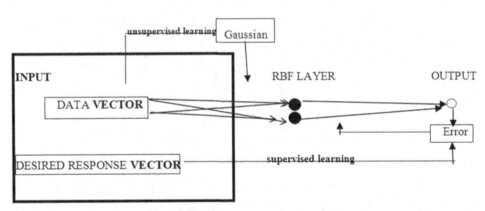

sional projection that preserves the topology of the input space as good as possible.

There are different ways of self-organizing a neural network. Most of these algorithms implement a kind of competition among neurons, in such a way that only those receiving the most similar input are activated in detriment of others receiving signals that are not as similar. Competitive learning is intrinsically a nonlinear operation. It can be divided into two basic types: hard and soft. Hard competition means that only one neuron wins; soft competition means that there is a clear winner, but its neighbors also shared a small percentage of the system resources (Rumelhart & Zipser, 1986). In the brain, competition between neurons leads to the *selection* of certain representations to become more strongly active, while others are weakened or suppressed. In analogy with the evolutionary process, the "survival of the fittest" idea is an

important forced in shaping both learning and processing to encourage neurons to be better adapted to particular situations, tasks, environments and so on (O'Reilly & Munakata, 2000).

Self-organization amounts to the use of competition between a set of receiving units as a way of conditioning the responses of these units. Thus, a given unit will become active to the extent that it is more strongly activated by the current input pattern than other units are. A self-organized map (SOM) is an unsupervised learning technique invented by Teuvo Kohonen. This algorithm reduces the dimensions of input data using soft competition among neurons at the output layer (Kohonen, 2001). *Vector quantization* is the process of dividing space into several connected regions, a task similar to clustering. That is to say, an appropriate algorithm divides the input space into local regions, each of which is associated with an output unit or neuron.

Figure 4.12. A self-organized map

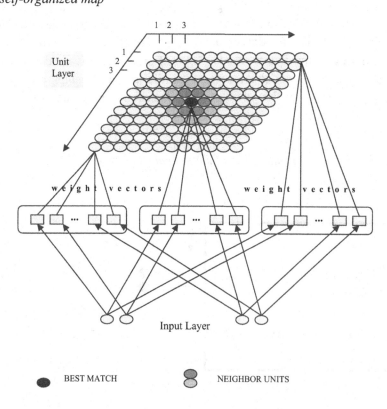

The basic architecture of this kind of neural network consists in just two layers of neurons or processing units: input and output, without any hidden layer. It is the output layer, which is usually called self-organized map or SOM for short (Figure 4.12). It is a planar (bidimensional) representation of interconnected neurons *quantizing* the input space, where neighboring regions in the input space are neighbors in the discrete output space. Every input unit is fully connected to the array of output units, which are also connected between themselves in terms of neighbor relationships (lateral connections). The strength of links between output units is directly proportional to the distance between them (nearest neighbors are strongest, while more distant nodes are linked more weakly).

The activation of these output neurons depend on the values coming from the input neurons, which contain external information (measures, descriptive features) like their counterparts in supervised learning (backpropagation networks), but also on the particular intensities arriving laterally from neighboring neurons. Remember that this is a competitive learning mechanism, in which an activated neuron strongly activates those units near it and inhibits those not so near. This inhibition is reduced as distance continues to increase, until there is no effect at all.

The use of "lateral" connections in the output or self-organized layer makes output values become ordered so that similar models are close to each other and dissimilar models far from each other, as if some meaningful nonlinear coordinate system for the different input features were being created over the network. Given that not only the winning neuron but also its *neighbors* on the output layer are allowed to self-organize, neighboring neurons will gradually specialize to represent similar inputs, and the representations will become *ordered* on the output neurons lattice. A kind of a division of labor emerges in the network when different neurons specialize to represent different types of inputs.

The specialization is enforced by competition among the neurons, what implies that the results offered by this unsupervised learning algorithm depend on the particular relationships allowed between the neurons in the output layer. We can organize them in different ways. The simplest way is as a line of elements, so each element only has two neighbors (the preceding and the following unit) (Figure 4.13).

A one-dimensional SOM can be thought of as a string of neurons, where each one is restricted to be near its two neighbors. In most cases, however, the output layer is more complex than a simple output vector. Output units can be organized as individual cells in a 2D space. There are two main options:

1. **Allowing for rectangular connections between neurons:** A non-border neuron has eight neighbors in a rectangular pattern (Figure 4.14).
2. **Allowing for hexagonal connections between neurons:** A non-border neuron has six neighbors in a hexagonal pattern (Figure 4.15).

In this way, the output layer represents regions or clusters in a kind of solution space, which has the characteristics of those spatial representations we are used to (maps). Feature-detecting units are arranged in spatial configurations in which nearby units represent similar inputs. For example in a

Figure 4.13. A simple one-dimensional self-organized map

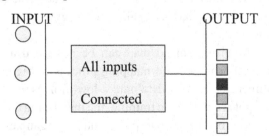

Figure 4.14. A bidimensional self-organized map with rectangular partial neighborhood

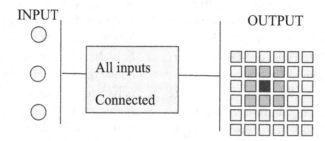

Figure 4.15. A bidimensional self-organized map with hexagonal full neighborhood

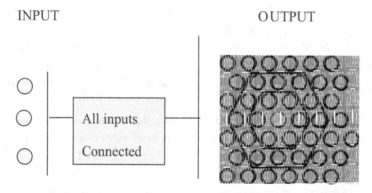

classification problem, the attributes for "object A" are mapped to a particular output unit or region, such that it yields the highest result value and is associated with that object, while the attributes for "object B" are mapped to different regions. New inputs can be mapped by simply running the new data through the map in a "testing" or "production" set and finding the winning processing element for each input. This winning processing element's location will determine which natural cluster it belongs.

Typically, a self-organized map is created of size $N \times N$ (where N is dependent upon the number of data points and the "resolution" of your desired mapping) and each logical cluster of input data is located in subsets of neurons in that $N \times N$ map. These dimensions determine not only the number of clusters, but also the distance between clusters derived by the SOM. For instance, a cluster can be in the top left region of the output layer -say

neurons (1,1) (1,2) (1,3) (2,1) and (2,2)-. Since clustering is unsupervised, there is no predefined number of clusters in the dataset and the clustering is left to the interpretation of the user. However, clusters of output units only reflect the ordering of the input patterns. If the various input points are distributed on a curved surface (for instance, archaeological sites on a real topographic surface, whose input values are x,y,z) they will be mapped onto the output layer on a flat plane. Distances between points will not be preserved, but their topology will. Input vectors that were adjacent to each other will still be adjacent to each other. This property has been called: topology-preserving mapping.

A self-organized map can be described as a nonlinear, ordered mapping process of high-dimensional input data onto a low-dimensional output array. During training, the map learns the position of the input data points and self-organizes following two goals: data representation and data set topology representation. Commonly, the Euclidean distance between the weight vector of the output neuron and the input vector serves as the activation function. In the next step, the weight vector of the node showing the highest activation (i.e., the smallest Euclidean distance) is selected as the winner and is modified to resemble more closely the presented input vector. Pragmatically speaking, the weight vector of the winner is moved towards the presented input signal by a certain fraction of the Euclidean distance as indicated by a time-decreasing learning rate. Thus, this neuron's activation will be even higher the next time the same input signal is presented. Furthermore, the weight vectors of nodes in the neighborhood of the winner are modified accordingly, yet to a less strong amount as compared to the winner. This learning procedure finally leads to a topologically ordered mapping of the presented input signals, that is, similar input signals are mapped onto neighboring regions of the map.

The learning procedure is as follows (Fort, 2006; Honkela, 1997; Kohonen, 2001; Kaski, 1997; Koua & Kraak, 2004; Kulkarni, 2001):

Step 1. Initialize elements of the weight matrix W to small random values. Element w_{ij} of matrix W represents the connection strength between unit j of the input layer, and unit i of the output layer.

Step 2. Present the input vector $x=(x_1, x_2, ..., x_n)^T$, and compute the activation of each output neuron, according the basic dot product.

$$Output = \sum w_{ij} - x_j \qquad (8)$$

Remember that all input units are connected to all output units, so we will obtain an output value for all units in the output layer.

Step 3. Select the output unit with the maximum activation level. This is the unit whose weight vector is most similar to the input vector. That means that for any input vector $x=(x_1, x_2, ..., x_n)^T$, we should compute the degree of mismatch for each unit in the output layer. The degree of mismatch is:

$$v_i = \sum (w_{ij} - x_j)^2 \qquad (9)$$

The weight with the shortest distance (lowest mismatch) is the winner. If there is more than one with the same distance, then the winning weight is chosen randomly among the weights with the shortest distance.

Step 4. Adapt all weight vectors, including those of the winning neuron, within the current neighborhood region. Those outside this neighborhood are left unchanged. The weight that is chosen is rewarded by being able to become more like the selected sample vector. In addition to this reward, the neighbors of that weight are also rewarded by being able to become more like the chosen sample vector. We can use the following general update rule:

$$W_{new} = W_{old} + \text{training constant (input - } W_{old}) \qquad (10)$$

At each time step, this rule is applied to the maximally responding unit and to all the units within the neighborhood of that unit. That is, we have to weight the effects of output units surrounding distances. The neighborhood could be homogenous (all neurons within this region should be updated by the same amount) or the effective change in the weight vectors within the neighborhood could be weighted, so that neurons close to the centre of the neighborhood are proportionally changed more than those at its boundary. The amount the output units learn will be governed by a neighborhood kernel h, which is a decreasing function of the distance of the units from the winning unit on the output layer. If the locations of units i and j on the map grid are denoted by the two-dimensional vectors r_i and r_j, respectively, then

$$h_{ij}(t) = h(\|r_i - r_j\|;t) \qquad (11)$$

where t denotes time. When considering neighborhood, the weight update rule is then

$$w_i(t+1) = w_i(t) + h_{ci}(t)[x(t) - w_i(t)] \qquad (12)$$

where $x(t)$ is the input at time t and $c = c(x(t))$ is the index of the winning unit. That means that the amount of neighbors decreases over time. This process is similar to coarse adjustment followed by fine-tuning. The individual function used to decrease the radius of influence has no importance as long as it decreases. In practice, the neighborhood kernel is chosen to be wide in the beginning of the learning process to guarantee global ordering of the map, and both its width and height decrease slowly during learning.

Step 5. Repeat Steps 2 to 4 for all input samples.

Without mathematical details, the algorithm goes through the following sequence. It chooses at random a given input. Then it selects from all output neurons organized in a lattice at the output layer the "best match" for the chosen input (i.e., selecting the one with the minimum Euclidean distance). Let us call that selected neuron the "winner." Next, the algorithm adjusts the winner's components according to the remaining difference between its current values and those of the current input. At the same time, all the other neurons on the output layer are also adjusted proportionally to their physical distance to the winner location. In each step, the operator decreases how much and how far away from the winner the adjustment is done.

Over the course of many repeated training steps, this leads to a replication of major topological structures existing in high-dimensional space.

One could also interpret the training process as density mapping, since larger congregations of input vectors in attribute space will cause the reinforcement of neuron weights for a large number of neighboring neurons. The opposite is true for portions of the attribute space that are barely occupied by actual input vectors. After neural network training, every one of these neurons is associated with an n-dimensional vector.

The result is a two dimensional grid containing a representation of high dimensional prototype vectors. However, it remains a challenging task to interpret such an output, because it remains a non-trivial task to elicit the features that are the most relevant and determining ones for a group of input data to form a cluster of output nodes. We need methods allowing the automatic assignment of labels describing every neuron in output layer or self-organized map. A simple approach consists in labeling each output neuron by assuming what relates the nearest input data vectors. Output neurons may be assigned multiple labels if they respond to multiple input vectors, thereby providing a measure of confusion between categories and concepts when the same input is grouped into multiple categories, each corresponding to a unique concept. This method, however, requires heavy manual interaction by examining each dimension separately and does thus not offer itself to automatic labeling self-organized output neurons.

Imagine we want to test a traditional typology with the neural network. Once the network has learnt how to organize similarity relationships between a number of initial artifacts, we fed the network with a new data sets containing arrow points of a known functional and chronology (Figure 4.16).

Furthermore, we can build a three-dimensional histogram on the output self-organized map to show how these known input vectors appear clustered on the SOM layer. The data histogram visualization shows how many vectors belong to a cluster defined by each neuron (Figure 4.17). We

Figure 4.16. Testing a Kohonen self-organized map using archaeological data (Nenet 1.1. software http://koti.mbnet.fi/~phodju/nenet/Nenet/General.html)

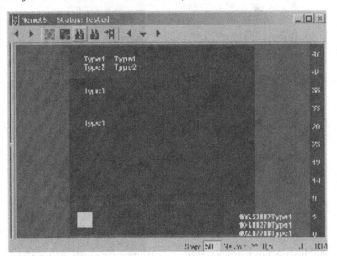

Figure 4.17. A 3 dimensional histogram on the output self-organized map from previous example (Nenet 1.1. software http://koti.mbnet.fi/~phodju/nenet/Nenet/General.html)

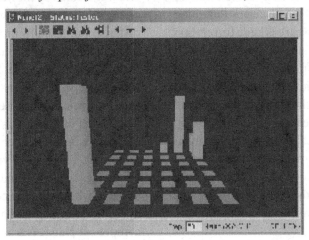

will proceed in this way, until we know the meaning of each neuron in the self-organized layer.

Because the self-organized map reflects the topology of the input data, visual inspection of the output layer should provide a cursory but effective indication of category clustering. Output values can be seen as z values (height) ordered spatially (x,y). The height is calculated as the sum of the distances to all immediate neighbors normalized by the largest occurring height. This value will be large in areas where no or few data points reside, creating mountain ranges for cluster boundaries. The sum will be small in areas of high densities, thus clusters are depicted as valleys. This graphical representation leads to an interpretable, 3-dimensional landscape of the self-organized map. This diagram is called Unified Distance Matrix or short U-matrix (De Bodt et al., 2002; Kaski et al., 1998; Kohonen, 2001; Takatsuka, 2001; Ultsch, 2003; Ultsch & Moerchen, 2005).

Figure 4.18. Ideal display of the U-matrix for a 40x40 units self-organized map

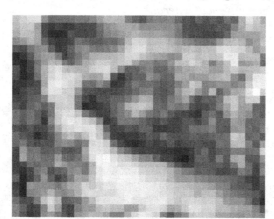

The U-matrix should be understood as the cluster structure revealed by all the variables together. The contribution of a variable can be measured as the share of the distances stemming from the variable. If the share is large in a certain area, the variable explains well the local cluster structure. A large share implies also that the types of data that nearby locations on the map represent differ predominantly in the values of the variable. Neurons that are in a meaningful cluster will be close to each other (because of the higher input density) and will be surrounded by neurons that are farther apart because of the lower input density between clusters. Thus, the U-matrix display will show low values inside a cluster and high values between the clusters.

To explore the similarity structure within the input data set we should interpret the landscape of the U-matrix in visual terms. Given an *n*-dimensional data set, the question is if there exists any structure in form of subsets that is, clusters of data that are very similar to each other. The U-matrix should be interpreted as follows: if a subset of input data falls into a valley surrounded by walls then this indicates a cluster containing similar vectors. In other words, there are valleys where the vectors in the lattice are close to each other and hills or walls where there are larger distances, indicating dissimilarities in the input data. The dissimilarity among the different clusters is indicated by the height of the walls or hills on the U-matrix. On the map display, each scaled distance value determines the grey level or color of the point that is in the middle of the corresponding neurons in the output layer. The light shading typically represents a small distance, and the dark shading typically represents a large distance. A black band of neurons is developed when cases are distant in weight, hence the cases being very dissimilar. This type of visualization is useful as long as clear cluster boundaries exist. The location of cases within and the corresponding make-up of the U-matrix are defined by the values of the component planes (variables).

To illustrate this visual approach to understanding the U-matrix, I will use Databionic ESOM Tools. In its U-matrix display, the cluster structures in the data are visualized as grey levels depicting the distances between model vectors connected to neighboring locations on the map lattice. It is the result of the self-organized clustering of artificially simulated 212 input items, which were measured according to three variables (C1, C2 and C3). The network contains then 3 input neurons, and 50x50 neurons in the self-organized output layer (Figure 4.19).

Figure 4.19. 50 x 50 neurons U-matrix, after processing 212 objects, using three different measures. Simulated data. (Using the Databionic ESOM Tool: http://databionic-esom.sourceforge.net)

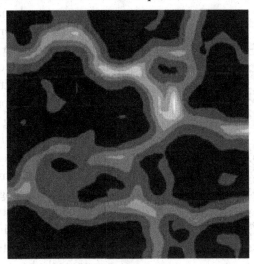

Figure 4.20. Different U-matrix solutions corresponding to each of the three variables defining the original input data set. (Using the Databionic ESOM Tool: http://databionic-esom.sourceforge.net)

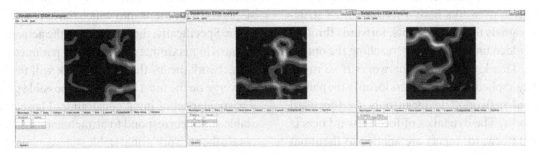

In this case, the grey gradient has been inverted for depicting results much clearer. The smallest height is mapped to the darkest value (black), the largest to the brightest (white). Darkest areas contain the identified clusters, separated by neurons where values are higher, and represented as grey or white. We can identify tentatively eight different clusters in the original data set of 212 items.

We also can explain the contribution of each input variable into the final clustering. The software allows us to update the U-matrix using each time a different variable or component (Figure 4.21). Here you have the result for each of the three input variables *C1, C2, C3*. In those images, we

see how different variables combinations generate different clustering structures.

Finally, given that individual cases can be named and labeled, we can convert an U-matrix with bestmatches depicted into a matrix with cluster symbols.

RECURRENT NETWORKS

The networks considered up to this point have no feedback connections, that is, they do not have "inverse" connections where weights extend from the outputs of a layer to its inputs. Backpropaga-

Figure 4.21. An ideal representation of clustering structure on a self-organized output layer

```
11112222222222222222222222222222222222222333333333
11112222222222222222222222222222222222222333333333
11112222222222222222222222222222222222222333333333
11112222222222222222222222222222222222222333333333
11112222222222222222222222222222222222222333333333
11112222222222222222222222222222222222222333333333
11112222222222222222222222222222222222222333333333
1111222222222222222222222222222222223333333333333333
1111222222222222222222222222222222223333333333333333
1111222222222222222222222222222222223333333333333333
444444444444444444444444444433333333333333333333333
444444444444444444444444444433333333333333333333333
444444444444444444444444444433333333333333333333333
444444444444444444444444444433333333333333333333333
444444444444444444444444444433333333333333333333333
444444444444444444444444444433333333333333333333333
444444444444444444444444444433333333333333333333333
44444444444444444444444444445555555555555555555555
66666444444444444444444444445555555555555555555555
66666444444444444444444444445555555555555555555555
66666444444444444444444444445555555555555555555555
```

tion is not a true feedback, because the inverse flow of errors does not arrive to the input. We say these networks have a *feed-forward* structure: signals flow from inputs, forwards through any hidden units, eventually reaching the output units. This kind of neural networks is so much widely applied, that some users identify the phrase "neural networks" to mean only feed-forward networks. The dynamics of feed-forward nets is straightforward: inputs are applied to the input neurons and subsequent layers evaluate their neuron outputs until the output layer is reached. This whole process is referred to as a *forward pass*. Conceptually, neurons in successively higher layers abstract successively higher-level features from preceding layers (Mehrotra et al., 1997, p. 20). The lack of feedback ensures that the networks are unconditionally stable. They cannot enter a mode in which the output wanders interminably from state to state, never producing a usable output.

Networks with feedback connections and/or inter-layer connections are said to be *recurrent* (Amari, 1993; Maes, 1989,). They are based on bidirectional excitatory connectivity (also known as *recurrence*). Such a system does not need a control structure. Who does what at what moment does not require an explicit decision. The schedule is, in a sense, a byproduct of the interactions of units with each other and the world. The notion of *attractor* provides a unifying framework for understanding the effects of bidirectional excitatory connectivity. An attractor is a stable activation state that the network settles into from a range of different starting states. The ranges of initial states that lead to the same final attractor state comprise the *attractor basin*. For example, we can think of pattern completion as the process of the network being attracted to the stable state of the complete pattern from any of a number of different partial initial states. Thus, the set of partial initial states that lead to the complete state constitute the basin of attraction.

We can relate the notion of attractor to constraint satisfaction ideas. Neural connections and synaptic weights literally constrain the possible stable configurations into which the network can settle. Specifically, the tendency of the activation updates to maximize some general parameter of the network means that the network will tend to converge on the most stable states possible given a particular set of input constraints. These most stable states correspond to attractor states. If we regard the network's final stable state as a solution, then the connections between inputs and outputs will represent conceptual constraints on the solution, and the stable state should be the state of the network that best satisfies these constraints.

Such a constraint satisfaction is a form of parallel search, where the network searches through a number of different possible states before finding one that satisfies the constraints optimally. The search proceeds in parallel instead of sequentially, visiting a huge number of distinct states in sequence. Although many stimuli (e.g., familiar ones) will result in the rapid settling of the network into a relatively optimal state in response to that stimulus, others may require more extended iterative "searching" for an appropriate activity state. In either case, the resulting activity state will not typically be the same each time the same stimulus is presented, due to a number of factors (e.g., learning, habituation, and sensitization). (O'Reilly & Munakata, 2000, p. 210).

The main advantage of recurrent networks is the possibility to include the previous state of the network in calculating the output. A purely feed-forward system cannot generate any vector sequences on its own. It is wholly dependent on its input. A recurrent network can generate complex sequences of activation vectors all by itself. It can be trained to discriminate a standard sequence of physical configurations. A recurrent network's primary unit of representation is not the point in activation space, but rather the *trajectory* in activation space. It is a temporally extended sequence of activation patterns. The virtue of such trajectories is that they can represent objective phenomena with a temporal profile.

Recognition occurs when something close to a prototypical activation vector unfolds the relevant population of neurons. The activation vectors carve out, over time, a special line, or path in the relevant space. That is to say, recurrent networks represent the world as unfolding in time, as something that contains prototypical processes, structured sequences, and standard causal pathways. Perceptual discrimination in these cases often consists in the perceptually initiated activation of an appropriate vector sequence, whose unfolding, however, is owed primarily to the recurrent activity of the trained network itself rather than to the external stimuli it receives (Churchland, 1995, 1998).

Therefore, we should consider a *recurrent network* as receiving an input sequentially and altering its response appropriately depending upon what information was received at previous steps in the sequence (recurrent activation). It does this by feeding a pattern achieved on a higher layer back into a lower layer, where it functions as a type of input. This is a sequential task, where a sequence of discrete events has to be learnt. The central problem in learning sequential tasks is

developing useful context representations that capture the information from previous events that is needed to produce an appropriate output or interpretation at some later period in time. In the simplest case, the only prior context necessary to predict the next step in the sequence is contained in the immediately preceding time step. An example of this is one where the context representation literally contains a copy of all prior states. Obviously, such a strategy is impossible with limited capacity memory systems.

Two closely related types of neural network models were developed by Jordan (1986) and Elman (1990, 1992), and are often called *Jordan and Elman networks*. The category that includes both models is known as a *simple-recurrent network*.

This kind of neural network differs from feed-forward networks in that it has one or more additional layers of nodes, known as *context neurons*, which consist of units that are fed by the hidden layer but that also feed back into the (main) hidden layer. It is a three-layer network with the customary feed-forward connections from input neurons to hidden neurons, and from hidden to output ones. There is an additional set of units

Figure 4.22. Recurrent flow of activations in a Jordan-Elman network

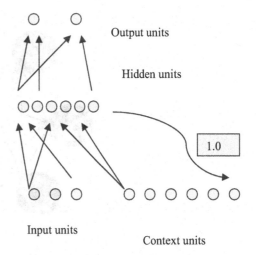

181

called context neurons, which provide for limited recurrence (and so this may be called a simple recurrent network). These context units are activated on a one-for-one basis by the hidden units, with a fixed weight of 1.0. In a Jordan network, the prior state was derived from the output units on the previous time cycle. In an Elman network, the prior state comes from the hidden neuron patterns on the previous cycle. Because the hidden units are not taught to assume specific values in the course of learning a task, they can develop representations encoding the temporal structure of that task (Figure 4.22). In other words, the hidden units learn to become a kind of memory, which is very task specific.

The result is that at each time cycle, the hidden unit activations are copied into the context units; on the next time cycle, the contexts combine with the new input to activate the hidden units. The hidden units therefore take on the job of mapping new inputs and prior states to the output; and because they themselves constitute the prior state, they must develop representations, which facilitate the input/output mapping.

A more complex example of recursive networks is the Hopfield network (Caudill & Butler, 1992; Haykin, 1999; Hopfield, 1982; Mehrota et al., 1997; Principe et al., 2000). It consists of a number of artificial neurons connected to every other neuron in the network. It is important that the weights connecting two units be at least roughly *symmetric*, so that those of the other unit reciprocate the influences of one unit. This symmetry enables the network to find a single consistent state that satisfies all of the units. If the weights were not symmetric, then one unit could be "satisfied" but the other "unsatisfied" with the same state, which would obviously not lead to a consistent global state.

The network has connections that allow activation to pass forward or backward: each unit sends its activation to each other neuron, and receives from all other ones. Importantly, the weights are symmetrical in that w_{ij} is equal to w_{ji}. A novel feature of the network is its asynchronous changes in the activation states of units. Each unit will adjust its state randomly in time at some average attempt rate.

Figure 4.23. An ideal model for a full recurrent network, where all neurons are connected to all other networks, without layers

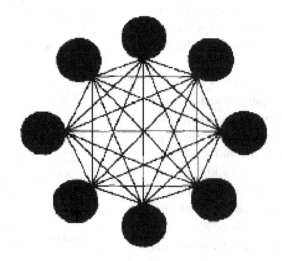

The mathematics of full recurrent networks is usually very complex. Do not panic! I am offering here only some very general ideas. Although the reader may not understand the mathematics, the way this technology works is very intuitive. Practical examples of this technique appear at the end of Chapter VIII and in Chapter IX.

This kind of recursive neural networks differs from the feed-forward ones in operation. Their inputs are applied simultaneously to all neurons and consist of a set of starting values, which can be either binary (0 or 1) or bipolar (-1 or + 1). The network cycles through a succession of states, until it converges on a stable solution. The output of the network is given by the value of all the neurons in this steady state. The activation rule is simple: unit i will be on and have an output of 1 only if the sum of its weighted input exceeds a threshold, otherwise it will have an output of 0. The learning rule is not the major focus of interest. Hopfield (1982) was primarily concerned to show that the collective action of the units, given some set of weightings, could be understood as analogous to energy minimization, when energy is expressed by some global measure. The standard form of the network energy function is as follows:

$$E= - \frac{1}{2}\sum_{j}\sum_{i} x_i w_{ij} x_j \qquad (14)$$

where x_i and x_j represent the sending and receiving unit activations, respectively, and w_{ij} is the weight connecting them. Note that each unit in the network appears as both a sender and a receiver in the double sum term. The change in the total "energy" E of the system that would result from a change in activation of neuron $i,$ is given thus:

$$\Delta E= -\Delta x_i \sum w_{ij} x_j \qquad (15)$$

The simple act of updating activations in the network generates the same kind of settling into a lower energy state by satisfying more constraints. The repeated application of the activation rule effectively reduces E to a minimum, as each ap-

plication of the rule will either leave E unchanged or reduce it. If activation state does not change, the global energy remains constant. If the activation state changes from 1 to 0 (Δx_i is -1), its total input ($\Sigma w_{ij} x_j$) is negative, thus the product of these two terms is positive and by the above equation there is a reduction in E. If the unit changes from an activation of 0 to 1(Δx_i is 1), its total input must be positive, again the product of these terms is positive and again E is reduced. The interactions between components impose the constraints on this system, and part of its energy is a function of how strong these constraints are and to what extent the system is obeying them or not. A system that is not obeying its constraints has higher energy, because it takes energy to violate the constraints. A system that has satisfied the constraints is at a lower level of energy, and nature always tries to settle into lower energy state by satisfying more constraints.

Training a Hopfield net involves lowering the energy of states that the net should "remember." This allows the net to serve as a content addressable memory system, that is to say, the network will converge to a "remembered" state given only part of the activation state.

A Hopfield network is created by supplying input data vectors, or pattern vectors, corresponding to the different classes. These patterns are called *class patterns*. In an n-dimensional data space, the class patterns should have n binary components {1,-1}. The network is then used to classify distorted patterns into these classes. When a distorted pattern is presented to the network, then it is associated with another pattern. If the network works properly, this associated pattern is one of the class patterns. In some cases (when the different class patterns are correlated), spurious minima can also appear. This means that some patterns are associated with patterns that are not among the pattern vectors.

For example, let us build a four-neuron Hopfield recursive network. That means 4 neurons fully interconnected, what produces a 4 x 4 weight matrix. The purpose of the network is to be used as an *associative network* to link a class pattern to each input pattern. The initial state of its weight matrix will be:

0	0	0	0
0	0	0	0
0	0	0	0
0	0	0	0

This initial matrix is empty (all zeros), because at the beginning the network has no knowledge. It should learn to recognize some pattern. We will enter an imaginary pattern vector corresponding to the characteristics of some archaeological artifact coded in binary terms. We have four input variables A= 1, B= 0, C=0, D=1. We use this single input to train the network. Using the previous recursive algorithm, the weight matrix finally finds a stable configuration:

0	-1	-1	-1
-1	0	1	-1
-1	1	0	-1
1	-1	-1	0

Now, if we reenter the input pattern 1001, the output will be "1001." The auto-associative network echoes the input when it recognizes it. If we enter the pattern 1000, the output will now be "1001." The neural network did not recognize "1000," but the closest thing it knew was "1001." It figured you made an error typing and attempted a correction! Now, notice a side effect. Enter "0110," which is the binary inverse of what the network was trained with ("1001"). Hopfield networks always get trained for the binary inverse too. Therefore, if you enter "0110," the network will recognize it. Likewise, if you enter "0100" the neural network will output "0110" thinking that is what you meant. One final test: we try "1111," which is totally off base and not close to anything the neural network knows. The neural network responds "?0000?," it did not try to correct, it has no idea what you mean!!

The importance of Hopfield networks in practical application is limited due to theoretical limitations of the network structure but, in certain situations, they may constitute interesting models. Hopfield networks are typically used for classification problems with binary pattern vectors. As we saw in the previous example, a binary Hopfield neural network can associate an input pattern to a previously learnt one. The learnt pattern associated to the input one is characterized by some proximity properties induced by the used metrics. Similarly to human memory, a Hopfield network is able to associate an output Y to a certain input X without the use of a difficult deductive process; it should also be able to associate the right output $Y = X$ to the input X corrupted by noise. The data and information necessary for a correct associative process should already be stored in the memory; that is, memory contains the prototypes of all the possible outputs Y that the network is able to recall. The network should also be able to:

- Associate an output prototype Y which is somehow "similar" to an input prototype X;
- Associate the right output prototype Y to incomplete input data X; and
- Associate a clear output prototype Y to a vague input X.

We shall say that an Hopfield system has a *capacity m* if it is able to recall *m* prototypes (outputs): *i = 1, 2, ..., m*, corresponding to different inputs.

More complex neural architectures and recursive algorithms will not be fully discussed here. Among them, we can mention ART Networks (Grossberg, 1988). ART stands for adaptive resonance theory. ART networks operate using a resonance process between inputs coming from the outside—sensory neurons receiving external stimuli—and those coming from the inside, that is, signals generated by a priori models. ART is a theoretical principle of the structure of adaptive robust feedback connections between two different layers. The output layer is cognitively "higher" than the other is. A single neuron at the output layer encodes patterns of neuron activities from the input layer, which has a lower cognitive level. Output neurons are conceptual units: they recognize an individual input in the lower level neuron activities. The lower level input pattern activates the higher-level output neurons, the synaptic connections of which it matches. The term "resonance" refers to a coherent dynamic state that arises from matching between an input lower level pattern and a stored prototype pattern. The stored pattern is represented at the synaptic connections from the output to the input layer and is activated by an output neuron. Perception corresponds to the resonant state between the concept and the data. When resonance occurs, both the bottom-up filter (recognized input) and the top-down prototype (conceptual output) are updated.

During a cycle of activity through an ART network, some external signal activates a particular pattern of activation in a set of input neurons, and this activity has the effect of inhibiting an additional arousal unit. Activation is then mapped from the input units through a set of learned weights to higher level output neurons, where a pattern of activity may be generated. These output units are competitive, so tending to favor a local representation of the input pattern. Activity in output neurons is subsequently recycled down through an additional set of weights to adjust activity in the input units, with there being inhibition of activity that mismatches that generated from the output layer. If there is no mismatch, a stable pattern of activity is generated in which the model "resonates" to the input. Normally, there are some changes over time in the activity values in the two layers of neurons (so that different representations, X^* and Y^*, are respectively

generated in the input and output units). If the initial representation (Y) in the higher level output neurons does not provide a good match to the input representation (X), then the top down feedback will inhibit the input representation. When this occurs, the orienting unit (A) is reactivated. This provides a non-specific signal that re-sets the classifier units, enabling a different classifier unit to "win" any competition if the same stimulus is subsequently presented.

Learning in ART networks involves changing the two sets of weights, from the input to the output layers, and from the output back to the input units: the bottom-up and the top-down weights. The weights are changed at a rate that reflects the activation values in (respectively) either the input or the output units (for the bottom-up and top-down weights). These changes operate relatively slowly (determined by a rate of change parameter), and so only come into effect when the network reaches a stable (resonating) change.

Applying this last kind of neural networks is even more difficult than other recursive algorithms. The reason is that they are more interesting as a model of brain functioning, than a practical algorithm for learning and classifying.

DIRECTIONS FOR FURTHER RESEARCH

In this chapter, only an introduction to neurocomputing has been presented. The most simple and frequently used algorithms have been explained, but there are many other alternatives. Given that the core of the book is not on neural networks alone, but they are only one technique to implement methods of automated learning in archaeology, more complex architectures and learning algorithms have not been presented. In any case, I suggest the reader to look for information about probabilistic neural networks and Oja's Principal Component Analysis-type learning. Some authors are also working with different learning algorithms adapted to network topologies without hidden neurons. These new algorithms seem to provide similar results as backpropagation in less time, and have fewer tendencies to bad convergence. Questions of space justify why I have not presented them in this chapter (Principe et al., 2000). The theory of recurrent networks also merits more investigation. The reader will find a bit more material about that at the end of the chapter on spatiotemporal analysis. In the recent years, many efforts are being addressed to expert systems and rule-based interfaces linked to neural networks. These hybrid systems contribute to reduce the "black box" character of any neural networks.

Many complex neurocomputational algorithms have not being designed as practical tools for classification or prediction, but as a models of brain functioning. Obviously, we are not interesting in simulating the archaeologist's brain. This is not a book on psychology, but on Archaeology and, perhaps, of philosophy of science. Therefore, I am not exploring how computer calculations mimic brain mechanisms, but on finding practical algorithms for computing nonlinear relationships. The reader can use the bibliographic references given throughout the chapter for studying algorithms that are more complex but they may seem out of purpose for the present discussion. Scientific reasoning is a kind of "artificial" way of reasoning for obtaining very specific kind of results. Therefore, simple and well documented algorithms like backpropagation (or radial basis functions), self-organized maps, simple recurrent networks or Hopfield algorithms are much more convenient than complex mechanisms that seem to act in the same way as our brain process information, but give too complex models of input-output relationship.

Neural networks technology opens to archaeologists an entirely new domain. Nevertheless, neural networks cannot provide the solution to archaeological problems by working individually. In this sense, they should be seen as a new

development within a rich and varied history of statistical models of scientific discovery and explanation. However, this techniques allow that learning the relationship between visual features and social explanations be no more conditioned by the nature of standard statistical tools, which tend to impose linear relationships, nor by the verbal nature of descriptive features. Modern views on social causality, which is described as a nonlinear, probabilistic and non-monotonic relationship fit exactly the neural network analogy. What we need to investigate now is not exactly new algorithms, but new ways of applying those methods to archaeological problems. We are far from those days in which archaeologists used pencil, paper, and common sense to interpret their data. We should think in terms of vectors and activations to understand how explanations are related to visual inputs. Furthermore, even in the case of self-organized neurocomputational algorithms, archaeological reasoning can be implemented in a way that transcend trivial clustering, incorporating experiments, controlled observations and simulated conditions.

REFERENCES

ALEKSANDER, I., & MORTON, H. (1993). *Neurons and symbols. The stuff that mind is made of.* London: Chapman and Hall.

AMARI, S.I. (1993). Mathematical aspects of neurocomputing. In O.E. Barndorff-Nielsen, J.L. Jensen & W.S. Kendall (Eds.), *Networks and chaos-statistical and probabilistic approaches* (pp. 1-39). London: Chapman and Hall.

BAILEY, D., & THOMPSON, D. (1990). How to develop neural networks. *AI Expert*, 5(6), 38-47.

BARCELÓ, J.A. (1995). Back-propagation algorithms to compute similarity relationships among archaeological artifacts. In J. Wilcock & K. Lockyear (Eds.), *Computer applications in archaeology* (pp. 165-176). Oxford: ArcheoPress.

BARCELÓ, J.A., & PIJOAN-LOPEZ, J. (2004). Cutting or scrapping? Using neural networks to distinguish kinematics in use-wear analysis. In Magistrat der Stadt Wien (Ed.), *Enter the past. The e-way into the four dimensions of culture heritage* (pp. 427-431). Oxford: ArcheoPress.

BARCELÓ, J.A., VILA, A., & GIBAJA, J. (2000). An application of neural networks to use-wear analysis. Some preliminary results. In K. Lockyear, T.J.T. Sly & V. Mihailescu-Birliba (Eds.), *Computer applications and quantitative methods in archaeology* (pp. 63-70). Oxford: ArchaeoPress.

BECHTEL, W., & ABRAHAMSEN, A. (1991). *Connectionism and the mind.* Cambridge, UK: Blackwell.

BISHOP, C.M. (1995). *Neural networks for pattern recognition.* Oxford, UK: Oxford University Press..

CAUDILL, M. (1991). Neural network training tips and techniques. *AI Expert,6*, 56-61.

CAUDILL, M., & BUTLER, C. (1992). *Understanding neural networks. Computer explorations.* Cambridge, MA: The MIT Press.

CHATER, N. (1995). Neural networks: The new statistical models of mind. In .P. Levy, D. Bairaktaris, J.A. Bullinaria & P. Cairns (Eds.), *Connectionist models of memory and language.* London: UCL Press.

CHURCHLAND, P.M. (1991). A deeper unity: Some feyerabendian themes in neurocomputational form. In P.M. Churchland & P.S. Churchland (Eds.), *On the contrary, critical essays, 1987-1997.* Cambridge, MA: The MIT Press.

CHURCHLAND, P.M. (1995). *The engine of reason, the seat of the soul. A philosophical journey into the brain.* Cambridge, MA: The MIT Press.

CHURCHLAND, P.M. (1998). Conceptual similarity across sensory and neural diversity. *The Journal of Philosophy, 95*(1), 5-32.

CLARK, A. (1993). *Associative engines. Connectionism, concepts, and representational change.* Cambridge, MA: The MIT Press.

DAWSON, M.R.W. (2004). *Minds and machines. Connectionism and psychological modeling.* Blackwell, London.

DE BODT, E., COTTRELL, M., & VERLEYSEN, M. (2002). Statistical tools to assess the reliability of self-organizing maps. *Neural Networks, 15*(8), 967-978.

DeCALLATAŸ, A. M. (1992). *Natural and artificial intelligence. Misconceptions about brains and neural networks.* Amsterdam: North Holland.

EGMONT-PETERSEN, M., DE RIDDER, D., & HANDELS, H. (2002). Image processing with neural networks—a review. *Pattern Recognition, 35*, 2279-2301.

ELLIS, R., HUMPHREYS, G. (1999). *Connectionist psychology.* London: Psychology Press,

ELMAN, J.L. (1990). Finding structure in time. *Cognitive Science, 14*, 179-211.

ELMAN, J.L. (1992). Grammatical structure and distributed representations. In S. Davis (Ed.), *Connectionism: Theory and practice.* Oxford (UK): Oxford University Press..

FINE, T.L. (1999). *Feedforward neural network methodology.* New York: Springer.

FORT, J.C. (2006). SOM's mathematics. *Neural Networks, 19*, 812–816.

GEVREY, M., DIMOPOULOS, & LEK, I. (2003). Review and comparison of methods to study the contribution of variables in artificial neural network models. *Ecological Modelling, 160*(3), 249-264.

GORMAN, R. P., & SEJNOWSKI, T. J. (1988). Analysis of hidden units in a layered network trained to classify sonar targets. *Neural Networks, 1*, 75-89.

GROSSBERG, S. (1988). *Neural networks and natural intelligence*. Cambridge, MA: The MIT Press.

HADLEY, R.F. (2000). Cognition and the computational power of connectionist networks. *Connection Science, 12*(2), 95-110.

HAGAN, M.T., DEMUTH, H.B., & BEALE, M. (1996). *Neural network design*. Boston, MA: PWS Publishing Company,

HAYKIN, S. (1999). *Neural networks. A comprehensive foundation* (2nd ed.). Upper Saddle River, NJ: Prentice Hall.

HINTON, G.E. (1986). Learning distributed representations of concepts. *Proceedings of the Eigth Annual Conference of the Cognitive Science Society* (pp. 1-12). Hillsdale, NJ: Lawrence Erlbaum,.

HINTON, G.E., & BECKER,S. (1992). Using coherence assumptions to discover the underlying causes of the sensory input. In S. Davis (Ed.), *Connectionism: Theory and practice.* Oxford, UK: Oxford University Press.

HONKELA, T. (1997). S*elf-organizing maps in natural language processing* (PhD. Dissertation) Helsinki Technical University. http://www.cis.hut.fi/~tho/thesis/index.html (File downloaded on September 2007).

HOPFIELD, J. (1982). Neural networks and physical systems with emergent collective computational abilities. *Proceedings of the National Academy of Sciences, 79*, 2554-2558.

HORNIK,K.,STINCHCOMBE,M.,&WHITE,H. (1989). Multilayer feedforward networks are universal approximators. *Neural Networks, 2*, 359-366.

JORDAN, M. I. (1986). *Serial order: A parallel distributed approach*. ICS Report 8604. San Diego, CA: University of California, Institute for Cognitive Science.

KASKI, S. (1997). *Data exploration using self-organizing maps*. Acta Polytechnica Scandinavica, Mathematics, Computing and Management in Engineering Series No. 82, Espoo, 57 pp. Published by the Finnish Academy of Technology.

KASKI, S. NIKKILÄ, J., & KOHONEN, T. (1998). Methods for interpreting a self-organized map in data analysis. In *Proceedings 6th European Symposium on Artificial Neural Networks (ESANN98)*. Bruges, Belgium: D-Facto.

KLIMASAUSKAS, C. (2002). Taking back-propagation to the extreme. *PC AI Magazine, January/February*, 31-35.

KOHONEN, T. (2001). *Self-organizing maps* (3rd ed.).*Berlin: Springer.*

KOUA, E.L., & KRAAK, M.J. (2004). An evaluation of self-organizing map spatial representation and visualization for geospatial data: Perception and visual analysis. In J. Dykes, , A.M. MacEachren & M. J. Kraak (Eds.), *Exploring geovisualization* (pp. 627-644). Amsterdam: Elsevier

LEUNG, Y. (1997). Feedforward neural network models for spatial data classification and rule learning. In M.M. Fischer & A.Getis (Eds.), *Recent developments in spatial analysis. Spatial statistics, behavioural modeling and computational intelligence*. Springer: Berlin.

MAES, P. (1989). How to do the right thing. *Connection Science, 1*, 291-323.

MARCUS, G.F. (2001). *The algebraic mind. Integrating connectionism and cognitive science.* Cambridge, MA: The MIT Press.

McCLOSKEY, M., & COHEN, N.J. (1989). Catastrophic interference in connectionist networks:

The sequential learning problem. In G.H. Brower (Ed.), *The psychology of learning and motivation* (vol. 24). New York: Academic Press.

O'REILLY, R.C., & MUNAKATA, Y, (2000). *Computacional explorations in cognitive neuroscience*. Cambridge, MA: The MIT Press.

OLDEN, J.D., JOY, M.K., & DEATH, R.G. (2004). An accurate comparison of methods for quantifying variable importance in artificial neural networks using simulated data. *Ecological Modelling*, 178(3-4), 389-397.

PENNY, W.D., & ROBERTS, S.J. (1999). Bayesian neural networks for classification: How useful is the evidence framework? *Neural Networks, 12*(6), 877-892.

PERLOVSKY, L.I. (2001). *Neural networks and intellect. Using model-based concepts*. New York: Oxford University Press.

PRINCIPE, J.C., EULIANO, N.R., & LEFEBVRE, W.C. (2000). *Neural and adaptive systems. Fundamentals through simulations*. New York: John Wiley.

QUINLAN, P. (1991). *Connectionism and psychology*. Hempstead: Harvester Wheatsheaf.

REED, R.D., & MARKS, R.J. (1999). *Neural smithing. Supervised learning in feedforward artificial neural networks*. The MIT Press.

RIPLEY, B.D. (1993). Statistical aspects of neural networks. In O.E. Barndorff-Nielsen, J.L. Jensen & W.S. Kendall (Eds.), *Networks and chaos-statistical and probabilistic approaches* (pp. 40-123). London: Chapman and May.

RUMELHART, D.E. (1989). The architecture of mind: A connectionist approach. In M.I. Posner (Ed.), *Foundations of cognitive science*. Cambridge, MA: The MIT Press.

RUMELHART, D.E., HINTON, G.E., & WILLIAMS, R.J. (1986). Learning internal representations by error propagation. In D.E. Rumelhart, J.L. McClelland, & the P.D.P. Research Group (Eds.), *Parallel distributed processing. Explorations in the microstructures of cognition*. Cambridge, MA: The MIT Press.

RUMELHART, D.E., & TODD, P.M. (1993). Learning and connectionist representations. In D.E. Meyer & S. Kornblum (Eds.), *.Attention and performance XIX*. Cambridge, MA: The MIT Press.

RUMELHART, D. E., & ZIPSER, D. (1986). Feature discovery by competitive learning. In D.E. Rumelhart, J.L. McClelland, & the P.D.P. Research Group (Eds.), *Parallel distributed processing. Explorations in the microstructures of cognition*. Cambridge, MA: The MIT Press.

SCHWENKER, F., KESTLER, H.A., & PALM, G. (2001). Three learning phases for radial-basis-Function Networks. *Neural Networks* 14, 4-5, pp. 439-458.

STASSOPOULOU, A., & PETROU, M. (1998). Obtaining the correspondence between Bayesian and neural networks. *International Journal of Pattern Recognition and Artificial Intelligence, 12*(7), 901-920.

STONE, G.O. (1986). An analysis of the Delta rule and the learning of statistical associations. In D.E. Rumelhart, J.L. McClelland, & the P.D.P. Research Group (Eds.), *Parallel distributed processing. Explorations in the microstructures of cognition*. Cambridge, MA: The MIT Press.

TAKATSUKA, M. (2001). An application of the self-organizing map and interactive 3-D visualization to geospatial data. *Proceedings of the 6th International Conference on GeoComputation*. University of Queensland, Brisbane, Australia. Retrieved June 2007 from http://www.geocomputation.org/2001/papers/takatsuka.pdf

ULTSCH, A. (2003). Maps for the visualization of high-dimensional data spaces, *Proceedings of Workshop on Self Organizing Maps WSOM03* (pp 225-230), Hibikino, Kitakyushu, Japan.

ULTSCH, A., & MOERCHEN, F. (2005). ESOM-Maps: Tools for clustering, visualization, and classification with Emergent SOM. *Technical Report Dept. of Mathematics and Computer Science, University of Marburg, Germany*, No. 46.

ZEIDENBERG, M. (1990). *Neural networks in artificial intelligence*. Chichester, UK: Ellis Horwood.

ZHOU, J., & CIVCO, D.L. (1996). Using genetic learning neural networks for spatial decision making in GIS. *Photogrametric Engineering and Remote Sensing*, 62(11), 1287-1295.

Section III
Practical Examples of Automated Archaeology

Chapter V
Visual and Non–Visual Analysis in Archaeology

FROM OBSERVABLE EFFECTS TO UNOBSERVABLE CAUSES

As we have discussed in previous chapters, an artificial neural network is an information-processing system that maps a descriptive feature vector into a class assignment vector. In so doing, a neural network is nothing more than a complex and intrinsically nonlinear statistical classifier. It extracts the *statistical central tendency* of a series of exemplars (the learning set) and thus comes to encode information not just about the specific exemplars, but about the stereotypical feature-set displayed in the training data (Churchland, 1989; Clark, 1989, 1993; Franklin, 1995). That means, it will discover which sets of features are most commonly present in the exemplars, or commonly occurring groupings of features. In this way, semantic features statistically frequent in a set of learning exemplars come to be both highly marked and mutually associated. "Highly marked" means that the connection weights about such common features tend to be quite strong. "Mutually associated" means that co-occurring features are encoded in such a way that the activation of one of them will promote the activation of the other.

As a learning mechanism, a neural network looks as if it explicitly generates and stores prototypes of, for example, the typical stone knife of this period, the typical burial practice in this community, the typical social organization in this period and place. However, there are no such explicit, stored items. What exist are sets of connection weights and synaptic efficacies, respectively. The prototype is not a thing stored at some specific place within the network; it is not an ideal representation of reality waiting to be retrieved by a stimulus. The extraction of the *prototype* arises as an emergent consequence of the proper selection of some characteristic features or input variables.

A prototype as formed within a neural network is by definition "general," in the same sense in which a property is general: it has many instances, and it can represent a wide range of diverse examples. However, this property does not mean that prototypes are universal generalizations. No prototype feature needs to be universal, or even nearly universal, to all examples in the class. Furthermore, prototypes allow us a welcome degree of looseness precluded by the strict logic of universal quantifier: not all *F*s need to be *G*s, but the standard or normal ones are, and the non-standard ones must be related by a relevant similarity relationship to these that properly are *G*.

Different neurons represent different "prototypical values" along the continuum, and respond with graded signals reflecting how close the current exemplar is to their preferred value. Note that what is really being stored is the degree to which one neuron, representing a micro-feature of the final concept or prototype, predicts another neuron or micro-feature. Thus, whenever a certain configuration of micro-features is present a certain other set of micro-features is also present (Rumelhart, 1989). This is important, because it means that the system does not fall into the trap of needing to decide which category to put a pattern in before knowing which prototype to average. The acquisition of the different prototypes proceeds without any sort of explicit categorization. If the patterns are sufficiently dissimilar, there is no interference among them at all.

It is clear that a single prototype represents a wide range of quite different possible inputs: it represents the extended family of relevant features that collectively unite the relevant class of stimuli into a single category. Any member of that diverse class of stimuli will activate the entire prototype. In addition, any other input stimulus that is *similar* to the members of that class, in part or completely, will activate a pattern that is fairly close to the prototype. Consequently, a prototype vector activated by any given visual stimulus will exemplify the accumulated interactions with all the possible sources of the same or similar stimuli in proportion to the frequency with which they have been experienced.

The ability to represent both prototypical information and information about specific instances is the basis of the neurocomputing success. We can activate two properties, and discover which outputs are most likely to fit that scenario. The network will initially produce higher activations in the output units which posses any of these properties, with those sharing both properties getting the highest activations. The units for the most widely shared properties also become the most active. Thus the network not only identifies which outputs shared the initial pair of properties, but what their other properties were likely to be, and which among those not possessing the initial pair show the best fit with those who did satisfy the initial pair of properties.

This is an important property of the model, but the importance of this property increases when we realize that the model can average several patterns in the same composite memory trace. Thus, one neural network can be trained to exhibit behavior appropriate to knowledge of a number of distinct prototypes, such as an arrow point, a settlement of a particular kind, or a kind of social organization. Interestingly, if the input is indeterminate between a stone knife and a stone scraper, for instance, the neural network will generate an overall pattern, as if it had an idea not just of knives and scrapers but also on stone tools. We see then that the talent of the system is used to generate a *typical* set of properties associated with some description, even though all the system directly knows about are individuals, none of whom needs to be a perfectly typical instantiation of the description in question.

This way of representing concepts is the consequence of *graded learning* in a neural network: a new concept emerges as the result of a number of different learning situations or the gradual differentiation of a single concept into two or more related ones. Therefore, as activation spreads from input to output, outputs *grade* according to how well they exemplify the existing training exemplars. Considering that several different prototypes can be stored in the same set of weights, a typical single prototype model may represent instances as sets of attributes (properties or features) with some numeric measure of both the importance of the attribute to that concept (sometimes called its weight) and the extent to which the attribute is present. In this way, neural networks adopt a *probabilistic view* to categorization. The idea of defining necessary of sufficient properties is replaced with that of the probable properties for a member of a given class. A probabilistic view accounts for graded class membership, since the "better" members will be those exhibiting more of the characteristic properties. Instead of representing several concrete instances in memory, we judge category membership by degree of connection to an abstract model or *prototype*.

An intriguing problem is in what way similarity is represented in a neural network. Some authors argue that similarities are *not computed* at all in the neural network, because they do not involve matching to a stored representation. The only thing to be "matched" within a network appears to be weight vectors, but they are not *matched*, that is, brought into correspondence with the input. The fact that similar inputs tend to produce similar outputs is a causal story, due to similarity between inputs in the sense of overlap of input representations and, thus, similar activation flow through the network (Curchland, 1989; Hahn & Chater, 1998).

More than an analogy with a universal database, our automated archaeologist should act as any of us by using an *associative memory*. This is a device storing not only associations among individual perceptual representations, but organizing "conceptual" information not directly derived from the senses (Kosslyn, 1994, p. 215).

Neural networks are used as associative memories. Pattern associators are constructed from the neurons and modifiable connections defined in the neural architecture. During a learning stage, the activation states of the input processing neurons are used to represent patterns to-be-recalled. The connection weights are then modified to store the association between the two patterns. It is a distributed representation because this association is stored throughout all the connections in the network, and because one set of connections can store several different associations. During the recall stage, a cue pattern is presented to the network by activating the input units. This causes signals to be set through the connections in the network and to activate the output processors. If the associative mechanism runs properly, then the pattern of activation in the output neurons will be the pattern that was originally associated with the cue pattern (Dawson, 2004). Therefore, the automated archaeologist will acquire some visual input in form of a vector of activity to the input neurons (feature detectors), which will be used as a cue pattern to retrieve its associated explanation, represented as a vector of activity in the memory's output neurons. The advantages are obvious:

- An automated archaeologist solves problems by recognizing something, and with the help of that result, recognizing further:
- When a previously stored (that is, "familiar") pattern is "seen" by the system, it is amplified, and it responds with a stronger version of the input pattern.
- When an unfamiliar pattern is "seen" by the system, it is dampened, and the response of the machine is shut down. This is a kind of unfamiliar response.
- When part of a familiar pattern is "seen," the system responds by "filling in" the missing parts. This is a kind of recall paradigm in which the part constitutes the retrieval cue, and the filling in is a kind of memory-reconstruction process.
- When a pattern similar to a stored pattern is "seen," the system responds by distorting the input pattern toward the stored pattern. This is a kind of assimilation response in which similar inputs are assimilated to similar stored events
- Finally, if a number of similar patterns have been stored, the system will respond strongly to the central tendency of the stored patterns,

even though the central tendency itself was never stored.

Such an associative memory, however, is not limited to the association of only those specific individual objects that the robot has seen before. If such were the case, the mechanisms underlying archaeological automatic explanation would be of limited use. As archaeologists, we must identify a range of novel visual data as corresponding to a given type of object. Generalization is part of our ability to identify objects and events; we typically can identify social actions having been performed in the past even when the visual appearance of its material consequences in the present does not exactly matches what we know of previously memorized cause/effect associations. The capability for archaeological recognition implies then the existence of some previous form of learning, in which the abstract potentially explanatory categories have been created and defined. The goal of recognition is to perform these identifications correctly, in the sense that identification reflects a meaningful property of the world that is independent of the particular data that is being interpreted.

We call this approach to archaeological reasoning *category-based* because explanatory elements are accessed through a process of categorization. It implies that the input reaching the automated archaeologist sensors is sorted out into discrete, distinct categories whose members somehow come to resemble one another more than they resemble members of other categories (Harnad, 1987). We have already seen that the categorization (or pattern recognition) approach proposes that two operations are involved. First, the system classifies an observable as being a member of a large number of known categories according to its input properties. Second, this identification allows access to a large body of stored information about this type of object, including its function and various forms of expectations about its future behaviors. This two-step schema has the advantage that any explanatory property can be associated with any object, because the relation between the form of an object and the information stored about its function, history, and use can be purely arbitrary, owing to its mediation by the process of categorization. That means that the responses of the automated archaeologist to the incoming input are not dependent of any particular attribute of the input. Rather, the solution to the archaeological problem will make sense only when considered as one component in a causal chain that generates responses entirely according to the probability distribution of the past significance of the same or related input. The answer provided by the intelligent machine exemplifies not the stimulus or its sources as such, but the accumulated interactions with all the possible sources of the same or similar stimuli in proportion to the frequency with which they have been experienced (see Chapter I).

IDENTIFICATION-BASED ANALYSIS

The easiest way of creating an associative memory for archaeological explanations is by assuming that there is a roughly fixed set or vocabulary of "supposed" descriptive regularities shared by a single population of objects, which are also distinctive enough. Partial identification of individualized parts of the input is carried out by lower-order neurons, processed, and eventually decoded by middle- and higher-order neurons. In this way, low-level neurons would respond selectively when particular local configurations are presented. Higher-level neurons represent particular solutions or explanatory concepts, looking for particular combinations of identified components from the low-level units. At the highest level, a decision mechanism selects the concept corresponding to that represented by the cognitive detector activated by the highest quantity of partial identifications.

In many cases, however, input neurons are not proper visual units, because the appropriate primitive visual features captured by the automated archaeologist sensors do not stimulate them. Instead, it is the human user, who feeds the network with an interpreted input, in which each feature contains the result of a previous inference. In this way, the receptive field of low-level neurons does not encode the salient features of the input image, but the previous knowledge the user has about the features characterizing the archaeological evidence. This kind of neural network is mostly similar to an expert system, as presented in Chapter II. The analysis of rock-art can be used as an appropriate example of identification-based analysis. Some other examples will be presented later in the chapter.

One of the first neural networks applied to archaeological data is a classification of Late Bronze Age warrior decorated *stelae,* dated between 1100 B.C. and 7th century B.C. in south-western Iberian Peninsula. In a preliminary experiment (Barceló, 1995a) input vectors contained:

* Total number of iconographic motives in a *stela*

* Iconographic relevance of human figure
* Iconographic relevance of the figure of a shield
* Number of "prestige" items in a *stela*
* Degree of schematism

Here the descriptive concepts "iconographic complexity," "relevance of human figure," "relevance of shield," and so forth were neither "seen" nor "recognized" by the machine. They were introduced in their final form as already identified terms. Additionally, for each representation, the chronology, the geographical situation, and the number of engraved imported items were also identified:

* Four chronological phases (Late Bronze Age II, Late Bronze Age III, orientalizing the historical *Tartessos* period, Post-Colonization period).
* Four geographical regions: Tajo Valley, Guadiana Valley, Zújar valley, and Guadalquivir valley).
* A so called "degree of colonization" measure, deduced from the quantity of imported

Figure. 5.1a. Graphical representation of a Late Bronze Age Warrior Stela, compared to the vectorial notation for input and output (Barceló 1995a).

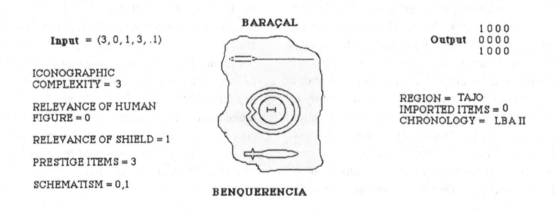

Figure. 5.1b. Graphical representation of another Late Bronze Age Warrior Stela, compared to the vectorial notation for input and output (Barceló 1995a).

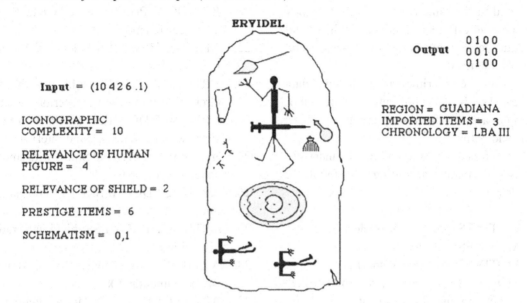

items depicted in the rock slab: >3, >5, >7, >9).

Some of the exemplars were chronologically ambiguous, because the items engraved had no clear chronological adscription. In those cases, exemplars were assigned a chronological output of 0.5 for two different consecutive phases.

The typical question that the automated archaeologist was supposed to solve is "are the iconographically most complex representations situated in the regions and chronological phases where Phoenician colonization was strongest?" This is a typical supervised learning example. In archaeological terms, the network has to generalize the relationship between iconography, geography, and chronology. The network was trained using only 38 exemplars.

The network converged to a MSE = 0.1176, classifying correctly 96 percent of training exemplars. Predicted output allowed in most cases the correction of ambiguous chronological de-

termination. For instance, a monument assigned simultaneously to the colonial and post-colonial period (0.5 for the desired output), obtained 0.7 for the colonial and 0.3 for post-colonial times, which is perfectly sound according to archaeological knowledge.

A test set of 12 exemplars were used to validate training. The automated archaeologist made some important mistakes when trying to predict the region, the number of imported items, and the chronology. However, it only misclassified contiguous regions. The program was also able to learn both extremes of the temporal range, having less good results for the intermediate phases.

All these *negative* results coincide with what we can expect from archaeological research in the area. We can explain chronology using similarities and iconographic data. The concept of "colonization," however, cannot be represented exclusively in terms of similarity between individual rock-art representations, because not all exemplars in the same region, with the same chronology and with the same number of imported items are similar in iconographic structure. In the same phase and in the same region, the iconography of rock-art is different, although the historical consequences of the colonization process were, probably, identical.

A successive experiment using the same data (Barceló, 1995b, 1997) presented a more elaborated approach, still based on externally identified inputs and outputs.

The 30 first neurons represent the binary descriptive information, according to the following variables:

1. MOTIVES: presence of shield
2. MOTIVES: presence of sword
3. MOTIVES: presence of spear
4. MOTIVES: presence of a "mirror like" object (or musical instrument?)
5. MOTIVES: presence of human figure
6. MOTIVES: presence of comb
7. MOTIVES: presence of fibula
8. MOTIVES: presence of chariot
9. MOTIVES: presence of helmet
10. MOTIVES: presence of more than one human figure
11. MOTIVES: presence of animal figures
12. MOTIVES: presence of bow and/or arrow
13. MOTIVES: presence of series of points (unknown meaning)
14. MOTIVES: presence of hair band
15. ICONOGRAPHIC STRUCTURE: Shield and human figure symmetrically in horizontal plane.
16. ICONOGRAPHIC STRUCTURE: Shield and human figure symmetrically in vertical plane
17. ICONOGRAPHIC STRUCTURE: Shield secondary positioned with respect to human figure
18. ICONOGRAPHIC STRUCTURE: Sword parallel to spear and flanking a central element
19. ICONOGRAPHIC STRUCTURE: Sword parallel and joint to spear

20. ICONOGRAPHIC STRUCTURE: Sword crossed on human figure
21. ICONOGRAPHIC STRUCTURE: Sword and spear independent
22. ARTIFACT DETAILS: Shield with V marks in all circles
23. ARTIFACT DETAILS: Shield with outer circle with V marks, and interior without.
24. ARTIFACT DETAILS: Shield with outer circle without V marks, and interior with
25. ARTIFACT DETAILS: Shield with smooth concentric circles
26. ARTIFACT DETAILS: Shield with parallel lines
27. ARTIFACT DETAILS: Shield with radial disposition
28. ARTIFACT DETAILS: Round smooth shield, without marks
29. ARTIFACT DETAILS: Horned helmet
30. ARTIFACT DETAILS: Crested helmet

These are typical external identifications, because the automated archaeologist does not know how to distinguish a shield from a human figure or the representation of a chariot or a sword. All those terms are introduced from outside in its definitive form by the human user, who has learnt to discriminate the representation of human figures and the recognition of objects and motives in the engraved lines.

The output layer has eight units.

1. CHRONOLOGY: LATE BRONZE AGE II
2. CHRONOLOGY: LATE BRONZE AGE III
3. CHRONOLOGY: PHOENICICAN CO-LOIZATION PERIOD
4. CHRONOLOGY: POST-COLONIZATION PERIOD
5. GEOGRAPHY: Tagus valley
6. GEOGRAPHY: Guadiana valley
7. GEOGRAPHY: Zújar valley
8. GEOGRAPHY: Guadalquivir valley

Again, these concepts are not generated by the system, but known to it in their final form.

The network has a three-layer feed forward topology with ten intermediate neurons (in the hidden layer). The network contains a total of 48 units or neurons. An initial set of 33 exemplars, with well-known chronology was used in the training mode, for 2,000 epochs.

In all training cases, the program assigned the correct chronology to the different rock-art representations. For instance, in the case of the Ategua Stelae, the network correctly determined chronology, although with some indeterminacy (Neuron 3: Colonial Period; Neuron 4: Post-orientalizing Period), and provenience: Guadalquivir (Neuron 8) (Figure 5.2).

In the case of the Arroyo Bonaval exemplar, the network correctly determined chronology also with some indeterminacy (Neuron 1: Late Bronze Age II; Neuron 2: Late Bronze Age III), and concluded correctly the region of provenience (Tagus valley: Neuron 5). Categorization was not perfect, however, when differences are too few between competing categories.

Once trained, the network has been used to classify fragmented rock-art monuments (Figure 5.3). The idea was to study the relevance of each variable, either jointly, or separately. The neural network is not activated with the full descriptions of the representation, but with some hypothetical descriptions, of the type:

- What would happen if the representation contained only a crest helmet?
- What would happen if the representation contained only a shield of concentric circles?
- What would happen if the representation contained only a mirror and a chariot?

Results are very interesting. As we supposed, the more usual attributes (sword, shield, etc., engraved in most rock-art representations) have poor discriminating power. Shield typology helps a little in distinguishing between chronological periods. On the other hand, the appearance of an isolated human figure, without other elements, suggests a late chronology (Post-Colonial times).

Iconographic variables, that is to say, those that describe the way in which the elements represented in the stelae are arranged provided little information. The most interesting feature comes from the way in which the sword and the spear are associated: when these elements flank the central figure (a human figure or a shield), the network

Figure. 5.2. Using a neural network to estimate the provenience and chronology of two Late Bronze Age Warrior Stelae (Ategua and Arroyo Bonaval) (Barceló 1995b)

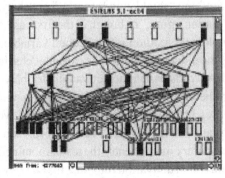

Ategua

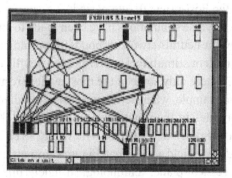

Arroyo Bonaval

5.3. Different activations of the trained neural network with fragmented monuments depicting only one feature (Barceló 1995b)

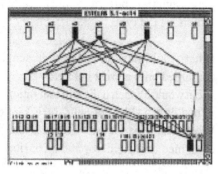

crested helmet

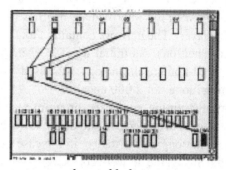

horned helmet

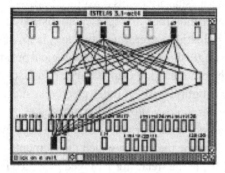

presence of human figure

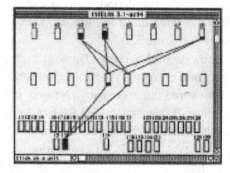

Presence of more than one human figure

suggests it is an old exemplar, with a chronology in the Late Bronze Age II or Late Bronze Age III. The most probable chronology is a later one (Post-Colonial times) when the sword and the spear are depicted parallel and together. A sword crossing a human figure is an ambiguous feature, because it can be assigned both to the Orientalizing and to the Post-orientalizing periods.

Diverse simulations have been made to study how the neural network responds to contradictory stimuli or stimuli that are reinforced. I will comment here only some of the most evident results. For example, when activating two contradictory variables in the input layer, as they are "fibula (safety-pin)" and "ICONOGRAPHIC STRUC-TURE: Shield and Human Figure symmetrically in vertical plane," chronological indeterminacy increases, since a rock-art representation with

those two variables in its description could not be assigned, with clarity, to a chronological period. In the case of "mirror" and "horned helmet" activated in the input layer, we observe that the joint result is similar to that we obtained when processing each one of the variables separately. The same happens in the activation of the variables "chariot" and "shield with V marks," or "chariot" and "human figure," although in the first case, the chronological fixation of the second variable reduces the indeterminacy of the variable "chariot." In other words, when the activated variables are contradictory, in some cases ambiguity really increases. On the contrary, whenever the network is activated with associated variables (present in contemporary monuments), the results obtained in the individual activation remain without relevant modifications, or they are reinforced.

The validation of all these results will depend on the trust we have on the ability of the neural network to learn. Certainly, we have based the reliability of the approach on the results of the first turn of simulations, that is to say, the experimentations with those rock-art representations, which were already interpreted. In all cases, the neural network provided the chronological and geographical associations that were expected from current archaeological knowledge. Nevertheless, the data used in the supervised learning phase can be partial or incomplete, or, the results of the archaeological investigation can surpass quickly what is known at a specific moment. For that reason, it is essential to insist on the fundamental character that the selection of initial data has.

A modern version of this kind of analysis is Di Ludovico and Ramazzotti's (2005) study of ancient glyptic, in particular the scenes cut on the surfaces of the cylinder seals dating to the Mesopotamian prehistory, specially the Akkadian, the Post-Akkadian and Ur III periods. The aim of the investigation was to understand the figurative organization of depicted scenes, what requires an in-depth study of their very complex iconographic lexicon. The whole study is mainly based on the idea that figurated scenes are expression of a formal language, which can be understood, in its essential outlines, by the simulating interaction of the elements isolated in it by a process of shape deconstruction. The first step of the analysis is the ideal breaking up of every scene in numerous pieces as the minimum signifying elements, which can be recognized in them: number of figures, sex, directions towards which they are oriented, their poses, their dresses, the objects serving as their attributes, etc.). In this way, each kind of feature empirically noticed has been translated into variables, the number of which agreed with the possible theoretical combinations between the features and the contexts to which they could belong.

Each seal has been translated into a string of 611 presence/absence attributes. A self-organized map neural network (Chapter IV) has led to the drawing of a multi-dimensional clustering in 16 classes. A test of the map related to the chronological distribution of the seals has pointed out how the classes have been divided coherently with the three traditional historic periods. The neural net has outlined inputs that can be partly related to the specific production of each period and partly to overlapping or transitional phases.

Another example of an identification-based analysis using neural networks, come from lithic use-wear studies. Van den Dries (1998) has tried to classify functionally lithic tools using subjectively identified use-wear descriptors. Such descriptors are qualitatively defined, and identified by a human expert in the microscope image; the researcher "sees" striations, polished areas, scars, particles, undifferentiated background. Even the "intensity" of a trace has also been determined subjectively, introducing attributes like "poor," "high," "developed," "greasy," and so forth. As in the previous rock-art example, input neurons are not proper visual units, because they are not stimulated directly by the input luminance values captured by the automated archaeologist sensors. Instead, it is the human user, who feeds the network with an interpreted input, in which each feature contains the result of a previous inference. The neural network (called WARP) has been trained to recognize the action that produced some degree of "polish" on the surface of the tool, provided the user is able to distinguish features like: distribution, texture, brightness, topography and the width of the polish. Those variables were translated into a presence/absence format, producing 31 binary variables like:

DISTRIBUTION A: scintillation
DISTRIBUTION C: reticulated
DISTRIBUTION E: thin line along the edge
TEXTURE A: smooth & matt
TEXTURE B: rough & greasy
BRIGHTNESS A: very bright
BRIGHTNESS C: dull

TOPOGRAPHY A: domed
TOPOGRAPHY B: flat
WIDTH A: 0-250 micron
WIDTH B: 251-500 micron
WIDTH C: 501-750 micron

Since WARP was meant to interpret wear traces generated by working activities with the tool, the output neurons represent the worked materials:

MATERIAL 1: dry hide
MATERIAL 2: fresh hide
MATERIAL 3: hard wood
MATERIAL 4: soft wood
MATERIAL 5: dry bone
MATERIAL 6: soaked bone
MATERIAL 7: dry antler
MATERIAL 8: soaked antler
MATERIAL 9: cereals
MATERIAL 10: butchering meat and fish
MATERIAL 11: pottery
MATERIAL 12: stone
MATERIAL 13: soil
MATERIAL 14: siliceous plants
MATERIAL 15: non-siliceous plants

The training set consisted of 160 examples of experimentally replicated tools used in laboratory to process the actions mentioned on the output neurons list.

Circa 38 exemplars (26.4 percent) were not correctly learnt. Some difficulty could have been expected because repeated attempts confirmed that the data contained various contradictory facts on which it would be difficult to train the network. For instance, the reference collection contained facts with a similar texture but a different functional interpretation and facts with a different texture but the same kind of use. This means that in one case WARP must learn that the use-wear features (attributes) *A, B,* and *C* relate to worked material *X*, while in another example these traces relate to material *Y*, while in another

example these traces relate to material *Y.* It is for a neural network even more confusing that material *X* can also be associated with attributes *D, E,* and *F,* while this does not hold for material *Y.*

It turned out that the network failed to learn 25 percent of the examples because it was more rigorous than necessary. Many answers were not wrong, but a matter of degree of certainty. Most of the differences resulted from the fact that the answers were not very persuasive. Consequently, many of them had a score that just misfit the training tolerance. Still, most answers corresponded with the expected answer and pointed at the right worked material. In fact, all "mistakes" included the right worked material in the answer. Moreover, eight of the "mistakes" consisted of two outputs with equal scores on similar materials like cereals and siliceous plants.

Subsequently, WARP was tested with 16 randomly selected testing data. Considering the degree of answer overlapping, only four (25 percent) were wrong. Van den Dries compared the performance of the network on experimental data, and on archaeological data (interpreted by a human analyst). Despite some unfortunate guesses, WARP performed rather well.

AN AUTOMATED ARCHAEOLOGIST, WHICH UNDERSTANDS SCIENTIFIC TEXTS

As another example of non-visual explanation, let us consider the classification of texts and documents, according to the words used to describe them. Given that most archaeological evidence is still described verbally, this can be a good example for evaluating artificial intelligence applications in archaeology. Consider a very large collection of textual descriptions of archaeological traces, such as the excavation field book, a site excavation monograph, or an encyclopedia.

WEBSOM is a method for organizing miscellaneous text documents onto meaningful maps

Table 5.1. The actually worked materials and archaeological artifacts (linear band ceramic objects. Neolithic) compared with the interpretations of the Neural Network (Van den Dries 1998 pp. 96-97)

COMPARISON WITH TRAINING DATA

TRAINING DATA	NEURAL NETWORK INTERPRETATION
soaked antler	dry antler/fresh bone
medium hard wood	soft wood
shell	soft plants
soft wood	soft wood
soaked antler	hard wood
soft wood	dry hide
soft wood	fresh bone
soft wood	fresh bone
fresh hide	fresh hide
fresh hide	fresh hide
fresh hide	fresh hide
hide with ochre	soft wood/dry antler
soft wood	soft wood
fresh hide	fresh hide
dry bone	fresh bone/dry antler

COMPARISON WITH ARCHAEOLOGICAL MATERIAL

	HUMAN EXPERT INTERPRETATION	NEURAL NETWORK INTERP.
1	dry hide	fresh hide
3a	dry hide	fresh hide
3b	bone	butchering
5	hide?	fresh hide
6	bone	butchering
10	fresh hide	fresh hide
19	wood	hard wood/soft wood
20	fresh hide	fresh hide
31	hide	fresh hide
34	antler	soaked antler

for exploration and search (Kohonen, 2001). This method orders a collection of textual items, say, documents according to their contents, and maps them onto a regular two dimensional array of map units. It is based on the SOM (self-organized map) algorithm (Chapter IV) to automatically organize the documents onto a two-dimensional grid (a U-Matrix), which serves as a graphical map display showing related documents close to each other. Documents that are similar based on their whole contents will be mapped to the same or neighboring SOM neurons, and at each unit, a link connects to the document database. Thus, the program can be used to locate interesting documents on the output map using a content-directed search.

WEBSOM encodes original documents as a histogram of word categories based on the similarities in the contexts of the words. This encoded information is used to learn the self-organized map on which nearby neurons refer to similar documents. Input data (stored documents) are represented as binary vectors whose components or input neurons correspond to words of a vocabulary. The value of the component is one if the respective word is found in the document; otherwise, the value is zero. Instead of binary values, real values can be used in which each component corresponds to some function of the frequency of occurrence of a particular word in the document. Each document is represented as a linear combination of the low-dimensional (typically between 100 and 200-dimensional) latent representations of the document vectors. If similar words can be clustered together, documents can be represented as histograms of word clusters rather than of individual words.

While the searching can be started by locating those documents that match best with the search expression, further relevant search results can be found on the basis of the pointers stored at the same or neighboring map units, even if they did not match the search criterion exactly. For instance, imagine the user has clicked an output layer region with the label 'bell-beaker,' obtaining a view of a section of the map with articles on archaeology in Western Europe around 2100 B.C., various shapes of potteries, individual burials, early metallurgical prototypes, and so forth. Searches performed on the map could confirm that also megalithic burials and dolmens can be found nearby. A topic of interest is thus displayed in a context of related topics. Examples have been published on seven million documents classification, viz. of all of the patent abstracts in the world that have been written in English and are available in electronic form (Kaski et al., 1998). In this case, the output map consists of about one million models (nodes). Another example using the Encyclopedia Britannica has been reported by Lagus et al. (2004). The collection consisted of about 68,000 articles from this publication, and additionally summaries, updates, and other miscellaneous material of about 43,000 items. Some of the articles were very long, and split into several sections. In total, about 115,000 text items were obtained, and each was regarded as a document to be organized by the WEBSOM. The total vocabulary consisted of 325,275 different words.

In this line of research, innovative technologies and methodologies have been developed that enable the exploration of large information repositories containing cultural heritage knowledge on a global scale. Díaz-Kommonen and colleagues (Avilés Collao et al., 2003; Díaz-Kommonen & Kaipainen, 2002) describe how to convert historical written sources into automated explanatory mechanisms. The authors have extracted a semantic space from two historical texts: *A Description of the Northern People*, 1555, and the *Carta Marina* of 1539. The semantic space is built from the analysis of relationships among linguistic object-such terms, sentences, or documents in, the entire documents collection. Through the pattern of co-occurrences of words, a latent semantic indexing algorithm is able to infer the structure of relationships between documents and terms.

THE ARCHAEOLOGICAL ANALYSIS OF VISUAL MARKS

At the beginning of the book, I argued that archaeology is a quintessentially visual discipline. Among all archaeological features, some of them, the most important for the recognition and/or explanation of the item, have a visual nature, that is to say, have something to do with how light arrives to the archaeologist's eyes or to the robot sensors. Mechanisms used to "automate" archaeological inference and reasoning can be based on this premise. Tasks such as identifying a pottery type, identifying decorative patterns or use-wear in archaeological materials, recognizing archaeological structures in a satellite or aerial image, identifying layers or buildings at the site, interpreting burials or settlement patterns can be considered to be within the purview of visual analysis.

Identification-based analysis or textual classification is a tricky way of solving this problem. In fact, it is not a visual analysis, because the original visual input is being "described" in non-visual terms (words). When processing rock-art paintings we fed the neural network not with the original images of those archaeological elements, but with subjectively defined descriptors like "zoomorphic representation," or "anthropomorphic," and so forth. Low-level recognitions are assumed to be known, but no criteria are given about their reliability. Is a "shield" really a "shield" or another iconographic symbol? If we program the automated archaeologist in such a way that it process the visual input by itself, many sources of subjectivity will be avoided.

Human beings have the ability to recognize and classify images, identifying interesting patterns and single objects in them. Computers and robots can do it, too. Computer vision has been defined as a process of recognizing elements of interest in an image, and it can be described as the automatic logical deduction of structures or properties of the three-dimensional objects from either a single image or multiple images and the recognition of objects with the help of these properties (Kulkarni, 2001). As such, computer vision should be considered as an *interpretive process*. Any reasonable sophisticated visual system must involve a set of processes that extract a variety of types of information from the input image about the visual scene it comes from. This information is captured in a variety of internal intermediate-level representations (neural networks, for instance) which form the basis for higher-level recognition processes.

The first task is to decide what sort of distinctive visual marks an automated archaeologist should seek to understand why what it sees is what it seems to be. Observable properties can be reduced to the *size, shape, texture, composition,* and *location* of material consequences of social activity. Relevant questions to an automated archaeologist are then:

- How can it be discovered what makes such a shape a container?
- How can it be discovered what makes that use-wear texture a knife?
- How can it be discovered what makes an artifact with that composition a foreign production?
- How can it be discovered what makes such locations an activity area?

The automated archaeologist should find the social *cause* (production, use, distribution) of what it "sees." Production, use, and distribution are the social processes, which in some way have caused *observed* differences and variability among characteristic features. Unfortunately, there is no universal method of searching for informative visual marks. Features can be extracted from any real image almost *ad infinitum*, but one usually fails to formalize the significant criterion for those features. An additional difficulty is that different features will almost definitely be of importance for different classifications (Shelley, 1996).

The approach we adopt here to build an automated archaeologist able to recognize the visual appearance of archaeological evidence is based on current computational theories of visual perception that tend to break down the perception of meaningful stimuli into three functional stages. It is now common to categorize visual process into low, intermediate, and high levels. Low-level information is typically about the spatial relationships among primitive, two-dimensional visual features such as observed shape, texture, and composition variability patterns. Intermediate information describes the properties arising from forms of organization of the low-level primitives, such as texture or shape differences, and may include descriptions of the three-dimensional spatial relationship (location) among visual properties.

In his most influential essay, David Marr (1982) suggested that there are different mechanisms by which any sensing agent (a human or a machine) transforms visual data into an identification of the cause of visual variation. He saw perception essentially as building larger and larger structures from elementary sensory features. First, primitive visual features (e.g., location of shape and texture components) are extracted from empirical data. Second, these features are used to construct a description of the structure of the input information (texture and/or compositional variation). Third, the constructed description is matched against stored descriptions. The line between perception and cognition should be drawn between stages two and three. Specifically, cognitively derived expectations and beliefs do not interact with visual processing up to the construction of a visual description, but may influence the matching stage, perhaps by modulating the threshold amount of activation necessary to trigger a match to a particular object type.

The idea is then to build the automated archaeologist "brain" in terms of a *hierarchy* of feature detectors and specialized problem-solvers. At the lowest level in the hierarchy, there is what we have called *input units*, or visual feature detectors.

These detectors encode primitive visual features, namely, shape or texture basic parts. The retinal units provide a vector description of the stimulus in terms of a spatial co-ordinate system. These units activate all appropriate mapping units to which they are connected, and in turn, the mapping units activate all of their super ordinate object-based units. The receptive field properties of low-level detectors would encode the salient features of the input image in order to generate a preliminary model of the external world. This first level encodes information, which will be processed and eventually decoded by middle and higher-order mechanisms. The middle-level contains mapping mechanisms building a mapping between image defined and explanation-centered descriptions. What the mapping mechanisms are doing is to impose a frame of reference on the visual features, so that these features can be matched up with the same features specified in the definition of explanations. Specialized problem-solvers (higher-level mechanisms) represent particular solutions or explanatory concepts looking for particular combinations of features from the feature detectors. At the highest level, a decision mechanism selects the concept corresponding to that represented by the specific problem-solver activated by the highest quantity of features.

When building a neural network in an archaeological domain, visual input activates a first layer of neurons and this activation propagates through the network, using the connections among neurons at other layers. At higher layers, a given neuron embodies certain local hypothesis about a part of an object in an image. In moving from lower to higher levels of neurocomputing, it is interesting to consider the application of constraint satisfaction to perceptual processing. The pattern of activation changes dynamically over time, and eventually settles into a stable pattern in which some nodes are highly active, and other not.

This approach to nonlinear pattern matching suggests that, instead of casting object recognition as a massive dynamic search problem, we can think of it in terms of gradual sequences of transformations (operating in parallel) that emphasize certain distinctions and collapse across others. If the result of this sequence of transformations retains sufficient distinctions to disambiguate different possible explanations, but collapses across irrelevant differences produced by individual variability, then functional determination has been achieved. This approach is considerably simpler because it does not try to recover the complete 3-D structural information or form complex internal models.

Archaeological visual explanation is then a gradual process that proceeds from the general to the specific and that overlaps with, guides, and constrains the derivation of a causal explanation from an image or visual representation of some archaeological evidence (Figure 5.4).

The overall explanatory process is thus broken down into the extraction of a number of different observable physical properties (low-level analysis: shape, texture, composition and location), followed by a final decision based on these properties (high-level analysis) (Figure 5.5).

Figure. 5.4. A schema showing the process of visual interpretation

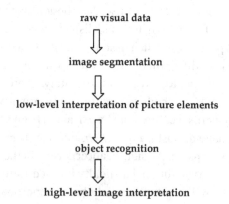

Figure.5.5. Flowchart of visual information processing

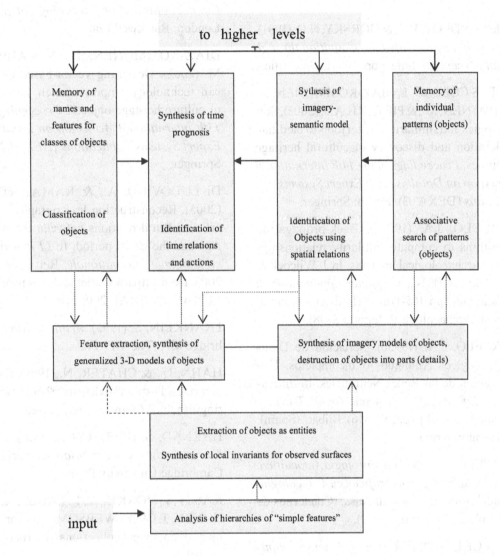

DIRECTIONS FOR FURTHER RESEARCH

The purpose of this chapter was only to introduce different archaeological domains where neural networks technology can be applied. Given the quintessential "visual" character of archaeological data, and the numeric and "vector" nature of neural networks, this chapter seemed necessary. I have

also included some examples of "non-visual" data processing, where the neural network was used as a supplement to more traditional approaches. Suggestions for further research appear in the following chapters. Especially relevant is also the last chapter, where some of the theoretical aspects on associative memories, here only sketched, are fully developed.

REFERENCES

ALEXANDROV, V.V., & GORSKY, N.D. (1991). *From humans to computers. Cognition through visual perception.* Singapore: World Scientific.

AVILES COLLAO, J., DIAZ-KOMMONEN, L., KAIPAINEN, M., & PIETARILA, J. (2003). Soft ontologies and similarity cluster tools to facilitate exploration and discovery of cultural heritage resources. *Proceedings of the 14th International Workshop on Database and Expert Systems Applications* (DEXA'03). Berlin: Springer.

BARCELÓ, J.A. (1995a). Back-propagation algorithms to compute similarity relationships among archaeological artifacts. In J. Wilcock & K. Lockyear (Eds.), *Computer applications in archaeology* (pp. 165-176). Oxford: ArcheoPress. (British Archaeological Reports S598).

BARCELÓ, J.A. (1995b). Seriación de Datos Arqueológicos Ambigüos o Incompletos. Una Aplicacion de las Redes Neuronales. In *Aplicaciones Informáticas en Arqueologia. Teoría y Sistemas* (vol. II.) (pp. 99-116) Bilbao (Spain): Denboraren Argia.

BARCELÓ, J.A. (1997). *Arqueología Automática. El uso de la Inteligencia Artificial en Arqueología.* Sabadell (Spain): Editorial Ausa, (Cuadernos de Arqueología Mediterránea, 2).

CHURCHLAND, P.M. (1989). *A neurocomputational perspective. The nature of mind and the structure of science.* Cambridge, MA: The MIT Press.

CLARK, A. (1989). *Microcognition: Philosophy, cognitive science, and parallel distributed processing.* Cambridge, MA: The MIT Press.

CLARK, A. (1993). *Associative engines. Connectionism, concepts and representational change.* Cambridge, MA: The MIT Press.

DAWSON, M.R.W. (2004). *Minds and machines. Connectionism and psychological modeling.* London: Blackwell Pub.

DÍAZ-KOMMONEN, L., & KAIPAINEN, M. (2002). Designing vector-based ontologies: can technology empower open interpretation of culture heritage objects? *Proceedings of the 13th International Workshop on Database and Expert Systems Applications (DEXA'02).* Berlin: Springer.

Di LUDOVICO, A., & RAMAZZOTTI, M. (2005). Reconstructing lexicography in glyptic art: Structural relations between the Akkadian Age and the Ur III period. In *LI Rencontre Assyriologique Internationale.* Retrieved October 2007 from http://www.let.leidenuniv.nl/rencontre/RAI_2005/RAI_2005.html

FRANKLIN, S. (1995). *Artificial Minds.* Cambridge MA: The MIT Press.

HAHN, U., & CHATER, N. (1998). Similarity and rules: Distinct? exhaustive? empirically distinguishable? *Cognition, 65,* 197-230.

HARNAD, S. (1987). *Categorical perception. The groundwork of cognition.* Cambridge, UK: Cambridge University Press.

KASKI, S., HONKELA, T., LAGUS, K., & KOHONEN, T. (1998). WEBSOM—self-organizing maps of document collections. *Neurocomputing, 21,* 101-117.

KOHONEN, T. (2001). *Self-organizing maps* (3rd ed.).Berlin: Springer.

KOSSLYN, S.M. (1994). *Image and brain. The resolution of the imagery debate.* Cambridge, MA: The MIT Press.

KULKARNI, A.D., (2001). *Computer vision and fuzzy neural systems.* Upper Saddle River, NJ: Prentice Hall.

LAGUS, K., KASKI, S., & KOHONEN, T. (2004). Mining massive document dollections by the WEBSOM method. *Information Sciences, 163*(1-3), 135-156.

MARR, D.H. (1982). *Vision. A computational investigation into the human representation and processing of visual information.* San Francisco, CA: W.II. Freeman.

RUMELHART, D.E. (1989). Towards a microstructural account of human reasoning. In S. Vosniadou & A. Ortony (Eds.), *Similarity and analogical reasoning.* Cambridge, UK: Cambridge University Press.

SHELLEY, C. P. (1996) Visual abductive reasoning in archaeology. *Philosophy of Science, 63,* 278-301.

Van den DRIES, M.H. (1998). *Archeology and the application of artificial intelligence. Case studies on use-wear analysis of prehistoric flint tools.* Archaeological Studies Leiden University No. 1., Faculty of Archaeology, University of Leiden (Holland).

Chapter VI
Shape Analysis

WHY ARCHAEOLOGICAL EVIDENCE HAS "SHAPE"?

In order to be able to acquire visual information, our automated "observer" is equipped with *range* and *intensity* sensors. The former acquire range images, in which each pixel encodes the distance between the sensor and a point in the scene. The latter are the familiar TV cameras acquiring grey-level images. That is to say, what the automated archaeologist "sees" is just the pattern of structured light projected on the scene (Trucco, 1997). To understand such input data, the spatial pattern of visual bindings should be differentiated into sets of marks (points, lines, areas, volumes) that express the position and geometry of perceived boundaries, and retinal properties (color, shadow, texture) that carry additional information necessary for categorizing the constituents of perception.

Currently, recognition of archaeological artifacts is performed manually by an expert. Generally, the expert attempts to find already recognized artifacts that are perceptually similar to the unclassified artifact. In order to recognize such artifacts, the human expert usually searches through a reference collection. A reference collection is a collection of reference artifacts, which is usually published as a set of formalized descriptions together with line drawings of the artifacts. Manual comparison of excavated artifacts with artifacts from a reference collection is a highly intuitive and uncontrollable process. In order to overcome these drawbacks, an automated archaeologist will use a kind of content-based shape retrieval system to find geometrically similar artifacts. Here "shape" appears as the key aspect for the mechanization of visual perception.

The attempts at defining the term *shape* usually found in the related literature are often based on the concept of "object properties invariant to translation, rotation and scaling" (Dryden & Mardia, 1998; Palmer, 1999; Small, 1996). While such definitions manage to capture an important property of shapes as perceived by humans, namely what relates the different appearances of the same object seen from different perspectives, they do not clearly specify what a *shape* is. An alternative and less conventional definition of shape has been advanced by Costa and Cesar (2001, p. 266): a shape can be understood as any "single," "distinct," "whole" or "united" visual entity. Fortunately, these terms can be formalized using the mathematical concept of *connectivity*, which leads to the following definition:

SHAPE is any connected set of points.

Consequently, shape is not an intrinsic property of observed objects, but it arises in images in different contexts: linear separation between regions of relative light and dark within an image, discontinuity in the surface depth, discontinuity in surface orientation, markings on the surfaces, and so forth, usually called "interfacial boundaries:" surfaces and/or contours. In other words, "shape" is the characteristic that delimits distinct spatial areas which appear when visual appearances are "significantly different" from one area to the next.

Shape analysis is more a task of discovery than plain description. It is essentially the operation of detecting significant local changes among luminance values in a visual scene. The method for "finding" connected sets of points in the images that represent archaeological observables can be approached by calculating the *luminance gradient* in the data array, that is, the direction of maximum rate of change of luminance values, and a scalar measurement of this rate. Following an earlier algorithm by Marr and Hildreth (1980), the automated archaeologist can extract shape information in a data array by finding the position of maximum variation in the map of luminance (grey or RGB-color levels). First-order differential operators compute the variation levels of such intensity function, and the algorithm finds the connectivity by detecting the highest value in the first derivative of the intensity function. A more economical algorithm for finding edges would be to detect *zero-crossings of the second derivative* of the intensity function. The second derivative of a function is just the slope of its previously calculated first derivative. The second derivative thus computes "the slope of the slope" of the original luminance function. Notice that in this second derivative function, the position of the interfacial boundary corresponds to the zero value in between a highly positive and a highly negative value. In any case, these are not the only ways of finding interfacial boundaries. There is huge literature, indeed an industry, concerned

with "edge detection" algorithms (Costa & Cesar, 2001; Heideman, 2005; Martin et al., 2004; Palmer, 1999; Sonka et al., 1994).

Nevertheless, conventional shape analysis techniques, being sensitive to (image) noise and intensity variations, often *do not* give us the true boundaries of objects in images. It is now generally acknowledged that, without a higher-level information of the object itself (such as the geometry of the object), such techniques produce erroneous results. Consequently, it seems a good idea to build an optimal edge detector by training a neural network with a certain predefined network structure with examples of edge and non-edge patterns.

In any case, we are not interested in the mechanical procedure of extracting shape connectivity among visual input, but in explaining shape information. Consequently, we are considering a higher-order definition, in which "shape" refers to the visual individualization of objects. The fact that a machine be able to individualize what it sees carries important clues about the structure of what is visible, and therefore it is the prime carrier of information in computer vision.

DIRECT SHAPE RECOGNITION

Let us consider the case, in which input neurons represent a matrix in which each row, and each column identify a point in the image and corresponding input neurons contain the intensity of light (grey or color level) at that point (pixel). In the case of bitmap images (black and white pictures), this is rather simple (Figure 6.1).

Díaz and Castro (2001) have used this approach to analyze the shape of rock-art symbols. The input data are real images (bitmaps), described in binary terms (1,0) (Figure. 6.2).

The neural network outputs the explanatory label of this visual input: abstract forms, zoomorphic and anthropomorphic motives. In this case, shape appears as an a priori defined verbal category. The neural network proceeds using a training set and the backpropagation algorithm to generalize known instances of rock-art symbols from visual data. In a related paper, the authors have also explored the possibilities of using Kohonen networks to clustering bitmap images of rock-art. Given a sample data for an archaeological

site, the unsupervised network was able to group most of the rock-art symbols in three main groups according to the elements complexity, but with some other assigned to single-element clusters, interpreted as marginal symbols (Castro & Díaz, 2004).

A very similar neural network has been used to recognize written characters in ancient documents, in numismatics and in epigraphy (Ailloli et al., 1999; Kashyap et al., 2003; Vezzosi et al., 2002). Assume that we want a network to recognize two patterns "T" and "H" (Figure 6.3). We might use an array of, say, nine sensors, each recording the presence or absence of ink in a small area of a single digit. The network would therefore need nine input units (one for each sensor), 2 output units (one for the "T" and another for the "H") and a number of hidden units. The associated patterns are all black and all white respectively, as shown in Figure 6.3.

In a real case, we would need a bigger array of sensors, say, 256 sensors or more, for encod-

Figure. 6.1. A bitmap image used to feed the input. Note that each pixel in the image (a number indicating the grey level associated with that pixel) activates one neuron in the input layer.

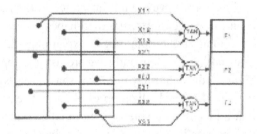

Figure. 6.2. A bitmap image of a rock-art symbol used to feed a neural network (Díaz and Castro 2001) Reprinted with permission from Damián Castro.

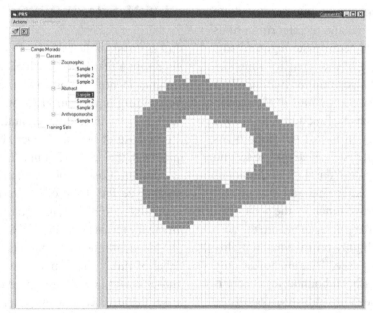

Figure. 6.3. Distributed representations of visual input for recognizing written characters

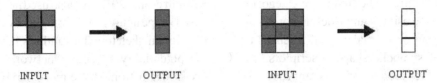

ing the digitalized image of each character. For instance, Kashyap and his collaborators report an artificial neural network for studying ancient Indian documents written in Kannada, a language of southern India, which is as old as 5th century A.D. (Kashyap et al., 2003). It constitutes an historical problem because fonts have evolved over the centuries, and it is difficult now to recognize the written characters in ancient documents. Characters from known texts dated from 3rd century B.C. to the present day are used for supervised learning. Data used for analysis were scanned epigraphic texts obtained from the Department of Epigraphy, Archaeological Survey of India, Mysore. Each letter was then converted to bitmap images. These images were scaled horizontally and vertically in proportion to fit a grid size of 10x14 pixels. This was followed by converting gray scale images to monochrome images. A preliminary neural network was trained using the backpropagation algorithm to identify ancient characters in terms of how well scanned images fit the known shape. The test character fed to the network was subsequently fed to a secondary probabilistic mechanism, which had prior data of known characters belonging to different centuries. The age of the character is the output of this second component.

Although in some simple cases this way of encoding shape information in terms of an exhaustive sampling of pixel values can be useful, in the more usual archaeological cases it does not work easily. Assuming that each pixel is an input neuron, we would need too many neurons in the input layer, and too many training exemplars to arrive to a gross approximation to original variability. Consider a low resolution image (640 x 480 pixels). Given that the image should be stored in the input layer, we need a computing neuron for each pixel; that means 307200 neurons in the input layer. We need a very powerful computer to run such a network. Even in the simple binary case reported by Díaz and Castro (2001), the network needed 24 hours of training for recognizing patterns in one of the shape explanatory categories: abstract, zoomorphic, anthropomorphic motives. Pixel-based shape input imposes a drastically reduction of the preliminary visual resolution so that neurocomputations can be generated in acceptable time.

Some essays have been published to reduce the complexity of neural network with digital images as input. Ji et al. (2005) have suggested using as input some measures (area, perimeter, area ratio, etc.) related to the area of the window in which the object lies, and not the full visual input.

If a fully distributed representation of the image in the input layer is computationally too demanding, we can encode the visual input in form of discrete shape parameters. This is a localized approach, which implies describing the shape in terms of geometric components, instead of using directly the visual information contained in the perceptual input. Feature based methods of shape description have been the typical approach used in classical classification frameworks. They can be divided into four categories according to the type of shape features used: (1) global features,

(2) global feature distributions, (3) spatial maps, and (4) local features. The first three categories represent a shape using a single descriptor. As an example we can quote Maloof and Michalski's (1997) use of symbolic shape descriptors. An archaeological example of this approach is Camiz and Venditti (2004), who have explored the possibilities of the automated classification of complex-shaped objects, like Egyptian scarabs. The authors suggest a qualitative code of shape information and stylistic features, and compare multiple correspondence analysis with neural networks.

This way of qualitatively describing shape is typical in bone analysis (both physical anthropology, archaeozoology and paleontology). Bell and Jantz (2002) have published the results of an interesting project to classify human bones remains using a neural network. The database contained shape descriptions of skulls representing 559 individuals from 25 sites occupied by the Arikara Indians located in the Middle Missouri region of South Dakota. Years represented ranged from AD 1600-1817. For each individual, 66 cranial features were reported. The output variables to be discriminated using shape differences were phase, period, and geographic location (bank of the river on which the site was located). That is to say, the goal was to distinguish the anatomic features of individuals from sites at both banks of river Missouri at different periods, given the assumption of different human populations at both areas, separated by the river. At a threshold of 75 percent, the neural models were able to predict period slightly better than chance (looking at the average percentage of correctly classified items). At the 0.60 threshold, geographic location was also predicted better than chance. Male and female skulls did not show any statistically significant differences. Thus, results suggest that the river was an effective barrier between sites and peoples since cranial measurements were sufficient to distinguish them.

Corsini and Schmitt (Corsini et al., 2005; Schmitt et al., 2001) have also used neural network based shape analysis to distinguish variability on the human skeleton. The authors have explored the potentiality of neural networks to predict age-at-death from shape morphology of human bones recovered from archaeological sites. They applied a neural network on the indicators from the pubic *symphysis* and the *sacropelvic* surface of the *illium* on 677 individuals from identified dry bone collections. In this study, neural inputs are discrete values (observation of the indicator, sex and collection). The output is a continuous numeric function of the age at death of individuals that the authors intent to map into age categories. The system obtained reliable classification that distinguishes three age intervals: 20-29, 32-59, and over 60 years old.

Morphometry is a way of describing the shape using relational geometric indexes as indicators. Among them, we can enumerate:

- **Circularity:** The degree of circularity of a solid. That is how much this object is similar to a circle. Where 1 is a perfect circle and 0.492 is an isosceles triangle. This shape is expressed by:

$$\frac{4\pi s}{p^2} \quad \begin{array}{l} \text{s: object area} \\ \text{p: object perimeter} \end{array}$$

- **Quadrature:** The degree of quadrature of a solid, where 1 is a square and 0.800 an isosceles triangle. This shape is expressed by:

$$\frac{p}{4\sqrt{s}}$$

- **Irregularity:** Measurement of the irregularity of a solid. It is calculated based on its perimeter and the perimeter of the surrounding circle. The minimum irregularity is a circle, corresponding at the value 1. A square is the maximum irregularity with a value of 1.402. This shape is expressed by:

$$\frac{p_c}{p}$$

- **Elongation:** The degree of ellipticity of a solid, where a circle and a square are the less elliptic shape. This shape is expressed by:

$$\frac{D}{d}$$ D: maximum diameter within an object
d: minimum diameter perpendicular at D

Alternatively, we can rely on the fact that the outer frame of the observed object may be enough to specify the type it belongs. In this approach, the outer frame, usually called *contour* or silhouette, is used as the most basic building block of visual shape. Contours provide a relatively compact way of representing the shape of an object, with the assumption that the region between the edges defining the contour is relatively homogenous. This is an increasingly used descriptive method in archaeology (Bendels et al., 2006; De Napoli et al., 2003; Halir & Fluzer, 1997; Kampel, Mara & Sablatnig, 2006; Kampel & Sablatnig, 2003; Leitao & Stolfi, 2002, 2005; Leymarie, 2003; Papaioannou & Karabassi, 2002; Papaioannou et al., 2001, 2003; McBride & Kimia, 2003; Mara & Sablatnig, 2005, 2006; Uçoluk & Toroslu, 1999; Willis et al., 2002).

For shape recognition, coordinates of detected contour points are in the input and interpreted "shapes" in the output. The problem is that we would need infinite coordinates to describe the outer frame of even the simplest object. We need to assume that the shape of any object is essentially captured by a finite subset of its contour points, so the input of the network contains just a selection of the points constituting the object's contour.

From here, there are two possibilities:

- Selected points along the contour should correspond to key-points, such as maxima of curvature or inflection points. "Salient" means that the point is in some way "special" or "distinct from its neighbors." Attempts to define what a salient point (SP) is suffer from the problem that an isolated pixel cannot be special by itself, but only in comparison to its neighbors. Hence, saliency makes sense only with respect to the surroundings. A suggested method is based on finding points of inflection (i.e., curvature zero-crossings) on a curve at varying levels of detail. The curvature k of a planar curve, at a point on the curve, is defined as the instantaneous rate of change of the slope of the tangent at that point with respect to arc length (for the general procedure, see Bebis et al., 1998, see also Heideman 2005),

- Selected points along the contour should not only correspond to key-points. We can select any points (usually 100 or more), provided we are sampling the shape with roughly uniform spacing (for the general procedure, see Belongie et al., 2002).

Let we consider some examples using this way of describing shape. In an archaeozoological and paleontological application, Paul Gibson (1993a, 1993b, 1996) has used neural networks and back-propagation learning to create a system for the ageing and interpretation of archaeozoological material. He has used modern day data for training the network. One approach to age-estimation is based on the eruption and wear stages of animal's teeth. A mammal dentition changes through a set of distinguishable stages as along as the animal matures. Archaeozoological analysis uses diagrams for each tooth that represent idealized wear stages. A tooth in a given mandible is compared against the diagram and the diagram that best matches with the tooth suggests the wear stage. This analysis results in a *tooth wear stage value*. These values are then used to produce a *mandible wear stage value* that represents the relative age of the sample. A sample of 22 modern sheep mandibles with varying stages of attrition and a number of tooth abnormalities was selected as training set. Such a data set had a combination of missing teeth, unerupted teeth, teeth in early stages of wear, and teeth in moderate stages of wear. Mandibles were "presented" to the computer as pre-processed images acquired through a video digitizer with a frame buffer of 640x480 pixels with 16 grey levels. Light and orientation of the mandibles and of the camera were strictly controlled. Sub-images were extracted from original ones, in such a way to obtain arrays of 120x80 pixels, which implied 9600 neurons in the input layer. From the tooth image, the neural network must identify which teeth are present as an indicator for the application of wear stage models. This means identifying the borders of the tooth and mapping their outline to one of the tooth descriptors. An algorithm was created that highlighted the approximate border of the teeth based on background information. The neural network was trained to distinguish between different teeth silhouettes. Each output from the network represented all possible wear stages. For example, for a tooth at wear stage "A" the network was taught to produce a "1" output for the first neuron in the output layer and "0" in the rest. The system was measured against estimations made by human experts and found to have an overall performance of 65 percent agreement. Like the human experts, the neural network appeared to have problems in assessing early wear stages whilst having greater success with later stages.

Eastham and Gwynn used neural networks in a similar way, for identifying bird egg-shells found at archaeological sites. Using a reference collection of photographs, the system was able to identify around 17 different species of birds, whose eggs were used by the neolithic populations of northern Britain (Eastham & Gwynn, 1997).

Sam Redfern has approached the recognition of megalith burial monuments, based on their morphological and topographic measurements made using aerial photography data. The goal of the analysis was a typology of 125 archaeological enclosures and sub-circular features visible in vertical aerial photographs of the Bruff area (Ireland). A set of morphological and topographic measurements regarding each of these monuments was generated using image-processing tools: circularity, rectangularity, elongation, area, slope, and aspect. The first four of these are generated from the objective outline tracing of a monument, while the last two are generated from the digital elevation model (DEM) of a monument, which is created through the application of digital photogrammetry techniques to stereo images. The data generated were submitted to an agglomerative cluster analysis using Ward's method in order to define objectively typological groups. This resulted in the definition of six groups, five of which were further divisible into sub-groups. A neural network was designed to calculate the mapping between remotely sensed topographic and shape features and explanatory morphological types. The neural network should learn the underlying patterns in the data, and then should be capable of accurately predicting a typological class given only a set of input values. Following investigations into the most suitable neural architecture for the task, it was found that a hierarchical collection of networks was most useful (Redfern, 1998a, 1998b, 1999).

Lohse is working on an archaeological auto classification system, which uses neural network technology to classify stone arrow points based on the geometrical information of their contours. The input layer consists of information pulled from an image of a projectile point, while the output layers give the classification of that tool, and a related information set. That is to say, the output contains a localized representation of archaeological types ("simple lanceolate," "side notched," "corner notched," etc.). Through training, the neural network can replicate the actions of archaeological experts in identifying types. When the silhouette of a new unknown lithic point is fed to the system, it answers with an estimate of the best match for such an item. The initial application uses projectile point specimens drawn from the Pacific Northwest cultural area, but the system is extensible to other cultural areas and other artifact classes (Lohse et al., 2004).

Bignon et al. (2005) use a 3D scanner to acquire three-dimensional coordinates of specific salient points along the contour of animal bones (prehistoric horse *metapoda*). The authors observed that contour coordinates, contrarily to distances, are sensitive to translation and rotation of the reference system. Accordingly, each object was therefore scaled to unit centroid size, centered and rotated in order to minimize its deviations from a reference object. The whole data set is represented by a size measure, a reference object called *consensus* corresponding to the mean object over the whole sample, and a residual matrix containing the shape parameters of each object. A feed forward neural network has been built for establishing the relationship between shape and geographic origin of the archaeozoological samples (three distinct areas: Switzerland Plateau, Paris Basin, and Charente, in France). The research tries to test the possibility of large migrations of wild horses between the North and the South of Western Europe during the Late Glacial, by determining whether the shape of bones from different areas have also different anatomical shapes. A neural network (input=shape parameters; output=region and/or site) has been used here to estimate the classification rates between regions and/or sites. Almost all horse bones are clearly separated between a northern group (Paris Basin) and a southern group (Switzerland Plateau and Charente). The latter group also shows important differences in shape, although unrelated to the preceding ones. Even if the observed differences are less genetically determined than the authors believe (and more under the influence of mechanical constraints), they clearly evidence a regional population fragmentation pattern for the studied Late Glacial horses of Western Europe.

The fragmentation of the Magdalenian *E. caballus arcelini* into regional populations would not be surprising, since present day large ungulates in the tundra display the same pattern. Today, this appears to be dependent on the existence of high demographic density and of course, from the absence of large scale migrations.

Zweig (2006) has classified whole vessels from the site of Tel es-Safi (the biblical Philistine town of Gath) and pottery sherds from Tel Batash (the biblical town of Timnah) defining the borders of different parts, such as lip, rim, shoulder, and base. Contours were automatically subdivided into elemental sections using different methods. Two of them were based on curve peaks; one was based on inflection points, and another on curvature changes in relation to the horizontal axis. Many attributes were calculated for each section, such as average curvature, average thickness, curvature skew, curvature kurtosis, section relative length, and so forth. Neural Networks were set to create prediction models for the various presumed functions and the temporary stratum number in which they were found. This actually created a set of fuzzy variables that defined the likeness of the vessel to the predicted trait.

Van der Maaten and colleagues have developed a content-based image retrieval system to aid the classification of historical glass objects. The authors have developed a content-based image retrieval system that compares photographs of artifacts with drawings from a reference collection, and take as a result the most similar, according to a machine learning algorithm. First, a shape profile has to be computed from the artifact photograph using an edge detector. This is necessary in order to compute outer shape features of the artifact. Once the outer shape profile is extracted from the photograph, a number of points is sampled from the boundary of the shape contour. The points are described as shape context descriptors. Shape context descriptors describe the distance and angle of a point to all other points in a discretized log-polar space. By means of this description, a set of shape context descriptors (i.e., a shape context) contains global information about the shape. After the computation of the shape context descriptors, a similarity measure is computed. The similarity measure is based on the dissimilarity between two shape contexts. Subsequently, the optimal matching between the shape context descriptors of two shapes is calculated. The costs of this matching provide a measure for the dissimilarity of the two shapes. Although the system does not perform well on highly degraded artifacts, the authors think it forms an important contribution to archaeology. Even when the retrieved artifacts are not perfect matches, the system provides an entry into the reference collection, allowing the archaeologist to classify artifacts faster and with a lower risk of errors. In addition, the system can be used for automatic shape analysis of entire reference collections. By performing the shape analysis on the entire reference collection, it is possible to present perceptually similar artifacts for every artifact in the reference collection (Van der Maaten et al., 2006).

The same authors have also developed a fast and reliable system for coin classification. Although the system was designed for classifying and sorting the heterogeneous coin collection of unsorted pre-Euro coins, it can be used also for archaeological and numismatic collections. COIN-O-MATIC performs automatic classification of coins in five stages: segmentation, feature extraction, pre-selection, classification, and verification. Segmentation is the separation of the coin from the background of the coin photograph. Feature extraction is the transformation of the segmented coin into an efficient and coin-specific representation. The coin stamp information is translated into edge-based statistical distributions, and used to train a classifier. Pre-selection is the selection of possible coin classes based on some of these edge-based statistical distributions. Classification is the process of mapping the feature representation onto one of the selected coin labels, based on information gathered from the training process.

Verification is checking whether two coin images have identical labels, based on visual comparison. Verification is necessary because the test sets contain unknown coins that are not available in the training set. The classification stage contains no explicit way to handle unknown coins (Van der Maaten & Boon, 2006).

Some other neurocomputing applications of shape recognition are only indirectly related to archaeology. For instance, we should mention that feed forward neural networks and the back-propagation algorithm have been used to classify different properties of wheat grains based on image morphology (Wang et al., 2002). Other relevant applications identify mineral inclusions and petrographic information from thin sections of geologic or archaeological samples (Fueten, 1997; Fueten et al., 2001; Thompson, Fueten & Blockus, 2001). Those examples give us a clue about how to apply neural networks for shape identification in paleobotanical or archaeometric analysis (for instance, microscopy recognition).

ADVANCED METHODS OF SHAPE ANALYSIS AND INTERPRETATION

Shape cannot be reduced to a *bi-dimensional* geometrical parameter. Archaeological observables are three-dimensional entities, and their bi-dimensional contour is but a crude surrogate of their real shape. Interfacial boundaries of real objects have the appearance of *surfaces*, more than *curves*. We may need then more sophisticated mechanisms for analyzing archaeological shapes in all their complexity. The advantages of using neural network for such a task are diverse (Peng & Shamsuddin, 2004):

- Neural networks with backpropagation technique are able to estimate the depth (z) of an object with higher accuracy than other methods. It also means that neural networks are able to reconstruct object from 2D image to 3D after training.

- This type of reconstruction is able to produce more points of an object or surface. Therefore, a neural network is able to reconstruct more complex object with smoother surface.
- Even with scattered or unorganized data of an object is provided, neural networks are able to regenerate the object when outliers are removed and the smoothness of the surface is maintained.

3D objects can be described using a variation of bidimensional feature based methods of shape description. Examples of such global descriptors are the statistical moments of volume, volume-to-surface ratio, or the Fourier transform of a surface. Other global features for 3D shape are bounding boxes, cords-based, moments-based and wavelets-based descriptors, convex-hull based indices like hull *crumpliness* (the ratio of the object surface area and the surface area of its convex hull), hull packing (the percentage of the convex hull volume not occupied by the object), and hull compactness (the ratio of the cubed surface area of the hull and the squared volume of the convex hull).

Neural networks can be used to build connected surfaces from edge and vertices input information. In general, such programs rely on coordinate information (x,y,z or longitude, width, height), that is to say, the spatial location of interfacial boundaries for *interpolating* a geometric mesh (see Gu & Yan, 1995; Peng & Shamsuddin, 2004; Piperakis & Kumazawa, 2001).

The difficulty involved in the problem of surface reconstruction from unorganized x,y,z points is in obtaining correct connectivity among the sample points. Correct connectivity can give us a reconstructed geometric model that faithfully represents the shape and topology of the original object from which the set of sample points were drawn. Different neurocomputational approaches try to solve this problem. Yu (1999) introduced the technique for surface reconstruction from unorganized points by applying Kohonen's self-organized map. This is a top-down approach where a geometric model with correct topology (connectivity) has already been given in advance with some help from the user, for example, the user can decide from the sample points whether the original object is topologically equivalent to a sphere or a torus. A similar approach has been published by Barhak and Fischer (2001), Knopf and Al-Naji (2001), Knopf and Kofman (2002).

In addition to point coordinates and geometric interpolation models, shading is a very useful cue for reconstruction of surface shape (Cho & Chow 1999; Wei & Hirzinger, 1996). The brightness of a point in an image $I(x,y)$, is a function of the incident illumination and the corresponding surface normal $n(x,y)$, given by the image irradiance. There are infinite numbers of normal vector fields that can give rise to an intensity image. This makes the problem extremely difficult. The problem would be better posed by enforcing additional constraints such as integrability by different means. Most shape from shading methods have been based on minimizing the average error in satisfying the image irradiance equation. This includes direct reconstruction of height by enforcing differential smoothness constraints, using line drawing interpretation to reconstruct piecewise smooth surfaces or using only local differential conditions.

Ben-Arie and Nandy (Ben-Arie & Nandy, 1998; Nandy & Ben-Arie, 2001) have proposed a neurocomputational method for extracting 3D shape information from shading. The input array in their system has a local receptive field in the image domain. The array of output units defines the reconstructed surface function corresponding to the local receptive field. The network should be able to estimate relative surface heights of neighboring pixels under varying conditions of illumination as well as variations of the surface type from being concave or convex, or ellipsoids, cylinders or hyperboloids.

Mostafa et al. (1999) presents a framework for integrating multiple sensory data, sparse range data, and dense depth maps from shape from shading in order to improve the 3D reconstruction of visible surfaces of 3D objects. The integration process is based on propagating the error difference between the two data sets by fitting a surface to that difference and using it to correct the visible surface obtained from shape from shading. A feed-forward neural network is used to fit a surface to the sparse data.

DECOMPOSING SHAPE

The alternative to 3D shape modeling is *volumetric representation,* which describe an object as a set of primitives plus a set of spatial connectivity relations among them. It implies both a decomposition approach and a constructive framework, which describe the shape of an object as a combination of primitive elements. This different approach is based on the idea that the shape of an object has an important aspect that cannot be captured by the description of its coordinates, edges, and interfacial boundaries: the fact that most complex objects are perceived as being composed of distinct parts. As we will use the term, a part is a restricted portion of an object that has semiautonomous status in visual perception. For instance, "a chair has four legs, a set, and a back." In addition to such decomposition in parts, object perceptions include the spatial relations among them (Palmer, 1999, p. 348). The part decomposition approach assumes that each object can be decomposed into a small set of generic components that combine to form units depending on the relationships between the components.

Consider the decomposition schema for a figurine; it has several parts as a head, a neck, a body, two arms, two legs. Each part has a characteristic shape and size: the head may be geometrically represented as a small triangular block, the neck a short cylinder, the body a large rectangular block, and the arms and legs long and slim cylinders. The parts are arranged in more

or less specific locations. The head is attached to one end of the neck, and its other end is attached to the body. The legs are attached to the bottom of the body to support it. All such information must be represented in order to recognize some visual input as an instance of a figurine.

In such a decomposition-based approach, the input variables are grouped into sets, where the relationships within each set are more accurately modeled than those across different sets. We refer to each such set as a *part*. For example, parts of a figurine's face, such as the eyes, nose, and mouth, can be considered as *parts* and modeled separately. However, it should be emphasized that *parts* need not have a natural meaning to us (such as a nose or an eye), but could be defined as a group of geometric units, that satisfy certain mathematical properties. In addition, these *parts* do not have to be composed from disjoint groups of variables; a variable can be re-used in multiple *parts*. A parts-based approach selects each *part* to represent a small group of variables that are known to be statistically dependent. Such an approach avoids devoting representational resources to weak relationships and instead allocates richer models to the stronger relationships (Schneidermann & Kanade, 2004).

A more formal decomposition may be obtained by a hierarchical graph representation that captures local curvature, distance between features and angles between features. Automated shape analysis of archaeological objects may be based on the decomposition of object shapes into discrete parts, followed by the identification of those parts and their spatial and temporal relationships. We have not to forget, however, that the relationship between parts (their configuration) is equally important. The intrinsic or extrinsic features of other parts may influence the internal descriptions of the parts themselves. The perception of shape will then depend critically not only on the part structure of objects and how its various parts are related to one another in terms of their relative positions, relative orientations, relative sizes, and so forth.

The hypothesis that parts have their own meaning and function to understand the complexities of a distinct shape, has led many researchers to assume that all shapes can be specified in terms of sets of parts; the idea of an alphabet of shape is then a prevalent one. Biederman (1987, 1995) called the primitive 3D components *geons*, which is a shortened form of *geometric units*. Each *geon* corresponds to an elementary universal shape component (e.g., a brick, a cylinder, a curved cylinder), and all shapes are represented by combinations of *geons*. Biederman defined a set of 36 qualitatively different universal geons by making distinctions in some variable dimensions: cross-sectional curvature, symmetry, axis curvature, and size variation. This produces a relatively small set of distinct primitive volumes from which a huge number of object representations can be constructed by putting two or more together. Because complex objects are conceived in Biederman's theory as configurations of two or more *geons* in particular spatial arrangements, they are encoded as structural descriptions that specify both the *geons* present and their spatial relationships. If geons are the alphabet of complex 3-D objects, then spatial relations among *geons* are analogous to the order of letters in words. Biederman uses structural descriptions in which 108 qualitatively different relations can be represented between two *geons*. Some of this connections concern how they are attached (e.g., SIDE-CONNECTED and TOP-CONNECTED); others concern their relational properties, such as relative size (e.g., LARGER-THAN, SMALLER-THAN). With these *geon* relations, it is logically possible to construct more than a million different two-*geon* objects. Adding a third *geon* and its relations to the other two geons pushes the number of combinations into the trillions.

Although geons are themselves volumetric entities, Biederman theory proposes that geons are identified directly from image-based features such as edges and vertices. Hummel and Biederman (1992) have built a complex neural architecture to represent how shape analysis can be performed automatically. The network has seven layers of neurons, and each one deals with a different class of visual or spatial feature. The First layer, *L1,* has a cluster of units for each region of an input array. Within a cluster, there are some units responding to the orientation of edges, some to their curvature, and some to the termination of an edge. Units in *L1* feed units in *L2*, each of which responds to edge groupings defining vertices, axes of parallelism, axes of symmetry, and elongated blobs. Both *L1* and *L2* are retinotopic in the sense that adjacent clusters of cells deal with adjacent regions of the input array. Together sets of units in *L1* and *L2* represent the set of representational, volumetric primitives (geons), and units in *L3* respond to properties of those geons such as their location, orientation, type of major axis and so forth. In *L4* and *L5* units code various spatial relations among geons ranging from location to "above." The units of *L6* receive input from *L3* and *L5* and so code a geon and its relations with others. Finally *L7* units integrate the *geons* signaled by *L6* and so respond to whole objects constituted by geon assemblies.

This kind of shape-decomposition approaches can be very useful as a general method of shape analysis for archaeological research. Some improvements and advances, however, have been proposed. Edelman (Edelman, 1994, Edelman & Intrator, 2000, 2002) has suggested giving up the classical compositional representation of shape by a fixed alphabet of crisp "all-or-none" explicitly tokened primitives (such as *geons*) in favor of a fuzzy, super positional coarse-coding by an open-ended set of image fragments. This alternative approach has met with considerable success in computer vision. For example, the system described by Nelson and Selinger (1998) starts by detecting contour segments, and determines whether their relative arrangement approximates that of a model object. Because none of the individual segment shapes or locations is critical to the successful description of the entire shape, this method does not suffer from the brittleness associated with the classical structural description models of recognition. Moreover, the tolerance to moderate variation in the segment shape and location data allows it to categorize novel members of familiar object classes (Nelson & Selinger, 1998).

Leow and Miikkulainen (1997) take a more or less similar approach based on the representation of structure in terms of schema hierarchies, implemented as laterally and vertically connected topological maps. They are interested not only in direct object recognition, but in scene understanding. The authors address the problem of recognizing different shapes, when a single input contains more than a single object. For instance, imagine that the visual input is a picture of some excavated area, showing the shape of a prehistoric dwelling in terms of remains of the walls, floors, and fallen roof elements. Pottery sherds and animal bones appear also in the scene. Is it possible to program a computer system, so it can be able to recognize the different "components" of this archaeological scene? Furthermore, such computer system must be able to process different scenes where the same components may appear in different spatial order, or some new components may be present. In order to solve this complex visual problem, the machine must be able to represent knowledge about the spatial structure. Leow and Miikkulainen's VISOR system (visual schemas for object recognition) accepts as input a modified picture containing edges and closed contours present in the original visual image. It contains three different subsystems: (1) the low-level visual module (LLVM) extracts positional and visual features information for the image (length, breadth, closure, vertical tilt, horizontal tilt, degree of expansion, curvature); (2) the schema module matches decomposition schemas with inputs, and (3) the response module generates the object and scene labels expected by the environment. Each module corresponds to a level in the schema hierarchy, with the scene schemas at the top, and the object schemas at the bottom.

LIMITATIONS IN SHAPE ANALYSIS AND RECOGNITION

Direct methods for shape recognition can generate oversimplified results, given that most original visual information is not taken into account when limiting visual input to shape geometry. Multi-resolution image representation and processing is a well-known image analysis methodology that has been used by many researchers to solve this kind of troubles (see Belongie et al., 2002; Young et al., 1997,). A multi-resolution image representation can be viewed as an image pyramid. An image pyramid is a data structure that includes the original full resolution input image as its base level, together with several increasingly lower resolution copies comprising the ascending levels of the pyramid. The search can start at a very coarse resolution level, on which the size of the data representation is small compared to the full resolution input. Matching results at each level guide the process at the next higher resolution level (lower level in descent through the image pyramid). This multilayer process is also called top–down matching, or hierarchical matching. In top-down matching, a coarse-to-fine matching strategy is used in which fine features, at higher resolution, are matched by using constraints induced by results of the coarse matching obtained at the lower resolution levels. The recursive constraints speed up the matching process, since they narrow the searching space at subsequent higher resolution levels containing features that are more abundant. All top–down matching procedures perform the matching in a hierarchical manner. Generally, hierarchical structures capture details about the objects of interest in sequentially increasing resolution levels. A major problem associated with this strategy is that if an error occurs at an early stage, then this low-resolution error is propagated into each subsequent higher resolution level and finally a mismatch would occur. This mismatch cannot be corrected by using the information at another level, because the information flows top–down in a feed-forward manner and there is no feedback from higher resolution levels. To address this problem, a technique called *coarse-and-fine* matching has been proposed, where top-down and bottom–up matching are concurrently performed for each pair of levels of the image pyramid in order to find the best matched features at each level pair simultaneously (Ullman, 1996).

All the examples presented up to now are based on the assumption that certain simple properties remain invariant under the transformations in the perception of an object. That is, we may believe that shape constancy occurs simply because we are able to recognize the same object from different perspective views by using different features. A vase can be seen from above or from the bottom, from the right or from the left, and if the object is not a perfect sphere, its 3D interfacial boundaries (contours or surfaces) will look different. To identify such a pot as an ancient container of wine, an intelligent robot should assume that for each shape definition stored in memory, there is a set of allowed transformations the object may undergo, as changes in position, scale, or orientation in space. The fact that each shape description should cover the range of possible viewing angles introduces a great deal of complexity in shape recognition, because to represent the entire object a huge number of descriptions for the same object are required. Therefore, an object should be represented for recognition purposes by a number of its views, rather than a single 3D representation. The implication is that combinations of a small number of stored views can approximate novel views, from new viewing directions.

Several novel network architectures have been developed specifically to cope with concomitant object variations in position (in-plane or out-of-plane), rotation, scale, or illumination. It is clear that a distinction needs to be made between invariant recognition in 2D (projection or perspective) images and in 3D volume images. An interesting approach that performs object recognition, which is invariant to 2D transla-

tions, in-plane rotation and scale, is the neural what-and-where filter (Carpenter et al., 1998). It combines a multi-scale oriented filter bank (*what*) with an invariant matching module (*where*). Other approaches rely on learning the variations explicitly by training. The general strategy seems to be the construction of different templates for each shape in every possible position, orientation, and size. The template with the best match to the target will be a reasonable approximation to their true "similarity" within this shape similarity scheme. Kulkarni explains how to use such kind of neural networks. A three-layered feed-forward network with backpropagation algorithm would use images with different degrees of rotation to train the network. During the training process, the rotated and scaled images would be used as input images. In general, such models work well with images with rotational and translational differences, but not quite well in recognizing objects with different scales (Kulkarni, 2001; Langner, 2001). Model-based object recognition solves the problem of invariant recognition by relying on stored prototypes at unit scale positioned at the origin of an object-centered coordinate system. Elastic matching techniques are used to find a correspondence between features of the stored model and the data and they can compute the parameters of the transformation the observed instance has undergone relative to the stored model.

A major disadvantage of these approaches is that object variations in rotation and scale have to be learned explicitly by the classifier. It calls for a very large, complete training set and a classifier that can generalize well (see discussion in Egmont-Petersen, 2002). An example has been proposed by Ullman (1996). His general idea is that given an input shape and a candidate model, a correspondence is first established between them. This means that a small number of features (including point wise features and lines) are identified as matching features in the image and the model. Based on the corresponding features, the transformation separating the model from the image is uniquely determined. The recovered transformation is then applied to the model. The image generated by the transformed model is then compared with the viewed object. Based on the degree of match, the candidate model is selected or rejected. To be accepted, the match must be sufficiently close, and better than that of competing models.

DIRECTIONS FOR FURTHER RESEARCH

I have just reviewed some basic aspects on the way shape information can be fed into a neural network to recognize the perceived archaeological object. It is impossible, however, to give in a few pages an exhaustive account of intelligent and automated shape analysis. Further details can be read in Caelli and Bischof (1997), Loncaric (1998), Belongie et al. (2002), Egmont-Petersen (2002), Osada et al. (2002), Rolls and Deco (2002), Tangelder and Veltkamp (2004).

Over the years, object recognition has attracted attention in many computational disciplines, including (but not limited to) robotics, computer vision, psychology, and artificial intelligence. A number of computational methods have been developed for extracting "meaning" from visual input (Bicici & St. Amant, 2003). These methods are based on shape analysis, as presented along this chapter, but also on knowledge about the way the object was used, the naive physical rules that govern the objects. DiManzo et al. (1989), for instance, regarded object recognition as the ability to integrate shape and function with the help of planning. It suggests that reasoning about the functionality of archaeological objects requires a cross-disciplinary investigation ranging from recognition techniques used in computer vision and robotics to reasoning, representation, and learning methods in artificial intelligence.

A different line of research is active vision. Active vision refers to the process of exploring an image or scene for relevant features, just as biological organisms do. The advantages of such systems are obvious, including attentive focus, which excludes processing of areas of the image that are irrelevant, and providing an elegant method of handling variance in location, scale, and rotation. Related to this new line of research are those approaches to object recognition, based not only on shape information, but also on the direct interaction between the user and the object. Haptic exploration, grasp planning, and physical perception through observing changes in objects are some of the techniques used in this area.

It can be difficult to apply in archaeology many of the examples mentioned here. Specially, in the active vision approach, archaeologists should realize that the only way to explain archaeological traces is by experimentation and careful replication of ancient techniques and production/use behaviors. In such a way, shape analysis, as any other way of visual analysis, can be seen as a constraint satisfaction problem where the mappings between form and meaning are actually many-to-many and recovering an object by matching previously recognized ones leads to combinatorial growth.

There are fast infinite suggestions for further research here. The domain of computer vision is one of the most dynamic in the recent years, and there is no day without a new algorithm or a new approach that brings some improvements. The reader is advised to not considering the methods here presented as the best ones, because the field is evolving at fast speed. Publications like *Pattern Recognition,* the *International Journal of Pattern Recognition and Artificial Intelligence*, and the *IEEE Transactions on Pattern Analysis and Machine Intelligence.*

REFERENCES

AILLOLI, F., SIMI, S., SONA, D., SPERDUTTI, A., & STARITA, A. (1999). SPI: A system for paleographic inspections. *AI*IA Notizie, 12*(4), 34-39.

BARHAK, J., & FISCHER, A. (2001). Parameterization and reconstruction from 3D scattered points based on neural network and PDE techniques. *IEEE Trans. on Visualization and Computer Graphics, 7*(1), 1-16.

BEBIS,G., PAPADOURAKIS,G., & ORPHANOUDAKIS, S. (1998). Recognition using curvature scale space and artificial neural networks. *Proceedings of the IASTED International Conference Signal and Image Processing, Las Vegas, Nevada – USA.*

BELL, S., & JANTZ, R. (2002). Neural network classification of skeletal remains. In G. Burenhult (Ed.), *.Archeological informatics: Pushing the envelope* (pp. 205-212). Oxford: ArchaeoPress.

BELONGIE, S., MALIK, J., & PUZICHA, J. (2002). Shape matching and object recognition using shape contexts. *IEEE Transactions on Pattern Analysis and Machine Intelligence, 24*(24), 509-522.

BEN-ARIE, J., & NANDY, D. (1998). A neural network approach for reconstructing surface shape from shading. *IEEE International Conference on Image Processing, Chicago Oct. 1998.*

BENDELS, G.H., GUTHE, M., & KLEIN, R., (2006). Free-form modelling for surface inpainting In *Proceedings of the 4th International Conference On Computer Graphics, Virtual Reality, Visualisation and Interaction in Africa (Afrigraph 2006)* (pp. 49-58). ACM Sigraph.

BICICI, E., & ST. AMANT, R. (2003). *Reasoning about the functionality of tools and physical artifacts.* Technical Report TR-2003-22, Department of Computer Science, North Carolina State University, April, 2003.

BIEDERMAN, I. (1987). Recognition-by-components: A theory of human image understanding. *Psychological Review, 94*(2), 115-147.

BIEDERMAN, I. (1995). Visual object recognition. In S. F. Kosslyn & D. N. Osherson (Eds.), *An invitation to cognitive science, (2nd ed) Volume 2. Visual cognition* (pp. 121-165). MIT Press.

BIGNON, O., BAYLAC, M., VIGNE, J.D., & EISENMANN, V. (2005). Geometric morphometrics and the population diversity of late glacial horses in western europe (Equus caballus arcelini): Phylogeographic and Anthropological Implications. *Journal of Archaeological Science, 32,* 375–391.

CAELLI, T., & BISCHOF, W.F. (1997). The role of machine learning in building image interpretation systems. In T. Caelli, P. Lam & H. Bunke (Eds.), *Spatial computing* (pp.143-168). Singapore: World Scientific.

CAMIZ, S., & VENDITTI, S. (2004). Unsupervised and supervised classifications of egyptian scarabs based on typology qualitative characters. In F. Nicolucci (Ed.), *Beyond the artefact. Computer applications in archaeology.* Budapest: ArchaeoLingua.

CARPENTER, G.A., GROSSBERG, S., & LESHER, G.W. (1998). The what-and-where filter—a spatial mapping neural network for object recognition and image understanding. *Computer Vision and Image Understand, 69*(1), 1–22.

CASTRO, D., & DIAZ, D. (2004). Kohonen networks applied to rincón del toro rock art site analysis. In F. Niccolucci (Ed.), *Beyond the artefact. Computer applications in archaeology.* Budapest: ArcheoLingua.

CHO, S. Y., & CHOW, T.W.S. (1999). Shape recovery from shading by new neural-based reflectance model. IEEE Transactions on Neural Networks, *10*(6), 1536-1541.

CORSINI, M.M., SCHMITT, A., & BRUZEK, J. (2005). Aging process variability on the human skeleton: Artificial network as an appropriate tool for age at death assessment. *Forensic Science International, 148,* 163-167.

COSTA, L.F., & CESAR, R.M., (2001). *Shape analysis and classification: Theory and practice.* Boca Raton, FL: CRC Press.

De NAPOLI, L., LUCHI, L., MUZZUPAPPA, M., & RIZZUTI, S. (2003). Recognition and classification of fragments from ceramic artefacts. In M. Doerr & A. Sarris (Eds.), *The digital heritage of archaeology. Computer applications and quantitative methods in archaeology* (pp. 295-300). Heraklion, Greeece: Archive of Monuments and Publications. Hellenic Ministry of Culture.

DIAZ, D. & CASTRO, D. (2001). Pattern recognition applied to rock art. In G. Burenhult (Ed.), *.Archaeological informatics: Pushing the envelope* (pp. 463-468). Oxford: ArchaeoPress.

DIMANZO, M., TRUCCO, E., GIUNCHIGLIA, F. & RICCI, F. (1989). FUR: understanding functional reasoning. *International Journal of Intelligent Systems, 4,* 431–457.

DRYDEN, I.L., & MARDIA, K., (1998). *Statistical shape analysis.* London: John Wiley.

EASTHAM, A., & GWYNN, I. A. (1997). Archaeology and the electron microscope. Eggshell and neural network analysis of images in the neolithic: methods. *Anthropozoologica, 25-26,* 85-94.

EDELMAN, S. (1999). *Representation and recognition in vision.* Cambridge, MA: The MIT Press.

EDELMAN, S., & INTRATOR, N. (2002). Visual processing of object structure. In M. A. Arbib (Ed.), *The handbook of brain theory and neural networks* (2nd ed.). Cambridge, MA: The MIT Press.

EDELMAN, S., & INTRATOR, N. (2003). Towards structural systematicity in distributed, statically bound visual representations. *Cognitive Science, 27,* 73-110.

EGMONT-PETERSEN, M., DE RIDDER, D., & HANDELS, H. (2002). Image processing with neural networks—A review. *Pattern Recognition, 35,* 2279-2301.

FUETEN, F. (1997). A computer controlled rotating polarizer stage for the petrographic microscope. *Computers and Geosciences, 23,* 203-208.

FUETEN, F., HYNES, K., & VANLUT-TIKHUISEN, R.L. (2001). An experimental setup for the analysis of analogue deformation experiments using the rotating polarizer stage. *Journal of Structural Geology, 24,* 241-245.

GU, P., & YAN, X. (1995). Neural network approach to the reconstruction of freeform surfaces for reverse engineering. *Computer Aided Design, 27*(1), 59-64.

HALIR, R., & FLUSSER, J. (1997). Estimation of profiles of sherds of archaeological pottery. *Proceedings 1997 Czech Pattern Recognition Workshop (CPRW'97),* (pp. 126-130).

HEIDEMAN, G. (2005). The long-range saliency of edge and corner-based salient points. *IEEE Transactions on Image Processing, 14*(11), 1701-1706.

HUMMEL, J.E., & BIEDERMAN, I. (1992). Dynamic binding in a neural network for shape recognition. *Psychological Review, 99*(3), 480-517.

JI, S., YUAN, Q., & ZHANG, L. (2005). Study of auto recognizing metal chips' shape based on RBF neural networks. *Journal of Information & Computational Science, 2*(1), 51-56.

KAMPEL, M., & SABLATNIG, R. (2003). An automated pottery archival and reconstruction system. *Journal of Visualization and Computer Animation, 14*(3), 111-120.

KAMPEL, M., MARA, H., & SABLATNIG, R. (2006). Automated investigation of archaeological vessels. In *Proc. of EUSIPCO 2006: 13th European Signal Processing Conference, Florence, Italy.*

KASHYAP, H.K., BANSILAL, P., & KOUSHIK, A.P. (2003). Hybrid neural network architecture for age identification of ancient kannada scripts. Proceedings of the 2003 IEEE International Symposium on Circuits and Systems (ISCAS 2003), Vol. 3, pp. 423-426.

KNOPF, G.K., & KOFMAN, J. (1999). Free-form surface reconstruction using Bernstein basis function networks. In C.H. Dagli et al. (Eds.), *Intelligent engineering systems through artificial neural networks (Vol. 9)* (pp. 797 – 802). ASME Press

KNOPF, G.K., & KOFMAN, J. (2002). Surface reconstruction using neural network mapping of range-sensor images to object space. *Journal of Electronic Imaging, 11*(2), 187-194

KNOPF, G.K., & AL-NAJI, R. (2001). Adaptive reconstruction of bone geometry from serial cross-sections. *Artificial Intelligence in Engineering, 15*, 227 - 239.

KULKARNI, A.D. (2001). *Computer vision and fuzzy neural systems*. Upper Saddle River, NJ: Prentice Hall,

LANGNER, D. (2001). Leaves recognition v 1.0. Neural network based recognition system for leafs images. Retrieved January 2007 from http://damato.light-speed.de/lrecog/

LEITAO, H., DA GAMA, D., & STOLFI, J. (2001). Digitization and reconstruction of archaeological artifacts. *In XIV Brazilian Symposium on Computer Graphics and Image Processing (SIBGRAPI'01)*. Retrieved January 2007 from http://csdl2.computer.org/comp/proceedings/sibgrapi/2001/1330/00/13300382.pdf

LEITAO, H., DA GAMA, D., & STOLFI, J. (2002). A multiscale method for the reassembly of two-dimensional fragmented objects. *IEEE Transactions on Pattern Analysis and machine Intelligence*, 24(9), 1239-1251.

LEOW, W.K., & MIIKULAINEN, R. (1997). Visual schemas in neural networks for object recognition and scene analysis. *Connection Science, 9*(2), 161-200.

LEYMARIE, F. (2003). *Three-dimensional shape representation via shock flows*, PhD thesis, Brown University. Retrieved August 2007 from http://www.lems.brown.edu/~leymarie/phd/

LOHSE, E.S., SCHOU, C., SCHLADER, R., & SAMMONS, D. (2004). Automated classification of stone projectile points in a neural network. In Magistrat der Stadt Wien-Referat Kulturelles Erbe-Städtarhchäologie Wien (Ed.), *Enter the past. The e-way into the four dimensions of culture heritage* (pp. 431-437). Oxford: ArcheoPress.

LONCARIC, S. (1998). A survey of shape analysis techniques. *Pattern Recognition, 31*, 983–1001.

MALOOF, M.A., & MICHALSKI, R. (1997). Learning symbolic descriptions Of shape for object recognition In x-ray images. *Expert Systems with Applications, 12*(1), 11-20.

MARA H., & SABLATNIG, R. (2005). 3D-vision applied in archaeology. *Forum Archaeologiae - Zeitschrift für klassische Archäologie*, 34(3).

MARA, H., & SABLATNIG, R. (2006). Orientation of fragments of rotationally symmetrical 3D-shapes for archaeological documentation. In M. Pollefeys & K. Daniilidis (Eds.), *Proc. of 3rd Intl. Symposium on 3D Data Processing, Visualization and Transmission (3DPVT), Chapel Hill, USA.*

MARR, D., & HILDRETH, E. (1980). Theory of edge detection, Proc. R. Soc. Lond. B, *207*, 187-217.

MARTIN, D.H., FOWLKES, CC., & MALIK, J. (2004). Learning to detect natural image boundaries using local brightness, color, and texture cues. *IEEE Transactions On Pattern Analysis And Machine Intelligence, 26*(5), 530-549.

MCBRIDE, J.C., & KIMIA, B.B. (2003). Archaeological fragment reassembly using curve-matching. In *Proc. of the IEEE/CVPR Workshop on Appls. of Computer Vision in Archaeology (ACVA'03)*.

MOSTAFA, M., YAMANY, S., & FARAG A. (1999). Integrating shape from shading and range data using neural networks. *IEEE Computer Society Conference on Computer Vision and Pattern Recognition* (CVPR'99) - Volume 2.

NANDY, D., & BEN-ARIE, J. (2001). Shape from recognition: A novel approach for 3-D face shape recovery. *IEEE Transactions On Image Processing*, *10*(2), 201-217.

NELSON, R.C., & SELINGER, A. (1998). A cubist approach to object recognition. In *Proc. International Conference on Computer Vision (ICCV98)*, (pp. 614-621), Bombay, India, January. Retrieved September 2007 from http://citeseer.ist.psu.edu/article/nelson98cubist.html

OSADA,R., FUNKHOUSER, T., CHAZELLE, B., & DOBKIN, D. (2002). Shape distributions. *Transactions on Graphics*, *21*(4), 807-832.

PALMER, S. (1999). *Vision science. Photons to phenomelogy*. Cambridge, MA: The MIT Press.

PAPAIOANNOU, G., & KARABASSI, E.A. (2003). On the automatic assemblage of arbitrary broken solid artefacts. *Image & Vision Computing*, *21*(5), 401–412.

PAPAIOANNIOU, G., KARABASSI, E., & THEOHARIS, T. (2001). Virtual archaeologist: Assembling the past. *IEEE Computer graphics and applications*, *21*(2), 53-59.

PAPAIOANNOU, G., KARABASSI, E.A., & THEOHARIS, T. (2002). Reconstruction of three dimensional objects through matching of their parts. *IEEE Trans. on Pattern Analysis and Machine Intelligence*, *24*(1), 114–124.

PENG, L.W., & SHAMSUDDIN, S.M. (2004). Modeling II: 3D object reconstruction and representation using neural networks. *Proceedings of the 2nd. International Conference on Computer graphics and interactive techniques in Australasia and Southeast GRAPHITE '04*. Published by the Academy of Computing Machinery Press.

PIPERAKIS,E., & KUMAZAWA, I., (2001). Affine transformations of 3D objects represented with neural networks. *3-D Digital Imaging and Modeling,Proceedings*, (pp. 213-223).

REDFERN, S. (1998a). An approach to automated morphological-topographical classification. *AARGnews*, 17.

REDFERN, S. (1998b). A framework for digital survey from aerial photographs. *The Journal of Irish Archaeology*, *9*, 135-150.

REDFERN, S. (1999). Digital wide-area survey from aerial photographs. In K. Fennema & H. Kamermans (Eds.), *Making the connection to the past. Computer applications in archaeology. Faculty of Archaeology* (pp. 103-106).. University of Leiden, Holland,.

ROLLS,E.T., & DECO, G. (2002). *Computational neuroscience of vision*. Oxford, UK: Oxford University Press.

SCHMITT, A., LE BLANC, B., CORSINI, M.M., LAFOND,C., & BRUZEK, J. (2001). Les résaux de neurones artificiels. Un outil de tratitement de donnés prometteur pour l'Anthropologie. *Bulletin et Mémoirs de la Société d'Anthropologie de Paris*, n.s., t. *13*(1-2), 143-150.

SCHNEIDERMANN, H., & KANADE, T. (2004). Object detection using the statistics of parts. *International Journal of Computer Vision*, *56*(3), 151–177.

SMALL, C.G. (1996). *The statistical theory of shape*. Berlin: Springer.

SONKA, M., HLAVAC, V., & BOYLE, R. (1994). *Image processing, analysis, and machine vision.* London: Chapman and Hall.

TANGELDER, J.W.H., & VELTKAMP, R.C. (2004). A survey of content based 3D shape retrieval methods. *Shape Modeling International,* Genova, Italy, June 2004.

THOMPSON, S., FUETEN, F., & BOCKUS, D. (2001). Mineral identification using artificial neural networks and the rotating polarizer stage. *Computers in Geosciences, 27,* 1081-1089.

TRUCCO, E. (1997). Active model acquisition and sensor planning. In V. Cantoni, S. Levialdi & V. Roberto (Eds.), *Artificial vision. Image description, recognition and communication.* San Diego: Academic Press.

UÇOLUK, G., & TOROSLU, I.H. (1999). Automatic reconstruction of broken 3D surface objects. *Computers & Graphics, 23*(4), 573-582.

ULLMAN, S. (1996). *High-level vision. Object recognition and visual cognition.* Cambridge, MA: The MIT Press.

Van Der MAATEN, L.J.P., & BOON, P.J. (2006). COIN-O-MATIC: A fast and reliable system for coin classification. In *Proceedings of the MUSCLE Coin Workshop 2006,* (pp. 7-17). Berlin, Germany.

Van Der MAATEN, L.J.P., BOON, P.J PAIJMANS, J.J., LANGE, A.G., & POSTMA, E.O. (2006). Computer vision and machine learning for archaeology. In *Proceedings of the Computer Applications in Archaeology Conference 2006,* Fargo (ND).

VEZZOSI, S., BEDINI, L., & TONAZZINI, A. (2002). An integrated system for the analysis and the recognition of characters in ancient documents. In *Document Analysis Systems V: 5th International Workshop, DAS 2002, Princeton, NY.* Berlin: Springer. Lecture Notes in Computer Science, Vol. 2423, 49-52.

WANG, J.Y., & COHEN, F.S. (1994). 3-D object recognition and shape estimation from image contours using B-splines, shape invariant matching, and neural network, *IEEE Transactions on Pattern Analysis And Machine Intelligence, 16*(I), 13-23.

WANG, N., DOWELL, F., & ZHANG, N. (2002). Determining wheat vitreousness using image processing and a neural network. *2002 ASAE International Annual Meeting/CIGR XVth. World Congress.*

WEI, G.Q., & HIRZINGER, G. (1996). Learning shape-from-shading by a multilayer network. IEEE Transactions on Neural Networks, *7*(4), 985-995.

WILLIS, A., ANDREWS, S., BAKER, J., CAO, Y., HAN, D., KANG, K. et al. (2002). Bayesian virtual pot-assembly from fragments as problems in perceptual-grouping and geometric-learning. *International Conference on Pattern Recognition (ICPR'02), Québec City, Canada.* IEEE Computer Society publ., Proc. of ICPR, vol. III, (pp. 297-302).

YOUNG, S.S., SCOTT, P.D., & NASRABADI, N.M. (1997). Object recognition using multilayer hopfield neural network, *IEEE Trans. Image Process, 6*(3), 357–372.

YU, Y. (1999). Surface reconstruction from unorganized points using self-organizing neural networks. *Proc. of IEEE Visualization'99 Late Breaking Hot Topics,* (pp.61-64) San Francisco, CA.

ZWEIG, Z. (2006). *Using data-mining techniques for analyzing pottery databases.* Master's Degree Dissertation. Department of Land of Israel Studies & Archaeology, Bar-Ilan University.

Chapter VII
Texture and Compositional Analysis in Archaeology

TEXTURE

What is the "Texture" of an Archaeological Evidence?

In this section, we will consider *archaeological textures* as the archaeological element's surface attributes having either tactile or visual variety, which characterize its appearance. The surfaces of archaeological objects, artifacts, and materials are not uniform but contain many variations; some of them are of visual or tactile nature. Such variations go beyond the peaks and valleys characterizing surface micro-topography, which is the obvious frame of reference for "textures" in usual speaking. Archaeological materials have variations in the local properties of their surfaces like albedo and color variations, uniformity, density, coarseness, roughness, regularity, linearity, directionality, frequency, phase, hardness, brightness, bumpiness, specularity, reflectivity, transparency, and so on. *Texture* is the name we give to the perception of these variations. What we are doing here is introducing a synonym for "perceptual variability" or "surface discontinuity." It is a kind of perceptual information complementing shape information.

Texture has always been used to describe archaeological materials. Maybe the most obvious texture example in archaeology is the surface irregularities due to the characteristics of the raw material. We can distinguish between different archaeological materials, because of the appearance of the raw material they are made of. For example, based on textural properties, we can identify a variety of materials such as carved lithic tools, stripped bones, polished wood, dry hide, painted pottery, and so on.

Furthermore, texture patterns are not only intrinsic to the solid itself. Beyond those physical, geological, or biological characteristics of the raw material, some visual features of an artifact's surfaces are consequences of the modifications having experimented that object along its history. After all, the surface of solids plays a significant role in any kind of dynamic processes. This study is usually called *tribology*: the science and technology of interacting surfaces in relative motion and the practices related thereto. Solids are rigid bodies and resist stress. When a force is applied, a solid deforms; the deformation determines its perceptual appearance largely. As a result, solid surfaces appear usually heterogeneous. The solid surfaces are generally not equipotential, because surface energy varies from point to point, given the number of asperities and irregularities (Lüth, 1993; Rao, 1972). That means that when a surface interact with another surface, texture is more intense, higher points have more intense effects (higher energy) than lower areas. When a surface is plane and uniform, there is a low quantity of texture, because all surface points have the same interfacial contribution, that is, all points have the same potential to induce changes on a contacting surface (energy).

When we analyze macro or microscopically an object's surface, we should *recognize* some differential features (striations, polished areas, scars, particles, undifferentiated background) which are the consequence of an action (human or bio-geological) having modified the original appearance of that surface (Figure 7.1). Consequently, the main assumption is that artifacts have surface properties because of the way they have been made, or the way they have been used. That is, we should distinguish two kinds of perceptual appearances, one of them is inherent to the artifact raw material, and the other one is the result of modifications on the surface generated by work activities.

For instance, making and/or using an instrument make important alterations in its surface features, so we can use a description of such changes to understand how the object was made and/or used. Texture variations due to human work are observable, and may vary according to different causal factors, among them:

- Movement: longitudinal (cutting), transversal (scrapping)
- Surface of friction: the effects of worked material (wood, bone, shell, fur, etc.)

In the same way, decoration should be understood in its physical nature, and not only stylistically. Engraved, carved or painted, decorative patterns are man-made modifications on the surface of some objects, and they can be considered as an example of induced texture (Maaten et al., 2006)

Preservation also alters surface features. It implies a third factor for texture origin: original visual appearances of raw material and man made surface modifications should not only be taken into account, but also taphonomic and post depositional modifications.

Therefore, it is easy to see that the problem of texture variation is a complex one. Texture analysis mainly aims to represent computationally an intui-

Figure 7.1. Altered surface properties as an example of archaeological texture in a lithic tool (Photograph by the author's research team)

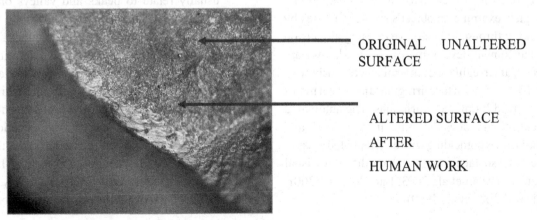

ORIGINAL UNALTERED SURFACE

ALTERED SURFACE

AFTER

HUMAN WORK

Figure 7.2. Texture differences between lithic tools used in different ways. A: Original andesite texture before using; B: Result of the alteration in surface A when the tool was used scrapping fur. C: A different raw material (obsidian) with texture features produced through wood scrapping (Photographs by the author's research team).

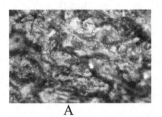  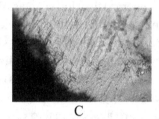

A   B   C

tive perception of visual irregularities and variations and to facilitate their automatic processing. The process of texture analysis needs some kind of numeric descriptions of texture, called texture features. They are perceived as a combined effect of light, shadow, topography, and edge.

Describing Texture

A robot with appropriated sensors can describe perceived textures in terms of the particular dispersion of luminance values in a surface, because light reflects according to surface attributes. That means that texture should be analyzed as a consequence of anisotropic reflection. The underlying assumption is that light waves undergo reflection when they encounter a solid interface (surface), and this reflection is irregular depending on the heterogeneity of the surface. When human archaeologists examine an object's surface features by looking through (naked) eye or using any vision enhancement device (microscope), what we are seeing are irregularities in luminance distribution, and we infer surface irregularities in terms of perceived luminance variations. The automated archaeologist does the same. It "sees" dark and bright areas coinciding with differentiated areas in the same surface; areas that have different visual features (Adán et al., 2003; Barceló et al., 2001; Pijoan-López et al., 1999).

Therefore, texture can be measured according to wavelength variability. In this case, we may distinguish two kinds of variations:

- *Roughness* includes wavelength irregularities of a surface. It defines how that surface feels, how it looks, how it behaves in a contact with another surface. For instance, in the case of human instruments use-wear, and according to the *size* of those wavelength irregularities, we can speak about the more widely spaced (longer wavelength) deviations (*waviness)*, or the finest (shortest) wavelength deviations (*roughness)*. The main parameter is here *spacing*, which refers to the distance between individuated areas with different perceptual features. The features that determine a spacing parameter usually relate to peaks and valleys or to average wavelengths, and so forth.

- *Lay* refers to the predominant direction of the surface texture. Ordinarily lay is determined by the particular production method and geometry used. Turning, milling, drilling, grinding, and other cutting processes usually produce a surface that has lay: striations or peaks and valleys in the direction that the tool was drawn across the surface. It is important to distinguish between the lay (or the lack thereof) of the raw material (stone, wood, bone, etc.), and the directionality of the wavelength irregularities which define roughness. This second source of direction-ality is related to the work movement made with the artifact. For instance, a smooth fin-ish will look rough if it has a strong lay. A rougher surface will look uniform if it has no lay (it will have more of a matte look).

Generally, there are two major approaches to translate image features into a numeric de-scription of texture variation: the *macro-texture* approach and the *micro-texture* approach. The macro-texture approach makes more emphasis on the space-organization of the visual constituents of an archaeological solid's surface. Such "con-stituents" are in fact texture primitives: regions in the image with uniform gray levels. Textures can be understood then as complex visual pat-terns composed of entities, or sub-patterns, that have characteristic brightness, color, slope, size, and so forth. Thus, texture can be regarded as a similarity grouping in an image. The idea then seems to be that of decomposing the luminance of the analyzed surface into regions that differ in the statistical variability of their constitutive visual features. Archaeological use-wear on the surface of lithic tools, for example, fast always shows an irregular pattern of different areas, each one with different shape edges and differ-ent luminance values. The textural character of the surface usually depends on the spatial size of such *texture primitives*, in such a way that coarse texture can be decomposed in large areas, while small areas give fine texture surfaces. Leung and Malik (2001) have developed further this decomposition approach by building a small, finite vocabulary of microstructures, which they call *3D textons*. Once such a universal vocabulary of 3D primitive components of texture are defined, the surface of any material such as marble, concrete, leather, or rug can be represented as a spatial ar-rangement (perhaps stochastic) of symbols from this vocabulary.

Macro-texture analysis demands combining pattern segmentation for the discrimination of different textures, and texture description, for the processing of the basic micro-patterns and the exact location of the texture constituents boundaries. Whenever a machine vision system is expected to perform this texture discrimination task, it has to solve the problem of segmenting the input image into statistically differentiated regions, locating the borders between different areas with homogenous visual features. In the case of use-wear textures on lithic tools, our goal is to segment those texture elements, in order to be able to study their variability in shape and spatial location. The input for such a task is a digitized microscopic image of the tool's active surface (Figure 7.3).

In the resulting matrix of grey values, a group of related pixels can be considered as a texture minimal unit, sometimes called *texel*—texture element—if a set of local statistics or other local properties of the average density function are con-stant, slowly varying, or approximately periodic. Surface alteration features are then represented as distinct areas with particular luminance in-tensity. By using image analysis, specific areas corresponding to concrete thresholds, within the usual grayscale of 256 values, can be separated from their neighboring zones. In this way, texture is characterized not only by the gray value at a given pixel, but also by the gray value pattern in a neighborhood surrounding the pixel (Jain & Karu, 1996). Thanks to this, it is possible to extract quantitative texture information from the digital image that remits us to certain characteristics of the surface alteration.

Once the texture elements are identified in the image, there are two major approaches for analyzing the texture. One computes statistical properties from the extracted texture elements and utilizes these as texture features. The other tries to extract the placement rule that describes the texture. The latter approach may involve geometric or syntactic methods of analyzing

Figure 7.3. Visual input for texture analysis. Micro-photograph of a stone tool (Photographs by the author's research team).

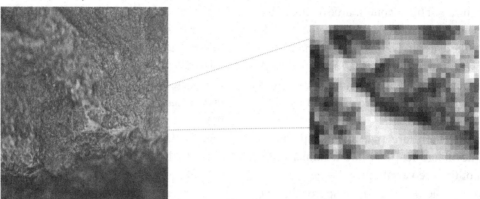

texture. Those methods can be synthesized in the following list:

- **Area measurements:** Total number of pixels with the same luminance or range of luminance. The edge is defined by the proximity of a grey level. Normally a simple operation of threshold is enough to define the area or areas of a discrete *texel*. In use-wear analysis, we can take area measurements to extract the extension of a micro-polish, the micro-scars size, and the linear features length. In the analysis of pottery thin-section, it is used for measuring the size of each mineral particle in the fabric.

- **Texels perimeter:** We can take the information about the size of a mineral particle or a linear feature length. This variable is used for calculating different ratios of the variables related to the perimeter shape. The *Euler-Poincaré* characteristic measures the ratio between the micro-topography and the micro-polish extension. This variable is not necessary in the thin-section analysis. The *frequency and entropy of brightness* within a texel is calculated using an histogram of grey levels The *frequency and entropy of contrast*: local change in brightness (ratio between average

brightness within the texel and the neighboring texels. It is used as an intermediate calculus to describe coarseness.

- **Perimeter shape and orientation:** To introduce the category of shape we can use the natural geometric shapes as indicators, to define the pattern of the geometric model of the sample, using the same relational geometric indexes used in shape analysis: circularity, quadrature, irregularity, and so forth. All those shape measurements measure the tendencies of the geometric pattern for describing the orientation and shapes of the micro-polish and the linear features, both in the use-wear analysis and mineral particles in thin-section analysis.

- **Orientation:** The orientation given by the angle of the detected linear features with the tool's edge is used in use-wear analysis to define the direction of the movement done with the tool.

- **Topology of texture:** Those measures are measured from relationships and associations between texels, and not at each texel.

- **Randomness:** Entropy of the number of textels within a modified surface. It can be used in use-wear for discriminating the area of the micro-polish from background.

- **Linearity:** Linear features can be represented using linear equations: $y = a + bx$, where y and x are co-ordinates, and a and b linear coefficients. We use both coefficients as quantitative variables in our study. We can also include some other numerical attributes such as the quantity of lines, and their longitude. The width of linear features can be measured on the three-dimensional representation, and included in the image quantification.
- **Directivity:** Entropy of the edge-direction histogram. Directional textures have an even number of significant peaks, direction-less textures have a uniform edge-direction histogram. This can be used in the description of linear features orientation.
- **Size:** Number of pixels corresponding to each contour in the image. It allows the study of micro-polish topography.

The advantage of this macro-textural approach is that it provides an understandable description of visual features variation in a surface; however, it faces at least two complex problems, one of which is the need to identify the textural primitives while the other is the description of the spatial relationships between these primitives. Additionally, when extracting primitive texture elements, it should be taken into account that detected relevant areas depend on the specific luminance intervals used or thresholds. It is easy to see that the elements of texture vary according to the concrete interval we analyze in the same image. The criterion for selecting a concrete luminance interval lies in our previous knowledge about the characteristics of surface alteration.

The micro-texture approach measures textures without identifying textural primitives. It is based on the pioneering work of Haralick (1979), which subsumes luminance reflection in the spatial variation of pixel intensities (gray values) across an image (macro- or microscopic) of some area of the studied surface. This is the basis for the so called *statistical approach* to texture analysis: texture properties are represented as a bi-dimensional mapping of points (p_i, q_i) with a specific luminance value (r_i). The resulting function is then $p_x q_x r$. Texture is then described as the relationships of luminance values in one pixel with luminance values in neighboring pixels. This approach has been useful in a variety of applications and it is subject of intense study by many researchers (Jain & Karu, 1996; Julesz, 1981; Malik & Perona, 1990; Materka & Strzelecki, 1998; Martin et al., 2004; Ruiz del Solar, 1998; Song, 2003; Turceryan & Jain, 1998).

There are two ways of studying the spatial variation of luminance effects across the surface (Adán et al., 2003):

- *First-order statistics* measure the likelihood of observing a gray value at a randomly chosen location in the image. First-order statistics can be computed from the histogram of pixel intensities in the image. These depend only on individual pixel values and not on the interaction or co-occurrence of neighboring pixel values. The average intensity in an image is an example of the first-order statistic. Consequently, texture features are computed based on tonal features such as mean, variance, skewness, and kurtosis of grey levels along with texture features computed from grey level co-occurrence matrices.
- *Second-order statistics* are defined as the likelihood of observing a pair of gray values occurring at the endpoints of a dipole (or needle) of random length placed on the image at a random location and orientation. These are properties of pairs of pixel values. Julesz (1981) conjectured that two textures are not distinguishable if their second order statistics are identical. Therefore, second-order statistics are usually much more important than first-order variation.

There are other ways to describe texture features using numbers. We can mention *model based* texture analysis, using fractal and stochastic models, and attempting to interpret an image texture by use of, respectively, a generative image model and a stochastic model. The parameters of the model should be previously estimated and then used for image analysis. In practice, the computational complexity arising in the estimation of stochastic model parameters is the primary problem, although the fractal model has been shown to be useful for modeling some natural textures. *Transform methods* of texture analysis, such as Fourier, Gabor, and wavelet transforms, represent an image in a space whose co-ordinate system has an interpretation that is closely related to the characteristics of a texture (such as frequency or size). Spectral techniques are based on properties of the Fourier spectrum and describe global periodicity of the grey levels of a surface by identifying high energy peaks in the spectrum.

Any approach to image-based texture analysis should take into account the fact that texture measured in an image of the object is not the same as the object's texture. Luminance variations and distinguishing differentiated texture elements are an effect of the perceptual acquisition mechanism (the microscope, the eye, the sensor), and consequently images not only show features of the object being analyzed but they mix this variation with variability coming from the context of observation and the mechanical characteristics of the observation instrument. There are always shadows and reflections, which are not the result of original irregularities at the surface, but generated by the light source, the instrument, or other objects in the scene. That means that an image texture not only contains the object surface irregularity data, but additional information which in the best cases is just random noise, and in many other cases makes difficult to distinguish what belongs to the object from what belongs to the observation process.

Modeling the physical process having modified the surface of an ancient tool is then very difficult. The automated archaeologist should rely on the assumption that texture can be characterized in terms of the bi-dimensional variations in the luminance intensities present in an *image* of the object whose texture we (or the robot) want to analyze. To recognize an artifact based on the original texture of its raw material, or use-induced modifications on its surfaces, the robot should be capable to delete all image features that are not related to surface variations. This is called a *texture classification problem*. The goal of texture classification involves deciding what texture category an observed image of an archaeological material belongs. In order to accomplish this, the automated archaeologist needs to have an *a priori* knowledge of the classes to be recognized. Once this knowledge is available and the texture features are extracted, one then uses classical pattern classification techniques in order to do the classification.

The conventional method of texture classification involves two main steps. The first step is obtaining prior knowledge of each class to be recognized. Normally this knowledge encompasses some sets of texture features of one or all of the classes. Once the knowledge is available and texture features of the observed image are extracted, then classification techniques can be used to make the decision. That is the second step. There are many examples of using neural networks as a classification tool for this task. Those examples range from meat quality determination based on lamb chop images, to use-wear detection in machine parts or ceramic tiles (Acebrón-Linuesa et al., 2002; Chandraratne et al., 2003; Jain & Karu, 1996; Kulkarni, 2001; Ruiz del Solar, 1998). More related to archaeological analysis is the essay of distinguishing decorative patterns in textiles (Bhakar et al., 2004; Mayorga & Ludeman, 1991, 1994; Valiente-González, 2001).

Van der Maaten et al. (2006; Van der Maaten & Boon, 2006) approached texture analysis in a numismatic investigation. Coins often contain very detailed pictures, which can be considered as the texture of the coin. The authors encode texture information using a procedure based on the Gabor wavelet. The training set contains 692 different coin types with 2,270 different coin faces. The system classifies approximately 78 percent of the coins in the test set correctly. Usually, misclassifications are due to very dirty coins or due to unknown coins.

Texture has also been used to identify vegetal remains from pollen data. Li and Flenley (1999) built a neural network for detection of light microscope images of pollen grains. The input data employed were Haralick texture measures, (i.e., angular second moment, contrast, entropy, inverse difference moment, and variance; masks with a 3×3 and 5×5 windows); and matrix measures. The authors compared neural network classification with some previously published statistical classifiers. Although both types of classifiers may work, the neural network results were apparently superior to the statistical methods in three ways: high success rates (100 percent in this case), small number of samples needed for training, and simplicity of features.

In material sciences, texture analysis of thin sections is used to identify the composition of some items. Marmo et al. (2005) have used more than 1,000 thin-section photos of ancient (Phanerozoic) carbonates from different marine environments (pelagic to shallow-water) to automatically identify carbonate textures unaffected by post depositional modifications (recrystallization, dolomitization, meteoric dissolution, and so on). The methodology uses, as input, 256 grey-tone digital image and by image processing gives, as output, a set of 23 values of numerical features measured on the whole image including the "white areas" (calcite cement). A feed-forward neural network takes as input these features and gives, as output, the estimated class. Principal component analysis (PCA) was used to reduce the dimensionality of feature spaces. The reduced

feature space, with geometric variables and texture features, was used to feed the input layer, rather that visual data directly. The authors used 532 images of thin sections to train the neural network, whereas to test the methodology 268 images taken from the same photo collection were used and 215 images from San Lorenzello carbonate sequence (Matese Mountains, southern Italy), Early Cretaceous in age. The neural network has shown 93.3 percent and 93.5 percent of accuracy to classify automatically textures of carbonate rocks using digitized images on the 268 and 215 test sets, respectively.

Drolon et al. (2003) have analyzed geological textures using also neural network technology. The shape of sedimentary particles has been recognized for a long time as being an important parameter in helping to improve the understanding of the geologic processes. The shape of quartz grains reflects the genesis of a given source and is distinct from the shape of quartz grains from other sources. Thus, it gives sedimentology information about the physical agent having fashioned the grain, about its transport and deposit conditions. The basic idea consists of characterizing the contour by one or several parameters, linking these parameters to a studied physical property: elongation, angularity, roughness, or roundness, and more generally the degree of wear of the particle. The notion of texture depends partly on the scale of observation. For this reason, most authors have attempted to isolate its different constituents which are the global aspect (texel sphericity, elongation) and details (angularity, roughness, or roundness) by characterizing them by independent coefficients. This decomposition in different levels of the information on the shape suggests that the notion of scale of observation is essential to characterize a particle. By using the harmonic wavelet transform, the authors developed a new shape descriptor, *the multiscale roughness descriptor*, which proves to be perfectly adapted to the description of particles. This descriptor acts as a mathematical microscope and allows the analyses of the contour of a grain and its roughness at different scales of resolution. Coefficients provided by this descriptor are invariant under translation, rotation, change of scale of the contour, and can therefore be used to compare sands stemming from a wide range of sedimentary environments. The basic idea is to use a feed-forward neural network to model wear and erosion phenomena acting on quartz grains. The network, which uses sigmoid functions, consists of 18 input units, six hidden units, and three output units, corresponding to the three classes (eolian, marine, and non worn). The database has been randomly divided into two sets: one for training the network (89 samples) and the other for testing the classifier (91 samples). After learning, the network classifies correctly 100 percent of samples. The network recognizes relatively well eolian and non-worn grains, with a classification rate superior to 93 percent. On the other hand, it has more difficulty to recognize grains of marine type (average rate of 87.5 percent of classification), and has a tendency to classify them as eolian (9.38 percent of grains). Nevertheless, the global correct classification rate (92.22 percent) indicates that the statistical model built by the network is perfectly valid. By using a neural network, it seems therefore possible to model wear phenomena acting on particles and thus to reconstitute the history of sands in sedimentary basins.

Related applications have been published by Kalliomäki et al. (2005) and Martínez-Aljarín et al. (2005).

The Analysis of Use-Wear in Prehistoric Lithic Tools

Archaeologists studying lithic remains usually wish to determine whether or not these stones have been used as tools and how they were used. The best way to do this is through the analysis of macro and microscopic traces of wear generated by the use of the tool. An identification-based

neural network solution to this problem (Van den Dries, 1998) was presented in Chapter V. Although. Van den Dries' results are impressive, we may question the use of qualitative presence/absence variables to describe texture. The network associated a subjective description of texture (TEXTURE A: smooth & matt, TEXTURE B: rough & greasy, BRIGHTNESS A: very bright), with an objective description of explanatory categories (experimental replication). Such *recognition* is then as subjective as its initial description, because it follows personal criteria, only relevant to the actual observer. The problem is that it is difficult to know if a texture pattern is "greasy" or "very brilliant." It is based on the assumption that there is a fixed set or vocabulary of "supposed" basic texture elements, distinctive enough, and easily identifiable.

If we want to go beyond this kind of identification-based analysis, we should find a way to introduce in the network luminance intensity data directly and not through a subjective identification. The PEDRA system is an example of how using macro and micro-texture analysis for the texture classification of lithic tools according to use-wear (*pedra* means "stone" in Catalan language, Adán et al., 2003; Barceló & Pijoan-López, 2003; Pijoan-López et al., 2002; Pijoan-López, 2007; Toselli et al., 2002). Instead of "types of use-wear," a computational system was designed based on image segmentation techniques associating pixels with the same grey level and defining areas with comparable luminance variance. The underlying idea was that extracted *texels* or texture elements corresponded to bumps or "large *plateaux*" seen on the lithic surface. Different gray-level thresholds were explored to obtain different image segmentations, but we selected finally 120 grey levels as the threshold to separate a texel from the tool's background.

In previous experiments with lithic tools (Pijoan-López et al., 2002; Toselli et al., 2002), we had observed that *texels* have different shapes when generated by different processes. *Texels* are different depending on the movement made with the tool (longitudinal or transversal), and according to the surface of friction (wood, shell and fur). For instance, surfaces of tools used for processing "hide" have more *texels*, but smaller than tools used for processing "wood." The tendency to differentiate textures generated by friction over hard and soft worked materials has been confirmed through experimental tests. For instance, we have found that shell and wood processing generate similar texture, very different to that generated when processing dry hide. Specifically, the *texels* on hide-generated textures are glossier than the *texels* associated with wood processing. Generally, alterations by use related to fur processing are the darkest in the series. Results for shell processing are between both (Figure 7.4).

To measure the differences between textures features associated to the kinematics (movement) of the working action, we should take into account other attributes: the angle of the major axis to the edge of the tool, and the shape of the *texel*, specifically its *elongation*, which is a "deformation" feature associated with kinematics (Barceló et al., 2001; Toselli, 2004). Texture is a phenomenon generated by a dynamic process. Consequently, the direction of the energy flux produced by movement determines the shape of texture elements. If the movement is longitudinal ("cutting"), then the energy generated by this movement will tend

to create elongated *texels*, and their orientation according to the original movement is clearer. Transversal movement ("scrapping") is much more irregular, and consequently energy flux is less focused at a single direction (Figure 7.5). The consequence is a higher dispersion and variability of *texel* shapes: elongated, and circular *texels* appear together.

In our experiments, not all *texels* were good indicators of the working movement, because not all of them were oriented to the direction of movement (transversal or longitudinal). Given that the *texel's* major axis can be in some cases parallel to the tool's edge or parallel to the *x* axis of the canvas, we observed that the longest *texels* were also the best oriented according to the working movement (along the edge of the tool when cutting, across the edge of the tool when scrapping). That means that surfaces of tools have parallel *texels* to the *x* axis when they were submitted to a longitudinal working movement and to the *y* axis when they experimented transversal working movement. In the same way, the more elongated the *texel's* shape, the more parallel to the major axis (Toselli et al., 2002).

We have designed a neural network for the texture classification of lithic tools according to their use (movement and worked material) (Figure 7.6). We wanted to verify whether the shape, composition, and size features are related to work

Figure 7.4. Determining use-wea texels using luminance thresholds. In this example, 120 grey levels have been selected as threshold.

ORIGINAL IMAGE   *THRESHOLDED IMAGE*   *TEXEL DEFINITION*

239

kinematics and the nature of worked material. It is the same goal explored by Van der Dries, but substituting the qualitative subjective texture input with objective quantitative measures of shape and luminance composition of *texels.*

Statistical analysis (Pijoan-López, 2007) has proved that there is no clear-cut rule that relates the shape and geometry of the *texture elements* and the work activity performed by the tool. It is important to remember that what we are describing as *texture* is just a light effect, that is to say, an indirect evidence of some irregularities on the active surface of the tool. The shape parameters of such texture constituents correspond to the edge or interfacial boundary defined by light reflection, and consequently they do not fit necessarily with the real texture. Neural network should allow us to discover whether there is enough evidence to establish some degree of nonlinear relationships between light reflection variability and micro-topographic features on the active surface of the lithic tool. Observed image texture depends on factors such as scene geometry and illumination conditions. Certain properties of flint surfaces have effects on the appearance of use-wear. Because grey values depend on shadows, and shadows depend on the position of light sources, if we do not care, the same object surface may have very different *texels* associated. In our experiments, we have controlled light sources, and the influence of the image acquisition device to be able to understand observed patterns, but additional control is necessary to select the luminance intervals selected for *texel* extraction.

We have replicated in laboratory more than 100 lithic tools using the same kind of flint. Three microphotographs were taken for each tool from different areas of the working surface. *Texels* were individually measured for their area, perimeter, axis length, and so forth.

A feed-forward neural network has been built. Input neurons read central tendency measures (mean and standard deviation) of all *texels* segmented at each microphotograph, obtaining a dataset of 496 microphotographs, described in terms of:

- Mean of Elongation/ Std. dev. of Elongation
- Mean of Circularity/ Std. dev. of Circularity
- Mean of Quadrature-Thinness/ Std. dev. of Quadrature-Thinness
- Mean of Ratio Compactness-Thinness/ Std. dev. of Ratio Comp.-Thin.

Figure 7.5. Longitudinal and transversally generated original surfaces (Photographs by the author's research team)

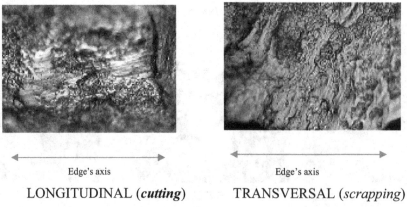

LONGITUDINAL (*cutting*) TRANSVERSAL (*scrapping*)

- Mean of Compactness/ Std. dev. of Compactness,
- Mean of Irregularity/ Std. dev. of Irregularity
- Mean of Rectangularity/ Std. dev. of Rectangularity,
- Mean of Ratio Perimeter/Elongation/Std. dev. of Rt. Per./Elong.
- Mean of Feret diameter/ Std. dev. of Feret diameter
- Mean of Minimum rectangularity/ Std. dev. of Minimum rectangularity

Central tendency values of composition among all *texels* identified at a single microphotograph:

- Mean of luminance means within a *texel*/ Std. dev. of lum. means
- Mean of luminance std.dev. within a *texel*/ Std. dev. of lum. st. dev.

- Mean of luminance modes within a *texel*/ Std. dev. of lum. modes
- Mean of luminance min.values within a *texel*/ Std. dev. of lum. min.va.

Central tendency values of size among all *texels* identified at a single micro-photograph size:

- Mean of Area of all *texels* within the image / Std. dev. of Area

In a preliminary investigation, we analyzed the relationship between texture variation at a single microphotograph and the experimented activity (cutting or scrapping bone, shell, meat, dry or fresh hide, dry or fresh wood). Therefore, the network has seven output units and a hidden layer with 144 neurons. Learning algorithm was backpropagation. Results are interesting. When comparing training data with network

Figure 7.6. A neural network to recognize visual textures as use-wear patterns in lithic tools

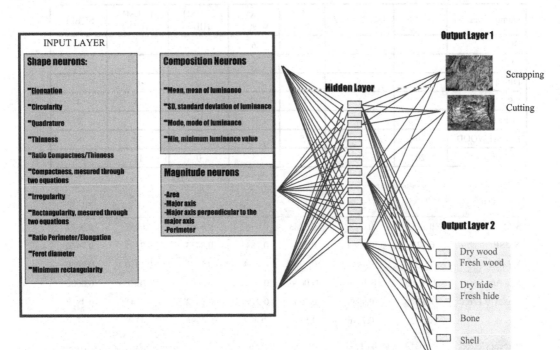

interpretation (see Table 7.1.), it is easy to see that the neural network correctly classifies most replicated tools according to the worked material. Only "bone" and "fresh wood" get a percentage of right classifications less than 50 percent. However, even these errors are understandable. Bone can be misclassified with shell, shell with bone, fresh wood with dry wood, butchery with fresh hide, but only similar worked materials can be confounded. Misclassification is just a result of hardness overly.

When comparing test data (15 percent of experimental replications not used in the training set) with network interpretation we obtain the results presented in Table 7.2.

Obviously, testing results are worst than training data results. The reason of the bad results for fresh hide is the size of the analyzed sample. In any case, errors are again within similar hardness categories. This fact can be used to explain what the neural network is really doing. It seems that it is able to "generalize" texture parameters characteristic of each work activity, but not precisely each worked material. The network could not find formally defined grammars for texture components placement rules, but it has had some success in creating an associative memory for similar hardness categories.

Results of texture analysis are even better, when analyzing the kinematics of the working activity. The experimental database contained replications of three different actions: cutting (longitudinal kinematics), scrapping (transversal kinematics), and butchery (a kind of kinematics that pretends to be longitudinal but given the soft nature of the worked material —meat—is at the end half longitudinal/half transversal). Using the same texture attributes in the input layer, three output units, and a hidden layer with 13 neurons, we obtain the results shown in Table 7.3.

Table 7.1.

Output / Desired	BONE	BUTCHERY	DRY HIDE	DRY WOOD	FRESH HIDE	FRESH WOOD	SHELL
BONE	55	0	0	6	1	3	10
BUTCHERY	8	43	4	2	5	1	0
DRY HIDE	13	4	46	6	0	6	3
DRY WOOD	13	1	12	43	1	13	4
FRESH HIDE	3	17	7	3	18	0	0
FRESH WOOD	10	1	5	6	0	28	8
SHELL	20	1	6	5	0	11	44

Performance	BONE	BUTCHERY	DRY HIDE	DRY WOOD	FRESH HIDE	FRESH WOOD	SHELL
MSE	0,1433	0,0626	0,0983	0,0962	0,0405	0,0852	0,0892
NMSE	0,7731	0,5364	0,7271	0,7844	0,8473	0,7795	0,7449
MAE	0,237	0,1455	0,1966	0,20543	0,1137	0,1910	0,1950
Min Abs Error	1,1E-05	8,2E-05	0,0006	0,0006	0,0002	2,7E-05	0,0002
Max Abs Error	1,0388	0,9980	0,9961	0,9779	0,9352	1,0341	0,9818
r	0,512	0,7116	0,5397	0,477	0,4998	0,4709	0,5119
Percent Correct	45,0819	64,1791	57,5	60,5633	72	45,1612	63,7681

Table 7.2.

Output / Desired	BONE	BUTCHERY	DRY HIDE	DRY WOOD	FRESH HIDE	FRESH WOOD	SHELL
BONE	10	0	0	3	0	0	2
BUTCHERY	2	5	1	0	2	0	0
DRY HIDE	4	1	5	1	0	5	1
DRY WOOD	2	0	2	8	0	4	3
FRESH HIDE	1	6	1	0	0	0	0
FRESH WOOD	3	1	0	3	0	4	2
SHELL	6	0	1	1	0	3	13

Performance	BONE	BUTCHERY	DRY HIDE	DRY WOOD	FRESH HIDE	FRESH WOOD	SHELL
MSE	0,189	0,0605	0,0819	0,1074	0,04058	0,1057	0,1151
NMSE	0,974	0,5631	0,9590	0,8387	2,192	0,8254	0,725
MAE	0,288	0,133	0,1761	0,2202	0,1109	0,2225	0,2392
Min Abs Error	0,005	2,4E-05	0,0006	0,00289	0,0005	0,0003	0,0003
Max Abs Error	1,015	0,9161	0,9882	0,9690	0,67488	0,8836	0,86803
r	0,318	0,7056	0,3194	0,422	0,28249	0,4213	0,5303
Percent Correct	35,71	38,4615	50	50	0	25	61,904

Butchery activity was correctly identified in all tested cases, and longitudinal and transversal kinematics was distinguished in a majority of cases! Nevertheless, these good results can be the consequence of a bad selection of the output categories. Longitudinal and Transversal kinematics have been replicated over different materials (shell, bone, dry wood, fresh wood, dry hide, fresh hide), but the third kind of kinematics was exclusive of a worked material (meat). It would be possible that the neural network had learnt to distinguish butchery from the other categories, but not the proper activity. To solve this problem we built a new network to distinguish only longitudinal from the transversal action, and deleted from the database all the butchery experiments. The network had the usual 35 central tendency inputs, 13 units in the hidden layer, and only two outputs. The activation function of those output neurons was adjusted so that it can be read as a probability measure (the joint activation of both units sum 1). The results for the experimental training set are shown in Table 7.4.

Using 20 percent of replicated tools not used for training as a test database, we obtain also excellent results, showing the ability of the network to learn to discriminate between the working activities, and hence, to discover the social cause behind the visual appearances of texture, excellent results (Table 7.5).

COMPOSITION

What is the "Composition" of Archaeological Evidence?

Compositional data are a special case of categorical data. It implies that some attribute be sorted out

Table 7.3.

Output / Desired	KYNEMAT(L)	KYNEMAT(T)	KYNEMAT(L(T))
KYNEMAT(L)	196	43	0
KYNEMAT(T)	39	125	0
KYNEMAT(L(T))	20	13	60

Performance	KYNEMAT(L)	KYNEMAT(T)	KYNEMAT(L(T))
MSE	0,159825824	0,147879337	0,042461323
NMSE	0,639813032	0,63808968	0,399318228
MAE	0,329403594	0,323901311	0,115223238
Min Abs Error	0,00045138	0,004611709	0,000183032
Max Abs Error	0,989362897	0,963606931	0,969773317
r	0,615687356	0,612099014	0,802275184
Percent Correct	76,8627451	69,06077348	100

Table 7.4.

Output / Desired	*KYNEMAT(T)*	*KYNEMAT(L)*
KYNEMAT(T)	143	86
KYNEMAT(L)	26	177

Performance	*KYNEMAT(T)*	*KYNEMAT(L)*
MSE	0,173922583	0,174325181
NMSE	0,730265892	0,731956322
MAE	0,360646928	0,361481759
Min Abs Error	0,000365206	0,000365206
Max Abs Error	0,962687106	0,962687106
r	0,61404546	0,61404546
Percent Correct	84,61538462	67,30038023

into discrete, distinct categories whose members somehow come to resemble one another more than they resemble members of other categories (Harnad, 1987). It is the kind of approach used when speaking about *decomposition*, a procedure describing an object in terms of a collection of primitive objects combined through a gluing operation (see also Chapter VI). When listing and describing the texture elements detected on the surface of a tool, when we enumerate the objects we have found inside a grave or inside a hut, or when we discuss the parts of a sword or the different spatial areas individualized at a settlement, we are speaking about the *composition* of such grave, hut, sword, or settlement.

However, not any categorization is the result of a true decomposition. Data should fulfill two conditions:

• The components should be "generic" in the sense that all objects can be described as different combinations of the same components.

Table 7.5.

Output / Desired	*KYNEMAT(T)*	*KYNEMAT(L)*
KYNEMAT(T)	40	29
KYNEMAT(L)	12	43

Performance	*KYNEMAT(T)*	*KYNEMAT(L)*
MSE	0,21612187	0,217864788
NMSE	0,887577423	0,894735306
MAE	0,402846942	0,406095708
Min Abs Error	0,0230306	0,0230306
Max Abs Error	0,981177104	0,981177104
r	0,4237645	0,4237645
Percent Correct	76,92307692	59,72222222

For instance, the components of a grave-good set can be decomposed in pottery, metal, organic material; the components of a room can be decomposed into walls, floor, ceiling and empty space, a village can be decomposed into houses, streets, non-urbanized areas, and so forth. It is necessary that the component be explicitly defined before the decomposition approach.

• To be true com*positional* data, it is necessary that a component be expressed as a proportion of the total sum of components, which defines the composition of the entity. Compositions should be expressed as vectors of data, which sum up to a constant, usually proportions or percentages. To say that there is a wall in the room, or that 6 vases compose the grave-good of a burial, is not a true decomposition of the room or the burial. Instead, we have to say that 13 percent of the room consists in wall or wall-like structures, and the remaining 87 percent is composed of free space. Similarly a true decomposition will specify that 60 percent of the grave-good is composed of pottery, a 15 percent of it is made of meat offerings, a 5 percent consists in metal objects, and 20 percent is composed of textiles. In both

cases, the components sum a constant (100), and composition is measured against this total. Each of the n components p_i of each data point $(p_1, ..., p_n)$ says what proportion (or "percentage") of a statistical unit falls into the ith category in a list of n categories (Aitchison, 1986, 1994, 1997; Aitchison & Barceló-Vidal, 2002; Billheimer et al., 1998).

Compositional Analysis of Archaeometric Data

Archaeometric data typically follow this schema so strictly that in most cases compositional data seem restricted to the listing of proportions of different chemical or mineralogical components within an archaeological sample. Here, a vector of chemical or mineralogical concentrations encodes each sample. Unsupervised and supervised neural networks can be implemented to process those vector data. In the case of unsupervised models, the archaeologist looks for a blind classification of samples based on similar compositions. The assumption seems to be that the same people, at the same place, produced archaeological artifacts with a similar composition in the same way. On the other hand, supervised approaches are based on prior knowledge about the production method, use, or provenance of the sample, associating each chemical or mineralogical input with some hypothesis. The goal is to find a nonlinear classification rule to be used to recognize and explain new archaeological evidence based on experimental analysis.

As an example of unsupervised neural networks for compositional analysis, we can quote the classification of ancient Roman glazed ceramics (López Molinero et al., 2000). Inductively coupled plasma-atomic emission spectroscopy analyzed clay ceramic bodies and the chemical composition obtained was processed by using a self-organized map. The results obtained provide two types information: firstly, differentiation between the elemental chemical information, and secondary, a classification of ceramic samples according to distinct provenance. Certain chemical elements allowed differentiating between provenance areas, whereas other elements give redundant information and do not contributed to sample differentiation. The studied ceramics were 68 ancient Roman glazed objects belonging to collections of the Museum of Zaragoza (Spain). A subset of eight chemical elements was retained for analysis: *Al, Ca, Fe, K, Mg, Mn, Na* and *Ti*. Measurement data were normalized using the *z*-Gaussian transformation so that each compositional variable has a mean of zero and a standard deviation of 1.The same eight compositional chemical data were taken as input variables and studied by the self-organized map-neural network algorithm. The best results were obtained with a 14x14 neuron map. "Best results" means: (a) reduction of the number of conflicts, and (b) reduction of the number of empty spaces in neural maps.

After training, the network showed the location of samples in three different areas or clusters. They correspond to ceramic samples with: *non-calcareous* bodies, *calcareous* ceramics, and a *third group* of undifferentiated ceramics. The identified groups and the samples ascribed are as follows:

- Non-calcareous bodies. This group was composed of samples with calcium oxide contents below three percent. Two subgroups can be differentiated. A common origin can be proposed for all these objects and this was confirmed by other archaeological features.
- Calcareous bodies, with a calcium oxide content above six percent. This group can also be divided into two subgroups. A common provenance for all these calcareous ceramics can also be proposed. The archaeological information suggests an Italian provenance.
- The third group of bodies is located on the edges of the map and has a wide dispersion of contents, particularly of aluminum and calcium. Their archaeological features are not common and consequently, it was difficult to assign their provenances.

The influence or significance of the different chemical elements was obtained by deducing the weight values of the neurons after the learning step of the network was complete. So, the first weight component in each neuron corresponds to the influence of the *Na* concentration, the second weight component gives the *K* influence, and so on for the remaining input variables. A sodium map shows a positive influence on the left of the map and a negative influence on the right which means that samples with a high *Na* concentration will tend to be located in this area. However, samples with a low *Na* concentration will appear on the right of the map. The potassium provides a similar map to that of sodium. That is, samples with a high *K* concentration tend to appear on the left of the map and samples with a low *K* concentration on the right. From the previous arguments, it can be concluded that *Na* and *K* influences are very similar because ceramics with the same concentration of *Na* or *K* (relative concentration level, that is, low or high concentration) tend to be located in the same area of the neural map. They provide redundant information and have the same capacity to distinguish between samples. Consequently, the sodium and potassium chemical compositions can be reduced as an input variable to one composition (*Na* or *K*) without a significant loss in their classification capacity. On the other hand, the neural maps corresponding to the concentrations of *Cr, Cu, Ni* and *Zn*, have a common characteristic. Most of the neurons have a negative influence. These elements are not very significant in the sample characterization and consequently their concentrations are therefore not useful for differentiation between ceramic samples.

Another archaeometric application of SOM networks is Fermo et al. (2004). In this work, about one hundred Etruscan pottery sherds from the archaeological excavation at *Pian di Civita* in Tarquinia (Central Italy), dating from the 8th to the 4th century B.C., have been analyzed by inductively coupled plasma optical emission spectrometry and flame atomic emission spectrometry. The aim of the investigation was to settle their provenance and to acquire knowledge about the ceramic production technology. The examined sherds belong to the class of the *depurata* pottery, a fine ware produced in Tarquinia over a long period. In order to assess the production centre it, archaeological samples were compared with so-called reference or control groups, which may be formed by local references (local clays or kiln remains) or imported, that is, non-locally made, objects. For this purpose, clays coming from the Tarquinia area and some imported objects have been analyzed together. The samples have been analyzed for fifteen elements (*Ca, Al, Mg, Fe, Ti, Cr, Cu, Ni, Zn, Mn, Zr, Sr, Na, K,* and *Rb)*. Analysis by self-organized maps networks allowed a deeper investigation of sample similarities. Several network architectures were evaluated; the final network was chosen with an architecture of 15×15 neurons, trained with 25 epochs. Results show that the class of *etrusco-geometrica* sherds can be split into different sub-groups. In fact the objects belonging to this class, even if quite homogeneous from the stylistic point of view, are characterized

by a more variable chemical composition probably because the raw material used, was not subjected to any further depuration procedure. Combining results from a principal component analysis with those from the unsupervised neural network, the authors conclude that only six fragments out of 92 analyzed had a non-local origin.

Similar applications to these ones are Novic et al. (2001), Chang et al. (2002), Lletí et al. (2003), Beardah and Baxter (2005), Baxter (2006). In those cases archaeological samples were screened for similarities (clusters) using unsupervised neural networks (SOM). The neural network was applied in order to map original dimensional objects (sampled variables or components) into two-dimensional space (typology).

Not only can the chemical or mineralogical composition of archaeological artifacts be analyzed using neural networks. Brodaric et al. (2000) used SOM to investigate the process of generalizing classes from geological field data. This example can also be of interest to archaeologists. The study data contained composition (rock type descriptions) and spatiotemporal disposition (structural type and measurement), each possessing several attributes, including an attribute denoting the dominance of the composition. Site descriptions typically consisted of multiple compositions and dispositions, many of which were related (i.e. dispositions were measured within specific compositions):

- Dominant compositions: descriptions of the dominant lithology at a site.
- Dominant composition and dispositions 1: dominant lithology and planar structural feature type (omitting orientation measurements).
- Dominant composition and dispositions 2: dominant lithology and planar structural measurements.
- Dominant composition and dispositions 3: dominant lithology and all structural measurements.

- Composition: all lithologies described at a site.
- Composition and disposition: all lithologies and all structural measurements at a site.

Unsupervised clustering results occupied three distinct areas in feature space, each characterized by one of three main rock composition types: plutonic, volcanic, and sedimentary. Overlap is evident in all areas, however. The geological explanation of the overlap argues that it is difficult to observe accurately the dominant rock composition in complex terrain, though it would appear to become easier with increased exposure to, and thus greater scientific knowledge of, the study area.

Supervised learning has been mostly used to explain compositional data in terms of the geographical provenance of archaeological samples. John Fulcher (1997) has applied this framework in an investigation on obsidian provenance. Obsidian has been quarried by the indigenous people of Papua New Guinea for around 20,000 years. Through the analysis of compositional data provenance studies, it has been tried to obtain some information about trading and exchange practices. Fulcher used proton induced x-ray emission (PIXE) data as input to the network and tried to classify into six provenance areas. Data were gathered from six different sites in West New Britain area of Papua New Guinea: Kutau, Gulu, Garala, Baki, Hamilton and Mopir. There were only a few obsidian rock samples from each site to be used as training exemplars (between four and seven). The neural network was defined with 31 input neurons (compositions), and six outputs (geographical areas), with a hidden layer composed of eight neurons. After data normalization and careful parameter selection, the model generated only nine percent of misclassification rate (most of which could be attributed to samples form either Garala or Baki). These results confirm the possibilities to use neural network to test provenance hypothesis based on archaeometric data.

Bell and Croson (1998) have published a very similar example. They analyze slag inclusions in iron currency. Sixteen input variables were used, Na_2O, MgO, Al_2O_3, SiO_2, P_2O_5, SO_3, K_2O, CaO, TiO_2, V_2O_5, Cr_2O, MnO, FeO, BaO, Ni and As, and three output units, three geographically separate sites were studied, labeled as Danebury, Gretton, and Beckford. After some experimentation, a network configuration with 40 hidden neurons was retained. In these experiments, a radial bases function network was the best classifier. Compared to backpropagation, this network was able to compensate for sparse data by extending the response field while the backpropagation network could not. The authors suggest that in archaeometrical analysis, it can be useful to perform a principal component analysis of original data, and then using PCA scores and input vectors for the RBF.

Petrelli et al. (2001, 2003) have followed a similar approach in the study of provenance of travertine from some of the most important monuments in Umbria (Italy). Provenance determination of travertine is a complex archaeometric problem due to the textural and chemical variability characterizing this material. This system is based on the use of geochemical data obtained by chemical analysis of travertine samples. Extensive sampling was carried out from important monuments of different ages in different localities in Umbria, and in outcrop from ancient quarries or zones of excavation mentioned in historical documents as sites of extraction of the stones employed in monuments. The samples were characterized by optical microscopy and X-ray fluorescence analysis. The network consists of 27 neurons, one for each analyzed chemical element. The network was trained using exclusively known quarry samples. To test the reliability of such a system, controls were performed exclusively on quarry samples randomly chosen from the original database. Results indicate a good discriminative power of the system able to recognize the exact provenance of more than 80 percent of samples. The system was then used to determine provenance of travertine samples from three historical monuments. Results point to a local origin, from Sabina quarry and from different outcrops within Orvieto District, for the samples from the Etruscan Arch (3rd century B.C.) and Orvieto Cathedral (1290-1532), respectively. On the other hand, provenance of samples from Fontana Maggiore (1277-1278) cannot univocally be determined since all the sampled quarries may be considered, in different extent, as probable sites of provenance of the travertine employed in the monument.

Grudzinski et al., (2003; Grudzinski & Karwowski, 2005) have compared the efficiency of backpropagation neural networks with other machine learning tools based on rule generalization. They used archaeometric data on La Tène period objects made of glass. In most of their experiments, neural networks achieved overall results of 80 percent of good classifications using testing data; those results were, in general, better than the other soft-computing comparative methods.

Kadar et al. (2004) have explored the supervised classification of ancient copper alloys fabrication techniques. Mechanical properties have been assessed for tin bronze archaeological objects and the influence of the variation of tin composition has been monitored by a trained neural network.

Other archaeometric applications to provenience studies are those by Ma et al. (2000), Ma (2003). The results show that archaeological evidence belongs to three categories, the Yellow River Valley (YR) region, the Yangtse River Valley (YV) region and other region (OR). This work reveals that the ANN seems to be more suitable than PCA in classifying such archaeological samples.

Not only can the chemical or mineralogical composition of archaeological artifacts be analyzed using supervised neural networks. Bell and Croson (1998) report an example of archaeological soils classification to determine if soil chemical composition has been impacted by human activity. Data associated with total acid dissolution

were selected. Soils classified as "controls" were assumed to be unaffected by human activities while those excavated from features (waste pit, hearth, and residence) were classified as impacted. Thus, desired outputs for the networks involved a simple binary output. Statistical analysis show that overlap exists between site and control samples, while refuse pits and hearth samples were clearly delineated. Thus, construction of a decision surface capable of separating them was expected to be difficult. The authors built a radial basis function network using 25 hidden units and the first two principal components as input (accounting for 71 percent of variance). In this network, none of the test vectors was misclassified.

A back propagation neural network has been successfully applied in predicting paleo-soil sequences using well log suites from two wells in a Cenozoic basin in southwestern Montana (Link, n.d.). The training set consists of neutron porosity, bulk density, and resistivity logs and the interpreted paleo-soil section. Training is accomplished using well log values over a range of depths rather than discrete depths. The trained network is used to predict paleo-soil occurrences in a neighboring well. Network prediction results show good agreement with paleo-soil interpretations.

Bursik and Rogova (2006) suggest building hybrid information processing systems for the compositional correlation of geologic layers. This method can also be useful for archaeological stratigraphic correlation. The working hypothesis is that the system can correctly correlate layers from one site to another even when data are sparse. The authors use a feature vector comprising data on maximum size of mineral inclusions, bed thickness, fraction of inclusions, and grading.

DIRECTIONS FOR FURTHER RESEARCH

Texture and compositional analysis have been here compared, because both derive from decompositional approaches. Compositional analysis is much more popular in archaeology, especially given its direct implication in archaeometry. By its characteristics, it is the prime domain for neurocomputational applications, maybe also because those applications are made by chemists of physicists, and not by archaeologists alone. This is a very dynamic subfield in mathematics and classification dealing with the specific characteristics of compositional data vectors. However, there is still much to be done in this domain, especially in supervised and unsupervised algorithms. Support vector machines is a relatively new classification method that should be explored in these domains.

The field of texture analysis seems to be poorly explored by archaeologists, although it has obvious interest. We need much more investigations on this area, both in the descriptive features, the data processing methods, and interpretive considerations. In some aspects, we can rely on tribology studies in related disciplines, to understand why and how the surface of objects is modified because of human activities with those objects. In this chapter, I have relied very much on my own work on use-wear analysis. The image-processing approach I have developed together with Jordi Pijoan-López take the most part of the chapter. We have adopted this way of describing textures because of its simplicity, although we know there are better ways to analyze texture patterns. The classical matrix approach by Haralick (1979) also merits that we explore its possible archaeological applications. This way of measuring texture irregularities have been integrated into open source image processing software like *ImageJ*. Some commercial computer programs for image processing, also include the possibility of integrating a neural network just by clicking a few buttons.

The next chapter on remote sensing applications of neurocomputing is also of interest as an example of texture and shape analysis.

The reader may think that there is very few of computational "intelligence" in these applications. What I have called shape, texture, and compositional analysis, is just classification or typology. I hope that the differences between the traditional approach and the one taken here are evident. Emphasis has been placed on supervised/unsupervised *generalization*, and not on using subjective experience, whose only reliability lies on the academic authority of the researcher. Experimentation and the nonlinear nature of the relationship between visual appearance (shape, texture, and composition) and archaeological explanation are the key aspects here.

There is a way of going beyond the apparently simple "classificatory" approach to the visual analysis presented in the last two chapters (Bicici & St. Amant, 2003). These methods are based on shape, texture, and compositional analysis but also on knowledge about the way the object was used, the naive physical rules that govern the objects.

Some interesting studies that may serve as starting points are the investigations of Ernest Davis, who has done considerable amount of work towards formalizing the physical world of objects through commonsense physical understanding. One of Davis's efforts deals with formalizing the kinematics of cutting solid objects. He shows the geometric aspects of various cutting operations: slicing an object in half, cutting a notch into an object, stabbing a hole through an object, and carving away the surface of an object (Davis, 1990, 1993).

This kind of integration of knowledge is essential for a robotic system to understand not only how the objects are and how they look like but also what they are made of, and why. Much more investigation is necessary along these lines. Rivlin and colleagues have investigated object recognition from the description of object's usage, that is, in terms of a sequence of images of a known object performing some action. The usage analysis results in several activity primitives and these are compared with previously known usage-to-explanation mappings (Duric et al., 1996; Froimovich et al., 2002; Rivlin et al., 1995; Pechuk et al., 2005). Stark and Bowyer's GRUFF (1996) is a function-based object recognition system that recognizes objects by classifying them into categories that describe the functionality they might serve. The system is based on computer vision techniques for recognizing functionality, and tries to achieve interactive recognition ability by observing the deformations that happen on objects when they are used. Green et al. (1994) take a comparable approach, in which kinematics properties are investigated. See also Bogoni and Bajcsy (1993), Bogoni and Bajcsy (1995), Cooper et al. (1995).

Peursum et al. present a method for finding and classifying objects within real-world scenes by using the activity of humans interacting with these objects to infer the object's identity. The premise of this approach is that since humans interact differently with objects that differ in their functionality, it should be possible to identify objects using their associated visual human interaction signatures. The advantage of such an approach is that it considers object recognition independent of the object's physical structure. Furthermore, the system can use an evidence-based framework to classify objects in an incremental manner, and thus should be flexible enough to adapt to the scene as it changes over time (Peursum et al., 2003, 2005, 2007).

Chaigneau et al. (2004, cf. also Barsalou et al., 2005) have proposed the HIPE model of functional reasoning. It uses causal modeling methods to represent the structure of functional senses. The idea is to build a causal model, a Bayesian network, for instance, cf. Chapter III, contains information about four components: the object's history, the agent's goal, the agent's action, and the object's physical structure. If the physical description of the object is somewhat vague, then what is known about the object's history can influence predictions about how to conceptualize its physical structure, which in turn can influence the outcome. If the

object's history is compromised, the machine may infer that the object's physical structure is likely to be somewhat flawed. This approach assumes that a linked set of causal states—a causal model—supports inferences about actual and imagined action.

All these new lines of research show how we can go well beyond description and using computer vision to explain the causal nature of archaeological evidence.

REFERENCES

ACEBRÓN-LINUESA F., LÓPEZ-GARCÍA, F., & VALIENTE-GONZÁLEZ, J.M. (2002). Surface defect detection on fixed ceramic tiles. *Proceedings of the Second IASTED International Conference on Visualization, imaging, and image processing.*

ADÁN, M., BARCELÓ, J.A., PIJOAN-LOPEZ, J.A., PIQUE, R., & TOSELLI, A. (2003). Spatial statistics in archaeological texture analysis. In M. Doerr & A. Sarris (Eds.), *The digital heritage of archaeology* (pp. 253-260). Published by the Archive of Monuments and Publications. Athens, Greece: Hellenic Ministry of Culture.

AITCHISON, J. (1986). *The statistical analysis of compositional data.* London: Chapman and Hall.

AITCHISON, J. (1994). Principles of compositional data analysis. In T.W. Anderson, I. Olkin, & K.T. Fang (Eds.), *Multivariate analysis and its applications* (pp. 73-81). Hayward, CA: Institute of Mathematical Statistics.

AITCHISON, J. (1997). The one-hour course in compositional data analysis or compositional data analysis is easy. In V. Pawlowsky Glahn (Ed.), *Proceedings of the 3rd Annual Conference of the International Association for Mathematical Geology* (pp. 3-35). Barcelona, Spain: CIMNE.

AITCHISON, J., & BARCELÓ-VIDAL, C. (2002). Compositional processes: A statistical search for understanding. In *Proceedings of the 8th Annual Conference of the International Association for Mathematical Geology.*

BARCELÓ, J.A., & PIJOAN-LOPEZ, J. (2004). Cutting or scrapping? Using neural networks to distinguish kinematics in use-wear analysis. In Magistrat der Stadt Wien (Ed.), *Enter the past. The e-way into the four dimensions of culture heritage* (pp. 427-431). Oxford: ArcheoPress.

BARCELÓ, J.A., PIJOAN-LÓPEZ, J.A., & VICENTE, O. (2001). Image quantification as archaeological description. In Z. Stancic & T. Veljanovski (Eds.), *Computing archaeology for understanding the past* (pp. 69-78). Oxford: ArcheoPress.

BARSALOU, L.W., SLOMAN, S.A., & CHAIGNEAU, S.E. (2005). The HIPE theory of function. In L. Carlson & E. Van der Zee (Eds.), *Representing functional features for language and space: Insights from perception, categorization and development* (pp. 131-147). Oxford UK: Oxford University Press.

BAXTER, M.J. (2006). A review Of supervised and unsupervised pattern recognition in archaeometry. *Archaeometry, 48*(4), 671–694

BEARDAH, C.C., BAXTER, M.J. (2005). An R library for compositional data analysis in archaeometry, In *2nd Compositional Data Analysis Workshop, CoDaWork'05* Girona.

BELL, S., CROSON, C. (1998). Artificial neural networks as a tool for archaeological data analysis. *Archeometry, 40*(1), 139-151.

BHAKAR, S., DUDEK, C.K., MUISE, S., SHARMAN, L., HORTOP, E., & SZABO, F. (2004). Textiles, patterns and technology: Digital tools for the geometric analysis of cloth and culture. *Textile: The Journal of Cloth and Culture, 2*(3), 308-327.

BICICI, E., & ST. AMANT, R. (2003). *Reasoning about the functionality of tools and physical artifacts.* Technical Report TR-2003-22, Department of Computer Science, North Carolina State University, April, 2003.

BILLHEIMER, D., GUTTORP, P., & FAGAN, W.F. (1998). *Statistical analysis and interpretation of discrete compositional data.* NRCSE Technical Report Series, NRSCE-TRS No. 011 (http://www.nrcse.washington.edu/pdf/trs11_interp.pdf) (File downloaded on September 2006).

BOGONI, L., & BAJCSY, R. (1993). An active approach to characterization and recognition of functionality and functional properties. In *AAAI Workshop on Reasoning about Function.* (pp. 9–16).

BOGONI, L., & BAJCSY, R. (1995). Interactive recognition and representation of functionality. *Computer Vision and Image Understanding, 62*(2), 194–214.

BRODARIC, B., GAHEGAN, M., TAKA-TUSKA, M., & HARRAP, R. (2000). Geocomputing with geological field data: Is there a 'ghost in the machine?' *Proceedings of the 5th International Conference on GeoComputation* University of Greenwich, United Kingdom. Retrieved May 2007 from http://www.geocomputation.org/2000/GC028/Gc028.htm

BURSIK, M., & ROGOVA, G. (2006). Use of neural networks and decision fusion for lithostratigraphic correlation with sparse data, *Computers & Geosciences, 32*, 1564–1572

CHAIGNEAU, S.E., BARSALOU, L.W., & SLOMAN, A. (2004). Assessing the causal structure of function *Journal of Experimental Psychology: General, 133*(4), 601–625.

CHANDRARATNE, M.R., SAMARASINGHE, S., KULASIRI., D., FRAMPTON, C., & BICKERSTAFFE, R. (2003). Determination of lamb grades using texture analysis and neural networks.

Proceedings of the 3rd IASTED International Conference VISUALIZATION, IMAGING AND IMAGE PROCESSING, Benalmadena, Spain.

CHANG, H-C., KOPASKA-MERKEL, D., & CHEN, H.C. (2002). Identification of lithofacies using kohonen self-organizing maps. *Computers & Geosciences, 28*, 223–229

COOPER, P. R., BIRNBAUM, L.A., & BRAND, M.E., (1995). Causal scene understanding. *Computer Vision and Image Understanding, 62*(2), 215–231.

DAVIS, F. (1990). *Representations in commonsense knowledge.* San Mateo, CA: Morgan Kaufmann Publishers.

DAVIS, E. (1993). The kinematics of cutting solid objects. *Annals of Mathematics and Artificial Intelligence, 9*(3/4), 253–305.

DROLON, H., HOYEZ, B., DRUAUX, F., & FAURE, A. (2003). Multiscale roughness analysis of particles: Application to the classification of detrital sediments. *Mathematical Geology, 35*(7), 805-817.

DURIC, Z., FAYMAN, J., & RIVLIN, E. (1996). Function from motion. *IEEE Transactions on Pattern Analysis and Machine Intelligence, 18*, 579–591.

FERMO, P., CARIATI, F., BALLABIO, D., CONSONNI, V., & BAGNASCO GIANNI, G., (2004). Classification of ancient etruscan ceramics using statistical multivariate analysis of data. *Applied Physics A Materials Science & Processing, 79*(2), 299-307.

FROIMOVICH, G., RIVLIN, E., & SHIMSHONI, I. (2002). Object classification by functional parts. *Proceedings of the First Symposium on 3D Data, Processing, Visualization and Transmission*, (pp. 648-655).

FULCHER, J. (1997). Neural networks for archaeological provenancing. In E. Fiesler & R. Beale

Handbook of Neural Computation. New York: Institute of Physics/Oxford University Press.

GREEN, K., EGGERT, D., STARK, L., & BOWYER, K. (1994). Generic recognition of articulated objects by reasoning about functionality. In *AAAI Workshop on Representing and Reasoning about Function.*

GRUDZINSKI K., KARWOWSKI M., & DUCH W. (2005). Computational intelligence study of the iron age glass data. *International Conference on Artificial Neural Networks (ICANN) and International Conference on Neural Information Processing (ICONIP), Istanbul.* Retrieved June 2007 from http://www.fizyka.ukw.edu.pl/publikacje/a_s_p.pdf

GRUDZINSKI, K., & KARWOWSKI, M. (2005, June 13-16). The analysis of the unlabeled samples of the iron age glass data. In Mieczyslaw A. Klopotek, Slawomir T. Wierzchon, & Krzysztof Trojanowski (Eds.), *Intelligent Information Processing and Web Mining, Proceedings of the International IIS: IIPWM'05* Conference held in Gdansk, Poland. Berlin: Springer (Advances in Soft Computing Series).

HARALICK, R.M. (1979). Statistical and structural approaches to texture, *Proceedings of the IEEE, 67*, 786-804.

HARNAD, S. (1987). *Categorical perception. The groundwork of cognition.* Cambridge, UK: Cambridge University Press.

JAIN, A.K., & KARU, K. (1996). Learning texture discrimination masks. *IEEE Transactions on Pattern Analysis And Machine Intelligence, 18*(2), 195-205.

JULESZ, B. (1981). A theory of preattentive texture discrimination based on first-order statistics of textons. *Biological Cybernetics, 41*, 131-138.

KADAR, M., ILEANA, I., & JOLDES, R. (2004). Artificial neural networks used in forms recognition of the properties of ancient copper based alloys. In F. Niccolucci (Ed.), *Beyond the artefact. Computer Applications in Archaeology.* Budapest: ArcheoLingua.

KALLIOMÄKI, I., VEHTARI, A., & LAMP-INEN, J. (2005). Shape analysis of concrete aggregates for statistical quality modeling. *Machine Vision and Applications, 16*(3), 197-201.

KULKARNI, A.D. (2001). *Computer vision and fuzzy neural systems.* Upper Saddle River, NJ: Prentice Hall.

LEUNG, T., & MALIK, J. (2001). Representing and recognizing the visual appearance of materials using three-dimensional textons. *International Journal of Computer Vision, 43*(1), 29–44.

LI, P., & FLENLEY, J.R. (1999). Pollen texture identification using neural networks. *Grana 38,* 59–64.

LINK, C.A. (n.d.). Artificial neural networks for Lithology prediction and reservoir characterization geophysical engineering. *Montana Tech of the University of Montana.* Retrieved august 20, 2006 from http://www.mtech.edu/GEOPHYS-ICS/RESEARCH/NeuralNetworks.htm

*LLETÍ, R. SARABIA,L.A., ORTIZ, M.C., TODE-SCHINI, R., & COLOMBINI, M.P. (*2003). Application of the kohonen artificial neural network in the identification of proteinaceous binders in samples of panel painting using gas chromatography-Mass Spectrometry, *Analyst,128,* 281-286.

LOPEZ MOLINERO, A., CASTRO, A., PINO, J., PEREZ-ARANTEGUI, J., & CASTILLO, J.R. (2000). Classification of ancient Roman glazed ceramics using the neural network of self-organizing maps. *Fresenius Journal of Analytical Chemistry, 367,* 586-589.

LÜTH, H. (1993). *Surfaces and interfaces of solids.* Berlin: Springer.

MA, Q. (2003). Application of EDXRF and artificial neural networks to provenance studies of the archaeological pottery sherds during neolithic age in Gansu Province, China. *Journal of Lanzhou University Natural Sciences, 39*(1), 47-53.

MA, Q.,YAN, A., & HU, Z. (2000). Principal component analysis and artificial neural networks applied to the classification of chinese pottery of neolithic age. *Analytica Chimica Acta, 406,* 247-256.

MARMO, R., AMODIO, S. TAGLIAFERRI, R., FERRERI, R., & LONGO, G. (2005). Textural identification of carbonate rocks by image processing and neural network: Methodology proposal and examples. *Computers & Geosciences, 31,* 649–659.

MARTIN, D.H., FOWLKES, C.C., & MALIK, J. (2004). Learning to detect natural image boundaries using local brightness, color, and texture cues. *IEEE Transactions On Pattern Analysis And Machine Intelligence, 26*(5), 530-549.

MARTINEZ-ALAJARIN, J.M., LUIS-DELGA-DO, J.D., & TOMAS-BALIBREA, L.M. (2005). Automatic system for quality-based classification of marble textures. *IEEE Transactions on Systems, Man, And Cybernetics—Part C: Applications And Reviews, 35*(4), 488-497.

MATERKA, A., & STRZELECKI, M. (1998). *Texture analysis methods – a review.* Technical University of Lodz, Institute of Electronics. Brussels (Belgium): COST B11 report.

MAYORGA, M.A., & LUDEMAN, L.C. (1991). Neural nets for determination of texture and its orientation. *ICASSP-91.*

MAYORGA, M.A., & LUDEMAN, L.C. (1994). Shift and rotation invariant texture recognition with neural nets. *IEEE World Congress on Computational Intelligence.*

NOVIČ, M., NOVIČ, M., ŽUPANČIČ, M., & SAKARA SUČEVIĆ, M. (2001). The application of the combination of chemical (ICP-OES and ICP-MS) and chemometric analytical procedures for the tracing of the geologically predetermined composition of archaeological pottery. *12th International Symposium Spectroscopy in Theory and Practice with Thinkshop In search of the Metrological Basis of Spectroscopic Measurements*, Bled, Slovenia.

PECHUK, M., SOLDEA, O., & RIVLIN, E. (2005). Function-based classification from 3D data via generic and symbolic models. Paper presented at The *20th National Conference on Artificial Intelligence (AAAI-05)*, Pittsburgh, Pennsylvania. Retrieved April 2007 from http://www.cs.technion.ac.il/~mpechuk/publications/oclsAAAI05.pdf

PETRELLI, M., PERUGINI, D., MORONI, B., & POLI, G. (2001). A simple system based on fuzzy logic and artificial neural networks to determine travertine provenance from ancient buildings. In L. Bordoni & G. Semeraro (Eds.), *Proceedings of the Workshop Artificial Intelligence for the Cultural heritage and Digital Libraries*. Dipartimento di Informatica, Università degli Studi di Bari. Associazione Italiana per l'Inteligenza Artificiale.

PETRELLI, M., PERUGINI, D., MORONI, B., & POLI, G. (2003). Determination of travertine provenance from ancient buildings using self-organizing maps and fuzzy logic *Applied Artificial Intelligence, 7*(8-9), 885-900.

PEURSUM, P., VENKATESH, S., WEST, G. & BUI, H.H. (2003). Object labeling from human action recognition. *IEEE International Conference on Pervasive Computing and Communications, Dallas-Fort Worth, Texas, 23-26 March 2003,* (pp. 399-406).

PEURSUM, P., BUI, H.H., VENKATESH, S., & WEST, G. (2005). Robust recognition and segmentation of human actions using HMMs with missing observations. *EURASIP Journal of Applied Signal Processing, 2005*(13), 2110-2126.

PEURSUM, P., VENKATESH, S., WEST, G. (2007). Tracking-as-recognition for articulated full-body human motion analysis. In *IEEE International Conference on Computer Vision and Pattern Recognition (CVPR)*. IEEE Press.

PIJOAN-LÓPEZ, J., BARCELÓ, J.A., BRIZ, I., VILA, A., & PIQUÉ, R. (1999). Image quantification in use-wear analysis. In K. Fennema & H. Kamermans (Eds.), *Making the connections to the past. CAA 1999.* Computer Applications in Archaeology (pp. 67-74). Holland: Leiden University.

PIJOAN-LÓPEZ, J., BARCELÓ, J.A., CLEMENTE, I., & VILA, A. (2002). Variabilidad Estadística en imágenes digitalizadas de rastros de uso: resultados preliminares. In I. Clemente, R. Risch, & J. Gibaja (Eds.), *Análisis Funcional. Su aplicación al estudio de sociedades prehistóricas.* (pp. 55-64). Oxford: ArcheoPress.

PIJOAN-LÓPEZ, J. (2007). *Quantificació de traces d'ús en instruments lítics mitjançant imatges digitalitzades: Resultats d'experiments amb Xarxes Neurals I Estadística.* PhD. Dissertation. Universitat Autonoma de Barcelona (Spain).

RAO, S.R. (1972). *Surface phenomena.* London, UK: Hutchinson Educational Ltd.

RIVLIN, E., DICKINSON, S., & ROSENFELD, A. (1995). Recognition by functional parts. *Computer Vision and Image Understanding, 62*(2), 164– 176.

RUIZ DEL SOLAR, J. (1998). TEXSOM: Texture segmentation using self-organizing maps. *Neural Networks, 21,* 7-18.

SONG, A. (2003). *Texture classification: A genetic programming approach.* PhD Dissertation, Department of Computer Science, RMIT, Melbourne, Victoria, Australia,

STARK, L., & BOWYER, K. (1996). *Generic object recognition using form and function, Vol. 10* of *Series in Machine Perception and Artificial Intelligence.* Singapore: World Scientific.

TOSELLI, A. (2004). *Identificación y descripción de trazas de uso en obsidiana mediante la experimentación.* Master Thesis. Universitat Autónoma de Barcelona (Spain).

TOSELLI, A., PIJOAN, J., & BARCELÓ, J.A. (2002). La descripción de las trazas de uso en materias primas no silíceas: resultados preliminares de un análisis estadístico descriptivo In *Análisis Funcional: su aportación al estudio de Sociedades Prehistóricas 1er Congreso de Análisis Funcional de España y Portugal* Oxford: British Archaeological Reports Archeopress.

VALIENTE-GONZÁLEZ, J.M, (2001). Object comparison in structural analysis of decorative patterns in textile design. *Preprints and Electronic Proceedings of 12th International Conference on Design Tools and Methods in Industrial Engineering, 1,* B1.

Van den DRIES, M.H. (1998). *Archeology and the application of artificial intelligence. Case studies on use-wear analysis of prehistoric flint tools.* Archaeological Studies Leiden University No. 1, Faculty of Archaeology, University of Leiden (Holland).

VAN DER MAATEN, L.J.P., & BOON, P.J. (2006). COIN-O-MATIC: A fast and reliable system for coin classification. In *Proceedings of the MUSCLE Coin Workshop 2006,* (pp. 7-17). Berlin, Germany.

VAN DER MAATEN, L.J.P., BOON, P.J., PAIJMANS, J.J., LANGE, A.G., & POSTMA, E.O. (2006). Computer vision and machine learning for archaeology. In *Proceedings of the Computer Applications in Archaeology Conference 2006,* Fargo (ND).

Chapter VIII
Spatiotemporal Analysis

THE ANALYSIS OF SPATIAL FREQUENCIES

As we have suggested many times throughout the book, the general form of an archaeological problem seems to be "*why* an archaeological site is the way it is?" If we translate it into the spatial domain, we should be asking "*where* social agents performed their actions and work processes on the basis of the observed relationships between the actual locations of the social action material traces?," or more precisely, "why those archaeological materials have been found *here* and not *elsewhere*?" Consequently, the automated archaeologist should *infer* where social agents performed their actions and work processes based on the observed relationships between the actual locations of the supposed material consequences of social action. This is the domain of application for a spatial analysis: to infer the location of what cannot be seen based on observed things that are causally related to the action to be placed. Knowing where someone made something based on what she did, is an inverse problem with multiple solutions, which can be solved using some of the methods and technologies already presented.

It is important to realize that "location" is a property of social acts, but it is not a *cause* in itself. Social action is produced *in* physical space, but it also contributes to the formation process of such

space. The characteristics of space as a dimension, rather than the properties of phenomena, which are located in space, are of central and overriding concern. Consequently, "place" can only be understood according to what is performed at each place and at each moment. Social actions should be analyzed as conditioned and/or determined by other actions, because they have been performed in an intrinsically better or worse spatiotemporal location for some purpose because of their position relative to some other location for another action or the reproduction of the same action (Barceló & Pallarés, 1998). Some of the actions performed near the location increase the chances of one type of action and decrease the chances of others. What we are looking for is whether what happens in one location is the cause of what happens in neighboring locations (Barceló, 2002, 2005; Barceló, Maximiano & Vicente, 2005; Mameli, Barceló & Estévez, 2002).

The automated archaeologist's objective is then to analyze where, when and why a social action "varies from one location (spatiotemporal) to another." Social action is never performed isolated or in an abstract vacuum. To solve this archaeological problem, the intelligent machine will correlate different social actions, and describe how the spatial distribution of material effects of some action, and hence the place where the action was originally performed, has an influence over the spatial distribution of the material effects of other(s) action(s).

In seeking to understand a spatial pattern in observed data, it is important to appreciate that it might arise either from region-wide 'trends' (first-order variation) or from correlation structures (second-order variation), or from a mixture of both. In the first order case, the spatial frequencies of archaeological features vary from location to location due to changes in the underlying properties of the local environment. For example, frequencies of archaeological artifacts may be influenced by variations in terrain. In the second order case, frequencies of archaeological data vary from location to location due to local interaction effects between observations. For example, material consequences of social action tend to happen in areas where the social action has been performed. We should assume a second order pattern in the data is due to some process that varies spatially. That means that patterns arise due to variations in social actions performed at discrete locations.

The question that also arises is whether the social action displays any systematic spatial pattern or departure from randomness either in the direction of *clustering* or *regularity*. Randomness at the spatial level can be the result of post depositional alteration, and should be detected before social action at the spatial level can be explained. We need tools and methods to differentiate diverse spatial ways in which an action can be performed at different places. Questions that are more interesting include:

- Is the observed clustering due mainly to natural background variation in the population from which intensities arise?
- Over what spatial scale does any clustering occur?
- Are *clusters* merely a result of some obvious a priori heterogeneity in the region studied?
- Are they associated with proximity to other specific features of interest, such the location

of some other social action or possible point sources of important resources?
- Is material evidence that aggregates in space also clustered in time?

All these sorts of questions serve to take us beyond the simple detection of non-randomness. Discriminating between random, clustered, and regular patterns of observed spatial frequencies of archaeological features is a fundamental concern, because it will help us to understand the nature of the causal process (social actions) involved. The actual evidence of the presence of a social action should be statistically different from the random location of its material traces through different spatial and temporal locations.

To infer the cause (social action performed at the spatial level) from the effect (the spatial frequency of material evidence measured at some finite set of locations), we have to rebuild the real frequency that was generated in the past by the social action. This theory forms the underpinnings of geostatistics. Geostatistics applies the theories of stochastic processes and statistical inference to spatial locations. It is a set of statistical methods used to describe spatial relationships among sample data and to apply this analysis to the prediction of spatial and temporal phenomena (Fotheringham et al., 2000; Haining, 2003; Lloyd & Atkinson, 2004).

NEURAL NETWORKS FOR SOLVING THE SPATIAL INTERPOLATION PROBLEM

If the intelligent robot has not previous information about how observed spatial frequencies of archaeological observables might have been formed, then estimates of the parameters defining the best function between input (frequency of material traces at the spatial level) and output (placement of the social action that caused such frequencies and spatial densities) must be generated from its actual observations (archaeological frequencies). If such a function can be calculated, then by using observations of archaeological frequencies made at some locations, an automated archaeologist will estimate the frequency of archaeological evidence at neighbor locations and the probabilities that a social action was performed at some place.

The result is an interpolated manifold (usually a surface), which can be understood as a probabilistic map for the placement of social actions performed in the past. In such a map, nearer things appear to be more related than distant things (Tobler's law), because the synchronicity of social actions states that, all else being equal, activities that occur at the same time will tend to increase the joint frequency of their effects. Using this model, the automated archaeologist assumes that the probability that a social action occurs at a specific location should be related someway to the frequency of its material effects (the archaeological record) at nearby locations. Therefore, when the frequency of an archaeological observable at some locations increases, the probability that the social action was performed in its neighborhood will converge towards the relative frequency at adjacent locations. Then, if the machine knows the relationship between the social action and its archaeological descriptor, the density probability function for the location of archaeological artifacts can be a good estimator for the spatial variability of the social action.

The purpose of any geostatistical investigation is to predict the value of the dependent variable at any imaginable spatiotemporal coordinate. Given a sample of observed frequencies at known locations, what the automated archaeologist needs to generalize is a nonlinear function that represents the probability density function of the social action original spatial modality. For example, suppose that we know the presence or absence of archaeological evidence for settlement at different places at different historical periods. Then spatial-temporal interpolation would estimate the probability of human settlement at un-sampled locations and times. Nevertheless, it is important that although the interpolated model allows us to go beyond the too simple description of the spatial modality of social action, the complexity of the model and its ability to find a solution will depend on the complexity of the spatial process. We should take into account that the interpolated function contains both the process that generated the original frequencies *prima facie*, and all post-depositional process that altered the original values. That means that we can never hope fully to characterize the archaeological spatial process.

A neural network can be used for calculating the nonlinear relationship between spatial inputs and social outputs. In a multilayer neural network, spatial coordinates (x, y) are fed to two input neurons. Outputs neurons will estimate the probability that different action was performed there. Training data are necessary in the form of locations, where we have some idea or confidence that the action was performed, given the quantity and the nature of archaeological evidence at that place (output=1).

In so doing, neural networks offer a non-algorithmic approach to geostatistical interpolation (Dowd & Sarac, 1994; Kanevski et al., 1997; Matsuda et al., 2003). The purpose of all such interpolation methods is to discover hidden spatial dependencies between observed frequencies at different places. Although spatial dependencies may be considered using traditional statistical tools, only neural network models rely on redundancy of representations in space and time. In other words, they normally disregard individual signal or pattern variables and concentrate on *collective properties* of sets of variables, for example, on their correlations, conditional averages, and so forth.

Additional advantages for using neural networks as spatial interpolators are:

- Highly non stationary spatial processes,
- Cartography of distribution functions, as opposed to cartography of the mean value, and

• User and data-driven parameterization for the discrimination between a stochastic trend and auto-correlated residuals, cartography of stochastic deviations related to advection-diffusion models.

However, it is important that we take into account some important experimental studies recently published (Martínez et al., 2004; Willmes et al., 2003): neither the standard spatial interpolators like kriging nor neural networks could clearly demonstrate an advantageous performance over an evolutionary optimization without meta-models. It is not surprising to observe that the prediction quality differs depending on the learning schedule. Some studies indicate that deductively generated spatial models can provide unexpected predictions on unseen data points while models trained with observed data give better predictions, which suggests that the construction of local meta-models is more practical and reliable than global models.

Interpolation and related methods only maximize available information from often sparsely distributed data. As such, it does not solve the archaeological problem of inferring the original location of the social action, nor why the materials are where they are, but gives us some information about the spatial modality of the social action based on the spread and density of its materials effects. We need to discover other aspects of the social action as it has been performed at a spatial scale.

We discussed at the beginning of the chapter, that another question that also arises is whether the social action displays any systematic spatial pattern or departure from randomness either in the direction of *clustering* or *regularity*. Unsupervised learning approaches can be very useful for detecting it. When archaeological data on a group of sites is introduced as input for the unsupervised network, these sites will be self-organized in the output in such a way that those with similar archaeological characteristics will be located

close to one another on a map. Imagine we have the spatial coordinates (x, y) of different archaeological observables, and we want to understand the density of findings in terms of the intensity of a social action (for instance, the number of residential units). Based on the density of findings, we can suggest the hypothetical existence of a number of clusters, for instance, three huts or activity areas. Consequently, we need as many units in the output layer as spatially relevant units we have hypothesized. When the neighborhood of output units is set as linear (one output unit after another), we can plot the output weights, which represent the cluster centers directly above the input data (Figure 8.1). In this case we have two channels from the input neurons (the input values x, y) and two channels from the output (the weights). We use these weights as coordinates, to compare the output spatial location with the input. What we would like to do is to plot the inputs (channels 0 and 1) as an x, y scatter, and the weights connected to a given output neuron as the other two x, y scatters.

The same problem has been solved in archaeology using standard *k-means* clustering (Blankholm, 1991; Kintigh & Ammermann, 1982). Although the *k-means* clustering algorithm and the SOM are very closely related (Openshaw & Turton, 1996), the ways of using them in data mining are probably different. Whereas in the *k-means* clustering algorithm the number of clusters should be chosen according to the number of clusters in the data, in the SOM the number of reference vectors can be chosen to be much larger, irrespective of the number of clusters. The difference is that in the SOM the distance of each input from all of the reference vectors is taken into account, weighted by the neighborhood kernel h. This gives the spatial nature of clusters, that is to say, their distance and topological ordering. The close relation between the SOM and the *k*-means clustering algorithm also hints at why the self-organized map follows rather closely the distribution of the data set in the input space: it is

Figure. 8.1. A self-organized map (SOM) solving a spatial clustering problem. The diagram plots the output weights representing the spatial cluster centers directly above the input data.

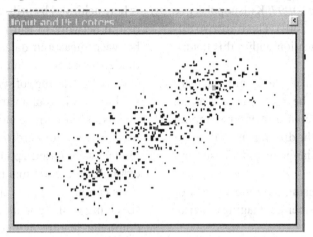

known for vector quantization that the density of the reference vectors approximates the density of the input vectors for high-dimensional data.

According to Brodaric et al. (2004) this last approach not always works. The actual encoding of site location in the input data vector to ensure actual nearest neighbors are proximal may cause them to dominate categorization, resulting in SOMs that reflect only geographic distribution of the data, and forgetting other kind of regularities. This aspect is out of question in supervised analysis (feed-forward networks that learn by backpropagation), but is so important in unsupervised approaches where distance can be a spatial feature *and simultaneously* a comparative procedure.

INTERPRETING REMOTE SENSING DATA: AN EXAMPLE OF SPATIAL INTERPOLATION

Remote sensing can be defined as the art and science of detecting, identifying, classifying, delineating, and analyzing spatial features and phenomena with imagery acquired from terrestrial, aircraft and satellite sensors (Civco, 1993).

Remote sensing has a long tradition in archaeology (Scollar, 1990). It is an example of spatial interpolation problem because they are based on estimating the where some features can be found based on a finite set of local observations.

Estimating global archaeological information from a handful of remote measurements is a very interesting approach to archaeological investigation. If we are interested in interpreting the social history of geographical regions, we need some kind of "general" information about the way material consequences of social action were spread over the study area. To excavate all those remains is an unattainable dream: there are not enough archaeologists, nor time nor funding for doing it in a reasonable period. Observations made without excavation maybe are not very detailed, but they provide information about many of the elements present at the region in a global sense. The quality of archaeological information derived from these measurements varies significantly depending on the strength and uniqueness of the visual features of archaeological evidence and mathematical methods applied to extract this information. Therefore, it would be interesting to develop methods to understand and explain these kinds of data.

Interpreting remote sensing data is a relevant field of application for neural network technology (Atkinson & Tatnall, 1997; Krasnopolsky & Shiller, 2003; Kulkarni, 2001). There are two different domains of application within this field:

- When remote sensing data are intensity measurements to be reconstructed as an image. This is the case of laser scanning (3D-scanners) or the different modalities of geoelectric/georadar/geomagnetic surveying.
- When remote sensing data are images or part of an image (satellite imaging or aerial pictures)

In the first case, artificial neural networks have been successfully applied to a number of geophysical modeling problems, including parameter prediction and estimation, classification, filtering and optimization (Al-Nuamy et al., 2000; Baan & Jutten, 2000; Calderón-Macías et al., 2000; Poulton et al., 1992). In archaeological geophysical surveying, neural networks can be used to interpolate the possible nonlinear spatial trend among magnetic differential measurements obtained in an archaeological geophysical survey and derive estimates of feature burial depths, allowing a three-dimensional reconstruction of buried subsurface remains to be made. The neural network approach potentially offers several advantages in terms of efficiency and flexibility over more conventional data interpolation techniques. An example has been published by Bescoby et al. (2006), who demonstrate how feed-forward neural networks can lead to an enhanced interpretation of magnetic survey data, allowing the combination with other geoarchaeological data to provide a clearer picture of settlement evolution within the context of landscape change. The aim of this research is to model the depth and shape of source anomalies from the magnetic measurements, providing an enhanced interpretation of the data through a subsurface reconstruction of archaeo-

logical features. The determination of a final shape model for the given set of magnetic measurements is here achieved by utilizing a simple multi-layer neural network to learn the nonlinear mapping between measured data and sub-surface shape model parameters. Suitable training data were derived from a range of synthetic models of buried wall foundations of a variety of types and burial depths and the corresponding magnetic responses produced via forward modeling. The synthetic models were based upon known archaeological examples recorded in a number of trial excavations conducted within the study area, in which surviving wall foundations were found to be the dominant feature of interest. Remotely sensed data was input into the network as a vector of magnetic field values, representing an effective 2 x 2 meters area above the buried walls. The corresponding target data consisted of a single value representing the depth below the surface to the estimated wall features, falling at the centre of the input magnetic field values. Subsequent training pairs were derived by moving the 2 x 2 meter input window sequentially over the modeled area.

In the second category of remote sensing data, the input is not an array of sensor measurements, but an aerial or a satellite image. Many relevant neural network models of remotely sensed image interpretation and analysis have been recently published (see among other Civco, 1993; Foody et al., 1995; Gong et al., 1996; Heermann & Khazenie, 1992; Lee & Lothrop, 2006; Paola & Schowengerdt, 1995; Wilkinson, 1997; Yoshida & Omatu, 1994).

Remotely sensed images are digital pictures composed of pixels showing grey-level values. In many satellite or remote sensing cases, such values are the intensities of specific spectra of electromagnetic radiation of either form of reflection or emission. Because different types of objects have different physical nature in terms of the reflection, absorption, and emission, these values of two or more layers are used to categorize the pixels into several groups. The idea is then to distinguish between the various categories of spatial features of interest to archaeologists. It can be a difficult task because archaeological features comprise a complex spatial assemblage of disparate land cover types—including built and/or linear structures, numerous vegetation types, bare soil and water bodies—each of which has different reflectance characteristics. Conventional image classification techniques assume that all the pixels within the image are pure, that is that they represent an area of homogenous cover of a single land cover class. This assumption is usually untenable with pixels of mixed land-cover composition.

By using neural network approaches, the idea is to use image data (brightness, greenness, wetness, and ratio indexes) and geographical information (forest, grass, water, archaeological elements, etc.) to train an input-output nonlinear relationship model. The resulting network can be exported and used for new satellite images, were map data have not been interpreted, and these geographical values may be predicted. The input data typically comprises a set of multi-spectral data, although it may also include measures of image texture or ancillary data. Supplemental information such as soils or elevation attributes, and even non-numerical data such as ground cover classes or soil types that might assist the classification, can be easily integrated. In the output layer, there is one unit for each class in the classification.

Neural network analysis of remotely sensed imagery involves either supervised or unsupervised classification. Unsupervised classification of imagery involves the analysis of color or black and white pixels of the image for the purposes of classifying image objects and entities, where tone, texture, and hue are used. Supervised classification is employed to tell whether a candidate image pixel is really an archaeological element or not by its spectral characteristics. This technique involves referencing the pixels to actual observed conditions in the ground. All supervised classifiers share a common objective, to allocate each case of unknown spatial class membership to a pre-defined class based on its spectral properties. The program should select groups of pixels representative of the spatial ground information of interest, extract the appropriate spectral reflectance parameters for those training areas, and use them to classify the entire image. The idea is to know where archaeological sites or any other spatial features are to be found in the satellite imagery, based on decision rules generalized from the mapping between a subset of known ground locations and the spectral properties of remotely sensed images. In addition to the spectral information, the spatial information of landscape can be integrated through a neural network classifier to provide improved classification accuracy over that obtained with spectral data alone.

Kim and Nevatia (2004) have published an interesting application. Although it is not an archaeological example, it deals with a relatively similar problematic: recognition of complex buildings from multiple images and range data (DEM—digital elevation models). This procedure can be applied to any archaeological remote sensing case, or even, to any essay of recognizing of interesting shape and texture features within an image. The authors present an approach for detecting and describing complex buildings with flat or complex rooftops by using multiple, overlapping images of the scene. The input consists of low-quality images. The system finds 3D rooftop boundary hypotheses from the line and junction features of the images by applying consecutive grouping procedures. It applies an hypothesize-and-verify paradigm, where lower-level features are grouped (hypothesized) into higher level ones, then filtered (verified) for the purpose of minimizing the computation (otherwise, the computation will be exponential). Usually, the DEM data are generated by stereo matching of the images, and used as auxiliary information to provide cues that help reduce the search spaces and validate feature matches.

In the case of un-supervised neural networks, the self-organized output layer is a matrix of cells or nodes that captures the topological relationships of the input data. In so doing, spectral classes that are adjacent in the input space are mapped as adjacent nodes in the SOM layer, in effect creating a Voronoi tessellation of cells (Baraldi & Parmiggiani, 1995; Martínez et al., 2001; Oka et al., 2000; Villmann, 1999).

As an example of unsupervised neural networks used to analyze archaeological remotely sensed images, we can mention the work by Cantero et al. (2005). The aim of this study is to self-organize a series of airborne photographs to detect automatically roads and buildings in an archaeological site formed by the remains of a Roman town founded during the era of Emperor Augustus in southwestern Spain. The main aim of this study was to cluster similar pixels in original airborne images taken in year 1956 in order to classify them in terms of three important areas in the archaeological site.

Of course, unsupervised results are not meaningful in themselves. They are just a cluster of similar pixels. Although a human expert might interpret the neural network results, these outputs can reveal hidden information, detect slopes and classify the color intensity with a better precision than human eye, together with the possibility of creating classes and arranging the information depending on the number of output neurons. The SOM network can be seen then as a mechanism to produce the input for a subsequent supervised learning study.

NEUROCOMPUTATIONAL SPATIAL MODELS IN ARCHAEOLOGY AND THE SPATIAL SCIENCES

If there is some evidence of a relationship between a location in the physical space and some action that was there performed, then we can program a robot to learn it. Even if the relationship changes over space, that can also be learned if it is encoded in the spatial examples presented.

The necessary neurocomputational model is formally very similar to the spatial interpolator presented in previous pages. The only differences concern the nature of variables and of the training set. In the interpolation problem the purpose was to estimate the probability of a spatial generalization based on known locations. Now we need to calculate a function able to estimate the occurrence of historical events at unknown locations, based on the evidence of related events at the same or neighbor locations.

Neural networks are being used for this kind of spatial modeling applications in domains like ecology (Aitkenhead et al., 2004; Gong et al., 1996; Hilbert & Ostendorf, 2001; Lek et al., 1996; Özesmi & Özesmi, 1999; Özesmi et al., 2006; Yang, 2005) and geography (German et al., 1997; Merwin et al., 2002; Openshaw, 1994; Rigol et al., 2001; Zhou & Civco, 1996). In such examples, a neural network is trained on sets of dependent variables (outputs) measured at known spatial locations (inputs) to generalize how such ecological or social aspects are spatially related. Ecological applications showed that neurocomputation was a viable technique and had advantages over linear models. Examples are very diverse, from the classification of soil structure based on soil sample data to the prediction of changes in the dominant species of grassland communities based on climatic input variables. Neural networks have been used to predict the presence, absence, or abundance of some species based on habitat variables.

Let us see a geographical example, which can be easily applied to the archaeological domain. More archaeological examples will be presented later in this chapter. We can begin with the following general case, adapted from an ecological study presented in Ripley (1993, p. 89-91, see also Mahiny & Turner, 2003). The goal is to know the cause of the geographical distribution of particular vegetation types of some geographical features.

Input neurons contain the predictor variables (hypothetical causal factors): latitude, longitude, month at which the observation was made, elevation, annual evaporation, annual rainfall, maximum of monthly mean temperature maxima, maximum of monthly mean temperature, average temperature over year, slope, aspect, topographic features, geology. Using a finite set of actual observations—the training set—the purpose is to generalize a vegetation index (Normalized Difference Index, NDI, very usual in satellite imaging) to estimate its most probable value at some precise locations of the space-time.

Spitz and Lek (1999) have analyzed the relationship between hunting and agriculture in the modern world. In their model, environmental characteristics appear in the input (elevation, topography, orientation, proximity to water source, proximity to a road, distance to the nearest inhabited place, number of inhabitants within a radius of 500 m., etc.). These spatial variables are used to understand the relationship between changing conditions in habitat and the decrease of wild animal in ecologically damaged areas. This is a classical feed-forward network, with one hidden layer, and just one output unit, trained using the backpropagation learning algorithm.

Brown and Chang (2001) also offer an ecological application of a feed forward neural network that can be easily understood by archaeologists. In this application, the output to be predicted is the spatial abundance of some feature (in their case of a grass kind), and the input is a series of independent spatial and environmental variables like:

Latitude (in UTM)
Longitude (in UTM)
Annual water balance
Annual days above 90° F
Percent of the geographical area stable uplands
   with soils of coarse texture
Percent of the geographical area stable uplands
   with soils of fine texture

Percent of the geographical area stable uplands
   with soils of medium texture
Distance to centers of probable grass origin (Major
   genetic diversity):
Southwestern Wyoming
Southwestern New Mexico
East Texas coast

The neural network allowed understanding how each spatial feature influenced on the dependent variable. In this case, latitude alone affected poorly. The climatic determinism variables performed much better, but the estimation was at times ambiguous, leading to examination of false patterns, and learning had to start over. Edaphic factors provided very good and consistent results. Location, either absolute or relative to competing dispersal resources, provided the best estimates. That fact suggests that the pattern of western wheatgrass is one of invasion and not in equilibrium with the present day climate. The combination of both the relative location and soils provided the greatest understanding by the artificial neural network. In every case where the climatic data were added, the artificial neural network found that the signal extracted was ambiguous relative to the grass pattern.

As an example of an explicitly "causal" spatial model, we can mention the investigation by Stassopoulou and Petrou (1998). The application they consider is that of assessing the degree of risk of desertification (output) of burned forest areas in the Mediterranean region, given some information (input) on the factors that influence desertification. The degree of land degradation (desertification) varies between different areas and depends on rock type (permeable, semi-permeable, impermeable), ground slope (gentle, middle, steep), soil depth (bare, shallow, deep), ground aspect (south, west/east, north), animal grazing (slightly, moderately, heavily grazed), risk of erosion (low, medium, high), regeneration potential (low, medium, high). The authors have created a Bayesian network for taking into consideration these factors in order to assess the risk of desertification of a burned forest. As we saw in Chapter III, a Bayesian network links should be quantified by conditional probability matrices, which derive from available evidence. The authors have used a neural network approach to calculate such conditional probabilities, and transforming the spatial input-ecological output relationship into a causal model. Here information regarding location has not been integrated as factors of the model, but just as a way to organize the training set, that is, different places have been observed, in which the there was enough evidence the factors had some contribution into the observed output. It is interesting to see how an interpretive spatial model can be formulated without strict location information, just with the qualitative information available for each observed location.

Self-organized maps (SOM) have also been used for spatial modeling in ecological studies designed to investigate the spatial distribution of animal of vegetal species. When using presence–absence data of species distributions at given locations, the input vectors to a SOM are binary, and the connection weights after learning are between 0 and 1. Using fuzzy set theory, Gevrey et al. (2006) present an approach to the interpretation of these weights. Taking an example from invasive species research, they show that in the case of presence/absence data, a connection weight can be interpreted as the probability that an event will occur at a given location. A SOM was used to model the species distribution, to determine geographic patterns and define the species correlations.

Those examples can help us to understand the proper nature of archaeological spatial modeling. The aim for our research should be that of estimating the probability of archaeological site presence as a function of other attributes, both geographical (including elevation, slope, vegetation, water resources, soil properties) or properly speaking "historical" (presence of other human populations, political borders, spatial social interaction, transportation networks, etc.). Traditionally, such problems have been solved using standard statistical techniques (Leusen, 2002; Beekman & Baden, 2005; Mehrer & Wescott, 2005; Wescott & Brandon, 1999; Zubrow & Robinson 2000). When data are very disperse and the spatial processes to be modeled are nonlinear and non-parametric, neural networks seem to be a better approach.

Let us review some examples of neurocomputational spatial models in archaeology. The simplest approach is the classification of archaeological sites to use the resulting classification rules as a basis for understanding why human settlements in some area are similar. Reeler (1999) reports on the application of a neural network/fuzzy logic hybrid system to spatial and other excavation data from Maori *pa* sites in New Zealand. The *pa* sites are defended sites, often situated on raised, easily defensible landforms where the natural defenses provided by the landscape were enhanced by the addition of artificial earthwork defenses. These sites were constructed primarily during the period from about 1500 A.D. to the early 1800s. In the early 1800s the European colonization of New Zealand and the increasing availability of firearms led to a change in site form and by the start of the 20th century, *pa* sites were no longer constructed. Twenty variables were defined describing each site, based on data collected from the excavation reports and digitized maps of the sites. Some of these variables included data provided by the GIS used in the project, such as total site area and area of features, area of defenses and topographic type. Neural networks were trained using a classification of those sites into similarity classes. The analysis of associations made by the neural networks suggested ways in which sites might be grouped into analytical units based on the interplay of a number of different variables. These variables suggest important patterns within the variables extracted from the sites. Several of the influential variables suggest the choices made by the prehistoric people who built the sites.

Ramazzotti (1999a, 1999b) analyzed the storical process on the territory of ancient Uruk using neural networks. A great number of surveyed Mesopotamian sites were described using chronological, culture-history, area and territorial variables. Eight historical periods were considered as output variables. The aim of the investigation was to discover the spatial and cultural features of sites belonging to each historical period. In this way, the main aspects of the historical process could be discovered and evaluating how the territory and the morphology of towns and villages changed throughout the social and economical transformations that let to state formation.

Ducke (2003) suggests the use of feed forward neural networks as a statistical system that maps geographic locations to archaeological site probabilities. His idea is to look for the way environmental and geographical features of archaeological sites (terrain geometry, height, slope and aspect angle, distance from surface water, ground water level, soil texture, and soil quality) can be correlated to the frequency of sites in different environmental feature sets to gain an estimation of archaeological potential for a specific landscape. Ducke compared standard clustering analysis, where locations were grouped (clustered) into patches of similar environments according to their attributes. In this way, each group (cluster) represents a particular type of environment. After analyzing the distribution of archaeological sites over these environment types, an estimation of archaeological potential could be gained for the rest of the area. The network consists of an input layer with predictor variables (location attributes), and an output layer with just two units. Training data corresponds to some survey projects in the state of Brandenburg in northeastern Germany. These correspond to the two possible cases "site present" and "no site present." In the published reports of this project, Ducke shows that the system was able to achieve a rough classification of archaeological sites based on locational attributes.

The overall picture gained from the output was rather "noisy." In addition, limiting the predictive model to just two output cases might not be what one expects of a useful model. Site absence is seldom recorded systematically and being sure about a site's absence is even more problematic that being sure about a site's presence.

Most of the above examples seem to be based on the traditional conception that defend the axiom that *physical space* determines *human settlement*, that is, that the location of social action is a consequence of the environmental features or spatial properties of natural resources. This can be useful in some cases but it is a too trivial explanation. Instead, we should base our analysis on the assumption that productive actions (hunting, fishing, gathering, herding, agriculture, etc.) determine the location of residential actions (settlement). We need descriptions of historical events at known locations, to estimate how the spatial location of some action or event influences (or influenced) the location of another action or event. That is to say, social actions are not *adapted* to the environment, but productive actions (hunting, fishing, and gathering) determine the location of residential actions (settlement).

For instance, let us consider the relationship between geographical distance, transport time and degree of technological complexity (input variables), and the spatial probabilities of being located at a specific place. To calculate this nonlinear relationship, the automated archaeologist would need archaeological data that relate the three variables. In the case of a supervised model, the quantity of non-local materials in a site S_0 with a known provenience from site S_1 will serve as an estimation of the probability of interaction between both. In the unsupervised case, an automated archaeologist would use the same number of output neurons as settlements in the training set. The purpose of a self-organized map would be to transform similarities in distance, transportation possibilities, and degree of technological complexity into an estimation of spatial probabilities given in terms of the activation signal of output neurons at different neighborhoods.

Consider an attempt to identify optimum locations for a hillfort. Factors considered in the analysis might include distance from centers of population, distance from the road network, the suitability of underlying geology, and so forth. There are also some further social, economical, cultural, and political constraints, which differentiates this problem from a simple site selection problem. For instance, it might be that no hillfort is within some pre-determined distance of any other hillfort site, nor it is too far from others and from populated areas. These non-environmental constraints increase the complexity of the analysis, since the value of a particular site can only be evaluated when considered with combinations of other selected sites. This type of problem is known as a combinational optimization problem since the number of combinations that must be considered increases dramatically with the number of sites to be located. Many "real world" spatial analysis problems are of this type. Not surprising that suitable functionality is not available within current GIS.

There are many examples of using neural networks to quantify spatial relationships that are important to explain the occurrence of social action at different places. For instance, White (1989) considered the placement of economic institutions as dependent from the population at each place, the distance among areas, and the pattern of connectivity (transportation) between such areas. Nijkmap and Reggiani (1998) consider different examples where transportation networks influence the placement of different social institutions. Shellito and Pijanowski (2003) use as location predictions different measures of "distance from." In this case, the output contains the location of the place to be predicted (in two coordinates, x and y, or *longitude, latitude*). The network has in the input different variables (neurons) that contain the known values of the distance from

cities with populations of less than 500 persons, more than 100,000 persons, local roads, places with special interest, and so forth. Once learned the relationship between spatial features and the geographical location of the city, such a network can be used to experiment with the influence of each spatial feature on the already known locations, or alternatively, to predict the location of unknown sites, based on simulated values in the input neurons.

There are some examples of this kind of explanatory spatial models in archaeology. We can quote the interesting study by Zupanek and Mlekuz (2001) who intend to understand the causes and consequences of social variability between two Roman cities: Emona and Poetovio in modern day Slovenia. They have approached social variation through a comparison of the religious backgrounds of both towns. Available data are in form of dedicatory inscriptions. Several attributes were recorded for each monument: name of the deity, social class of the dedicator, date, and original location of the monument, and so forth. Two samples have been used: 77 inscriptions from Poetovio and only 23 from Emona. Percentage and numerical diagrams of deities from both towns show considerable differences between the Emona and Poetovio. For neurocomputing, each town, social class (citizen, soldier, and slave) and date (1st century, 2nd century, 3rd century) was used as input variables. The class of deity was the resulting output unit; deities were classified according to their respective origins and/or functions into the following groups: Roman, Eastern, and Local deities. Known cases (based on the inscription contents) were then presented to the neural network. Results show that in the Emona sample citizens in the first century had equal preference for local and Roman deities, while in the second century Roman deities were by far preferred. By the 3rd century, the scarce data indicate the growing popularity of the local deities. As for slaves, chiefly Roman deities are preferred in Emona during the first two centuries, whereas an increase of local deities is detectable in the third century. The citizens of Poeotvio held Roman deities ion the highest esteem in the second century, with local and eastern deities coming in second place. In the third century, Eastern deities are first in line with local following and Roman far behind. The ratio of local deities worshipped by the slave class in Poetovio is similar during both the second and third centuries. The ratio of eastern deities then rises in the third century, and the Roman ones declines. Therefore, the religious backgrounds of both towns differ significantly, and researchers are tempted to interpret the difference in the sample sizes as a reflection of different populations in both towns. However, it could also be the result of varying religious habits in the local population, or simply a consequence of different economic backgrounds.

Deravignone is trying to build a neurocomputational spatial model of medieval settlement in Central Italy (Deravignone, 2006). In this project, a neural network calculates a nonlinear function between historical and archaeological data of ancient castles and hillforts in medieval Tuscany and their spatial location. Point coordinates are used as input, whereas the output adopts the aspect of raster map. In this way, specific points of a territory (input) are being related to thematic maps containing geomorphological and environmental data. The spatial contexts of castles and hillforts documented in historical sources or through archaeological excavations are then used as training data. To use the neural network means to introduce the coordinates of some place in the input, and obtaining as a result an interpretation of social actions or natural process that took place at that location.

Recurrent networks are also an interesting method for spatial explanation. Let us consider the following simulated archaeological problem (adapted from Murnion, 1996). Suppose that the spatial frequencies of archaeological traces allow an estimation of the number of people having worked at specific locations of a surveyed area.

We have some population estimates, measured in a 10 x 10 grid, where each cell has three km of side. We want to study the potential locations of residential units within such an area. We have some prior knowledge about social dynamics at that territory:

1. No social agent will walk more than one grid from a residential point to working area (location of subsistence resources), so the demographic base of a settlement shall include the grid square of that settlement and the surrounding eight squares.

2. Social agents will always go use the nearest settlement to their resource catchments area.

3. If N possible settlement locations are equally distant from a grid square then the number of social agents going to each settlement will be the population of the grid square divided by N.

A Hopfield network can be used to solve this recursive problem (see Chapter IV), where each cell in the 10 x 10 grid is a neuron. When the network has stabilized to a solution, neurons that are "on" are considered appropriate locations for optimum settlements. The higher the spatial frequency of archaeological evidence at a site, the more likely that site is to switch "on." The network cycles through various states until a static or dynamic equilibrium is reached. In the equilibrium state, the spatial frequencies of the sites switched "on" will be sufficient to counteract the negative first term of the motion equation. However, in this case, the automated archaeologist is only interested in the optimum locations for human settlement. In order to achieve this, the probability of i activation is increased with each iteration. Eventually only the optimum sites will remain switched on. Since there are so many locations competing for the proper placement of the settlement, the catchment area of each site will be small. Since large numbers of sites are "on" and catchment areas are small, many sites switch "off." In the next iteration, there are few sites, so catchment areas are large and many sites switch "on." The network oscillates repeatedly between many-sites/few-sites states.

If prehistoric people living in that area decided to place two new settlements such that the demographic base of the two sites in total is maximized, then the problem becomes non-trivial. In general, for a twin site selection in a grid of N sites there will be $N (N - 1)$ possible ways to place the two settlements. Using common sense, the number of possible choices can be reduced, for example the optimum locations for the two sites is unlikely to involve the four corner sites in the 10x10 grid (0,0), (0,9), (9,0) and (9,9). In a more complicated problem, this sort of reduction may not be possible and the automated archaeologist may well have to resort to the "brute force" method of processing every possible combination. An alternative sub-optimum method would be to choose the best site for the first settlement and then having fixed the position of the first one, choose the best site from the remaining sites for the second settlement. This method is much faster but is not guaranteed to arrive at an optimum solution.

The reader may think that in archaeology we do not have enough "explanatory" variables, or the necessary training cases to go beyond a mere spatial description of archaeological evidence. Let us consider an example that shows how more explanatory social investigations can be made possible. It is an investigation of the origins of the city in the Etrurian area of Central Italy between 11th and 6th centuries BC (Barceló, Pelfer & Mandolesi, 2001). Research goals are:

- The archaeological correlates for *generators* of capital accumulation, and
- The archaeological correlates for *restraints* on capital accumulation.

Such correlates can be calculated by measuring qualitatively the presence/absence of social actions (settlement, resources acquisition, labor action, distributive/exchange activities, ritual action). Among others, observational inputs would be:

- Presence/absence of colonial import goods
- Presence/absence of indigenous import goods (pottery, metal)
- Presence/absence of locally produced valuable pottery
- Presence/absence of weapons
- Presence/absence of metallurgical activities
- Presence/absence of store buildings and structures
- Presence/absence rich burials
- Presence/absence of complex residential structures (multi-room houses)
- Presence/absence of subsistence activities (farming, husbandry, etc.)

The attraction force exerted by a city core area is directly proportional to the number or intensity of interactions between periphery locations and the center and the squared distance between both entities, and inversely proportional to the attraction force exerted by alternative periphery locations. Local factors may be understood in terms of locally accumulated mobile capital (for instance, quantity of colonial imported goods, presence/absence of metallurgical luxury objects). To represent the process of capital accumulation at the city, we need to estimate the volume of wealth accumulated directly proportional to the level of dominance or power of the city over the surrounding rural area, plus the frictional effects due to the cost of coercion, and inversely proportional to the total amount of capital accumulated at the periphery. The more productive is a location, and the more independent are their local elites, the most difficult is to ensure dominance and capital transfers from periphery to core areas. Consequently, among the possible outputs or dependent spatial variables, we can mention:

- *SPATIAL DENSITY OR SETTLEMENT CONCENTRATION*. It can be empirically measured in terms of a spatial probability density measure associated to each location, based on the geographical proximity with neighboring locations. Concentration maps, however, can be misleading. The causal mechanism of urban emergence is not physical proximity, nor spatial density. The real cause should be explained in terms of the "influence" capital accumulated at a location has over the residence or productive actions performed at other locations in the proximity.

- *GLOBAL INTERACTION*. If settlement concentration is a relevant variable, then *distance* is one of the main dynamic factors determining the process of city formation. Spatial Interaction is related to distance, in such a way that the less distance between social agents, the higher the probabilities of social interaction. The definition of such *distances* is very complex:

  o Distance produced by the diversity of resources at different locations
  o Distance produced by the diversity of production activities at different locations
  o Distance produced by the differences in the volume of produced goods at different locations
  o Distance produced by the diversity of non productive activities—consumption—at different locations
  o Distance produced by the differences in the volume of non productive activities—consumption—at different locations
  o Distance produced by the differences of the nature of social agents at different locations
  o Distance produced by the differences and diversity of social interactions between different locations

- *DOMINANCE AND COERCION*. The automated archaeologist also needs to estimate the inequality and directionality of interaction flows. In other words, it has to integrate into the model the hierarchy between social cores and peripheries, that is to say, the differentiation between the emergent urban core and the exploited rural periphery, for instance. This allows understanding capital accumulated in the center *as a function of* capital extracted from the periphery. Therefore, if power and dominance may be analyzed in terms of spatial attraction, then the inequality of interaction from core to periphery is directly proportional to capital generated in both points, and inversely proportional to the cost of coercion and domination. The neural network model can explains this nonlinear function.

More details about spatial modeling in the social domain are discussed on Chapter IX.

THE ANALYSIS OF TEMPORAL SERIES AND CHRONOLOGICAL DATA

Unlike object recognition and spatial analysis, where all observable features are simultaneously present in the input, there are a number of tasks, notably in historical research, where the observations to be explained consist of a sequence of individual features arranged over a limited period of time (Bairaktaris, 1995). Such data configure time series, mathematically described as:

$$Y = f(t), \text{ where } t = t_0, t_1, t_2, ..., t_N$$

What has to be analyzed is how the dependent variable (Y) depends on time. That means that to process temporal data, the principle is to associate a previous state with some external input and to learn how a subsequent state is produced:

Old State and New Pattern → New State

Every spatiotemporal system can be defined by two components: one that computes the new internal state of the system based on the input and previous state, and one that computes the output of the system based on the new state (Kremer, 2001). Therefore, the temporal problem the automated archaeologist wants to solve refers to the relationship that may exist between the past and the future state of a single process. In the case of heterogeneous, multivariate, time varying processes, the task is to discover dependency patterns, and their changes. Dependency patterns are combinations of past lagged values of a set of time series, which when used as arguments of a suitable prediction function, produce high values of a chosen model quality measure.

The evolution through a sequence of changes of state, where stable states of different natures are separated by the corresponding transient states, is a situation typical in most complex systems, including human societies. Historical events refer to the behavior of social agents under certain spatiotemporal states. A sequence of historical events s can be expressed as a tri-tuple (s, t_s, t_e). The set $s = \{(A_1, t_1), (A_2, t_2) \dots (A_n, t_n)\}$, is an ordered events set. The variable A_i ($i = 1, 2, \dots n$) represents the event, and its attributes <*attribute* i_1, *attribute* i_2,... *attribute* i_m>; t_s and t_e represent starting and ending time; t_i is the occurring time of an event, $t_s \leq t_i < t_e < t_i < t_i + 1$ ($i = 1, 2, \dots n-1$). The temporal distribution of those events is intimately controlled by local circumstantial and contextual characteristics. At different time, the change of the context will lead to some phenomena happening at same place or at different places. In order to find the main factors explaining the actual occurrence of a specific event and the association relationship among these local and circumstantial factors, we need to build a decision table (in the format of transactional records) (Zhai et al., 2005). According to prior knowledge, we assume that the behavior of the social actor is affected by factors $f_1, f_2, \dots f_n$, at different time t_1, $t_2, \dots t_n$. The long-term behavior of these actors can be regarded as a sequence of historical events and form a decision table including values of the attribute and states.

There are various ways to model this relationship. One can make a recursive prescription for extrapolating the most recent data points based on the success of previous extrapolations. One can also parameterize the time dependences of the various statistical moments and time derivatives of the time series of interest. Alternatively, one can try to find a single function that gives a future value of the observable as its output when some set of past observables is supplied as its input. This last model can be implemented using a neural network (Vemuri & Rogers, 1994).

To fit a mathematical function that closely resembles the temporal variation of the dependent variable values, an automated archaeologist should interpolate the observed longitudinal variation. In this sense, the temporal problem is identical to the spatial problem. Traditionally, archaeologists have relied on linear interpolation, based mainly on looking at frequency trends, moving averages, and certain graphical patterns, for performing predictions and subsequently understanding the temporal dynamics of the process. Most of these linear approaches have shortcomings. It is easy to see that temporal analysis should not be limited to fitting a regression line between the dependent variable values estimated at different time intervals. Input data should represent a statistical population, and each event is a temporal sample produced by a stochastic process. In the same way as we considered in the spatial case, a temporal analysis pretends to build a model of the stochastic process that produced the observed series. Following Wold's theorem, this process may be represented by the following expression:

DATA = DETERMINISTIC COMP. + STOCHASTIC COMP. + RANDOM COMP.

The theorem states that a temporal process may be modeled as the sum of two independent processes: the first is *deterministic* and the other is characteristically *non-deterministic* (also called *stochastic* or *probabilistic*). The objective of the analysis will be to decompose the series variance in deterministic components and stochastic ones. The deterministic component reflects consistent effects through time, and it includes other kinds of systematic variation:

- SECULAR VARIATION or *trend*, which represents the general orientation followed by the series of samples through time.
- SEASONAL VARIATION *or cycles*, which represents fluctuations of trend at periodic intervals.

The stochastic component usually reflects the effects of *serial* dependency: the degree of dependence between contiguous points in a sequence. In a time series, however the value of a variable in a specific time point can be independent of the values this variable has had before or will have thereafter (Badran & Thiria 1997; McDowell et al., 1980).

There is nearly always some degree of deterministic trend in any temporal sequence of values. Archaeological cases are not an exception, but we cannot observe them, because such a temporal trend is hidden by sampling differences in the data. The purpose of temporal analysis will be, then to *extract* this deterministic component, as if *sampling* differences and error introduced by the way an archaeological variable has been measured at different time steps may be deleted.

The goal of such a temporal interpolation is to separate the data into a smooth component and a rough component:

DATA = SMOOTH + ROUGH

The *rough* should contain as little structure as possible. In our case, the percentage of total variance explained by the rough component is greater that the percentage explained by the smooth component, but the latter is a real model of deterministic temporal variation in the stratigraphic order. Its relevance as a source of variation was originally greater, but it has been reduced because we are not analyzing the material effects of social action as they were generated, but probably unrelated archaeological samples ordered stratigraphicaly.

Neural networks can be used for such fitting a temporal function not based on global trends but on information available at each discrete time moment. In fact, one of their main characteristics is that they are usually trained and tested over historical data. The networks generating the most accurate predictions are saved, modified, and retested over additional historical data until the most efficient model with respect to accuracy of predictions is obtained (Badran & Thiria, 1997; Berardi & Zhang, 2003; Castillo & Melin, 2002; Cawley et al., 2007; Chakraborty et al., 1992; Elsner, 1992; Sumpter & Bulpitt, 1998; Sharda & Patil, 1992; Tang et al., 1991; Vemuri & Rogers, 1994; Weigend et al., 1990).

Under ideal conditions, there is little difference in predictability efficiency between regression models, for instance, and neural networks. However, under less than ideal conditions (in the presence of an outlier, or in the presence of multicollinearity or model misspecifications), the neural network do a better job (Denton, 1995). The main advantage of neural networks as nonlinear interpolators is that we do not need to specify the structure of a model *a priori*, which is clearly needed in the linear interpolation. In addition, nonlinear techniques can approximate more easily complex dynamical systems, than simple statistical models. Of course, there are also disadvantages in using these models instead of the more classical ones. In classical regression, we can use the information given by the parameters to understand the process, that is, the coefficients of the model can represent the causal influence of some event in transforming a historical trajectory. This is not so easy in the case of a nonlinear, adaptive and recursive model, because the model appears some times as black box, with too many parameters of very difficult interpretation.

For the purposes of time series analysis, a neural network can be thought of as a general nonlinear mapping between some subset of the past time series values and a future time series value. The specific mapping performed by the network depends on the architecture of the network (number of neurons, number of hidden layers, and the manner in which neurons are connected, and so on) and the values of the connection weights between neurons. For specific network architecture, training can be thought of as the process of adjusting the weight parameters to achieve a mapping that approximates the underlying relationship between past and future values. The time delay can be understood as output error: the averaged sum of the differences between the network outputs and the actual time series values they are supposed to predict. Training a neural network can be viewed as an optimization problem: the minimization of the time delay with respect to the weights (Badran & Thiria, 1997; Vemuri & Rogers, 1994; Weigend et al., 1990).

When the idea is that of approximating a temporal function by means of a multilayer feedforward neural network, the output neuron of the network may indicate the value of a variable to be predicted at time *t+1* or at time *t-1*, while the inputs of the network are values of that variable at times < *t*. The network should provide directly the estimation of the time series at instant k_{h+1} from the information at instant k_{+1}. That means that the network uses a sequence of numbers to infer the next row of numbers in line. It uses historical data from a definite interval of time to calculate future or past possibilities beyond the interval used for training.

The additional advantage of a neural network is the possibility of testing the interpolated temporal function. To test for short-term accuracy, the network should be given actual time series values from the test data set as the input and the resulting output is compared with the next time series point. This is done for every point in the test data set, and an error statistic is calculated. The ability of the network to learn longer-term temporal dynamics can also be tested. To do this, the network is given an input vector from near the beginning of the test data set. The output of the network, which is the predicted future value, is then used as part of the next input vector. The ouput from the second interval is likewise used as part of the third input vector. Continuing the process in this way, the network recursively propagates the time series forward in time to test the validity of the learned function many time steps ahead. The divergence of the prediction from the actual time series as a function of the number of time steps indicates how far into the future the network predictions can be used. Often the short and long-term prediction properties of neural networks are very different, so this is a useful test to perform before making predictions longer than one time step into the future (Vemuri & Rogers, 1994).

These ideas have been organized by Peter Halls (Halls & Miller, 1996; Halls et al., 1999). He and his colleagues proposed to describe the rate and direction of temporal variance, in terms of a time curve (or "worm") linking each observation (or "tode") to its temporal neighbors. This time curve is controlled by the measured, or acceptable, rate of change. It allows predicting the nature of intermediate unmeasured locations from the recorded data. It would also be possible to investigate the effects of changes to rates, confidence factors, and so forth, upon the relative 'fit' of the curve and so further assess the accuracy of observations. A curve fitting technique based on neural networks was proposed by the authors to generate curves based upon a number of temporal nodes, or todes, plus associated information on their relative precision and the effect this should have upon constraining the curve-fitting algorithm.

A classical example of time analysis suitable for an archaeological application is the kind of study usually carried out in the geosciences, where some variable with paleoecological or paleo-environmental interest varies temporally across stratigraphy (Iloghalu, 2003; Martínez et al., 2004; Valdes & Bonham-Carter, 2006). This kind of problem has been analyzed in archaeological literature as "assemblage diversity through time" or "frequency seriation" (Barceló & Mameli, 2004; Baxter, 2001, 2003; Djindjian, 1990; Lyman & O'Brien, 1999; 2003, 2006).

Kroeber used frequency seriation for the first time in 1916 to measure the passage of time. It has been traditionally defined as a relative dating method, which relies principally on measuring changes in the proportional abundances measured among finds. Archaeological formation processes had been described in terms of *accumulation,* what led to general principles like *Nelson's law* (1909): there is a direct relationship among the population size at a site, the site occupation span, and the amount of material discarded by its inhabitants. In such a way, the changing frequency of archaeological materials along stratigraphic order measures time effects. In its simplest form, this approach implies a longitudinal record of depositional events as a mark of time.

Assuming that artifacts' characteristics follow a bell curve, archaeologically observed frequency values start slowly growing to a peak and then dying away as other characteristics become more frequent. This also assumes that descriptive features will be broadly similar from assemblage to assemblage within the same time span. Following these rules, an assemblage of objects can be placed onto sequence so that sets with the most similar proportions of certain characteristics are always together.

The idea is then that of converting a longitudinal record of hypothetically consecutive archaeological accumulations into a coherent temporal trajectory, or site formation process. It must be assumed that the frequency and diversity of items within an assemblage vary according to the process responsible for the accumulation. Other necessary assumptions are:

- Garbage disposal is a random accumulation around the residential and/or domestic unit,
- The nature of the accumulation does not change for all the history of the site,
- The amount of residues accumulated in a single event depends on the number of people generating garbage, the time during which they have been producing garbage, and the social way of disposing garbage (Varien & Mills, 1997, p. 143).

The frequency of archaeological observables and their diversity are also affected by element use-life through time. Schiffer (1987) labels the problem as the "Clarke effect" to describe "the statistical tendency for the variety of discarded artifacts to increase directly with a settlement's occupation span." This principle indicates that previous assumptions are over specific, and that real archaeological data do not follow them. Artifact use-life, differential temporal duration and the different nature of accumulations within the same site formation process can: (1) produce variation in assemblage composition that might be erroneously attributed to different activities, (2) affect seriations in non-chronological ways, and (3) cause archaeological frequencies to differ from systemic frequencies.

To address the problem posed by the Clarke effect, the automated archaeologist has to examine some determinants of differential temporal duration. It will regard archaeological assemblages as the interaction of temporal duration and stratigraphic order. An alternative would be to assume some characteristic or set of characteristics associated with the assemblage that produced the apparent accumulative effect. The problem then becomes one of identifying the appropriate characteristic or set of characteristics of the accumulation, what is a theoretical, rather than a methodological problem.

ASSEMBLAGE= PERIOD (stratigraphic order) – DURATION

Furthermore, the accumulation of archaeological items in observed depositional events not always is the result of purposeful human activity. The archaeological record may be patterned, but it does not follow that the patterning of the items and the patterning of the human behavior that produced it are identical. An aggregation may not reflect past human social action nor its temporal duration, but rather post depositional process: fluvial, transport, solifluction, rodent activity, contemporary farming, and so forth.

Therefore, if time in archaeology will be measured in terms of aggregates of individual elements, it is important to take into account the agents of modification and their considerable potential for variation in the traces depositional events ultimately may bear. For instance, a single depositional process can give rise to materials in different deposits, and a single deposit can contain the products of many different depositional processes. In view of these possibilities, one must acknowledge that most archaeological accumulations do not neatly bound the products of a discrete depositional event or process.

We will use frequency/diversity seriation to describe patterns of change, and to establish the direction and magnitude of causal relationships (Baxter, 2001, 2003). Data are counts of the occurrence of class i (archaeological evidence of the ith category) in assemblage j (each one of the j stratigraphic episodes or temporal periods). Plotting each frequency count against each value of time order yields a graphical representation of the sequence of states. The automatic archaeologist should be able to recall the archaeological items in the original temporal seriation. This problem involves investigating the *stationarity* of the frequency series, the existence of linear and/or nonlinear trends in the stratigraphically ordered sequence. However, the stationarity, lack of stationarity or discontinuities associated with this pattern of change are not only a consequence of a social process correlated to time, but the result of sampling or the specificity of some depositional units. For instance, a discontinuity in any time interval may be explained as a "temporal" change in the social process that produced the archaeological depositional event, or as an individual property of that depositional unit, where some material was accumulated differentially due to a different function, a different post depositional process (preservation) or a different sampling procedure.

Let us analyze a real example. First pottery vases appeared in the Near East once production economy had been consolidated, in full sedentary societies. Chronologically, the earliest pottery remains should be dated in the period ranging from the 9th Millennium B.P. to the beginnings of the 8th. Early pottery is in all those sites a scarce material, typologically not much diverse, and coarsely manufactured. The purpose of the investigation is not to explain how pottery was invented, but to discover the degree of correlation between time and the abundance of deposited archaeological materials. This analysis has been done with data from the Neolithic site of Tell Halula, located in the middle Euphrates valley (Barceló & Faura, 1997).

The initial assumption was that the quantity of unconnected sherds in a depositional unit was a consequence of the diversity and repetition of cleaning practices performed at successive occupation floors. The investigation looks for: (1) determining the temporal trajectory (historical tendency) of rubbish accumulation all over the site, and (2) how the rate of change in material accumulations is related to economic and social transformation.

We used radiocarbon dates for estimating time order. The trouble is that radiocarbon dates cannot be represented as fixed points, but as intervals.

Consequently, we have introduced two different time points for each archaeological observation: one for the oldest extreme in the two-sigma interval and another for the newest. For instance:

DEPOSITIONAL UNIT	DATE	Total Pottery
S7-iv	-7034	5
S7-iv	-6465	5
S7-vi	-7727	25
S7-vi	-5596	25
S7-viii	-6415	35
S7-viii	-6119	35
S7-xii	-6779	539
S7-xii	-6200	539

…/…

Radiocarbon estimates are negative years, given that they are "before our era" dates. Each frequency measure is input twice: the first representing the oldest possible date and the second the newest. In such a way, all points within the temporal interval are assumed to provide the same information.

A very simple feed-forward neural network has been built and is shown in Figure 8.2.

The input unit contains "time" values (transformed into a 0.1 scale, that is, 6200 is represented as 0.6200) and the output unit contains frequencies (also transformed). Backpropagation was used to learn this network (see details in Barceló & Faura, 1997). In this case, the Neural Network learns correctly the negative correlation between time (negative values because we are in B.C. years) and quantity of pottery.

Once trained, we used the network to predict quantities of pottery at different time moments, filling the holes in the observed sequence at the site.

We obtain a description of the accumulation of pottery rubbish at the Tell Halula site as it "moves through time." It seems that the global frequency of pottery sherds accumulations after cleaning grows trough time. This tendency is not linear, however. Although at the beginning there are very few occupational floors with pottery, and it is also very scarce, at the end of the series (late phases), there are contemporary occupational floors with pottery and others without pottery. The better explanation for this fact is that the nature of accumulation (and not only *quantity*) changed with time. Not only frequency increases, but also the variability of depositional process. At the beginning of the historical trajectory, pottery was scarce and rubbish was placed at random; at the end of the sequence (once pottery manufacture and use consolidated), there are a lot of vessels in circulation; rubbish accumulation does not appear as a random action of discard, but as a result of intentional actions which vary spatially. Garbage accumulation becomes specialized and spatialized.

The abundance of pottery items at a depositional event is a consequence of some social and economic processes, but only some of these

Figure 8.2. A simple neural network topology to infer temporal relationships

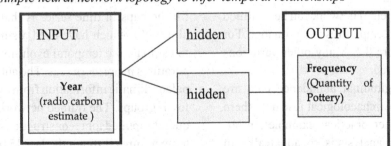

Figure 8.3. Changes in the absolute frequencies of ancient pottery in the Tell Halula site, as estimated by a neural network (Barceló and Faura 1997)

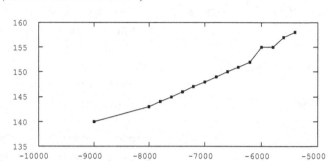

processes may be positively correlated to time. Pottery remains have not been discovered in primary contexts, but as apparently random spreads of discard material. They are not the result of *in situ* fragmentation, that is, we do not have broken vessels, but accumulations of unconnected sherds. Consequently, an important problem in the investigation is to prove whether there is some correlation between the quantity of pottery accumulated at some site and general qualitative changes not related to post-depositional processes. The automated archaeologist cannot propose a simple correlation between pottery production/consumption and time, but it should limit itself to correlate time with rubbish formation. Rubbish is the result of some social actions, which are indirectly linked with production and consumption. Therefore, it can be assumed that any change in the nature of rubbish is related to changes in consumption (there is an increase of refuse material from most commonly used pottery), which are also related to changes in productive systems (technology) and social demand.

The previous neural network can be modified to fit a much more complex research situation. For instance see Figure 8.4. Many other variations can also be explored.

Although longitudinal abundance data are very important to archaeological research, there are not many other practical examples, probably because time analysis is, paradoxically, an under explored domain in archaeology. We need much more research in the domain of frequency seriation, both using stratigraphic ordering and radiocarbon estimates.

The Tell Halula case can also be considered as an example of the filling of gaps in an archaeological time series by means of an artificial neural network. Here, a simple neural model fits a nonlinear function between abundance data and time, expressing time in absolute (radiocarbon) or relative (stratigraphy) terms. A somewhat related example has been published by Dergachev et al. (2001). The investigation is of relevance for obtaining a radiocarbon calibration curve, based the correlation between solar irradiance variations (Wolf index) and cosmogenic isotope ^{14}C. The usual procedure—the Stuiver-Pearson calibration curve—is based on linear regression between dendrochronological and ^{14}C estimates; Dergachev and colleagues suggest the use of a neural network to fit a nonlinear curve between Wolf index estimates, and radiocarbon data.

Another use of neural networks as a tool to fill the gaps in time series is that of Cortese et al. (2005), which have used a similar approach to estimate the temporal evolution of paleotemperatures in northern seas. The authors extracted paleo-climatic information from different microfossil groups. The trained networks were subsequently applied for reconstructions of sea surface temperatures through the last 15,000 years. The

Figure 8.4. A more sophisticated neural network topology to infer temporal relationships

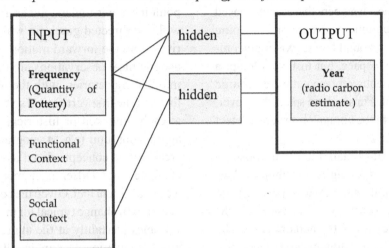

reconstructed paleo-temperature was quite high during the Bølling–Allerød, when it reached values only found later during the warmest phase of the Holocene. The climatic transitions in and out of the Younger Dryas were very rapid and involved a change, which took place over 440 and 140 years, respectively. Paleo-temperature remains at a maximum during the early Holocene, and this Radiolarian Holocene Optimum Temperature Interval predates the commonly recognized middle Holocene Climatic Optimum. During the -8200 event, paleo-temperatures decreased, and this episode marked the establishment of a cooling trend, roughly spanning the middle Holocene (until ca. 4200). Successively, since then and through the late Holocene, paleo-temperature follows instead a statistically significant warming trend.

Bhattacharya and Solomatine (2006) have applied neural networks to model sedimentation as the consequence of a temporal process. Paruelo and Tomasel (1997) tested the potential of neural networks as predictive tools in ecology. Other ecological examples have been reported by Spitz and Lek (1999).

Demographic data are typically represented in a manner that is both spatially and temporally discrete, at well-delineated, stable, spatial locations and fixed moments in time. How can an automated archaeologist visually represent the temporal change of spatially fixed geographic objects, for example, the historical transformation of social attributes for a number of geographical areas? One answer would be to compute and explicitly visualize attribute differentials using a change map, for example, a map of population growth from Phase *A* to Phase *B*. Another common approach relies on map comparison by creating multiple maps using the same underlying base map. For example, maps showing social features for Bronze Age and Iron Age would be placed side-by-side. The GeoVISTA (http://www.geovista.psu.edu) research group has extended the principles underlying such side-by-side comparisons of distinct temporal layers to three-dimensional self-organized maps (Gahegan et al., 2002; Takatsuka, 2001). They describe two methods for visualizing historical change. One method called *chronological cluster analysis* creates a different SOM and visualization for every time interval. The other method called "temporal cluster analysis" trains a single SOM with data from all temporal periods as input then creates different visualizations by applying the trained

SOM to data from different time intervals. The primary difference between these SOM-based approaches and common cartographic mapping is that they are not bound by the existing geometry of geographic space, but instead attempt a holistic, simultaneous representation of a large number of variables in attribute space. However, they still leave it to the human observer to detect changes visually.

Skupin and Hagelman (2005) propose to explicitly represent changing attribute values of spatio temporal features as movement of these objects across the two-dimensional SOM surface. The core idea of the authors is that the explicit delineation of n-dimensional trajectories in a two-dimensional display space may add to our understanding of demographic change. The demographic data set utilized in this experiment includes 254 areas (aggregated units: settlement, village, town or territory) with 32 sample socio-economic attributes for three temporal phases, what makes 762 n-dimensional input vectors ($n = 32$). The SOM trained output layer consists of 100 x 100 providing the ability to replicate both "global" and "regional" patterns existing in the data set. After neural network training, every one of these neurons is associated with one settlement, village, or area (input vector), socially and demographically described. One simple form of investigating temporal patterns in the trained SOM layer would be to visualize the year corresponding to each location. Remember that spatial locations where introduce three times, one for each temporal moment. For instance, it seems that certain portions of the output map were "abandoned" during the time between phase A and phase C, as indicated by the lack of any post phase A observations in some regions of the SOM. However, this still does not indicate whether geographical areas developed in similar ways after being similar at some moment in time. Knowing the specific path taken by individual counties and groups of counties can provide such information. The location of a settlement, village, or territory at a particular point in time is understood as a temporal vertex within a directed graph, in which direction derives from the forward motion of time. The 762 geographical observations are thus transformed into 254 trajectories, with the phase A location forming the first vertex, and so forth. In this way, at each time-step or historical period, a given aggregation unit (e.g., a geographically defined area) can be conceptualized as a locus in some attribute space. Different moments in time would lead to different loci. Given the continuous nature of temporal change typical for most demographic variables (certainly at the aggregation levels at which population data are handled by historians and archaeologists) and the natural order of time, different loci for the same unit can be linked to form a trajectory. In a visualization, the most natural representation of that trajectory would be through a directed, non-branching graph. When one says that two areas exhibit parallel patterns of development, this would assume somewhat similar (though not necessarily identical) loci at the same moments in time, which over multiple temporal periods leads to parallel trajectories. On the other hand, diverging development will correspond to trajectories that start with early loci in relative proximity, but later loci that are far apart. When individual loci or whole trajectories are then linked to additional social, political, or economic events, then relationships between trajectories and specific socioeconomic developments may become expressed quite explicitly.

Although multilayer feed-forward networks trained both in a supervised way (backpropagation) and in an unsupervised way (SOM) provide interesting results, it is true that the mapping performed is static (Gupta et al., 2000; Kremer, 2001). In fact, they are not describing a temporal process, but they classify temporal patterns by transforming the temporal domain into a spatial domain. For example, consider the following two vectors:

011100000
000111000

Suppose these two vectors are different but they were generated by the same temporal process, that is, they are contemporaneous. A neural network can be trained to treat these two patterns as similar, that is to say, to infer the same time step, although input values are clearly different. The similarity is a consequence of an external teacher, and not of the similarity structure of the patterns themselves, and the desired temporal pattern does not generalize easily to novel patterns.

Recently, interest has increased in the application of neural networks to learn historical trajectories, and to the identification and/or control of dynamic systems. In such cases, it is natural to use the networks involving dynamic elements, in the form of feedback connections, which are known as recurrent neural networks (see Chapter IV). If having a feed-forward neural architecture is what allows one to discriminate instances of prototypical things, then having a recurrent neural architecture is what provides one with the further capacity to discriminate instances of prototypical processes. What is interesting for a temporal recognition mechanism is that recognition occurs when something close to a prototypical sequence of activation vectors unfolds across the relevant population of neurons, when the activation vector carve out, over time, a special line or path in the relevant space (Churchland, 1995).

Several forms of recurrent networks have been proposed and they may be classified as fully recurrent or simple recurrent networks (Berthouze & Tijsseling, 2006; Chappelier & Grumbach, 1998; Ermentrout, 1998; Kremer, 2001; Serpen, 2004; Sumpter & Bulpitt, 1998; Tijsseling & Berthouze, 2001). Boné et al. (2002, 2004) has tried to integrate the best aspects of recursive networks with the well-known learning properties of back propagation algorithm. Just by adding some delay-connections and by adjusting the learning algorithm to learn directly the delay between connections. In fully recurrent networks, any unit may be connected to any other unit in the network and individual units may be input units, output units, or both. A temporal sequence of patterns can be stored in a Hopfield network, for instance, by using Hebbian learning that partially stores each pattern and partly stores the association between previous patterns and subsequent patterns. The network can be made to cycle through the various stored patterns in order (Ellis & Humphreys, 1999).

Examples of recurrent networks include networks trained using: (a) backpropagation through time, (b) recurrent backpropagation, and (c) real-time recurrent learning rules. Backpropagation through time is a training method for fully recurrent networks which allows backpropagation with weight sharing to be used to train an unfolded feed-forward non-recurrent version of the original network. Once trained, the weights from any layer of the unfolded net are copied into the recurrent network, which, in turn, is used for the temporal mapping task.

Aihara and Ichinose (1999) consider the possibility of computational dynamics with spatiotemporal chaos in neural networks as an example of a relation between deterministic chaos and computation. Properties of excitable dynamics with deterministic chaos and asynchronous updating in biological neurons should generate rich spatiotemporal nonlinear phenomena at the level of neural networks. Their model is able to generate various complex phenomena with spatiotemporal chaos at the level of neural networks. Such global chaos self-organizes through nonlinear interaction among elemental neurons with their own chaotic dynamics at the level of single neurons, while the behavior of each neuron is influenced by the global behavior of the network due to sensitive dependence on perturbations and fine bifurcation structure in the chaotic dynamics of each neuron. This hierarchical feedback between global spatiotemporal chaos at the network level and elemental chaos at the single neuron level produces spatiotemporal dynamics with the ability of computation.

In Chapter IV, I presented a simple recursive architecture, which can be very interesting to our purpose: the Jordan and Elman network (Elman, 1990, 1992; Jordan, 1986), which allows time to be represented by the effect it has on processing. This means giving the processing system dynamic properties that are responsive to temporal sequences. In short, the network must be given memory. This alternative approach uses a recurrent architecture in which the output from the network at time t is fed back as part of the input at time $t+1$. This gives the network access to its past states, so that associations may be learnt between subsequent states. A system of this type is able to learn temporal sequences of states as a chain of associations. The training regime involved presenting each input vector, one at a time, in sequence. The task for the network is to predict the next input. The sequence wraps around, in such a way that the first pattern is presented after the last. For instance, imagine that some archaeological context can be described in terms of the presence/absence of four different Boolean variables. The contexts are input to the machine in their original stratigraphic order.

Input	output
01101	00001
00001	01110
01110	11001
11001	11001
11001	00101
00101	?

The task is simply for the network to take the successive value from the input stratigraphic sequence and to calculate the subsequent value by producing it on the output layer. After each time step is introduced, the output is compared with the actual next value in the training set, and the backpropagation algorithm is used to adjust the network weights. Results: the network is not able to predict the precise order of specific values, but it recognizes that (in this corpus) there is a class of contexts typically following the previous ones.

Although the resulting temporal process is characteristically non-deterministic, it is also true that it is also not random or unconstrained. For any given sequence of temporal positions, there are a limited number of possible successors. Under these circumstances, it would seem more appropriate to ask whether the network has learned the class of valid successors at each point in time. We therefore might expect that the network should learn to activate the output nodes to some value proportional to the probability of occurrence of each value in that consecutive order. Therefore, to evaluate the final network performance we can compare the output with the probability of occurrence of possible successors. These values can be derived empirically from the training database; such calculation yields a "likelihood output vector" which is appropriate for each input and which reflects the context-dependent expectations given the training base (where context is defined as extending from the beginning of the series to the input). Note that it is appropriate to use the likelihood vectors only for the evaluation phase. Training must be performed on the actual successor values, because the point is to force the network to learn the context dependent probabilities for itself.

Recursive networks also constitute an interesting alternative to traditional approaches to evolutionary archaeology. Phylogenetic methods such as cladistics are routinely borrowed from biology and applied to material culture, assuming that similarity reflects homology; two artefacts are similar because they are ancestrally related. One may be descendent from the other, in which case the shared traits are inherited through vertical transmission. Or they may be descend from a 'common ancestor' in which case the common ancestor is depicted as a branching point (Lipo et al., 1997; Lyman & O'Brien, 2003; Mace, Holden, & Shennan, 2005; Maschner, 1996; O'Brien et al., 2001; Shennan, 2000; Shennan & Wilkinson, 2001). However, artifacts may arise independently yet be similar because they are alternative solutions within similar design constraints. Thus, similarity needs not reflect homology. Furthermore, whether or not two artifacts "share a common ancestor" can be quite arbitrary. The statistical approach to evolutionary seriation is then misguided. Recent advances in using graph models can revert this situation (Gabora, 1995; Lipo 2006). Even more interesting would be the use of genetic algorithms (cf. Chapter III, p. 106ff) or "cultural algorithms," cf. Reynolds, 1999, Franklin & Bergerman, 2000), Bayesian networks (see also Chapter III, p. 122ff) or even recurrent neural networks, as we have presented here.

UNDERSTANDING THE FUTURE: TOWARDS HISTORICAL PREDICTION

Time fluctuations are due to an almost infinite variety of social actions produced by agents that act independently from each other, and reproduce their actions without any apparent relationship with what they did before. However, even in the middle of the apparently chaotic changes of social activities through time, an automated archaeologist may see some appearance of order. If it can fit a neural network to the observed temporal variation among data, can an intelligent machine not only "predict" the next time step, but also "explain" how social action will be in the future?

This task is the forecasting side of any kind of historical research. For purposes of this discussion, a forecast is simply a statement that a particular event—ideally one that has been specified un-ambiguously—will occur (or might occur, with some unambiguous probability) at a point in the future (Schrodt, 2002, 2004). The "event" is usu-ally the value of a continuous variable but they can also concern a discrete occurrence chosen from a relatively small set of possible events (e.g.,

Barcelona Football Club will or will not win the Championship; I will or will not lose my job after writing a book like this). As observed by Weigend et al. (1990), understanding the future, hinges on two types of knowledge: knowledge of underly-ing laws, and the discovery of strong empirical regularities on observations of a given system.

There are two different types of forecasting with very different properties. *Unconditional* forecasts seek simply to predict the future under a *ceteris paribus* condition. The exercise is one of simple extrapolation: if things continue on the current track, then X, Y and Z will occur. This is the classical crystal ball problem; the most appropriate natural science analogy would be meteorology. Of greater interest is the *contingent forecast*—the "what if" question. The appropri-ate natural sciences analogy here is chemistry (or applied physics, "engineering"), where vari-ables are continually manipulated to establish true causal relationships. In other words, there are two kinds of historical predictions. The first one supposes to predict the future occurrence of some event from fixed factors; that is, "given these circumstances, what will happen?"' The second one could be expressed as "if this is what characterizes this condition, and this is how the circumstances have changed, so what will hap-pen?" (Schrodt, 2004)

The single greatest criticism of unconditional forecasting is that it can be trivialized as mere "data-mining:" take a very large number of vari-ables, cram them into a generic model, crunch the numbers, and then accept the results irrespective of whether they make any theoretical sense. The data-mining approach is tempting because it is easy, it looks impressive, and it actually works in applications where one is interested only in unconditional forecasts to the exclusion of ex-planatory theory or manipulation of the underlying variability. Contingent forecast is a much more difficult problem because contingent forecasts will only be correct if the model has identified true causal mechanisms; correlation is not sufficient.

For example, suppose a hypothesis indicates that infant mortality is a strong correlate of technological evolution, but in fact, infant mortality is simply a surrogate indicator for a cluster of other variables that are the "true" causes. In these circumstances, efforts to determine the degree of infant mortality in cemetery data will have only limited effects on predict the technological level of that society. This confusing of correlation and causality is probably one of the main reasons that forecasting has gotten such a bad name.

How does our intelligent robot go about making such historical predictions? Ideally, it must use past data to construct a set of basic rules, like Newton's laws, that can be used to make predictions under very general circumstances. Unfortunately, this approach cannot always be carried out in practice. In some cases, the underlying principles are not known or are poorly understood because the system of interest is very complicated. This is the case in the social sciences, in which relationships between various parameters are not known, and some of the relevant parameters, such as intention or goal-oriented action, may not be accessible to the automated archaeologist or quantifiable. Another problem with this approach is that often, even when the basic laws are known, direct solution of the equations is not possible without detailed information about initial values and boundary conditions.

To use a neural network for historical prediction means that the temporal problem is solved by using error-correction learning since the training examples are drawn from previous, present of future realizations of the historical process itself (Weigend et al., 1990). Let $t'(n)$ denote the one-step prediction produced by the neural network at time n. An error signal $e(n)$ is defined as the difference between $t(n)$ and $t'(n)$, which is used to adjust the free parameters of the neural network. Based on a quantification of such error signals, predictions may be seen as a form of model building in the sense that the smaller the automated archaeologist makes the prediction error $e(n)$ in a statistical sense, the better the network serves as a model of the physical or social process responsible for generating the data. When this process is *nonlinear*, the use of a neural network provides a powerful method for solving the prediction problem, because of the nonlinear processing units that could be built into its construction. The only possible exception to the use of nonlinear processing units, however, is the output unit of the network: if the dynamic range of the time series is unknown, the use of a linear output unit is the most reasonable choice.

A typical example of historical prediction though a neural network is Patricia Cerrito's forecasting of the success or failure of historical revolutions (Cerrito, 1996). She looks for the identification of patterns in the historical development of revolutions. She defines a revolution as a public uprising against the established government, which may have success (change the established government) or not. Seven variables are considered as initial conditions at the start of any rebellion:

Opponent
 1= established government is an external force
 0= established government is an internal force
Ideals
 2= republican or democratic government
 1= dictatorship
 0= no plan (or overthrow existing order only)
Outside pressures
 1= external force supporting rebels
 -1= external force supporting existing order
 0= no external force
Economic stability of rebels
 2= very strong
 1= strong
 -1= weak
 -2= very weak

Economic stability of established order
    2= very strong
    1= strong
    -1= weak
    -2= very weak
Stability of government of rebels
    2= very strong
    1= strong
    -1= weak
    -2= very weak
Stability of government of existing order
    2= very strong
    1= strong
    -1= weak
    -2= very weak
      1= established government is an external force

To complete the model, an output variable must also be defined. Its values are $Y=1$ if the rebellion is successful and $Y=0$ otherwise.

The author used historical data from well studied revolutions, from the American Independence, to Soviet Revolution. The complete list of historical events used for training the neural network are: Maccabees (Judea), Zealots (Judea), Medieval England Magna Carta, Cromwell 1649, Scottish Rebellion of Bonnie Prince Charlie, French Revolution 1789, American Independence, South America Independence Wars, French Revolution 1848, German Revolution 1848, Hungary 1848, Bohemia 1848, Italy 1848, American Civil War, Various Indian Rebellions in United States, Mexican Revolution, Russian Revolution of 1917, Irish Rebellion of 1921, Spanish Civil War (1936-1939), the Frente Sandinista in modern Nicaragua.

The purpose of the analysis was not a classification of social facts but predicting the consequences of social uprisings. As Cerrito explains in her analysis (1996), once learned using the appropriate data from historical sources, the Neural network was able to predict the most probable outcome of recent social uprisings in Eastern Europe (the example of Bosnia, for instance), when introduced a description of political situation and social circumstances in the input.

Of related interest is Lagazio and Russett (2004; Lagazio, 2006) work, which used backpropagation neural network for predicting interstate conflict in actual times. The historical event to be predicted (dispute), or network output, is one if a militarized interstate dispute had begun and is zero otherwise. Only the initial year of the militarized conflict is included because the authors' concern is to predict the onset of a conflict. Input variables include allies, geographical contingency, distance between the two states' capitals, political information (if either one or both states in the dyad are a major power). Democracy is another input variable coded as a 21-point scale variable measuring the level of democracy in the less democratic state in each dyad. Dependence is a continuous variable measuring the level of economic interdependence (dyadic trade as a portion of a state's gross domestic product) of the less economically dependent state in the dyad. Their model correctly recognized 82.4 percent and 64 percent of cold war era and pre-cold war era military disputes respectively; it also correctly predicted 72.2 percent and 65.5 percent of cold war and pre-cold war era non-military disputes respectively. This is an example of mixed predictive power from the backpropagation algorithm.

Let us present some examples of automated systems that try to explain future behavior of dynamic systems. Mann and Benwell (1996) built a neural network able to predict the probability of land degradation in the future. Degradation is multifactor in origin, spatially heterogeneous, temporally variable, and affected by land management. Thus, any measure of land condition must reflect a large number of contributing factors, and a parametric expression for such a measurement would be obscure. The neural network had 31 input neurons about ecological features, topography, grazing at different periods, rabbit population, frequency of burns in 25 years, and so forth. The purpose of the neurocomputational approach was to predict the percentage of bare ground (degraded land) at different time steps. The network output was a kind of "thermometer" encoding scheme where ten outputs encoded the ten intervals of bare ground percentage (between 0 and 10, between 10 and 20, etc.). Time information was not explicitly coded as a factor, but an historical database consisting in ecological records from 164 sites was available, totaling 1276 observations. The resulting neural model correctly predicted the training data, and correctly generalized to test information gathered for additional sites. The model was then used to interpolate non-recorded years, obtaining a characteristic nonlinear mapping of time/land degradation. Such a mapping was then used to simulate ecological history, simulating, for instance, the occurrence of a big fire, the temporal dynamics of natural recovery of degraded land in those circumstances.

Openshaw and Turner (2000) used a neural network for forecasting global climatic change impacts on Mediterranean agricultural land use in the 21st Century. The authors employed a mix of GIS, neurocomputing, and fuzzy logic technologies to attempt the prediction of agricultural land degradation risk under various climate change scenarios.

Due to the extreme complexity of any social system, few predictive models have been built which truly represent the dynamics of settlement growth and which can provide consistent results with what we know about such changes. The goal of these models is to establish functional relationships between a set of spatial predictor variables that are used to predict the locations of temporal change on the landscape. The variable values and actual instances of land use change are typically observed from historical data and used to establish functional relationships that can be used to extrapolate land use change probabilities into the future. Examples of this line of research come from the simulation and prediction of the changing pattern of land uses (Almeida & Gleriani,

2005; Diappi et al., 2002, 2004; Li & Yeh, 2002; Liu et al., 2005; Pijanowski et al., 2002).

Neural networks designed to predict land use dynamics are supervised learning models using historical data to predict the future use of some specific area. This means that the network learns from a set of spatiotemporal events where land use at different moments of the past is known, the connections between the final state at time $t+1$ (the target) and the local and neighboring conditions at time t. The input describes the urbanized state of the area and of its neighborhood at the time t, the output variables represent only the cell state at the time $t+1$. Once the learning and testing phase has been concluded, the averaged weight matrix is processed with a data set of cells "potentially" in urbanization in the next time lag. The resulted pattern shows a probable scenario where prevailing urbanization process may take place.

Some of these examples make evident the strong relationship between time and space. Time and space are not different ways of considering the nature of social activity. Temporal processes influence the spatial position of social acts, in the same way the spatial processes influence the temporal reproduction of the same actions. Therefore, the analysis of archaeological events necessarily implies to consider both space and time, because things happen at precise locations and moments. The intentionality of social actions performed in the past should be explained not only in terms of the spatiotemporal "influence" an action performed at some place *and* at some moment has over all actions in the same spatiotemporal proximity. That means that any archaeological pattern existing at one moment of time is the result of the operation of processes that have differential spatial impacts. A spatiotemporal analysis will be based on an examination of:

- How the spatial distribution of an action has an influence over the spatial distribution of other(s) action(s),

- How the temporal displacement of an action has an influence over the spatial distribution of other(s) action(s),
- How the temporal displacement of an action has an influence over the temporal displacement of other(s) action(s), and
- How the spatial distribution of an action has an influence over the temporal displacement of other(s) action(s).

Predicting the future implies that social action can generate the reproduction of similar actions, or it can prevent any other similar action in the same spatiotemporal vicinity. Some of the actions performed *here* and *now* increase the chances of one type of action and decrease the chances of others *there* and *then*. The automated archaeologist is looking for whether what happened in the past is the cause of what *will* happen in a neighboring future (Barceló, 2002). Its analysis then pretends to examine if the characteristics in one spatiotemporal location have anything to do with characteristics in a neighboring location, through the definition of a general model of spatiotemporal dependencies.

A neural network does not discover *always* an historical trend. The inputs to the network may not contain sufficient information about the temporal sequence in order to predict that time point. That is, the input vector, *t(k),...,t(k-m)*, may be very distant in the time from the prediction horizon, and it may not have any relation with that historical moment of the trajectory. A neural network has only sense when a relation exists between the information available at current instant and the prediction horizon. However, in many cases, it will forecast the future of a system with very few errors. It is unclear what is being estimated when neurocomputational smoothing functions are fitted to time series data. No simple parametric function is employed, and the use of different learning algorithms could easily yield markedly dissimilar functions. This criticism is especially relevant in our case. If an automated archaeolo-gist arrives to compute the existence of trend in the historical data using a neural network, should we conclude that it has discovered the source of variation related to time?

DIRECTIONS FOR FURTHER RESEARCH

Archaeology is one among the other GeoSciences. In fact, there are not many differences between geography and our discipline. Maybe, the only way of differentiating both sciences is because archaeology studies "finished" social actions, whereas in geography the action is still being performed. Therefore, in the case of archaeology, the spatiality and the temporality of social actions cannot be observed but inferred from indirect evidence. Archaeologists cannot see the social actor, and everything should be explained from some of the consequences of what he and she did. This strong similarity between both disciplines makes that geographers and archaeologists can learn from the other discipline.

We have seen in this chapter that neurocomputational applications in geography and other geosciences are more numerous and interesting than in archaeology. Archaeologists have only applied some simple techniques in very trivial problems. However, there is considerable room for improving these applications. After all, the nature of the spatial problem is nearly the same. Only data are somewhat different.

We need more theoretical investigations on the assumptions of spatial models. The very idea of spatial causality has to be analyzed, because we do not know if "space" can be integrated in an explanation as a causal factor, or is it a descriptive dimension of human action. Only by developing these theoretical questions, new neurocomputational and artificial intelligence techniques will prove their utility. In this chapter, I have advanced some elements for modeling the spatial modalities of social actions as a kind of input-output mechanism. Further research is needed, however. In the same way, the "spatial" nature of self-organized maps has to be further explored to build more sophisticated representations of social "spaces."

We can complaint about the underdeveloped nature of spatial questions and tools in archaeology, but temporal analysis is even in a worst condition. This is a paradox, given that the very name of our discipline *archeo*-logy implies the notion of time. What is time? How a temporal model should be defined? These questions still wait to be asked.

The research domain that can interest more to present day archaeologists is the linking between neural networks and geographical information systems. I am not referring to the simple GIS systems usually available, that are no more than a database and some cartographic representations, but complex spatiotemporally related knowledge bases. In the same way that a lot of effort is doing nowadays in temporal GIS, we need to integrate data about how spatial and temporal locations of social action vary in a neurocomputational framework. Such integration would provide the advantages of nonlinearity, non-assumptions based and non-monotonic character of neural networks to the domain of spatial and temporal processing (www.geovista.org, Gahegan et al, 2002).

A similar approach is being developed in geography, especially around the GeoVista project and its GeoVista Studio software program.

REFERENCES

AIHARA, K., & ICHINOSE, N. (1999). Modeling and complexity in neural networks. *Artificial Life Robotics, 3*, 148-154.

AITKENHEAD, M. J., MUSTARD, M. J., & MCDONALD, A.J.S. (2004). Using neural networks to predict spatial structure in ecological systems. *Ecological Modelling, 179*(3), 393-403.

AL-NUAIMY, W., HUANG, Y., NAKHKASH, M., FANG, M.T.C., NGUYEN, V.T., & ERIKSEN, A. (2000). Automatic detection of buried utilities and solid objects with GPR using neural networks and pattern recognition. *Journal of Applied Geophysics, 43*, 157-165.

ATKINSON, P.M., & TATNALL, A.R.L. (1997). Neural networks in remote sensing—introduction. *International Journal of Remote Sensing, 18*(4), 699–709.

BADRAN, F., & THIRIA, S. (1997). Neural network smoothing in correlated time series contexts. *Neural networks, 10*, 1445-1453.

BAIRAKTARIS, D. (1995). Temporal chunking and synchronization using a modular recurrent network architecture. In J.P. Levy, D. Bairaktaris, J.A. Bullinaria & P. Cairns (Eds.), *Connectionist models of memory and language.* London: UCL Press.

BARALDI, A., & PARMIGGIANI, F. (1995). A neural network for unsupervised categorization of multivalued input patterns: An application to satellite image clustering. *IEEE Transactions on Geoscience and Remote Sensing, 33*(2), 305-16.

BARCELÓ, J.A. (2002). Archaeological thinking: Between space and time. *Archeologia e Calcolatori, 13*, 237-256.

BARCELÓ, J.A.,(2005). Multidimensional Spatial Analysis in Archaeology. Beyond the GIS Paradigm. In *Reading the Historical Spatial Information in the World -Studies for Human Cultures and Civilizations based on Geographic Information System-* Edited by K. Ono. Kyoto (Japan): Institute for Japan Studies.

BARCELÓ, J.A., & FAURA, M., (1997). Time series and neural networks in archaeological seriation. An example on early pottery from the near east. In L. Dingwall, S. Exon, V. Gaffney, S. Laflin, M. Leusen (Eds.), *Archaeology in the age of internet* (pp. 91-102). Oxford: ArcheoPress.

BARCELÓ, J.A., & MAMELI, L. (2004). Frequency seriation and temporal order. A zooarchaeological study. In F. Nicolucci & S. Hermon (Eds.), *Beyond the artefact. Computer applications in archaeology.* Budapest, Hungary: ArcheoLingua.

BARCELÓ, J.A., MAXIMIANO, A., & VICENTE, O. (2004). La Multidimensionalidad del Espacio Arqueológico: Teoría, Matemáticas, Visualización. In I. Grau (Ed.), *La aplicación de los SIG en la arqueología del paisaje.* Alicante, Spain: Publicaciones de la Universidad de Alicante.

BARCELÓ, J.A., & PALLARES, M. (1998). Beyond GIS. The archaeological study of social spaces. *Archeologia e Calcolatori, 9,* 47-80.

BARCELÓ, J.A. PELFER, G., & MANDOLESI, A (2002). The origins of the city. From social theory to archaeological description. *Archeologia e Calcolatori, 13,* 41-64.

BAXTER, M. J. (2001). Methodological issues in the study of assemblage diversity. *American Antiquity, 66*(4), 715-725.

BAXTER, M.J. (2003). *Statistics in archaeology.* London: Arnold Publ.

BEECKMAN, C.S., & BADEN, W.W. (eds.). (2005). *Nonlinear Models for Archaeology and Anthropology: Continuing the Revolution* London: Ashgate Publishing.

BERARDI, V.L., & ZHANG, G.P. (2003). An empirical investigation of bias and variance in time series forecasting: Modeling considerations and error evaluation. *IEEE Transactions on Neural Networks, 14*(3), 668- 679.

BERTHOUZE, L., & TIJSSELING, A. (2006). A neural model for context-dependent sequence learning. *Neural Processing Letters, 23,* 27–45.

BESCOBY, D.C., CAWLEY, G.C., & CHROSTON, P.N. (2006). Enhanced interpretation of magnetic survey data from archaeological sites using artificial neural Networks. *Geophysics, 71*(5), 45-53.

BHATTACHARYA, B., & SOLOMATINE, D.P. (2006). Machine learning in Sedimentation modelling. *Neural Networks, 19,* 208–214.

BLANKHOLM, H.P. (1991). *Intrasite spatial analysis in archaeology.* Aarhus, Danemark: University of Aarhus Press.

BONÉ, R., CRUCIANU, M., & ASSELIN DE BEAUVILLE, J.-P. (2002). Learning long-term dependencies by the selective addition of time-delayed connections to recurrent neural networks. *NeuroComputing, 48,* 251-266.

BONÉ, R., & CRUCIANU, M. (2004). Multi-step-ahead prediction with neural networks. *European Journal of Economic and Social Systems (Neural Networks Special Issue), 17,* 85-98.

BRODARIC, B., GAHEGAN, M., & HARRAP, R. (2004). The art and science of mapping: Computing geological categories from field data. *Computers & Geosciences, 30,* 719–740.

BROWN, D. A., & CHANG, K. C. (2001). *Artificial neural networks, paradigms, and western wheatgrass geography.* Retrieved June 2006 from http://cla.umn.edu/grasslands/wwANNabst.htm.

CANTERO, M.C., MARTÍNEZ, P., PÉREZ, R.M., PANIAGUA, J., DEL RÍO, L.M., CERRILLO, E., et al. (2005). Archaeological Sites Studies Based On Neural Computation Techniques. *Proc. of the 3rd ESA CHRIS/Proba Workshop, 21–23 March, ESRIN, Frascati, Italy, (ESA SP-593, June 2005).* Retrieved October 2006 from http://earth.esa.int/workshops/chris_proba_05/papers/27_cante.pdf

CASTILLO, O., & MELIN, P. (2002). Hybrid intelligent systems for time series prediction using neural networks, fuzzy logic, and fractal theory. *IEEE Transactions on Neural networks 13*(6), 1395- 1408.

CAWLEY, G.C., JANACEK, G.J., HAYLOCK, M.R., & DORLING, S.R. (2007). Predictive uncertainty in environmental modeling. *Neural Networks, 20, 537–549.*

CERRITO, P. (1996). Using neural networks to study and predict historical structure. *Mathematical Connections,*4(1).

CHAKRABORTY, K., MEHROTRA, K., MOHAN, C.K., & RANKA, S. (1992). Forecasting the behavior of multivariate time series using neural networks. *Neural networks, 5*(6), 961-970.

CHAPPELIER, J.C., & GRUMBACH, A. (1998). RST: A connectionist architecture to deal with spatiotemporal relationships. *Neural Computation, 10*, 883–902.

CHURCHLAND, P.M. (1995). *The engine of reason, the seat of the soul. A philosophical journey into the brain.* Cambridge, MA: The MIT Press.

CIVCO, D.L. (1993). Artificial neural networks for landcover classification and mapping. *International Journal of Geographic Information Systems, 7*, 173-186.

CORTESE, G., DOLVEN, J.K., BJØRKLUND, K.R., & MALMGREN, B.A. (2005). Late pleistocene–holocene radiolarian paleotemperatures in the norwegian sea based on artificial neural networks. *Palaeogeography, Palaeoclimatology, Palaeoecology, 224*, 311– 332.

De ALMEIDA, C.M., & GLERIANI, J.M. (2005, April 16-2*1*). Cellular automata and neural networks as a modeling framework for the simulation of urban land use change. *Anais XII Simpósio Brasileiro de Sensoriamento Remoto, Goiânia, Brasil, ,* INPE, (pp. 3697-3705).

DERAVIGNONE, L. (2006). *Intelligenza artificiale: sviluppo metodologico e applicativo nell'archeologia del territorio.* Dipartimento di Archeologia e Storia delle Arti di la Università degli Studi di Siena. Retrieved October 2006 from http://archeologiamedievale.unisi.it/NEW-PAGES/TESTIprogetti/deravignone.pdf.

DERGACHEV, V.A., GORBAN, A.N., ROSSIEV, A.A., KARIMOVA, L.M., KUANDYKOV, E.B., MAKARENKO, N.G. et al. (2001). The filling of gaps in geophysical time series by artificial neural networks. *Radiocarbon, 43*(2A), 365-371.

DIAPPI, L., BOLCHI, P., FRANZINI, L., BUSCEMA, M., & INTRALIGI, M. (2002, August 27-31). The Urban Sprawl Dynamics: Does a Neural Network Understand the Spatial Logic Better than a Cellular Automata*? 42nd ERSA Congress – Dortmund., 2002.* Retrieved February 2007 from http://www.ersa.org/ersaconfs/ersa02/cd-rom/papers/033.pdf

DIAPPI, L., BOLCHI, P., & BUSCEMA, M. (2004). Improved understanding of urban sprawl using neural networks. In J.P. Van Leeuwen & H.J.P. Timmermans (Eds.), *Recent advances in design and decision support systems in architecture and urban planning* (pp. 33-49). Kluwer Academic Publishers.

DJINDJIAN, F. (1990). *Les méthodes de l'archéologie.* Paris: Armand Colin.

DOWD, P.A., & SARAC, C. (1994). A neural network approach to geostatistical simulation. *Mathematical Geology, 26*(4).

DUCKE, B. (2003). Archaeological predictive modelling in intelligent network structures. In M. Doerr & A. Sarris (Eds.), *The digital heritage of archaeology. Computer applications and quantitative methods in archaeology.* Heraklion, Greece: Hellenic Ministry of Culture, Archive of Monuments and Publications.

ELLIS, R., & HUMPHREYS, G. (1999). *Connectionist psychology.* London: Psychology Press.

ELMAN, J.L. (1990). Finding structure in time. *Cognitive Science, 14*, 179-211.

ELMAN, J.L. (1992). Grammatical structure and distributed representations. In S. Davis (Ed.), *Connectionism: Theory and practice.* Oxford, UK: Oxford University Press.

ELSNER, J.B. (1992). Predicting time series using a neural network as a method of distinguishing chaos from noise. *Journal of Physics A: Mathematical and General, 25*, 843–850.

ERMENTROUT, B. (1998). Neural networks as spatiotemporal pattern-forming systems. *Reports on Progress in Physics, 61*, 353–430.

FOODY, G.M., McCULLOCH, M.B., & YATES, W.B. (1995). Classification of remotely sensed data by an artificial neural network: Issues relating to data characteristics. *Photogrametric Engineering and Remote Sensing, 61*, 391-401.

FOTHERINGHAM, A.S., BRUNSDON, C., & CHARLTON, M.E. (2000). *Quantitative geography: Perspectives on spatial data analysis.* Sage Publications.

FRANKLIN, B., & BERGERMAN, M. (2000). Cultural algorithms: Concepts and experiments. *Evolutionary Computation, 2*, 1245–1251.

GABORA, L. (1995). Meme and variations: A computer model of cultural evolution. In L. Nadel & D. Stein (Eds.), *1993 lectures in complex systems* (pp. 471-486). Reading, MA: Addison-Wesley.

GAHEGAN, M., TAKATSUKA, M., WHEELER, M., & HARDISTY, F. (2002). Introducing GeoVISTA studio: An integrated suite of visualization and computational methods for exploration and knowledge construction in geography. *Computers, Environment and Urban Systems, 26*, 267-292.

GERMAN, G., GAHEGAN, M., & WEST, G. (1997). Predictive assessment of neural network classifiers for applications in GIS. *Presented at the 2nd annual conference of GeoComputation '97 & SIRC '97, University of Otago, New Zealand,* Retrieved September 2006 from http://www.geocomputation.org/1997/papers/german.pdf

GEVREY, M., WORNER, S., KASABOV, N., PITT, J., & GIRAUDEL, J.L. (2006). Estimating risk of events using SOM models: A case study on invasive species Establishment. *Ecological Modelling, 197*(3-4), 361-372.

GONG, P., PU, R., & CHEN, J. (1996). Mapping ecological land systems and classification uncertainties from digital elevation and forest-cover data using neural networks. *Photogrametric Engineering and Remote Sensing, 62*(11), 1249-1260.

GUPTA, L., MCAVOY, M., PHEGLEY, J.M. (2000). Classification of temporal sequences via prediction using the simple recurrent neural network. *Pattern Recognition, 33*, 1759-1770.

HAINING, R. (2003). *Spatial data analysis. Theory and practice.* Cambridge, UK: Cambridge University Press.

HALLS, P.J., & MILLER, A.P. (1996). Of todes and worms: An experiment in bringing time into arc/info. *Proceedings of the 1996 ESRI European Users Conference*, Watford UK.

HALLS, P.J., POLACK, F.A.C., & O'KEEFE, S.A.M., (1999). A new approach to the spatial analysis of temporal change using todes and neural nets. *Cybergeo,* article 139. Retrieved July 2007 from http://www.cybergeo.eu/index911.html

HEERMANN, P.D., & KHAZENIE, N. (1992). Classification of multispectral remote sensing data using a backpropagation network. *IEEE Transactions on geoscience and Remote Sensing, 30*(1), 81-88.

HILBERT, D.W., & OSTENDORF, B. (2001). The utility of artificial neural networks for modeling the distribution of vegetation in past, present and future climates. *Ecological Modelling, 146*(1-3), 311-327 .

ILOGHALU, E.M. (2003). Application of neural networks technique in lithofacies classifications used for 3D reservoir geological modeling and exploration studies. A novel computer-based methodology for depositional environment interpretation. *AAPG Annual Convention* May 11-14, 2003, Salt Lake City, Utah. Retrieved July 2007 from http://www.searchanddiscovery.com/documents/abstracts/annual2003/extend/75734.PDF

JORDAN, M.I. (1986). *Serial order: A parallel distributed approach. ICS Report 8604.* San Diego, CA: University of California, Institute for Cognitive Science.

KANEVSKI, M., MAIGNAN, M., DEMYANOV, V., & MAIGNAN, M.F. (1997). How neural network 2d interpolations can improve spatial data analysis: Neural network residual kriging. *IAMG 97 Int. Assoc. Mathematical Geology,* (pp. 549-554).

KIM, Z.W., & NEVATIA, R. (2004). Automatic description of complex buildings from multiple images. *Computer Vision and Image Understanding, 96,* 60–95.

KINTIGH, K., & AMMERMAN, A. (1982). Heuristic approaches to spatial analysis in archaeology. *American Antiquity, 47*(1), 31-63.

KREMER, S.C. (2001). Spatiotemporal connectionist networks: A taxonomy and review. *Neural Computation, 13,* 249–306

KRASNOPOLSKY, V.M., & SCHILLER, H. (2003). Some neural network applications in environmental sciences. Part I: Forward and inverse problems in geophysical remote measurements. *Neural Networks, 16*(3-4), 321-334.

KULKARNI, A.D. (2001). *Computer vision and fuzzy neural systems.* Upper Saddle River, NJ: Prentice Hall.

LAGAZIO, M. (2006) Assessing different Bayesian neural network models for militarized interstate dispute outcomes and variable influences. *Social Science Computer Review, 24*(1).

LAGAZIO, M., & RUSSETT, B. (2004). A neural network analysis of militarized disputes, 1885-1992: Temporal stability and causal complexity. In P. Diehl (Ed.), *The scourge of war: New extensions on an old problem,* (pp. 28-62). Ann Arbor, MI: University of Michigan Press.

LEE, S., & LATHROP, R.G. (2006). Subpixel analysis of landsat ETM+ using self-organizing map (SOM) neural networks for urban land cover characterization. *IEEE Transactions on Geoscience and Remote Sensing, 44*(6), 1642-1654.

LEK, S., DELACOSTE, M., BARA, P., DIMOPOULOS, I., LAUGA, J. & AULAGNIER, S. (1996). Application of neural networks to modeling nonlinear relationships in ecology. *Ecological Monitoring, 90,* 39-52.

Van LEUSEN, P.M., (2002). *Pattern to process: Methodological investigations into the formation and interpretation of spatial patterns in archaeological landscapes,* PhD thesis, University of Groningen.

LI, X., & YEH, A.G.O. (2002). Neural network-based cellular automata for simulating multiple land use changes using GIS. *International Journal of Geographical Information Science, 16*(4), 323-343.

LIPO, C. P. (2006). The resolution of cultural phylogenies using graphs. In R. L. Lyman & M. J. O'Brien (Eds.), *Mapping our ancestors: Phylogenetic approaches in anthropology and prehistory.* New York: Aldine.

LIPO, C. P., MADSEN, M., DUNNEL, R., & HUNT, T. (1997). Population Structure, Cultural Transmission, and Frequency Seriation. *Journal of Anthropological Archaeology, 16,* 301-333.

LIU, W., SETO, K.C., & SUN, Z. (2005). Urbanization prediction with an ART-MMAP neural network based spatiotemporal data mining method. *International Archives of Photogrammetry, Remote Sensing and Spatial Information Sciences,* XXXVI(8)/W27.

LLOYD, C.D., & ATKINSON, P.M. (2004) Archaeology and geostatistics. *Journal of Archaeological Science, 31*(2), 151-165.

LYMAN, R.L., & O'BRIEN, M. (1999). *Seriation, stratigraphy, and index fossils: The backbone of archaeological dating.* New York: Kluwer Academic/Plenum.

LYMAN, R.L., & O'BRIEN, M. (2003). *Cladistics and archaeology.* Salt Lake City, UT: University of Utah Press.

LYMAN, R.L., & O'BRIEN, M. (2006) Seriation and cladistics: The difference between anagenetic and cladogenetic evolution. In R. L. Lyman & M. J. O'Brien (Eds.), *Mapping our ancestors: Phylogenetic approaches in anthropology and prehistory* (pp. 65-88). New York: Aldine.

MACE, R. C., HOLDEN, J., & SHENNAN, S. (2005). *Evolution of cultural diversity: A phylogenetic approach.* London: UCL Press.

MAHINY, A.S., & TURNER, B. J. (2003, September 8-10). Modeling past vegetation change through remote sensing and G.I.S: A comparison of neural networks and logistic regression methods. In *Proceedings of the 7th International Conference on GeoComputation* University of Southampton, United Kingdom. Retrieved July 2007 from http://www.geocomputation.org/2003/Papers/Mahiny_Paper.pdf

MAMELI, L., BARCELÓ, J., & ESTÉVEZ, J. (2001). The statistics of archaeological deformation processes. An archaeozoological case. In G. Burenhult (Ed.), *Archaeological informatics: Pushing the envelope* (pp. 221-230). Oxford: ArcheoPress.

MANN, S., & BENWELL, G.L. (1996). The integration of ecological, neural and spatial modeling for monitoring and prediction for semi-arid landscapes. *Computers & Geosciences, 22*(9), 1003-1012.

MARTINEZ, A., SALAS, J.D. & GREEN, T.G. (2004). Sensitivity of spatial analysis neural network training and interpolation to structural parameters, *Mathematical Geology, 36*(6), 721-742.

MARTÍNEZ, P., GUALTIERI, J.A., AGUILAR, P.L., PÉREZ, R.M., LINAJE, M., PRECIADO, J.C., et al. (2001). Hyperspectral image classification using a self-organizing map, *Summaries of the XI JPL Airborne Earth Science Workshop.*

MASCHNER, H. D. G., (Ed.) (1996). *Darwinian archaeologies.* New York: Plenum Press.

MATSUDA, S., KOIKE, K., & OHMI, M. (2003). Spatial estimation of geologic data using a neural network and detection of influence factors on their distribution, *Journal of the Mining and Materials Processing Institute of Japan, 19*(6/7), 359-369.

McDOWELL, D., McCLEARY, R., MEIDINGER, E.E., HAY, R.A. (1980). *Interrupted time series analysis.* Newbury Park, CA: Sage Publ.

MEHRER, M.W., & WESCOTT, K.L. (2005). *GIS and archaeological site location modeling.* London: Taylor & Francis.

MERWIN, D.A., CROMLEY, R.G., & CIVCO, D.L. (2002). Artificial neural networks as a method of spatial interpolation for digital elevation models. *Cartography and Geographical Information Systems, 29*(2), 99-110.

MURNION, S.D. (1996). Spatial analysis using unsupervised neural networks. *Computers & Geosciences, 22*(9), 1027-1031.

NIJKAMP, P., REGGIANI, A. (1998). *The economics of complex spatial systems.* Amsterdam: Elsevier.

O'BRIEN, M. J., DARWENT, J., & LYMAN, R. L. (2001). Cladistics is useful for reconstructing archaeological phylogenies: Paleoindian points from the Southeastern United States. *Journal of Archaeological Science, 28*, 1115-1136.

OKA, S., TAKEFUJI, Y., & SUZUKI, T., (2000). Feature extraction of IKONOS images by self-organization topological map. *Proceedings of the International Conference on Imaging Science, Systems, and Technology. CISST'2000* Vol. 2, (pp. 687-91). Athens, GA: CSREA Press - Univ. Georgia.

OPENSHAW, S. (1994). Neuroclassification of spatial data. In B.C. Hewitson & R.G. Crane (Eds.), *Neural nets: Applications in archaeology.* Dordrecht, Holland: Kluwer Academic Publ.

OPENSHAW, S., & TURNER, A. (2000). Forecasting global climatic change impacts on mediterranean agricultural land use in the 21st century, *Cybergeo, article 120*, Retrieved July 2007 from http://www.cybergeo.eu/index2255.html

OPENSHAW, S., & TURTON, I. (1996). A parallel kohonen algorithm for the classification of large spatial datasets. *Computers & Geosciences, 22*(9), 1019-1026.

OZESMI, S.L., & OZESMI, U. (1999). An artificial neural network approach to spatial habitat modeling with interspecific interaction. *Ecological Modelling, 116*, 15-31.

ÖZESMI, S.L., TAN, C.O., & ÖZESMI, U. (2006). Methodological issues in building, training, and testing artificial neural networks in ecological applications. *Ecological Modelling, 195*(1-2), 83-93.

PAOLA, J.D., & SCHOWENGERDT, R.A. (1995). A detailed comparison of backpropagation neural network and maximum likelihood classifiers for urban land use classification. *IEEE Transactions on Geoscience and Remote Sensing, 33*(4), 981-996.

PIJANOWSKI, B.C., BROWN, D.G., SHELLITO, B. A., & MANIK, G. A. (2002). Using neural networks and GIS to forecast land use changes: A land transformation model, *Computers, Environment and Urban Systems, 26*, 553–575.

POULTON, M.M., STERNBERG, B.K., & GLASS, C.E. (1992). Location of subsurface targets in geophysical data using neural networks. *Geophysics, 57*(12), 1534–1544.

RAMAZZOTTI, M. (1999a). Analisi qualitative dei depositi archeologici come indice guida nelle ricerche a sclara territoriale In M. Buscema & Semeion Group (Eds.), *Reti Neurali Artificiali e Sistemi Socieli Complessi. Teoria-Modelli-Aplicazioni.* Milan, Italy: FrancoAngeli Editore.

RAMAZZOTTI, M. (1999b). *La Bassa Mesopotamia come laboratorio storico. Le reti neurali artificiali come strumento di ausilio alle ricerche di archeologia territoriale.* Contributi e Materiali di Archeologia Orientale, VIII. Università di Roma la Sapienza. Italy.

REELER, C. (1999). Neural networks and fuzzy logic analysis in archaeology. In L. Dingwall, S. Exon, V. Gaffney, S. Laflin & M. Van Leusen (Eds.), *Archaeology in the age of the internet.* Oxford: ArcheoPress (BAR Int. Series S750).

REYNOLDS, R.G. (1999). An overview of cultural algorithms, *Advances in Evolutionary Computation.* McGraw Hill Press.

RIGOL, J.P., JARVIS, C.H., & STUART, N. (2001). Artificial neural networks as a tool for spatial interpolation. *International Journal of Geographical Information Science,*15(4), 323-343.

RIPLEY, B.D. (1993). Statistical aspects of neural networks. In O.E. Barndorff-Nielsen, J.L. Jensen & W.S. Kendall (Eds.), *Networks and chaos-statistical and probabilistic approaches* (pp. 40-123). London: Chapman and Hall.

SCHIFFER, M. (1987). *Formation Processes of the Archaeological Record.* Alburqueque (NM): University of New Mexico Press.

SCHRODT, P.A. (2002). Forecasts and Contingencies: From Methodology to Policy. *Paper presented at the theme panel Political Utility and Fundamental Research: The Problem of Pasteur's Quadrant at the American Political Science Association meetings, Boston, 29 August - 1 September 2002.* Retrieved July 2007 from http://www.ukans.edu/~keds/papers.html

SCHRODT, P.A. (2004). *Patterns, rules and learning: Computational models of international behavior* (2nd Edition). Parus Analytical Systems, Vinland, Kansas, USA. Retrieved July 2007 from http://www.ku.edu/~keds/books.html

SCOLLAR, I. (1990). *Archaeological prospecting and remote sensing.* Cambridge, UK: Cambridge University Press.

SERPEN, G. (2004). Managing spatiotemporal complexity in hopfield neural network simulations for large-scale static optimization source. *Mathematics and Computers in Simulation, 64*(2), 279–293.

SHARDA, R., & PATIL, R.S. (1992). Connectionist approach to time series prediction: An empirical test. *Journal of Intelligent Manufacturing, 3*(5), 317-323.

SHELLITO, B.A., & PIJANOWSKI, B.C. (2003). Using neural nets to model the spatial distribution of seasonal homes. *Cartography and Geographic Information Science, 30*(3), 281-290.

SHENNAN, S. J. (2000). Population, culture history, and the dynamic of culture change. *Current Anthropology, 41*, 811-835.

SHENNAN, S. J., & WILKINSON, J. R. (2001). Ceramic style change and neutral evolution: A case study from neolithic europe. *American Antiquity, 56*, 577-594.

SKUPIN, A., & HAGELMAN, R. (2005). Visualizing demographic trajectories with self-organizing maps. *GeoInformatica, 9*(2), 159–179,

SPITZ, F., & LEK, S. (1999). Environmental impact prediction using neural network modeling. *Journal of Applied Ecology, 36*, 317-326.

STASSOPOULOU, A., & PETROU, M. (1998). Obtaining the correspondence between Bayesian and neural networks. *International Journal of Pattern Recognition and Artificial Intelligence, 12*(7), 901-920.

SUMPTER, N., & BULPITT, A. (1998). *Learning spatiotemporal patterns for predicting object behaviour.* Technical report, University of Leeds, School of Computer Studies.

TAKATSUKA, M. (2001). An Application of the Self-Organizing Map and Interactive 3-D Visualization to Geospatial Data. *Proceedings of the 6th International Conference on GeoComputation.* University of Queensland, Brisbane, Australia. Retrieved October 2005 from http://www.geo-computation.org/2001/papers/takatsuka.pdf

TANG, Z., ALMEIDA, C., & FISHWICK, P.A. (1991). Time series forecasting using neural networks vs. box-jenkins methodology. *Simulation, 57*(5), 303-310.

TIJSSELING, A., & BERTHOUZE, L. (2001). A Neural Network for Temporal Sequential Information. *Proceedings of the 8th International Conference on Neural Information Processing, Shanghai, China* (pp. 1449-1454).

VALDES, J.J., & BONHAM-CARTER, G. (2006). Time dependent neural network models for detecting changes of state in complex processes: Applications in earth sciences and astronomy. *Neural Networks, 19*, 196–207.

Van der BAAN, M., & JUTTEN, C. (2000). Neural networks in geophysical applications. *Geophysics, 65*(4), 1032–1047.

VARIEN, M.D., & MILLS, B.J., (1997). Accumulations Research: Problems and Prospects for Estimating Site-Occupation Span. *Journal of Archaeological Method and Theory*, vol. 4 (2), pp. 141-191.

VEMURI, V.R., & ROGERS, R.D. (1994). Time series and the forecasting problem. In V.R. Vemuri

& R.D. Rogers (Eds.), *Artificial neural networks: Forecasting time series.* Los Alamitos, CA: IEEE Computer Society Press.

VILLMANN, T., (1999). Benefits and Limits of the Self-Organizing Map and its Variants in the Area of Satellite Remote Sensoring Processing. *Proc. of European Symposium on Artificial Neural Networks (ESANN'99),* pp. 111-116.

WEIGEND, A.S., HUBERMAN, B., & RUMELHART, D. (1990). Predicting the future. A connectionist approach. *Int. Journal of Neural Systems, 1,* 193-210.

WESCOTT, K.L., & BRANDON, R.J. (1999). *Practical applications of GIS for archaeologists: A predictive modeling toolkit.* London: Taylor & Francis.

WHITE, R.W. (1989). The artificial intelligence of urban dynamics: Neural network models of urban structure. *Papers of the Regional Science Association, 67,* 43-53.

WILKINSON, G. (1997). Neurocomputing for earth observation-recent developments and future challenges. In M.M. Fischer & A.Getis (Eds.), *Recent developments in spatial analysis. Spatial statistics, behavioural modeling and computational intelligence.* Berlin: Springer.

WILLMES, L., BACK, T., YAOCHU, J., & SENDHOFF, B. (2003). Comparing neural networks and kriging for fitness approximation in evolutionary optimization. *CEC '03. The 2003 Congress on Evolutionary Computation, 2003, 1,* 663- 670.

YANG, X. (2005). *Implementation of neural network interpolation in ArcGIS and case study for spatial-temporal interpolation of temperature.* Master Project. The University of Texas at Dallas, GIS Program POEC 6389.

YOSHIDA, T., & OMATU, S. (1994). Neural network approaches to landcover mapping. *IEEE Transactions on Geosciences and Remote Sensing, 32,* 1103-1109.

ZHAI, L., TANG, X., LI L., & JIANG, W. (2005, August 27-29). Temporal association rule mining based on T-apriori algorithm and its typical application. *Proceedings of the International Symposium on Spatiotemporal Modeling, Spatial Reasoning, Analysis, Data Mining and Data Fusion,* Peking University, China.

ZHOU, J., & CIVCO, D.L. (1996). Using genetic learning neural networks for spatial decision making in GIS. *Photogrametric Engineering and Remote Sensing, 62*(11), 1287-1295.

ZUBROW, E. B.W. (2003). The archaeologist, the neural network, and the random pattern: problems in spatial and cultural cognition. In M. Forte and P.R. Williams (Eds.) F. El Baz & J. Wiseman (Co-Eds.), *The reconstruction of archaeological landscapes through digital technologies Italy-United States Workshop, Boston, Massachusetts.* Oxford: ArcheoPress.

ZUBROW, E. B.W., & ROBINSON, J. (2000) Between spaces: Interpolation in archaeology. In M. Gilling, D. Mattingly, & J. Van Dalen (Eds.), *Geographic information systems and landscape archaeology* (pp. 65-84). Oxford: Oxbow Press.

ZUPANEK, B., & MLEKUZ, D. (2001). Counting the uncountable: A quantitative approach to the religious differences between the roman towns of Emona and Poetovio. In Z. Stancic & T. Veljanovski (Eds.), *Computing archaeology for understanding the past.* Oxford: ArchaeoPress.

Chapter IX
An Automated Approach to Historical and Social Explanation

NEUROCLASSIFICATION AS SOCIAL EXPLANATION

Since the beginning of the book, we know that solving archaeological problems implies answering a *double causality* question:

- Given the perception of visual inputs, the automated archaeologist should explain *what* social activity produced in the past the evidence perceived in the present.
- Once it knows what social activity was performed, where, and when, the automated archaeologist should explain *why* such activities were performed there and then, and in what way.

It is obvious that answering the first question is a condition to solve the second. In the same way as human archaeologists, the automated archaeologist needs to know what, where and when before explaining why some social group made something, and how. That is to say, only after having explained why archaeological observables are the way they are in terms of the consequence of some social activity or bio-geological process performed in the past or in the present, the automated archaeologist will try to explain more abstract causal processes.

In previous chapters, we have been dealing, for the most part, with the first kind of problem. Automated discovery programs allow describing the action or process, which most probably caused the actual appearance of the archaeological record. Nevertheless, the automated archaeologist has not yet discovered *why* that activity took place there and then. Things become a bit more difficult when the automated archaeologist moves from the explanation of objects to the explanation of action and social behavior, because it should take into account people and people motivations.

The simplest way of understating social behavior is by classifying it. That means an automated archaeologist will explain people and social acts by recognizing them as members of some previously defined classes of people or events. Social explanation would then consist in the apprehension of the individual case as an instance of a general type, a type for which the intelligent machine should have a detailed and well-informed representation. Such a representation allows the system to anticipate aspects of social activity so far unperceived.

It is usual in the social sciences to classify people according to social attributes. Computational intelligence tools can help in such a classification. In the social sciences, a neural network can classify a population into homogenous groups using factors such as age, sex, and other socio-economic variables to infer social status or position. A classical example is that of Meraviglia (1996, 2001) on social mobility, where input variables "gender," "father's education," "father's class position when age of respondent is 14," and so on, are used to predict "son's (or daughter's) current class position." Although this can be a good example of social explanation, no any causal explanation should be generated in that way. After all, we have already examined many examples of causal explanation based on alternative approaches, and we will present some other ways at the end of the chapter. In any case, we can explore the explanatory possibilities of "social classification" beyond trivial associations.

The most obvious way of classifying people to understand social dynamics in archaeology can be done in burial analysis. By studying the differences between graves according to the material remains of funerary rituals, an automated archaeologist can understand how social personality was built by a human group in the past. Wealth and poverty in acient times, prehistoric social elites and inequality, past evidence of social marginality can be discovered by studying the quantity and diversity of archaeological grave goods, ways of body manipulation, etc. In general, the quantity of labor invested in a funerary ritual is a good estimation of the social importance of the buried individual.

Davino et al. (1999) have studied the Iron Age Italian cemetery of Sala Consilina. 173 graves were selected and described using as input variables the following nominal variables: preservation, burial length, sex/age, depth, quantity of grave goods, most frequent grave goods category (clay, metals), and type (according to the presence/absence of weapons and other features). The goal was to calculate a classification rule for age/sex, based on grave attributes. A neural network was so created using 24 inputs (one for each qualitative value), three outputs (male, female, and child), and one hidden layer made of eight units. The network was trained with 110 graves whose skeletons were determined according sex and age, and used using the remaining 63. With training data, the network obtained 90.26 percent of correct classification, so it was used with the unclassified data, and was able to determine 39 male burials, 15 female, and nine children.

Although rather simple, this example is not trivial. It explains how we can explain the different social personality of women and men in Italian peninsula during 9th-7th centuries B.C. The limitations of the approach lie on the supervised nature of the neural network. The only "known" category to be predicted is "sex" or "age," because there is an independent instrument for measuring them (physical anthropology analysis). If we could find additional known categories, a social classification approach would be very interesting for understanding social personality. For instance, if we estimate the quantity of labor invested in making some burials, we would build an input-output function relating the presence/absence of some funerary symbols, predicting how they relate (in a nonlinear way) with social status, measured in terms of the quantity of labor invested in the burial. Additionally, we can use general information about a human group (productive mechanisms, degree of inequality, kinship, exchange, etc.) and build a neural network correlating observed material culture items (archaeological record) with interpreted social categories.

On the other hand, we can follow an unsupervised approach, that is to say, trying to build a general classificatory framework to explain observed differences. Let us consider the following simulated example. Suppose the automated archaeologist investigates a Late Bronze Age cemetery from Western Europe. 65 graves have been identified from three different historical phases, which can be ordered consecutively (Phase *A*, Phase *B*, Phase *C*). Hypothetically, this society evolved slowly towards increasing complexity and inequality, in such a way that during the two first phases, burials are relatively similar and homogenous, and that beginning in Phase *C*, social elites appear, together with social exclusion practices. We want to explore this situation with a description of grave goods discovered at different burials (six different kinds of pottery vases, the quantity of bronze, gold and iron, the quantity of animal bones, and the typology of the burial itself (type of ritual, type of grave). Given that this is an unsupervised analysis, we will build a self-organized map. I have used for this example the Databionics ESOM freeware tool.

The network contains 17 input units (one for each variable describing the archaeological record of burial practices documented at the simulated site). The SOM layer has been defined as an array of 20x20 neurons in a rectangular neighborhood configuration (see details on Chapter IV). After 50 iterations, the corresponding U-Matrix is the following one (Figure 9.1).

As it was presented in Chapter IV, the U-matrix should be understood as the cluster structure revealed by all the variables together. It should be interpreted as follows: a group of similar burials falls into a light grey or white in the U-matrix surrounded by black areas. The dissimilarity among the different clusters is indicated by the intensity of grey level on the U-matrix. In this case, we can suggest a minimum of six groups.

Let us explain this social clustering by activating relevant components separately. A common first step in investigating unsupervised classification results is to inspect vector weights for all the neurons, one component plane (i.e., variable) at a time. Through these component planes we can realize emerging patterns of data distribution on SOM's grid (Kohonen, 2001), detect correlations among variables and the contribution of each one to the SOM differentiation.

Figure 9.1. Self-organized map of simulated burial data (U-Matrix)

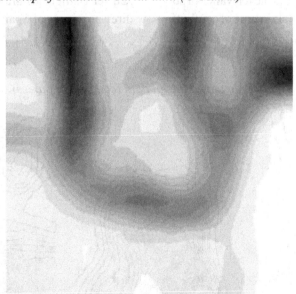

Figure 9.2 gives three of the component planes in a grey level representation, where the darker the color, the higher the contribution of that factor. In the case of "bronze" and "iron," both prestige items, there is a region in the self-organized map were burials classified there show high values. It coincides with the detected cluster in the inferior left sector of the U-matrix (Figure 9.1), represented as a light-grey area. If we consider now some non-prestige items like "decorated pottery," they concentrate on another region of the SOM, which distinguishes itself from the group of social elite burials.

In this way, the SOM layer configures a conceptual space for social categories. We can label different areas using appropriate social classification labels. That means that, by relating component displays, an automated archaeologist can explore and make interpretations of relationships and patterns in the dataset. New knowledge can be found by this hypothesis formulation, exploration, and by the association between several representations of attributes.

The treatment of the dead during conflict may vary significantly with the conventional behaviors associated with mortuary customs. Stephanie Spars (2005) has investigated the relevance of social variability among burials in time of conflicts.

She intends to explore the treatment of war dead across time, space, and culture by identifying characteristics of anomalous sites/behaviors at burial sites within conflict areas and suggesting possible explanations for those deviations from normative practice. She has build a SOM neural network using as input the military or civilian status of the individual, the presence of normative container associated with the individual, the cause of death (related to combat, extrajudicial, disease, natural), the mutilation of the corpse, the normative position of the body, presence of ritual markers, grave marker, cloth, presence/absence of grave goods, permanent or temporary cemetery, intentional obscuration. The author analyzed five datasets from seven different conflict episodes spanning from the 15th century to the late 20th century. Each data set represents a different century, type of conflict, culture (including social and/or political groups), and grave type. The five data sets are: the battle of Towton mass grave (Medieval England); the Snake Hill mass grave (Canada, War of 1812); the remnants of four graves from the American Civil War battle of Antietam; six individual graves from Ox Hill, Virginia, dated on U.S. Civil War; the battle of Little Big Horn (Custer Battlefield) graves; four mass graves in three provinces of Spain from the Spanish Civil

Figure 9.2. Self-organized map of simulated burial data (component planes)

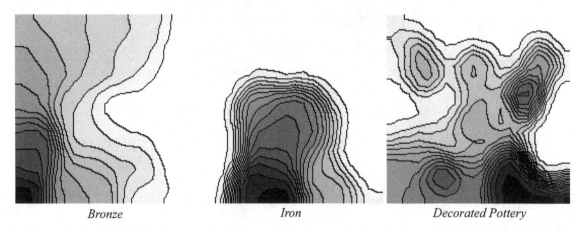

| *Bronze* | *Iron* | *Decorated Pottery* |

War (1936-1939); graves from the United Nations military engagement in the Korea peninsula; and several small graves from conflicts in the Balkans, one site in Bosnia-Herzegovina and another site in Croatia. Additional data sets contain a description of normative burials at each historical situation. The SOM method was used to create clusters of data, representing the three conflict types, friendly, neutral, and hostile, and to examine correlations between variables within the data set as a whole. Standard statistical clustering methods produced good differentiation of normative versus conflict burials, although these tools showed their incapability of extracting mining from the diversity of data, geographic regions, and conflict type. The SOM also shows clearly two main groups: normative burials vs. conflict burial, based on cemetery type. These two parts are then further divided into six smaller clusters, which identify subtle variations in both normative and conflict behavior, based on the presence/absence of ritual markers (characteristic of 19th century American data), and on the relevance of hostile burials, that is, civilians killed extra-judicially without any normative grave goods or markers.

Those examples allow us to consider how SOM clustering of social groups provides a good representation of the natural levels of fuzziness that seem to characterize social data (Astrom & Vencatasawmy, 2001; Lobo et al., 2004; Openshaw, 1994). Many social features vary in size and thus the level of precision and resolution of the data varies geographically. The main problem in social classifications is the "sense" that cluster labels should have, that is, their correspondence with what we know about socio-economic and demographic structure, and on the degree to which the variables and data selected as input deliver results that are perceived to be useful at the end of the process (Openshaw et al., 1995).

Going a bit beyond social groups in the past, a similar approach has been used to build a universal conceptual map of the concepts of welfare and poverty (Kaski & Kohonen, 1996; Kohonen, 1989).

Here the data consisted of World Bank statistics of countries in 1992. Altogether, 39 indicators describing various quality-of-life factors, such as state of health, nutrition, educational services, etc, were used. The complex joint effect of these factors can be visualized by organizing the countries using the self-organized map. Countries that had similar values of the indicators found a place near each other on the map.

Social scientists are using self-organized networks in this way for categorizing social groups. Winter and Hewitson (1994) used social data from South African census to investigate racial and economic separation after the apartheid era. The resulting SOM layer was used as a classification of the spectrum of social characteristics. Among the overall patterns that emerge in this layer, the racial stratification is readily noticeable in the U-matrix: the "white" group is dominant in the lower right hand side of the image but is noticeably absent to the center of the image. By contrast, the "colored" group dominates the center.

Diapi et al. (1999) have used a neural network approach to study how various social factors (i.e., criminality, low cultural level, youth unemployment, low housing quality) affect sustainability. In their model, the authors used three kinds of indicators: the first group of features is used to estimate how the quality of human life is supported by the functional-environmental structure that offers possibilities for social interaction, but also risks of social and environmental degradation. The second group concerns the complex relationships between residence, labor, and income of the population, and the third group is designed to measure the economic vitality of the community, the efficiency of the urban structure. Negative externalities include the risks of economic stagnation, reduction of investments and building degradation.

Ponthieux and Cottrell (2001) proposed to use the Kohonen algorithm first to describe how the elements of living conditions at modern households are combined, and secondly to classify households according to their living conditions. The main interest is to analyze not only quantitative differences in the "levels" of living conditions, but also qualitative differences within similar "levels." Living conditions are described by variables about the dwelling itself, and about the environment. In a first step, the authors classify only the modalities, in order to obtain a good description of living conditions: how the characteristics of the environments and the opinion of people about their homes are combined. In a second step, the authors classify the observations, searching for a consistent grouping of households described only by their living conditions. The classifications obtained tend to confirm that beyond differences in the "level" of (bad) living conditions, there are significant within level differences in the nature of the difficulties. At first glance, the resulting SOM layer shows a first social category grouping very serious living conditions (low standard dwelling, absence of very common durable goods, and privations in elementary consumptions), a second one corresponding mainly to other problems relating to the dwelling and environmental disadvantages and a last group, at the "frontier" between "negative" and "neutral" conditions, characterized by the inability to afford one week's holidays or replacing worn out furniture that suggest a particular status for these items. Similar investigations have been published by Koua and Kraak (2004), Lobo et al. (2004), Silva et al. (2004), Skupin and Hagelman (2005), Ju et al. (2006).

All those examples contribute to emphasize a very important aspect of the "classification as explanation" approach. Even in the case of unsupervised learning, we need some prior knowledge in order to experiment with the resulting classification and be able to transform it in a real conceptual space. In all those cases, authors had some knowledge that allowed making relevant questions to the classification, for instance: "where in the self-organized map can be placed "poor" countries, or "negative living conditions." In the case of archaeological explanation, it is important

to consider this fact. Applying artificial intelligence algorithms to excavation data is a futile task, because observed data are not knowledge to be transformed into explanations, it is perceptual knowledge waiting to be explained in causal terms. If we want to create a conceptual map, then we need an exhaustive list of observations, in such a way that all variation is included. We need to know what "poor" means, before recognizing some elements of the archaeological record as "poor," or "rich," or anything similar. That is, we need observed causal events in an exhaustive set of different situations to obtain predictions before explaining. Only once you have obtained the knowledge, you or your automated machine will explain observed data.

TOWARDS A NEUROCOMPUTATIONAL APPROACH TO SOCIAL DYNAMICS

Besides being valuable tools for pattern recognition and functional inference, neural networks possess another interesting property: they can be viewed as complex systems, in which the low-level interaction of many simple components produces some observable order without any intervention of a higher order factor. Consequently, if we interpret highly interconnected neurons as social agents, and connections as interaction flows between people, we will have a model of social dynamics, whose behavior is described not by a system of coupled differential equations, but by a neural network.

When using the neurocomputational analogy, we are implicitly assuming that at some level of the abstraction, the functioning of society may be regarded as analogous to the functioning of a nervous system (Makarenko, 2006; Minsky, 1985; Nijkamp & Reggiani, 1998; Parisi & Nolfi, 2005; Puljic & Kozman, 2005; Schrodt, 2004; Szilagyi, 1991). Whereas, the nervous system is composed of individual neurons connected by synapses, and the state of each neuron depends on the signal arriving across synapses from other neurons, society is composed of individuals (or social roles), interlinked by social relationships. People's feelings, cognitions, and actions depend on the social context of each individual, which in turn is composed of other individuals.

Obviously, the neural network is only an analogy: social agents clearly do more than adding information they see and listen. However, the organizational structures of human societies resemble neural networks more than they resemble regression or expected utility equations. Neural and social networks have several common features. Both can be represented by a labeled directed graph structure, consisting of a set of nodes and a set of links connecting pairs of nodes. It is the pattern of interconnections what it is represented mathematically as a weighted, directed graph. The vertices or nodes represent basic computing elements (social agents), the links or edges represent the connections between agents (social relationships), the weights represent the strengths of these connections, and the directions establish the flow of information. The meaning of nodes (the "personality" of each social agent) plays no direct role in the computation: the social model is based only on the activation values of social agents and not on the individual characteristics of each one. However, labeling social agent nodes play an important indirect role, because the nature of the input to the model depends on the labels and the output of a model depends on its input.

To model a human society using this particular kind of network, we need to declare how the social agents process information arriving at the incoming links and disseminate the information on the outgoing links. Connections in network models represent influences arriving at each site from the rest of the sites in the network. That is, social agents mutually influence each other as participants in a group. People continuously develop their relationships by connecting or disconnecting with others. The competition for connection space

is intense, and success in finding and maintaining a connection depends on the activation of relationships. Therefore, by using a neurocomputational model of a society in which inhibitive links and excitative ones can coexist, it can be shown how the sole structure of social influence can originate stabilization or endogenous fluctuations in the state of the agents. In this way, non-convergent dynamics are derived from a quantitative effect, which is the number of neighbors. At the level of the individual agent, the network's architecture of connections and the weights of the individual connections can change because of the agent's interactions with the external environment, and these changes translate into changes in behavior (learning). At the population level, a social agent is a member of an evolving population of individually different agents and the architecture of connections and/or the connection weights of the agent's neural network are encoded in the agent's inherited class membership. Social identity and group membership reproduce selectively and with the constant addition of new variants (social change, social mobility) and it results in neural/ behavioral changes in successive generations of agents (evolution). This neural representation of social dynamics may serve then as a bridge between micro-and macro-levels of descriptions of social reality. The stable solutions of the system of interconnected people could represent stable formations in society. The network parameters like "energy," "learning rate," "temperature" could be translated as ideas of social energy and social temperature, that is to say, as emergent social properties produced by the interactions between individuals. Changes in society would then be explained as redistributions of the connections between the units (Szilagyi, 1991).

There are different levels of abstractions for neural and social network models. One abstraction would represent a human society as a multilayer organization: the input layer consists of information that enters from the external environment (Schrodt, 2004). This information is well organized (the number of neurons and input channels), but each social agent at the middle layer (or layers) integrates different information and knowledge about other people and circumstances, weighing the reported information positively, negatively or ignoring it altogether. Each of these social agents has access to all of the collected information, but they use it differently. For example the member of a social and political elite interested in recommending military activity in a conflict might positively weight information on power disparities, negatively weight the presence of social conflict in his/her collectivity, and ignore information on the cause of social conflict. These individuals are finally involved in some collective behaviors (output units), which modify the environment and the knowledge each individual has about the other people and their circumstances. Activation would flow from knowledge to behavior, from information to activity in different cycles, modifying interaction flows between individual at each time step, modifying potential behavior, and even the relationships between the individuals. In this particular example, and contrary to what happens in the majority of feed-forward networks, the units representing social agents (neurons at the middle layer or layers) are all interconnected by weighted links that simulate power relationships.

Alternatively, a human society can also be represented using a competitive network (Situngkir, 2003). In such a neural network, every neuron represents human actions and the social system evolves in the way each agent competes to survive, while the winning agents are imitated by the losing ones. The bounded input and mechanism to produce certain behaviors can be viewed as a legitimization of the norms or morality.

Bellomo et al. (2007) offer a much more developed analogy. They describe a social system as constituted by a large population of interacting individuals. Their number is constant in time. Individuals are divided into several social levels characterized by different social states, where the lowest level corresponds to extreme poverty and the highest to the maximum level social state. The key point in this model is that interactions modify social status. They have to be precisely regarded not as individual based interactions, but as the output of complex mechanisms such as social conflicts, welfare politics, taxation politics, economical decisions, and so on. The overall wealth is known and is preserved, as a global quantity, in the evolution. Political management may operate in different ways. Specifically, it is important in modeling to distinguish between interactions where high-level classes operate to help low-level classes to improve their state, or in contrast, situations where high-level classes exploit lower level classes.

Based on what is now known about the properties of neural networks, these different approaches provide at least three advantages in explaining social activity (Schrodt, 2004). First, in contrast to a finite set of social principia or laws, a human society represented as a neural network has some associative recall, error correction, insensitivity to missing information, and resistance to systemic failure. Because in social groups individuals may fail randomly—inexperienced or incompetent leaders, blindness for long term consequences of each action, insistence on self-profit above any other "rational" decision or the effect of isolation, this property of insensitivity to individual failure is particularly important. Those capabilities derive from the networked structure of the organization, not from the cognitive capabilities of its individual members. Second, a network structure is an effective means of dealing with social organization bandwidth limitations. Units at the input level act as feature detectors: in deciding whether to raise concerns about an issue, agents at the middle layer can use their high bandwidth associative and sub-cognitive capabilities to infer complex motives, draw historical analogies, and deal with multiple counterfactuals and contingencies. They weight the information coming from the exterior and continually adjust those weights. On the contrary, the information that must be transmitted through the limited organizational bandwidth is simple: one needs only to know whether individuals are sending "on" or "off" signals, and the only decision one must transmit is one's own resulting state.

Let us review some analogies between neural networks and social dynamics. A very simple example is Hinton's model of kinship knowledge and reasoning (Hinton, 1986). A neural network was designed and trained, so it learned how an individual could be *socially related* to another individual. Consider for instance the case of *kinship* where a kind of automated anthropologist has to calculate that *person1* is-the-mother-of *person2*. Hinton designed a multi-layered network to carry out a reasoning task involving the kinship relations between 24 individuals. The input contains two neurons, one for depicting people, and another for containing the different social relationships (mother, father, son, daughter, etc.). The output neuron should contain the name (or label) of the person that maintains the relationship with the person introduced in the input. The input units use a localized encoding for *person1* and the relationship (one neuron for each possible relationship). The fact that the 24 units coding for *person1* must feed their activity pattern through a bottleneck of six units forces the network to find a distributed representation of the different individuals that extracts the relevant features for inferring *person2*. Backpropagation learning was used to train the network on available triplets *<Person1, relationship, Person2>*. Given some combination of *person1* and relationship as input, the system is expected to signal the appropriate *person2* (or set of such individuals) which fits this description. The ability to respond correctly to new cases indicates that the network has found a way of representing, in its weights, the relationships among the family members.

This anthropological example can be very relevant in an archaeological investigation where the social agents are not observable, but inferred from indirect evidence or from ethnological analogy. For instance, in our ethno-archaeological research in Tierra del Fuego (the southernmost part of America), we have ethnographical and ethno-historical data on the way indigenous Yamana populations performed labor, what men and women did, and even, the labor activities carried on by children and seniors. We can configure a network with the following neurons in the input layer:

- One unit for each described labor activity: hunting, butchering, cooking, cleaning, tool manufacture, baby care, education, health, etc.
- Some other units for describing the quantity of work (time, task complexity, number of people involved) for each activity.
- Four different units for social agents that performed that action: man, woman, boy, girl.

In the output layer, we would need:

- Some units for representing the social agents that took some benefit by the action: man, woman, boy, girl.
- A unit for measuring the social value that Yamana Society gave to this action (irrelevant, important, basic, etc).

The purpose of the network would be to generalize the relationship between quantity of work, social value, and the nature of the agent that made the action. Preliminary results for such an investigation have already been published (Barceló et al., 1999, 2006). This work is being done by a joint research team of the Universitat Autònoma de Barcelona and the Institució Milà i Fontanals (CSIC), Spain, under the coordination of Jordi Estévez and Assumpció Vila.

The *<agent, relationship, agent>* triplet can also be expressed in terms of an influence diagram, giving weight to the influences in term of Bayesian functions, as we discussed at the end of Chapter III. It would be interesting to integrate a Bayesian network with a neural network. Kim et al. (1999) have explored how to build influence diagrams using neural networks. Their results show, however, that it may be an appropriate way to solve the problem in the topological level, but the generated causal representations are not usually well-formed influence diagrams. It needs further modification to be applicable to real decision problems.

Neural weighted links can do much more than represent interpersonal connections. A relevant example is the analysis of the social organization of a medieval peasant community before the Hundred Years' War perfomed by Villa and Boulet (2007). The authors use textual data about agrarian contracts from the Castelnau-Montratier seignory (Lot, South West of France) between 1240 and 1350. Based on this database, the authors constructed a weighted graph having 226 vertices (the peasants) which are linked together if they appeared in the same contract. The weights were simply the number of common contracts in which two peasants appeared together. The aim of the investigation was to extract social tendencies in the graph linking "economically" medieval peasants, using a variant self organizing map, the Dissimilarity SOM algorithm, which is able to process non-vector data, only described by a dissimilarity measure. Every class found by the dissimilarity SOM corresponds to one or several connected communities. Results emphasize the fact that family links are more important than geographical ones.

In Geography, the data needed for a social interaction explanation at the spatial level consists of a Flow Matrix, which indicates the start and end of some social movement or transference (Nijkamp & Reggiani, 1992).

TO DESTINATION			
FROM	*Location 1*	*Location 2*	*Location 3*
Location 1	a	b	c
Location 2	d	e	f
Location 3	g	h	i

Matrix values represent here intensities (a measure of the frequency and/or importance of interaction). Total flows leaving location 1 is the row sum ($a+b+c$), whereas total movements to location 2 is the column sum ($a+d+g$). The key inputs to a spatial interaction model are then, the sum of flows (O_i), the sum of movements (D_j), the observed matrix of flows(T_{ij}), and the cost of travel (or distance) between locations(c_{ij}):

$$T_{ij} = O_i D_j c_{ij}^{\ \beta}$$

A neural network set up for this problem would include three input neurons (flow produced, flow attracted and flow length), one hidden layer with and one output layer, the observed flows (Openshaw, 1994, 1997; White, 1995). In our case, T_{ij} is the output value, $O_i D_j c_{ij}$ are the inputs and β is a bias unit.

In archaeology, it is not easy to distinguish between "from" and "to." We may build distance models and neighborhood relationships, but we lack the "directionality" component on any *flow* or transference action. However, we may consider that any *attraction* force is directly proportional to the number or intensity of interactions between "peripheral social locations" and a "central core location," and inversely proportional to the attraction force exerted by alternative periphery social locations. Therefore, if we can distinguish between people located at the periphery and the centre, then we can use a variation of the same flow matrix. Consequently, in the archaeological case, T_{ij} can be described in the following terms: it is the amount of similarity or frequency of interactions from origin *i* to destination *j*. c_{ij} is the cost or distance between *i* and *j* (geographical or "social" distance, i.e., dependence). O_i is the size of peripheral locations, D_j is the size of core areas (Barceló, 2001). According to Black (1995), such a the network would have three inputs: (a) number of flows produced at each site; (b) number of flows attracted at each site; (c) flow length. The network also has one output, (d) number of observed flows.

Other examples of neurocomputational models of social interaction at the spatial level have been published by Manfred Fischer and colleagues (Fischer & Gopal, 1993; Fischer & Reismann, 2002; Gopal & Fischer, 1996). The authors tried to predict the intensity of interaction between social entities. The input is a 32x32 matrix, whose values represent distances between spatial locations. As we have seen, those can be measured as geographical distances or as any other measure of difference between two social units. The output is also a 32x32 matrix showing the intensity of interaction flows. In this application, this is actually a measure of interregional telecommunications flow, but for our purposes, it can be any other measure of interaction strength. The idea is that a feed-forward neural network can learn a mapping between geographical distance (or similarity/difference relationships), and the intensity of interaction. Obviously, this is a supervised approach, so we would need observed instances where some distance measure is related to some interaction strength. An archaeological adaptation of this example would be using geographical distances and measures of differences in the frequency of different artifact categories (imported pottery, imported raw materials, locally made metallurgy, etc.) as input, and estimations of the interaction strength between both settlements based on the quantity of objects with a similar origin. Many variations from this assumption can be imagined.

Klüver and Stoica (Klüver et al., 2005; Stoica & Klüver, 2007) describe a computational model for the simulation of the emergence of social order. The model is theoretically based on the theory of social typifying by Berger and Luckmann. Social order is the result of mutual typifying processes of at least two interacting agents. Social rules emerge via "habitualization," that is, by the iterative application of the same action strategies the agents have successfully used during previous interactions. "Successfully" refers to the fact that the agents try to make the best of the action situation. They do not simply try to maximize their own profit but they try to obtain rules of interaction that can be accepted by both agents. This process of establishing mutually obligatory rules of interaction is not necessarily symmetric, because emerging social order may frequently be a hierarchical one. Klüver's model consists of interacting artificial individuals (agents), each one represented by two neural networks, an action net, and a perception net. The action network whose task is the generation of adequate rules of action is a multilayered feed-forward network. The input layer of the action network represents the personality of each agent, written as a vector $X_i = (x_1, ..., x_s)$. The output layer $Y = (y_1, ..., y_s)$ represents components of social activity such as coming near, escaping, working together to produce the same item, stealing, exchanging, paying tribute, obeying or disobeying an order, and the like. These vectors are social rules in the sense "if A meets B, then A acts according to the vector Y_{AB}," and vice versa. When A for the first time meets B, both have to evaluate the other, that is, they have to find mutually a behavior Y_A and Y_B that is suitable for oneself and for the other. The neurocomputational models representing agent A and agent B start with random weight matrices with the described restrictions. "Starting" means that each activation network gets its respective X-vectors as input, that is the X-vectors of their own personalities and social characteristics and generate a Y-vector of possible social actions. A behavior that is satisfying for both is reached when the relation between the personalities is nearly the same as the relation between the actions. The reason for this definition is that a person tends to act rather "strongly" in those characteristics where he or she is good or even superior in relation to others; in turn, other agents accept this type of action if they perceive that the first agent is indeed superior in this respective aspect. To be sure, an agent may be in error whether he is indeed good in some aspects. Then the mutual adjusting process forces the agent to correct his internal structure, the weight matrix, at least in this aspect. If this is the case, i.e., if the first actions are not satisfactory, the backpropagation algorithm is used for the changing of the internal structure of both agents. Now this process of establishing rules of interactions is repeated with the other agents. As a result, we have a social group where each agent is connected with each other agent by a specific Y-vector Y_{NM} for two persons N and M. The set of all Y-vectors is the social order of this group, generated by the perception and evaluation of the other agents.

The perception network (PN) is a hetero-associative net with two or more layers. The input layer of the PN of a person A is the X-vector of a person B, which the person A meets. The output layer is the Y-vector of A with respect to the person B. Y_{AB} is again the action vector of A with respect to person B. A and B mutually generate action vectors Y with respect to one another, as was described above. These vectors are rules of interaction insofar as A and B always act according to their vectors when they meet again. When these rules are established, the PNs of both agents are trained to associate the X-vector of the other agent B with the own vector Y_{AB} (in the case of A); the same is the case after A has established a mutual rule with C, D, and E. A then has four rules at its disposal that are "stored" in its PN by the training processes of associating a certain X-vector with the corresponding action vector. When A meets a new person F, there are two possibilities:

1. F is not similar to any member of the group (in the perception of A). In this case, the PN of A will not recognize F; A and F will have

to establish specific rules of behavior according to the procedure described previously.

2. F is similar to a member of the group, say D. Then the PN of A will generate the vector Y_{AD} when receiving the X-vector of F. In this case, F will be perceived by A as the same type as D, although F is not identical with D (F is another person or agent).

When A acts with Y_{AD}, F has to adjust his own Y-vector with respect to A; the adjusting process is not mutual but only the task of the newcomer F. The reason for this is the consideration that members of an already established group only typify a newcomer, whereas the newcomer has to adjust his behavior with respect to all members of the group. Now the rules of interaction become general rules in the sense that they are valid not only for a particular agent B but also with respect to all other agents that belong to the same type as B. In sociological terms, the rules are valid for all agents that belong to the same social type, that is, that occupy the same social role. Nevertheless, that is just one possibility of interpretation. In any case, the agents now are able to typify, that is, to abstract from individual peculiarities of other agents and to perceive them as representatives of a certain type. Y-vectors mean, as described, social rules of interaction. The group is socially structured in the sense that each actor knows how to behave toward another actor when meeting him again. This is done by the PN. In addition, it is possible to generate a social structure of the group in the sense that the group members are placed onto a social hierarchy. The model described so far represents the emergence of social structure in a group of actors or agents respectively.

Bainbridge took a different approach (Bainbridge, 1995; Bainbridge et al., 1994). He has built one particular kind of network, based on maximization of variance across categories in a category (varimax nets), to study how religious beliefs emerge in a human population. The key idea in this approach is that humans seek explanations because they are valuable. Tragically, many of the rewards that humans seek are very difficult to obtain. Bainbridge assumed that when the individual does not have access to the reward it needs, he or she turns towards religion, because religions are postulates of reward that are not readily susceptible to unambiguous evaluation. Bainbridge built a scenario of 24 individuals exchanging rewards. The idea of such a neural network was to simulate the impossibility of most individual human beings to create religion in isolation from other believers. The simulated individuals (neurons) learn that gods can be good exchange partners in some conditions. This is a somewhat strange example: the neural networks should learn something that does not exist, but in some circumstances, what cannot be proved (religion, supernatural beings) is the only learnable category.

Nowak and colleagues (Nowak & Vallacher, 1998, 2002; Nowak et al., 1998) have applied the theory of recursive neural networks to the analysis of social interaction. This theory explicitly goes beyond what we have seen up to now, allowing the explanation of how patterns of incoming information about the social environment can produce dynamics of interactions between individuals. As we discussed in precedent chapters, a recursive neural network is characterized by massive feedback loops between neurons, without separate layers. Every neuron is connected to every other neuron. The central idea of this kind of neural network model is that the relation between individuals or specific tokens of information is bidirectional. In the social interpretation of such a neural topology, "learning" the social environment would correspond to the formation or dissolution of relationships (i.e., connections) among individuals (i.e., neurons) in a group. Positive connections represent relationships in which the two individuals influence one another to have similar behavior, moods, attitudes, and so forth, whereas negative connections represent reactance-like influences between the two indi-

viduals. If the interaction between two individuals is positive, it means that one unit reinforces the other's activity (cooperation). Positive connections typically correspond to relations with positive valence (i.e., friendship, solidarity, reciprocity, help, collaborative work), and negative connections correspond to relationships with negative valence (dislike, hostility, resentment, etc.). In case of a negative matrix element, one unit tries to suppress the other's activity (competition). In some situations, however, the sign of connection represents strategic decisions concerning coalition formation, rather than an affective quality. It is also imaginable that coercion can be modeled as a positive connection from the dominated to the dominant, balanced with a negative connection from the dominant to the dominated. In reality, of course, everyone is influenced by more than one other person. Social interactions rarely are the sole source of personal change. Each individual's activity depends on many other factors. The joint effect of all such factors has been represented by Nowak et al. as a random influence on each individual. In recursive neural networks, such random influences are commonly referred to as *noise*. The introduction of noise can qualitatively change the dynamics of processes in networks. In particular, it can make a given individual change his or her opinion in a way that is contrary to social influence. The greater the proportion of outside and random influences on agent's activity, the weaker the role of equilibriums produced by the structure of social relations within the group.

To analyze recursive neural networks as models of dynamic social networks, it is important to distinguish two fundamentally different types of dynamics. The first type occurs in neural networks during recognition and involves changes in states of neurons, with the connections among neurons remaining stable. Such network dynamics correspond to the convergence of the state of the network to one of its attractors. It may be described socially as social agents trying to adjust their activity to the total influence they receive from interactions with other people, from the environment, and random influences. The general rule is that if the sum of all inputs from other neurons exceeds a certain threshold, the neuron adopts an excited state. Otherwise, it adopts a low value, corresponding to a non-excited state. Interpreted in terms of social networks, the dynamics of the neurons correspond to individuals' changing their activity because of influence through existing social ties with other individuals. The model of a social group then undergoes evolution, with each social agent (neuron) adjusting to the influence (activation) arriving from other social agents in the group. Eventually, the dynamics of the group reaches some equilibrium state, so called attractor, in which the network's flow of activations stabilizes.

The second type of dynamics occurs during learning and involves changes in the connections with the neurons remaining stable. The dynamics of connections are defined in terms of a learning algorithm that guarantees that the desired configuration of links and weights functions as an attractor. In the social interpretation, such dynamics correspond to the formation and dissolution of social relation based on the concrete behavior of individuals. Because such changes converge on attractors, only certain configurations of social activity and so forth are likely to be observed for a given social relationship.

The assumption is that if two individuals are in the same state simultaneously, the connection between them will become more positive, whereas if two individuals are in a different state at the same time, the connection between them will become more negative (inhibitory). Suppose the neurons represent different social categories (men, women, boys, girls), and we have some ethnographic or archaeological information about social inequalities on different issues among them. For instance, we know the time individuals from each category dedicate to different productive and reproductive activities or the relationship quantity of labor/received benefit from labor. Such social information

will be represented as different activations pattern. The purpose of the analysis is to create a recursive network that finds such attractors (each social situation in which we have measured some degree of inequality), in terms of positive and negative connections. Through the appropriated learning algorithm, it will be established a structure for the network such that the above configurations would correspond to an attractor. We assume that the connection between two elements is proportional to the correlation between their respective states. To allow for variation in the strength of different equilibriums, one can introduce a weight for each pattern, such that the more important patterns have higher weights. In the social interpretation, the greater the proportion of issues on which individuals share the same inequalities, the more positive the relationship between the individuals, and hence the more positive the influence they have over one another. In effect, the social position of every individual are anchored on the similarity of labor activities with which he or she has positive social relations. If the number of situations in which there is some inequality increases, a negative social relationship develops. As differences in labor appear are discovered, the positive ties will weaken and eventually negative ties will develop. The strength of negative ties is proportional to the number of dissimilarities minus the number of similarities. Influence to the context of such inhibitory connections is likely to be manifest as reactance.

Louzon and Atlan (2007) take a different approach to the complex systems analogy between human societies and neural networks. Instead of reproducing social interaction in terms of neuron-weighted connections, they intend to show that "intentional" activity within such a model is not required to explain what we spontaneously attribute to conscious decisions. The social properties that we saw emerged from social interaction patterns were in fact the result of relatively simple constraints, deterministic or stochastic at the level of the individual parts. The architecture of the network and some learning rules are established directing the process of social order emergence. Only the detailed evolution of the units and connections is not explicitly programmed and is self-organized in that sense. Thus, some internal dynamics leads to the detection of non-obvious hidden rules or regularities in the data. A step further would be the building of self-organized social networks able to create the meaning of their agent behavior in the form of functional goals not previously programmed and achieved further repeatedly, even with possible variations. The authors suggested that some memory device should be used so that the functional meaning of social activity within the network would result from self-observation, i.e. an internal comparison between previous states and the current one. This kind of self-organization would be appropriately "intentional," at least in the minimal sense of an intentional action directed by an internally specified goal. Such intentionality is obviously limited when compared with human intentionality with all its aspects of long term planning, and the so-called creative intelligence. In this study, the meaning of "intentions" has been limited to conscious decisions to act towards goals, defined as such by the previous self-organized functioning of the network.

Louzon and Atlan describe a network that defines its own goals. It is achieved by transforming non-intentional causal sequences of states into procedures to reach a goal. Practically, the model is made of two related networks. The first one is a self-organized recurrent network. It evolves from any input initial state towards a steady state, defined as its output (a stable attractor exhibiting some macroscopic structure). As in the case of standard pattern recognition systems, this final state may be associated with some functional behavior, provided some observer may be aware of it and find it meaningful. In this model, this observer is the system itself. This is partially achieved by the storage of a link between final and original states. One more element is needed,

as a kind of satisfaction function, to weigh the value of different outputs, in order to choose and define them as interesting (or desired goals). The second network assumes the function that is working as non-supervised learning network. The satisfaction function is provided from inside by the self-organized recurrent neural network and the most frequent occurrences of what has been learned in the first network. More precisely, it results from the history of exposures of this network to random external inputs from its environment and of responses to these inputs produced by its internal evolving structure. It is this history, which provides the satisfaction function in a dynamic way. The set of states kept as "desired" goals is the set of most frequently learned goals at each stage of this history.

This example is indeed compatible with a worldview where free will is seen as an illusion based in our ignorance of the real causes of our voluntary actions. Nevertheless, it does not exclude a sort of negative free will, based on the capacity to consciously inhibit and prevent some actions, initiated unconsciously, in the process of their execution.

BEYOND THE "NEURAL" ANALOGY: BUILDING AN ARTIFICIAL SOCIETY

Neurons after all, are not people. In human organizations, the information transmitted from person to person is frequently more complicated than a yes/no decision, or an intensity measure, a weight. The neural network analogy indicates that we can reduce human transmission bandwidth to be as narrow as a single bit without impeding robust decision-making, and the emergence of many interesting social properties. The doubt, however, remains whether the neural interconnectivity is the proper analogy for representing how people contact other people, exchange information in a collective way, and modify its activity because of the activity of other social agents.

For this reason, we have to explore those computer models, in which social agents and all other factors are not represented by a single neuron, but by a full expert system or even more, by a full neural network. In this way, we can move from the simple network of interconnected units, to a full artificial society.

Artificial Life is an attempt of studying all phenomena of life by reproducing them in artificial systems, either simulated in a computer or physically realized in robots and other physical artifacts (Bonabeau, 2002; Conte & Gilbert, 1995; Gilbert, 1998, 2000; Edmonds, 1998, 2000; Klüver et al., 2003; Thalmann, 2001). In those simulations, an agent is just any entity capable of self-controlled goal directed activity. The goals of the agent must be inherent to the agent, rather than being assigned according to a pragmatic 'stance' of an observer. A goal-directed action is under an agent's control if (*i*) the goal normally comes about as the result of the agent's attempt to perform the action, (*ii*) the goal does not normally come about except as the result of the agent's action, and (*iii*) the agent could have not performed the action (Wobcke, 1998).

Simulated agents are "living" in a simulated environment that is an abstraction of the original environment and thus part of the model (Castelfranchi, 2000; Klügl et al., 2005). This global entity may carry some global state variables like its own dynamics. These dynamics also can be so complex, for example, containing production of new entities, that one may assign some form of behavior with the simulated environment. Every environmental dynamic that is model-specific can be counted to it.

The simulated environment is unique for a specific multi-agent simulation. The most basic form of a simulated environment is an "empty world." In this case, the simulation model itself just consists of a society of simulated agents; the simulated environment possesses no specific state, nor dynamics. Such an empty simulated environment may only be used in very abstract simulation models. Any simulation model replicating detailed aspects of the real world requires a reproduction of some aspects of the agents' context. As the real world constrains the structure and behavior of the real agents, the simulated context plays that role for the simulated agent system. The perceptions of the simulated agents need to have some origin in all factors external to that agent, and it has to be represented in a specific environmental model. Thus, complex agent models require rich contextual models that cannot be abstracted to the empty environment without loosing the necessary complexity of the simulated agents.

Virtual social agents "live" in an environment populated by many other agents, so the successful completion of their tasks is subject to the decision and actions of others. On the one hand, agents may interfere with each other due to a mere side effect of their activities. Coordination, in a sense, occurs when agents adapt their activities in the face of those interactions. Coordination makes autonomous agents act as a distributed system, that is to say, as a society of autonomous problem solving agents from whose interactions coordinated activities emerge (Sawyer, 2005; Sun, 2006).

The model should consist then of intentional agents, making choices that depends on their individual preferences, expectations, and beliefs as well as upon incomplete knowledge of the environment. Patterns of cooperation emerge from individual choices at certain threshold values. An agent will cooperate with the fraction of the group perceived as cooperating exceeds a critical threshold. Critical threshold depend on group size and the social organizational structure emerging from the pattern of interdependencies among individuals. The potential for cooperative solutions of social dilemmas increases if groups are allowed to change their social structure.

An artificial prehistoric society is then a complex set of computational reactive units simulating how a group of people behaved in the past. There are an increasing number of examples in the specialized literature. Most of them are based on pioneering work by Jim Doran, whose EOS system simulated the emergence of social order at the end of Middle Paleolithic Times (Doran, 1997, 1999, 2000; Doran et al., 1994; Doran & Palmer 1995a, 1995b). This is a computer exploration of the explanatory model specified by Paul Mellars for the growth of social complexity around the time of the last glacial maximum in Southwestern France. Mellars's model relates changing features of the natural environment to the emergence within the human population of centralized decision-making and other related social phenomena. The main features of the system are:

- A two-dimensional simulated environment or "landscape" with a population of mobile agents and changing resources providing "energy" for the agents. If an agent does not sufficiently regularly acquire energy by "harvesting" and "consuming" resources, its energy level falls below its target satisfaction level and if the level falls to zero then the agent "dies," that is, disappears from the simulation. Agents can also be "born" during a simulation trial.
- The agents are structured as production systems with rules that "reactively connect environmental resources with social actions (hunting, gathering, consumption). In addition, there are other rules implementing inter-agent communication, generating, maintaining, and updating simple plans for execution. In fact, inter-agent relationship is expressed by beliefs within the social models of the agents concerned. For example, to say that Agent X and Y are in a leader/follower relationship means that Agent X believes that Agent Y is its leader and vice versa. This relationship comes into existence whenever one agent agrees to join another's plan.
- A variety of adjustable parameters, including those that specify the behavior of the resources in the environment.

Although very simple in their contents, the collective execution of agent plans implies that each individual plan affects the plans of other agents, and is affected by them in a recursive way. For instance, by observation of which agent first acquired each resource, agents came to recognize particular resources as "owned" by particular agents or groups. Agents then plan first for the acquisition of their own resources. Since resources are immobile, this implied that a form of territoriality was displayed.

Successive ameliorations of the model lead to consider an alternative explanation to that of Mellars, put forward by Clive Gamble. Although both authors seemingly disagree about what actually happened, when building the computer model there is no conflict between their views of the processes involved, because they are proposing different socio-cultural reactions to different environmental circumstances. In the new system, the environment has been programmed with lowering resource availability, without resource concentration and with unpredictable variation in richness of individual resources, which leads to greater number of alliances. Consequently, agents must be able to plan the coordination of many agents, and not to simple acquire complex resources, as in the previous version. This requires them to undertake a more complex form of planning. Agents decide the resources to target, the number of agents needed to acquire them, and then seek to make an agreed allocation of agents to resources.

As simulated, agents create and execute plans of behavior concurrently and asynchronously. The adoption of plans for execution is a complex matter. Agents select and invite other agents to join the plans they have created, selecting first their own followers and allies. Agents adopt those plans that they judge most potentially beneficial to themselves in terms of their own current beliefs: either they persist with their own plan, or they join another agent to execute its plan. The effect is that, with some delay, the more highly rated plans are adopted wholly or partially for execution by groups of agents. One of the agents in each group is the originator of the plan, and is therefore viewed by the others in the group as, potentially, a leader. After multiple instances of cooperation between two agents, an alliance will be formed. When two agents are in an alliance, they exchange information about their needs, and give priority to incorporating one another in their plans. In these new conditions, an instance of a leader/follower relationship, however, will come into being when cooperation is consistently "one-way." If Agent X is constantly recruited to Agent Y's plans over a limited period, then both X and Y will come to see themselves as in a leader/follower relationship with Y as the leader. Note that a leader/follower relationship can evolve from an alliance, and that both types of relationship can break down if the agents involved lose contact with one another for a sufficient time.

Running this computer model of an artificial society simply amounts to instantiate the simulated populations of people, letting the agents interact, and monitoring what emerges. What *emerges* from the collective execution of rules packaged in form of agents is a gradual updating of agent's beliefs and the concomitant modification of their plans, arriving at some form of *social order*. This should be conceived as any form of systemic structuring which is sufficiently stable, to be considered the consequence of social self-organization and self-reproduction through the actions of the agents, or consciously orchestrated by (some of) them (Castelfranchi, 2000; Sawyer, 2000). It can be studied as a non-accidental and non-chaotic (thus, relatively predictable, repeated and stable) pattern of interactions in a given system of interfering agents. Dynamic social order occurs when the stable macro-pattern or equilibrium is maintained thanks to an incessant local (micro) activity of its units, able to restore or reproduce the desired features. In any case, the basic point is that social order is not the sum

of single intentions, but the collective result of nonlinear interactions.

In the case of EOS, a group of 16 agents was subjected to the following resource regime: a brief initial period of ample available resource energy followed by a substantial period of very low available resource energy and then sustained ample resource energy again. The resources were spatially semi-distributed: randomly scattered over an area of 500x500 distance units within a 1,000x1,000 environment. Resources could be harvested by a single agent, and renewed every 30 cycles. Each agent consumes one energy unit per cycle. They all begin with energy levels of 1,000 and they all have a fixed target satisfaction level of 1,000. Agent's awareness range is set at 200 units of distance, and an agent's movement in each cycle is at most 50 units. In the initial phase (200 runs) the agent community survives easily without any complex activity nor alliance. As the reduction in resources impacts, from about 500 cycles, agents begun to build more elaborate coordination plans and leadership structures appear. Soon after 1,000 cycles, deaths began to cause instability in the structures. However, the agents continue with high levels of coordination planning, even long after resource availability has returned to normal, because their current energy levels have dropped well below their target level with the result that a very substantial hierarchy peak occurs around 2,500-3,000 cycles. Hierarchy persists, with some decline, over the next 5,000 runs.

Many other experiments have been run with this artificial society, although the implications of all the variants of the model have been nowhere near fully explored (Doran, 1997). In any case, this agent-based simulation is far more sophisticated than traditional explanations of hunter-gatherer societies. Doran's approach has been pursued by many other scholars, which have modeled different hypotheses about foraging behavior and social reproduction in small-scale societies. For instance, Parisi and Nolfi (2005) simulate a collection of agents living in the same environment, which contains food elements randomly distributed. A neural network controls each agent's behavior. Input units encode the position of the single food element nearest to the agent. Output units represent the agent behavior possibilities in the environment. The neural networks of all agents have the same architecture but at the beginning of the simulation, each individual agent is assigned a genotype encoding a different random set of connection weights for the agent's neural network. Each agent lives for a total number of time units (input/output cycles of its neural network) which is identical for all individuals. At birth, each individual has zero energy but its energy is incremented by one unit each time the individual by moving in the environment reaches (eats) a food element. When the energy of the individual reaches a threshold, the individual generates a new individual (offspring) which inherits the same genotype of its (single) parent, with the addition of some random changes to the quantitative value of some of the weights. The offspring is placed near its parent and the parent's energy returns to zero. At the beginning of the simulation, the agents are not very good at reaching food because of the random connection weights. The selective reproduction of those individuals better able to reach food and to increase their energy, and the constant addition of new variability to the pool of genotypes because of the random variations in the inherited connection weights, lead to an improvement in the average ability to reach food in the population with each successive generation. After an initial transient phase, population size stabilizes at a value reflecting the quantity of food present in the environment (carrying capacity). Food is periodically re-introduced to compensate for the food eaten, and the carrying capacity of the environment, and therefore, population size, are functions of the length of the interval between successive food re-introductions. The results of the simulation show that if food is re-introduced sufficiently frequently, the population distributes

itself homogeneously in the environment. However, if food is reintroduced less frequently, an interesting collective phenomenon emerges with respect to the spatial distribution of the agents: one observes oscillatory migratory waves of the agents in the environment. Agents may concentrate in a particular zone of the environment but, after a while, the population leaves the zone and disperses in the environment, with different individuals going in different directions. When the agents reach the wall that limits the environment, they remain near the wall for a while and then they slowly return to the initial zone in which they concentrate again. This oscillatory movement repeats itself periodically until the end of the simulation.

The agents in this simulation do not even perceive each other. Their respective neural networks are able to perceive only the food elements and made movement decisions consequently. It responds to input from the nonsocial environment (food) with output behavior, which is uniquely directed to the nonsocial environment (eating the food). However, such output behavior alters the physical environment, and hence the input the neural network will receive on the next cycle. In this way, individual agents can have an indirect influence on other individuals since each agent responds to an environment altered by the behavior of other agents. This can produce emerging collective phenomena in the spatial distribution of the population. The agents periodically modify their output behavior (spatial aggregation and disaggregation) when they *learn to predict* how the action at a previous step modifies the input at the next step. Many individuals can end up near each other simply because they tend to approach the same localized resource such as food or a water source. In these circumstances too, the agents' behavior resulting in social aggregation has not evolved for that function. Each individual approaches food or water for eating or drinking, not for social purposes. However, even if it is a simple by-product of learning nonsocial behaviors, social aggregation can be a favorable pre-condition for the emergence of social behaviors such as communication and economic exchange among individuals that happen to find themselves near each other. In other circumstances, however, social aggregation may not be simply a by-product of behavior emerged for other purposes but is the result of behavior which has emerged exactly because it produces spatial aggregation.

Of related interest are simulations of hominid behavior, using relevant archaeological and paleoecological data to test specific hypotheses (Janssen et al., 2005; Mithen & Reed, 2002; Newton, 2007; Premo, 2005; Reynolds et al., 2001; Sept et al., 2007). Additional experiments on small-scale societies have been published by Lake (2000a, 2000b), Costopoulos (1999, 2001, 2002), and Read (2003). Also, within the same domain, Brantingham (2003) has simulated how raw material procurement by a hunter-gatherer society is dependent only upon random encounters with stone sources and the amount of available space in the mobile toolkit. Bentley et al. (2005) have tried to follow from raw material acquisition to full economic exchange networks within a similar agent-based approach.

Going beyond forager behavior, and moving towards the explanation of the emergence of social complexity, we can mention the studies by Caldas and Coelho (1999). These authors have shown with their simulation that what we call today "institutions" were in fact solutions to recurring problems of social interaction in small-scale societies, and should be understood as preconditions for social life, unintended outcomes, and human devised constraints. Younger (2005) has simulated the emergence of violence in this kind of societies. In this model, a population of 100 agents inhabited a landscape of 20x20 squares containing five sources of food. Agents moved about the landscape in search of food, shared, stole, mated, produced offspring, and ultimately died of old age. Violence and revenge reduced the survival probability and, for surviving popula-

tions, replaced hunger as the second leading cause of death after old age. Excluding large segments from violence and revenge significantly improved survival rates. Tolerance to transgressions reduced the number of agents killed in revenge attacks. Higher population density increased the number of revenge deaths but also increased the survival rate of the total population. Decreasing the food supply for a fixed initial set of agents resulted in more deaths due to violence and revenge. Flight from known aggressors enhanced the survival of the total population, at the expense of social cohesion. When killing had a positive social value the survival rate increased as the number of revenge killings decreased.

Artificial societies are also being programmed for studying the origins of agriculture. Some researchers have reconstructed the dynamics of landscape change during the Mesolithic period, just before the spread of agriculture (Ch'ng & Stone 2006). Alexandra Figueiredo and Gonçalo Velho (2001) have programmed a system based on three different kinds of agents: cattle, hunters, and farmers. These agents compete for natural resources (plants). The success of each type of agent is determined not only by the availability of the natural resource but also by the capability of other agents to gather those resources for themselves. Running the model consists of creating a landscape and introducing initial populations of animal and hunters. The initial group of hunters follows the cattle around killing them whenever possible. The killing rule relates the energy of the animal to the number of humans in spatial units around it. So the kills are determined by the patterns of movements of animals and hunters. As the animals follow the concentration of plants, and hunters the concentration of animals, the two groups move close together. Farming disturbs the natural availability of resources. Farmers are located in the same locations were animals eat. Cattle are competitors for farmers, hunters are competitors for hunters, farming increase the number of cattle. Vaart et al. (2006) used a similar approach to understand the consequences of the different social mechanisms related to the management of wild preys and domesticated cereals. Parisi et al. (2003; Cecconi et al., 2006) follow a different approach within the same problem using cellular automata, which can be seen as a simplified version of an agent-based model. They have simulated the agricultural colonization of Europe from the VII to the IV millennium, and its possible similarity with the prehistoric differentiation of European languages. A similar simulation has been developed by Drechsler and Tiede (2007) in the case of the spread of Neolithic herders within the Near East, towards the Arabian Peninsula. In the model, environmental local features influence a global innovation diffusion pattern. Here, computational agents represent mobile populations. The spreading process itself is simulated by a repeated generation of random agents in space. The random component represents the archaeologically incomprehensible decisions that lead to human displacements. Because it is more likely that "wandering groups" populate nearby places than far away places, the possibility for the adoption on an innovation like agriculture is highest in the direct neighborhood of prior acceptance of innovation. Therefore, the random agents cluster spatially more frequently around the "parent" nodes. The spreading surface represents a combination of environmental parameters that are considered fundamental to the dispersal of Neolithic herders across the Arabian Peninsula. These parameters were evaluated for their influence on the movement of human groups, reclassified, and combined to obtain a spreading surface that represents local resistance to the process of spreading. As a result:

- Every place in each generation decreases the underlying raster value simulating the drain on resources and its exploitation value.
- The number of descendants at each place in each generation depends on the value of the underlying raster. The higher the value

("better conditions"), the greater will be the number of descendents in the next generation.

- The actual spreading distance ("how far a new generation will go") also depends on the underlying raster value. The lower the raster value at a specific point, the higher the spreading distance.

Kuznar and Sedlmeayer (2005) have developed a flexible agent-based computer simulation of pastoral nomad/sedentary peasant interaction that can be adapted to particular environmental and social settings. The authors focus on how environmental and material factors condition individual agent response, allowing the modeling of how collective behaviors (mass raiding, genocide) can emerge from individual motives and needs. Many factors influence tribal conflict in the modern world (ethnicity, global politics). However, these simulations reinforce the analyses of some social scientists that argue such conflicts are the inevitable result of the breakdown of land use in the face of growing populations, marginal habitats, and an unprecedented ecological crisis.

Bentley et al. (2005) have explored how an exchange network coevolves with the changing specializations of the agents within it. Through simulation, the authors keep track of who is connected to whom through a mapping of the network and the specializations of each agent, and they test the effects of simplified individual motivations for exchange, the make-up of the initial population of agents, and abstract representations of basic ideological dispositions such as the belief in private ownership. The aim was to test whether specialization and wealth inequalities are natural, self-organizing qualities of a small-scale economy.

An interesting phenomenon that can be studied with these methods is the emergence of specialization, in which different individual agents spontaneously assuming different roles in the execution of the task (Parisi & Nolfi, 2005). The most effective strategy includes primitive forms of "situated" specialization in which identical individuals play different roles according to the circumstances such as leading or following the group. These forms of functional specialization seem to be due to the need to reduce interference between potentially conflicting sub-goals such as moving toward the rest of the group to maintain aggregation and moving toward the target. Imagine a group of agents that has to reach a target in the environment but to be rewarded they must approach the target by maintaining reciprocal proximity. If the agents are initially dispersed in the environment, they may be unable to perceive each other and therefore they may be unable to aggregate and then move together toward the target. The solution is to evolve some signaling behavior that allows the group to aggregate.

Within the research domain of agricultural societies, the VIRTUAL ANASAZI project (Axtell et al., 2002; Dean et al., 2000; Gummermann et al., 2003) is another example of agent-based modeling designed to investigate where prehistoric people of the American Southwest would have situated their households based on both the natural and social environments in which they lived. The idea was to define nuclear families (households, the smallest social unit consistently definable in the archaeological record) as agents, and loosed them on landscapes, which have been archaeologically studied for different historical periods, and plenty of paleo-productivity data exist. The model is used to predict individual household responses to changes in agricultural productivity in annual increments based on reconstructions of yearly climatic conditions, as well as long-term hydrologic trends, cycles of erosion and deposition, and demographic change. The performance of the model is evaluated against actual population, settlement, and organizational parameters. By manipulating numbers and attributes of households, climate patterns, and other environmental variables, it is possible to evaluate the roles of these factors in prehistoric culture change. Here, the household is a

theoretical construct but it moves on a historically defined environment, which is the most precise available archaeological data allow.

Simulated population levels closely follow the historical trajectory. In the first 200 years, the model understates the historical population, whereas the peak just after 1100 A.D. is somewhat too high in the model. The historical clustering of settlements along the valley zonal boundaries is nicely reproduced. Although the ability of the model to predict the actual location of settlements varies from year to year, the progressive movement of the population northward over time, clear in the historical data, is also reproduced in the simulation. Long House Valley was abandoned after 1300 A.D.. The agent model suggests that even the degraded environment between 1270 and 1450 could have supported a reduced but substantial population in small settlements dispersed across suitable farming habitats located primarily in areas of high potential crop production in the northern part of the valley. The fact that in the real world of Long House Valley, the supportable population chose not to stay behind but to participate in the exodus from the valley indicates the magnitude of socio-cultural "push" or "pull" factors that induced them to move. Thus, comparing the model results with the actual history helps differentiate external (environmental) from internal (social) determinants of cultural dynamics. It also provides a clue—in the form of the population that could have stayed but elected to go—to the relative magnitude of those determinants.

The evolution of the Virtual Anasazi project can be seen in the very similar "Village Ecodynamics" project by Tim Kohler and his colleagues (Johnson et al., 2005; Kohler, 2003; Kohler & Carr, 1997; Kohler & Yap, 2003; Kohler et al., 2000, 2005, 2007). The authors began by entering paleoenvironmental data on a digitized map of the area, and then placed the agents—simulated households—randomly on the map. The primary area of research is the study of the effect of exchange relationships upon the formation of larger social groups. Since agricultural yields varied greatly from year to year, farmers needed to adapt mechanisms to reduce their uncertainty of future yields. One such mechanism thought to be important is reciprocity between households. After a reasonable model of agent planting was constructed, agents were endowed with balanced reciprocity behaviors and adaptive encodings of exchange, placing the households into a social and an economic network or other (related and unrelated) households. This network is flexible enough to evolve according to agent interactions and changes in the world environment. The authors are also trying to include the natural production and human degradation of what they consider critical natural resources into the agent-based simulation modeling of household settlement patterns. By demonstrating the ease with which populations could have depleted fuels in this environment, for instance, the simulation builds a context in which changes in food preparation, craft production, architecture, frequency of axes, and so forth, which might be responsive to fuel scarcity, become more plausibly interpreted as having been intended to do so (Johnson et al., 2005).

In recent simulations, the authors have extend the previous model by adding the ability of agents to perform symmetrically initiated or asymmetrically initiated generalized reciprocal exchange (Kobti & Reynolds, 2005; Reynolds, Kobti & Kohler, 2004a, 2004b, 2005). According to this model, the decision made by the group is not a consensus based upon the weights and opinions of the members, but the individual knowledge is pooled and used by a central decision maker to produce a decision (Reynolds & Peng, 2005). Selected individuals contribute to the cultural knowledge, which is stored and manipulated based on individual experiences and their successes or failures.

A small world social network emerged and the resultant agent populations were shown to be more resilient to environmental perturbations. When allowing agents more opportunities to exchange resources, the simulation produced more complex network structures, larger populations, and more resilient systems. Furthermore, allowing the agents to buffer their requests by using a finite state model improved the relative resilience of these larger systems. Introducing reciprocity that can be triggered by both requestors and donors produced the largest number of successful donations. This represents the synergy produced by using the information from two complementary situations within the network. Thus, the network has more information with which it can work and tended to be more resilient than otherwise.

Researchers at the University of Chicago and Argonne National Laboratory (Altaweel et al., 2006; Altaweel & Christiansen, 2005; Christiansen & Altaweel, 2004, 2006a, 2006b) have modeled the trajectories of development and demise of Bronze Age settlement systems for both the rain-fed and irrigated zones of Syria and Iraq. Investigators intend to demonstrate that urban systems of ancient Near Eastern cities co-evolved in an intimate relationship with their social and economic environment, primarily by means of the aggregation through time of smaller fundamental units (e.g., households). The model allows for the scaling up of a settlement from a single household to a village, and ultimately to an urban center with its appropriate array of subsidiary and neighboring settlements. Agrarian production (specifically in light of environmental stresses) and social interaction is modeled at a mutually consistent, fairly detailed level that will support a realistic representation of feedback processes, nonlinear behavior mechanisms, and some degree of self-organization in Bronze Age settlement systems. Emphasis is on the development of the household model and its transformation into higher-order settlements. Everyday decisions in farming are also being incorporated into the model (e.g., when to plant, whether to fallow or crop annually, etc.), as well as social factors such as the pooling of resources. Moreover, the full model includes mechanisms that allow for the growth of social differentiation and that enable some households to grow and others to become subordinate.

Some other relevant applications of agent-based methodologies for building historical artificial societies have been published in the domain of Roman History. Bob Reynolds and colleagues (Reynolds & Lazar, 2002; Reynolds, Lazar & Kim, 2002) are designing a computational model of the origins of the Zapotec State, centered at Monte Alban, in the Valley of Oaxaca, Mexico. Graham (2005, 2006) has tried to understand the geography of the Roman Empire from the point of view of a person traveling through ancient roads. The author takes the lists in the historical written *Itineraries*, and recast them as networks of interconnected cities. The purpose is to know whether there are any significant differences between provinces' connective network topography in terms of the transmission of information. One agent is given a piece of 'knowledge,' which it may or may not share with those it encounters. The rate at which knowledge is transmitted therefore depends on the chance of transmission in any given encounter, and on the topology of the itinerary network. By controlling for the different variables, significant differences in how the different provinces' networks facilitated the transmission of information may be inferred.

By implementing social events as computational agents and their mutual influences as interactions, the automated archaeologist assumes that collective action is accentuated by continuous transitions and transformations between subjects. The explanatory model also takes into account needs, motivations, goals, behavior, signs, tools, rules, community, division of labor, and the embedded hierarchical levels of collective motivation-driven activity and individual goal-driven action. The term *contradiction* can be used then to indicate a misfit within the components of social action, that is, among subjects, needs, motivations, goals, actions and operations, and even mediating artifacts (division of labor, rules, institutions, etc.). The explanatory framework assumes there

is a global tendency to resolve underlying tension and contradictions by means of changing the way of performing the activity and transforming the context and circumstances in which the activity took place.

Social agents are not static entities, with a precise position, nor a fixed impulse. They have always different possibilities for action, according to the characteristics of the context and circumstances in which the action or actions takes place. Social action is the joint result of the modalities of the action, the other social agents who act in their spatiotemporal neighborhood, the forms of collaboration or lack of collaboration between social agents, the power relations which prevent to conduct certain actions or force to execute others, and so on.

A multi agent-based simulation has important advantages compared to more traditional simulation techniques:

- It supports modeling and implementation of pro-active behavior, which is important when simulating humans (and animals) able to take initiatives and act without external stimuli. In short, it is often more natural to model and implement humans as agents than objects.

- It supports distributed computation in a very natural way. Since each agent is typically implemented as a separate piece of software corresponding to a process (or a thread), it is straightforward to let different agents run on different machines. This allows for better performance and scalability.

Since each agent typically is implemented as a separate process and is able to communicate with any other agent using a common language, it is possible to add or remove agents during a simulation without interruption. It is even possible to swap an agent for the corresponding simulated entity, for example, a real person during a simulation. This enables extremely dynamical simulation scenarios.

Nevertheless, an important criticism can be mentioned about those examples of artificial societies. Most of these examples have been considered as nothing more than a traditional "rational-choice" explanation where each agent individually assesses its situation and makes decisions based on a fixed set of condition-action rules (Gulyas, 2002). That makes many agent-based models nothing more than a discrete planning for expressing descriptions of intended courses of action. It seems as if some designer (be a human or a god) needs to know the society before modeling it. Environmental determinism appears then as an obvious consequence, but only because it is easier to model such a system, given that archaeologists have more data about the landscape itself, than about how people lived at such landscape. Social dynamics is a more complex problem, and the diversity of hypothesis makes more difficult to find the proper simulation approach. In any case, there are many artificial societies replicating complex social interactions, like the emergence of inequality and hierarchy, conflict, class struggle, coercion, and so on.

Among the agent-based models that explicitly take into account social inequality and conflict, we can mention Smith and Choi (2007), who have simulated the emergence of inequality in small-scale societies. The model is predicated on the assumption that a limited number of asymmetries, such as differential control over productive resources, can explain the emergence of institutionalized inequality. They also draw on contemporary evolutionary theory in order to avoid the pitfalls of naïve functionalism and teleology. Their approach is not to deny any possibility of collectively beneficial outcomes or directionality to sociopolitical evolution, but rather to show how it emerges from the interaction of individual agency, social structure, and environmental constraints. In their computer simulation, some agents (depicted as "patrons") control limited areas with greater per capita resource endowments, and can trade access to these for services from less

fortunate agents (depicted as "clients"). There is also an additional set of isolated agents which simply defend richer patches for their exclusive use, while others (depicted as "doves") share any resources on their patch with other non-territorial agents (doves or clients). In the initial simulation, all agents are doves, randomly distributed over an heterogeneous environment, so each agent has different probabilities to become a patron or a client depending on its behavior and the productivity of the area it is placed. Under default parameter values, non-territorial strategies dominate, split equally between dove and client types, and isolated and patron types are about equally represented in the remaining areas. However, a stable patron-client regime emerges in about one third of all runs, and takes over the population about 10 percent of the time. Obviously, environmental heterogeneity is critical, as Patrons capitalize on their relatively rich patch endowments to participate in exchanges with clients, and hence variation in property endowment, provides the initial opportunity for the emergence of inequality. Yet this is not sufficient, nor can this be glossed as "environmental determinism," since alternative strategies, interacting with similar resource heterogeneity do not generate socioeconomic inequality. Demographic parameters have also a strong effect on the relative success of territorial and non-territorial strategies. When mortality is high or reproductive rate low, the initial (all-dove) population expands slowly so that isolated and patron agents are able to spread and control rich patches, effectively keeping dove and client numbers low at equilibrium. Conversely, low mortality or high reproductive rate allows doves to proliferate rapidly, and territorial agents are locked out (with clients arising in modest numbers through mutation and drift). Increased mutation rates are favorable to the spread of client and patron strategies, but only because this retards the initial proliferation of doves.

Although the model may be considered as too restricted and limited, it allows exploring the hypothesis that a limited number of asymmetries can explain most cases of emergence of institutionalized inequality. These might include asymmetries in control over productive resources, control over external trade, differential military ability (and resultant booty and slaves), or control of socially significant information. As the simulation suggest, these asymmetries need not be employed coercively, as long as they are economically defensible and can provide an advantage in bargaining power sufficient to allow the concentration of wealth and/or power in the hands of a segment of the social group or polity. The modeling indicates that such asymmetries can be self-reinforcing, and thus quite stable to moderate perturbations over time. Because most of the social transactions based on them are mutual rather than coercive, it may be suggested that such systems are likely to be more stable than the stratified social systems (e.g., nation states) that eventually succeed them.

Dwight Read (2002, 2003) has followed a very similar approach and shows how competition is shown to play a critical role in the way interaction—among decision-making, demographic parameters, and social units that organize resource ownership and procurement—either promotes or inhibits change in social organization.

Specially relevant for evaluating the possibilities of studying alternative approaches to social explanation, Cioffi-Revilla's computational theory for the emergence of social complexity accounts for the earliest formation of systems of government (pristine polities) in prehistory and early antiquity. The theory is based on a fast process of stressful crises and opportunistic decision-making through collective action. This core iterative process is canonical in the sense of undergoing variations on a main recurring theme of problem solving, adaptation and occasional failure. When a group is successful in managing or overcoming serious situational changes (endogenous or exogenous to the group, social or physical) a probabilistic phase transition may occur, under a well-specified set of conditions, yielding a long-term (slow) process of emergent political complexity and development. A reverse process may account for decay. Formally, the canonical theory is being implemented through an agent-based model. Empirically, it is testable with the datasets on polities developed by the Long-Range Analysis of War (LORANOW) Project (Cioffi-Revilla, 2004, 2005).

Some other ways of avoiding the "environmental determinism" and "rational choice" assumptions can be mentioned. Saam and Harrer have simulated the way social norms controlling aggression reduce social inequality. Their results show that this hypothesis holds only in quite egalitarian societies (Saam & Harrer, 1999, see also Verhagen, 2001). Suleiman and Fischer (2000) studied how hierarchical decision-making can affect inter-group conflicts. Pedone and Conte (2001) have analyzed the dynamics of status symbols in hierarchically ordered societies. Impullitti and Rebmann (2002) have investigated the consequences of wealth distribution in artificial societies. Different authors are simulating the emergence of violence, conflict and war (Clements & Hughes, 2004; Ilachinski, 2004; Taylor et al., 2004; Younger, 2005), and there are also some published simulation on the emergence of gender stratification (Robinson-Cox et al., 2007). Consequently, the lack of more "social" and conflictive aspects is not a shortcoming of the technique, but more of a subjective decision from the modelers themselves, who in many cases build the computational surrogates of social agents as rational individual.

A more sophisticated artificial society is being built by the "NewTies" project, in which societies of agents are expected to develop autonomously because of individual, population, and social learning. These societies are expected to be able to solve environmental challenges by acting collectively. The challenges are intended to be analogous to those faced by early, simple, small-scale human societies (Gilbert et al., 2006).

Building artificial societies inside a computer allows us to understand that social reality is not capricious. It has been produced somehow, although not always the same cause produces the same effect, because social actions are not performed isolated, but in complex and dialectical frameworks, which favor, prevent, or modify the capacity, propensity, or tendency the action has to produce or to determine a concrete effect. Obviously, the automated archaeologist should take into account the existence of weak or strong activities, partial implications, or the appearance of self-determination, when the instability between the components of social activity causes a qualitative or quantitative change in the way the activity is performed or in related activities. The assumption is, however, that indeterminacy is out of the social worlds. By definition, everything a human does (and did) is determined in some way by something. Everything that exists, has existed, or will exist has, has had, or will have a cause, by complex or apparently weak that this one is or can seem to an independent observer.

DIRECTIONS FOR FURTHER RESEARCH

This way of understanding social dynamics is still in its infancy. Although many social kinds of social behavior have been already simulated, there are many, many aspects of the methodology that still wait to be investigated.

We need new investigation looking for alternative ways of exploring social mechanisms. Agent-based or distributed simulation is a rather new technology that has allowed going beyond traditional simulations in terms of linear systems. This technology has generated the actual effervescence to the discipline. However, in some aspects, it is a kind of coming back to traditional computer programming in terms of rules and expert systems. Of course, I am not saying that anything created

20 years ago is necessarily out-fashioned, but we know the theoretical and practical limitations of such mechanisms. Although in some small simulations current technology performs quite well, if we would like to simulate full-scale social systems, we need better implementations, using neural networks as agents, or hybrid systems integrating the best from all worlds.

Obviously, the problems are not only methodological and technical. Once we know that simulating a society is possible, we need to review all we thought to know about social dynamics. The real matter is not only "how to simulate?," but rather "what needs to be simulated?." Too many aspects of social knowledge were taken for granted, and most of them were never analyzed as mechanisms. Social mechanization has still a bad reputation, and simulation approaches inspire fear to many scientists. Many of them think that not everything is mechanizable, others think that there is nothing to be gained by such efforts. Consequently, theoretical and even philosophical work on these subjects is the most necessary.

REFERENCES

ALTAWEEL, M., PAULETTE, T., & CHRISTIANSEN, J. (2006). Modeling dynamic human ecologies: Examples from northern mesopotamia *BANEA conference*, Edinburgh. Retrieved July, 2007 from http://oi.uchicago.edu/OI/PROJ/MASS/papers/PresentationBanea.pdf

ALTAWEEL, M., & CHRISTIANSEN, J. (2004). Simulating a bronze age city state under stress. *Modeling Long-Term Culture Change Workshop at the Santa Fe Institute, October 2004. Retrieved July 2007 from* http://oi.uchicago.edu/OI/PROJ/MASS/papers/SFI2004_MASS_2.pdf

ASTROM, M., & VENCATASAWMY, C.P. (2001). Incorporating artificial intelligence in microsimulation. *Geografiska Annaler, 83B*, 53-65.

BAINBRIDGE, W. (1995). Neural network models of religious belief. *Sociological perspectives, 38*, 483-494.

BAINBRIDGE, W. S., BRENT E., CARLEY K., HEISE D., MACY M., & MARKOVSKY, J. (1994). Artificial social intelligence. *Annual Review of Sociology, 20*, 407-436.

BARCELÓ, J.A. (2001). Técnicas de Inteligencia Artificial en Arqueología. Su uso en el studio de las formas de interacción social durante la Edad del Bronce. In M. Ruiz-Gálvez (Ed.), *La edad del bronce, ¿Primera edad de oro de españa?* (pp. 55-86). Barcelona, Spain: Editorial Crítica.

BARCELÓ, J.A., VILA, A., & ARGELES, T. (1994). KIPA. A computer program to analyze the social position of women in hunter-gatherer societies. In I. Johnson (Ed.), *.Methods in the mountains*. Proceedings of the UISPP IV Meeting, Mount Victoria. Sydney, Australia. University Archaeological Methods Series, No. 2.

BARCELÓ, J.A., BRIZ, I., CLEMENTE, I., ESTEVEZ, J., MAMELI, L., MAXIMIANO, A., et al. (2006). Análisis etnoarqueológico del valor social del producto en sociedades cazadoras-recolectoras. In *Etnoarqueología de la Prehistoria: más allá de la analogía* (pp. 189-209). *Serie Treballs d'Etnoarqueologia, 6*. Madrid, Spain: CSIC.

BELLOMO, N., BERTOTTI, M.L., & DELI-TALA, M. (2007). From the kinetic theory of active particles to the modeling of social behaviors and politics. *Quality and Quantity, 41*, 545–555.

BENTLEY, R.A., LAKE, M.W., & SHENNAN, S.J. (2005). Specialisation and wealth inequality in a model of a clustered economic network. *Journal of Archaeological Science, 32*, 1346-1356.

BONABEAU, E. (2002). Agent-based modeling: Methods and techniques for simulating human systems. *Proc. National Academy of Sciences, 99*(suppl. 3), 7280-7287.

BRANTINGHAM, J. (2003). A neutral model of stone raw material procurement. *American Antiquity, 68*(3), 487–509.

CALDAS, J.C., & COELHO, H. (1999). The origin of institutions: Socio-economic processes, choice, norms and conventions. *Journal of Artificial Societies and Social Simulation, 2*(2).

CASTELFRANCHI, C. (2000). Engineering social order. In A. Omicini, R. Tolksdorf, & F. Zambonelli (Eds.), *Engineering societies in the agents world*. Berlin: Springer. (Lecture Notes in Computer Science, No. 1972).

CECCONI, F., PARISI, D., ANTINUCCI, F., & NATALE, F. (2006). Simulating the expansion of farming and the differentiation of european languages. In B. Laks (Ed.), *Origin and evolution of languages: Approaches, models, paradigms*. Oxford, UK: Oxford University Press.

CH'NG, E., & STONE, R.J. (2006). Enhancing virtual reality with artificial life: Reconstructing a flooded european mesolithic landscape. *Presence: Teleoperators & Virtual Environments, 15*(3), 341-352.

CHRISTIANSEN, J., & ALTAWEEL, M. (2005). Agent-based holistic simulations of bronze age mesopotamian settlement systems. In A. Figueiredo & G. Velho (Eds.), *The world is in your eyes. Computer applications in archaeology 2005 Proceedings*. Tomar, Portugal: CAA-Protugal.

CHRISTIANSEN, J., & ALTAWEEL, M. (2006a). Understanding ancient societies: A new approach using agent-based holistic modeling. *Structure and Dynamics: eJournal of Anthropological and Related Sciences, 1*(2), Article 7.

CHRISTIANSEN, J., & ALTAWEEL, M. (2006b). Simulation of natural and social process interactions: An example from bronze age mesopotamia. *Social Science Computer Review, 24*(2), 209-226.

CIOFFI-REVILLA, C. (2005). A canonical theory for the emergence and development of social complexity, *Journal of Mathematical Sociology,* 29(2), 33–153.

CIOFFI-REVILLA, C. (2004). Mnemonic structure and sociality: A computational agent-based simulation model. In D. Sallach & C. Macal (Eds.), *Proceedings of the Agent 2004 Conference on Social Dynamics: Interaction, Reflexivity and Emergence.* University of Chicago, Argonne National Laboratory.

CLEMENTS, R.R., & HUGHES, R.L. (2004). Mathematical modelling of a mediaeval battle: The battle of Agincourt, 1415. *Mathematics and Computers in Simulation, 64*(2), 259 – 269.

CONTE, R., & GILBERT, N. (1995). Computer simulation for social theory. In N. Gilbert, & R. Conte (Eds.), *Artificial societies: The computer simulation of social life* London: UCL Press.

COSTOPOULOS, A. (1999). *Modeling and simulation for anthropological archaeology: the logic of long-term change.* Ph.D. Dissertation held at Oulu University, Finland.

COSTOPOULOS, A. (2001). Evaluating the impact of increasing memory on agent behaviour: Adaptive patterns in an agent-based simulation of subsistence. *Journal of Artificial Societies and Social Simulation,* 4(4).

COSTOPOULOS, A. (2002). Playful agents, inexorable process: Elements of a coherent theory of iteration in anthropological simulation, *Archeologia e Calcolatori, 13,* 259-266.

DAVINO, C., Di MARTINO, R., MOLA, F., & VISTOCCO, F. (1999). Riconoscimento automatico di Forma en archeologia: il caso delle necropoli di Sala Consilina. *Workshop Intelligenza Artificiale per i Beni Culturali* Bologna. Retrieved February 2007 from http://studi131.casaccia.enea.it/enea/apps/aiia/consili.pdf

DIAPPI, L., BOLCHI, P. & FRANZINI, L. (1999). Urban sustainability: Complex interactions and the measurement of risk. *CyberGeo,* 98(28). Retrieved May 2007 from http://www.cybergeo.presse.fr/suger/lidiapi/parigi.htm

DORAN, J. E. (1997). Distributed artificial intelligence and emergent social complexity. In S. E. Van de Leeuw & J. McGlade (Eds.), *Time, process and structured transformation in archaeology. One World Archaeology series, 26,* 283-297. London: Routledge.

DORAN, J. E. (1999). Prospects for agent-based modelling in archaeology. *Archeologia e Calcolatori, 10,* 33-44.

DORAN J.E. (2000). Trajectories to complexity in artificial societies. In A. Kohler & G. Gumerman (Eds.), *Dynamics in human and primate societies.* New York: Oxford University Press.

DORAN, J. E., & PALMER, M. (1995a). The EOS project: Integrating two models of palaeolithic social change. In N. Gilbert & R. Conte (Eds.), *Artificial societies: The computer simulation of social life* (pp. 103-125). London: UCL Press.

DORAN, J. E., & PALMER, M. (1995b). The EOS project: Modelling prehistoric sociocultural trajectories. In *Aplicaciones informaticas en Arqueologia: Teoria y Sistemas* Vol I Proceedings of First International Symposium on Computing and Archaeology (pp 183-198), Paris 1991. Bilbao, Spain.: Danboraren Argia.

DORAN, J., PALMER, M., GILBERT, N., & MELLARS, P. (1994). The EOS project: Modelling upper paleolithic social change. In G. N. Gilbert & J. Doran (Eds.), *Simulating societies: The computer simulation of social phenomena.* London: UCL Press.

DRECHSLER, P., & TIEDE, D. (2007). The spread of neolithic herders—a computer aided modeling approach. In A. Figueiredo & G. Velho (Eds.), *The world is in your eyes. Computer applications in archaeology* (pp. 231-236). Tomar, Portugal: CAA Portugal.

EDMONDS, B. (1998). Modelling socially intelligent agents. *Applied Artificial Intelligence, 12*(7), 667-669.

EDMONDS, B. (2000). The use of models—making MABS more informative. In S. Moss & P. Davidsson (Eds.), *Multi-agent-based simulation.* Berlin: Springer (Lecture Notes in Computer Science, No. 1979).

FIGUEIREDO, A., & VELHO, G.L.C. (2002). Complexity in action: The emergence of agro-pastoral societies. In Z. Stancic & T. Veljanovski (Eds.), *Computing archaeology for understanding the Past.* Oxford: ArchaeoPress.

FISCHER, M.M., & GOPAL, S. (1993). Neuro-computing—a new paradigm for geographical information processing. *Environment and Planning A, 25*, 757-760.

FISCHER, M.M., & REISMANN, M. (2002). A methodology for neural spatial interaction modelling. *Geographical Analysis, 34*(3), 207-228.

GILBERT, N. (1998). Simulation: An introduction to the idea. In P. Ahrweiler & N. Gilbert (Eds.), *Computer simulations in science and technology studies* (pp. 1-14). Berlin: Springer.

GILBERT, N. (2000). The simulation of social processes. In N. Ferrand (Ed.), *Modèles et Systèmes Multi-Agents pour la Gestion de l'Environment et des Territoires* (pp. 121 – 137). Clermont-Ferrand, France: Cemagref Editions.

GILBERT, N., DEN BESTEN, M., BONTOVICS, A., CRAENEN, B.G.W., DIVINA, F., EIBEN, A.E., GRIFFIOEN, R. et al. (2006). Emerging artificial societies through learning. *Journal of Artificial Societies and Social Simulation, 9*(2)

GOPAL, S., FISCHER, M.M. (1996). Learning in single hidden-layer feedforward network models. *Geographical Analysis, 28*(1), 38-55.

GRAHAM, S. (2005b). Agent based modeling, archaeology and social organisation: The robust-ness of Rome. *The Archaeological Computing Newsletter, 63*, 1-6.

GRAHAM, S. (2006). Networks, agent-based modeling, and the Antonine itineraries. *The Journal of Mediterranean Archaeology, 19*(1), 45-64.

GULYÁS, L. (2002). On the transition to agent-based modeling: Implementation strategies from variables to agents. *Social Science Computer Review, 20*, 389-399.

HINTON, G.E. (1986). Learning distributed representations of concepts. *Proceedings of the Eigth Annual Conference of the Cognitive Science Society* (pp. 1-12). Hillsdale, NJ: Lawrence Erlbaum,

ILACHINSKI, A. (2004). *Artificial war: Multi agent-based simulation of combat: Multi agent-based simulation of combat.* Singapore: World Scientific.

IMPULLITTI, G., & REBMANN, C.M. (2002). *An agent-based model of wealth distribution.* CEPA Working Paper 2002-15. Retrieved July 2007 http://www.newschool.edu/cepa/papers/archive/cepa200215.pdf

JANSSEN, M.A., SEPT, J.M., & GRIFFITH, C.S. (2005). Foraging of *Homo Ergaster* and *Australopithecus Boisei* in East African environments. *NAACSOS Conference 2005, June 26-28, 2005, Notre Dame, Indiana, USA, Annual Conference of the North American Association for Computational Social and Organizational Science.*

JOHNSON, C. D., KOHLER, T.A., & COWAN, J.A. (2005). Modeling historical ecology, thinking about contemporary systems. *American Anthropologist, 107*, 96-108.

JU, W., LAM, N.S.N., & CHEN, J. (2006). Application of kohonen self-organizing map for urban structure analysis. *2006 IEEE International Conference on Granular Computing*, (pp. 118- 123).

KASKI, S. & KOHONEN, T. (1996). Exploratory data analysis by the self-organizing map: Structures of welfare and poverty in the world. In A.P.N. Refenes, Y. Abu-Mostafa, J. Moody & A. Weigend (Eds.), *Neural networks in financial engineering* (pp. 498–507). Singapore: World Scientific.

KIM, J.K., LEE, J.K., & KIM, S.H. (1999). An interactive approach to building an influence diagram based on neural networks. *Journal of Decision Systems*, 8(3), 389-405.

KLÜGL, F., FEHLER, M., & HERRLER, R. (2005). About the role of the environment in multi-agent simulations. In D. Weyns, H. Van Dyke Parunak, F. Michel (Eds.), *Environments for multi-agent systems*. Berlin: Springer. (Lecture Notes in Computer Science, No. 3374).

KLÜVER, J., STOICA, C., & SCHMIDT, J. (2003). Formal models, social theory and computer simulations: Some methodical reflections *Journal of Artificial Societies and Social Simulation, 6*(2).

KLÜVER, J., SCHMIDT, J., STOICA, C. (2005). The emergence of social order by processes of typifying: A computational model. *Journal of Mathematical Sociology*, 29, 1–21.

KOBTI, Z., &REYNOLDS, R.G. (2005). Modeling protein exchange across the social network in the village multi-agent simulation. *IEEE International Conference on Systems, Man and Cybernetics, 4*(10-12), 3197–3203.

KOHLER, T. (2003). Agent-based modeling of Mesa Verde region settlement systems: introduction. *Paper presented in Symposium Building Models for Settlement Systems in the Late Prehispanic Mesa Verde Region: An Interdisciplinary Approach 68th Annual Meeting of the Society for American Archaeology*. Milwaukee. Retrieved March 2007 http://www.wsu.edu/%7Evillage/Kohler%20SAA%20%2703.pdf

KOHLER, T.A., & CARR, E. (1997). Swarm-based modeling of prehistoric settlement systems in southwestern north america. In I. Johnson & M. North (Eds.), *Proceedings of Colloquium II, UISPP, XIIIth Congress, Forli, Italy, Sept 1996. Sydney University Archaeological Methods Series 5*. Sydney, Australia: Sydney University.

KOHLER, T., & GUMMERMAN, G. (editors). (2000). *Dynamics in human and primate societies: Agent-based modeling of social and spatial processes*. Santa Fe Institute Studies in the Sciences of Complexity, New York: Oxford University Press.

KOHLER, T.A., KRESL, J., VAN WEST, C.R., CARR, E., & WILSHUSEN, R. (2000). Be there then: A modeling approach to settlement determinants and spatial efficiency among late ancestral pueblo populations of the Mesa Verde region, U.S. Southwest. In T. A. Kohler & G. J. Gumerman (Eds.), *Dynamics in human and primate societies: Agent-based modeling of social and spatial processes* (pp. 145-178). Santa Fe Institute Studies in the Sciences of Complexity, New York: Oxford University Press.

KOHLER, T. A., & GUMERMAN, G.A., REYNOLDS, R.G. (2005). Simulating ancient societies. *Scientific American, 293*, 77-84.

KOHLER, T.A., & YAP, L. (2003) *Modeling reciprocal exchange in southwestern societies. Paper presented at the 68th Annual Meeting of the Society for American Archaeology, Milwaukee, WI*. Retrieved from July 2007 http://www.wsu.edu/%7Evillage/Kohler%20&%20Yap%20SAA%202003.pdf

KOHLER, T.A., JOHNSON, C.D., VARIEN, M., ORTMAN, S., REYNOLDS, R., KOBTI, Z., COWAN, J. et al (2007). Settlement Ecodynamics in the Prehispanic Central Mesa Verde Region. In T.A. Kohler & S. E. Van der Leeuw (Eds.), *Model-based archaeology of socionatural systems*. Santa Fe, NM: SAR Press.

KOHONEN, T. (1989). *Self-organization and associative memory.* Berlin: Springer.

KOHONEN, T. (2001). *Self-organizing maps* (3rd ed.). Berlin: Springer.

KOUA, E.L., & KRAAK, M.L. (2004). An evaluation of self-organizing map spatial representation and visualization for geospatial data: Perception and visual analysis. In J. Dykes, A.M. MacEachren & M. J. Kraak (Eds.), *Exploring geovisualization.* (pp. 627-644) Elsevier: Amsterdam.

KUZNAR, L.A., & SEDLMEYER, R. (2005). Collective violence in Darfur: An agent-based model Of pastoral nomad/sedentary peasant interaction. *Mathematical Anthropology and Cultural Theory: An International Journal, 1*(4).

LAKE, M. W. (2000a). MAGICAL computer simulation of mesolithic foraging. In T. A. Kohler, and G. J. Gumerman (Eds.), *Dynamics in human and primate societies: Agent-based modelling of social and spatial processes* (pp. 107-143). Santa Fe Institute Studies in the Sciences of Complexity, New York: Oxford University Press.

LAKE, M. W. (2000b). MAGICAL computer simulation of mesolithic foraging on islay. In S. J. Mithen (Ed.), *Hunter-gatherer landscape archaeology: The southern hebrides mesolithic project, 1988-98, (vol. 2): Archaeological fieldwork on colonsay, computer modelling, experimental archaeology, and final interpretations,* (pp. 465-495). Cambridge, UK: The McDonald Institute for Archaeological Research.

LOBO, V., BAÇÃO, F., & PAINHO, M. (2004, April 29-May 1). The self-organizing map and it's variants as tools for geodemographical data analysis: The case of Lisbon's metropolitan area. In *7th AGILE Conference on Geographic Information Science, Heraklion, Greece. Parallel Session 4.1- Geographic Knowledge Discovery.*

LOUZOUN, Y., & ATLAN, H. (2007). The emergence of goals in a self-organizing network:

A non-mentalist model of intentional actions. *Neural Networks, 20*, 156–171.

MAKARENKO, A. (2006). Neural networks for modelling of large social systems. approaches for mentality, anticipating and multivaluedness accounting. *International Journal Information Theories & Applications, 13*, 371-376.

MERAVIGLIA, C. (1996) Models of representation of social mobility and inequality systems. A neural network Approach. *Quality and Quantity, 30*, 231-252.

MERAVIGLIA, C. (2001). *Le reti neurali nella ricerca sociale.* Milan, Itlay: FrancoAngeli.

MINSKY, M. (1985). *The society of mind.* New York: Simon and Schuster.

MITHEN, S.J. & REED, M. (2002). Stepping out: A computer simulation of hominid dispersal from Africa. *Journal of Human Evolution, 43*, 433-462.

NEWTON, A. (2007). Modelling the behavioural of *Paranthropus* and *Homo Habilis.* In *Layers of Perception. Computer Applications in Archaeology Proceedings.* Berlin (in press).

NIJKAMP, P. & REGGIANI, A. (1992). *Interaction, evolution and chaos in space.* Berlin: Springer.

NIJKAMP, P. & REGGIANI, A. (1998). *The economics of complex spatial systems.* Elsevier: Amsterdam.

NOWAK, A., & VALLACHER, R.R. (1998). Toward computational social psychology: Cellular automata and neural network models of interpersonal dynamics. In S.J. Read & L.C. Miller (Eds.), *Connectionist models of social reasoning and social behavior* (pp. 277-311). London: Lawrence Erlbaum.

NOWAK, A., & VALLACHER, R.R. (2002). Computational models of social processes. In *En-*

cyclopedia of cognitive science. London: Nature Publishing Group (Macmillan Publishers).

NOWAK, A., VALLACHER, R.R., & BURNSTEIN, E. (1998). Computational social psychology: A neural network approach to interpresonal dynamics. In W.B.G. Liebrand, A. Nowak and R. Hegselmann (Eds.), *Computer modelling of social processes*. London: Sage Publications.

OPENSHAW, S. (1994). Neuroclassification of spatial data. In B.C. Hewitson & R.G. Crane (Eds.), *Neural nets: Applications in archaeology*. Dordrecht, Holland: Kluwer Academic Publ.

OPENSHAW, S. (1997). Building fuzzy spatial interaction models. In M.M. Fischer & A.Getis (Eds.), *Recent developments in spatial analysis. Spatial statistics, behavioural modeling and computational intelligence*. Berlin: Springer.

OPENSHAW, S., BLAKE, M., & WYMER, C. (1995). Using neurocomputing methods to classify Britain's residential areas. In P. Fisher (Ed.), *Innovations in GIS 2*. London: Taylor & Francis.

PARISI, D., & NOLFI, S. (2005). Sociality in embodied neural agents. In R. Sun (Ed.), *Cognition and multi-agent interaction*. Cambridge, UK: Cambridge Univerity Press.

PARISI, D., CECCONI, F., & NATALE, F. (2003). Cultural change in spatial environments: The role of cultural assimilation and of internal changes in cultures. *Journal of Conflict Resolution, 47*, 163-179.

PEDONE, R., & CONTE, R. (2001). Dynamics of status symbols and social complexity. *Social Science Computer Review, 19*(3), 249-262.

PONTHIEUX, S., & COTTRELL, M. (2001). Living conditions: Classification of households using the kohonen algorithm. *European Journal of Economic and Social Systems, 15*(2), 69-84.

PREMO, L. S. (2005) Patchiness and prosociality: An agent-based model of plio/pleistocene hominid

food sharing. In P. Davidsson, K. Takadama, & B. Logan (Eds.), *Multi-agent and multi-agent-based simulation*. Berlin: Springer. *Lecture Notes in Artificial Intelligence, 3415*, 210-224.

PULJIC, M., & KOZMA, R. (2005). Activation clustering in neural and social networks. *Complexity, 10*(4), 42-50.

READ, D.R. (2002). A multitrajectory, competition model of emergent complexity in human social organization. In *Adaptive Agents, Intelligence, and Emergent Human Organization: Capturing Complexity through Agent-Based Modeling*, Proceedings National Academy of Sciences, U S A. (vol. 99) (Suppl 3), 7251–7256.

READ, D. (2003). Emergent properties in small-scale societies. *Artificial life, 9*(4), 419–434.

REYNOLDS, R.G., LAZAR, A., & KIM, J. (2002). Agent-based simulation of the evolution of archaic states. *Agent 2002 Social Agents: Ecology, Exchange & Evolution (Agent 2002)*, Chicago, October 11-12.

REYNOLDS, R.G., LAZAR, A., & KIM, J. (2002, May 12-17). Simulating the evolution of archaic states. *2002 Congress on Evolutionary Computation (WCII 2002)*. Hilton Hawaiian Village, Honolulu, HI.

REYNOLDS, R. G., & PENG, B. (2005). Knowledge learning and social swarms in cultural algorithms. *Journal of Mathematical Sociology, 29*, 1-18.

REYNOLDS, R., WHALLON, R., & GOODHALL, S. (2001). Transmission of cultural traits by emulation: An agent-based model of group foraging behavior. *Journal of Memetics - Evolutionary Models of Information Transmission*, 4. Retrieved August 2007 from http://jom-emit.cfpm.org/2001/vol4/reynolds_r&al.html

REYNOLDS, R. G., KOBTI, Z., & KOHLER, T. (2004a). The effect of culture on the resilience of social systems in the village multi-agent simulation. *IEEE International Congress on Evolutionary Computation, Portland, OR.* (pp. 1743-1750).

REYNOLDS, R.G., KOBTI, Z., & KOHLER, T. (2004b). The effects of generalized reciprocal exchange on the resilience of social networks: An example from the prehistoric Mesa Verde region, *Journal of Computational and Mathematical and Organization Theory*, (pp. 229-254).

REYNOLDS, R. G., KOBTI, Z., & KOHLER, T. (2005). Learning in dynamic multi-layered social networks: A mesa verde example. In *Proceedings of Geo-Computation 2005*.

ROBISON-COX, J.F., MARTELL, R.F., & EMRICH, C.G. (2007). Simulating gender stratification. *Journal of Artificial Societies and Social Simulation, 10*(3).

SAAM, N.J., & HARRER, A. (1999). Simulating norms, social inequality, and functional change in artificial societies. *Journal of Artificial Societies and Social Simulation, 2*(1)

SAWYER, R.K. (2000). Simulating emergence and downward causation in small groups. In S. Moss & P. Davidsson (Eds.), *Multi-agent-based simulation*. Berlin: Springer. (Lecture Notes in Computer Science, No. 1979).

SAWYER, R.K. (2005). *Social emergence: Societies as complex systems*. Cambridge: Cambridge University Press.

SCHRODT, P.A. (2004). *Patterns, rules and learning: Computational models of international behavior* (2nd ed.). Parus Analytical Systems, Vinland, Kansas, USA. Retrieved July 2007 from http://www.ku.edu/~keds/books.html

SEPT, J.M., GRIFFITH, C.S., & LONG, B. (2007). HOMINIDS: An agent based model of plio-pleistocene hominid foraging behaviour. In *Layers of Perception. Computer Applications in Archaeology 2007 Berlin Conference proceedings*.

SILVA, M., MONTEIRO, A., & MEDEIROS, J. (2004). Visualization of geospatial data by component planes and u-matrix. In *Brazilian Symposium on GeoInformatics – GEOINFO*. Edited by Cirano Iochpe e Gilberto Câmara. São José dos Campos, Brasil: INPE.

SITUNGKIR, H. (2003). Emerging the emergence sociology: The philosophical framework of agent-based social studies. *Journal of Social Complexity, 1*(2), Bandung Fe, India: Institute Press.

SKUPIN, A., & HAGELMAN, R. (2005). Visualizing demographic trajectories with self-organizing maps. *GeoInformatica, 9*(2), 159–179.

SMITH, E.A., & CHOI, J.K. (2007). The emergence of inequality in small-scale societies: Simple scenarios and agent-based simulations. In T. A. Kohler & S. E. Van der Leeuw (Eds.), *Model-based archaeology of socionatural systems*. Santa Fe, NM: SAR Press.

SPARS, S.A. (2005). *Interpreting conflict mortuary behaviour: Applying non-linear and traditional quantitative methods to conflict burials*. Ph.D. Thesis. University of Glasgow. Department of Anthropology.

STOICA, C., & KLÜVER, J. (2007). Interacting neural networks and the emergence of social structure. *Complexity, 12*(3), 41-52.

SULEIMAN, R., & FISCHER, I. (2000). When one decides for many: The effect of delegation methods on cooperation in simulated inter-group conflicts *Journal of Artificial Societies and Social Simulation, 3*(4),

SUN, R. (2006). *Cognition and multi-agent interaction: From cognitive modeling to social simulation*. Cambridge, UK: Cambridge University Press.

SZILAGYI, M. (1991). A neural approach to the simulation of human society. *Quality and Quantity, 25*, 211-2210.

TAYLOR, G., FREDERIKSEN, R., VANE, R.R., & WALTZ, E. (2004). Agent-based simulation of geo-political conflict. Paper Presented at *Innovative Applications of Artificial Intelligence (IAAI) July 2004*. Retrieved July 2007 from http://www.soartech.com/pubs/IAAI04-GTaylor-AGILE.pdf

THALMANN, D. (2001). The foundations to build a virtual human society In A. de Antonio, R. Aylett, & D. Ballin (Eds.), *Intelligent virtual agents*. Berlin: Springer. (Lecture Notes in Computer Science, No. 2190).

VAN DER VAART, E., HANKEL, A., DE BOER, B., & VERHEIJ, B. (2006). Agents adopting agriculture: Modeling the agricultural transition. *From Animals to Animats 9, 9th International Conference on Simulation of Adaptive Behavior, SAB 2006, Rome, Italy, September 25-29, 2006. Proceedings* (pp. 750-761). Berlin: Springer. (Lecture Notes in Computer Science: Vol. 4095).

VERHAGEN, H. (2001). Simulation of the learning of norms. *Social Science Computer Review, 19, 296 - 306.*

VILLA, N., & BOULE, R. (2007, April 25-27). Clustering a medieval social network by SOM using a kernel based distance measure. *European Symposium on Artificial Neural Networks. Advances in Computational Intelligence and Learning* Bruges (Belgium). Retrieved March 2007 from (http://hal.archives-ouvertes.fr/docs/00/14/51/17/PDF/villa_boulet_ESANN2007_final.pdf)

WHITE, W.R. (1995). Spatial interaction modeling using artificial neural networks. *Journal of Transport Geography, 3*(3), 159-166.

WINTER, K., & HEWITSON, B.C. (1994). Self-organizing maps—applications to census data. In B.C. Hewitson & R.G. Crane (Eds.), *Neural nets: Applications in archaeology*. Dordrect, Holland: Kluwer Academic Publ.

WOBCKE, W. (1998). Agency and the logic of ability. In W. Wobcke, M. Pagnucco, & C. Zhang (Eds.), *Agents and multi-agent systems: Formalisms, methodologies, and applications*. Berlin: Springer. (Lecture Notes of Computer Science, 1441).

YOUNGER, S. (2005). Violence and revenge in egalitarian societies. *Journal of Artificial Societies and Social Simulation, 8*(4).

Section IV
Conclusions:
The Computational Philosophy
of Archaeology

Chapter X
Beyond Science Fiction Tales

...by performing better and cheaper, the robots will displace humans from essential roles. Rather quickly, they could displace us from existence.

I'm not as alarmed as many by the latter possibility, since I consider these futures machines our progeny, "mind children" built in our image and likeness, ourselves in more potent form. Like biological children of previous generations, they will embody humanity's best chance for a long term future. It behaves us to give them every advantage and to bow out when we can no longer contribute. (Moravec, 1998, p. 13)

THE AUTOMATED ARCHAEOLOGIST AS A TIME MACHINE

We have already argued that an automated archaeologist cannot understand past social actions by enumerating *every* possible outcome of *every* possible social action. The need to insert *all* the world within the automated archaeologist's brain and then maintain every change about is impossible. However, if we cannot introduce the world inside the robot, we may introduce the robot inside the world. What the automated archaeologist would need then is to be situated in the past,

and then using observation and attention to learn from human action, because of the complexities of the past, which resist modeling. It leads to a modification of the aphorism espoused by Rodney Brooks (1989): "the past itself should be its own best model." Consequently, the automated archaeologist must travel to the past to be able to understand why it happened. Only by being situated directly in the past, the automated archaeologist would understand what someone did and why she did it there or elsewhere.

This is the classical time machine analogy. If situated in the past, the automated archaeologist would interact with the precise context in which social activity was performed because it would be an integral part of it. Wonderful! Now, the bad news. There is no way of actually going back into the past to test a historical hypothesis. The automated archaeologist exists only in the present, then any activity or action or behavior that happened in the past is now out of its reach. It cannot see in the present what was performed in the past. It can examine only what it perceives within the present, the material objects that surround it, here and now, and, only from these objects, the cognitive robot should infer what it has undergone. Of course, the automated archaeologist can perceive the *effects* of social activity performed in the past, but these are its *actual* effects. Social activity in the past cannot be perceived in the present, and then, our machine cannot be situated in the context in which the action was performed.

The impossibility of seeing the past affects not only archaeologists but also any discipline dealing with *cause* and *effect*. The past should be transferred to the present if someone pretends to explain the cause of an effect observed in the present. When a pediatrician asks the child's father what his son ate *yesterday*, she is doing "history," because she investigates a temporal dimension to solve a *why* question: why the child has *now* stomachache. The pediatrician uses what the father says (a narration in the present about something he saw in the past) to "see" in the present what the child's ate yesterday. Like medical histories, social researchers have at their disposal texts containing narrative memories existing in the present, but written in the past by real (or supposed) witnesses of past events. In so doing, historians are not traveling themselves to the past, but they build a surrogate of the past, which they interrogate. They are situated in a virtual world extracted from a narration -supposed to be true-, written (or told) by an individual having seen someone doing something in the past, or explaining her intentions when acting. The past is then accessible through the filter of a surrogate built indirectly from personal narratives, written or told in the past and preserved in our present.

In Archaeology, we do not have any personal witnesses. We do not have descriptions of past facts, or explanations of motivations, intentions, nor goals. The only we have are some material traces for some (not all) outcomes of social activities performed in the past. Even in the case of human bodies found in burials, we do not have the *actors* of past activities; they are, in some sense, products, or material consequences of what others did with them. Even in those circumstances, the past can be transferred, partially, to the present.

In general, the automated archaeologist assumes that some initial event in the past has been

modified, and what it perceives *in the present* is just some of those modifications, which have been preserved in some way. In that sense, archaeological sites can be considered as puzzling traces (effects) of long-past events, because all outcomes of social activity have been created and transformed during the development of some activity and they carry with them a historical residue of that development.

Michael Leyton (1992, 2005) argues that a trajectory of changes (a history) can be described as a discontinuous sequence composed of a minimal set of distinguishable actions. The key idea is that what appears to be different in the present speaks about some action in the past that generated such a difference. Variability in the present is understood as having arisen from variability in the formation processes. In an archaeological data set with no variability, nor any differences among its elements, the best hypothesis is that the corresponding causal process has the least amount of variation. If a property is invariant (unchanged) under an action, then one cannot infer from the property that the action has taken place. Any cognitive agent (be a human or a machine) cannot explain the history of water in a lake, because water is spatially and temporally undifferentiated. However, if we can distinguish variation (curvature, or surface irregularity) along the basin lake perimeter, we can follow the geological transformation of this landscape. Therefore, the automated archaeologist should regard the complexity of the spatiotemporal trajectory of visually apparent differences as a measure of the amount of social activity needed to produce perceivable variation.

The automated archaeologist will use perceived "variation" in shape, size, texture composition and spatiotemporal location values to "run time backwards" and *explain* how those variations were *caused*. Distinctions between successive stages of an archaeological trajectory of changes and modifications point to a past event where variation did not exist; sufficiently far back, no difference existed. An automated archaeologist will explain a trajectory of changes by imposing a temporal *slicing* on archaeologically perceived *discontinuities*. The intention for such a slicing will be to represent visually the transitions between events. In this way, the automated archaeologist would simulate the actual occurrences of the events in an historical sequence. Such a trajectory of events would be "explanatory" because the same occurrence of an event within the trajectory, and its spatiotemporal relationship with the preceding and successive event would serve as the *explanandum* of what happened in the past.

The true nature of social activity is expressed in such *directivity* of the sequence chain of human induced changes between spatiotemporal successive events. Directivity is the result of interpreting a persisted state or the discovery of an order in a sequence or trajectory of multiple different states. Consequently, the explanation of specific social activities should be studied in terms of their causal contributions to final states, and not as the immediate effect of some individual decision. This only means that social events are always understood in historical terms, that is, according to what changed at each place and at each moment.

Therefore, it should be assumed that the past will be "seen" within the present, if and only if some different states within the present can be distinguished, and *these states are ordered according some kind of temporal directivity*. This last assumption is very important, because not any observed difference in the present speaks about the past.

That means that historical (and archaeological) explanation depends on the actual occurrences of the events in the explanatory sequence. There is no single law that constrains these occurrences; it is the same occurrence, which serves as the *explanandum*.

"SEEING" THE PAST IN THE PRESENT

What our time machine should perceive at an archaeological site are not stones, walls, buildings, pottery sherds, animal carcasses, but a chronologically ordered sequence of changes and modifications acting over the consequence of former changes and modifications (Barceló 2007). Consequently, the intelligent robot should be programmed to look for material entities whose changing properties it may assume it is able to trace.

In order to be able to acquire visual information (shape), our automated "observer" is equipped with *range* and *intensity* sensors. The former acquire range images, in which each pixel encodes the distance between the sensor and a point in the scene. The latter are the familiar TV cameras acquiring grey-level images. That is to say, the automated archaeologist may use a CCD camera to observe a pattern of structured light projected on the scene (e.g., a beam of laser light, or a grid of lines). The resulting data is only a spatial pattern of visual bindings, which can be subdivided into sets of marks (points, lines, areas, volumes) that express the position and the shape of perceived boundaries, and their visual properties (texture). In addition, the automated archaeologist should acquire information on the frequency variation of different materials (composition) at different spatiotemporal locations.

The job of the automatic archaeologist sensors is not to provide with a representation of the world in abstract but to generate the information that the robot needs to interact with the world. The spatial location of archaeological features, and the characteristics relevant to its explanation, must be recognized and represented in the robot's "brain" in such forms that they can be used in the planning of epistemic actions. Perceptual features are treated as evidence and their estimation accuracy should be directly correlated to their power to resolve alternative hypotheses. That accuracy in turn depends upon feature extraction methods. It can be carried out by means of specialized feature detectors, which pick up information specifying, for instance, some shape invariants of real objects in the external word (lines and angles). Other detectors may capture both the feature and other parameters. By this account, hierarchies of feature detectors are combined together in ways given by coactivity of the underlying detectors and necessary knowledge structures necessary to integrate them. Complex association structures are formed when simple feature detectors and prior knowledge structures become associated through repeated sequential fixations of the corresponding features.

The next step implies going beyond the partition of perceived input into a set of non-overlapping, uniform connected conceptual entities. Events themselves are higher-level entities, integrated in historical trajectories, which should be constructed using mechanisms that are more complex. Subsequent levels of processing are needed to represent the higher-level correlations that arise when archaeological events are finally categorized.

Information processing in a robot should be organized on different levels of cognition, covering the handling of sensor streams, holistic processes (neural level), knowledge processing, and dealing with mathematical models, in a kind of *subsumption* architecture (Brooks 1999, Rachermacher 1996).

Seeing the past in the present is then a gradual task that proceeds from the general to the specific and that overlaps with, guides, and constrains the derivation of a causal explanation from the visual input acquired at the archaeological site and at the laboratory. The overall explanatory process is thus broken down into the extraction of a number of different observable physical properties (low-level analysis), followed by a final decision based on these properties (high-level analysis). Low-level processes typically concern the extraction of relevant features (form and frequency, shape and composition) characterizing the individuality of each archaeological event (see Figure 10.1).

Each level is implemented by a distinctly engineered layer. That is to say, explanatory-

Figure 10.1. The gradual process of seeing the past in the present and recognizing it.

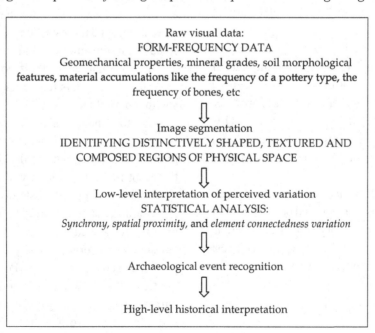

achieving tasks should be represented as separate layers of the same mechanism. In its purest sense, the explanatory device should permit communication between layers, but they will be heavily restricted. We can imagine a first layer processing *signals*. It is a series of mechanisms receiving information from sensory systems and filtering out "features." The second layer would be the *feature* level. Here features would be aggregated "to arrive at the basic building blocks of level 3 of the hierarchy considered, namely concepts and notions to be communicated to a higher level of representation. Layer four deals with knowledge processing, where the information content from level two is further interpreted and reduced, leading to symbolic concepts. Layer five is the *theory* level, which represents information in the form of formal theories or models, often using mathematical tools.

Initially, low-level processing is activated when it is stimulated by the "recognition" of spatiotemporally distributed discontinuities in shape, texture, and composition. This layer then activates all appropriate higher-level mechanisms to which they are connected, and in turn activates all of their super ordinate explanatory processes. In the case of a neural network approach, the receptive field properties of low-level neurons would encode the salient features of the input data in order to generate a preliminary model of the external world. This encoded information would then be processed and eventually decoded by middle-and higher-order neurons. In this way, feature detectors (low-level neurons) would respond selectively when particular local configurations are presented. Cognitive detectors (higher-level neurons) represent the outcomes of particular simulations of hypothetical causal processes. At the highest level, a decision mechanism selects the concept corresponding to that represented by the cognitive detector activated by the highest quantity of features.

In principle, the automated archaeologist can see the past in the present without semantic criteria for comparison. That is to say, it can be programmed so that its ability to discriminate among archaeological events will depend on low-level, data-driven mechanisms that use visual features sensed at the site. It should be stressed, however, that visual features give not a clean line to distinguish the effects of social action.

"CONCEPTUALIZING" THE PAST IN THE PRESENT

The problem the automated archaeologist must solve can be defined in formal terms as the transformation of an incoming sensory vector into an appropriate conceptual vector, which should be consistent with a hypothetical causal model of the input vector (Churchland 1995). That is, given a description of archaeologically observable features and a set of already known mechanisms corresponding to hypothetical social activities, actions, and/or behavior models known to the automatic archaeologist, it should assign correct causal explanations to what it has seen in the present, as they were the material consequences of social actions performed in the past.

We can say then that an automated archaeologist "perceives" some reality because it recognizes input information according to previously learnt categories. The goal of explanation is to perform relevant associations between input and output correctly, in the sense that the recognition reflects a meaningful property of the world in terms of what has been already learnt of its formation process through previous experiments or controlled observations, and which is independent of the particular data that is being interpreted. First, a visual sub-system has classified the percept as being a member of one of a large number of results from known causal processes according to visible properties, such as its shape, size, color, and location, and relations between them. Second, this identification allows access to a large body of stored information about this type of object, including its function and various forms of expectations about its future behaviors. This two-step schema has the advantage that any functional property can be associated with any object, because the relation between the visual characteristics of an object and the information stored about its function, history, and use can be purely arbitrary, owing to its mediation by the process of categorization.

Minsky (2000) believes that we all have powerful "commonsense" knowledge that helps us to predict the possible behavior of what we see. He claims that: "The secret of what X means to us lies in how our representations of X connect to the other things we know." He also mentions the need for classifying objects according to what they can be used for or which goals they can help us achieve (Minsky 1991). This procedure seems to ascribe to any cognitive machine an organized "library" of internal representations of various prototypical perceptual situations, to which the results of perceptions are associated. Explanatory understanding consists then in the apprehension of the problematic case as an instance of a general type. Such a representation would allow the machine to anticipate aspects of the case so far unperceived, and to deploy practical techniques appropriate to the case at hand. Consequently, automated understanding can be understood as the generator of a set of descriptions of the actual physical world that might be sufficient (perhaps in concert with other contextual information) to identify instances of social actions performed in the past, according to what the robot knows about them from the laboratory experiments, computer simulations or ethnoarchaeological analogies.

The suggestion that scientific reasoning might simply consist in a sequence of input-output or perception-action associations has been developed, among others, by Howard Margolies (1987) and Paul Churchland (1989) (see also Abelson and Lalljee 1988, Latour and Teil 2005). Scientific reasoning does not involve any introspection into the process of thinking, but rather is itself a process of pattern recognition. A priori models account for any deterministic variability, whereas deviations from the model are random and statistically independent for different subsets. They represent an expected, deterministic aspect of the data, although the deterministic uncertainties can be implemented in terms of unknown model parameters. Models should be specified a priori; the adaptation or learning is achieved by estimating model parameters from the available data. Perlovsky (2001, pp. 161) has suggested that understanding is only possible through the combination of sophisticated a priori knowledge with adaptive learning in the presence of perceptual uncertainties of a diverse nature. That is to say, an automated archaeologist should be able to integrate what it knew before experience (predefined rules) and what it should learn through intervention in the real world.

However, it is important to remark that the inner knowledge to be learnt by the robot is not a store of associations constituted as a large database (Typology), but concepts (input-output functions) created from a variety of experiences. It is the nonlinear and adaptive way of learning what allows for the formation of scientific concepts. Automated conceptualization shares three characteristics with explanatory concepts formed by humans: (a) the boundaries of learned concepts should be fuzzy in that no single feature is required to distinguish one concept from another; (b) the formation of learned concepts should be path-dependent in that the final properties of the concept vary with the details of the learner's selection history, and (c) the cumulative effect of selection should cause the epistemic system to function *as if* a general concept has been formed.

This is a *depictive representation* of archaeological explanations. A depictive representation is a type of picture, which specifies the locations and values of configurations of points in space-time (Kosslyn 1994). In a depictive representation, each entity is represented by a pattern of points, and the spatial relations among these patterns in the conceptual space correspond to the similarities among the concepts themselves. Furthermore, depictive representations do not represent predicates explicitly; instead, the relation between arguments emerges from the spatial positions of the depicted objects and parts. In this form of representation, the basic element is a point placed on a certain location, as opposed to an abstract symbol. This is precisely the definition of a *conceptual space*. The intuition around this word is a spatial analogy: a concept can be represented in terms of its relationships to the most relevant concepts that are located in the neighborhood in the ordered "representation space" (Kohonen 2001, Aisbett and Gibbon 2001).

According to Gärdenfors (2000), a conceptual space is a set of quality dimensions with a geometrical or topological structure for one or more domains. The key notion in this framework is that of a *conceptual* dimension. The fundamental role of such dimensions is to build up the domains needed for representing concepts, that is to say, they correspond to the different ways stimuli are judged to be similar or different. The dimensions form the framework used to assign *properties* to objects and to specify *relationships* among them. Thus, shape concepts, for instance, belong to one dimension, concepts for textures to a second, the composition of archaeological observables to a third, and so on. Additional examples of conceptual dimensions are sensory-derived qualities such as time or the three ordinary spatial dimensions of height, width, and depth; qualities of an abstract non-sensory character, such as integrity or complexity; or internally derived features such as social inequality. A domain is represented through a set of integral dimensions, which are distinguishable from all other dimensions. Gärdenfors defines a *domain* as a set of related dimensions that are separable from all other dimensions. Accordingly, a *conceptual space* will be defined as collection of one or more domains.

This view is also coherent with a conception of scientific theories as a structure that serves to pick a specific model out of a set of possible models. The outcomes of preliminary low-level explanations (recognitions) should be combined to obtain global patterns serving as new input patterns to higher-level inferences. Thus, our automated archaeologist will solve problems by recognizing something, and with the help of that result, explaining further.

Neural networks, as used through this book, exemplify this approach. In the neural network, visual input activates the first layer of neurons -the input "feature" nodes- and this activation propagates throughout the network via the connections among neurons. In a neural network almost all knowledge is *implicit* in the structure of the device that carries out the task, rather than *explicit* in the states of units themselves. Knowledge is not directly accessible to interpretation, but it is built into the processor itself. It determines directly the course of processing. It is acquired through tuning of connections as these are used in processing, rather than formulated and stored as declarative facts (Rumelhart 1989).

As it was described in preceding chapters, explanatory concepts become activated to a degree that depends both on available knowledge at each moment (the level of activation in all the neurons to which it is connected) and on the association between individual knowledge bits (the strength or weight of connections among neurons), which can be either positive or negative. Furthermore, in contrast with discrete Aristotelian logics, neural network models are more *graded*. Neurons integrate information from a large number of different input sources, producing a continuous, real valued number that represents something like the relative *strength* of these inputs (compared to other inputs it could have received). The neuron then communicates another graded signal (its rate of firing, or *activation*) to other neurons as a function of this relative strength value. These graded signals can convey something like the *probability* of the cause in some specifically constrained circumstances.

Neurocomputing suggests that, instead of casting automated explanation as a massive dynamic search problem, we can think of it in terms of a gradual sequence of nonlinear transformations (operating in parallel) that emphasize certain features and collapse across others. If the result of this sequence of transformations retains sufficient information to disambiguate different possible explanations, but collapses across irrelevant differences produced by individual variability, then explanation has been achieved. Neural networks implement the capability to organize explanations into a memory for coordinated, interacting processes, not for descriptions of them per se.

In this way, the automated archaeologist does not learn discrete responses to discrete facts, and there is no assumption that the world consists of a finite body of facts. Rather, the world consists of a rich body of information, some of which crosses the sensory thresholds of the problem solving machine. The information that is captured in the activation of input units in the connectionist processing system provides a broad spectrum about the environment in which the cognitive robot, some of which may be regarded as contextual, depending upon what task the machine is performing. It is up to the machine to learn to identify objects in the environment by learning responses to patterns. One advantage of this way of viewing the system's responsiveness to the environment is that the particular response of the system may be influenced by a variety of different factors. Some of them may be only indirectly related to the problem, but they are able to influence the patterns of activation arising inside the system.

The most important characteristic of connectionist systems is that they simultaneously evaluate multiple constraints among a number of sources of information (Thagard and Verbeurgt 1998, Read and Miller 1998, Ranney and Schank 1998). Explanation is conceived as a gradual process that is continuously updated rather than a final judgment at the end of a series of observations are assumed by the probabilistic approach. Each neuron represents a hypothesis of some sort and in which each connection represents constraints among the hypothesis. Additionally, the neurons in such a model are organized in layers, with each layer corresponding to a different level of analysis. The nodes can be thought of as representing hypotheses about the presence or absence specific features or concepts at that level (Read and Miller 1998), or alternatively, each active neuron can represent a "micro-feature" of an item, and the connection strengths stand for plausible "micro-inferences" between micro-features. Any particular pattern of activity of the units will satisfy some of the micro-inferences and violate others. Links between neurons are excitatory when micro-features are consistent or support one another and inhibitory when they are inconsistent. Thus, for example, if explanation *B* is expected to be relevant whenever feature *A* is present, there should be a positive association from the neuron corresponding to the hypothesis that *A* is present to the neuron representing the hypothesis that *B* is expected. Similarly, if there is a constraint that whenever *A* is present *B* is *not* expected, there should be a negative connection from *A* to *B*. If the constraints are weak, the weights should be small. If the constraints are strong, then the weights should be large. The inputs to such a network can also be thought of as constraints. A positive input to a particular neuron means that there is evidence from the outside that the relevant feature is present. A negative input to a particular neuron means that there is evidence from the outside that the feature is not present.

It has been argued, however, that neural networks are just a technology—a set of tools and methods which can be applied to a wide variety of practical and modeling tasks, and not an architecture for an intelligent agent. Neural networks are just a family of number crunching algorithms and without a theory of meaning, whether explicit or implicit, it would be impossible to view connectionist systems as problem-solver mechanisms

(Christiansen and Chater 1992, Marcus 2001). Connectionist networks seem to allow "for the possibility of constructing intelligence without first understanding it."

Connectionism has been equated with trivial "associationism," and many scientists from different disciplines view connectionism as a revival of the radical empiricist approach that dominated the "dark ages" in social sciences. In that behavior-functionalist era, explanation amounted to accounts of environmental information and of the observable behaviors they produced. In many respects, the computational approach to neural networks echoes this endeavor. Neural networks would be just rote memorizers in the tradition of associationism or behaviorism, incapable to match the performance of human in higher-level cognitive abilities.

Connectionist learning has also been attacked. The claim that connectionist systems are capable of capturing sufficiently rich empirical generalizations has been strongly contested. The general theme of these critiques is that neural networks capture some, but not all, of the empirical regularities thought to be critical to understanding the social phenomena being modeled. Fodor and Pylyshyn (1988) have dismissed learning in connectionist systems for being merely "frequency sensitive," as if the machine was able to learn only the probability of occurrence of events it has seen. Perceptual learning in connectionist models merely amounts to becoming familiar with the statistics of input patterns. Therefore, despite showing holistic traits, connectionism still has an impoverished understanding of "context" which is reduced to the coincidence of contingent features, and according to which relationships in the cognitive system are established in a bottom-up manner by simply correlation rules (Engel and König 1998).

Furthermore, in simple connectionist models, the categories to be learned (from the observer's perspective) are already implicit in the features by which an experimenter defines the inputs for the program. Storing a sequence of inputs with given output places simple connectionist learning squarely back in the associationist camp (Clancey 1997). Although the system has certain input-output knowledge, it is incapable of expressing in words what this way of using explanatory concepts is. A neural network is a system knowing its way around in a certain domain yet lacking, in an important sense the concepts we might use to describe *what* it knows.

The main trouble seems to be that while the correlation approach at least promises to provide an account of how internal states of a network can represent propositions, it provides no account at all concerning how they can represent properties. Fundamentally, connectionists attach meaning to the states of a network on the basis of what those states correlate with, and there are serious philosophical problems concerning not only a connectionist semantics based on causal correlation but also, in general, the adequacy of correlation semantics as the basis of any theory of meaning. Since concepts are mental representations standing for situational contexts, this means that the correlation view provides no account of what it is for an internal state to correspond to a concept. What is learned by a neural network are not internally constructed experiences but input-output pairings provided by the experimenter, and what is related are not *interacting processes* but predefined features by which inputs are described.

A further problem for causal/correlation accounts of meaning is explaining the origin of the meaning of explanatory terms such as FREEDOM or JUSTICE, which have no real instances and hence cannot be learnt, or correlated to internal states. These symbols cannot be "grounded" by some state of a network, which comes to correlate the presence of utopia in the social environment; for these are never present in the environment— they don't exist. Problems with non-existent universals have plagued philosophy since Hume. The only proposed solution for a causal/correlation view is that the meaning of non-existents is composed out of the meaning of more primitive terms, which do exist. Therefore, the story goes, freedom means absence of coercion power, and since this can be observed and measured, "freedom" inherits its meaning from the contexts where coercion power is absent. This view presupposes that terms for things, which do not exist can be defined in terms of things that do. Therefore, it seems that we must conclude that every term must be definable in terms of other terms.

The connectionist response to such criticisms is to moderate their claims about the possibilities of the technology. They argue that because of practical limitations, the networks that they create should not be expected to capture all of the relevant empirical generalizations. However, because these simple systems can account for some interesting data, it is argued that they warrant serious consideration. The suggestion is that as networks become larger and more sophisticated, they will be able to account for a broader range of empirical phenomena.

Sophisticated connectionist models overcome the limitations of the simple association mechanism in at least two ways. First, their representations are structured, not only in the sense that they manage to represent complex structured entities such as causal laws, but also because they have an internal structure which determines how they are handled in the system. This internal structure is not, of course, *syntactic* structure (i.e., it is not the result of combining primitive symbolic tokens according to grammatical rules). This structure is a particular configuration of activation values, which *locates* the representation in the state space and hence determines how the system will treat it. Second, connectionist systems are not simple mechanisms for recording a set of discrete associative links between elements. The training process is, to be sure, one of getting the network to duplicate the specific regularities presented in the training environment. It does this, however, only by constructing a particular dynamical sys-

tem, whose behavior is defined only over the set of instances ("associations") to which it has been exposed, but rather over the full range of possible input (or hidden) states. That is, a connectionist system generating an appropriate response to a certain fixed range of inputs is automatically one that generates *some* response to the full range of possible inputs. It will generate the *correct* response to the full range of possible inputs if the training process succeeds in discovering a distributing transformation from input to internal representations, which gives the space of internal representations the right kind of intricate hierarchical structure. In other words, although the automatic archaeologist implemented as a neural network has no single or literal idea of the meaning of, say, "chiefdom," "hunting," "animal prey," "activity area," or "tool," it has some ideas about the circumstances in which the use of this concepts seems appropriate.

There is certainly merit in this position, but it should be recognized for what it is: a promissory note. The enthusiastic predictions about the future performance of an automated archaeologist based on larger networks should be tempered by the knowledge that the advantages of small neural networks often disappear when their size is scaled up.

The most important limitations of neurocomputing only arise when connectionism is applied to higher-level cognitive functions such as reasoning in the same way human archaeologists really do. The major points of controversy in the philosophical literature on connectionism have to do with whether connectionists provide a viable and novel paradigm for understanding the mind. The mere fact that a network can be trained to perform a task does not provide any understanding of how the mind performs the task, since it does not offer any insights into the inner workings of the mind. It should be taken into account that in this book, I have not pretended to simulate the real human archaeologist, but I have tried to look for ways to mechanize scientific reasoning. Although the most important part of the criticism is addressed to the connectionist pretension to replicate human mind, in general, some points are also relevant in our restricted case.

"UNDERSTANDING" THE PAST IN THE PRESENT

The automated archaeologist does not "see" the past as it once was. In other words, when we say that the automated archaeologist has perceived a buried "wall," this is not entirely true. The real matter is that it has detected some texture variation between the nature of the sediment covering accumulations of stones and other material, and the stones that once formed part of that wall. It has perceived that the differences between the sediment area and the stone accumulation area are patterned, and an edge can be traced contouring the limits of the discontinuity between both areas. It will be able to understand such a discontinuity in terms of one component of a house, if it knows the specific operation that accumulated stones at that place and not elsewhere, and the process that explains the unordered accumulation of sediment above a previous ordered accumulation of stones. That is to say, if our automated archaeologist knows how to build a wall, and how stonewalls collapse and become a ruin, it will able to explain a perceived and measured accumulation of stones as a wall. Otherwise, the detected discontinuity will remain unexplained.

The very idea of distributed or adaptive learning has also been attacked. This approach has been called the *affordances* view of perceptual explanation, because it can be traced back to Gibson's formulation of affordance theory (Gibson 1979). The relationship between an agent and its environment afforded by a potential action is termed an *affordance*. On this view, the explanation of any observable thing reflects the actions that can be performed on it (and with it), given both its physical structure and the physical structure of the agent interacting with it. In other words, the a priori contents of the problem-solver are not concepts, but a kind of "pre-concepts" having dynamic, adaptive nature. They are a bridge between the mind and the experience. Concepts-as-potentialities belong to the a priori content of the mind, whereas concepts-as-actualities come immediately close to the world of experience (Perlovsky 2001).

An automated archaeologist understands archaeological observables in terms of a priori *affordances*: relationships between observed properties and the inferred properties/abilities of people having generated those properties. The affordances of any archaeological evidence become obvious in its use and/or formation process. Both involve establishing and exploiting constraints (between the user/producer and the material evidence of his/her action, the user/producer and the natural environment, and the material evidence and the natural environment). Physical affordances, closely related to constraints, are mutual relationships that involve both the agent and the material elements she/he manipulates (and the environment he/she operates). The constraints that are relevant in function of the archaeological entity fall into different categories, which would include the following (St. Amant 2002, Bicici and St. Amant 2003):

- *Spatial* constraints describe the spatial relationships associated with a tool and its use in an environment. For example, to use a hammer one needs enough room to swing it.
- *Physical* constraints describe physical relationships in the use of the tool, such as weight or size.
- *Dynamic* constraints describe movement- or force-related properties of tool use. For example, one needs to swing a hammer with appropriate speed in its use.

Defining archaeological affordances as functional explanations is not as straightforward as it might seem. If the definition proposed by the automated archaeologist is too specific, it may need to include a large number of exceptions; if it is too general, it may end up including many inutile features. In the Artificial Intelligence literature of functional analysis, the example of a chair is often used to illustrate these problems. One functional explanation for a chair is "something that you can sit on." However, because you can sit on almost anything, this definition is too general, including such things as floor, animals, and other people. At the same time, an explanation such as "a chair has a sit-able structure that is held between a backing structure and a legged support structure not much taller than the legs of a human" is too specific. It excludes physical objects we might like to include, such as overturned pails and appropriately shaped rocks. We have already found these kinds of problems, and we have suggested solving it in terms of conceptual spaces, associative memories, and potential fields.

Therefore, understanding those elements of the past that have been seen in the present assumes that the perceived strength of causes is directly stored in memory under the form of mental connections between the *potential cause* and the observed effect (Van Overwalle and Van Rooy 1998). The robot will only learn when perceived events violate their previous expectations, and it assumes that an increasing number of comparison cases with a similar outcome will cause an increase in the perceived influence of the context.

For this sort of cognitive task to work, the automated archaeologist has to know what precipitating conditions generate an increase in the probability of occurrence of an effect. Beyond a simple addition of individual random decisions, social activity should be defined in terms of social *dispositions* or *capacities* within a system of subjects, intentions, activities, actions and operations, some of them rational, others clearly indeterminate, impulsive or unconscious. The

fact that the performance of some social action A, in circumstances T, has a probability P of causing a change Y in some entity N (social agent, community of social agents or the nature itself), is a property of the social action A. It is a measurement of the intensity of the propensity, tendency, or inclination of certain events to appear in determined causal circumstances. Thus, the primary *explanandum* of archaeological theory is social capacities: the capacity to work, to produce, to exchange, to interact, to obey, to impose something or someone.

This approach is based on the idea that the probability of an event is the inversely proportional relation between the occurrence of the effect and the capacity of the cause to produce the effect. Then the probability would not be more than a measurement of the regularity; that is, of the frequency whereupon the performance of a social action is associated with a material outcome. More specifically, the probability is usually identified with the limit towards which it tends the relative frequency of the effect as long as the cause has acted. If in a finite number of cases in which cause C was present the automated archaeologist has observed some effect E with a relative frequency h_n, it can be postulated that in a greater number of cases not yet observed, the frequency of observation of the effect will tend to a value limit around h_n. Therefore, when the number of observed cases increases, the probability that the next case be effect of the most probable cause will converge towards the relative frequency of cases with the characteristics produced by that cause and not by another one. What allows the automated archaeologist to assure that C causes Y in circumstances T is not the increase of probability of Y with C in T, but the fact that in T some Cs regularly cause E.

Capacities are best understood as the causal disposition to contribute to something (Cummins 1975, 2000, 2002, Treur 2005). For each of type of observable change in the materiality of archaeological evidence, a specific type of potentiality should be considered; e.g., the potentiality of a flint pebble with shape S to become a scraper with shape S'. S is the consequence of a geologic process responsible for the material origin of the stone, S' is the consequence of a work operation which transformed a raw material into an instrument. In general, if the potentiality (occurring in a state S) to have state property X has led to a state S' where indeed X holds, then this state property X of state S' is called the fulfillment or actualization of the potentiality for X occurring in state S.

"SIMULATING" THE PAST IN THE PRESENT

The implementation of such causal affordances or potentialities inside a machine to explain what it "sees, is usually called computer "simulation" of a causal process (Gilbert 1996, Axelrod 2005, Becker et al. 2005). History runs only once. However, in the computer, it can run over and over again. We can explore (by altering the variables) the entire possible range of outcomes for different behaviors. The simulation either may provide a test of the models and its underlying theory, if any, or may simply allow the experimenter to observe and record the behavior of the target system. As the emphasis shifts from describing the behavior of a target system in order to understand natural social systems the better to exploit the behavior of a target for its own sake, so the objective of the research changes to the observation and experimentation with *possible social worlds*.

Therefore, the starting point of the explanation of social systems by means of computer simulation is not the simulation of one particular system but the investigation of the mathematically possible development of specific classes of model systems (potentialities). This way of explaining what happened in the past requires the problem solver (human being or machine) to simulate in the present, perhaps in very sketchy terms, a *mechanism*, which, given the properties of the constituent

components and of the environment, gives rise to the phenomena of interest. "Mechanisms are entities and activities organized such that they are productive of regular changes from start or set-up to finish or termination conditions" (Machamer et al., 2000, p.3). They describe the causal process underlying the activity to be explained (Glennan, 2002), and consequently translate a *why*-question into a *what-is-it-for* question. Obviously, the word "mechanism" is here a parable of how social intentions, goals and behaviors are causally connected. It should explain how social activity worked, rather than why the traits contributing to these activities or workings are there (Bechtel & Abrahamsen, 2005; Bechtel & Richardson 1993). In this way, the building blocks for explanations in the social domain are products (people, goods, information), production (human labor, social action), and events (the context in which production took place) organized such that they are productive of some changes, regular or irregular, from start-up to finish or termination conditions. The termination conditions are the effects explained by an account of the workings of the social mechanisms producing them. Such explanatory mechanisms are more than static beginning and end-points. The stages are dynamically connected via intermediate operators. It is the ability of such operators to *produce* the subsequent changes in the social mechanism that keep the process going (Carver, 2001; Darden, 2002; Machamer, 2002; Machamer et al., 2000). The simulation happens when the automated archaeologist executes this social mechanism in a controlled way. Running such a model simply amounts to instantiate agent populations, letting the agents interact, and monitoring what emerges. That is, executing the model—spinning it forward in time—is all that is necessary in order to "solve" it. Since the model is "solved" merely by executing it, there results an entire dynamical history of the process under study.

With the possibility of simulating virtual social systems, a new methodology of scientific inquiry becomes possible. In this model of research, the target is no more a natural society but an artificial one, existing only in the mind of the automated archaeologist, and the researcher behind it. A new target, the artificial system, is created with its own structure and behavior (the simulation itself).

By simulating social activity, an automated archaeologist can explain social causality at the micro and macro levels. In the first case, it explicitly attempts to model specific behaviors of specific individuals. A micro-simulation consists of individual agents, commonly implemented in software as objects. Agent objects have states and rules of behavior. The behavior of those individual units may have huge numbers of degrees of freedom and can be neither forecast nor traced back for each point of time in the future and past. At macroscopic scale, there are social patterns emerging from the apparently unorganized interaction of low-level units. The behavior of the whole system, that is, its dynamics is an "emergent" result of the strictly locally defined interactions between single elements. Emergence occurs when interactions among objects at one level give rise to different type of objects at another level. More precisely, social explanation is emergent if it requires new categories to describe it, which are not required to describe the behavior of their underlying components. This property allows to observe at some aggregate level, processes and characteristics which cannot necessarily been explained by a simple generalization from the behavior of a single agent, and which in turn may influence the agent's behavior at the micro level. Theoretically and methodologically, such approaches allow constructing the model from the level of processes that are immediately empirically observable, namely the local interactions of single elements.

The automated archaeologist will not study how social activities took place by trying to understand the intentions or motivations of individual agents alone, no matter how detailed the knowledge of those individuals might be. It

will study a subset of social activity: collective action, *why* different people made the same action, or different actions at the same place and at the same time. The negative side of this approach is that there is no possibility of knowing why an individual person made something somewhere at some moment. However, it does not presuppose the implicit randomness, subjectivity, or indeterminism of social action. The goal should be to explain the sources or causes of that variability, and not exactly the inner *intentions* of individual action. The real issue is precisely that intentional actions of the agents give rise to functional, unaware collective phenomena (e.g., the division of labor).

A FINAL COMMENT ON AUTOMATED EXPLANATION

Simulating is a conscious process of recollecting previous experience. What is simulated depends on the associated context, or better, what has been experienced depends on the associated context. Isolated, inputs are not merely noted and stored; rather the machine learns a relationship between a given input and the total set of simulated experiences. Reconstructing experience—simulating—involves establishing a new coordination, which reuses previous perceptions, ways of expressing, and conceptions. Thus, automatic explanation is not a mere retrieving of memorized concepts but reestablishing an association, a way of coordinating perceptions, ideas, and actions.

That is, information is not stored in form of simple condition-action pairs, but according to all possibilities for association. Explanation can be described as a procedure that relates the *history* of what has previously simulated to the current perception. Our intelligent machine models experience as a cumulative, contextual effect and not as discretely stored and tagged events. That means that the explanation active at any particular moment is appropriate to the machine's internal and external circumstances.

Automated problem solving is then an action-oriented cognitive task, cast in action-relative, and even, action inviting terms. That means that, what is archaeologically explained, will be always known in terms directly related to an agent's current possibilities for future action. In such a way, the automated archaeologist perceive "possibilities for explanation," when studying an historical situation. It does not name or identify blindly, but recognize circumstances to apply what it has previously learnt and experimented.

Thus, an automated archaeologist explains the archaeological record according to what it expects about social activity. It is able to produce those expectations because it has simulated the potentialities of such an action in terms of an input-output relationship. It has a memory for coordinated, interacting processes, not for descriptions of them per se. What we call here a memory is an ability to *act similarly* to the way the robot has acted before. Memory is best viewed as a set of skills serving perception and action. That is, it is a *capability* to organize explanations into a configuration relating perceptions to potentialities for action.

In other words, the solutions to an archaeological problem are *indexical relations* between the problem solver and its actual activity. These solutions relate what the program has just been doing—experienced in a simulated world—and what is sensing now. An indexical relation is always relative to the robot's frame of reference. The meaning of an indexical relation is a relation between the agent and the world formed within an ongoing activity. Nor are internal states stored pointers to things. Rather, these designators are ongoing historical relations between the sensor and explanations, which exist only while the robot is learning to explain. The system's history determines what produces an informative configuration and what is mere noise. The system's history determines what a pattern in the environment is.

Anticipatory schemas play a crucial role in providing both the direction and context for interaction with the past. Perception and explanation can only be generated through the interaction between signals coming from within the "mind" and from the outside world. It is a fundamental departure from trivial inductive approaches, which emphasize learning from data (signals coming from outside). It also is contrary to the strict deductive approach emphasizing the role of previously defined rule-based (signals coming from within the mind of the problem-solver). Our approach combines the interaction of existing explanatory models (mental) and agent's intervention in the world. Note that one of the functions of the intelligent system is to "interpret" the world, that is, to develop internal representations of the world, and establish the correspondence between the world and the interpreter's representations.

The automated archaeologist appears then as an embedded evolved associative engine capable of actively simulating some of the environments from which it has received teaching inputs. Thus, instead of describing the kinds of knowledge needed to explain archaeological observables according to content (e.g., implicit, declarative, spatial, visual, etc.), an automated archaeologist should distinguish the different components of knowledge according to the properties of their simulated mechanisms. The assumption is that knowledge to solve archaeological problems is not acquired, but created using basic knowledge of a domain that predisposes to certain types of hypotheses. This is the classical assumption of a true scientific method.

Scientific activity is more construction than discovery; construction of models that must be adequate to the phenomena, and not of discovery of truth concerning the unobservable. Explanations, meanings produced by the machine, will then be understood in terms of the computational mechanisms that led to its construction and guide its use. The meaning of an explanation resides in its functional role, which is determined by its production mechanism and use. Explanation will not be fixed by definitions. Rather its role will depend on the history of its use. The general point is that the use of the concept in all possible contexts constitute the meaning of the concept, as opposed to have merely a single word standing for "activity area," "chiefdom," "knife" or anything similar, regardless of the possible contexts. What determines the meaning of any term is the peculiar cluster of beliefs in which the term figures, and the peculiar pattern of inferences they make possible. This situational ontology implies that what we can archaeologically perceive are not context-invariant entities, but rather, they are individuated according to the situation's demands and according to the task. Concepts, in this view, do not correspond to specific internal states or structures within the automated archaeologist. They must be equated with the ability to use a skill: that of deploying the concept in a convincing range of relevant situations. Even after an agent has learned a concept, the meaning of the concept very often changes because of new experiences. Problem solving never ends, because a solution is not the last state, but a particular state which impulses towards new states.

The approach exposed here challenges the received picture of an explanation as an invariant structure. Solving archaeological problems is an activity. We have to change the way we understand explanatory concepts. There are not verbal labels we attach to some percepts by means of a previously existing rule but a cognitive action, or a requisite to a next action. Explanations should be based on purposeful, goal-directed mechanisms emerging from a dynamical system that has been calibrated by learning (trial and error, experimentation, analogy) to make the right choices in the proper circumstances. What I am suggesting is that when explaining, our automated archaeologist conceptually navigates in a potential field of explanations looking for attractors (goals) and repulsions (constraints). Upon

detecting the goal, the explanation moves toward it, executes it and then follows until another goal or constraint is found. It repeats this sequence of actions until it has returned all attractors in the potential field. Since the robot does not manipulate propositions, any account of automated explanation that would draw on connectionist principles would not be able to limit itself to principles of logical inference in describing how some belief was arrived at. Rather, it is necessary to rely on something like the notion of maximal satisfaction of soft constraints to describe how the a machine behaves cognitively, and in *evaluating* its performance we would presumably consider whether the constraints it satisfied in arriving at its output state were the appropriate constraints. This would lead us into an evaluation of how an automated archaeologist has learnt, specifically, whether its training had resulted in ways that enabled it to respond to inputs in a manner that was most likely to meet its needs in the environment. This would constitute a major change, since epistemology has generally been pursued through conceptual analysis, not empirical inquiry (Bechtel & Abrahamsen, 2005).

This shift in perspective from *knowledge as stored* artifact to knowledge as *constructed capability-in-action* is inspiring a new generation of cyberneticists in the fields of situated robotics (Anderson, 2003; Brooks, 1989, 1991, 1999; Brooks et al., 1998, 1999; Clark, 1993, 1997; Clancey, 1997; Franklin, 1995; Engel & König, 1998; Hendriks-Jansen, 1996; Iyida et al. 2004; Pfeiffer & Scheier 1999; Winograd & Flores 1986). *Situated* means the robot is an integral part of the world. A robot has its own goals and intentions. When a robot acts, it changes the world, and receives immediate feedback about the world through sensing. What the robot senses affects its goals and how it attempts to meet them, generating a new cycle of actions.

Situated robotics demonstrates the usefulness of viewing intelligent machine construction as a problem of designing an *interactive system-in-its-context*. That is to say, we do not simply ask, "What knowledge structures should be placed on the head of the robot?" but rather, "What sensory-state coupling is desired, and what machine specification brings this about?" These concerns are extremely important, because we can assume that building a "Marxist" robot, a "functionalist," "historic-cultural," "positivist," or "structuralist" one is the wrong way. Instead of storing Marx, Weber, Levi-Strauss, or similar theoretical knowledge in the robot's memory, we should build a machine able to think formally, and which produces knowledge rationally, that is, according to some goals. Of course, the "goals" are ideologically mediated, in the sense that a "marxist" robot will have some historical materialist goals, but it will proceed formally from observation to goal conclusion. In the same way, a "structuralist" robot may have different goals, but the knowledge it produces when trying to attain them, is not "structuralist," but proceed following the same inference mechanism as in the case of attaining Marxist goals. At the end, we can compare the results obtained with different goals, and probably we will find some surprises, in the sense, that Marxist explanations can be integrated with functionalist ones in those cases in which they come from different, but related goals.

Goals are based on beliefs about some domain. Correct beliefs result in sensible behavior; incorrect beliefs can cause peculiar actions. When a robot analyzes its own behavior using these models, it creates beliefs about its own goals. Goals, beliefs, and intentions are then arbitrary interpretations of physical events. They do not exist as explicit sentences. Rather, the machine should be aware of those things that are playing a prominent role in constraining the global constraint satisfaction settling process within the brain.

What constitutes an automated consciousness is not just the intrinsic character of the reasoning system itself, but also the rich matrix of relations it bears to the other problem-solvers (humans or machines), practices, and institutions. Any explanatory account of robotic consciousness must take into account the manner in which the cognitive core of the agent comes to represent not just the gross features of the world (physical or simulated) but also the character of the other cognitive creatures with which it interacts, and the details of the social world in which they act.

In so assuming, the automated archaeologist does not appear as a social determinist. Social explanation is produced in a determined way, but not in a deterministic way, because the causal process is fast never predictable in a simple way. Social actions are not fully predictable, rational, and machine-like. It also means that certain social actions are more probable that others, at certain situations. The robot is able to explain the past performance of human actions and historical events, but it is not an oracle knowing the Truth.

This perspective tells us that we have to take the reasoning mechanism in its entirety into account. However, the view that the brain is the sole factor responsible for intelligence is hard to eradicate. In science, the idea of enormously powerful computers, of *superbrains* that will exceed human intelligence by far, is still common (Moravec, 1998). The idea of such a superbrain seems to be based on a misunderstanding of the nature of intelligence. Information processing is very powerful in virtual worlds like chess, but it is not sufficient to make sense of the real world. Information arises from data, and knowledge can be said to emanate from information. Then knowledge is information in context, organized so that it can be readily applied to solving problems, perception, and learning.

I sustain the view that archaeological explanation should be considered as a complex relational system that links social structure, intention, settings, action, and change history. We can argue that archaeological functional statements should provide an answer to the question "how does

S work?" where S is a goal-directed system in which the material entity whose function we are interested in appears. That means that what has to be determined, is the history of social actions causally related with a particular observable property at different circumstances. The automated archaeologist must explain not only why the property is there, and why it has this visual appearance, but its disposition to contribute causally to the output capacity of a complex system of interrelated social agents and actions.

Thus, an archaeological entity should be explained by the particular causal structure in which it is supposed to participate. The knowledge of some perceived material element should reflect the causal interactions that someone has or can potentially have with needs, goals, and products in the course of using such elements (Chaigneau et al., 2004; Kitamura & Mizogouchi, 1999).

Formally speaking, all "explanations" should be represented as complex relational structures. An explanation is not a simple unitary feature of an object. As research in artificial intelligence demonstrates, representing the full structure of a functional sense requires an integrated set of conceptual relations (e.g., Chandrasekaran & Josephson, 2000).

Relational systems that underlie the role of some material element within a given social activity will be used to categorize, to name, to guide inferences, and to fill gaps in the explanation of the element's function. The automated archaeologist will attribute meanings to observed material elements because it can be proved that they may exhibit certain behaviors under the appropriate conditions. Two objects will be functionally equivalent (or analogous) if they *do* the same (or similar) things in the same (or similar) systems in the same (or similar) environment. The key is the emphasis on the word "do." No other features of the archaeological materials are relevant other than the fact that they *do* the same things under certain conditions, in order words, it is their behavior what matters.

TOWARDS A "COMPUTATIONAL PHILOSOPHY OF SCIENCE"

The very idea of a *computational philosophy of science* has been called "the most self-contradictory enterprise in philosophy since business ethics." I am using a direct reference to Paul Thagard's book *Computational Philosophy of Science* (1988), where he presented a challenge to the philosophical community: philosophical theories of scientific method, if they are worth their salt, should be represented as computer programs. Computational philosophy of science is a kind of experimental epistemology. It investigates methods for representing knowledge and for modeling reasoning strategies that can manipulate that knowledge. Once one has a working system, one can experiment with "what if" scenarios, adding or removing strategies to determine their effects (Alai, 2004; Humphreys, 2004; Darden, 1997; De Jong & Rip, 1997; Fernández, 2003; Magnani, 2004; Magnani & Dossena, 2006; Peschl, 1996; Shrager & Langley, 1990; Stary & Peschl, 1995).

Such an approach can be characterized as "understanding by building" (Adams et al., 2000; Dawson, 2004; Drennan, 2005; Doyle, 2006; Holland & McFarland, 2001; Fernandez, 2003). It is based upon the general assumption that theory building would be better served by synthesis (simulation) than analysis (logics). Here, the problem-to-be-solved is translated into a design issue: How can we design an *artificial archaeologist* so that it will exhibit the desired epistemic behaviors? Making a computational model forces us to be explicit about exactly how the relevant process actually works below the level of consciousness. Such explicitness carries with it many potential advantages. As such, it should provide novel sources of insight into the archaeologist's reasoning and behavior. It should allow a way to deal with complexity in ways that usual verbal arguments cannot, producing satisfactory explanations of what would otherwise just be vague hand-wavy arguments. Explicitness can contribute to a greater appreciation of the complexities of otherwise seemingly simple process. Furthermore, by integrating cognitive development into robot engineering a system comes to know new things about its environment, integrates those with what it already knows, and utilizes that knowledge.

It has been said that artificial intelligence is philosophy underneath (Agre, 2005), because these endeavor can be seen as an effort to work out and develop, through its characteristic technical means, the philosophical systems it inherits. Computational Intelligence formal methodology renders explicit the hidden difficulties and allows them to surface.

This approach owes much to the work of David Marr on computational psychology (see Marr, 1982). According to his suggestion, theories of computation, and an automatic archaeology is just a theory of computation, are at the top of a three-level hierarchy. At the highest, most abstract level, there is the fundamental problem we want to solve. An intermediate level describes one solution to that problem, particularly in terms of the representations and operations required for the solution. The lowest description is concerned with the physical implementation of the algorithm to generate the solution.

The top level can be equated with the *knowledge-level* (Newell, 1982), where a number of predisposed cognitive actions are specified. The knowledge level is a level of abstractions where we can consider what the problem solver knows, without necessarily knowing anything about how to reason. The components are goals and actions. You should imagine this level as containing terms, which are assumed to correspond to the "knowledge" archaeologists deal with. Given a specific goal, specific input to work with, and specific assumptions about the world, one may hope that there might be only one set of computations allowing a system to produce the required output. In other words, one assumes that it is possible to identify the "optimal" computation or function performed by any archaeologist in a given context. Whatever the archaeologist does, it must somehow accomplish the same optimal computation. Under this view, it does not really matter how the archaeologist perform his or her task, because it is ultimately driven by the optimality criterion of matching expected demands for items, which in turn is assumed to follow general laws. The additional difficulty is that optimality can rarely be defined in purely "objective" terms, and so often, what is optimal in a given situation depends on the detailed circumstances.

For this reason, if the first level is a theory of what should be computed, the next level down is a theory of the algorithm, which specifies *how* a computation should be performed, and specifies the conditions where the procedure can generate valid results. The theory of the algorithm specifies an explicit set of steps that will guarantee a given output when provided with a given input. Such an intermediate level describes the performed function in terms abstracted from the details of the system's physical implementation (the human brain or the mechanic hardware circuitry). Typically, many different algorithms can carry out a computation, so we need a lower level, where all the actions are described without giving an explicit account of what overall function is performed. Note that while the higher levels are about what the agent—human or machine—believes about the external world and what its goals are in terms of the outside world), the lower levels are about what goes inside an agent in order to reason about the external world.

Consequently, whether a theory of computation can be seen as a description of the problem, a theory of the algorithm is a description of a particular solution. The *knowledge* level, or the theory of the computation may be treated as paramount because it characterizes the problem that must be solved by a system, and until one understands what a system does in specific circumstances, one cannot specify the details of how the system works. We can place the algorithm at a lower level of the hierarchy because it does not characterize a problem, but rather specifies a possible solution to a problem that is characterized at the more abstract level.

Such an implementation of knowledge within a computer can be seen as the action of embedding a model of behavior within another model, where the notion of embedding may be envisioned as a logical or causal relation.

This book pretends to give some indications about the first two layers, given only some basic aspects of the technicalities of the lowest level. Given that automated archaeologists do not exist, I have preferred to discuss how to design it (knowledge level or theory of the computation) rather that its possible implementation (physical level).

In this book's preface, I predicted that after reading it, some of you will say that we do "not yet" have automatic archaeologists, but we should hurry up to the engineering department and build them for having someone able to substitute us in the tedious task of studying ourselves and our past. Other readers will claim: "fortunately, such a machine will never exist!" "Why we need such an awful junk? Computers cannot *emulate* humans." These critics seem to think that computer programs are guilty of excessive simplification, of forcing knowledge, or distorting it, and of failing to exploit fully the knowledge of the expert, but it seems to me that it is archaeology, and not computer programs, what is "narrow minded." The saddest thing is that archaeologists do not know how they know what they believe to know. Does it mean that archaeology is even impossible for humans? Maybe we must re-invent archaeology. Simulating or reproducing the way archaeologists think today is not the guide to understand archaeology, because *we are doing archaeology in the wrong way!* Computable archaeology, if you do not like the expression "automatic archaeology," is the proper way of exploring new ways of thinking old concepts.

Computer programs do work in real science, not only in archaeology. Consequently, the discussion is between what is considered an *artificial* way of reasoning (computer programs), and a supposed *natural* way of reasoning. Critics of computationalism insist that we should not confound scientific statements with predicate logic operations, since discursive practices or argumentations observed in a scientific text are not "formal." By that reason, they are tributary, to a certain extent, from the narrative structure (literary) of which scientific texts derive. I take the opposite approach: scientific problem solving stems from the acquisition of knowledge from a specific environment, the manipulation of such knowledge, and the intervention in an appropriately simulated world with the manipulated knowledge. The more exhaustive and better structured the knowledge base, the more it emulates a scientific theory and the easier will be the solution to the scientific problem, and more adequate the interpretations we get.

Throughout the book, I have imagined an *automated* or *artificial archaeologist* as a machine able to act as any of us, human archaeologists, learning through experience to associate archaeological observations to explanations, and using those associations to solve archaeological problems. It should have its own "cognitive core" and should interact with some explicitly simulated world to make changes or to sense what is happening (Murphy, 2002, pp. 3-4).

This automated archaeologist has been described as a *cognitive robot*. Ronald Arkin gives the following definition: "an intelligent robot is a machine able to extract information from its environment and use knowledge about its world to move safely in a meaningful and purposive manner" (Arkin, 1998, p. 2, see also Stein, 1995). By substituting "moving" by "solving archaeological problems," we get a perfect working definition for our automated archaeologist. "Intelligent" implies that the robot does not work in a mindless, repetitive way; it is the opposite of the connotation from factory automation. An artificial archaeologist should be then a *"physically instantiated... system that can perceive, understand... and interact with its environment, and evolve in order to achieve human-like performance in activities requiring context-(situation and task) specific knowledge"* (European Commission Framework 6 objective for 'Cognitive Systems'). Here I am assuming that *explanations* are for our automatic archaeology machine a form of *activity* (Kirsch & Maglio, 1995).

It is easy to see that the purpose of an *android epistemology* (see Ford et al., 1995 for the meaning of the term) is not to study machines in themselves, but *human cognition*. Everybody is aware of the enormous complexity of a human being. If we look at something comparatively simple like a robot, we may be surprised how complicated it is, all the topics and issues one has to think about, design, and build before anything goes. Therefore, I am not arguing that "natural" archaeology can be fully described in terms of an "automated" archaeology. I am suggesting that we can adapt our philosophy, ontology, and sociology as far as possible to what computers can do; that is to say, statistics about the counting of labeled occurrences. Instead of making computers intelligent, I accept the elementary stupidity of computers, and I build the logics and ontology that work at their level of stupidity. Imitating the *Hume Machine* by Latour and Teil (2005), if we would like to build really an automated archaeologist, we must take the computer for what it is without imposing anthropomorphic projections and epistemological beliefs on it. I am not talking about imitating human archaeologists. We have to work with computers and their own way of being in the world.

My aim throughout the book has been to develop in a regressive manner of reasoning the methodical process of the self-organization of information in archaeological knowledge by way of analyzing and reconstructing the internal mechanisms. This strategy involves one assumption and one precondition that are worth noting.

One underlying assumption of this approach is that social activity is computable. This is actually a rather strong and daring assumption. Most dynamical systems defined in human societies cannot be characterized by equations that specify a computable function.

A necessary precondition is that archaeological reasoning be analyzable. In these *post-modern* days, this is a provocation. Some readers may think that archaeology is just what archaeologists do, and there is no formal basis except the personal subjectivities of the archaeologist. The approach adopted here has a distinct *processualist* flavor: there is a reality out here, and it can be analyzed in terms of the causal processes having generated it. However, I have found that there is no way to program an automated archaeologist, without taking into account some of the classical topics of *post-processualist* criticism, notably, the nature of context, goals, intentions, and motivations.

The successful applications we have reviewed in this book points out to the possibility of building an intelligent system in mechanical terms, that is, as a mere number crunching algorithm dedicated to vector transformations. Such transformation would imply the explicit association between what the system perceives, and what it assumes to be a probable explanation to it.

In other scientific domains, the performance of humans at a particular task has been used to design a robot that can do the same task in the same manner (and as well) (Bryant et al., 2001; Datteri & Tamburrini, 2006; Florian, 2002; King et al., 2004; Kovacs & Ueno, 2005; Moravec, 1998; Murphy, 2002; Nolfi & Floreano, 2000; Santore & Shapiro, 2004; Tamburrini & Datteri, 2005; Trafton et al., 2004). It has been shown how 'robot scientists' can interpret experiments without any human help. Such robots generate a set of hypotheses from what it is known about a scientific domain, and then design experiments to test them. That is, a robot scientist can formulate theories, carry out experiments, and interpret results. Consequently, the design of an automated archaeologist should not be considered a mere science fiction tale. It is a technological reality. Research in cognitive robotics is concerned with endowing robots and software agents with higher level cognitive functions that enable them to reason, act and perceive in changing, incompletely known, and unpredictable environments. Such robots must, for example, be able to reason about goals, actions, when to perceive and what to look for, the cognitive states of other agents, time, collaborative task execution, and so forth. In short, cognitive robotics is concerned with integrating reasoning, perception, and action within a uniform theoretical and implementation framework. The question of whether it is possible to such machines to automate the scientific process should be of both great theoretical interest and increasing practical importance because, in many scientific areas, data are being generated much faster than they can be effectively analyzed.

Intelligent robots are here, around us. I have never heard of a claim against wash machines selecting "intelligently" the best way to wash a specific tissue, or a photo camera with an "intelligent" device measuring luminance and deciding by itself the parameters to take the picture. So, why do we fear of a machine classifying a prehistoric tool and deciding "intelligently" its origin, function, and/or chronology? The so-called "intelligent" machines incite instinctive fear and anger by resembling ancestral threats -a rival for our social position as more or less respected specialists. Nevertheless, it is important to remember (Chapter I) that any formal definition of an *automaton* includes both human beings and the "intelligent" robots within the same reference class. People are indeed mechanical, in both mind and body, but are not necessarily machines or material machines (Doyle, 2006).

Maybe the real question is not whether machines think but whether archaeologists do.

DIRECTIONS FOR FURTHER RESEARCH

What new directions in the domain of automated explanation of social events should be explored? All of them. This book suggests only some directions that the reader can explore, but everything is still to be made. The only I wanted to stress is that the mechanization of scientific explanation in the Humanities is perfectly possible, and that there are many different ways of doing it. What has been here presented is for the moment only tentative.

Therefore I cannot suggest new directions for further research, because all approaches here sketched are still open, and we must explore some alternative ways, which I have had no time nor space to cover here.

We do not know where the solution is, but we have begun to formulate the question in its proper way.

REFERENCES

ABELSON, R.P., & LALLJEE, M. (1988). Knowledge structures and causal explanation. In D.J. Hilton Brighton (Ed.), *Contemporary science and natural explanation. Commonsense conceptions of causality* (pp. 175-203). UK: Harvester Press.

ADAMS, F.R. (1979). A goal-state theory of function attributions. *Canadian Journal of Philosophy, 9,* 493-518.

ADAMS, B., BREAZEAL, C., BROOKS, R.A., & SCASSELLATI, B. (2000). Humanoid robots: A new kind of tool. *IEEE Intelligent Systems and Their Applications: Special Issue on Humanoid Robotics*, 15(4), 25-31.

AGRE, P. (2005). The soul gained and lost: Artificial intelligence as a philosophical project. In S. Franchi & G. Güzeldere (Eds.), *Mechani-*

cal bodies, computational minds (pp. 153-174). Cambridge, MA: The MIT Press.

AISBETT, J., & GIBBON, G. (2001). A general formulation of conceptual spaces as a meso level representation. *Artificial Intelligence, 133*(1-2), 189 – 232.

ALAI, M. (2004) A.I., scientific discovery and realism. *Minds and Machines, 14*, 21–42.

AMANT, R.S. (2002). *A preliminary discussion of tools and tool use. NCSU technical report* TR-2002-06. Retrived September 2006 from http://www.csc.ncsu.edu/faculty/stamant/papers/ tools-summary.pdf

ANDERSON, M.L. (2003). Embodied cognition: A field guide . *Artificial Intelligence, 149*, 91-130.

ARKIN, R.C. (1998). *Behavior-based robotics.* Cambridge,MA: The MIT Press.

AXELROD, R. (2005). Advancing the art of simulation in the social sciences. In Jean-Philippe Rennard (Ed.), *Handbook of research on nature inspired computing for economy and management.* Hersey, PA: Idea Group.

BARCELÓ, J.A. (2007). Automatic archaeology: Bridging the gap between virtual reality, artificial intelligence, and archaeology. In F. Cameron & S. Kenderdine (Eds.), *Theorizing digital cultural heritage* (pp. 437-456). Cambridge,MA: The MIT Press.

BECHTEL, W., & ABRAHAMSEN, A. (2005). Explanation: A mechanistic alternative. *Studies in History of Philosophy of the Biological and Biomedical Sciences, 36*, 421-441.

BECHTEL, W., & RICHARDSON, R.C. (1993). Discovering complexity. Decomposition and localization as strategies in scientific research. Princeton: Princeton University Press.

BECKER, J., NIEHAVES,B., & KLOSE,K. (2005). A framework for epistemological perspectives on simulation. *Journal of Artificial Societies and Social Simulation, 8*(4).

BICICI, E., & ST. AMANT, R. (2003). *Reasoning about the functionality of tools and physical artifacts.* Technical Report TR-2003-22, Department of Computer Science, North Carolina State University.

BROOKS, R. A. (1989). How to build complete creatures rather than isolated cognitive simulators. In K. VanLehn (Ed.), *Architectures for intelligence* (pp. 225–239). Hillsdale,NJ: Erlbaum.

BROOKS, R. A. (1991). Intelligence without representation. *Artificial Intelligence Journal 47*, 139-160.

BROOKS, R. (1999). *Cambrian intelligence: The early history of the new AI.* Cambridge,MA: The MIT Press.

BROOKS, R.A., BREAZEAL (FERRELL), C., IRIE,R.,KEMP,C.,MARJANOVIC,M.,SCAS-SELLATI, B., & WILLIAMSON, M. (1998). Alternate Essences of Intelligence , *Proceedings of the Fifteenth National Conference on Artificial Intelligence (AAAI-98)* (pp. 961-976). Madison, Wisconsin.

BROOKS, R.A., BREAZEAL (FERRELL), C, MARJANOVIC, M., SCASSELLATI, B., & WILLIAMSON, M. (1999). The cog project: Building a humanoid robot. In C. Nehaniv (Ed.), *Computation for metaphors, analogy, and agents.* New York: Springer. Lecture Notes in *Artificial Intelligence, 1562*, 52–87.

BRYANT,C.H.,MUGGLETON,S.H.,OLIVER, S. G., KELL, D. B., REISER, P., & KING, R. D. (2001). Combining inductive logic programming, active learning and robotics to discover the function of genes. *Electronic Transactions on Artificial Intelligence, 5*, 1–36.

CRAVER, C.F. (2001). Role functions, mechanisms and hierarchy. *Philosophy of Science 68*, 31-55.

CHAIGNEAU, S.E., BARSALOU, L.W. & SLOMAN, A. (2004) Assessing the causal structure of function. *Journal of Experimental Psychology: General, 133*(4), 601–625.

CHANDRASEKARAN, B., & JOSEPHSON, J. R. (2000). Function in device representation. *Engineering With Computers, 16*, 162–177.

CHRISTIANSEN, M., & CHATER, N. (1992). Connectionism, learning and meaning. *Connectionism, 4*, 227-252.

CHURCHLAND, P.M. (1989). *A neurocomputational perspective. The nature of mind and the structure of science.* Cambridge, MA: The MIT Press.

CHURCHLAND, P.M. (1995). *The engine of reason, the seat of the soul. A philosophical journey into the brain.* Cambridge, MA: The MIT Press.

CLANCEY, W.J. (1997). *Situated cognition: On human knowledge and computer representations.* Cambridge, UK: Cambridge University Press.

CLARK, A. (1993). *Associative engines. Connectionism, concepts and representational change.* Cambridge, MA: The MIT Press.

CLARK, A. (1997). *Being there: Putting brain, body and world together again.* Cambridge, MA: The MIT Press.

CUMMINS, R. (1975). Functional analysis. *Journal of Philosophy, 72/20*, 741-765.

CUMMINS, R. (2000). How does it work vs. what are the laws? Two conceptions of psychological explanation. In F. Keil & R. Wilson (Eds.), *Explanation and cognition* (pp 117-145). Cambridge, MA: The MIT Press.

CUMMINS, R. (2002). Neo-teleology. In A. Ariew, R. Cummins & M. Perlman (Eds.), *Functions. New essays in the philosophy of psychology and biology.* Oxford: Oxford University Press.

DARDEN, L. (1997). Anomaly-driven theory redesign: Computational philosophy of science experiments. In T. W. Bynum & J. Moor (Eds.), *Digital phoenix: How computers are changing philosophy.* Oxford: Blackwell.

DARDEN, L. (2002). Strategies for discovering mechanisms: Schema instantiation, modular subassembly, forward/backward chaining. *Philosophy of Science, 69*, 354-365.

DATTERI, E., & TAMBURRINI, G. (2006). Bio-robotic experiments and scientific method. In L. Magnani & R. Dossena (Eds.), *Computing, philosophy and cognition* (pp. 397-41). London: College Publications.

DAWSON, M.R.W. (2004). *Minds and machines. Connectionism and psychological modeling.* London: Blackwell Pub.

DE JONG, H., & RIP, A. (1997). The computer revolution in science: Steps towards the realization of computer-supported discovery environments. *Artificial Intelligence, 91*, 225-256.

DOYLE, J. (2006). *Extending mechanics to minds. The mechanical foundations of psychology and economics.* Cambridge, UK: Cambridge University Press.

DRENNAN, M. (2005). The human science of simulation: A robust hermeneutics for artificial societies. *Journal of Artificial Societies and Social Simulation, 8*(1).

ENGEL, A.K., & KÖNIG, P. (1998). Paradigm shifts in the neurobiology of perception. In U. Ratsch, M.M. Richter & I.-O. Stamatescu (Eds.), *Intelligence and artificial intelligence. An interdisciplinary debate.* Berlin: Springer.

FERNANDEZ, J. (2003). Explanation by computer simulation in cognitive science. *Minds and Machines, 13*, 269–284,

FLORIAN, R.V. (2002). Why it is important to build robots capable of doing science. In C. G. Prince, Y. Demiris, Y. Marom, H. Kozima, & C. Balkenius (Eds.), *Proceedings of the Second International Workshop on Epigenetic Robotics: Modeling Cognitive Development in Robotic Systems* (pp. 27-34). Lund University Cognitive Studies, 94.

FODOR, J., & PYLYSHYN, Z. (1988) Connectionism and cognitive architecture. *Cognition, 28*, 3-71.

FORD, K.M., GLYMOUR, C., & HAYES, P.H. (eds.), (1995). *Android epistemology.* Menlo Park/Cambridge/London: AAAI Press/the MIT Press.

FRANKLIN, S. (1995). *Artificial minds.* Cambridge,MA: The MIT Press.

GÄRDENFORS, P. (2000). *Conceptual spaces. The geometry of thought.* Cambridge, MA: The MIT Press.

GIBSON, J.J. (1979). *The ecological approach to visual perception.* Boston, MA: Houghton Mifflin.

GILBERT, N. (1996). Simulation as a research strategy. In K. G. Troitzsch, U. Mueller, G. N. Gilbert & J. E. Doran (Eds.), *Social science microsimulation* (pp. 448-454). Berlin: Springer.

GLENNAN, S. (2002). Rethinking mechanistic explanation. *Philosophy of Science, 69,* 342-353.

HENDRIKS-JANSEN, H. (1996). *Catching ourselves in the act. Situated activity, interactive emergence, evolution, and human thought.* Cambridge, MA: The MIT Press.

HOLLAND, O. E., & MCFARLAND, D. (2001). *Artificial ethology.* Oxford: Oxford University Press.

HUMPHREYS, P. (2004). *Extending ourselves. Computational science, empiricism and scientific method.* Oxford: Oxford University Press

IYIDA, F., PFEIFFER, R., STEELS, L., & KUNIYOSHI, Y. (Eds.), (2004). *Embodied artificial intelligence.* Berlin: Springer.

KING, R.D., WHELAN, K.E., JONES, F.M., REISER, P.G.K., BRYANT, C.H.K, MUGGLETON, S.H., KELL D.B., & OLIVER S G. (2004). Functional genomic hypothesis generation and experimentation by a robot scientist. *Nature, 427*, 247–252.

KIRSCH, D., MAGLIO, P. (1995). On distinguishing epistemic from pragmatic action. *Cognitive Science, 18,* 513-549.

KITAMURA, Y., MIZOGOUCHI, R. (1999). An ontology of functional concepts of artifacts. *Artificial Intelligence Research Group. The Institute of Scientific and Industrial Research. Osaka University.* Retrieved July 2005 from http://www.ei.sanken.osaka-u.ac.jp/pub/kita/kita-tr9901.pdf

KOHONEN, T. (2001). *Self-organizing maps* (3rd ed). Berlin: Springer.

KOSSLYN, S.M. (1994). *Image and brain. The resolution of the imagery debate.* Cambridge,MA: The MIT Press.

KOVÁCS, A.I., & UENO, H. (2005, February 4-6). The case for radical epigenetic robotics. *Proceedings of the 10th International Symposium on Artificial Life and Robotics (AROB 2005).* Beppu, Oita, Japan. Retrieved October 2005 from http://www.alexader-kovacs.de/kovacs05arob.pdf

LATOUR, B., & TEIL, G. (2005). The Hume machine: Can association networks do more than formal rules? In S. Franchi & G. Güzeldere (Eds.), *Mechanical bodies, computational minds* (pp. 307-325). Cambridge, MA: The MIT Press.

LEYTON, M. (1992). *Symmetry. Causality, mind.* Cambridge, MA: The MIT Press.

LEYTON, M. (2005). Shape as memory storage. In C. Young (Ed.), *Ambient intelligence for scientific discovery.* Berlin: Springer.

MACHAMER, P. (2002). Activities and causation. *Philosophy of Science Assoc. 18th Biennial Mtg - PSA 2002: PSA 2002 Workshops.* Retrieved October 2005 from http://philsci-archive.pitt.edu/archive/00000864/

MACHAMER, P., DARDEN, L., & CRAVER, C. (2000). Thinking about mechanisms. *Philosophy of Science, 67,* 1-25.

MAGNANI, L. (2004). Conjectures and manipulations. Computational modeling and the extratheoretical dimension of scientific discovery. *Minds and Machines, 14,* 507–537.

MAGNANI, L., & DOSSENA, R. (2006). *Computing, philosophy and cognition.* London: College Publications.

MARCUS, G.F. (2001). *The algebraic mind. Integrating connectionism and cognitive science.* Cambridge, MA: The MIT Press.

MARGOLIES, H. (1987). *Patterns, thinking and cognition. A theory of judgement.* Chicago University Press.

MARR, D.H. (1982). *Vision, a computational investigation into the human representation and processing of visual information.* San Francisco: W.H. Freeman.

MINSKY, M. (1991). Logical versus analogical or symbolic versus connectionist or neat versus scruffy. *AI Magazine, 12*(2), 34–51.

MINSKY, M. (2000). Deep issues: Commonsense-based interfaces. *Communications of the ACM, 43*(8), 66–73.

MORAVEC, H. (1999). *Robot. Mere machines to trascend mind.* New York: Oxford University Press.

MURPHY, R.R. (2002). *Introduction to AI robotics.* Cambridge, MA: The MIT Press.

NEWELL, A. (1982). The knowledge level. *Artificial Intelligence, 18,* 87-127.

NOLFI, S., & FLOREANO, D. (2000). *Evolutionary robotics. The biology, intelligence, and technology of self-organizing machines.* Cambridge, MA: The MIT Press.

PERLOVSKY, L.I. (2001). *Neural networks and intellect. Using model-based concepts.* Oxford: Oxford University Press.

PESCHL, M.F. (1996). The development of scientific concepts and their embodiment in the representational activities of cognitive systems. Neural representation spaces, theory spaces, and paradigmatic shifts. *Philosophica, 57*(1),131-172.

PFEIFFER, R., SCHEIER, C. (1999). *Understanding intelligence.* Cambridge, MA: The MIT Press.

RADERMACHER, F.J. (1996). Cognition in systems. *Cybernetics and Systems, 27,* 1-41.

RANNEY, M., & SCHANK, P. (1998). Toward an integration of the social and the scientific: Observing, modelling, and promoting the explanatory coherence of reasoning. In S. J. Read & L. C. Miller (Eds.), *Connectionist models of social reasoning and social behavior* (pp. 245-276). London: Lawrence Erlbaum Associates.

READ, S.J., & MILLER, L.C. (1998). On the dynamic construction of meaning: An interactive activation and competition model of social perception. In S. J. Read & L.C. Miller (Eds.), *Connectionist models of social reasoning and social behavior* (pp. 27-68). London: Lawrence Erlbaum Associates.

RUMELHART, D.E. (1989). Towards a microstructural account of human reasoning. In S. Vosniadou & A. Ortony (Eds.), *Similarity and analogical reasoning.* Cambridge, UK: Cambridge University Press.

SANTORE, J.F., & SHAPIRO, S.C. (2004). A cognitive robotics approach to identifying perceptually indistinguishable objects. In A. Schultz (Ed.), *The intersection of cognitive science and robotics: From interfaces to intelligence, Papers from the 2004 AAAI Fall Symposium* (pp. 47-54). Menlo Park, CA: AAAI Press.

SHRAGER, J., & LANGLEY,P. (1990). *Computational models of scientific discovery and theory formation.* San Francisco,CA: Morgan Kaufmann.

STARY, C., & PESCHL, M.F. (1995). Towards constructivist unification of machine learning and parallel distributed processing. In K.M. Ford, C. Glymour & P.J. Hayes *Android Epistemology.* Menlo Park/Cambridge/London: AAAI Press/the MIT Press.

STEIN, L. A. (1995). Imagination and situated cognition. In K.M. Ford, C. Glymour & P.J. Hayes *(Eds.), Android epistemology.* Menlo Park/Cambridge/London: AAAI Press/the MIT Press.

TAMBURRINI, G., & DATTERI, E. (2005). Machine experiments and theoretical modelling: From cybernetic methodology to neuro-robotics. *Minds and Machines, 15*(3-4), 335-358.

THAGARD, P. (1988). *Computational philosophy of science.* Cambridge, MA: The MIT Press.

THAGARD, P. & VERBEURGT, K. (1998). Coherence as constraint satisfaction. *Cognitive Science, 22,* 1-24.

TRAFTON, J. G., SHULTZ, A. C., PERZANOWSKI, D., BUGAJSKA, M. D., ADAMS, W., CASSIMATIS, N. L. et al. (2004). Children and robots learning to play hide and seek. *Cognitive Systems Journal.*

TREUR, J. (2005). A unified perspective on explaining dynamics by anticipatory state properties. In J. Mira & J. R. Álvarez (Eds.), *Mechanisms, symbols, and models underlying cognition: First International Work-Conference on the Interplay Between Natural and Artificial Computation,* (pp. 27–37) IWINAC 2005, Las Palmas, Canary Islands, Spain, , Part I. Berlin, Springer-Verlag.

VAN OVERWALLE, F., & VAN ROOY, D. (1998). A connectionist approach to causal attribution. In S. J. Read & L. C. Miller (Eds.), *Connectionist models of social reasoning and social behavior* (pp. 143-171). London: Lawrence Erlbaum Associates.

WINOGRAD, T., & FLORES, F. (1985). *Understanding computers and cognition: A new foundation for design.* Norwood, NJ: Ablex Publ.

Glossary

Abduction (*abductive reasoning*). It is a thinking procedure establishing some relation between different knowledge units, in such a way that the established relationship should not necessarily be based on the deep nature of the associated units, but on an external criterion established by the scientist or by merely a practical reason.

Activity Area. This is the label received by any distinctive part of an *archaeological site* where it has been proved that some specific activity was performed.

Activity Theory. It is a social theory focusing on social actions as *practiced* by human actors in reference to other human actors and emphasizing human motivation and purposefulness. It was originally suggested by Leont'ev.

Adaptive algorithms. Instead of being defined a priori from specification, this kind of computer programs uses external data to set automatically their parameters. This means that they are made "aware" of their output through a performance feedback loop, so that the program output improves with respect to the desired *goal*.

Agent-Based Modeling. It is a computational modeling paradigm, in which phenomena are modeled as dynamical systems of interacting "agents". Each agent is just a computer program, usually implemented as an *Expert System* or a *Neural Network*. It is then a computer program made of interacting computer programs.

Analogy. We refer with this name to the cognitive process of transferring information from a particular subject (the analogue or source) to another particular subject (the target). In a narrower sense, analogy is an *inference* from a particular to another particular. The word *analogy* can also refer to the relation between the source and the target themselves, which is often, though not necessarily, a *similarity* relationship.

A Priori. It refers to the state of some internal model prior to the current learning experience. It contrasts a classical usage of the term, which refers to "God-given" unmodifiable contents that transcend all experience.

Archaeological Data. Data are composed by the subset of *recognized* elements having been *observed* at an archaeological situation. It is the result of a rational thinking operation on what can be seen at the archaeological site.

Archaeological Record. It is the generic set of all potentially sensed elements perceived at an archaeological situation (*archaeological site* excavation, museum collection, laboratory *experiment*). Once those *observables* are recognized as particular elements, they become *archaeological data*.

Archaeological Site. The place in physical space where social action was once performed, and some of their material consequences are still preserved, although indirectly.

Archaeometry. Archaeometric data are sets of measurements possible on *archaeological data*. In general, they are referred as chemical and physical determinations of any archaeological *artifact*.

Archaeozoology. The scientific study of animal bones found at archaeological sites. It includes taxonomic determinations, ecological inferences, and social practices of hunting, herding, butchery, and meat consumption.

Artifact. It is any material consequence of human intentional *action*. Pots and knives are artifacts, as huts, settlements, political territories, and socially modified landscapes. The unconscious material consequences of social action constitute another important category of *archaeological data*, but they are not *artifacts*.

Associationism. This is the name given to the theory that thinking and reasoning are performed in accordance with the law of association, only in terms of simple and ultimate elements derived from sense experiences.

Associative Memory. Content-addressed or associative memory refers to a memory organization in which the memory is accessed by its content (as opposed to an explicit address). Thus, reference clues are "associated" with actual memory contents until a desirable match (or set of matches) is found.

Automata. They are information-processing machines transforming *inputs* into *outputs*. Simply stated, an automaton is a discrete processing mechanism, characterized by internal states.

Automated Archaeologist. It is a machine able to act as any of us, human archaeologists, learning through experience to associate archaeological observations to explanations, and using those associations to solve archaeological problems. It should have its own "cognitive core" and should interact with some explicitly simulated world to make changes or to sense what is happening. In this book, it has been described as a cognitive *robot*.

Bayes Theorem (*also known as Bayes' rule or Bayes' law*). It is a result in probability theory, which relates the conditional and marginal probability distributions of random variables. The probability of an event A conditional on another event B is generally different from the probability of B conditional on A. However, there is a definite relationship between the two, and Bayes' theorem is the statement of that relationship.

Bayesian Network. Bayesian networks are directed acyclic graphs whose nodes represent variables, and whose arcs encode the conditional dependencies between the variables. The arcs specify the independence assumptions that must hold between the random variables. These independence assumptions determine what probability information is required to specify the probability distribution among the random variables in the network. According to authors like Pearl and Glymour, they have a causal interpretation. In this case, we are assuming that there is an arrow from X to Y in a causal graph involving a set of variables V just in case X is a direct cause of Y relative to V. The model consists in the causal graph together with the probability distribution of each variable conditional on its direct causes.

Bronze Age. In Europe, it is a chronological period from 2000 B.C. until 700 B.C. It is the time where bronze metallurgy spreads to all this geographical areas. In the Near East, Bronze Age chronology is a bit earlier, from 4000 B.C. until 1200 B.C..

Boolean. This adjective, coined in honor of George Boole, is used along the book to a measurement that results in one of the truth-values 'true' or 'false', often coded 1 and 0, respectively.

Burial Analysis. The name usually refers to the archaeological study of ancient graves and cemeteries, including the study of human bones, the architecture of the graves, and the nature, frequency and spatial position of grave-goods. The goal is to infer the social organization from the differences in observed funerary practices.

Case-Based Learning. It is a kind of instance-based learning, which represents knowledge in terms of specific cases or experiences and relies on flexible matching methods to retrieve previously memorized cases and apply them to new situations. Decisions are made based on the accumulated experience of successfully solved cases.

Categorization. It is the process in which ideas and objects are *recognized*, differentiated, and *understood*. *Categorization* implies that objects are grouped usually for some specific purpose. Ideally, each group or category illuminates a relationship between the subjects and objects of knowledge. *Classification* and *Clustering* are kinds of categorization.

Cause (*causality*). It has been defined as "the way an entity becomes what it is".

Chiefdom. In social evolution, this is a level of social organization, which is just before the formation of state and complex societies. Although such societies have some characteristics of complex structures, like inequality, they are still far from the characteristics of full-scale complex societies, like class-struggle, coercitive power, capital accumulation, etc.

Classification. It is a form of categorization where the task is to take the descriptive attributes of an observation (or set of observations) and from this to label or identify the observation within a different phenomenological domain. The task of a classifier is to partition this feature space into disjoint regions that each represents a particular class, cluster, or pattern.

Clustering. It is the process of grouping input samples in similarity classes. Clustering algorithms partition the input space so that diversity may be explicitly recognized and encoded.

Computer Vision. It has been defined as a process of *recognizing* elements of interest in an image, and it can be described as the automatic logical deduction of structures or properties of the three-dimensional objects from either a single image or multiple images and the recognition of objects with the help of these properties.

Computational Intelligence. Computational Intelligence is a discipline domain within computer science and cognitive studies, which is based on the hypothesis that reasoning can be realized using computation.

Conceptual Space. This is an analogy that allows understanding a concept as represented in terms of its relationships to the most relevant concepts that are located in the neighborhood in the ordered "representation space". Consequently, it is defined by a set of quality dimensions, which form the framework used to assign properties to concepts and to specify relationships among them.

Connectionism. Connectionism is a movement in cognitive science, which hopes to explain human intellectual abilities using artificial *neural networks*.

Constraint. In Artificial Intelligence, they are the expressly allowed values for variables. In some cases, problem solving methods are implemented as an evaluation or search that satisfies a restricted set of expressly allowed values.

Composition. It is said of the elements an entity is made of. Not any enumeration of constitutive elements is a *composition*. It is necessary that each component be expressed as a proportion of the total sum of components. Compositions should be expressed as vectors of data, which sum up to a constant, usually proportions or percentages.

Curve Fitting. This is the procedure of finding a curve, which matches a series of data points and possibly other *constraints*, in which the function must go exactly through the data points.

Deduction. In logic, it is a rigorous proof, or derivation, of one statement (the conclusion) from one or more statements (the premises)—*i.e.,* a chain of statements, each of which is either a premise or a consequence of a statement occurring earlier in the proof.

Distributed Representation. This is the most characteristic representation format in a *neural network*, where concepts appear as ephemeral patterns of activation across an entire set of units rather than as individuated elements or symbols. Different patterns capture different aspects of the content of the concepts in a partially overlapping fashion. Alternative concepts are simply alternative patterns of activation.

Emergence. It refers to the way complex systems and patterns arise out of a multiplicity of relatively simple interactions "Emergent" entities (properties or substances) 'arise' out of more fundamental entities and yet are 'novel' or 'irreducible' with respect to them.

Entropy. In information theory, it is a measure of the uncertainty associated with a random variable.

Epistemic Action. According to most dictionaries, "epistemic" is an adjective meaning "knowledge", "cognitive"; therefore, an epistemic action is some operation involving the creation or transformation of knowledge. *Problem solving* is an example of a series of epistemic actions.

Ethnoarchaeology. This is the study of material consequences of social action as perceived at an observed controlled situation, like in an ethnographic context. It usually implies the use of archaeological tools and methods for studying social *evidence* whose function and origin are known because they have been seen how a living population produced and used them.

Evidence. In its broadest sense, it refers to anything that is used to determine or demonstrate the truth of an assertion. In scientific research, evidence is accumulated through observations of phenomena that occur in the natural world, or which are created as experiments in a laboratory. Archaeological evidence usually goes towards supporting or rejecting a hypothesis. In some cases, it can be used as a synonym for *archaeological record*, or archaeological observables.

Experimentation. This is a scientific method, which tests through repeated controlled experiences the likelihood of some hypothesis. It is usually distinguished from mere observation, because experiences are not merely "observed", but performed by the observer (the experimentalist).

Expert System. The name refers to a computer program implementing a series of Production Rules (If...Then pairs), which is used to solve diagnostic problems.

Explanandum (*Latin*). In a *problem*, it is the statement that needs to be explained

Explanans (*Latin*). In a *problem*, it is the statement that explains the problem.

Explanation. This is a statement pointing to causes, context, and consequences of some object, process, state of affairs, etc. An explanation can only be given once *understanding* has been reached.

Function. In this book, this term refers to two different concepts. In logics, mathematics, and computer science, it is an abstract entity that associates an input to a corresponding output according to some rule. In Archaeology and biology, it has been argued that to ascribe a *function* to something means to relate it to the "intended" use of something else, or the role it should play in bringing something about. A functional predicate is a logical symbol that may be applied to an object term to produce another object term.

Fuzzy logic. It is derived from fuzzy set theory dealing with reasoning that is approximate rather than precisely deduced from classical predicate logic. Fuzzy truth values represent membership in vaguely defined sets.

Generalization. What is true for a set of elements should be true for all elements that are similar to the prior set, or are related in some way. It is used as a synonym for *induction*.

Genetic Algorithm. This is a computing search technique used to find exact or approximate solutions to optimization problems. It uses analogies inspired by evolutionary biology such as inheritance, mutation, selection, and crossover. Genetic algorithms are implemented as a computer simulation in which a population of abstract representations of candidate solutions evolves toward better solutions.

Geostatistics. It is a brand of statistics that deal specifically with spatial relationships. It involves the analysis and prediction of spatial or temporal phenomena, and it implies a class of techniques used to analyze and predict values of a variable distributed in space or time.

GIS (Geographic Information System). This is a computer program integrating a spatial database and a cartographic representation, in such a way that spatial data are automatically visualized cartographically, and database queries can be formulated by selecting geographic areas in the map representation.

Goal. This is usually a synonym of an objective or desired outcome. We refer to goals as desired state of affairs of a person or of a system, that is to say, a state of the domain of activity of an intelligent entity which she/he/it tries to achieve.

Gradient. It is the direction of maximum rate of some quantitative values, and a scalar measurement of this rate.

Grave-Goods. The objects and materials placed at a grave and supposed to accompany the dead person.

Heuristic. This is a reasoning procedure based on simple, efficient rules, instead of formal proofs, which have been proposed to explain how people make decisions, come to judgments, and solve problems. Although such rules hardly generate "true" results, they allow obtaining good enough results under most circumstances.

Holocene. This epoch is a geological period, which began approximately 11,550 calendar years BP (about 9600 B.C.) and continues to the present.

Household. More than a synonym of "house", we use this term in archaeology and anthropology to indicate all activities and work operations usually performed at a domestic level.

Hunter-Gatherer. A kind of human society whose subsistence is satisfied without the cultivation of plants or animal husbandry, but just in terms of hunting wild animals and gathering wild plants.

Iconography. This word literally means "image writing", and is used to indicate the identification, description and the interpretation of the content of images. Discussing imagery as iconography implies a critical "reading" of imagery that often attempts to explore social and cultural values.

Induction. It can be defined as the way of concluding that facts similar to those observed are true in cases not examined. Inductive learning tools are trained to recognize patterns or to predict outcomes by *generalizing* from a group of measurements for which the desired outcome is known (training data) to a larger set of circumstances.

Inequality. Applied to a social context, it refers to the degree of social differences in a human community, where not all individuals have the same access to resources or to social life means.

Inference. It is the act or process of deriving a consequence based solely on what one already knows.

Influence Diagram. This is a directed graph, where an arrow denotes an influence expressing available knowledge about the "relevance" of one variable to explain another.

Input. It refers to external information entering into a system.

Intelligence. It refers to any goal-directed functioning.

Intention. An agent's *intention* in performing an action is their specific purpose in doing so, the end or *goal* they aim at, or intend to accomplish.

Interaction. It is a kind of action that occurs as two or more entities have an effect upon one another. Social interaction can be broadly defined as social relationships generated through the movement of people, commodities, capital, and/or information over geographic space.

Interface. In this book, the term is used to indicate a boundary between two entities. It has also been used to indicate the ways to link entities that may be related, but are not properly connected, for instance, a computer and its human user.

Interpolation. This is a method of constructing new data points from a discrete set of known data points.

Inverse Reasoning. Inverse problems refer to problems in which one has observations on the response, or part of the response, of a system and wishes to use this information to ascertain properties that are more detailed. Inverse reasoning entails determining unknown *causes* based on observation of their effects.

Kinematics. It refers to the study of movements that can be made using a tool or an object.

Labor. In this book, it refers to work of any kind.

Learning. It refers to the acquisition and development of memories and behaviors, including skills, knowledge, understanding, values, and wisdom. It is the product of experience.

Lithics. It refers to those tools made of stone (flint, quartz, obsidian, etc.), which were the only cutting and scrapping tools before the invention of metallurgy.

Localized Representation. This is the most usual representation format, where concepts appear as individuated elements or symbols: one word for each concept.

Luminance. It is a photometric measure of the density of luminous intensity in a given direction. It describes the amount of light passing through or emitted from a particular area.

Machine. It is simply a device, which given a particular input, generates a corresponding output. In other words, it transforms an input signal into an output response.

Machine Learning. This is a discipline concerned with programming computers to optimize a performance criterion using example data or past experience.

Mapping. In mathematics and related technical fields, the term *map* is often a synonym for *function.* In many branches of mathematics, the term denotes a function with a property specific to that branch. In formal logic, the term is sometimes used for a *functional predicate,* whereas a function is a model of such a predicate in set theory.

Mechanism. It is a device designed to perform a particular function. When used out of its proper meaning, this term can be used as an analogy to elements or processes connected in such a way that they produce outputs. Throughout the book, the word it is used to refer to a set of computations designed to bring about a certain outcome.

Megalithism. We refer with this word to different prehistoric phenomena produced since the *Neolithic*: (a) monumentality (great monuments, of stone, earth, or wood); (b) multiple sepultures; (c) megaliths themselves (from Greek: *mega* great, *lith* stone). These phenomena (if they appeared) could have been simultaneous in specific areas or just one or two of them could have taken place. They have enough in common to be referred to with the same word, although in many cases they are different historical events. In Western Europe, megaliths are usually dated from 4500 to 2100 B.C. Some of these monuments could have remained at certain areas until 1000 B.C.

Mesolithic. It is the historical period that preceded the *Neolithic*, and the origin of agriculture and husbandry. In Western Europe, this period is usually dated from 10000 B.C to 5000 B.C.

Modeling. A *model* is a pattern, plan, representation, or description designed to show the structure or workings of an object, system, or concept. Scientific modeling is the process of generating explanatory models of perceived phenomena.

Morphometry. It refers to the measurement and quantitative analysis of *shape* features.

Monotonic. In mathematics, a monotonic function (or monotone function) is a *function,* which tend to move in only one direction as x increases or decreases, and therefore is either entirely nonincreasing or nondecreasing.

Neolithic. This is the historical period in which agriculture and animal domestication were discovered. Its chronology is very variable in different parts of the world, ranging from 9000 B.C. in the Near East, to 5000 B.C. or even 3000 B.C. in other regions.

Neural Network. An Artificial Neural Network (ANN) is an information processing paradigm that is inspired by the way biological nervous systems process information. The key element of this paradigm is that information is processed by a large number of *neurons* working in unison to solve specific problems. ANNs, like people, learn by example, adjusting the synaptic connections that exist between the *neurons*. In more practical terms neural networks are nonlinear statistical data modeling or decision making tools. They can be used to model complex relationships between inputs and outputs or to find patterns in data.

Neurocomputing. It is the field of research that deals with behavior of artificial neurons and artificial neural networks.

Neuron. An artificial *neuron* is a mere input-output computing mechanism, where the output is a weighted transformation of incoming input. Throughout the book, the terms *neuron, unit,* and *node* are used indistinctly to indicate the same.

Non-Monotonic. This term covers a family of formal frameworks devised to capture and represent *defeasible inference,* i.e., that kind of *inference* of everyday life in which reasoners draw conclusions tentatively, reserving the right to retract them in the light of further information. Such inferences are called "non-monotonic" because the set of conclusions warranted on the basis of a given knowledge base does not increase (in fact, it can shrink) with the size of the knowledge base itself.

Observation. It is the activity of *sensing*, which assimilates the knowledge of a phenomenon in its framework of previous knowledge and ideas. Observation is more than the bare act of seeing: To perform observation, an agent must seek to add to its knowledge.

Output. The outcome of any function, process, or mechanism.

Parallel Distributed Processing. The prevailing *connectionist* approach today was originally known as Parallel Distributed Processing (PDP). PDP was a neural network approach that stressed the parallel nature of neural processing, and the distributed nature of neural representations.

Perception. In psychology and the cognitive sciences, *perception* is the process of acquiring, interpreting, selecting, and organizing sensory information.

Pixel. A *pixel* (short for picture element) is a single point in a graphic image. Each such information element is not really a dot, nor a square, but an abstract sample. A pixel is generally thought of as the smallest complete sample of an image.

Planning. It refers to the process of thinking about the activities required to create a desired future on some scale. This thought process is essential to the creation and refinement of a plan, or integration of it with other plans. The term is also used to describe the formal procedures used in such an endeavor, the objectives to be met, and the strategy to be followed.

Post Depositional. All kind of disturbance processes that altered the original location and characteristics of archaeological materials after they were originally placed as a consequence of some *social action*.

Problem. We have a problem, when we are in a situation at which an *intention* or *goal* cannot be achieved directly.

Problem Solving. It is any directed sequence of rational cognitive operations intended to achieve some objective.

Processualism. Processual archaeology is a form of archaeological theory advocating the study of processes, that is to say, the way humans did things, and the way things decayed, in terms of an explicitly scientific methodology. Although the processualists are often criticized as omitting the social aspects of human behavior, they were the first archaeologists who re-created archaeology as the study of human behaviors and social processes. The critical reaction to processualism borne in the 1990s is called post-processualism, which is largely based on a critique of the scientific method for studying human and social phenomena. The general critique is that archaeology is not an experimental discipline. Since theories on social behavior cannot be independently verified experimentally then what is considered "true" is simply what seems the most reasonable to archaeologists as a whole. Since archaeologists are not perfectly objective then the conclusions they reach will always be influenced by personal (and social, political) biases.

Prototype. It is an original type, form, or instance of some entity serving as a typical example, for other entities of the same category. When the regularities extracted for a given archaeological data share a common set of attributes, this set can be said to define a prototype.

Recognition. It is a process that occurs in thinking when some event, process, pattern, or object recurs. Thus, in order for something to be recognized, it must be familiar. When the recognizer has correctly responded, this is a measure of *understanding*.

Recursive. A data structure that is partially composed of other instances of the data structure.

Recursive functions are characterized by the process in virtue of which the value of a function for some argument is defined in terms of the value of that function for some other arguments, as well as the values of certain other functions. In order to get the whole process started a certain class of functions needs to be singled out, whose values do not in turn depend of their values for smaller arguments. These are called the *initial* functions.

Remote sensing. In the broadest sense, remote sensing is the short or large-scale acquisition of information of an object or phenomenon, by the use of either recording or real-time sensing device(s) that is not in physical or intimate contact with the object (satellite imaging, magnetic resonance, Laser ranger, etc.)

Robot. It is a mechanical or virtual, artificial agent, which, by its appearance or behavior, conveys a sense that it has *intentions* or agency of its own. The word *robot* can refer to both physical and virtual software agents.

Self-Organizing. The internal organization of a system increases in complexity without being guided or managed by an outside .

Seriation. Formally speaking, it is a way of situating an object within a series. In archaeology, *seriation* is a relative dating method in which artifacts from numerous sites, in the same culture, are placed on chronological order.

Shape. This term refers to the external configuration of some thing — in contrast to the matter, content, or substance of which it is composed. In geometry, two sets have the same shape if one can be transformed to another by a combination of translations, rotations, and uniform scaling. In other words, the *shape* of a set is all the geometrical information that is invariant to location, scale, and rotation. Shape can also be more loosely defined as the "outline", silhouette, contour, or surface. This definition is consistent with the above, in that the shape of a set does not depend on its position, size

or orientation. However, it does not always imply an exact mathematical transformation.

Similarity. This is the degree of resemblance between two objects or entities. Given that resemblance can be defined as the correspondence in appearance or superficial qualities, similarity can be equated with a measure of correspondences between two entities.

Small-Scale Society. Generally, it is a society of a few dozen to several thousand people who live by foraging wild foods, herding domesticated animals, or non-intensive horticulture on the village level. Such societies lack cities as well as complex economies and governments.

Social Action. It can be defined in terms of purposeful changing of natural and social reality. In fact, it is the pattern of interactions between social agents with the world. Social actions are goal-directed processes that must be undertaken to fulfill some need or motivation. They are conscious (because one holds a goal in mind), and different actions may be undertaken to meet the same goal. However, an action can be an intentional action without the actor having to be aware of the intention from moment to moment.

Soft Computing. It differs from conventional (hard) computing in that, unlike hard computing, it is tolerant of imprecision, uncertainty, partial truth, and approximation. In effect, the role model for soft computing is the human mind. The guiding principle of soft computing is: "exploit the tolerance for imprecision, uncertainty, partial truth, and approximation to achieve tractability, robustness and low solution cost".

Spatial Analysis. This is the study of spatial location of archeological observations. It tries to discover the existence of regularities and dependencies between places in physical space where archaeological data have been recognized.

Supervised Learning. It is a *machine learning* technique for creating a *function* from training data, consisting of pairs of *input* objects, and desired *outputs*. The aim is to predict a class label of the input object (called *classification*) after having seen a number of training examples (i.e. pairs of input and target output). To achieve this, the learner has to *induce* from the presented data to unseen situations.

Taphonomy. It is the study of a decaying organism over time. Although the term was introduced to paleontology, it can be used to describe the study of the transition of remains, parts, or products of social action, from its original context, to the archaeological record *i.e.* the creation of fossil assemblages. The primary motivation behind the study of taphonomy is to better understand biases present in the fossil or archaeological record.

Taxonomy. In biology, it is the practice and science of species determination. Taxonomies, or taxonomic schemes, are composed of taxonomic units known as taxa (singular taxon), arranged frequently in a hierarchical structure.

Texture. Visual properties of a surface. It usually corresponds to observed irregularities in color, shape, roughness, etc.

Truth. There is no single definition of truth about which the majority of philosophers agree. A practical definition would be "the way the world really is, and not what I suppose it is".

Typology. It literally means the study of types. In archaeology, it refers to the *taxonomy* of artifacts according to their characteristics.

Understanding. It is a cognitive process related to an abstract or physical object, such as, evidence, person, situation, or message whereby one is able to think about it and use concepts to deal adequately with that object. Understanding is a set of concepts in the systems cognitive core along with interrelationships between them. The degree of understanding is related to the complexity of a system and to the richness of connections of a given concept to the entire body of knowledge available to the system.

Unsupervised Learning. It is a *machine learning* technique where a model is fit to observations. It is distinguished from *supervised learning* by the fact that there is no *a priori* *output*. In unsupervised learning, *input* samples are grouped in similarity classes (*clustering*), and in so doing, *prototypes* are built as surrogates for learned concepts.

Vector. Informally speaking, any object that may be scaled and added. It is an array of numbers specifying the dimensionality of some entity.

Vector Quantization. This is a general term used to describe the process of dividing space into several connected regions, using spatial neighborhood as an analogue of similarity.

Compilation of References

ABELSON, R.P., & LALLJEE, M. (1988). Knowledge structures and causal explanation. In D.J. Hilton Brighton (Ed.), *Contemporary science and natural explanation. Commonsense conceptions of causality* (pp. 175-203). UK: Harvester Press.

ACEBRÓN-LINUESA F., LÓPEZ-GARCÍA, F., & VALIENTE-GONZÁLEZ, J.M. (2002). Surface defect detection on fixed ceramic tiles. *Proceedings of the Second IASTED International Conference on Visualization, imaging, and image processing.*

ADAMS, B., BREAZEAL, C., BROOKS, R.A., & SCASSELLATI, B. (2000). Humanoid robots: A new kind of tool. *IEEE Intelligent Systems and Their Applications: Special Issue on Humanoid Robotics,* 15(4), 25-31.

ADAMS, F.R. (1979). A goal-state theory of function attributions. *Canadian Journal of Philosophy, 9,* 493-518.

ADÁN, M., BARCELÓ, J.A., PIJOAN-LOPEZ, J.A., PIQUE, R., & TOSELLI, A. (2003). Spatial statistics in archaeological texture analysis. In M. Doerr & A. Sarris (Eds.), *The digital heritage of archaeology* (pp. 253-260). Published by the Archive of Monuments and Publications. Athens, Greece: Hellenic Ministry of Culture.

ADELSON, E.H. (2001). On seeing stuff: The perception of materials by humans and machines. In B. E. Rogowitz & T. N. Pappas (Eds.), *Human vision and electronic imaging VI.* Proceedings of the SPIE, Vol. 4299, (pp. 1-12).

AGRAWAL, R., IMIELINSKI, T., & SWAMI, A. (1993). Mining association rules between sets of items in large databases. In *ACM SIGMOD Int. Conference on Management of Data* (pp. 207-216). Washington DC, USA.

AGRE, P. (2005). The soul gained and lost: Artificial intelligence as a philosophical project. In S. Franchi &

G. Güzeldere (Eds.), *Mechanical bodies, computational minds* (pp. 153-174). Cambridge, MA: The MIT Press.

AIHARA, K., & ICHINOSE, N. (1999). Modeling and complexity in neural networks. *Artificial Life Robotics, 3,* 148-154.

AILLOLI, F., SIMI, S., SONA, D., SPERDUTTI, A., & STARITA, A. (1999). SPI: A system for paleographic inspections. *AI*IA Notizie, 12*(4), 34-39.

AISBETT, J., & GIBBON, G. (2001). A general formulation of conceptual spaces as a meso level representation. *Artificial Intelligence, 133*(1-2), 189 – 232.

AITCHISON, J. (1986). *The statistical analysis of compositional data.* London: Chapman and Hall.

AITCHISON, J. (1994). Principles of compositional data analysis. In T.W. Anderson, I. Olkin, & K.T.Fang (Eds.), *Multivariate analysis and its applications* (pp. 73-81). Hayward, CA: Institute of Mathematical Statistics.

AITCHISON, J. (1997). The one-hour course in compositional data analysis or compositional data analysis is easy. In V. Pawlowsky Glahn (Ed.), *Proceedings of the 3rd Annual Conference of the International Association for Mathematical Geology* (pp. 3-35). Barcelona, Spain: CIMNE.

AITCHISON, J., & BARCELÓ-VIDAL, C. (2002). Compositional processes: A statistical search for understanding. In *Proceedings of the 8th Annual Conference of the International Association for Mathematical Geology.*

AITKENHEAD, M. J., MUSTARD, M. J., & MCDONALD, A.J.S. (2004). Using neural networks to predict spatial structure in ecological systems. *Ecological Modelling, 179*(3), 393-403.

ALAI, M. (2004) A.I., scientific discovery and realism. *Minds and Machines, 14,* 21–42.

ALEKSANDER, I., & MORTON, H. (1993). *Neurons and symbols. The stuff that mind is made of.* London: Chapman and Hall.

ALEXANDROV, V.V., & GORSKY, N.D. (1991). *From humans to computers. Cognition through visual perception.* Singapore: World Scientific.

AL-NUAIMY, W., HUANG, Y., NAKHKASH, M., FANG, M.T.C., NGUYEN, V.T., & ERIKSEN, A. (2000). Automatic detection of buried utilities and solid objects with GPR using neural networks and pattern recognition. *Journal of Applied Geophysics, 43*, 157-165.

ALPAYDIN, E. (2004). *Introduction to machine learning.* Cambridge, MA: The MIT Press.

ALTAWEEL, M., & CHRISTIANSEN, J. (2004). Simulating a bronze age city state under stress. *Modeling Long-Term Culture Change Workshop at the Santa Fe Institute, October 2004. Retrieved July 2007 from* http://oi.uchicago.edu/OI/PROJ/MASS/papers/SFI2004_MASS_2.pdf

ALTAWEEL, M., PAULETTE, T., & CHRISTIANSEN, J. (2006). Modeling dynamic human ecologies: Examples from northern mesopotamia *BANEA conference*, Edinburgh. Retrieved July, 2007 from http://oi.uchicago.edu/OI/PROJ/MASS/papers/PresentationBanea.pdf

AMANT, R.S. (2002). *A preliminary discussion of tools and tool use. NCSU technical report* TR-2002-06. Retrived September 2006 from http://www.csc.ncsu.edu/faculty/stamant/papers/tools-summary.pdf

AMARI, S.I. (1993). Mathematical aspects of neurocomputing. In O.E. Barndorff-Nielsen, J.L. Jensen & W.S. Kendall (Eds.), *Networks and chaos-statistical and probabilistic approaches* (pp. 1-39). London: Chapman and Hall.

ANDERSON, J.R. (1980). *Cognitive psychology and its implications.* New York: W.H. Freeman.

ANDERSON, J.R. (1983). *The architecture of cognition.* Cambridge, MA: Harvard University Press.

ANDERSON, J.R. (1990). *The adaptive character of thought.* L. Hillsdale, NJ: Erlbaum Associates.

ANDERSON, M.L. (2003). Embodied cognition: A field guide . *Artificial Intelligence, 149*, 91-130.

ARENTZE, T. A., BORGERS, A. W. J., & TIMMERMANS, H. J. P. (1996a). An efficient search strategy for

site-selection decisions in an expert system. *Geographical Analysis, 28*(2), 126–146.

ARKIN, R.C. (1998). *Behavior-based robotics.* Cambridge, MA: The MIT Press.

ASTROM, M., & VENCATASAWMY, C.P. (2001). Incorporating artificial intelligence in microsimulation. *Geografiska Annaler, 83B*, 53-65.

ATKINSON, P.M., & TATNALL, A.R.L. (1997). Neural networks in remote sensing—introduction. *International Journal of Remote Sensing, 18*(4), 699–709.

AVILES COLLAO, J., DIAZ-KOMMONEN, L., KAIPAINEN, M., & PIETARILA, J. (2003). Soft ontologies and similarity cluster tools to facilitate exploration and discovery of cultural heritage resources. *Proceedings of the 14th International Workshop on Database and Expert Systems Applications* (DEXA'03). Berlin: Springer.

AXELROD, R. (2005). Advancing the art of simulation in the social sciences. In Jean-Philippe Rennard (Ed.), *Handbook of research on nature inspired computing for economy and management.* Hersey, PA: Idea Group.

BADRAN, F., & THIRIA, S. (1997). Neural network smoothing in correlated time series contexts. *Neural networks, 10*, 1445-1453.

BAILEY, D., & THOMPSON, D. (1990). How to develop neural networks. *AI Expert, 5*(6), 38-47.

BAINBRIDGE, W. (1995). Neural network models of religious belief. *Sociological perspectives, 38*, 483-494.

BAINBRIDGE, W. S., BRENT E., CARLEY K., HEISE D., MACY M., & MARKOVSKY, J. (1994). Artificial social intelligence. *Annual Review of Sociology, 20*, 407-436.

BAIRAKTARIS, D. (1995). Temporal chunking and synchronization using a modular recurrent network architecture. In J.P. Levy, D. Bairaktaris, J.A. Bullinaria & P. Cairns (Eds.), *Connectionist models of memory and language.* London: UCL Press.

BALACHANDRAN, C.S, FISHER, P. F., & STANLEY, M.A. (1989). An expert system approach to rural development: A prototype (TIHSO). *Journal of Developing Areas, 23*, 259-270.

BANERJEE, S. (1986). Reproduction of social structures: An artificial intelligence model. *The Journal of Conflict Resolution, 30*, 221-252.

BARALDI, A., & PARMIGGIANI, F. (1995). A neural network for unsupervised categorization of multivalued input patterns: An application to satellite image clustering. *IEEE Transactions on Geoscience and Remote Sensing, 33*(2), 305-16.

BARCELÓ, J. A. (1997). *Arqueología Automática. El uso de la Inteligencia Artificial en Arqueología.* Sabadell (Spain): Editorial Ausa, (Cuadernos de Arqueología Mediterránea, 2).

BARCELÓ, J.A. (1995). Back-propagation algorithms to compute similarity relationships among archaeological artifacts. In J. Wilcock & K. Lockyear (Eds.), *Computer applications in archaeology* (pp. 165-176). Oxford: ArcheoPress.

BARCELÓ, J.A. (1995a). Back-propagation algorithms to compute similarity relationships among archaeological artifacts. In J. Wilcock & K. Lockyear (Eds.), *Computer applications in archaeology* (pp. 165-176). Oxford: ArcheoPress. (British Archaeological Reports S598).

BARCELÓ, J.A. (1995b). Seriación de Datos Arqueológicos Ambigüos o Incompletos. Una Aplicacion de las Redes Neuronales. In *Aplicaciones Informáticas en Arqueología. Teoría y Sistemas* (vol. II.) (pp. 99-116) Bilbao (Spain): Denboraren Argia.

BARCELÓ, J.A. (1996). Heuristic classification and fuzzy sets. New tools for archaeological typologies. *Acta Praehistorica Leidensia, 28*, 155-164.

BARCELÓ, J.A. (1996). Heuristic classification and fuzzy sets. New tools for archaeological typologies. *Acta Praehistorica Laidensia, 28*, 155-164.

BARCELÓ, J.A. (1997). *Arqueología Automática. El uso de la Inteligencia Artificial en Arqueología.* Sabadell (Spain): Editorial Ausa, (Cuadernos de Arqueología Mediterránea, 2).

BARCELÓ, J.A. (2000) Visualizing what might be. An introduction to virtual reality in archaeology. In J.A.Barcelo, M. Forte & D. Sanders (Eds.), *Virtual reality in archaeology* (pp. 9-36). Oxford: ArcheoPress. British Archaeological Reports (S843).

BARCELÓ, J.A. (2001). Técnicas de Inteligencia Artificial en Arqueología. Su uso en el studio de las formas de interacción social durante la Edad del Bronce. In M. Ruiz-Gálvez (Ed.), *La edad del bronce, ¿Primera edad de oro de españa?* (pp. 55-86). Barcelona, Spain: Editorial Crítica.

BARCELÓ, J.A. (2001). Virtual reality for archaeological explanation. Beyond picturesque reconstruction *Archeologia e Calcolatori,12*, 221-244.

BARCELÓ, J.A. (2002). Virtual archaeology and artificial intelligence. In F. Nicolucci (Ed.), *Virtual archaeology* (pp. 21-28). Oxford: ArchaeoPress. BAR International Series S1075..

BARCELÓ, J.A. (2007). A science fiction tale? A robot called archaeologist. In A. Figueiredo & G. Velho. Tomar (Eds.), *The wolds is in your eyes. Proceedings of the XXXIII Computer Applications and Quantitative Applications in Archeology Conference* (pp. 221-230). Portugal: CAA Portugal.

BARCELÓ, J.A. (2007). Automatic archaeology: Bridging the gap between virtual reality, artificial intelligence, and archaeology. In F. Cameron & S. Kenderdine (Eds.), *Theorizing digital cultural heritage* (pp. 437-456). Cambridge,MA: The MIT Press.

BARCELÓ, J.A. PELFER, G., & MANDOLESI, A (2002). The origins of the city. From social theory to archaeological description. *Archeologia e Calcolatori, 13*, 41-64.

BARCELÓ, J.A. (2002). Archaeological thinking: Between space and time. *Archeologia e Calcolatori, 13*, 237-256.

BARCELÓ, J.A., & FAURA, M., (1997). Time series and neural networks in archaeological seriation. An example on early pottery from the near east. In L. Dingwall, S. Exon, V. Gaffney, S. Laflin, M. Leusen (Eds.), *Archaeology in the age of internet* (pp. 91-102). Oxford: ArcheoPress.

BARCELÓ, J.A., & MAMELI, L. (2004). Frequency seriation and temporal order. A zooarchaeological study. In F. Nicolucci & S. Hermon (Eds.), *Beyond the artefact. Computer applications in archaeology.* Budapest, Hungary: ArcheoLingua.

BARCELÓ, J.A., & PALLARES, M. (1998). Beyond GIS. The archaeological study of social spaces. *Archeologia e Calcolatori, 9*, 47-80.

BARCELÓ, J.A., & PIJOAN-LOPEZ, J. (2004). Cutting or scrapping? Using neural networks to distinguish kinematics in use-wear analysis. In Magistrat der Stadt Wien (Ed.), *Enter the past. The e-way into the four dimensions of culture heritage* (pp. 427-431). Oxford: ArcheoPress.

BARCELÓ, J.A., BRIZ, I., CLEMENTE, I., ESTEVEZ, J., MAMELI, L., MAXIMIANO, A., et al. (2006). Análisis etnoarqueológico del valor social del producto en sociedades cazadoras-recolectoras. In *Etnoarqueología de la Prehistoria: más allá de la analogía* (pp. 189 209). *Serie Treballs d'Etnoarqueologia, 6*. Madrid, Spain: CSIC.

BARCELÓ, J.A., MAXIMIANO, A., & VICENTE, O. (2004). La Multidimensionalidad del Espacio Arqueológico: Teoría, Matemáticas, Visualización. In I. Grau (Ed.), *La aplicación de los SIG en la arqueología del paisaje*. Alicante, Spain: Publicaciones de la Universidad de Alicante.

BARCELÓ, J.A., PIJOAN-LÓPEZ, J.A., & VICENTE, O. (2001). Image quantification as archaeological description. In Z. Stancic & T. Veljanovski (Eds.), *Computing archaeology for understanding the past* (pp. 69-78). Oxford: ArcheoPress.

BARCELÓ, J.A., VILA, A., & ARGELES, T. (1994). KIPA. A computer program to analyze the social position of women in hunter-gatherer societies. In I. Johnson (Ed.), *.Methods in the mountains*. Proceedings of the UISPP IV Meeting, Mount Victoria. Sydney, Australia. University Archaeological Methods Series, No. 2.

BARCELÓ, J.A., VILA, A., & GIBAJA, J. (2000). An application of neural networks to use-wear analysis. Some preliminary results. In K. Lockyear, T.J.T. Sly & V. Mihailescu-Birliba (Eds.), *Computer applications and quantitative methods in archaeology* (pp. 63-70). Oxford: ArchaeoPress.

BARCELÓ, J.A.,(2005). Multidimensional Spatial Analysis in Archaeology. Beyond the GIS Paradigm. In *Reading the Historical Spatial Information in the World -Studies for Human Cultures and Civilizations based on Geographic Information System-* Edited by K. Ono. Kyoto (Japan): Institute for Japan Studies.

BARHAK, J., & FISCHER, A. (2001). Parameterization and reconstruction from 3D scattered points based on neural network and PDE techniques. *IEEE Trans. on Visualization and Computer Graphics, 7*(1), 1-16.

BARSALOU, L.W., SLOMAN, S.A., & CHAIGNEAU, S.E. (2005). The HIPE theory of function. In L. Carlson & E. Van der Zee (Eds.), *Representing functional features for language and space: Insights from perception, categorization and development* (pp. 131-147). Oxford UK: Oxford University Press.

BAXTER, M. J. (2001). Methodological issues in the study of assemblage diversity. *American Antiquity, 66*(4), 715-725.

BAXTER, M.J. (2003). *Statistics in archaeology*. London: Arnold Publ.

BAXTER, M.J. (2006). A review of supervised and unsupervised pattern recognition in archaeometry. *Archaeometry, 48*(4), 671–694.

BAXTER, M.J., & JACKSON, C.M. (2001). Variable selection in artefact compositional studies. *Archeometry, 43*(2), 253-268.

BEARDAH, C.C., BAXTER, M.J. (2005). An R library for compositional data analysis in archaeometry, In *2nd Compositional Data Analysis Workshop, CoDaWork'05* Girona.

BEAVER, J.E. (2004). Identifying necessity and sufficiency relationships in skeletal-part representation using fuzzy-set theory. *American Antiquity, 69*(1), 131-140.

BEBIS,G., PAPADOURAKIS,G., & ORPHANOUDAKIS, S. (1998). Recognition using curvature scale space and artificial neural networks. *Proceedings of the IASTED International Conference Signal and Image Processing, Las Vegas, Nevada – USA.*

BECHTEL, W., & ABRAHAMSEN, A. (1991). *Connectionism and the mind*. Cambridge, UK: Blackwell.

BECHTEL, W., & ABRAHAMSEN, A. (2005). Explanation: A mechanistic alternative. *Studies in History of Philosophy of the Biological and Biomedical Sciences, 36*, 421-441.

BECHTEL, W., & RICHARDSON, R.C. (1993). *Discovering complexity. Decomposition and localization as strategies in scientific research. Princeton: Princeton University Press.*

BECKER, J., NIEHAVES,B., & KLOSE,K. (2005). A framework for epistemological perspectives on simulation. *Journal of Artificial Societies and Social Simulation, 8*(4).

BEECKMAN, C.S., & BADEN, W.W. (eds.). (2005). *Nonlinear Models for Archaeology and Anthropology: Continuing the Revolution* London: Ashgate Publishing.

BEER, R.D. (1990). *Intelligence as adaptive behavior: An experiment in computational neuroethology*. New York: Academic Press.

BEL, L., LAURENT, J.-M., BAR-HEN, A., ALLARD, D., & CHEDDADI, R. (2005). A spatial extension of CART: application to classification of ecological data. In P. Renard, H. Demougeot-Renard, & R. Fridevaux (Eds.), *Proc. Vth Eur. Conf. Geostatistics for Environmental Applications* (pp. 99-109). Berlin: Springer.

BELL, S., & JANTZ, R. (2002). Neural network classification of skeletal remains. In G. Burenhult (Ed.), *.Archeological informatics: Pushing the envelope* (pp. 205-212). Oxford: ArchaeoPress.

BELL, S., CROSON, C. (1998). Artificial neural networks as a tool for archaeological data analysis. *Archeometry, 40*(1), 139-151.

BELLOMO, N., BERTOTTI, M.L., & DELITALA, M. (2007). From the kinetic theory of active particles to the modeling of social behaviors and politics. *Quality and Quantity, 41*, 545–555.

BELONGIE, S., MALIK, J., & PUZICHA, J. (2002). Shape matching and object recognition using shape contexts. *IEEE Transactions on Pattern Analysis and Machine Intelligence, 24*(24), 509-522.

BEN-ARIE, J., & NANDY, D. (1998). A neural network approach for reconstructing surface shape from shading. *IEEE International Conference on Image Processing, Chicago Oct. 1998.*

BENDELS, G.H., GUTHE, M., & KLEIN, R., (2006). Free-form modelling for surface inpainting In *Proceedings of the 4th International Conference On Computer Graphics, Virtual Reality, Visualisation and Interaction in Africa (Afrigraph 2006)* (pp. 49-58). ACM Sigraph.

BENFER, R.A., & FURBEE, L. (1989). Knowledge acquisition in the Peruvian Andes: Expert systems and anthropology. *AI Expert, 4*(11), 22-30.

BENFER, R.A., FURBEE, L., & BRENT, L.E. (1996). Expert systems and the representation of knowledge. *American Ethnologist, 23*(2), 416-420

BENTLEY, R.A., LAKE, M.W., & SHENNAN, S.J. (2005). Specialisation and wealth inequality in a model of a clustered economic network. *Journal of Archaeological Science, 32,* 1346-1356.

BERARDI, V.L., & ZHANG, G.P. (2003). An empirical investigation of bias and variance in time series forecasting: Modeling considerations and error evaluation. *IEEE Transactions on Neural Networks, 14*(3), 668- 679.

BERTHOUZE, L., & TIJSSELING, A. (2006). A neural model for context-dependent sequence learning. *Neural Processing Letters, 23*, 27–45.

BESCOBY, D.C., CAWLEY, G.C., & CHROSTON, P.N. (2006). Enhanced interpretation of magnetic survey data from archaeological sites using artificial neural Networks. *Geophysics, 71*(5), 45-53.

BEZDEK, J.C., & PAL, S.K. (1992). *Fuzzy systems for pattern pecognition.* Piscataway, NJ: IEEE Press.

BHAKAR, S., DUDEK, C.K., MUISE, S., SHARMAN, L., HORTOP, E., & SZABO, F. (2004). Textiles, patterns and technology: Digital tools for the geometric analysis of cloth and culture. *Textile: The Journal of Cloth and Culture, 2*(3), 308-327.

BHATTACHARYA, B., & SOLOMATINE, D.P. (2006). Machine learning in Sedimentation modelling. *Neural Networks, 19*, 208–214.

BICICI, E., & ST. AMANT, R. (2003). *Reasoning about the functionality of tools and physical artifacts.* Technical Report TR-2003-22, Department of Computer Science, North Carolina State University, April, 2003.

BIEDERMAN, I. (1987). Recognition-by-components: A theory of human image understanding. *Psychological Review, 94*(2), 115-147.

BIEDERMAN, I. (1995). Visual object recognition. In S. F. Kosslyn & D. N. Osherson (Eds.), *An invitation to cognitive science, (2nd ed) Volume 2. Visual cognition* (pp. 121-165). MIT Press.

BIGGS, D., DE VILLE, B., & SUEN, E. (1991). A method of choosing multiway partitions for classification and decision trees. *Journal of Applied Statistics, 18*, 49-62.

BIGNON, O., BAYLAC, M., VIGNE, J.D., & EISENMANN, V. (2005). Geometric morphometrics and the population diversity of late glacial horses in western europe (Equus caballus arcelini): Phylogeographic and Anthropological Implications. *Journal of Archaeological Science, 32*, 375–391.

BILLHEIMER, D., GUTTORP, P., & FAGAN, W.F. (1998). *Statistical analysis and interpretation of discrete compositional data.* NRCSE Technical Report Series, NRSCE-TRS No. 011 (http://www.nrcse.washington.edu/pdf/trs11_interp.pdf) (File downloaded on September 2006).

BINFORD, L. R. (1968). Methodological considerations of the archaeological use of ethnographic data. In L.R.

Binford (Ed) *An archaeological perspective.* New York, Academic Press.

BINFORD, L.R. (1981). Behavioural archaeology and the Pompeii premise. *Journal of Archaeological Research,* 37, 195-208.

BINFORD, L.R. (2001a). Where do research problems come from? *American Antiquity, 66*(4), 669-678.

BINFORD, L.R. (2001b). *Constructing frames of reference: An analytical method for archaeological theory building using hunter-gatherer and environmental data sets.* University of California Press.

BISHOP, C.M. (1995). *Neural networks for pattern recognition.* Oxford, UK: Oxford University Press..

BISHOP, M.C., & THOMAS, J. (1984). BEAKER—An expert system for the BB.C. micro. *Computer Applications in Archaeology, 12,* 49-55.

BLANKHOLM, H.P. (1991). *Intrasite spatial analysis in archaeology.* Aarhus, Danemark: University of Aarhus Press.

BOGONI, L., & BAJCSY, R. (1993). An active approach to characterization and recognition of functionality and functional properties. In *AAAI Workshop on Reasoning about Function.* (pp. 9–16).

BOGONI, L., & BAJCSY, R. (1995). Interactive recognition and representation of functionality. *Computer Vision and Image Understanding, 62*(2), 194–214.

BOLLA, D. (2007). Associative multilingual classification architecture for historical artefact. In A. Figueiredo & G. Velho (Eds.), *The world is in your eyes. Computer Aplicatioins in Archaeology* (pp. 85-94). Tomar,Portugal: CAAPortugal.

BONABEAU, E. (2002). Agent-based modeling: Methods and techniques for simulating human systems. *Proc. National Academy of Sciences, 99*(suppl. 3), 7280-7287.

BONÉ, R., & CRUCIANU, M. (2004). Multi-step-ahead prediction with neural networks. *European Journal of Economic and Social Systems* (*Neural Networks Special Issue*), *17,* 85-98.

BONÉ, R., CRUCIANU, M., & ASSELIN DE BEAU-VILLE, J.-P. (2002). Learning long-term dependencies by the selective addition of time-delayed connections to recurrent neural networks. *NeuroComputing, 48,* 251-266.

BORODKIN, L. (1999). Defining agricultural regions in Russia: Fuzziness in multivariate classification of historical data. *History and Computing, 11*(1-2), 31-42.

BORODKIN, L.I., & GARSKOVA, (1995). Analytical procedure for multidimensional hierarchical data. In *Statistical Analysis of Burial Customs of the Sarmatian Period in Asian Sarmata (6th -4th Centuries B.C.* pp. 63-114.). Napoli: Istituto Universitario orientale.

BOWES, J., NEUFELD, E., GREER, J.E., & COOKE, J. (2000). A Comparison of Association Rule Discovery and Bayesian Network Causal Inference Algorithms to Discover Relationships in Discrete Data. In *Advances in Artificial Intelligence: 13th Biennial Conference of the Canadian Society for Computational Studies of Intelligence, AI 2000, Montréal, Quebec, Canada, May 2000. Proceedings* Berlin: Springer Lecture Notes in Computer Science, Vol 1822.

BRADY, M. (1985). Artificial intelligence and robotics. *Artificial Intelligence and Robotics, 26,* 79-121.

BRANTINGHAM, J. (2003). A neutral model of stone raw material procurement. *American Antiquity, 68*(3), 487–509.

BREIMAN, L. (2001). Random forests. *Machine Learning, 45*(1), 5-32.

BREIMAN, L., FRIEDMAN, J.H., OLSHEN, R.A., & STONE, C.J. (1984). *Classification and regression trees.* Belmont, CA: Wadsworth.

BRENT, E. (1989). Designing social science research with expert systems. *Anthropological Quarterly, 62*(3), 121.

BRIGHT, J.R. (1958). *Automation and management.* Graduate School of Business Administration, Boston: Harvard University.

BRODARIC, B., GAHEGAN, M., & HARRAP, R. (2004). The art and science of mapping: Computing geological categories from field data. *Computers & Geosciences, 30,* 719–740.

BRODARIC, B., GAHEGAN, M., TAKATUSKA, M., & HARRAP, R. (2000). Geocomputing with geological field data: Is there a 'ghost in the machine?' *Proceedings of the 5th International Conference on GeoComputation* University of Greenwich, United Kingdom. Retrieved May 2007 from http://www.geocomputation.org/2000/GC028/Gc028.htm

BRON, C., CORFU-BRATSCHI, P., & MAOUENE, M. (1989). Hephaistos bacchant ou le cavalier comaste:

simulation de raisonnement qualitatif par le langage informatique LISP. *Annali Istituto Universitario Orientale (Archeologia e Storia Antica).* vol. XII: 155-172.

BRON, C., ROGGER, A., & VIRET BERNAL, F. (1991a). Iconographie et Intelligence Artificielle: du signe au sens; compréhension et interprétation d'image. *Aplicaciones Informáticas en Arqueología,* (vol. 1). Bilbao, Spain: Denboraren Argia.

BRON, C., VIRET BERNAL, F., BERARD, A., OBERLIN, A., ROGGER, A., & DE WERRA, D. (1991b). Heraclès chez T.I.R.E.S.I.A.S: Traitement Informatique de Réconnaissance des Elements Semiologiques pour l' Idéntification Analytique des Scènes. *Hephaistos. Kritische Zeitschrift zu Theorie und Praxis der Archäologie, Kunstwissenschaft und angrenzender Gebiete, 10,* 21-33.

BROOKS, R. (1999). *Cambrian intelligence: The early history of the new AI.* Cambridge: The MIT Press.

BROOKS, R. A. (1989). How to build complete creatures rather than isolated cognitive simulators. In K. VanLehn (Ed.), *Architectures for intelligence* (pp. 225–239). Hillsdale, NJ: Erlbaum.

BROOKS, R. A. (1991). Intelligence without representation. *Artificial Intelligence Journal 47,* 139-160.

BROOKS, R.A., BREAZEAL (FERRELL), C, MARJANOVIC, M., SCASSELLATI, B., & WILLIAMSON, M. (1999). The cog project: Building a humanoid robot. In C. Nehaniv (Ed.), *Computation for metaphors, analogy, and agents.* New York: Springer. Lecture Notes in *Artificial Intelligence, 1562,* 52–87.

BROOKS, R.A., BREAZEAL (FERRELL), C., IRIE, R., KEMP, C., MARJANOVIC, M., SCASSELLATI, B., & WILLIAMSON, M. (1998). Alternate Essences of Intelligence , *Proceedings of the Fifteenth National Conference on Artificial Intelligence (AAAI-98)* (pp. 961-976). Madison, Wisconsin.

BROOKS, R.A., C. BREAZEAL (FERRELL), R., IRIE, C., KEMP, M., MARJANOVIC, B., SCASSELLATI et al. (1998). Alternate essences of nitelligence. *Proceedings of the 15th National Conference on Artificial Intelligence (AAAI-98)* (pp. 961-976). Madison, Wisconsin.

BROUGH, D.R., & PARFITT, N. (1984). An expert system for the ageing of a domestic animal. *Computer Applications in Archaeology,* 49-55.

BROWN, D. A., & CHANG, K. C. (2001). *Artificial neural networks, paradigms, and western wheatgrass geography.* Retrieved June 2006 from http://cla.umn.edu/grasslands/wwANNabst.htm.

BROWN, D.C., & CHANDRASEKARAN, B. (1989). *Design problem solving. Knowledge structures and control strategies.* London: Pitman.

BRYANT, C. H., MUGGLETON, S. H., OLIVER, S. G., KELL, D. B., REISER, P., & KING, R. D. (2001). Combining inductive logic programming, active learning and robotics to discover the function of genes. *Electronic Transactions on Artificial Intelligence, 5,* 1–36.

BUCK, C.E., CAVANAGH, W.G., & LITTON, C. (1996). *Bayesian approach to intrepreting archaeological data.* London: John Wiley.

BUNGE, M. (1959). *Causality. The place of causal principle in modern science.* Cambridge, MA: Harvard University Press.

BUNGE, M. (2006). *Chasing reality: Strife over realism.* University of Toronto Press.

BUNTINE, W., & NIBLETT, T. (1992). A further comparison of splitting rules for decision-tree induction. *Machine Learning, 8,* 75-86.

BURSIK, M., & ROGOVA, G. (2006). Use of neural networks and decision fusion for lithostratigraphic correlation with sparse data, *Computers & Geosciences, 32,* 1564–1572

CAELLI, T., & BISCHOF, W.F. (1997). The role of machine learning in building image interpretation systems. In T. Caelli, P. Lam & H. Bunke (Eds.), *Spatial computing* (pp.143-168). Singapore: World Scientific.

CALDAS, J.C., & COELHO, H. (1999). The origin of institutions: Socio-economic processes, choice, norms and conventions. *Journal of Artificial Societies and Social Simulation, 2*(2).

CAMIZ, S., & VENDITTI, S. (2004). Unsupervised and supervised classifications of egyptian scarabs based on typology qualitative characters. In F. Nicolucci (Ed.), *Beyond the artefact. Computer applications in archaeology.* Budapest: ArchaeoLingua.

CANAL, E., & CAVAZZONI, S. (1990). Antichi insediamenti antropici nella laguna di Venezia: analisi multivariata di tipo fuzzy C-means clustering. *Archaeologia e Calcolatori, 1,.* 165-177.

CANTERO, M.C., MARTÍNEZ, P., PÉREZ, R.M., PANIAGUA, J., DEL RÍO, L.M., CERRILLO, E., et al. (2005). Archaeological Sites Studies Based On Neural Computation Techniques. *Proc. of the 3rd ESA CHRIS/Proba Workshop, 21–23 March, ESRIN, Frascati, Italy, (ESA SP-593, June 2005).* Retrieved October 2006 from http://earth.esa.int/workshops/chris_proba_05/papers/27_cante.pdf

CARLEY, K. (1988). Formalizing the social expert's knowledge. *Sociological Methods and Research, 17,* 165-232.

CARPENTER, G.A., GROSSBERG, S., & LESHER, G.W. (1998). The what-and-where filter—a spatial mapping neural network for object recognition and image understanding. *Computer Vision and Image Understand, 69*(1), 1–22.

CASTELFRANCHI, C. (2000). Engineering social order. In A. Omicini, R. Tolksdorf, & F. Zambonelli (Eds.), *Engineering societies in the agents world.* Berlin: Springer. (Lecture Notes in Computer Science, No. 1972).

CASTILLO, E., GUTIÉRREZ, J.M., & HADI, A.S. (1997). *Expert systems and probabilistic network models.* New York: Springer-Verlag.

CASTILLO, O., & MELIN, P. (2002). Hybrid intelligent systems for time series prediction using neural networks, fuzzy logic, and fractal theory. *IEEE Transactions on Neural networks 13*(6), 1395- 1408.

CASTRO, D., & DIAZ, D. (2004). Kohonen networks applied to rincón del toro rock art site analysis. In F. Niccolucci (Ed.), *Beyond the artefact. Computer applications in archaeology.* Budapest: ArcheoLingua.

CAUDILL, M. (1991). Neural network training tips and techniques. *AI Expert,6,* 56-61.

CAUDILL, M., & BUTLER, C. (1992). *Understanding neural networks. Computer explorations.* Cambridge, MA: The MIT Press.

CAWLEY, G.C., JANACEK, G.J., HAYLOCK, M.R., & DORLING, S.R. (2007). Predictive uncertainty in environmental modeling. *Neural Networks, 20,* 537–549.

CECCONI, F., PARISI, D., ANTINUCCI, F., & NATALE, F. (2006). Simulating the expansion of farming and the differentiation of european languages. In B. Laks (Ed.), *Origin and evolution of languages: Approaches, models, paradigms.* Oxford, UK: Oxford University Press.

CERRITO, P. (1996). Using neural networks to study and predict historical structure. *Mathematical Connections,4*(1).

CH'NG, E., & STONE, R.J. (2006). Enhancing virtual reality with artificial life: Reconstructing a flooded european mesolithic landscape. *Presence: Teleoperators & Virtual Environments, 15*(3), 341-352.

CHAIGNEAU, S.E., BARSALOU, L.W. & SLOMAN, A. (2004) Assessing the causal structure of function. *Journal of Experimental Psychology: General, 133*(4), 601–625.

CHAIGNEAU, S.E., BARSALOU, L.W., & SLOMAN, A. (2004). Assessing the causal structure of function *Journal of Experimental Psychology: General, 133*(4), 601–625.

CHAKRABORTY, K., MEHROTRA, K., MOHAN, C.K., & RANKA, S. (1992). Forecasting the behavior of multivariate time series using neural networks. *Neural networks, 5*(6), 961-970.

CHANDRARATNE, M. R., SAMARASINGHE, S., KULASIRI., D., FRAMPTON, C., & BICKERSTAFFE, R. (2003). Determination of lamb grades using texture analysis and neural networks. *Proceedings of the 3rd IASTED International Conference VISUALIZATION, IMAGING AND IMAGE PROCESSING*, Benalmadena, Spain.

CHANDRASEKARAN, B., & JOSEPHSON, J. R. (2000). Function in device representation. *Engineering With Computers, 16,* 162–177.

CHANG, H-C., KOPASKA-MERKEL, D., & CHEN, H.C. (2002). Identification of lithofacies using kohonen self-organizing maps. *Computers & Geosciences, 28,* 223–229

CHAOUKI M., & GAILDRAT, V.,(2005). Automatic classification of archaeological potsherds. In *The 8th International Conference on Computer Graphics and Artificial Intelligence,* 3IA'2005 (pp. 135-147) Limoges, France, 11 mai 12 mai 2005. Edited by Dimitri Plémenos, MSI Laboratory.

CHAPPELIER, J.C., & GRUMBACH, A. (1998). RST: A connectionist architecture to deal with spatiotemporal relationships. *Neural Computation, 10,* 883–902.

CHATER, N. (1995). Neural networks: The new statistical models of mind. In J.P. Levy, D. Bairaktaris, J.A. Bullinaria & P. Cairns (Eds.), *Connectionist models of memory and language.* London: UCL Press.

CHEESEMAN, P. (1990). On finding the most probable model. In J. Shrager & P. Langley (Eds.), *Computational models of scientific discovery and theory formation*. San Francisco, CA: Morgan Kaufmann.

CHO, S. Y., & CHOW, T.W.S. (1999). Shape recovery from shading by new neural-based reflectance model. IEEE Transactions on Neural Networks, *10*(6), 1536-1541.

CHRISTIANSEN, J., & ALTAWEEL, M. (2005). Agent-based holistic simulations of bronze age mesopotamian settlement systems. In A. Figueiredo & G. Velho (Eds.), *The world is in your eyes. Computer applications in archaeology 2005 Proceedings*. Tomar, Portugal: CAA-Protugal.

CHRISTIANSEN, J., & ALTAWEEL, M. (2006a). Understanding ancient societies: A new approach using agent-based holistic modeling. *Structure and Dynamics: eJournal of Anthropological and Related Sciences*, 1(2), Article 7.

CHRISTIANSEN, J., & ALTAWEEL, M. (2006b). Simulation of natural and social process interactions: An example from bronze age mesopotamia. *Social Science Computer Review, 24*(2), 209-226.

CHRISTIANSEN, M., & CHATER, N. (1992). Connectionism, learning and meaning. *Connectionism, 4*, 227-252.

CHURCHLAND, P.M. (1989). *A neurocomputational perspective. The nature of mind and the structure of science*. Cambridge, MA: The MIT Press.

CHURCHLAND, P.M. (1991). A deeper unity: Some feyerabendian themes in neurocomputational form. In P.M. Churchland & P.S. Churchland (Eds.), *On the contrary, critical essays, 1987-1997*. Cambridge, MA: The MIT Press.

CHURCHLAND, P.M. (1995). *The engine of reason, the seat of the soul. A philosophical journey into the brain*. Cambridge, MA: The MIT Press.

CHURCHLAND, P.M. (1998). Conceptual similarity across sensory and neural diversity. *The Journal of Philosophy, 95*(1), 5-32.

CIOFFI-REVILLA, C. (2004). Mnemonic structure and sociality: A computational agent-based simulation model. In D. Sallach & C. Macal (Eds.), *Proceedings of the Agent 2004 Conference on Social Dynamics: Interaction, Reflexivity and Emergence*. University of Chicago, Argonne National Laboratory.

CIOFFI-REVILLA, C. (2005). A canonical theory for the emergence and development of social complexity, *Journal of Mathematical Sociology, 29*(2), 33–153.

CIVCO, D.L. (1993). Artificial neural networks for land-cover classification and mapping. *International Journal of Geographic Information Systems, 7*, 173-186.

CLANCEY, W. (1984). Heuristic classification. *Artificial Intelligence, 27*, 289-350.

CLANCEY, W. J. (1983). The epistemology of a rule-based expert system—a framework for explanation. *Artificial Intelligence, 20*, 215–251.

CLANCEY, W.J. (1997). *Situated cognition: On human knowledge and computer representations*. Cambridge, UK: Cambridge University Press.

CLARK, A. (1989). *Microcognition: Philosophy, cognitive science, and parallel distributed processing*. Cambridge, MA: The MIT Press.

CLARK, A. (1993). *Associative engines. Connectionism, concepts and representational change*. Cambridge, MA: The MIT Press.

CLARK, A. (1997). *Being there: Putting brain, body and world together again*. Cambridge, MA: The MIT Press.

CLARK, P., & NIBLETT, T. (1989). The CN2 induction algorithm, *Machine Learning, 3*(4), 261-283.

CLARK, A. (1993). *Associative engines. Connectionism, concepts, and representational change*. Cambridge, MA: The MIT Press.

CLARKE, D.L. (1972). Models and paradigms in contemporary archaeology. In D.L. Clarke (Ed.), *Models in archaeology* (pp. 1-61). London: Methuen and Co.

CLARKE, D.L. (1973). Archaeology: The loss of innocence. *Antiquity, 47*, 6-18.

CLELAND, C.E. (2002). Methodological and epistemic differences between historical science and experimental science. *Philosophy of Science, 69*, 474-496.

CLEMENTS, R.R., & HUGHES, R.L. (2004). Mathematical modelling of a mediaeval battle: The battle of Agincourt, 1415. *Mathematics and Computers in Simulation, 64*(2), 259 – 269.

COLLINS, H., & KUSCH, M. (1998). *The shape of actions. What human and machines can do*. Cambridge, MA: The MIT Press,

CONLEY, J., GAHEGAN M., & MACGILL, J. (2005). A genetic approach to detecting clusters in point datasets. *Geographical Analysis, 37*(3), 286-314.

CONTE, R., & GILBERT, N. (1995). Computer simulation for social theory. In N. Gilbert, & R. Conte (Eds.), *Artificial societies: The computer simulation of social life* London: UCL Press.

COOPER, D. B., WILLIS, A., ANDREWS, S., BAKER, J., CAO, Y., HAN, D. et al. (2002). Bayesian pot-assembly from fragments as problems in perceptual-grouping and geometric-learning. *Proceedings of the 16th International Conference on Pattern Recognition, 3*, 30927–30931.

COOPER, P. R., BIRNBAUM, L.A., & BRAND, M F., (1995). Causal scene understanding. *Computer Vision and Image Understanding, 62*(2), 215–231.

CORSINI, M.M., SCHMITT, A., & BRUZEK, J. (2005). Aging process variability on the human skeleton: Artificial network as an appropriate tool for age at death assessment. *Forensic Science International, 148*, 163-167.

CORTESE, G., DOLVEN, J.K., BJØRKLUND, K.R., & MALMGREN, B.A. (2005). Late pleistocene–holocene radiolarian paleotemperatures in the norwegian sea based on artificial neural networks. *Palaeogeography, Palaeoclimatology, Palaeoecology, 224*, 311– 332.

COSTA, L.F., & CESAR, R.M., (2001). *Shape analysis and classification: Theory and practice.* Boca Raton, FL: CRC Press.

COSTOPOULOS, A. (1999). *Modeling and simulation for anthropological archaeology: the logic of long-term change.* Ph.D. Dissertation held at Oulu University, Finland.

COSTOPOULOS, A. (2001). Evaluating the impact of increasing memory on agent behaviour: Adaptive patterns in an agent-based simulation of subsistence. *Journal of Artificial Societies and Social Simulation, 4*(4).

COSTOPOULOS, A. (2002). Playful agents, inexorable process: Elements of a coherent theory of iteration in anthropological simulation, *Archeologia e Calcolatori, 13*, 259-266.

COX, E. (1993). *The fuzzy systems handbook. A practitioner's guide to building, using and maintaining fuzzy systems.* New York: Academic Press.

CRAVER, C.F. (2001). Role functions, mechanisms and hierarchy. *Philosophy of Science 68*, 31-55.

CRESCIOLI, M., D'ANDREA, A., & NICOLUCCI, F. (2000). A GIS-based analysis of the Etruscan cemetery of Pontecagnano using fuzzy logic. In G. Lock (Ed.), *Beyond the map: Archaeology and spatial technologies.* Amsterdam (Holland); IOS Press.

CROWTHER, P., & HARTNETT, J. (1997). Eliciting knowledge with visualization—instant gratification for the expert image classifier who wants to show rather than tell. *Paper presented at the second annual conference of GeoComputation '97 & SIRC '97,*University of Otago, New Zealand. Retrieved April, 2006, from http://www.geocomputation.org/1997/papers/crowther.pdf

CUMMINS, R. (1975). Functional analysis. *Journal of Philosophy, 72/20*, 741-765.

CUMMINS, R. (2000). How does it work vs. what are the laws? Two conceptions of psychological explanation. In F. Keil & R. Wilson (Eds.), *Explanation and cognition* (pp 117-145). Cambridge, MA: The MIT Press.

CUMMINS, R. (2002). Neo-teleology. In A. Ariew, R. Cummins & M. Perlman (Eds.), *Functions. New essays in the philosophy of psychology and biology.* Oxford: Oxford University Press.

DA MONTEIRO, M. C. (1993). Female Figures of the Upper Paleolithic: One Interpretation through an Expert System. *Aplicaciones Informáticas en Arqueología*, vol. 2. Denboraren Argia, Bilbao (Spain), pp. 335-355.

DAMS, W.Y., & ADAMS, E.W. (1991). *Archaeological typology and practical reality.* Cambridge, UK: Cambridge University Press.

DARDEN, L. (1997). Anomaly-driven theory redesign: Computational philosophy of science experiments. In T. W. Bynum & J. Moor (Eds.), *Digital phoenix: How computers are changing philosophy.* Oxford: Blackwell.

DARDEN, L. (2002). Strategies for discovering mechanisms: Schema instantiation, modular subassembly, forward/backward chaining. *Philosophy of Science, 69*, 354-365.

DARDEN, L., MOBERG, D., THADANI, S., & JOSEPHSON, J. (1992). *A computational approach to scientific theory revision: The TRANSGENE experiments* (Tech. Rep. 92-LD-TRANSGENE). Laboratory for Artificial Intelligence Research. Columbus, OH: Ohio State University.

DATTERI, E., & TAMBURRINI, G. (2006). Bio-robotic experiments and scientific method. In L. Magnani & R.

Dossena (Eds.), *Computing, philosophy and cognition* (pp. 397-41). London: College Publications.

David, N. (1992). Integrating ethnoarchaeology: A subtle realist perspective. *Journal of Anthropological Archaeology, 11*, 330-359.

DAVID, N., & KRAMER, C. (2001). *Ethnoarchaeology in action.* Cambridge, UK: Cambridge University Press.

DAVINO, C., Di MARTINO, R., MOLA, F., & VISTOCCO, F. (1999). Riconoscimento automatico di Forma en archeologia: il caso delle necropoli di Sala Consilina. *Workshop Intelligenza Artificiale per i Beni Culturali* Bologna. Retrieved February 2007 from http://studi131.casaccia.enea.it/enea/apps/aiia/consili.pdf

DAVIS, E. (1990). *Representations in commonsense knowledge.* San Mateo, CA: Morgan Kaufmann Publishers.

DAVIS, E. (1993). The kinematics of cutting solid objects. *Annals of Mathematics and Artificial Intelligence, 9*(3/4), 253–305.

DAVIS, J.R. & NANNINGA, P.M. (1985). GEOMYCIN: Towards a geographic expert system, for resource management, *Journal of Environmental Management, 21*, 377-390.

DAVYDOV, V. (1999). The content and unsolved problems of activity theory. In Y. Engeström, R. Miettinen, & R.L. Punamäki (Eds.), *Perspectives on activity theory.* Cambridge, UK: Cambridge University Press,

DAWSON, M.R.W. (2004). *Minds and machines. Connectionism and psychological modeling.* London: Blackwell Pub.

DAWSON, M.R.W. (2004). *Minds and machines. Connectionism and psychological modeling.* London: Blackwell Pub.

De ALMEIDA, C.M., & GLERIANI, J.M. (2005, April 16-21). Cellular automata and neural networks as a modeling framework for the simulation of urban land use change. *Anais XII Simpósio Brasileiro de Sensoriamento Remoto, Goiânia, Brasil,* , INPE, (pp. 3697-3705).

DE BODT, E., COTTRELL, M., & VERLEYSEN, M. (2002). Statistical tools to assess the reliability of self-organizing maps. *Neural Networks, 15*(8), 967-978.

DE JONG, H., & RIP, A. (1997). The computer revolution in science: Steps towards the realization of computer-supported discovery environments. *Artificial Intelligence, 91*, 225-256.

De NAPOLI, L., LUCHI, L., MUZZUPAPPA, M., & RIZZUTI, S. (2003). Recognition and classification of fragments from ceramic artefacts. In M. Doerr & A. Sarris (Eds.), *The digital heritage of archaeology. Computer applications and quantitative methods in archaeology* (pp. 295-300). Heraklion, Greeece: Archive of Monuments and Publications. Hellenic Ministry of Culture.

DeCALLATAŸ, A. M. (1992). *Natural and artificial intelligence. Misconceptions about brains and neural networks.* Amsterdam: North Holland,

DELLAPORTAS, P. (1998). Bayesian classification of Neolithic tools, *Applied Statistics, 47*, 279-297.

DERAVIGNONE, L. (2006). *Intelligenza artificiale: sviluppo metodologico e applicativo nell'archeologia del territorio.* Dipartimento di Archeologia e Storia delle Arti di la Università degli Studi di Siena. Retrieved October 2006 from http://archeologiamedievale.unisi.it/NEWPAGES/TESTIprogetti/deravignone.pdf.

DERGACHEV, V.A., GORBAN, A.N., ROSSIEV, A.A., KARIMOVA, L.M., KUANDYKOV, E.B., MAKARENKO, N.G. et al. (2001). The filling of gaps in geophysical time series by artificial neural networks. *Radiocarbon, 43*(2A), 365-371.

Di LUDOVICO, A., & RAMAZZOTTI, M. (2005). Reconstructing lexicography in glyptic art: Structural relations between the Akkadian Age and the Ur III period. In *LI Rencontre Assyriologique Internationale.* Retrieved October 2007 from http://www.let.leidenuniv.nl/rencontre/RAI_2005/RAI_2005.html

DIAPPI, L., BOLCHI, P. & FRANZINI, L. (1999). Urban sustainability: Complex interactions and the measurement of risk. *CyberGeo, 98*(28). Retrieved May 2007 from http://www.cybergeo.presse.fr/suger/lidiapi/parigi.htm

DIAPPI, L., BOLCHI, P., & BUSCEMA, M. (2004). Improved understanding of urban sprawl using neural networks. In J.P. Van Leeuwen & H.J.P. Timmermans (Eds.), *Recent advances in design and decision support systems in architecture and urban planning* (pp. 33-49). Kluwer Academic Publishers.

DIAPPI, L., BOLCHI, P., FRANZINI, L., BUSCEMA, M., & INTRALIGI, M. (2002, August 27-31). The Urban Sprawl Dynamics: Does a Neural Network Understand the Spatial Logic Better than a Cellular Automata? *42nd ERSA Congress – Dortmund., 2002.* Retrieved February

2007 from http://www.ersa.org/ersaconfs/ersa02/cd-rom/papers/033.pdf

DIAZ, D. & CASTRO, D. (2001). Pattern recognition applied to rock art. In G. Burenhult (Ed.), .*Archaeological informatics: Pushing the envelope* (pp. 463-468). Oxford: ArchaeoPress.

DÍAZ-KOMMONEN, L., & KAIPAINEN, M. (2002). Designing vector-based ontologies: can technology empower open interpretation of culture heritage objects? *Proceedings of the 13th International Workshop on Database and Expert Systems Applications (DEXA'02).* Berlin: Springer.

DIMANZO, M., TRUCCO, E., GIUNCIIIGLIA, F. & RICCI, F. (1989). FUR: understanding functional reasoning. *International Journal of Intelligent Systems, 4,* 431–457.

DING, J.M., WANG, Y.H., & DING L.X. (2006). Significance of expansive soil classification indexes analysed by rough sets. *Rock And Soil Mechanics, 27*(9), 1514-1518.

DJINDJIAN, F. (1990). *Les méthodes de l'archéologie.* Paris: Armand Colin.

DONAHUE, J.W., & PALMER, D.C. (1994). *Learning and complex behaviour.* Boston: Allyn and Bacon,

DORAN J. E. (1970a). Systems theory, computer simulations and archaeology. *World Archaeology, 1*(3), 289-298.

DORAN J. E. (1970b). Archaeological reasoning and machine reasoning. In J.C. Gardin (Eds.), *Archaeologie et Calculateurs* (pp 57-67). Paris: CNRS.

DORAN J.E. (2000). Trajectories to complexity in artificial societies. In A. Kohler & G. Gumerman (Eds.), *Dynamics in human and primate societies.* New York: Oxford University Press.

DORAN, J. E. (1972). Computer models as tools for archaeological hypothesis formation. In D.L. Clarke (Ed.), *Models in archaeology* (pp 425-451). London: Methuen and Co.

DORAN, J. E. (1977) Automatic generation and evaluation of explanatory hypotheses. In M. Borillo, W. Fernandezde la Vega, & A Guenoche (Eds.), *Raisonnement et methodes mathematiques en archaeologie* (pp. 172-181). Paris: CNRS.

DORAN, J. E. (1997). Distributed artificial intelligence and emergent social complexity. In S. E. Van de Leeuw & J. McGlade (Eds.), *Time, process and structured transformation in archaeology. One World Archaeology series, 26,* 283-297. London: Routledge.

DORAN, J. E. (1999). Prospects for agent-based modelling in archaeology. *Archeologia e Calcolatori, 10,* 33-44.

DORAN, J. E., & PALMER, M. (1995a). The EOS project: Integrating two models of palaeolithic social change. In N. Gilbert & R. Conte (Eds.), *Artificial societies: The computer simulation of social life* (pp. 103-125). London: UCL Press.

DORAN, J. E., & PALMER, M. (1995b). The EOS project: Modelling prehistoric sociocultural trajectories. In *Aplicaciones informaticas en Arqueologia: Teoria y Sistemas* Vol I Proceedings of First International Symposium on Computing and Archaeology (pp 183-198), Paris 1991. Bilbao, Spain.: Danboraren Argia.

DORAN, J., & HODSON,F.R. (1975). *Mathematics and computers in archaeology.* Edinburgh, UK: Edinburgh University Press,

DORAN, J., PALMER, M., GILBERT, N., & MELLARS, P. (1994). The EOS project: Modelling upper paleolithic social change. In G. N. Gilbert & J. Doran (Eds.), *Simulating societies: The computer simulation of social phenomena.* London: UCL Press.

DORAN, J.R. (1988). Expert systems and archaeology: What lies ahead? *Computer Applications in Archaeology* (BAR International Series, 393) 237-241.

DOWD, P.A., & SARAC, C. (1994). A neural network approach to geostatistical simulation. *Mathematical Geology, 26*(4).

DOYLE, J. (2006). *Extending mechanics to minds. The mechanical foundations of psychology and economics.* Cambridge, UK: Cambridge University Press.

DRAP, P., SEINTURIER, J., & LONG, L. (2003). A photogrammetric process driven by an expert system: A new approach for underwater archaeological surveying applied to the 'grand ribaud F' etruscan wreck. *Conference on Computer Vision and Pattern Recognition Workshop,1,* 16.

DRECHSLER, P., & TIEDE, D. (2007). The spread of neolithic herders—a computer aided modeling approach. In A. Figueiredo & G. Velho (Eds.), *The world is in your eyes. Computer applications in archaeology* (pp. 231-236). Tomar, Portugal: CAA Portugal.

DRENNAN, M. (2005). The human science of simulation: A robust hermeneutics for artificial societies. *Journal of Artificial Societies and Social Simulation, 8*(1).

DREYFUSS, H.L. (1972). *What computers can't do.* New York: Harper and Row.

DROLON, H., HOYEZ, B., DRUAUX, F., & FAURE, A. (2003). Multiscale roughness analysis of particles: Application to the classification of detrital sediments. *Mathematical Geology, 35*(7), 805-817.

DRYDEN, I.L., & MARDIA, K., (1998). *Statistical shape analysis.* London: John Wiley.

DUBOIS, D., PRADE, H., & SMETS, D. (1994). Partial truth is not uncertainty. fuzzy logic versus posibilistic logic. *IEEE Expert. Intelligent Systems and their applications,9*(4), 15-19.

DUCKE, B. (2003). Archaeological predictive modelling in intelligent network structures. In M. Doerr & A. Sarris (Eds.), *The digital heritage of archaeology. Computer applications and quantitative methods in archaeology.* Heraklion, Greece: Hellenic Ministry of Culture, Archive of Monuments and Publications.

DUNNELL, R. (1971). *Systematics in prehistory.* New York: The Free Press.

DURIC, Z., FAYMAN, J., & RIVLIN, E. (1996). Function from motion. *IEEE Transactions on Pattern Analysis and Machine Intelligence, 18*, 579–591.

EASTHAM, A., & GWYNN, I. A. (1997). Archaeology and the electron microscope. Eggshell and neural network analysis of images in the neolithic: methods. *Anthropozoologica, 25-26*, 85-94.

EDELMAN, S. (1999). *Representation and recognition in vision.* Cambridge, MA: The MIT Press.

EDELMAN, S., & INTRATOR, N. (2002). Visual processing of object structure. In M. A. Arbib (Ed.), *The handbook of brain theory and neural networks* (2nd ed.). Cambridge, MA: The MIT Press.

EDELMAN, S., & INTRATOR, N. (2003). Towards structural systematicity in distributed, statically bound visual representations. *Cognitive Science, 27*, 73-110.

EDMONDS, B. (1998). Modelling socially intelligent agents. *Applied Artificial Intelligence, 12*(7), 667-669.

EDMONDS, B. (2000). The use of models—making MABS more informative. In S. Moss & P. Davidsson

(Eds.), *Multi-agent-based simulation.* Berlin: Springer (Lecture Notes in Computer Science, No. 1979).

EGMONT-PETERSEN, M., DE RIDDER, D., & HANDELS, H. (2002). Image processing with neural networks—a review. *Pattern Recognition, 35*, 2279-2301.

EGMONT-PETERSEN, M., DE RIDDER, D., & HANDELS, H. (2002). Image processing with neural networks—A review. *Pattern Recognition, 35*, 2279-2301.

ELLIS, R., & HUMPHREYS,G. (1999). *Connectionist psychology.* London: Psychology Press.

ELLIS, R., HUMPHREYS,G. (1999). *Connectionist psychology.* London: Psychology Press,

ELMAN, J.L. (1990). Finding structure in time. *Cognitive Science, 14*, 179-211.

ELMAN, J.L. (1992). Grammatical structure and distributed representations. In S. Davis (Ed.), *Connectionism: Theory and practice.* Oxford (UK): Oxford University Press..

ELSNER, J.B. (1992). Predicting time series using a neural network as a method of distinguishing chaos from noise. *Journal of Physics A: Mathematical and General, 25*, 843–850.

ENGEL, A.K., & KÖNIG,P. (1998). Paradigm shifts in the neurobiology of perception. In U. Ratsch, M.M. Richter & I.-O. Stamatescu (Eds.), *Intelligence and artificial intelligence. An interdisciplinary debate.* Berlin: Springer.

ENGESTRÖM, Y. (1987). *Learning by expanding. An activity-theory approach to developmental research.* Helsinki: Orienta-Konsultit.

ENGESTRÖM, Y. (1999). Activity theory and individual social transformation. In Y. Engeström, R. Miettinen, & R.L. Punamäki (Eds.), *Perspectives on activity theory.* Cambridge, UK: Cambridge University Press.

ERGIN, A., KARAESMEN,E., ICALLEF, A., & WILLIAMS, A.T. (2004). A new methodology for evaluating coastal scenery: Fuzzy Logic Systems. *Area, 36*, (4).

ERMENTROUT, B. (1998). Neural networks as spatiotemporal pattern-forming systems. *Reports on Progress in Physics, 61*, 353–430.

ESTES, J. E. (1986). Applications of artificial intelligence techniques to remote sensing. *The Professional Geographer, 38*, 133-141.

ESTEVEZ, J., & VILA, A. (1995). Etnoarqueología: el nombre de la cosa. In J. Estevez & A. Vila. Treballs d'Etnoarqueologia (Eds.), *Encuentros en los conchales fueguinos* (pp. 17-23). 1. CSIC-UAB, Bellaterra (Spain).

FALKENHEIMER, B.C. (1990). Explanation and theory formation. In J. Shrager & P. Langley (Eds.), *Computational models of scientific discovery and theory formation*. San Francisco, CA: Morgan Kaufmann.

FAN, Y., & BROOKS, S. (2000). Bayesian modeling of prehistoric corbelled domes. *The Statistician, 49*, 339-354.

FARINETTI, E., HERMON, S., & NICOLUCCI, F. (2004). Fuzzy logic application to survey data in a GIS environment. In *Beyond the artefact. Computer applications in archaeology*. Budapest (Hungary): ArcheoLingua.

FARRINGTON, O.S., & TAYLOR, N.K. (2004). Machine learning applied to geo-archaeological soil data. In Magistrat der Stadt Wien-Referat Kulturelles Erbe-Stadtarchäologie Wien (Ed.), *Enter the past. The e-way into the four dimensions of cultural heritage* (pp. 456-459). Oxford: ArchaeoPress (BAR International Series, 1227),

FERMO, P., CARIATI, F., BALLABIO, D., CONSONNI, V., & BAGNASCO GIANNI, G., (2004). Classification of ancient etruscan ceramics using statistical multivariate analysis of data. *Applied Physics A Materials Science & Processing, 79*(2), 299-307.

FERMÜLLER, C., & ALOIMONOS, Y. (1995). Vision and action. *Image and Vision Computing, 13*, 725-744.

FERNÁNDEZ MARTÍNEZ, V., & GARCÍA DE LA FUENTE, M. (1991). El tratamiento informático de datos funerarios cualitativos: análisis de correspondencias y algoritmo ID3 de Quinlan. *Complutum, 1*, 123-131.

FERNANDEZ, J. (2003). Explanation by computer simulation in cognitive science. *Minds and Machines, 13*, 269–284,

FIGUEIREDO, A., & VELHO, G.L.C. (2002). Complexity in action: The emergence of agro-pastoral societies. In Z. Stancic & T. Veljanovski (Eds.), *Computing archaeology for understanding the Past*. Oxford: ArchaeoPress.

FILIS, I.V., SABRAKOS, M., YIALOURIS, C.P., SIDERIDIS, A.B., & MAHAMAN, B. (2003). GEDAS: An integrated geographical expert database system. *Expert Systems with Applications, 24*, 25–34.

FINDIKAKI, I. (1990). SISES: An expert system for site selection. In T. J. Kim, J. R. Wiggins, & Wright (Eds.), *Expert systems: Applications to urban planning*. New York: Springer.

FINDLER, N.V. (1992). Automatic rule discovery for field work in anthropology. *Computers and the Humanities, 25*, 285-392.

FINDLER, N.V., & BICKMORE, T. (1996). On the concept of causality and a causal modeling system for scientific and engineering domains, CAMUS. *Applied Artificial Intelligence, 10*, 455-487.

FINDLER, N.V., & DHULIPALLA, S., (1999). A decision support system for automatic rule discovery in anthropology. *Social Networks, 21*, 167-185.

FINE, T.L. (1999). *Feedforward neural network methodology*. New York: Springer.

FISCHER, M. D. (1985). Expert systems and anthropological analysis. *BICA: Bullettino. Istituto di Corrispondenza Archaeologica, 4*, 6-14.

FISCHER, M.M., & GOPAL, S. (1993). Neurocomputing—a new paradigm for geographical information processing. *Environment and Planning A, 25*, 757-760.

FISCHER, M.M., & REISMANN, M. (2002). A methodology for neural spatial interaction modelling. *Geographical Analysis, 34*(3), 207-228.

FLORENZANO, M.J., BLAISE, J.Y., & DRAP, P. (1999) PAROS. Close range photogrametry and architectural models. In L. Dingwall, S. Exon, V. Gaffney, S. Laflin, M., & Van Leusen (Eds.), *Archaeology in the age of the internet. CAA 1997*. Oxford: British Archaeological Reports (Int. Series, S750).

FLORIAN, R.V. (2002). Why it is Important to Build Robots Capable of Doing Science. In C. G. Prince, Y. Demiris, Y. Marom, H. Kozima, & C. Balkenius (Eds.), *Proceedings of the Second International Workshop on Epigenetic Robotics: Modeling Cognitive Development in Robotic Systems* (pp. 27-34). Lund University Cognitive Studies 94.

FODOR, J., & PYLYSHYN, Z. (1988). Connectionism and cognitive architecture. *Cognition, 28*, 3-71.

FOLEY, J., & RIBARSKY, B. (1994). Next-generation data visualization tools. In L. Rosenblum et al. (Eds.), *Scientific visualisation. advances and challenges* (pp. 103-127). New York: Academic Press.

FOODY, G.M. (2003). Uncertainty, knowledge discovery and data mining in GIS. *Progress in Physical Geography, 27*(1), 113-121.

FOODY, G.M., McCULLOCH, M.B., & YATES, W.B. (1995). Classification of remotely sensed data by an artificial neural network: Issues relating to data characteristics. *Photogrametric Engineering and Remote Sensing, 61,* 391-401.

FORD, K.M., GLYMOUR, C., & HAYES, P.H. (eds.), (1995). *Android epistemology.* Menlo Park/Cambridge/London: AAAI Press/the MIT Press.

FORSYTH, H. (2000). Mathematics and computers: The classifier's ruse. In G. Lock & K. Brown (Eds.), *On the theory and practice of archaeological computing* (pp. 31-39). Oxford, UK: Oxford University Committee for Archaeology.

FORT, J.C. (2006). SOM's mathematics. *Neural Networks, 19,* 812–816.

FOTHERINGHAM, A.S., BRUNSDON, C., & CHARLTON, M.E. (2000). *Quantitative geography: Perspectives on spatial data analysis.* Sage Publications.

FRANCFORT, H.P. (1987). Un système expert pour l'analyse archéologique de societés proto-urbaines. Premier étape: le cas de Shortugai. *Informatique et Sciences Humaines, 74,* 73-91.

FRANCFORT, H.P. (1990). Modélisation de raisonnements interprétatifs en archéologie à l'aide de systèmes experts: conséquences d' une critique des fondements des inférences. In J.C. Gardin & R. Ennals (Eds.), *Interpretation in the humanities: perspectives from artificial intelligence.* The British Library Publications. Library and Information Research Report, 71.

FRANCFORT, H.P. (1991). Palamede—application of expert systems to the archaeology of prehistoric urban civilisations. In K. Lockyear & S. Rahtz (Eds.), *Computer applications and quantitative methods in archaeology-1990.* Oxford: British Archaeological Reports (International Series 565),

FRANCFORT, H.P. (1997). Archaeological interpretation and nonlinear dynamic modelling: Between metaphor and simulation. In S.E Van der Leeuw & J. McGlade (Eds.), *Time, process and structured transformation in archaeology.* Routledge: London.

FRANCFORT, H.P., LAGRANGE, M.S., & RENAUD, M. (1989). *PALAMEDE. Application des systèmes experts*

à *l'archéologie de civilisations urbaines protohistoriques.* Paris: C.N.R.S.-U.P.R. 315. Technical report.

FRANKLIN, B., & BERGERMAN, M. (2000). Cultural algorithms: Concepts and experiments. *Evolutionary Computation, 2,* 1245–1251.

FRANKLIN, S. (1995). *Artificial Minds.* Cambridge MA: The MIT Press.

FROIMOVICH, G., RIVLIN, E., & SHIMSHONI, I. (2002). Object classification by functional parts. *Proceedings of the First Symposium on 3D Data, Processing, Visualization and Transmission,* (pp. 648-655).

FUETEN, F. (1997). A computer controlled rotating polarizer stage for the petrographic microscope. *Computers and Geosciences, 23,* 203-208.

FUETEN, F., HYNES, K., & VANLUTTIKHUISEN, R.L. (2001). An experimental setup for the analysis of analogue deformation experiments using the rotating polarizer stage. *Journal of Structural Geology, 24,* 241-245.

FULCHER, J. (1997). Neural networks for archaeological provenancing. In E. Fiesler & R. Beale *Handbook of Neural Computation.* New York: Institute of Physics/Oxford University Press.

FURBEE, L. (1989). A folk expert system: Soils classification in the colca valley, Peru. *Anthropological Quarterly, 62*(2), 83-102.

GABORA, L. (1995). Meme and variations: A computer model of cultural evolution. In L. Nadel & D. Stein (Eds.), *1993 lectures in complex systems* (pp. 471-486). Reading, MA: Addison-Wesley.

GAHEGAN, M. (2000). On the application of inductive machine learning tools to geographical analysis. *Geographical Analysis, 32*(1), 113-139.

GAHEGAN, M. (2003). Is inductive machine learning just another wild goose (or might it lay the golden egg)? *International Journal of Geographical information Science, 17*(1), 69-92.

GAHEGAN, M., TAKATSUKA, M., WHEELER, M., & HARDISTY, F. (2002). Introducing GeoVISTA studio: An integrated suite of visualization and computational methods for exploration and knowledge construction in geography. *Computers, Environment and Urban Systems, 26,* 267-292.

GALLAY, A. (1989). Logicism: A french view of archaeological theory founded in computational perspective. *Antiquity, 63*, 27-39

GANASCIA, J.C., MENU, M., & MOHEN, J.P. (1986). RHAPSODE: un système expert en archéologie *Bulletin de la Societé Préhistorique Française, 83*(10), 363-371.

GANDARA, M. (1990). La analogía etnográfica como heurística: lógica muestrela, dominios ontológicos e historicidad. In Y. Sugiera & M.C. Sierra (Eds.), *Etnoarqueología: Primer Coloquio Bosch-Gimpera*. México: UNAM.

GANDARA, M. (2006). La inferencia por analogía: más allá de la analogía etnográfica. In *Etnoarqueología de la Prehistoria. Más allá de la analogía* (pp. 14-23). Treballs d'Etnoarqueologia, No. 6, CSIC-UAB, Barcelona (Spain).

GÄRDENFORS, P. (2000). *Conceptual spaces. The geometry of thought*. Cambridge, MA: The MIT Press.

GARDIN, J.C. (1980). *Archaeological constructs*. Cambridge, UK: Cambridge University Press.

GARDIN, J.C. (1991). *Le Calcul et la Raison. Essais sur la formalisation du discours savant*. Paris, France : Editions de l'Ecole des Hautes Etudes en Sciences Sociales..

GARDIN, J.C. (1993). Les embarrass du naturel. *Archives Européennes de Sociologie XXXIV, 152-165.*

GARDIN, J.C. (1994). Informatique et progrès dans les sciences de l'homme *Revue Informatique et Statistique dans les Sciences Humaines, 30*(1-4),11-35.

GARDIN, J.C. (1998). Cognitive issues and Problems of Publication in Archaeology ." In W.Hensel, S. Tabczynski, & P. Urbanczyk (Eds.), *Theory and practice of archaeological research*. Warszawa: Institute of Archaeology and Ethnology. Polish Academy of Sciences.

GARDIN, J.C. (2003). Archaeological discourse, conceptual modelling and digitalisation: an interim report of the logicist program. In M. Doerr & A. Sarris (Eds.), *The digital heritage of archaeology*. Archive of Monuments and Publications. Hellenic Ministry of Culture.

GARDIN, J.C., GUILLAUME, O., HERMAN, P.O., HESNARD, A., LAGRANGE, M.S., RENAUD, M.et al. (1987). *Systèmes experts et sciences humaines. Le cas de l' archéologie*. Paris, France: Eyrolles.

GARGANO, M.L., & EDELSON, W. (1996). A genetic algorithm approach to solving the archaeology Seriation problem, *Congressus Numerantium, 119*, 193-203.

GARGANO, M.L., & LURIE, L. (2006). A hybrid evolutionary approach to solving the archaeological Seriation problem. *Congressus Numerantium, 180*, 43-53.

GEGERUN, A.P., PISLARY, I.A., & POPOVA, T.G. (1990). Archaeological classification and expert systems. In A. Voorrips (Ed.), *New tools from mathematical archaeology*. Krakow, Poland: Polish Academy of Sciences.

GERMAN, G., GAHEGAN, M., & WEST, G. (1997). Predictive assessment of neural network classifiers for applications in GIS. *Presented at the 2nd annual conference of GeoComputation '97 & SIRC '97, University of Otago, New Zealand*, Retrieved September 2006 from http://www.geocomputation.org/1997/papers/german.pdf

GEVREY, M., DIMOPOULOS, & LEK, I. (2003). Review and comparison of methods to study the contribution of variables in artificial neural network models. *Ecological Modelling, 160*(3), 249-264.

GEVREY, M., WORNER, S., KASABOV, N., PITT, J., & GIRAUDEL, J.L. (2006). Estimating risk of events using SOM models: A case study on invasive species Establishment. *Ecological Modelling, 197*(3-4), 361-372.

GEY, O. (1991). COCLUSH: Un générateur de classification d'objets structure's suivant différents points de vue. *Actes des 6 Journeés Françaises de l'Apprentissage.*

GIARRATANO, J., & RILEY, G. (2004). *Expert systems. Principles and programming*. Boston: PWS-KENT Publishing Company,

GIBBINS, P. (1990). BACON bytes back. In J. E. Tiles, G.T. McKee, & G.C. Dean *Evolving knowledge in natural science and artificial intelligence*. London, UK: Pitman.

GIBSON, J.J. (1979). *The ecological approach to visual perception*. Boston, MA: Mifflin.

GILBERT, N. (1996). Simulation as a research strategy. In K. G. Troitzsch, U. Mueller, G. N. Gilbert & J. E. Doran (Eds.), *Social science microsimulation* (pp. 448-454). Berlin: Springer.

GILBERT, N. (1998). Simulation: An introduction to the idea. In P. Ahrweiler & N. Gilbert (Eds.), *Computer simulations in science and technology studies* (pp. 1-14). Berlin: Springer.

GILBERT, N. (2000). The simulation of social processes. In N. Ferrand (Ed.), *Modèles et Systèmes Multi-Agents pour la Gestion de l'Environment et des Territoires* (pp. 121 – 137). Clermont-Ferrand, France: Cemagref Editions.

GILBERT, N., DEN BESTEN, M., BONTOVICS, A., CRAENEN, B.G.W., DIVINA, F., EIBEN, A.E., GRIF-FIOEN, R. et al. (2006). Emerging artificial societies through learning. *Journal of Artificial Societies and Social Simulation, 9*(2)

GILLIES, D. (1996). *Artificial intelligence and the scientific method.* Oxford, UK: Oxford University Press.

GIZA, P. (2002). Automated discovery systems and scientific realism. *Minds and Machines, 12*, 105–117,

GLENNAN, S. (1996). Mechanisms and the nature of causation. *Erkenntnis, 44*, 49-71.

GLENNAN, S. (2002). Rethinking mechanistic explanation. *Philosophy of Science, 69*, 342-353.

GLYMOUR, C. (2001). *The mind's arrows. Bayes nets and graphical causal models in psychology.* Cambridge, MA: The MIT Press.

GOLDBERG, D.E. (1989). *Genetic algorithms in search. Optimization and machine learning.* Redwood City, CA: Addison-Wesley.

GONG, P., PU,R., & CHEN,J. (1996). Mapping ecological land systems and classification uncertainties from digital elevation and forest-cover data using neural networks. *Photogrametric Engineering and Remote Sensing, 62*(11), 1249-1260.

GONZALEZ, A.M., & MAICAS, R. (1991). DENTALIA, un système expert pour la classification de restes osseux. *Aplicaciones Informáticas en Arqueología,* (vol. 1). Bilbao, Spain: Denboraren Argia.

GOPAL, S., FISCHER, M.M. (1996). Learning in single hidden-layer feedforward network models. *Geographical Analysis, 28*(1), 38-55.

GORMAN, R. P., & SEJNOWSKI, T. J. (1988). Analysis of hidden units in a layered network trained to classify sonar targets. *Neural Networks, 1*, 75-89.

GOULD, R.A. (1980). *Living archaeology.* Cambridge, UK: Cambridge University Press.

GRACE, R. (1989). *Interpreting the function of stone tools: The quantification and computerisation of microwear analysis.* Oxford, UK: Archeopress, B.A.R. international series 474.

GRACE, R. (1993). The use of expert systems in lithic Analysis. In *Traces et fonction: les geste retrouvés* (pp. 389-400) Eraul 50, (vol. 2). Liege, Belgium.

GRAHAM, S. (2005b). Agent based modeling, archaeology and social organisation: The robustness of Rome. *The Archaeological Computing Newsletter, 63*, 1-6.

GRAHAM, S. (2006). Networks, agent-based modeling, and the Antonine itineraries. *The Journal of Mediterranean Archaeology, 19*(1), 45-64.

GREEN, K., EGGERT, D., STARK, L., & BOWYER, K. (1994). Generic recognition of articulated objects by reasoning about functionality. In *AAAI Workshop on Representing and Reasoning about Function.*

GROSSBERG, S. (1988). *Neural networks and natural intelligence.* Cambridge, MA: The MIT Press.

GRUDZINSKI K., KARWOWSKI M., & DUCH W. (2005). Computational intelligence study of the iron age glass data. *International Conference on Artificial Neural Networks (ICANN) and International Conference on Neural Information Processing (ICONIP), Istanbul.* Retrieved June 2007 from http://www.fizyka.ukw.edu.pl/publikacje/a_s_p.pdf

GRUDZINSKI, K., & KARWOWSKI, M. (2005, June 13-16). The analysis of the unlabeled samples of the iron age glass data. In Mieczyslaw A. Klopotek, Slawomir T. Wierzchon, & Krzysztof Trojanowski (Eds.), *Intelligent Information Processing and Web Mining, Proceedings of the International IIS: IIPWM'05* Conference held in Gdansk, Poland. Berlin: Springer (Advances in Soft Computing Series).

GRUDZINSKI, K., KARWOWSKI, M., & DUCH, W. (2003). Computational Intelligence Study of the Iron Age Glass Data. *International Conference on Artificial Neural Networks (ICANN) and International Conference on Neural Information Processing (ICONIP).* Istanbul, June 2003, 17-20. Retrieved Agust 2007 from http://www.fizyka.ukw.edu.pl/publikacje/a_s_p.pdf

GU, P., & YAN, X. (1995). Neural network approach to the reconstruction of freeform surfaces for reverse engineering. *Computer Aided Design, 27*(1), 59-64.

GUILLET, D. (1989a). Expert systems applications in anthropology, part one. *Anthropological Quarterly, 62*(2), 57-105.

GULYÁS, L. (2002). On the transition to agent-based modeling: Implementation strategies from variables to agents. *Social Science Computer Review, 20*, 389-399.

GUPTA, L., MCAVOY, M., PHEGLEY, J.M. (2000). Classification of temporal sequences via prediction using the simple recurrent neural network. *Pattern Recognition, 33*, 1759-1770.

GURECKIS, T.M., & LOVE, B.C. (2003). Human unsupervised and supervised learning as a quantitative distinction *International Journal of Pattern Recognition and Artificial Intelligence, 17*(5), 885-901.

HADLEY, R.F. (2000). Cognition and the computational power of connectionist networks. *Connection Science, 12*(2), 95-110.

HAGAN, M.T., DEMUTH, H.B., & BEALE, M. (1996). *Neural network design.* Boston, MA: PWS Publishing Company,

HAHN, U., & CHATER, N. (1998). Similarity and rules: Distinct? exhaustive? empirically distinguishable? *Cognition, 65*, 197-230.

HAINING, R. (2003). *Spatial data analysis. Theory and practice.* Cambridge, UK: Cambridge University Press.

HAJ-YEHIA, B., & PELED, A. (2004). Rule-based system for updating spatial data-base, *XXth ISPRS Congress,* (Vol. XXXV), part B2. Istanbul ,Turkey.

HALIR, R., & FLUSSER, J. (1997). Estimation of profiles of sherds of archaeological pottery. *Proceedings 1997 Czech Pattern Recognition Workshop (CPRW'97),* (pp. 126-130).

HALLS, P.J., & MILLER, A.P. (1996). Of todes and worms: An experiment in bringing time into arc/info. *Proceedings of the 1996 ESRI European Users Conference,* Watford UK.

HALLS, P.J., POLACK, F.A.C., & O'KEEFE, S.A.M., (1999). A new approach to the spatial analysis of temporal change using todes and neural nets. *Cybergeo,* article 139. Retrieved July 2007 from http://www.cybergeo.eu/index911.html

HAN, J., & KAMBER, M. (2001). *Data mining. Concepts and techniques.* San Francisco, CA: Morgan Kaufmann.

HAND, D., MANNILA, H., & SMYTH, P. (2001). *Principles of data mining.* Cambridge, MA: The MIT Press.

HARALICK, R.M. (1979). Statistical and structural approaches to texture, *Proceedings of the IEEE, 67,* 786-804.

HARNAD, S. (1987). *Categorical perception. The groundwork of cognition.* Cambridge, UK: Cambridge University Press.

HATZINIKOLAOU, E., HATZICHRISTOS, T., SIOLAS, A., & MANTZOURANI, E. (2003). Predicting archaeological site locations using GIS and fuzzy logic. In M. Doerr & A. Sarris (Eds.), *The digital heritage of archeology. Computer applications and quantitatiuve methods in archaeology 2002* (pp. 169-178). Archive of Monuments and Publications. Hellenic Ministry of Culture, Heraklion (Greece),

HAWARAH, L., SIMONET, A., & SIMONET, M. (2003). A probabilistic approach to classify incomplete objects using decision trees. In *Database and expert systems applications* (pp. 77 – 87). Berlin: Springer Verlag.

HAYKIN, S. (1999). *Neural networks. A comprehensive foundation* (2nd ed.). Upper Saddle River, NJ: Prentice Hall.

HEBB, D.O. (1949). *The organization of behavior.* New York: John Wiley.

HEERMANN, P.D., & KHAZENIE, N. (1992). Classification of multispectral remote sensing data using a backpropagation network. *IEEE Transactions on geoscience and Remote Sensing, 30*(1), 81-88.

HEIDEMAN, G. (2005). The long-range saliency of edgeand corner-based salient points. *IEEE Transactions on Image Processing, 14*(11), 1701-1706.

HENDRIKS-JANSEN, H. (1996). *Catching ourselves in the act. Situated activity, interactive emergence, evolution, and human thought.* Cambridge, MA: The MIT Press.

HENSEL, E. (1991). *Inverse theory and applications for engineers.* Englewood Cliffs, NJ: Prentice-Hall.

HERMAN, P.Q. (1987). Cas n° 3: Que les ancêtres des figurines chypriotes lèvent le bras. In Gardin, J et al. (ed.), *Systèmes Experts et Sciences Humaines: le cas de l'Archéologie.*

HERMON, S., & NICCOLUCCI, F. (2002). Estimating subjectivity of typologists and typological classification with fuzzy logic. *Archeologia e Calcolatori, 13,* 217-232.

HERMON, S., & NICCOLUCCI, F. (2003). A fuzzy logic approach to typology in archaeological research. In M. Doerr & A. Sarris (Eds.), *The digital heritage of archeology. Computer applications and quantitatiuve methods in archaeology 2002.* Edited by. Archive of Monuments and Publications. Hellenic Ministry of Culture, Heraklion (Greece), (pp. 307-312).

HILBERT, D.W., & OSTENDORF, B. (2001). The utility of artificial neural networks for modeling the distribution of vegetation in past, present and future climates. *Ecological Modelling, 146*(1-3), 311-327 .

HINTON, G.E. (1986). Learning distributed representations of concepts. *Proceedings of the Eigth Annual Conference of the Cognitive Science Society* (pp. 1-12). Hillsdale, NJ: Lawrence Erlbaum.

HINTON, G.E., & BECKER,S. (1992). Using coherence assumptions to discover the underlying causes of the sensory input. In S. Davis (Ed.), *Connectionism: Theory and practice.* Oxford, UK: Oxford University Press.

HITCHCOCK, C., & SOBER, E. (2004). Prediction versus accomodation and the risk of overfitting. *British Journal for the Philosophy of Science, 55*, 1-34.

HOFFMAN, J. (1996). Visual object recognition. In W. Priz & B. Bridgeman (Eds.), *Handbook of perception and action. Volume 1* (pp. 297-344). New York: Academic Press.

HOLLAND, J.H., HOLYOAK, K.J., NISBETT, R.E., & THAGARD, P.R. (1986). *Induction. Processes of inference, learning, and discovery.* Cambridge, MA: The MIT Press.

HOLLAND, O. E., & MCFARLAND, D. (2001). *Artificial ethology.* Oxford: Oxford University Press.

HOLYOAK, K.J.. (1990). Problem solving. In D.N. Osherson & E.E. Smith (Eds.), *Thinking. An invitation to cognitive science* (Vol. 3) (pp. 117-146), Cambridge, MA: The MIT Press.

HONKELA, T. (1997). S*elf-organizing maps in natural language processing* (PhD. Dissertation) Helsinki Technical University. http://www.cis.hut.fi/~tho/thesis/index. html (File downloaded on September 2007).

HOOKER, J. (2002). *Coriosolite Expert System* Retrieved March, 2006, from. http://www.writer2001. com/exp0002.htm

HOPFIELD, J. (1982). Neural networks and physical systems with emergent collective computational abilities. *Proceedings of the National Academy of Sciences, 79*, 2554-2558.

HORNIK, K., STINCHCOMBE,M., & WHITE,H. (1989). Multilayer feedforward networks are universal approximators. *Neural Networks, 2*, 359-366.

HUGGET, J., & BAKER, K. (1986). The computerized archaeologist: The development of expert systems *Science and Archaeology, 27*, 3-12.

HÜLLERMEIER, E. (2007). *Case-based approximate reasoning.* New York/Berlin: Springer-Verlag.

HUMMEL, J.E., & BIEDERMAN, I. (1992). Dynamic binding in a neural network for shape recognition. *Psychological Review, 99*(3), 480-517.

HUMPHREYS, P. (2004). *Extending ourselves. Computational science, empiricism and scientific method.* Oxford: Oxford University Press.

HUNT, E. B. (1962). *Concept learning: An information processing problem.* New York: John Wiley.

ILACHINSKI, A. (2004). *Artificial war: Multi agent-based simulation of combat: Multi agent-based simulation of combat.* Singapore: World Scientific.

ILOGHALU, E.M. (2003). Application of neural networks technique in lithofacies classifications used for 3D reservoir geological modeling and exploration studies. A novel computer-based methodology for depositional environment interpretation. *AAPG Annual Convention* May 11-14, 2003, Salt Lake City, Utah. Retrieved July 2007 from http://www.searchanddiscovery.com/documents/abstracts/annual2003/extend/75734.PDF

IMPULLITTI, G., & REBMANN, C.M. (2002). *An agent-based model of wealth distribution.* CEPA Working Paper 2002-15. Retrieved July 2007 http://www.newschool. edu/cepa/papers/archive/cepa200215.pdf

IYIDA, F., PFEIFFER, R., STEELS, L., & KUNIYOSHI, Y. (Eds.), (2004). *Embodied artificial intelligence.* Berlin: Springer.

JACKSON, K.F. (1983). *The art of solving problems: Bulmershe-comino problem-solving project.* Reading, UK: Bulmershe College.

JACKSON, S.T., & WILLIAMS, J.W. (2004). Modern analogs in quaternary paleoecology: Here today, gone yesterday, gone tomorrow? *Annual Review of Earth and Planetary Sciences, 32*, 495-537.

JAIN, A.K., & KARU, K. (1996). Learning texture discrimination masks. *IEEE Transactions on Pattern Analysis And Machine Intelligence, 18*(2), 195-205.

JAIN, R., KASTURI,R., & SCHUNK,B.G. (1995). *Machine vision*. New York: Prentice Hall, Inc.

JANSSEN, M.A., SEPT, J.M., & GRIFFITH, C.S. (2005). Foraging of *Homo Ergaster* and *Australopithecus Boisei* in East African environments. *NAACSOS Conference 2005, June 26-28, 2005, Notre Dame, Indiana, USA, Annual Conference of the North American Association for Computational Social and Organizational Science*.

JENSEN, F. V. (2001). *Bayesian networks and decision graphs*. Berlin: Springer.

JERAJ, M., SZERASKO, D., TODOROVSKI, L., & DEBALJAK, M. (2004). Machine learning methods to Paleocological data. In *4th European Conference on Ecological Modelling* September 27 - 29, 2004, Bled, Slovenia. Retrieved February 2007 from http://www-ai.ijs.si/SasoDzeroski/ECEMEAML04/presentations/039-Jeraj.pdf

JI, S., YUAN, Q., & ZHANG, L. (2005). Study of auto recognizing metal chips' shape based on RBF neural networks. *Journal of Information & Computational Science, 2*(1), 51-56.

JOHNSON, C. D., KOHLER, T.A., & COWAN, J.A. (2005). Modeling historical ecology, thinking about contemporary systems. *American Anthropologist, 107*, 96-108.

JOHNSON-LAIRD, P.N. (1988). *The computer and the mind* Cambridge, MA: Harvard University Press.

JORDAN, M. I. (1986). *Serial order: A parallel distributed approach*. ICS Report 8604. San Diego, CA: University of California, Institute for Cognitive Science.

JORDAN, M. I. (Ed.) (1999). *Learning in graphical models*. Cambridge, MA: The MIT Press.

JORDAN, M.I. (1986). *Serial order: A parallel distributed approach*. *ICS Report 8604*. San Diego, CA: University of California, Institute for Cognitive Science.

JORDAN, M.I., & JACOBS, R.A. (1992). Modularity, unsupervised learning, and supervised learning. In S. Davis (Ed.), *Connectionism: theory and practice*. Oxford: University Press.

JOSEPHSON, J.R., CHANDRASEKARAN, B., SMITH, J.W., & TANNER, M.C. (1987). A mechanism for forming composite explanatory hypotheses. *IEEE Transactions on Systems, Man and Cybernetics, 17*, 445-454.

JU, W., LAM, N.S.N., & CHEN, J. (2006). Application of kohonen self-organizing map for urban structure analysis. *2006 IEEE International Conference on Granular Computing*, (pp. 118- 123).

JULESZ, B. (1981). A theory of preattentive texture discrimination based on first-order statistics of textons. *Biological Cybernetics, 41*, 131-138.

KADAR, M., ILEANA, I., & JOLDES, R. (2004). Artificial neural networks used in forms recognition of the properties of ancient copper based alloys. In F. Niccolucci (Ed.), *Beyond the artefact. Computer Applications in Archaeology*. Budapest: ArcheoLingua.

KAELBLING, L.P. (1993). *Learning in embedded systems*. Cambridge, MA: The MIT Press.

KAIPIO, J., & SOMERSALO, E., (2004). *Statistical and computational inverse problems*. Berlin: Springer.

KALLIOMÄKI, I., VEHTARI, A., & LAMPINEN, J. (2005). Shape analysis of concrete aggregates for statistical quality modeling. *Machine Vision and Applications, 16*(3), 197-201.

KAMPEL, M., & MELERO, F.J. (2003). Virtual vessel reconstruction from a fragment's profile. In D. Arnold, A. Chalmers, & F. Nicolucci (Eds.), *VAST2003 proceedings of the 4th International Symposium on Virtual reality, Archaeology, and Intelligent Cultural heritage* (pp. 79-88). Edited by. The Eurographics Association, Aire-la-Ville (Switzerland),

KAMPEL, M., & MELERO, F.J. (2003). Virtual vessel reconstruction from a fragment's profile. In D. Arnold, A. Chalmers, & F. Nicolucci (Eds.), *VAST2003 4th International Symposium on Virtual reality, Archaeology and Intelligent Cultural heritage* (pp. 79-88). The Eurographics Association, Aire-la-Ville (Switzerland).

KAMPEL, M., & SABLATNIG, R. (2002). Computer aided classification of ceramics. In F. Niccolucci (Ed.), *Virtual archaeology*. Oxford: ArcheoPress. (BAR Int. Series 1075).

KAMPEL, M., & SABLATNIG, R. (2003). An automated pottery archival and reconstruction system. *Journal of Visualization and Computer Animation,14*(3), 111-120.

KAMPEL, M., & SABLATNIG, R. (2003). An automated pottery archival and reconstruction system. *Journal of Visualization and Computer Animation,14*(3), 111-120.

KAMPEL, M., & SABLATNIG,R. (2004). New achievments on pottery reconstruction. In Magistrat der Stadt Wien-Referat Kulturelles Erbe-Stadtarchäeologie Wien (Eds.), *Enter the past. The e-way into the four dimensions of cultural heritage.* Oxford: ArcheoPress, (BAR Int. Series, 1227).

KAMPEL, M., MARA, H., & SABLATNIG, R. (2006). Automated investigation of archaeological vessels. In *Proc. of EUSIPCO2006: 13th European Signal Processing Conference, Florence, Italy.*

KANEVSKI, M., MAIGNAN, M., DEMYANOV, V., & MAIGNAN, M.F. (1997). How neural network 2d interpolations can improve spatial data analysis: Neural network residual kriging. *IAMG 97 Int. Assoc. Mathematical Geology,* (pp. 549-554).

KARP, P.D. (1990). Hypothesis formation as design. In J. Shrager & P. Langley (Eds.), *Computational models of scientific discovery and theory formation* (pp. 275-317). San Francisco, CA: Morgan Kaufmann.

KASHYAP, H.K., BANSILAL, P., & KOUSHIK, A.P. (2003). Hybrid neural network architecture for age identification of ancient kannada scripts. Proceedings of the 2003 IEEE International Symposium on Circuits and Systems (ISCAS 2003), Vol. 3, pp. 423-426.

KASKI, S. & KOHONEN, T. (1996). Exploratory data analysis by the self-organizing map: Structures of welfare and poverty in the world. In A.P.N. Refenes, Y. Abu-Mostafa, J. Moody & A. Weigend (Eds.), *Neural networks in financial engineering* (pp. 498–507). Singapore: World Scientific.

KASKI, S. (1997). *Data exploration using self-organizing maps.* Acta Polytechnica Scandinavica, Mathematics, Computing and Management in Engineering Series No. 82, Espoo, 57 pp. Published by the Finnish Academy of Technology.

KASKI, S. NIKKILÄ, J., & KOHONEN, T. (1998). Methods for interpreting a self-organized map in data analysis. In *Proceedings 6th European Symposium on Artificial Neural Networks (ESANN98).* Bruges, Belgium: D-Facto.

KASKI, S., HONKELA, T., LAGUS, K., & KOHONEN, T. (1998). WEBSOM—self-organizing maps of document collections. *Neurocomputing, 21,* 101-117.

KAUFMAN, K., & MICHALSKI, R. S. (2000). An adjustable rule learner for pattern discovery using the AQ methodology. *Journal of Intelligent Information Systems, 14,* 199-216.

KERSTEN, D., MAMASSIAN, P., & YUILLE, A. (2004). Object perception as Bayesian inference. *Annual Review of Psychology, 55,* 271-304.

KESELMAN, Y., & DICKINSON, S. (2005). Generic model abstraction from examples. *IEEE Transactions on Pattern Analysis and Machine Intelligence, 27*(7).

KIM, J.K., LEE, J.K., & KIM, S.H. (1999). An interactive approach to building an influence diagram based on neural networks. *Journal of Decision Systems, 8*(3), 389-405.

KIM, Z.W., & NEVATIA, R. (2004). Automatic description of complex buildings from multiple images. *Computer Vision and Image Understanding, 96,* 60–95.

KING, R.D., WHELAN, K.E., JONES, F.M., REISER, P.G.K., BRYANT, C.H.K, MUGGLETON, S.H., KELL D.B., & OLIVER S.G. (2004). Functional genomic hypothesis generation and experimentation by a robot scientist. *Nature, 427,* 247–252.

KINTIGH, K., & AMMERMAN, A. (1982). Heuristic approaches to spatial analysis in archaeology. *American Antiquity, 47*(1), 31-63.

KIRKBY, S. D. (1996). Integrating a GIS with an expert system to identify and manage dryland salinization. *Applied Geography, 16,* 289–302.

KIRSCH, A. (1996). *An introduction to the mathematical theory of inverse problems.* Berlin: Springer.

KIRSCH, D., & MAGLIO, P. (1995). On distinguishing epistemic from pragmatic action. *Cognitive Science, 18,* 513-549.

KIRSCH, D., MAGLIO, P. (1995). On distinguishing epistemic from pragmatic action. *Cognitive Science, 18,* 513-549.

KITAMURA, Y., & MIZOGOUCHI, R. (2004). Ontology-based systematization of functional knowledge. *Journal of Engineering Design, 15*(4), 327-351.

KITAMURA, Y., MIZOGOUCHI, R. (1999). An ontology of functional concepts of artifacts. *Artificial Intelligence Research Group. The Institute of Scientific and Industrial Research. Osaka University.* Retrieved July 2005 from http://www.ei.sanken.osaka-u.ac.jp/pub/kita/kita-tr9901.pdf

KLAHR, D., & DUNBAR,K. (1988). Dual space search during scientific reasoning. *Cognitive Science, 12*(1), 1-55.

KLAHR, D., FAY, A.L., & DUNBAR, K. (1993). Heuristics for scientific experimentation: A developmental study. *Cognitive Psychology, 13*, 113-148.

KLAHR,D. (2000). *Exploring science: The cognition and development of discovery processes*. Cambridge, MA: The MIT Press.

KLIMASAUSKAS, C. (2002). Taking backpropagation to the extreme. *PC AI Magazine, January/February*, 31-35.

KLÜGL, F., FEHLER, M., & HERRLER, R. (2005). About the role of the environment in multi-agent simulations. In D. Weyns, H. Van Dyke Parunak, F. Michel (Eds.), *Environments for multi-agent systems*. Berlin: Springer, (Lecture Notes in Computer Science, No. 3374).

KLÜVER, J., SCHMIDT, J., STOICA, C. (2005). The emergence of social order by processes of typifying: A computational model. *Journal of Mathematical Sociology, 29*, 1–21.

KLÜVER, J., STOICA, C., & SCHMIDT, J. (2003). Formal models, social theory and computer simulations: Some methodical reflections *Journal of Artificial Societies and Social Simulation, 6*(2).

KNOPF, G.K., & AL-NAJI, R. (2001). Adaptive reconstruction of bone geometry from serial cross-sections. *Artificial Intelligence in Engineering, 15*, 227 - 239.

KNOPF, G.K., & KOFMAN, J. (1999). Free-form surface reconstruction using Bernstein basis function networks. In C.H. Dagli et al. (Eds.), *Intelligent engineering systems through artificial neural networks (Vol. 9)* (pp. 797 – 802). ASME Press

KNOPF, G.K., & KOFMAN, J. (2002). Surface reconstruction using neural network mapping of range-sensor images to object space. *Journal of Electronic Imaging, 11*(2), 187-194

KOBTI, Z., &REYNOLDS, R.G. (2005). Modeling protein exchange across the social network in the village multi-agent simulation. *IEEE International Conference on Systems, Man and Cybernetics, 4*(10-12), 3197–3203.

KOHLER, T. (2003). Agent-based modeling of Mesa Verde region settlement systems: introduction. *Paper presented in Symposium Building Models for Settlement Systems in the Late Prehispanic Mesa Verde Region: An Interdisciplinary Approach 68th Annual Meeting of the Society for American Archaeology*. Milwaukee.

Retrieved March 2007 http://www.wsu.edu/%7Evillage/Kohler%20SAA%20%2703.pdf

KOHLER, T. A., & GUMERMAN, G.A., REYNOLDS, R.G. (2005). Simulating ancient societies. *Scientific American, 293*, 77-84.

KOHLER, T., & GUMMERMAN, G. (editors). (2000). *Dynamics in human and primate societies: Agent-based modeling of social and spatial processes*. Santa Fe Institute Studies in the Sciences of Complexity, New York: Oxford University Press.

KOHLER, T.A., & CARR, E. (1997). Swarm-based modeling of prehistoric settlement systems in southwestern north america. In I. Johnson & M. North (Eds.), *Proceedings of Colloquium II, UISPP, XIIIth Congress, Forli, Italy, Sept 1996. Sydney University Archaeological Methods Series 5*. Sydney, Australia: Sydney University.

KOHLER, T.A., & YAP, L. (2003) *Modeling reciprocal exchange in southwestern societies. Paper presented at the 68th Annual Meeting of the Society for American Archaeology, Milwaukee, WI*. Retrieved from July 2007 http://www.wsu.edu/%7Evillage/Kohler%20&%20Yap%20SAA%202003.pdf

KOHLER, T.A., JOHNSON, C.D., VARIEN, M., ORTMAN, S., REYNOLDS, R., KOBTI, Z., COWAN, J. et al (2007). Settlement Ecodynamics in the Prehispanic Central Mesa Verde Region. In T.A. Kohler & S. E. Van der Leeuw (Eds.), *Model-based archaeology of socio-natural systems*. Santa Fe, NM: SAR Press.

KOHLER, T.A., KRESL, J., VAN WEST, C.R., CARR, E., & WILSHUSEN, R. (2000). Be there then: A modeling approach to settlement determinants and spatial efficiency among late ancestral pueblo populations of the Mesa Verde region, U.S. Southwest. In T. A. Kohler & G. J. Gumerman (Eds.), *Dynamics in human and primate societies: Agent-based modeling of social and spatial processes* (pp. 145-178). Santa Fe Institute Studies in the Sciences of Complexity, New York: Oxford University Press.

KOHONEN, T. (1989). *Self-organization and associative memory*. Berlin: Springer.

KOHONEN, T. (2001). *Self-organizing maps* (3rd ed). Berlin: Springer.

KOLODNER, J. (1993). *Case-based reasoning*. San Francisco, CA: Morgan Kaufmann.

KOSKO, B. (1992). *Neural networks and fuzzy systems. A dynamical systems approach to machine intelligence.* Englewood Cliffs, NJ: Prentice Hall.

KOSKO,B. (1993). *Fuzzy thinking: The new science of fuzzy logic.* New York: Hyperion.

KOSSLYN, S.M. (1994). *Image and brain. The resolution of the imagery debate.* Cambridge, MA: The MIT Press.

KOUA, E.L., & KRAAK, M.J. (2004). An evaluation of self-organizing map spatial representation and visualization for geospatial data: Perception and visual analysis. In J. Dykes, , A.M. MacEachren & M. J. Kraak (Eds.), *Exploring geovisualization* (pp. 627-644). Amsterdam: Elsevier

KOVÁCS, A.I., & UENO, H. (2005, February 4-6). The case for radical epigenetic robotics. *Proceedings of the 10th International Symposium on Artificial Life and Robotics (AROB 2005).* Beppu, Oita, Japan. Retrieved October 2005 from http://www.alexander-kovacs.de/kovacs05arob.pdf

KRASNOPOLSKY, V.M., & SCHILLER, H. (2003). Some neural network applications in environmental sciences. Part I: Forward and inverse problems in geophysical remote measurements. *Neural Networks, 16*(3-4), 321-334.

KREMER, S.C. (2001). Spatiotemporal connectionist networks: A taxonomy and review. *Neural Computation, 13,* 249–306

KROEPELIEN, B. (1998). Image databases in art history: An expert system for norwegian silver. *Computers and the History of Art Journal, 8*(1), 17-38.

KULKARNI, A.D. (2001). *Computer vision and fuzzy neural systems.* Upper Saddle River, NJ: Prentice Hall,

KULKARNI, D., & SIMON, H.A. (1988). The processes of scientific discovery. The strategy of experimentation. *Cognitive Science, 12,* 139-176.

KUZNAR, L.A., & SEDLMEYER, R. (2005). Collective violence in Darfur: An agent-based model Of pastoral nomad/sedentary peasant interaction. *Mathematical Anthropology and Cultural Theory: An International Journal, 1*(4).

LAGAZIO, M. (2006) Assessing different Bayesian neural network models for militarized interstate dispute outcomes and variable influences. *Social Science Computer Review,* 24(1).

LAGAZIO, M., & RUSSETT, B. (2004). A neural network analysis of militarized disputes, 1885-1992: Temporal stability and causal complexity. In P. Diehl (Ed.), *The scourge of war: New extensions on an old problem,* (pp. 28-62). Ann Arbor, MI: University of Michigan Press.

LAGRANGE, M.S. (1989a) Les systèmes experts et la récherche en archéologie et sciences humaines. Un point de vue pragmatique. *Documentaliste,26*(1), 11-15.

LAGRANGE, M.S. (1989b). *VANDAL. Un Système expert d' aide a l' étude de la provenance de ceramiques fondé sur des données archéometriques. Manuel d' Utilisation.* Paris: C.N.R.S.-U.P.R. 315, Technical Report.

LAGRANGE, M.S. (1992). Symbolic data and numerical processing: A case study in art history by means of automated learning techniques. In J.C. Gardin & C. Peebles (Eds.), *Representations in archaeology* (pp. 330–356). Bloomington, IN: Indiana University Press,

LAGRANGE, M.S., & RENAUD, M. (1984). *SUPERIKON. Un essai de six expertises en iconographie: érudition ou trivialité?* Document de Travail n. 6. C.N.R.S-UPR 315, Paris.

LAGRANGE, M.S., & RENAUD, M. (1983). *Simulation du raisonnement archéologique: SNARK, sept archéologues et une pierre gravée.* Document de travail n° 2. CNRS (UPR 315). Paris.

LAGRANGE, M.S., & RENAUD, M. (1985). Intelligent knowledge-based systems in archaeology: A computerized simulation of reasoning by means of an expert system. *Computers and the Humanities, 19*(1), 37-52.

LAGRANGE, M.S., & RENAUD, M. (1987). Cas n° 6, Superikon, essai de cumul de six expertises en iconographie. In *Systèmes Experts et Sciences Humaines. Le cas de l' Archéologie.* Edited by Gardin et al. (1987). Paris: Eyrolles.

LAGRANGE, M.S., & RENAUD, M. (1987). *TRINITA: un étude de cas en histoire de l' art à l'aide d'un programme d'apprentissage.* Document de Travail n° 7. C.N.R.S.-U.P.R., 315, Paris (France).

LAGUS, K., KASKI, S., & KOHONEN, T. (2004). Mining massive document dollections by the WEBSOM method. *Information Sciences, 163*(1-3), 135-156.

LAKE, M. W. (2000a). MAGICAL computer simulation of mesolithic foraging. In T. A. Kohler, and G. J. Gumerman (Eds.), *Dynamics in human and primate societies: Agent-based modelling of social and spatial processes* (pp. 107-143). Santa Fe Institute Studies in the Sciences of Complexity, New York: Oxford University Press.

LAKE, M. W. (2000b). MAGICAL computer simulation of mesolithic foraging on islay. In S. J.Mithen (Ed.), *Hunter-gatherer landscape archaeology: The southern hebrides mesolithic project, 1988-98, (vol. 2): Archaeological fieldwork on colonsay, computer modelling, experimental archaeology, and final interpretations,* (pp. 465-495). Cambridge, UK: The McDonald Institute for Archaeological Research.

LANGLEY, P. (1996). *Elements of machine learning.* San Francisco, CA: Morgan Kaufmann.

LANGLEY, P., & ZYTKOW, J. (1989). Data-driven approaches to empirical discovery. *Artificial Intelligence, 40,* 283-312.

LANGLEY, P., SIMON, H.A., BRADSHAW, G.L., & ZYTKOV, J.M. (1987) *Scientific discovery. Computational explorations of the creative process.* Cambridge, MA: The MIT Press.

LANGNER, D. (2001). Leaves recognition v 1.0. Neural network based recognition system for leafs images. Retrieved January 2007 from http://damato.light-speed.de/lrecog/

LATOUR, B., & TEIL, G. (2005). The Hume machine: Can association networks do more than formal rules? In S. Franchi & G. Güzeldere (Eds.), *Mechanical bodies, computational minds* (pp. 307-325). Cambridge, MA: The MIT Press.

LAZAR, A., & REYNOLDS, R.G. (2002). Heuristic knowledge discovery for archaeological data using cultural algorithms and rough sets. In A. Ruhul, S. Sarker, Hussein A. Abbass, & Charles S. Newton (Eds.), *Heuristics and optimization for knowledge discovery (Vol. 2.)* Hershey, PA: Idea Group Publishing.

LAZAR, A., & REYNOLDS, R.G. (2005). Evolution-based learning of ontological knowledge for a large-scale multi-agent simulation. In M. Grana, R.J. Duro, A.D. Aryou, & P.P Wang, (Eds,), *Information processing and evolutionary algorithms-from industrial applications to academic speculation.* Berlin: Springer-Verlag.

LEE, S., & LATHROP, R.G. (2006). Subpixel analysis of landsat ETM+ using self-organizing map (SOM) neural networks for urban land cover characterization. *IEEE Transactions on Geoscience and Remote Sensing, 44*(6), 1642-1654.

LEITAO, H. D. DA GAMA, & STOLFI, J. (2002). A multiscale method for the reassembly of two-dimensional fragmented objects. *IEEE Transactions on Pattern Analysis and machine Intelligence, 24*(9), 1239-1251

LEITAO, H., DA GAMA, D., & STOLFI, J. (2001). Digitization and reconstruction of archaeological artifacts. *In XIV Brazilian Symposium on Computer Graphics and Image Processing (SIBGRAPI'01).* Retrieved January 2007 from http://csdl2.computer.org/comp/proceedings/sibgrapi/2001/1330/00/13300382.pdf

LEITAO, H., DA GAMA, D., & STOLFI, J. (2002). A multiscale method for the reassembly of two-dimensional fragmented objects. *IEEE Transactions on Pattern Analysis and machine Intelligence,* 24(9), 1239-1251.

LEK, S., DELACOSTE, M., BARA, P., DIMOPOULOS, I., LAUGA, J. & AULAGNIER, S. (1996). Application of neural networks to modeling nonlinear relationships in ecology. *Ecological Monitoring, 90,* 39-52.

LENAT, D. B. (1995a). Steps to sharing knowledge. In N.J.I. Mars (Ed.), *Toward very large knowledge bases.* Amsterdam: IOS Press,

LENAT, D. B. (1995b) Cyc: A large-scale investment in knowledge infrastructure. *Communications of the ACM, 38(*11).

LENAT, D.B., & GUHA, R.V. (1990). *Building large knowledge-based systems.* Reading, MA: Addison-Wesley.

LENIHAN, J.M., & NEILSON, R.P. (1993). A rule-based vegetation formation model for canada. *Journal of Biogeography, 20(*6), 615-628.

LEONT'EV, A. (1974). The problem of activity in psychology. *Soviet Psychology, 13*(2), 4-33.

LEOW, W.K., & MIIKULAINEN, R. (1997). Visual schemas in neural networks for object recognition and scene analysis. *Connection Science, 9*(2), 161-200.

LEUNG, T., & MALIK, J. (2001). Representing and recognizing the visual appearance of materials using three-dimensional textons. *International Journal of Computer Vision, 43*(1), 29–44.

LEUNG, Y. (1997). Feedforward neural network models for spatial data classification and rule learning. In M.M. Fischer & A.Getis (Eds.), *Recent developments in spatial analysis. Spatial statistics, behavioural modeling and computational intelligence.* Springer: Berlin.

LEWIS, R., & SÉGUIN,C. (1998). Generation of 3D building models from 2D architectural plans. *Computer aided Design, 30*(10), 765-769.

LEYMARIE, F. (2003). *Three-dimensional shape representation via shock flows*, PhD thesis. Brown University. Retrieved August, 2007 from http://www.lems.brown.edu/~leymarie/phd/

LEYMARIE, F. (2003). *Three-dimensional shape representation via shock flows*, PhD thesis, Brown University. Retrieved August 2007 from http://www.lems.brown.edu/~leymarie/phd/

LEYTON, M. (1992). *Symmetry. Causality, mind.* Cambridge, MA: The MIT Press.

LEYTON, M. (2005). Shape as memory Storage. In C. Young (Ed.), *Ambient intelligence for scientific discovery* Berlin: Springer.

LI, P., & FLENLEY, J.R. (1999). Pollen texture identification using neural networks. *Grana 38*, 59–64.

LI, X., & YEH, A.G.O. (2002). Neural network-based cellular automata for simulating multiple land use changes using GIS. *International Journal of Geographical Information Science, 16*(4), 323-343.

LIAO, S.H. (2003). Knowledge management technologies and applications—literature review from 1995 to 2002. *Expert Systems with Applications, 25*, 155–164

LIAO, S.H. (2005). Expert system methodologies and applications—a decade review from 1995 to 2004. *Expert Systems with Applications, 28*, 93–103

LIBEROPOULOU, L. (1999). An expert system for the conservation of archeological iron. *Workshop Intelligenza Artificiale per i Beni Culturali.* Bologna (Italy), 14 Settembre 1999

LIEBOWITZ, J. (1997). *Handbook of applied expert systems.* Boca Raton, FL: CRC Press.

LINK, C.A. (n.d.). Artificial neural networks for Lithology prediction and reservoir characterization geophysical engineering. *Montana Tech of the University of Montana.* Retrieved august 20, 2006 from http://www.mtech.edu/GEOPHYSICS/RESEARCH/NeuralNetworks.htm

LIPO, C. P. (2006). The resolution of cultural phylogenies using graphs. In R. L. Lyman & M. J. O'Brien (Eds.), *Mapping our ancestors: Phylogenetic approaches in anthropology and prehistory.* New York: Aldine.

LIPO, C. P., MADSEN, M., DUNNEL, R., & HUNT, T. (1997). Population Structure, Cultural Transmission, and Frequency Seriation. *Journal of Anthropological Archaeology, 16*, 301-333.

LIU, W., SETO, K.C., & SUN, Z. (2005). Urbanization prediction with an ART-MMAP neural network based spatiotemporal data mining method. *International Archives of Photogrammetry, Remote Sensing and Spatial Information Sciences, XXXVI*(8)/W27.

LLETÍ, R. SARABIA,L.A., ORTIZ, M.C., TODESCHINI, R., & COLOMBINI, M.P. (2003). Application of the kohonen artificial neural network in the identification of proteinaceous binders in samples of panel painting using gas chromatography-Mass Spectrometry, *Analyst,128*, 281-286.

LLOYD, C.D., & ATKINSON, P.M. (2004) Archaeology and geostatistics. *Journal of Archaeological Science, 31*(2), 151-165.

LOBO, V., BAÇÃO, F., & PAINHO, M. (2004, April 29-May 1). The self-organizing map and it's variants as tools for geodemographical data analysis: The case of Lisbon's metropolitan area. In *7th AGILE Conference on Geographic Information Science, Heraklion, Greece. Parallel Session 4.1- Geographic Knowledge Discovery.*

LOHSE, E.S., SCHOU, C., SCHLADER, R., & SAMMONS, D. (2004). Automated classification of stone projectile points in a neural network. In Magistrat der Stadt Wien-Referat Kulturelles Erbe-Städtarhchäologie Wien (Ed.), *Enter the past. The e-way into the four dimensions of culture heritage* (pp. 431-437). Oxford: ArcheoPress.

LONCARIC, S. (1998). A survey of shape analysis techniques. *Pattern Recognition, 31*, 983–1001.

LOOTS, L., NACKAERTS, K., & WAELKENS, M. (1999). Fuzzy viewshed analysis of the hellenistic city. Defence system at sagalassos. In L. Dingwall, S.Exon, V. Gaffney, S. Laflin & M. Van Leusen (Eds.), *Archaeology in the age of internet. Computer applications and quantitative methods in archaeology 1997* (pp. 63-65). Oxford: ArcheoPress.

LOPEZ MOLINERO, A., CASTRO, A., PINO, J., PEREZ-ARANTEGUI, J., & CASTILLO, J.R. (2000). Classification of ancient Roman glazed ceramics using the neural network of self-organizing maps. *Fresenius Journal of Analytical Chemistry, 367*, 586-589.

LOUZOUN, Y., & ATLAN, H. (2007). The emergence of goals in a self-organizing network: A non-mentalist model of intentional actions. *Neural Networks, 20,* 156–171.

LOVE, B. C. (2002). Comparing supervised and unsupervised category learning. *Psychonomic Bulletin & Review, 9,* 829-835.

LOWE, D.G. (1990). Visual recognition as probabilistic inference from spatial relations. In A. Blake & T. Troscianko (Eds.), *AI and the eye.* New York: John Wiley.

LUCKMAN,P.G., GIBSON, R.D., & CHAMARTI, R.R. (1997). A hybrid rule-object spatial modeling tool for catchment analysis. *Paper presented at the second annual conference of GeoComputation '97 & SIRC '97,*University of Otago, new Zealand.

LUGER, G.F. (2005). *Artificial intelligence: Structures and strategies for complex problem solving,* (5th Ed). Reading, MA: Addison-Wesley.

LÜTH, H. (1993). *Surfaces and interfaces of solids.* Berlin: Springer.

LYMAN, R.L., & O'BRIEN, M. (1999). *Seriation, stratigraphy, and index fossils: The backbone of archaeological dating.* New York: Kluwer Academic/Plenum.

LYMAN, R.L., & O'BRIEN, M. (2003). *Cladistics and archaeology.* Salt Lake City, UT: University of Utah Press.

LYMAN, R.L., & O'BRIEN, M. (2006) Seriation and cladistics: The difference between anagenetic and cladogenetic evolution. In R. L. Lyman & M. J. O'Brien (Eds.), *Mapping our ancestors: Phylogenetic approaches in anthropology and prehistory* (pp. 65-88). New York: Aldine.

MA, Q. (2003). Application of EDXRF and artificial neural networks to provenance studies of the archaeological pottery sherds during neolithic age in Gansu Province, China. *Journal of Lanzhou University Natural Sciences,* 39(1), 47-53.

MA, Q.,YAN, A., & HU, Z. (2000). Principal component analysis and artificial neural networks applied to the classification of chinese pottery of neolithic age. *Analytica Chimica Acta, 406,* 247-256.

MACE, R. C., HOLDEN, J., & SHENNAN, S. (2005). *Evolution of cultural diversity: A phylogenetic approach.* London: UCL Press.

MACHAMER, P. (2002). Activities and causation. *Philosophy of Science Assoc. 18th Biennial Mtg - PSA 2002:*

PSA 2002 Workshops. Retrieved October 2005 from http://philsci-archive.pitt.edu/archive/00000864/

MACHAMER, P., DARDEN, L., & CRAVER, C. (2000). Thinking about mechanisms. *Philosophy of Science, 67,* 1-25.

MAES, P. (1989). How to do the right thing. *Connection Science, 1,* 291-323.

MAGNANI, L. (2004). Conjectures and manipulations. Computational modeling and the extra-theoretical dimension of scientific discovery. *Minds and Machines, 14,* 507–537.

MAGNANI, L., & DOSSENA, R. (2006). *Computing, philosophy and cognition.* London: College Publications.

MAHINY, A.S., & TURNER, B. J. (2003, September 8-10). Modeling past vegetation change through remote sensing and G.I.S: A comparison of neural networks and logistic regression methods. In *Proceedings of the 7th International Conference on GeoComputation* University of Southampton, United Kingdom. Retrieved July 2007 from http://www.geocomputation.org/2003/Papers/Mahiny_Paper.pdf

MAÍCAS, R. (1989). Ejemplos de aplicación de inteligencia artificial en arqueología. *Cuadernos de Prehistoria y Arqueología de la Universidad Autónoma de Madrid,16,* 73-80.

MAKARENKO, A. (2006). Neural networks for modelling of large social systems. approaches for mentality, anticipating and multivaluedness accounting. *International Journal Information Theories & Applications, 13,* 371-376.

MALOOF, M.A., & MICHALSKI, R. (1997). Learning symbolic descriptions Of shape for object recognition In x-ray images. *Expert Systems with Applications, 12*(1), 11-20.

MAMELI, L., BARCELÓ, J., & ESTÉVEZ, J. (2001). The statistics of archaeological deformation processes. An archaeozoological case. In G. Burenhult (Ed.), *Archaeological informatics: Pushing the envelope* (pp. 221-230). Oxford: ArcheoPress.

MAMELI, L., ESTÉVEZ, J., & GOODALL, N. (2002). An expert system to help taxonomic classification in avian archaeozoology: A first attempt with bird species from tierra del fuego. *Acta Zoologica Cracoviensa, 45,* 383-391

MANN, S., & BENWELL, G.L. (1996). The integration of ecological, neural and spatial modeling for monitoring and prediction for semi-arid landscapes. *Computers & Geosciences*, 22(9), 1003-1012.

MANNILA, H., TOIVONEN, H., KORHOLA, A., & OLANDER, K. (1998) Learning, mining, or modeling? A case study from paleoecology. In A. Setsuo & M. Hiroshi (Eds.), *Discovery science* (Vol. 1532, pp. 12-24). Berlin: Springer

MARA H., & SABLATNIG, R. (2005). 3D-vision applied in archaeology. *Forum Archaeologiae - Zeitschrift für klassische Archäologie*, 34(3).

MARA, H., & SABLATNIG, R. (2006). Orientation of fragments of rotationally symmetrical 3D-shapes for archaeological documentation. In M. Pollefeys & K. Daniilidis (Eds.), *Proc. of 3rd Intl. Symposium on 3D Data Processing, Visualization and Transmission (3DPVT), Chapel Hill, USA*.

MARCOT, B.G., STEVENTON, J.G.D., SUTHERLAND, G.D., & MCKANN, R.K. (2006). Guidelines for developing and updating Bayesian belief networks applied to ecological modelling and conservation. *Canadian Journal of Forestal Research, 36*, 3063-3074.

MARCUS, G.F. (2001). *The algebraic mind. Integrating connectionism and cognitive science*. Cambridge, MA: The MIT Press.

MARCUS, G.F. (2001). *The algebraic mind. Integrating connectionism and cognitive science*. Cambridge, MA: The MIT Press.

MARGOLIES, H. (1987). *Patterns, thinking and cognition. A theory of judgement*. Chicago University Press.

MARKEL, J.L. (1987). *Archaeology and the computer technology revolution*. Ph.D. Dissertation. State University of New York, Buffalo (NY). Ann Arbor, MI: University Microfilms International.

MARMO, R., AMODIO, S. TAGLIAFERRI, R., FERRERI, R., & LONGO, G. (2005). Textural identification of carbonate rocks by image processing and neural network: Methodology proposal and examples. *Computers & Geosciences, 31*, 649–659.

MARR, D., & HILDRETH, E. (1980). Theory of edge detection, Proc. R. Soc. Lond. B, *207*, 187-217.

MARR, D.H. (1982). *Vision, a computational investigation into the human representation and processing of visual information*. San Francisco: W.H. Freeman.

MARTIN, D.H., FOWLKES, C.C., & MALIK, J. (2004). Learning to detect natural image boundaries using local brightness, color, and texture cues. *IEEE Transactions On Pattern Analysis And Machine Intelligence, 26*(5), 530-549.

MARTINEZ, A., SALAS, J.D. & GREEN, T.G. (2004). Sensitivity of spatial analysis neural network training and interpolation to structural parameters, *Mathematical Geology, 36*(6), 721-742.

MARTÍNEZ, P., GUALTIERI, J.A., AGUILAR, P.L., PÉREZ, R.M., LINAJE, M., PRECIADO, J.C., et al. (2001). Hyperspectral image classification using a self-organizing map, *Summaries of the XI JPL Airborne Earth Science Workshop*.

MARTINEZ-ALAJARIN, J.M., LUIS-DELGADO, J.D., & TOMAS-BALIBREA, L.M. (2005). Automatic system for quality-based classification of marble textures. *IEEE Transactions on Systems, Man, And Cybernetics—Part C: Applications And Reviews, 35*(4), 488-497.

MASCHNER, H. D. G., (Ed.) (1996). *Darwinian archaeologies*. New York: Plenum Press.

MATERKA, A., & STRZELECKI, M. (1998). *Texture analysis methods – a review*. Technical University of Lodz, Institute of Electronics. Brussels (Belgium): COST B11 report.

MATSUDA, S., KOIKE, K., & OHMI, M. (2003). Spatial estimation of geologic data using a neural network and detection of influence factors on their distribution, *Journal of the Mining and Materials Processing Institute of Japan, 19*(6/7), 359-369.

MAYORGA, M.A., & LUDEMAN, L.C. (1991). Neural nets for determination of texture and its orientation. *ICASSP-91*.

MAYORGA, M.A., & LUDEMAN, L.C. (1994). Shift and rotation invariant texture recognition with neural nets. *IEEE World Congress on Computational Intelligence*.

MCBRIDE, D.G., DIETZ, M.J., VENNEMEYER, M.T., MEADORS, S.A., BENFER, R.A., & FURBEE, N.L. (2001). Bootstrap methods for sex determination from the *Os Coxae* using the ID3 Algorithm. *Journal of Forensic Sciences, 46*, 427-431.

MCBRIDE, J.C., & KIMIA, B.B. (2003). Archaeological fragment reassembly using curve-matching. In *Proc. of the IEEE/CVPR Workshop on Appls. of Computer Vision in Archaeology (ACVA'03)*.

McCLOSKEY, M., & COHEN, N.J. (1989). Catastrophic interference in connectionist networks: The sequential learning problem. In G.H. Brower (Ed.), *The psychology of learning and motivation* (vol. 24). New York: Academic Press.

McDOWELL, D., McCLEARY, R., MEIDINGER, E. F., HAY, R.A. (1980). *Interrupted time series analysis.* Newbury Park, CA: Sage Publ.

MCKEOWN, D.M, HARVEY, W.A & MCDERMOTT, J. (1985). Rule based interpretation of aerial imagery *IEEE Tran. On Pattern Analysis and Machine Intelligence* , *1*(5), 510-585.

MCKEOWN, D.M. (1987). The role of artificial intelligence in the integration of remotely sensed data with geographic information systems, *IEEE Trans. On Geoscience and Remote Sensing, 25,* 330-348

MEHRER, M.W., & WESCOTT, K.L. (2005). *GIS and archaeological site location modeling.* London: Taylor & Francis.

MELERO, F.J., LEON, A.J., CONTRERAS, F., & TORRES, J.C. (2004). A new system for interactive vessel reconstruction and drawing. In Magistrat der Stadt Wien-Referat Kulturelles Erbe-Stadtarchäeologie Wien (Eds.), *Enter the past. The e-way into the four dimensions of cultural heritage.* Oxford: ArcheoPress, (BAR Int. Series, 1227).

MELLO, E., & ARIAS, C. (1996). Un sistema esperto a supporto della scelta di intervento conservativo su beni culturali. *Archeologia e calcolatori, 7,* 963-972.

MENNIS, J., & LIU, J. (2003). Mining association rules in Spatiotemporal data, *Proceedings of the 7th International Conference on GeoComputation,* Southampton UK: University of Southampton.

MEPHU NGUIFO, E., LAGRANGE, M.-S., RENAUD, M., & SALLANTIN, J. (1998). PLATA: An application of LEGAL, a machine learning based system, to a typology of archaeological ceramics. *Computers and the humanities, 31*(3), 169-187.

MERAVIGLIA, C. (1996) Models of representation of social mobility and inequality systems. A neural network Approach. *Quality and Quantity, 30,* 231-252.

MERAVIGLIA, C. (2001). *Le reti neurali nella ricerca sociale.* Milan, Itlay: FrancoAngeli.

MERWIN, D.A., CROMLEY, R.G., & CIVCO, D.L. (2002). Artificial neural networks as a method of spatial interpolation for digital elevation models. *Cartography and Geographical Information Systems, 29*(2), 99-110.

METZLER, P.J., & MARTINCIC, C.J. (1998). QUE: Explanation through exploration. *expert systems with applications, 15,* 253–263

MICHALEWICZ, Z. (1996). *Genetic algorithms + data structures=evolution programs.* Berlin: Springer.

MICHALSKI, R. S., & KAUFMAN, K. (2001). Learning patterns in noisy data: The AQ approach. In G. Paliouras, V. Karkaletsis & C. Spyropoulos (Eds.), *Machine learning and its applications* (pp. 22-38). Berlin: Springer.

MICHALSKI, R. S., Generating Alternative Hypotheses in AQ Learning, *Reports of the Machine Learning and Inference Laboratory,* MLI 04-6, Fairfax (VA): George Mason University.

MINSKY, M. (1968). *Semantic information processing.* Cambridge, MA: The MIT Press.

MINSKY, M. (1985). *The society of mind.* New York: Simon and Schuster.

MINSKY, M. (1991). Logical versus analogical or symbolic versus connectionist or neat versus scruffy. *AI Magazine, 12*(2), 34–51.

MINSKY, M. (2000). Deep issues: Commonsense-based interfaces. *Communications of the ACM, 43*(8), 66–73.

MISSIKOFF, O. (1996). Application of an object oriented approach to the formalization of qualitative (and quantitative) data. *Analecta Praehistorica Leidensia, 28*(I), 263-271.

MISSIKOFF, O. (2003). Ontologies as a reference framework for the management of knowledge in the archaeological domain. In Magistrat der Stadt Wien-referat kulturelles Erbe-Städtarchäologie Wien (Ed)., *Enter the past. The e-way into the four dimensions of cultural heritage* (pp. 35-40). Oxford: ArcheoPress (BAR Int. Series, S1227).

MITCHELL, M. (1996). *An introduction to genetic algorithms.* Cambridge, UK: Cambridge University Press.

MITCHELL, T.M. (1982). Generalization as search. *Artificial Intelligence, 18,* 203-226.

MITCHELL, T.M. (1987). *Machin Learning.* WCB/MC-Graw Hill.

MITHEN, S.J. & REED, M. (2002). Stepping out: A computer simulation of hominid dispersal from Africa. *Journal of Human Evolution, 43,* 433-462.

MOM, V. (2007). SECANTO-The section analysis tool. In A. Figueiredo & G. Velho (Eds.), *The world is in your eyes. Computer applications in archaeology* (pp. 95-102). Tomar, Portugal: CAA Portugal.

MOON, H.S., YOU, T., YOO, H.W., SOHN, M.H., & JANG, D.S. (2005). A recovery system of broken relics using least squares fitting and vector similarity techniques. *Expert Systems with Applications, 28*, 469–481

MORAVEC, H. (1999). *Robot. Mere machines to trascend mind*. New York: Oxford University Press.

MOSTAFA, M., YAMANY, S., & FARAG A. (1999). Integrating shape from shading and range data using neural networks. *IEEE Computer Society Conference on Computer Vision and Pattern Recognition* (CVPR'99) - Volume 2.

MOURRE, J. (1985). *Le Système Expert SILEX*. Rapport DESS, INRIA, Sophia-Antipolis (France). ISI. Laboratoire pour l'Analyse de Scènes.

MULDER, N.J., MIDDELKOOP, H., & MILTENBURG, J.W. (1988). Progress in Knowledge Engineering for image interpretation and classification. Kyoto: *ISPRS Congress*

MURNION, S.D. (1996). Spatial analysis using unsupervised neural networks. *Computers & Geosciences, 22*(9), 1027-1031.

MURPHY, R.R. (2002). *Introduction to AI robotics*. Cambridge, MA: The MIT Press.

NANCE, J.D. (2000). Elemental composition studies of lithic materials from western Kentucky and Tennessee. *Midcontinental Journal of Archaeology, 25*, 83-100.

NANDY, D., & BEN-ARIE, J. (2001). Shape from recognition: A novel approach for 3-D face shape recovery. *IEEE Transactions On Image Processing, 10*(2), 201-217.

NARDI, B.A. (1996). Studying context: A comparison of activity theory, situated action models and distributed cognition. In B.A. Nardi (Ed.), *Context and consciousness. Activity theory and human-computer interaction*. Cambridge, MA: The MIT Press.

NEAPOLITAN R.E. (1990). *Probabilistic reasoning in expert systems*. New York: Wiley.

NEAPOLITAN, R.E. (2003). *Learning Bayesian networks*. Upper Saddle River, NJ: Prentice Hall.

NELSON, R.C., & SELINGER, A. (1998). A cubist approach to object recognition. In *Proc. International Conference on Computer Vision (ICCV98)*, (pp. 614-621), Bombay, India, January. Retrieved September 2007 from http://citeseer.ist.psu.edu/article/nelson98cubist.html

NEWELL, A. (1982). The knowledge level. *Artificial Intelligence, 18*, 87-127.

NEWELL, A., & SIMON, H.A. (1972). *Human problem solving*. Englewood Cliffs, NJ: Prentice Hall.

NEWTON, A. (2007). Modelling the behavioural of *Paranthropus* and *Homo Habilis*. In *Layers of Perception. Computer Applications in Archaeology Proceedings*. Berlin (in press).

NICOLUCCI, N., D'ANDREA, A., & CRESCIOLI, M. (2001) Archaeological applications of fuzzy databases. In Z. Stancic & T. Veljanovski (Eds.), *Computing archaeology for understanding the past* (pp. 107-116). Oxford: ArcheoPress.

NIJKAMP, P. & REGGIANI, A. (1992). *Interaction, evolution and chaos in space*. Berlin: Springer.

NIJKAMP, P. & REGGIANI, A. (1998). *The economics of complex spatial systems*. Elsevier: Amsterdam.

NIJKAMP, P., REGGIANI, A. (1998). *The economics of complex spatial systems*. Amsterdam: Elsevier.

Nilsson, N.J. (1998). *Artificial intelligence: A new synthesis*. San Francisco, CA: Morgan Kaufmann Publishers, Inc.

NOË, A. (2004). *Action in perception*. Cambridge, MA: The MIT Press.

NOLFI, S., & FLOREANO, D. (2000). *Evolutionary robotics. The biology, intelligence, and technology of self-organizing machines*. Cambridge, MA: The MIT Press.

NOLFI, S., & FLOREANO, D. (2000). *Evolutionary robotics. The biology, intelligence, and technology of self-organizing machines*. Cambridge, MA: The MIT Press.

NOVIČ, M., NOVIČ, M., ŽUPANČIČ, M., & SAKARA SUČEVIĆ, M. (2001). The application of the combination of chemical (ICP-OES and ICP-MS) and chemometric analytical procedures for the tracing of the geologically predetermined composition of archaeological pottery. *12th International Symposium Spectroscopy in Theory and Practice with Thinkshop In search of the Metrological Basis of Spectroscopic Measurements*, Bled, Slovenia.

NOWAK, A., & VALLACHER, R.R. (1998). Toward computational social psychology: Cellular automata and neural network models of interpersonal dynamics. In S.J. Read & L.C. Miller (Eds.), *Connectionist models of social reasoning and social behavior* (pp. 277-311). London: Lawrence Erlbaum.

NOWAK, A., & VALLACHER, R.R. (2002). Computational models of social processes. In *Encyclopedia of cognitive science*. London: Nature Publishing Group (Macmillan Publishers).

NOWAK, A., VALLACHER, R.R., & BURNSTEIN, E. (1998). Computational social psychology: A neural network approach to interpresonal dynamics. In W.B.G. Liebrand, A. Nowak and R. Hegselmann (Eds.), *Computer modelling of social processes*. London: Sage Publications.

O'BRIEN, M. J., DARWENT, J., & LYMAN, R. L. (2001). Cladistics is useful for reconstructing archaeological phylogenies: Paleoindian points from the Southeastern United States. *Journal of Archaeological Science, 28*, 1115-1136.

O'REGAN, J.K., NOË, A. (2001). A sensorimotor account of vision and visual consciousness. *Behavioral and Brain Sciences, 24*, 939–1031.

O'REILLY, R.C., & MUNAKATA, Y. (2000). *Computational explorations in cognitive neuroscience*. Cambridge, MA: The MIT Press.

O'SHEA, J. (2004). The identification of shipwreck sites: A Bayesian approach. *Journal of Archaeological Science, 31*, 1533-1552.

OBERLIN, A., ROGGER, A., DE WERRA, D., BRON-PURY, C., VIRET-BERNAL, F., & BÉRARD, C. (1991). Identifying mythological scenes with artificial intelligence. *Science & Archaeology, 33*, 18-27.

OKA, S., TAKEFUJI, Y., & SUZUKI, T., (2000). Feature extraction of IKONOS images by self-organization topological map. *Proceedings of the International Conference on Imaging Science, Systems, and Technology. CISST'2000* Vol. 2, (pp. 687-91). Athens, GA: CSREA Press - Univ. Georgia.

OLDEN, J.D., JOY, M.K., & DEATH, R.G. (2004). An accurate comparison of methods for quantifying variable importance in artificial neural networks using simulated data. *Ecological Modelling,*178(3-4), 389-397.

OPENSHAW, S. (1994). Neuroclassification of spatial data. In B.C. Hewitson & R.G. Crane (Eds.), *Neural nets: Applications in archaeology*. Dordrecht, Holland: Kluwer Academic Publ.

OPENSHAW, S. (1997). Building fuzzy spatial interaction models. In M.M. Fischer & A.Getis (Eds.), *Recent developments in spatial analysis. Spatial statistics, behavioural modeling and computational intelligence*. Berlin: Springer.

OPENSHAW, S., & TURNER, A. (2000). Forecasting global climatic change impacts on mediterranean agricultural land use in the 21st century, *Cybergeo, article 120*, Retrieved July 2007 from http://www.cybergeo.eu/index2255.html

OPENSHAW, S., & TURTON, I. (1996). A parallel kohonen algorithm for the classification of large spatial datasets. *Computers & Geosciences, 22*(9), 1019-1026.

OPENSHAW, S., BLAKE, M., & WYMER, C. (1995). Using neurocomputing methods to classify Britain's residential areas. In P. Fisher (Ed.), *Innovations in GIS 2*. London: Taylor & Francis.

ORLANDI, T. (1997). Informatica, formalizzazione e discipline umanistiche. In T. Orlandi (Ed.), *Discipline umanistiche e informatica. Il problema della formalizzazione*, (pp. 7-17). Roma,

ORLANDI, T. (2002). Is humanities computing a discipline? *Jahrbuch für Computerphilologie, 4*, 51-58

OSADA, R., FUNKHOUSER, T., CHAZELLE, B., & DOBKIN, D. (2002). Shape distributions. *Transactions on Graphics, 21*(4), 807-832.

OZESMI, S.L., & OZESMI, U. (1999). An artificial neural network approach to spatial habitat modeling with interspecific interaction. *Ecological Modelling, 116*, 15-31.

ÖZESMI, S.L., TAN, C.O., & ÖZESMI, U. (2006). Methodological issues in building, training, and testing artificial neural networks in ecological applications. *Ecological Modelling, 195*(1-2), 83-93.

PALMER, S. (1999). *Vision science. Photons to phenomelogy*. Cambridge, MA: The MIT Press.

PALMER, S.E., & KIMCHI, R. (1986). The information processing approach to cognition. In T.J. Knap & L.C. Robertson (Eds.), *Approaches to cognition: Contrasts and controversies*. Hillsdale, NJ: Erlbaum Publ.

PAOLA, J.D., & SCHOWENGERDT, R.A. (1995). A detailed comparison of backpropagation neural network and maximum likelihood classifiers for urban land use classification. *IEEE Transactions on Geoscience and Remote Sensing, 33*(4), 981-996.

PAPAIOANNIOU, G., KARABASSI, E., & THEO-HARIS, T. (2001). Virtual archaeologist: Assembling the past. *IEEE Computer graphics and applications, 21*(2), 53-59.

PAPAIOANNOU, G., & KARABASSI, E.A. (2003). On the automatic assemblage of arbitrary broken solid arte-facts. *Image & Vision Computing, 21*(5), 401–412.

PAPAIOANNOU, G., & KARABASSI, E.A. (2003). On the automatic assemblage of arbitrary broken solid artefacts. *Image & Vision Computing, 21*(5), 401–412.

PAPAIOANNOU, G., KARABASSI, E.A., & THEO-HARIS, T. (2002). Reconstruction of three dimensional objects through matching of their parts. *IEEE Trans. on Pattern Analysis and Machine Intelligence, 24*(1), 114–124.

PARISI, D., & NOLFI, S. (2005). Sociality in em-bodied neural agents. In R. Sun (Ed.), *Cognition and multi-agent interaction*. Cambridge, UK: Cambridge Univerity Press.

PARISI, D., CECCONI, F., & NATALE, F. (2003). Cul-tural change in spatial environments: The role of cultural assimilation and of internal changes in cultures. *Journal of Conflict Resolution, 47*, 163-179.

PATEL, J., & STUTT, A. (1988). *KIVA: An archaeologi-cal interpreter*. Human Cognition Research Laboratory Technical Report, No. 35. Milton Keynes, UK: The Open University.

PATEL, J., & STUTT, A. (1989). Beyond classification: The use of artificial intelligence techniques for the interpretation of archaeological data. In S.P.Q. Rahtz and J. Richards (Eds.), *Computer Applications and Quantitative Methods in Archaeology*. Oxford: BAR International Series (S548).

PAWLAK, Z. (1991). *Rough sets: Theoretical aspects of reasoning about data*. Dordrecht (Holland): Kluwer Academic Publishers.

PEARL, J. (1988). *Probabilistic reasoning in intelligent systems*. San Mateo, CA: Morgan Kaufmann.

PEARL, J. (2000). *Causality. Models, reasoning and inference*. New York: Cambridge University Press.

PECHUK, M., SOLDEA, O., & RIVLIN, E. (2005). Function-based classification from 3D data via generic and symbolic models. Paper presented at The *20th Na-tional Conference on Artificial Intelligence (AAAI-05)*, Pittsburgh, Pennsylvania. Retrieved April 2007 from http://www.cs.technion.ac.il/~mpechuk/publications/oclsAAAI05.pdf

PEDONE, R., & CONTE, R. (2001). Dynamics of status symbols and social complexity. *Social Science Computer Review, 19*(3), 249-262.

PENG, L.W., & SHAMSUDDIN, S.M. (2004). Modeling II: 3D object reconstruction and representation using neural networks. *Proceedings of the 2nd. International Conference on Computer graphics and interactive techniques in Australasia and Southeast GRAPHITE '04*. Published by the Academy of Computing Machin-ery Press.

PENNY, W.D., & ROBERTS, S.J. (1999). Bayesian neural networks for classification: How useful is the evidence framework? *Neural Networks, 12*(6), 877-892.

PERLOVSKY, L.I. (2001). *Neural networks and intel-lect. Using model-based concepts*. New York: Oxford University Press.

PESCHL, M.F. (1996). The development of scientific concepts and their embodiment in the representational activities of cognitive systems. Neural representation spaces, theory spaces, and paradigmatic shifts. *Philo-sophica, 57*(1),131-172.

PETRELLI, M., PERUGINI, D., MORONI, B., & POLI, G. (2001). A simple system based on fuzzy logic and artificial neural networks to determine travertine provenance from ancient buildings. In L. Bordoni & G. Semeraro (Eds.), *Proceedings of the Workshop Artifi-cial Intelligence for the Cultural heritage and Digital Libraries*. Dipartimento di Informatica, Università degli Studi di Bari. Associazione Italiana per l'Inteligenza Artificiale.

PETRELLI, M., PERUGINI, D., MORONI, B., & POLI, G. (2003). Determination of travertine provenance from ancient buildings using self-organizing maps and fuzzy logic *Applied Artificial Intelligence, 7*(8-9), 885-900.

PEUQUET, D.J. & GUO, D. (2000). Mining spatial data using an interactive rule-based approach. *GIScience*, 152-153.

PEURSUM, P., BUI, H.H., VENKATESH, S., & WEST, G. (2005). Robust recognition and segmentation of human actions using HMMs with missing observations. *EURASIP Journal of Applied Signal Processing, 2005*(13), 2110-2126.

PEURSUM, P., VENKATESH, S., WEST, G. & BUI, H.H. (2003). Object labeling from human action recognition. *IEEE International Conference on Pervasive Computing and Communications, Dallas-Fort Worth, Texas, 23-26 March 2003,* (pp. 399-406).

PEURSUM, P., VENKATESH, S., WEST, G. (2007). Tracking-as-recognition for articulated full-body human motion analysis. In *IEEE International Conference on Computer Vision and Pattern Recognition (CVPR).* IEEE Press.

PFEIFFER, R., & SCHEIER,C. (1999). *Understanding intelligence.* Cambridge, MA: The MIT Press.

PIERCE, C. (1878). Deduction, induction and hypothesis. *Popular Science Monthly, 13,* 470-82.

PIJANOWSKI, B.C., BROWN, D.G., SHELLITO, B. A., & MANIK, G. A. (2002). Using neural networks and GIS to forecast land use changes: A land transformation model, *Computers, Environment and Urban Systems, 26,* 553–575.

PIJOAN-LÓPEZ, J. (2007). *Quantificació de traces d'ús en instruments lítics mitjançant imatges digitalitzades: Resultats d'experiments amb Xarxes Neurals I Estadística.* PhD. Dissertation. Universitat Autonoma de Barcelona (Spain).

PIJOAN-LÓPEZ, J., BARCELÓ, J.A., BRIZ, I., VILA, A., & PIQUÉ, R. (1999). Image quantification in use-wear analysis. In K. Fennema & H. Kamermans (Eds.), *Making the connections to the past. CAA 1999.* Computer Applications in Archaeology (pp. 67-74). Holland: Leiden University.

PIJOAN-LÓPEZ, J., BARCELÓ, J.A., CLEMENTE, I., & VILA, A. (2002). Variabilidad Estadística en imágenes digitalizadas de rastros de uso: resultados preliminares. In I. Clemente, R. Risch, & J. Gibaja (Eds.), *Análisis Funcional. Su aplicación al estudio de sociedades prehistóricas.* (pp. 55-64). Oxford: ArcheoPress.

PIPERAKIS,E., & KUMAZAWA, I., (2001). Affine transformations of 3D objects represented with neural networks. *3-D Digital Imaging and Modeling,Proceedings,* (pp. 213-223).

PIQUÉ, R., & PIQUÉ, J.M. (1993). Automatic recognition and classification of archaeological charcoals. In J.

Andresen, T. Madsen & I. Scollar (Eds.), *Computing the past. Computer applicatons and quantitative methods in archaeology.* Aarhus, Denmark: Aarhus University Press.

PIZLO, Z. (2001). Perception as viewed as an inverse problem. *Vision Research, 41*(25), 3145-3161.

PONTHIEUX, S., & COTTRELL, M. (2001). Living conditions: Classification of households using the kohonen algorithm. *European Journal of Economic and Social Systems, 15*(2), 69-84.

POP, H.F., DUMITRESCU, D., & SARBU, C. (1995). A study of roman pottery (terra sigillata) using hierarchical fuzzy clustering. *Analitica Chimica Acta, 310,* 269-279.

POPPER, K. (1963). *Conjectures and refutations: The growth of scientific knowledge.* London: Routledge & Kegan Paul.

POST, E.L. (1943). Formal reductions of the general combinatorial decision problem, *American Journal of Mathematics, 65,* 197-215.

POULTON, M.M., STERNBERG, B.K., & GLASS, C.E. (1992). Location of subsurface targets in geophysical data using neural networks. *Geophysics, 57*(12), 1534–1544.

PREMO, L. S. (2005) Patchiness and prosociality: An agent-based model of plio/pleistocene hominid food sharing. In P. Davidsson, K. Takadama, & B. Logan (Eds.), *Multi-agent and multi-agent-based simulation.* Berlin: Springer. *Lecture Notes in Artificial Intelligence, 3415,* 210-224.

PRINCIPE, J.C., EULIANO, N.R., & LEFEBVRE, W.C. (2000). *Neural and adaptive systems. Fundamentals through simulations.* New York: John Wiley.

PULJIC, M., & KOZMA, R. (2005). Activation clustering in neural and social networks. *Complexity, 10*(4), 42-50.

PULLAR, D. (1997) Rule-based modelling. In GIS, *Geo-Computation, 97.* Retrieved August, 2007, from *http://www.geocomputation.org/1997/papers/pullar.pdf*

PURVES, D., & LOTTO, R.B. (2003). *Why we see what we do. An empirical theory of vision.* Sunderland, MA: Sinauer Associates, Inc.

PUYOL-GRUART, J. (1999). Computer science, artificial intelligence and archaeology. In J.A. Barceló, I. Briz &

A. Vila (Eds.), *New techniques for old times* (pp. 19-27). Oxford: ArchaeoPress, (BAR International series, 757.

QUINLAN, J. R. (1986). Induction of decision trees. *Machine Learning, 1*, 81-106.

QUINLAN, J.R. (1993). *C4.5: Programs for machine learning* San Francisco, CA: Morgan Kaufmann.

QUINLAN, P. (1991). *Connectionism and psychology.* Hempstead: Harvester Wheatsheaf.

RADERMACHER, F.J. (1996). Cognition in systems. *Cybernetics and Systems, 27*, 1-41.

RAGIN, C. (2000). *Fuzzy-set social science.* Chicago, IL: University of Chicago Press.

RAJAMONEY, S. (1990). A computational approach to theory revision. In J. Schrager & P. Langley (Eds.), *Computational models of scientific discovery and theory formation* (pp. 225-253). San Francisco, CA: Morgan Kaufmann.

RAMACHANDRAN, V.S. (1990). Visual perception in people and machines. In A. Blake & T. Troscianko (Eds.), *AI and the eye* (pp. 21-77). John Wiley: New York.

RAMAZZOTTI, M. (1999a). Analisi qualitative dei depositi archeologici come indice guida nelle ricerche a sclara territoriale In M. Buscema & Semeion Group (Eds.), *Reti Neurali Artificiali e Sistemi Socieli Complessi. Teoria-Modelli-Aplicazioni.* Milan, Italy: FrancoAngeli Editore.

RAMAZZOTTI, M. (1999b). *La Bassa Mesopotamia come laboratorio storico. Le reti neurali artificiali come strumento di ausilio alle ricerche di archeologia territoriale.* Contributi e Materiali di Archeologia Orientale, VIII. Università di Roma la Sapienza. Italy.

RANNEY, M., & SCHANK, P. (1998). Toward an integration of the social and the scientific: Observing, modelling, and promoting the explanatory coherence of reasoning. In S. J. Read & L. C. Miller (Eds.), *Connectionist models of social reasoning and social behavior* (pp. 245-276). London: Lawrence Erlbaum Associates.

RAO, S.R. (1972). *Surface phenomena.* London, UK: Hutchinson Educational Ltd.

READ, D. (2003). Emergent properties in small-scale societies. *Artificial life, 9*(4), 419–434.

READ, D.R. (2002). A multitrajectory, competition model of emergent complexity in human social organization. In *Adaptive Agents, Intelligence, and Emergent Human Organization: Capturing Complexity through Agent-Based Modeling,* Proceedings National Academy of Sciences, U S A. (vol. 99) (Suppl 3), 7251–7256.

READ, S.J., & MILLER, L.C. (1998). On the dynamic construction of meaning: An interactive activation and competition model of social perception. In S. J. Read & L.C. Miller (Eds.), *Connectionist models of social reasoning and social behavior* (pp. 27-68). London: Lawrence Erlbaum Associates.

REDFERN, S. (1998a). An approach to automated morphological-topographical classification. *AARGnews,* 17.

REDFERN, S. (1998b). A framework for digital survey from aerial photographs. *The Journal of Irish Archaeology, 9*, 135-150.

REDFERN, S. (1999). Digital wide-area survey from aerial photographs. In K. Fennema & H. Kamermans (Eds.), *Making the connection to the past. Computer applications in archaeology. Faculty of Archaeology* (pp. 103-106).. University of Leiden, Holland,.

REED, R.D., & MARKS, R.J. (1999). *Neural smithing. Supervised learning in feedforward artificial neural networks.* The MIT Press.

REED, S., & LENAT, D. (2002). Mapping ontologies into cyc. In *AAAI 2002 Conference Workshop on Ontologies For The Semantic Web,* Edmonton, Canada,

REELER, C. (1999). Neural networks and fuzzy logic analysis in archaeology. In L. Dingwall, S. Exon, V. Gaffney, S. Laflin & M. van Leusen (Eds.), *Archaeology in the age of the internet.* Edited by. Oxford: ArcheoPress.

REELER, C. (1999). Neural networks and fuzzy logic analysis in archaeology. In L. Dingwall, S. Exon, V. Gaffney, S. Laflin & M. Van Leusen (Eds.), *Archaeology in the age of the internet.* Oxford: ArcheoPress (BAR Int. Series S750).

REYNOLDS, R. G. (1986) An adaptive computer model for the evolution of plant collecting and early agriculture in the eastern valley of Oaxaca. In K. V. Flannery (Ed.), *Guila naquitz: Archaic foraging and early agriculture in Oaxaca, Mexico* (pp. 439-500). New York: Academic Press.

REYNOLDS, R. G., & PENG, B. (2005). Knowledge learning and social swarms in cultural algorithms, *Journal of Mathematical Sociology, 29*, pp. 1-18.

REYNOLDS, R. G., & PENG, B. (2005). Knowledge learning and social swarms in cultural algorithms. *Journal of Mathematical Sociology, 29,* 1-18.

REYNOLDS, R. G., KOBTI, Z., & KOHLER, T. (2004a). The effect of culture on the resilience of social systems in the village multi-agent simulation. *IEEE International Congress on Evolutionary Computation, Portland, OR.* (pp. 1743-1750).

REYNOLDS, R. G., KOBTI, Z., & KOHLER, T. (2005). Learning in dynamic multi-layered social networks: A mesa verde example. In *Proceedings of Geo-Computation 2005.*

REYNOLDS, R., WHALLON, R., & GOODHALL, S. (2001). Transmission of cultural traits by emulation: An agent-based model of group foraging behavior. *Journal of Memetics - Evolutionary Models of Information Transmission,* 4. Retrieved August 2007 from http://jom-emit.cfpm.org/2001/vol4/reynolds_r&al.html

REYNOLDS, R.G. (1979). *An adaptive computer model of the evolution of agriculture in the valley of Oaxaca, Mexico,* Ph.D. Thesis, University of Michigan, Ann Arbor, MI: University Microfilms.

REYNOLDS, R.G. (1999) The impact of raiding on settlement patterns in the northern valley of Oaxaca: An approach using decision trees. In T.A. Kohler & G.J. Gumerman (Eds.), *Dynamics in human and primate societies. Agent based modeling of social and spatial processes.* Oxford University Press (Santa Fe Institute Studies in the Sciences of Complexity).

REYNOLDS, R.G. (1999). An overview of cultural algorithms, *Advances in Evolutionary Computation.* McGraw Hill Press.

REYNOLDS, R.G., & CHUNG, C. (1997). A cultural algorithm to evolve multi-agent cooperation using cultural algorithms. In P. J. Angeline, R. G. Reynolds, J. R. McDonnell, & R. Eberhart (Eds.), *Evolutionary Programming VI* (pp. 323-334). New York: Springer.

REYNOLDS, R.G., & SALEEM, S. (2005). The impact of environmental dynamics on cultural emergence. In L. Booker, S. Forrest, M. Mitchell, & R. Riolo (Eds.), *Perspectives on adaptation in natural and artificial systems: Essays in honor of John Holland* (pp. 253-280). New York: Oxford University Press..

REYNOLDS, R.G., KOBTI, Z., & KOHLER, T. (2004b). The effects of generalized reciprocal exchange on the resilience of social networks: An example from the prehistoric Mesa Verde region, *Journal of Computational and Mathematical and Organization Theory,* (pp. 229-254).

REYNOLDS, R.G., LAZAR, A., & KIM, J. (2002). Agent-based simulation of the evolution of archaic states. *Agent 2002 Social Agents: Ecology, Exchange & Evolution (Agent 2002),* Chicago, October 11-12.

REYNOLDS, R.G., LAZAR, A., & KIM, J. (2002, May 12-17). Simulating the evolution of archaic states. *2002 Congress on Evolutionary Computation (WCII 2002).* Hilton Hawaiian Village, Honolulu, HI.

REYNOSO, C., & JEZIERSKI,E. (2002). A genetic algorithm problem solver for archaeology. In G. Burenhult (Ed.), *Archaeological informatics: Pushing the envelope CAA 2001* (pp. 507-510). Oxford: ArchaeoPress.

RIGOL, J.P., JARVIS, C.H., & STUART, N. (2001). Artificial neural networks as a tool for spatial interpolation. *International Journal of Geographical Information Science,* 15(4), 323-343.

RIPLEY, B.D. (1993). Statistical aspects of neural networks. In O.E. Barndorff-Nielsen, J.L. Jensen & W.S. Kendall (Eds.), *Networks and chaos-statistical and probabilistic approaches* (pp. 40-123). London: Chapman and May.

RIVLIN, E., DICKINSON, S., & ROSENFELD, A. (1995). Recognition by functional parts. *Computer Vision and Image Understanding, 62*(2), 164– 176.

ROBERTSON, S.I. (2001). *Problem solving.* Hove: Psychology Press.

ROBISON-COX, J.F., MARTELL, R.F., & EMRICH, C.G. (2007). Simulating gender stratification. *Journal of Artificial Societies and Social Simulation,* 10(3).

RODRIGUEZ-BACHILLER, A., & GLASSON, J. (2004). *Expert systems and geographic information systems for impact assessment.* London: Taylor & Francis.

ROLLS, E.T., & DECO, G. (2002). *Computational neuroscience of vision.* Oxford, UK: Oxford University Press.

ROOT-BERNSTEIN, R.S. (1989). *Discovery: Inventing and solving problems at the frontiers of scientific knowledge.* Cambridge, MA: Harvard University Press.

ROSS, S. (1989). Expert systems for databases in the historical sciences: a case study from archaeology. In

Sciences Historiques, Sciences du Passé et Nouvelles technologies de l' Information. Bilan et Evaluation. Actes du Congrès International de Lille(France): Centre de Recherches sur la Documentation et l' Information.

RUIZ DEL SOLAR, J. (1998). TEXSOM: Texture segmentation using self-organizing maps. *Neural Networks, 21*, 7-18.

RUMELHART, D. E., & ZIPSER, D. (1986). Feature discovery by competitive learning. In D.E. Rumelhart, J.L. McClelland, & the P.D.P. Research Group (Eds.), *Parallel distributed processing. Explorations in the microstructures of cognition.* Cambridge, MA: The MIT Press.

RUMELHART, D.E. (1989). The architecture of mind: A connectionist approach. In M.I. Posner (Ed.), *Foundations of cognitive science.* Cambridge, MA: The MIT Press.

RUMELHART, D.E., & TODD, P.M. (1993). Learning and connectionist representations. In D.E. Meyer & S. Kornblum (Eds.), *.Attention and performance XIX.* Cambridge, MA: The MIT Press.

RUMELHART, D.E., HINTON, G.E., & WILLIAMS, R.J. (1986). Learning internal representations by error propagation. In D.E. Rumelhart, J.L. McClelland, & the P.D.P. Research Group (Eds.), *Parallel distributed processing. Explorations in the microstructures of cognition.* Cambridge, MA: The MIT Press.

RUSSELL, B. (1967) (1912). *The problems of philosophy.* Oxford, UK: Oxford University Press.

RUSSELL, S., & NORVIG, P. (2003). *Artificial intelligence. A modern approach* (2nd. Ed.) Englewood Cliffs, NJ: Prentice Hall.

RUTKOWSKA, J.C. (1993). *The computational infant.* London: Harvester Wheatsheaf.

SAAM, N.J., & HARRER, A. (1999). Simulating norms, social inequality, and functional change in artificial societies. *Journal of Artificial Societies and Social Simulation, 2*(1)

SABATIER, P.C. (2000). Past and future of inverse problems *Journal of Mathematical Physics, 41*, 4082-4124

SALLANTIN, J., SZCZECINIARZ, J.J., BARBOUX, C., LAGRANGE, M.S., & RENAUD, M. (1991). Théories semiempiriques: conceptualisation et illustrations. *Revue d'Intelligence Artificielle, 5*(1), 9–67.

SALSKI, A. (1992). Fuzzy knowledge-based models in ecological research. *Ecological Modelling, 63*, 103-112.

SALSKI, A. (1996). Fuzzy approach to ecological modelling and data analysis. In *Proceedings of FUZZY'96, Fuzzy Logic in Engineering and Natural Sciences* (pp. 316-325). Zittau (Poland).

SALSKI, A. (2002). Ecological applications of fuzzy logic. In F. Recknagel (Ed.), *Ecological informatics* (pp. 3-14). Berlin: Springer.

SALSKI, A., FRÄNZLE, O., & KANDZIA, P. (Eds). (1996) Fuzzy logic in ecological modelling. *Ecological Modelling, special issue, 85*(1).

SALSKI, A., & KANDZIA, P. (1996). Fuzzy sets and fuzzy logic in ecological modelling. *EcoSys, 4*, 85-97.

SANTORE, J.F., & SHAPIRO, S.C. (2004). A cognitive robotics approach to identifying perceptually indistinguishable objects. In A. Schultz (Ed.), *The intersection of cognitive science and robotics: From interfaces to intelligence, Papers from the 2004 AAAI Fall Symposium* (pp. 47-54). Menlo Park, CA: AAAI Press.

SAWYER, R.K. (2000). Simulating emergence and downward causation in small groups. In S. Moss & P. Davidsson (Eds.), *Multi-agent-based simulation.* Berlin: Springer. (Lecture Notes in Computer Science, No. 1979).

SAWYER, R.K. (2005). *Social emergence: Societies as complex systems.* Cambridge: Cambridge University Press.

SCHIFFER, M. (1987). *Formation Processes of the Archaeological Record.* Alburqueque (NM): University of New Mexico Press.

SCHIØTZ, I.G., & PÈTI, M. (2003). Rule based geoecological mapping on a local scale geography. *Roskilde University Research Report* No. 125. Publications from Geography, Department of Geography and International Development Studies, Roskilde University, Denmark.

SCHMITT, A., LE BLANC, B., CORSINI, M.M., LAFOND, C., & BRUZEK, J. (2001). Les résaux de neurones artificiels. Un outil de tratitement de donnés prometteur pour l'Anthropologie. *Bulletin et Mémoirs de la Société d'Anthropologie de Paris*, n.s., t. *13*(1-2), 143-150.

SCHNEIDER, D., MATUSZEK, C., SHAH, P., KAHLERT, R., BAXTER, D., CABRAL, J. et al. (2005). Gathering and managing facts for intelligence analysis.

In *Proceedings of the 2005 International Conference on Intelligence Analysis,* McLean, Virginia.

SCHNEIDERMANN, H., & KANADE, T. (2004). Object detection using the statistics of parts. *International Journal of Computer Vision, 56*(3), 151–177.

SCHRODT, P.A. (2002). Forecasts and Contingencies: From Methodology to Policy. *Paper presented at the theme panel Political Utility and Fundamental Research: The Problem of Pasteur's Quadrant at the American Political Science Association meetings, Boston, 29 August - 1 September 2002.* Retrieved July 2007 from http://www.ukans.edu/~keds/papers.html

SCHRODT, P.A. (2004). *Patterns, rules and learning: Computational models of international behavior* (2nd Edition). Parus Analytical Systems, Vinland, Kansas, USA. Retrieved July 2007 from http://www.ku.edu/~keds/books.html

SCHWENKER, F., KESTLER, H.A., & PALM, G. (2001). Three learning phases for radial-basis-Function Networks. *Neural Networks* 14, 4-5, pp. 439-458.

SCOLLAR, I. (1990). *Archaeological prospecting and remote sensing.* Cambridge, UK: Cambridge University Press.

SEPT, J.M., GRIFFITH, C.S., & LONG, B. (2007). HOMINIDS: An agent based model of plio-pleistocene hominid foraging behaviour. In *Layers of Perception. Computer Applications in Archaeology 2007 Berlin Conference proceedings.*

SERPEN, G. (2004). Managing spatiotemporal complexity in hopfield neural network simulations for large-scale static optimization source. *Mathematics and Computers in Simulation, 64*(2), 279–293.

SHARDA, R., & PATIL, R.S. (1992). Connectionist approach to time series prediction: An empirical test. *Journal of Intelligent Manufacturing, 3*(5), 317-323.

SHELLEY, C. P. (1996) Visual abductive reasoning in archaeology. *Philosophy of Science, 63,* 278-301.

SHELLITO, B.A., & PIJANOWSKI, B.C. (2003). Using neural nets to model the spatial distribution of seasonal homes. *Cartography and Geographic Information Science,30*(3), 281-290.

SHENNAN, S. J. (2000). Population, culture history, and the dynamic of culture change. *Current Anthropology, 41,* 811-835.

SHENNAN, S. J., & WILKINSON, J. R. (2001). Ceramic style change and neutral evolution: A case study from neolithic europe. *American Antiquity, 56,* 577-594.

SHENNAN, S.J., & STUTT, A. (1989). The nature of archaeological arguments. *Antiquity, 64*(245), 766-777.

SHI, T., & HORVATII, S. (2006) Unsupervised learning with random forest predictors. *Journal of Computational and Graphical Statistics, 15*(1), 118-138.

SHRAGER, J., & LANGLEY,P. (1990). *Computational models of scientific discovery and theory formation.* San Francisco,CA: Morgan Kaufmann.

SILVA, M., MONTEIRO, A., & MEDEIROS, J. (2004). Visualization of geospatial data by component planes and u-matrix. In *Brazilian Symposium on GeoInformatics – GEOINFO.* Edited by Cirano Iochpe e Gilberto Câmara. São José dos Campos, Brasil: INPE.

SIMON, H.A. (1996). *The sciences of the artificial* (3rd Ed.). Cambridge, MA: The MIT Press.

SIMON, H.A., & LEA,G. (1974). Problem solving and rule induction. A unified view. In L.W. Gregg (Ed.), *Knowledge and cognition.* Hillsdale, NJ: Lawrence Erlbaum Ass.

SIROMONEY, G. CHANDRASEKARAN, R. & SURESH, D. (1985). Developing an expert system for Indian epigraphy. Retrieved July 2006 from http://www.cmi.ac.in/gift/Epigraphy/epig_expertsystem.htm

SITUNGKIR, H. (2003). Emerging the emergence sociology: The philosophical framework of agent-based social studies. *Journal of Social Complexity, 1*(2), Bandung Fe, India: Institute Press.

SKIDMORE, A.K. (1989). Expert system classifies eucalypts forest types using thematic mapper data and a digital terrain model, *Photogrammetric Engineering and Remote Sensing, 55,* 1449-1464.

SKUPIN, A., & HAGELMAN, R. (2005). Visualizing demographic trajectories with self-organizing maps. *GeoInformatica, 9*(2), 159–179.

SLOMAN, A. (1987). Motives, mechanisms, and emotions. *Cognition and Emotion,* 1(3), 217-33.

SLOMAN, S. (2005). *Causal models. How people think about the world and its alternatives.* New York: Oxford University Press.

SMALL, C.G. (1996). *The statistical theory of shape.* Berlin: Springer.

SMITH, E.A., & CHOI, J.K. (2007). The emergence of inequality in small-scale societies: Simple scenarios and agent-based simulations. In T. A. Kohler & S. E. Van der Leeuw (Eds.), *Model-based archaeology of socionatural systems.* Santa Fe, NM: SAR Press.

SMITHSON, M. (1988). Fuzzy set theory and the social sciences: The scope for applications. *Fuzzy sets and systemsk, 16,* 4.

Soh, L. K., Tsatsoulis, C., Gineris, D., & Bertoia, C. (2004) ARKTOS: An intelligent system for SAR sea ice image classification. *IEEE Transactions on Geoscience and Remote Sensing, 42,* 229–248.

SONG, A. (2003). *Texture classification: A genetic programming approach.* PhD Dissertation, Department of Computer Science, RMIT, Melbourne, Victoria, Australia,

SONKA, M., HLAVAC, V., & BOYLE, R. (1994). *Image processing, analysis, and machine vision.* London: Chapman and Hall.

SPARS, S.A. (2005). *Interpreting conflict mortuary behaviour: Applying non-linear and traditional quantitative methods to conflict burials.* Ph.D. Thesis. University of Glasgow. Department of Anthropology.

SPAULDING, A.C.M. (1953). Statistical techniques for the discovery of artifact Types. *American Antiquity, 18,* 305-313.

SPIRTES, P., GLYMOUR,C., & SCHEINES, R. (2000). *Causation, prediction and search.* New York: Springer.

SPITZ, F., & LEK, S. (1999). Environmental impact prediction using neural network modeling. *Journal of Applied Ecology, 36,* 317-326.

STARK, L., & BOWYER, K. (1996). *Generic object recognition using form and function, Vol. 10 of Series in Machine Perception and Artificial Intelligence.* Singapore: World Scientific.

STARY, C., & PESCHL, M.F. (1995). Towards constructivist unification of machine learning and parallel distributed processing. In K.M. Ford, C. Glymour & P.J. Hayes (Eds.), *Android epistemology.* Menlo Park/Cambridge/London: AAAI Press /The MIT Press.

STARY, C., & PESCHL, M.F. (1995). Towards constructivist unification of machine learning and parallel

distributed processing. In K.M. Ford, C. Glymour & P.J. Hayes *Android Epistemology.* Menlo Park/Cambridge/London: AAAI Press/the MIT Press.

STASSOPOULOU, A., & PETROU, M. (1998). Obtaining the correspondence between Bayesian and neural networks. *International Journal of Pattern Recognition and Artificial Intelligence, 12*(7), 901-920.

STASSOPOULOU, A., & PETROU, M. (1998). Obtaining the correspondence between Bayesian and neural networks. *International Journal of Pattern Recognition and Artificial Intelligence, 12*(7), 901-920.

STECKNER, C. (1993). Quantitative methods with qualitative results in expert system. Physical qualities in historical shape design. In *Aplicaciones Informáticas en Arqueología. Teorías y Sistemas* (pp. 486-499). Bilbao, Spain: Denboraren Argia.

STEIN, L. A. (1995). Imagination and situated cognition. In K.M. Ford, C. Glymour & P.J. Hayes *(Eds.), Android epistemology.* Menlo Park/Cambridge/London: AAAI Press/the MIT Press.

STOICA, C., & KLÜVER, J. (2007). Interacting neural networks and the emergence of social structure. *Complexity,12*(3), 41-52.

STONE, G.O. (1986). An analysis of the Delta rule and the learning of statistical associations. In D.E. Rumelhart, J.L. McClelland, & the P.D.P. Research Group (Eds.), *Parallel distributed processing. Explorations in the microstructures of cognition.* Cambridge, MA: The MIT Press.

STUTT, A. (1988). Second generation expert systems. Explanations, arguments and archaeology. In S.P.Q. Rahtz (Ed.), *Computer applications and quantitative methods in Archaeology.* Oxford: BAR International Series (S446).

STUTT, A. (1990). Argument support programs: Machines for generating interpretation. In D.S. Miall (Ed.), *Humanities and the computer. New directions.* Oxford: Clarendon Press.

STUTT, A.(1989). *Argument in the humanities: A knowledge-based approach.* HCRL Technical Report No. 49. Milton Keynes (UK): The Open University (Human Cognition Research Laboratory).

SULEIMAN, R., & FISCHER, I. (2000). When one decides for many: The effect of delegation methods on cooperation in simulated inter-group conflicts *Journal of Artificial Societies and Social Simulation, 3*(4),

SUMPTER, N., & BULPITT, A. (1998). *Learning spatiotemporal patterns for predicting object behaviour*. Technical report, University of Leeds, School of Computer Studies.

SUN, R. (2006). *Cognition and multi-agent interaction: From cognitive modeling to social simulation*. Cambridge, UK: Cambridge University Press.

SUTTON, R. S., & BARTON, A.G. (1998). *Reinforcement learning: An introduction* Cambridge MA: The MIT Press.

SZILAGYI, M. (1991). A neural approach to the simulation of human society. *Quality and Quantity, 25*, 211-2210.

TAKATSUKA, M. (2001). An application of the self-organizing map and interactive 3-D visualization to geospatial data. *Proceedings of the 6th International Conference on GeoComputation*. University of Queensland, Brisbane, Australia. Retrieved June 2007 from http://www.geocomputation.org/2001/papers/takatsuka.pdf

TAMBURRINI, G., & DATTERI, E. (2005). Machine experiments and theoretical modelling: From cybernetic methodology to neuro-robotics. *Minds and Machines, 15*(3-4), 335-358.

TANAKA, K. (2004). *An introduction to fuzzy logic for practical application*. Berlin: Springer.

TANG, Z., ALMEIDA, C., & FISHWICK, P.A. (1991). Time series forecasting using neural networks vs. box-jenkins methodology. *Simulation, 57*(5), 303-310.

TANGELDER, J.W.H., & VELTKAMP, R.C. (2004). A survey of content based 3D shape retrieval methods. *Shape Modeling International*, Genova, Italy, June 2004.

TARANTOLA A, (2005). Inverse problem theory. *Society for Industrial and Applied Mathematics*. Retrieved February 2007 from http://www.ipgp.jussieu.fr/%7Etarantola/Files/Professional/SIAM/index.html

TAWFIK, A. Y., (2004). Inductive reasoning and chance discovery. *Minds and Machines, 14*, 441–451.

TAYLOR, G., FREDERIKSEN, R., VANE, R.R., & WALTZ, E. (2004). Agent-based simulation of geo-political conflict. Paper Presented at *Innovative Applications of Artificial Intelligence (IAAI) July 2004*. Retrieved July 2007 from http://www.soartech.com/pubs/IAAI04-GTaylor-AGILE.pdf

TERRAS, M., & ROBERTSON, P. (2005). Image and interpretation: Using artificial intelligence to read ancient roman texts. *HumanIT, 7*(3). Retrieved July 2007 from http://www.hb.se/bhs/ith/3-7/mtpr.pdf

THAGARD, P. & VERBEURGT, K. (1998). Coherence as constraint satisfaction. *Cognitive Science, 22,* 1-24.

THAGARD, P. (1988). *Computational philosophy of science*. Cambridge, MA: The MIT Press.

THALMANN, D. (2001). The foundations to build a virtual human society In A. de Antonio, R. Aylett, & D. Ballin (Eds.), *Intelligent virtual agents*. Berlin: Springer. (Lecture Notes in Computer Science, No. 2190).

THOMPSON, S., FUETEN, F., & BOCKUS, D. (2001). Mineral identification using artificial neural networks and the rotating polarizer stage. *Computers in Geosciences, 27,* 1081-1089.

THORNTON, C. (2000). *Truth from trash. How learning makes sense*. Cambridge, MA: The MIT Press.

TIJSSELING, A., & BERTHOUZE, L. (2001). A Neural Network for Temporal Sequential Information. *Proceedings of the 8th International Conference on Neural Information Processing, Shanghai, China* (pp. 1449-1454).

TOSELLI, A. (2004). *Identificación y descripción de trazas de uso en obsidiana mediante la experimentación*. Master Thesis. Universitat Autónoma de Barcelona (Spain).

TOSELLI, A., PIJOAN, J., & BARCELÓ, J.A. (2002). La descripción de las trazas de uso en materias primas no silíceas: resultados preliminares de un análisis estadístico descriptivo In *Análisis Funcional: su aportación al estudio de Sociedades Prehistóricas 1er Congreso de Análisis Funcional de España y Portugal* Oxford: British Archaeological Reports Archeopress.

TRAFTON, J. G., SHULTZ, A. C., PERZANOWSKI, D., BUGAJSKA, M. D., ADAMS, W., CASSIMATIS, N. L. et al. (2004). Children and robots learning to play hide and seek. *Cognitive Systems Journal*.

TREUR, J. (2005). A unified perspective on explaining dynamics by anticipatory state properties. In J. Mira & J. R. Álvarez (Eds.), *Mechanisms, symbols, and models underlying cognition: First International Work-Conference on the Interplay Between Natural and Artificial Computation*, (pp. 27–37) IWINAC 2005, Las Palmas, Canary Islands, Spain, , Part I. Berlin, Springer-Verlag.

TRUCCO, E. (1997). Active model acquisition and sensor planning. In V. Cantoni, S. Levialdi & V. Roberto (Eds.), *Artificial vision. Image description, recognition and communication*. San Diego: Academic Press.

TSAGANOU,G., GRIGORIADOU,M. CAVOURA,T., & KOUTRA, D. (2003). Evaluating an intelligent diagnosis system of historical text comprehension. *Expert Systems with Applications, 25,* 493–502.

TSOTSOS, J.K. (1990). Analyzing vision at the complexity level, *behavioral and brain sciences, 13*(3), 423 - 445.

TSOTSOS, J.K. (2001). Motion understanding: Task-directed attention and representations that link perception with action, *International Journal of Computer Vision, 45*(3), 265-280.

TYLER, A.R. (2007). *Expert systems research trends.* Hauppauge, NY: Nova Science Pub Inc.

UÇOLUK, G., & TOROSLU, I.H. (1999). Automatic reconstruction of broken 3D surface objects. *Computers & Graphics, 23*(4), 573-582.

ULLMAN, S. (1996). *High-level vision. Object recognition and visual cognition.* Cambridge, MA: The MIT Press.

ULTSCH, A. (2003). Maps for the visualization of high-dimensional data spaces, *Proceedings of Workshop on Self Organizing Maps WSOM03* (pp 225-230), Hibikino, Kitakyushu, Japan.

ULTSCH, A., & MOERCHEN, F. (2005). ESOM-Maps: Tools for clustering, visualization, and classification with Emergent SOM. *Technical Report Dept. of Mathematics and Computer Science, University of Marburg, Germany*, No. 46.

VALDES, J.J., & BONHAM-CARTER, G. (2006). Time dependent neural network models for detecting changes of state in complex processes: Applications in earth sciences and astronomy. *Neural Networks, 19,* 196–207.

VALDÉS-PEREZ, R.E. (1995). Machine discovery in chemistry: New results. *Artificial Intelligence, 65*(2), 247-280.

VALDÉS-PEREZ, R.E. (1996). Computer science research on scientific discovery. *Knowledge Engineering Review, 11,* 57-66.

VALDÉS-PEREZ, R.E. , ZYTKOW,J., SIMON, H.A. (1993). Scientific-model building as search in matrix spaces *Proceedings AAAI-93.* Washington,D.C. [quoted in Wagman 2002].

VALDES-PĚRZ, R.E. (1995). Machine discovery in chemistry: New results. *Artificial Intelligence, 65*(2), 247-280.

VALDES-PĚRZ,R.E.(1996a). Computer science research on scientific siscovery *Knowledge Engineering Review,* 11, 57-66.

VALDES-PĚRZ, R.E. (1996b). A new theorem in particle physics enabled by machine discovery. *Artificial Intelligence, 82*(1-2), 331-339.

VALDES-PĚRZ, R.E. (1999). Discovery tools for science applications. *Communications of the ACM, 42*(11), 37-41.

VALIENTE-GONZÁLEZ, J.M, (2001). Object comparison in structural analysis of decorative patterns in textile design. *Preprints and Electronic Proceedings of 12th International Conference on Design Tools and Methods in Industrial Engineering, 1,* B1.

VAN BALEN, K.E.P. (2001) Learning from damage of masonry Structures. Expert systems can help. In P.B. Lourenço & P. Roca (Eds.), *Historical constructions 2001: Possibilities of numerical and experimental techniques.* Guimarães, Portugal: Publicaçoes de Universidade do Minho.

VAN DEN DRIES, M.H. (1998). *Archeology and the application of artificial intelligence. Case studies on use-wear analysis of prehistoric flint tools.* Archaeological Studies Leiden University No. 1. Holland: Faculty of Archaeology, University of Leiden

Van der BAAN, M., & JUTTEN, C. (2000). Neural networks in geophysical applications. *Geophysics, 65*(4), 1032–1047.

Van Der MAATEN, L.J.P., & BOON, P.J. (2006). COIN-O-MATIC: A fast and reliable system for coin classification. In *Proceedings of the MUSCLE Coin Workshop 2006,* (pp. 7-17). Berlin, Germany.

Van Der MAATEN, L.J.P., BOON, P.J PAIJMANS, J.J., LANGE, A.G., & POSTMA, E.O. (2006). Computer vision and machine learning for archaeology. In *Proceedings of the Computer Applications in Archaeology Conference 2006,* Fargo (ND).

VAN DER MAATEN, L.J.P., BOON, P.J., PAIJMANS, J.J., LANGE, A.G., & POSTMA, E.O. (2006). Computer vision and machine learning for archaeology. In *Proceedings of the Computer Applications in Archaeology Conference 2006*, Fargo (ND).

VAN DER VAART, E., HANKEL, A., DE BOER, B., & VERHEIJ, B. (2006). Agents adopting agriculture: Modeling the agricultural transition. *From Animals to Animats 9, 9th International Conference on Simulation of Adaptive Behavior, SAB 2006, Rome, Italy, September 25-29, 2006. Proceedings* (pp. 750-761). Berlin: Springer. (Lecture Notes in Computer Science: Vol. 4095).

VAN DER MAATEN, L.J.P., & BOON, P.J. (2006). COIN-O-MATIC: A fast and reliable system for coin classification. In *Proceedings of the MUSCLE Coin Workshop 2006*, (pp. 7-17). Berlin, Germany.

Van LEUSEN, P.M., (2002). *Pattern to process: Methodological investigations into the formation and interpretation of spatial patterns in archaeological landscapes*, PhD thesis, University of Groningen.

VAN OVERWALLE, F., & VAN ROOY, D. (1998). A connectionist approach to causal attribution. In S. J. Read & L. C. Miller (Eds.), *Connectionist Models of Social Reasoning and Social Behavior* (pp. 143-171). London: Lawrence Erlbaum Associates.

VARIEN, M.D., & MILLS, B.J., (1997). Accumulations Research: Problems and Prospects for Estimating Site-Occupation Span. *Journal of Archaeological Method and Theory*, vol. 4 (2), pp. 141-191.

VEMURI, V.R., & ROGERS, R.D. (1994). Time series and the forecasting problem. In V.R. Vemuri & R.D. Rogers (Eds.), *Artificial neural networks: Forecasting time series*. Los Alamitos, CA: IEEE Computer Society Press.

VERHAGEN, H. (2001). Simulation of the learning of norms. *Social Science Computer Review, 19, 296 - 306*.

VEZZOSI, S., BEDINI, L., & TONAZZINI, A. (2002). An integrated system for the analysis and the recognition of characters in ancient documents. In *Document Analysis Systems V: 5th International Workshop, DAS 2002, Princeton, NY*. Berlin: Springer. Lecture Notes in Computer Science, Vol. 2423, 49-52.

VIERRA, R. K. (1982). Typology, classification, and theory building. In R. Whallon and J. A. Brown (Eds.), *Essays on archaeological typology* (pp. 162-175). Evanston, IL: Center for American Archaeology Press.

VILA, A. (2006). Propuesta de elaboración de la metodología arqueológica. In *Etnoarqueología de la Prehistoria: más allá de la analogía* (pp. 61-76). Treballs d'Etnoarqueologia, 6. CSIC-UAB (Barcelona, Spain).

VILLA, N., & BOULE, R. (2007, April 25-27). Clustering a medieval social network by SOM using a kernel based distance measure. *European Symposium on Artificial Neural Networks. Advances in Computational Intelligence and Learning* Bruges (Belgium). Retrieved March 2007 from (http://hal.archives-ouvertes.fr/docs/00/14/51/17/PDF/villa_boulet_ESANN2007_final.pdf)

VILLMANN, T., (1999). Benefits and Limits of the Self-Organizing Map and its Variants in the Area of Satellite Remote Sensoring Processing. *Proc. of European Symposium on Artificial Neural Networks (ESANN'99)*, pp. 111-116.

VISION, G. (1997). *Problems of vision. Rethinking the causal theory of perception*. Oxford, UK: Oxford University Press.

VITALI, V., & LAGRANGE, M.S. (1988). VANDAL: An expert system for the provenance determination of archaeological ceramics based on INAA Data. In S.P.Q.Rahtz (Ed.), *Computer applications and quantitative methods in archaeology 1988.* . Oxford: BAR International Series (S446).

WAGMAN, M. (2000). *Scientific discovery process in humans and computers*. Westport, CN: Praeger Publishers.

WAGMAN, M. (2002). *Problem-solving processes in humans and computers. Theory and research in psychology and artificial intelligence*. Westport, CN: Praeger Publ.

WANG, J.Y., & COHEN, F.S. (1994). 3-D object recognition and shape estimation from image contours using B-splines, shape invariant matching, and neural network, *IEEE Transactions on Pattern Analysis And Machine Intelligence, 16*(I), 13-23.

WANG, N., DOWELL, F., & ZHANG, N. (2002). Determining wheat vitreousness using image processing and a neural network. *2002 ASAE International Annual Meeting/CIGR XVth. World Congress*.

WARNER, T. A., LEVANDOWSKI, D. W. BELL, R. & CETIN, A. (1994). Rule-based geobotanical classification of topographic, aeromagnetic and remotely sensed vegetation community data. *Remote Sensing of Environment, 50*, 41 – 51.

WEI, G.Q., & HIRZINGER, G. (1996). Learning shape-from-shading by a multilayer network. IEEE Transactions on Neural Networks, *7*(4), 985-995.

WEIGEND, A.S., HUBERMAN, B., & RUMELHART, D. (1990). Predicting the future. A connectionist approach. *Int. Journal of Neural Systems, 1*, 193-210.

WEISS, S.M., & KULIKOWSKI, C.A. (1991). *Computer systems that learn*. San Francisco, CA: Morgan Kaufmann.

WESCOTT, K.L., & BRANDON, R.J. (1999). *Practical applications of GIS for archaeologists: A predictive modeling toolkit*. London: Taylor & Francis.

WHITE, R. (2003). The epistemic advantage of prediction over accomodation. *Mind, 112*, 653-683.

WHITE, R.W. (1989). The artificial intelligence of urban dynamics: Neural network models of urban structure. *Papers of the Regional Science Association, 67*, 43-53.

WHITE, W.R. (1995). Spatial interaction modeling using artificial neural networks. *Journal of Transport Geography, 3*(3), 159-166.

WICHERT, A. (2000). A categorical expert system 'Jurassic.' *Expert Systems with Applications, 19*, 149–158

WILCOCK, J. (1986). A review of expert systems: Their shortcomings and possible applications in archaeology *Computer Applications in Archaeology, 13*, 139-144.

WILCOCK, J. (1990). A critique of expert systems, and their past and present use in archaeology. In J.C. Gardin & R. Ennals (Eds.), *Interpretation in the humanities: Perspectives from artificial intelligence*. Library and Information Research Report, 71. The British Library Publications, Wetherby (UK).

WILKINSON, G. (1997). Neurocomputing for earth observation-recent developments and future challenges. In M.M. Fischer & A.Getis (Eds.), *Recent developments in spatial analysis. Spatial statistics, behavioural modeling and computational intelligence*. Berlin: Springer.

WILLIAMSON, J. (2004). A dynamic interaction between machine learning and the philosophy of science. *Minds and Machines, 14*, 539–549.

WILLIAMSON, J. (2005). *Bayesian nets and causality: Philosophical and computational foundations*. New York: Oxford University Press.

WILLIS, A., ANDREWS, S., BAKER, J., CAO, Y., HAN, D., KANG, K. et al. (2002). Bayesian virtual pot-assembly from fragments as problems in perceptual-grouping and geometric-learning. *International Conference on Pattern Recognition (ICPR'02), Québec City, Canada*. IEEE Computer Society publ., Proc. of ICPR, vol. III, (pp. 297-302).

WILLMES, L., BACK, T., YAOCHU, J., & SENDHOFF, B. (2003). Comparing neural networks and kriging for fitness approximation in evolutionary optimization. *CEC '03. The 2003 Congress on Evolutionary Computation, 2003, 1*, 663- 670.

WINDER, W. (1996). Texperts. *TEXT Technology*, 6.3. Wright State University.

WINOGRAD, T., & FLORES, F. (1985). *Understanding computers and cognition: A new foundation for design*. Norwood, NJ: Ablex Publ.

WINTER, K., & HEWITSON, B.C. (1994). Self-organizing maps—applications to census data. In B.C. Hewitson & R.G. Crane (Eds.), *Neural nets: Applications in archaeology*. Dordrect, Holland: Kluwer Academic Publ.

WITLOX, A. (2005). Expert systems in land-use planning: An overview. *Expert Systems with Applications, 29*, 437–445.

WITTEK, I.H., & FRANK, E. (2005). *Data mining: Practical machine learning tools and techniques* (Second Edition). San Francisco, CA: Morgan Kaufmann.

WOBCKE, W. (1998). Agency and the logic of ability. In W. Wobcke, M. Pagnucco, & C. Zhang (Eds.), *Agents and multi-agent systems: Formalisms, methodologies, and applications*. Berlin: Springer.

WOBCKE, W. (1998). Agency and the logic of ability. In W. Wobcke, M. Pagnucco, & C. Zhang (Eds.), *Agents and multi-agent systems: Formalisms, methodologies, and applications*. Berlin: Springer. (Lecture Notes of Computer Science, 1441).

WOODBURY, K.A. (2002) *Inverse engineering handbook*. Boca Raton, FL: CRC Press.

WOODWARD, J. (2003). *Making things happen. A theory of causal explanation*. New York: Oxford University Press.

WYLIE, A. (1985). The reaction against analogy. *Advances in Archaeological Method and Theory, 8*, 63-111.

YANG, X. (2005). *Implementation of neural network interpolation in ArcGIS and case study for spatial-temporal interpolation of temperature.* Master Project. The University of Texas at Dallas, GIS Program POEC 6389.

YAO, M., MENG, H.Y., ZHANG, L., HUANG,Y., PEI, M., HUANG, Z.J. et al.(2001). Towards improvement in locating of underground tomb relics using EM radar signals and genetic algorithms, *Genetic And Evolutionary Computation Conference Late-Breaking Papers* (pp. 493-498). San Francisco, CA.

YELLEN, J.E. (1977). *Archaeological approaches to the present: Models for reconstructing the past.* New York: Academic Press.

YIALOURIS, C., KOLLIAS, V., LORENTZOS, N., KALIVAS, D., & SIDERIDIS, A. (1997). An integrated expert geographical information system for soil suitability and soil evaluation. *Journal of Geographic Information and Decision Analysis, 1*(2), 90–100.

YOSHIDA, T., & OMATU, S. (1994). Neural network approaches to landcover mapping. *IEEE Transactions on Geosciences and Remote Sensing, 32*, 1103-1109.

YOUNG, S.S., SCOTT, P.D., & NASRABADI, N.M. (1997). Object recognition using multilayer hopfield neural network, *IEEE Trans. Image Process, 6*(3), 357–372.

YOUNGER, S. (2005). Violence and revenge in egalitarian societies. *Journal of Artificial Societies and Social Simulation, 8*(4).

YU, Y. (1999). Surface reconstruction from unorganized points using self-organizing neural networks. *Proc. of IEEE Visualization '99 Late Breaking Hot Topics,* (pp.61-64) San Francisco, CA.

ZADEH, L.A. (1965). Fuzzy sets. *Information and Control. 8,* 338-353.

ZADEH, L.A., KLIR, G.J., Yuan, B (eds.). (1996). *Fuzzy sets, fuzzy logic, and fuzzy systems: Selected Papers by Lotfi A. Zadeh (Advances in Fuzzy Systems - Applications and Theory, Vol 6.* Singapore: World Scientific.

ZEIDENBERG, M. (1990). *Neural networks in artificial intelligence.* Chichester, UK: Ellis Horwood.

ZHAI, L., TANG, X., LI L., & JIANG, W. (2005, August 27-29). Temporal association rule mining based on T-apriori algorithm and its typical application. *Proceedings of the International Symposium on Spatiotemporal Modeling, Spatial Reasoning, Analysis, Data Mining and Data Fusion,* Peking University, China.

ZHANG, C., CAO, C., GU, F., & SI, J. (2002). A domain-specific formal ontology for archaeological knowledge sharing and reusing. In D. Karagiannis & U. Reimer (Eds.), *Practical aspects of knowledge management*: 4th International Conference, PAKM 2002 vol. 2569 (pp. 213-225). Vienna, Austria. Proceedings. Berlin: Springer. Lecture Notes in Computer Science.

ZHANG, Q., & WANG, J, (2003). A rule-based urban land use inferring method for fine resolution multispectral imagery. *Canadian Journal of Remote Sensing, 29*(1), 1-13.

ZHOU, J., & CIVCO, D.L. (1996). Using genetic learning neural networks for spatial decision making in GIS. *Photogrametric Engineering and Remote Sensing, 62*(11), 1287-1295.

ZIARKO, W. (1994). *Rough sets, fuzzy sets and knowledge discovery.* Berlin: Springer.

ZINCHENKO, V.P. (1996). Developing activity theory: The zone of proximal development and beyond. In B.A. Nardi (Eds.), *Context and consciousness. Activity theory and human-computer interaction.* Cambridge, MA: The MIT Press.

ZUBROW, E. B.W. (2003). The archaeologist, the neural network, and the random pattern: problems in spatial and cultural cognition. In M. Forte and P.R. Williams (Eds.) F. El Baz & J. Wiseman (Co-Eds.), *The reconstruction of archaeological landscapes through digital technologies Italy-United States Workshop, Boston, Massachusetts.* Oxford: ArcheoPress.

ZUBROW, E. B.W., & ROBINSON, J. (2000) Between spaces: Interpolation in archaeology. In M. Gilling, D. Mattingly, & J. Van Dalen (Eds.), *Geographic information systems and landscape archaeology* (pp. 65-84). Oxford: Oxbow Press.

ZUPANEK, B., & MLEKUZ, D. (2001). Counting the uncountable: A quantitative approach to the religious differences between the roman towns of Emona and Poetovio. In Z. Stancic & T. Veljanovski (Eds.), *Com-*

puting archaeology for understanding the past. Oxford: ArchaeoPress.

ZWEIG, Z. (2006). *Using data-mining techniques for analyzing pottery databases.* Master's Degree Dissertation. Department of Land of Israel Studies & Archaeology, Bar-Ilan University.

ZYTKOW, J.M., BAKER, J. (1991) Interactive mining of regularities in databases. In. G. Piatetsky-Shapiro & W.J. Frawley (Eds.), *Knowledge discovery in databases* Menlo Park, CA: AAAI Press/The MIT Press.

About the Author

Juan Antón Barceló i Àlvarez is reader in the Department of Prehistory, Universitat Autònoma de Barcelona (Catalonia, Spain), where he teaches undergraduate and graduate courses on archaeological theory and methods. He is currently head of the laboratory for quantitative archaeology and computer applications, providing curricular support and technology training for faculty, staff, and students. In addition to his research in the applications of classical statistical tools, and the development of new methodologies from geostatistics, artificial intelligence and virtual reality, he has worked extensively on historical and archaeological investigations about social dynamics in Bronze Age times, Phoenician colonization in the Mediterranean, the origins of agriculture and social complexity in the Near East, and economic resource management and social organization in hunter-gatherer societies in the southernmost parts of America: Patagonia and Tierra del Fuego. He is now investigating long-term dynamics of Patagonian hunter-gatherer societies, with funding from the Spanish Ministry for Education and Research. He has authored a previous book on artificial intelligence applications in archaeology (in Spanish), and another book on statistical methods. He has also edited books on computer applications in archaeology and about virtual reality technologies. He is the author or co-author of more than 100 papers and publications. His Web page can be found at: http://antalya.uab.cat/prehistoria/Barcelo.

Index